Advance Praise for *Pictures o...*

"San Francisco has battened from its birth on instant wealth, high tech weaponry, and global commerce, and the present age is little different. Gold, silver, and sleek iPhones—they all glitter in the California sun and are at least as magnetic as the city's spectacular setting, benign climate, and laissez-faire lifestyles. The cast of characters changes, but the hustlers and thought-shapers eternally reign over the city and its hinterland, while in their wake they leave a ruined landscape of exorbitant housing, suburban sprawl, traffic paralysis, and delusional ideas about a market free enough to rob the majority of their freedom. Read all about it here, and weep."
—Gray Brechin, author of *Imperial San Francisco: Urban Power, Earthly Ruin*

"Too many studies of cities dwell on their peculiarities; this fascinating book balances the dramatic story of the Bay Area against a profound understanding of urbanization. It eschews a descriptive narrative in favor of hard-hitting critical analysis. The book is not only about the inherently contradictory development of the San Francisco region, but also about where it stands in relation to the rest of the United States, even the world and why it matters so much. No one but Richard Walker combines such an intimate knowledge one city with the theoretical insights necessary to make sense of it."
—Kevin Cox, author of *The Politics of Urban and Regional Development and the American Exception*

"Debunking the Horatio Alger promotional blather of self-flattering tech moguls, the real Bay Area comes into view, based on nurses and teachers, drivers and clerks, homeless and the desperate. Real estate bubbles have given way to tech bubbles which have given way to housing bubbles, and now have given way to a chimerical prosperity that is as fragile as any of the prior ones."
—Chris Carlsson, San Francisco historian and cofounder of Critical Mass

Pictures of a Gone City

Bay Area from space (NOAA)

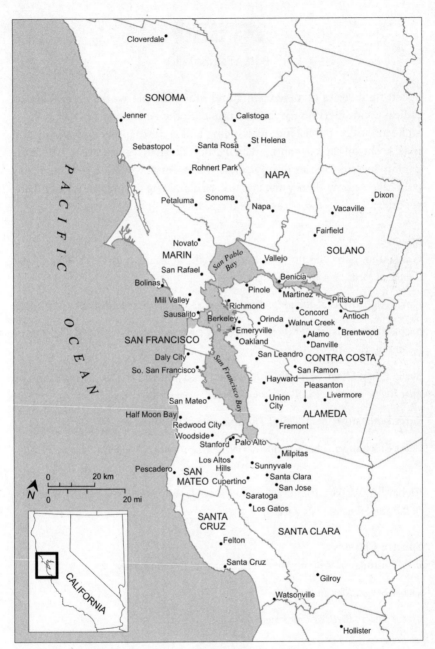

Map of Bay Area with 10 Counties and Select Cities

Editor: Sasha Lilley

Spectre is a series of penetrating and indispensable works of, and about, radical political economy. Spectre lays bare the dark underbelly of politics and economics, publishing outstanding and contrarian perspectives on the maelstrom of capital—and emancipatory alternatives—in crisis. The companion Spectre Classics imprint unearths essential works of radical history, political economy, theory and practice, to illuminate the present with brilliant, yet unjustly neglected, ideas from the past.

Spectre

Greg Albo, Sam Gindin, and Leo Panitch, *In and Out of Crisis: The Global Financial Meltdown and Left Alternatives*

David McNally, *Global Slump: The Economics and Politics of Crisis and Resistance*

Sasha Lilley, *Capital and Its Discontents: Conversations with Radical Thinkers in a Time of Tumult*

Sasha Lilley, David McNally, Eddie Yuen, and James Davis, *Catastrophism: The Apocalyptic Politics of Collapse and Rebirth*

Peter Linebaugh, *Stop, Thief! The Commons, Enclosures, and Resistance*

Peter Linebaugh, *The Incomplete, True, Authentic, and Wonderful History of May Day*

Richard A. Walker, *Pictures of a Gone City: Tech and the Dark Side of Prosperity in the San Francisco Bay Area*

Spectre Classics

E.P. Thompson, *William Morris: Romantic to Revolutionary*

Victor Serge, *Men in Prison*

Victor Serge, *Birth of Our Power*

Pictures of a Gone City

Tech and the Dark Side of Prosperity in the San Francisco Bay Area

Richard A. Walker

Pictures of a Gone City: Tech and the Dark Side of Prosperity in the San Francisco Bay Area
Richard A. Walker
© PM Press 2018

ISBN: 978-1-62963-510-1
Library of Congress Control Number: 2017964729

Cover by John Yates/Stealworks
Interior design by briandesign

10 9 8 7 6 5 4 3 2 1

PM Press
PO Box 23912
Oakland, CA 94623
www.pmpress.org

Printed in the USA by the Employee Owners of Thomson-Shore in Dexter, Michigan.
www.thomsonshore.com

The world is a beautiful place
to be born into
if you don't mind happiness
not always being
so very much fun
if you don't mind a touch of hell
now and then
just when everything is fine
because even in heaven
they don't sing
all the time

The world is a beautiful place
to be born into
if you don't mind some people dying
all the time
or maybe only starving
some of the time
which isn't half bad
if it isn't you

Oh the world is a beautiful place
to be born into
if you don't much mind
a few dead minds
in the higher places
or a bomb or two
now and then
in your upturned faces
or such other improprieties
as our Name Brand society
is prey to
with its men of distinction

and its men of extinction
and its priests
and other patrolmen
and its various segregations
and congressional investigations
and other constipations
that our fool flesh
is heir to

Yes the world is the best place of all
for a lot of such things as
making the fun scene
and making the love scene
and making the sad scene
and singing low songs and having inspirations
and walking around
looking at everything
and smelling flowers
and goosing statues
and even thinking
and kissing people and
making babies and wearing pants
and waving hats and
dancing
and going swimming in rivers
on picnics
in the middle of the summer
and just generally
"living it up"

Yes
but then right in the middle of it
comes the smiling
mortician

Lawrence Ferlinghetti,
"Pictures of the Gone World" (1951)

CONTENTS

Preface

WHEN I TELL PEOPLE I HAVE WRITTEN A BOOK ON THE SAN FRANCISCO BAY AREA, they invariably ask, "Yes, but what is it *about?*" For most people, a metropolitan region is a vague idea, too all-encompassing, sprawling, and unbounded to be a proper object of inquiry. To me, the Bay Area is a real thing, a living, breathing entity with its own character, anatomy, and biography, and very much worthy of serious investigation. Mine is a geographer's view of the world in all its immense diversity of places, societies, and landscapes—in spite of the homogenizing effects of markets, modernization, nation building, and globalization.

To be sure, seeing a city as a whole is not obvious. Most people are not used to thinking of metropolitan areas as entities in the same way as well-bordered units such as towns, states, and countries. While almost everyone has a strong sense of their neighborhood and daily realm of movement, and the accompanying sights, smells, and surroundings, at larger scales the geography quickly becomes unfamiliar. Moreover, there is a lot of honest confusion about what is meant by the word "city": does it refer to a municipality like Berkeley, an urban realm like Silicon Valley, or a megaregion such as the Bay Area? The latter now stretches about one hundred miles in every direction from San Francisco, encompassing twelve counties and a population of 8.5 million. Even worse, the definition of the region keeps changing as it grows.

Furthermore, cities are hellishly complex systems, consisting of economic bases, social orders, political practices, and much, much more. It is hard, of course, to come to grips with nation-states, but at least they are familiar entities. Big city-regions are not, except in casual references marked by a lot of hand-waving generalizations. At least for countries or the state of California, the researcher can turn to libraries full of books and reams of official data, often with the imprimatur of a recognized disciplinary field, such as American history. Such is not the case for a single metropolis, and urban studies is not a discipline with deep roots and a strong presence in the universities.

This is not an ethnographic inquiry into the lives of people living in the Bay Area, an economic study of the tech industry, a sociology of popular movements, or a political analysis of electoral campaigns. It is all of those, to a degree, yet not exactly any one of them. While I realize the importance of such approaches, my take on the city is more sweeping. I want to know *how* the Bay Area as a whole is distinctive, *why* it came to be so, and *what difference* that makes to the life of its residents. That means taking on board a huge number of thorny topics and drilling down into this one place to get at its foundations.

It also means reflecting on how this city relates to others, to the country, and to the world—how is it influenced from outside and how, in turn, it gestates ideas and practices that end up having an impact elsewhere. Looking intensely at a single place can, in fact, open a window on the world through which the picture comes more clearly into focus. Yet trying to do all this makes geography the thorniest of social sciences.

I intentionally avoid the national political scene as much as possible, despite the way it occupies so much attention for the dangers posed by the current administration on every front: immigration, democracy, environment, and more. My purpose is to focus on the Bay Area and not be unduly diverted by current events, but I am well aware of what is happening and it is there in the background—and sometimes moves to the foreground.

★ ★ ★

This is a book aimed at the general public. Some will read it as a way of understanding the place they live in. Others will read it as a guide to the tech capital of the world. Still others will look for comparisons to their own cities, from Shanghai to New York. I am not a journalist or popular writer, but I am a teacher and I write in a way reasonable people can readily understand.

Nevertheless, I believe in the power of theory to cut beneath the surface of the everyday and the necessity of coming up with explanations that go beyond common sense and popular ideology. My reflections on the Bay Area are backed up by years of work in urban studies, economic geography, sociology of race and class, political science, and so forth, but I bury that quietly in the footnotes for those who care.

Neither theory nor facts speak for themselves. Grand theory and weighty categories alone do not go very far in accounting for a complex reality, and there have to be a great many tools in a thinker's kit bag; middle-level concepts and complimentary theories are required to home in on any specific problem. Equally essential is a recourse to the facts at hand—empirical observation, data, and all manner of evidence—so this book is loaded up with a goodly number of charts and citations to information in business reports, academic studies, and newspaper accounts.

I offer this book as one person's attempt at a well-rounded portrait of the San Francisco Bay Area and as a piece of the larger puzzle of understanding the United States and capitalism at the present time. Many readers will know more than I about this or that topic, and the perils of writing about contemporary affairs are many, because history is a moving target. While mine is a partial view of the whole, one of the virtues of studying a single place is that it is possible to remain grounded, know a familiar terrain well, and not give flight to fanciful claims. I make no absolute claim to truth and rectitude, but if I make the reader think harder about this city and question further the era we are currently living through, then I will have succeeded.

★　★　★

My take on the Bay Area is decidedly leftist. Some readers may be uncomfortable with my use of certain terms of a radical provenance, such as *capitalism*, *working class*, *ruling class*, *ideology*, *exploitation*, and other old-fashioned, foundational concepts in political economy. Yet I am convinced that these classic ideas still reveal essential aspects of the contradictions of our present time.

Readers who cringe at the idea of being pummeled with criticisms of their beloved Bay Area can take heart, because I, too, love the place—warts and all. I do my best to present the positives about the region's successes and virtues, which makes some of my radical friends cringe. While I am not quite that oxymoron, "a Marxist booster," as one friend calls me, I do believe in laying out the case for and against the indicted and letting the court of public opinion decide.

If, in the end, my take on the Bay Area grates against conventional boosterism, so much the better. Mainstream thinking has helped deliver this country to its present fate by the refusal to recognize many deep and disturbing truths about American society. In too much of everyday U.S. ideology, "class" is a dirty word, the individual is king, racism is a matter of bad thoughts and not the social order, capitalism is confused with market exchange, and markets never fail, only governments. If we are to learn from the best that American society has to offer—some of which is right here under our collective noses in the San Francisco Bay Area—then we had best learn from its defects, as well.

Donald Trump is not the cause of our distress so much as a symptom of a deeper disease. Let's find a cure together—leftists, liberals, anarchists, libertarians, conservatives, and everyone else who cares about reason, democracy, and justice and the future of this city and country.[1]

★ ★ ★

I want to thank my editor, Sasha Lilley, for insisting that I write a book on the Bay Area and pushing me to make it a critical study that goes to the heart of contemporary capitalism. I greatly appreciate the willingness of Ramsey Kanaan and PM Press to take on the job of publishing the book and to do so with alacrity and enthusiasm. Thanks to everyone at PM for their stellar work: designers, copy editors, printers, and others hidden from my view. A special note of thanks goes to cartographer Molly Roy and graphics specialist Linda Herman for preparing the figures. All graphics and maps were redrawn by Roy and Herman unless specified otherwise.

I am delighted that PM Press accepted my preferred system for footnotes and references, which might be called the "Berkeley System." It combines the best of the Chicago System of footnotes and the Harvard System of a consolidated bibliography, without the former's inclusion of full references in footnotes and the latter's intrusion of citations in the body of the text. The Berkeley System provides references (and comments) at a glance in footnotes along with the convenience of a consolidated bibliography.

Hearty thanks are due to friends who willingly took on the labor of reading drafts of the book and individual chapters, and who were unstinting in their critical evaluations. This honor roll includes Joseph Matthews, Joan Greer, Wendy Brown, Chris Carlsson, Louise Mozingo, Michael Watts, Jim Brook, Matt Williams, Shelley Kessler, Zelda Bronstein, David Loeb, Stacey Murphy, Mike Pyatok, Fern Tiger, and Peter Cohen. The final result is much the better for their attentions.

This book is dedicated to my beloved daughter, Zia Walker-Chinoy, and her companion, Autumn McCloskey, who are also my housemates in a tight property market in Berkeley. They are the ones who will have to live with what the Bay Area and the country are becoming, but they embody the best of today's young people, who give me so much hope for the future, in spite of it all.

---

[1]   I try to use well-known political and economic terms with care, even though they are, by nature, imprecise and loaded with meaning. Capitalism and exploitation will be explained more fully in chapters 1 and 2. Classes will be sorted out in chapter 3 and races in chapter 4. The competing territorial definitions of the Bay Area are confronted in chapters 5 and 7. The ideology of the Tech World is expanded on in chapter 9. Political terms, like "leftist" and "neoliberal," are tackled in chapter 10.

I want to say a sad farewell to our fantastic furry family member of so many years, Alucia the Wonder Poodle, who accompanied me on so many walks, sat patiently through long hours of writing, and helped immeasurably with the hard work of parenting.

Lastly, I salute Joan for believing so fully in this project and its author, and for her radiant presence over morning cups of tea and coffee.

Introduction

THIS BOOK RESTS ON THE CLAIM THAT THE SAN FRANCISCO METROPOLIS IS ONE OF the most important places in the world today. This may sound like a shocking assertion, but it is assuredly true. The Bay Area is rarely listed among the top global cities because it has only one-third the population of monster urban regions like Tokyo. Los Angeles bubbles over with mass entertainment, missiles, and immigrants; New York signifies worldwide finance, corporate headquarters, and high culture; and Shanghai shouts industrialization, consumerism, and boom times of the age of globalization. Instead of such muscular imagery, San Francisco seems a nice little city with pretty views, a bunch of low-slung suburbs around a capacious bay, and perhaps the cultural counterpoint to conventional America. But it is much, much more than that.

The San Francisco metropolis is a place of virtually unparalleled prosperity and dynamism in our time, and its global connections and influence are far out of proportion to its size. As the global heartland of the new information technology, what comes out of the Bay Area affects the daily lives of billions of people. As a growth center, it is one of the most dynamic economies in the world; California is the world's fifth-largest economy and the Bay Area, the mother lode of the Golden State, is in the top twenty. The bay region is one of the prime generators of new wealth on the planet, and home to many of the largest and richest corporations astride the globe. It is, moreover, a place in the vanguard of many political and cultural movements, sending forth ideas that are changing life far beyond its borders. It is, for many, the best hope for capitalism and its promise of human progress and an ever-better future—even as the old complaints have resurfaced about capitalism's gilded elite, corrosion of democracy, and inability to deliver the goods to the mass of humanity, not to mention its danger to the fate of the earth.

I do not go so far as to claim that the Bay Area can stand in for the whole of contemporary capitalism, but it does represent just about the best possible case for it, especially the American version. It is dynamic, extremely rich, and relatively high wage; it is remarkably open to new people and ideas; it is politically and intellectually in continual ferment; and it repeatedly reveals new possibilities of human achievement and social justice. It even nurtures perhaps the most powerful environmental movement on earth. Like London in the eighteenth century, Paris in the nineteenth and Detroit in the early twentieth, it is a city that captures the imagination of an era and embodies the spirit of the times. As the capital of the Digital Age it is a key player in the twenty-first century and a place to be taken very seriously, indeed.

Yet the Bay Area reveals the perils of capitalist prosperity in the midst of a world-beating economy and a digital information revolution. The bay region suffers from a host of persistent problems, such as wildly gyrating growth, shamefully unaffordable housing, ghastly homelessness, a plethora of low-wage work, and severe air pollution. This list of failures is not short. They are not just externalities or passing flaws in an otherwise meritorious system, things that can be easily fixed. On the contrary, they are inseparable parts of the social machinery that delivers the goods, creates the jobs, and grows the city. Or, if you prefer less mechanical metaphors, they are endemic diseases of the body politic which cannot be cured without reconfiguring the economy, the urban system, and the class structure that breeds them.

The Bay Area is capitalism's shining star today, but such good fortune is always marked by its opposite. Capitalism delivers lots of goods, to be sure, but they come packaged in a social order full of nasty surprises. In consequence, contemporary San Francisco generates a kind of schismatic outlook, which this book tries to embrace in all its fullness—meaning that its observations will surely bother both sides of the political spectrum. On one hand, it makes the case for the relative brilliance of the Bay Area; on the other, it roundly denounces the seamy side of success. This is unlikely to please either the upbeat promoters of the wonders of Tech World or the downbeat critics of the current order of a monstrous city devouring its own.

There is no reason to think that trying to wrap one's head around the contradictions of twenty-first-century capitalist urbanism is any easier than the task faced by writers of the past. *A Tale of Two Cities* resonates with the two-faced nature of today's Bay Area as the heartland of the IT revolution. Dickens was grappling with the political hopes raised by the French Revolution and the failed revolutions of 1830 and 1848 during his own lifetime, which had to be set against the heartbreaking results for those caught under the wheels of history. The same was true for Karl Marx and Frederick Engels writing *The Communist Manifesto*, which featured the fundamental contradiction of the new capitalist order: never before had there been greater power to transform the world for human good and never was there a more brutal regime driving the machinery of production and grinding down the working people.

Americans might well regard those times as ancient history, but capitalism and rapid urbanization are still the indelible foundations of modern life. Of course, much has changed, but the vast economic growth, geographic expansion, and modernization of life have been driven by the logic of capital accumulation and led by big cities for several centuries now. Historians, by contrast, might complain that San Francisco cannot hold a candle to the twin capitals of the European world at the height of its powers, London and Paris.

The answer is that the tech revolution of our time is in many ways as earth-shaking as the Industrial Revolution, and the Bay Area is unanimously recognized as the world center of IT; greater San Francisco is the Manchester of the new digital world and the leading edge of capitalist development. Yes, China and its massive cities are in other ways the Great Frontier of today's industrial world, but Chinese factories are frequently manufacturing products designed on the West Coast, while companies like Alibaba grow rich by replicating the digital revolution in Chinese characters. This is an excellent time and place to observe what globalized markets, unceasing technological change, and capital accumulation have unleashed, and there is no reason to think that the contradictions of the capitalist order have been contained.

★   ★   ★

The case for the significance of the Bay Area rests on several pillars. First, it is the global center of information technology—all those smartphones, web searches, and social media that no one can do without today. The tech industry occupies the opening chapter of the book, which lays out the reasons why it is so successful in the bay region. Second, the Bay Area is one of the leading growth centers of the contemporary world economy, and while the tech industry is the principal driver, it is far from alone. The bay economy, like an army, marches on many legs—and its stomach—as shown in chapter 2.

At the same time, the Silicon Gold Rush has brought the region a volcanic eruption of wealth that generates more billionaires per square foot than anywhere else and fills the coffers of some of the world's most valuable corporations. Thanks to this mountain of money, average incomes and wages are higher than in any other big city in the country, if not the world, providing a nice payoff for tech professionals and many less-skilled working people as well. Meanwhile, a racially diverse working class has been created that holds the promise of truly interracial society. These are the subjects of chapters 3 and 4.

Fifth, the bay metropolis is undergoing one of the most dramatic urban makeovers in the country, providing a prime example of how building booms transform city skylines and urban life in the centers of the New Urbanity—at least for those with the money to afford the benefits of cosmopolitanism.

Chapter 5 tackles those trends. At the same time, bay housing markets have skyrocketed to the top of the charts, accompanied by a tsunami of gentrification—which some people regard as an upgrade to the city. That will be dealt with in chapter 6. The Bay Area also offers an excellent case of the growing dominance of the largest urban regions, as it has become the fourth-largest megacity in the United States, redefining itself far beyond the old San Francisco–Oakland core. Chapter 7 tells that story.

An eighth reason why the Bay Area is worth a close look is its legacy as a Green City and the home of the country's—if not the world's—strongest environmental movement in the twentieth century. Chapter 8 notes the progress made in patrolling the impacts of monstrous growth and adapting to the contingencies of climate change. Another claim to fame of the San Francisco region is its role as the Mother Church of the digital age, singing hosannas to the tech revolution and networked society. As chapter 9 argues, this resonates with deep American cultural proclivities and the relentless Futurism of capitalist modernity.

Finally, the Bay Area continues to be a political lodestar of progressivism, wearing its mantle as the Left Coast of America with pride. It has repeatedly authored new initiatives in local politics and altered the terms of national political debate, on everything from combating racism to limiting sugary soda drinks. It continues to show how the finest tendencies of American politics bubble up from below. Chapter 10 wraps up the book's excursion through the "best of the bay."

★   ★   ★

But be not deluded: the preceding highlights of the Bay Area's accomplishments amount to a lovely ride on the tour bus to the Golden Gate, but everyone is going to have to get off and walk through the mean streets of the city in order to see beyond the beautiful views. There they will find a place that despite all its good fortunes thrives on some of the worst tendencies of today's capitalism and mega-urbanism. In the end, this book will not be a paean to prosperity but a warning to those who don't know that Silicon Valley fever is a disease of a social body infected with the overheated pursuit of riches and expansion.

Every theme of the rapturous hymns widely sung to celebrate the Bay Area's blessings has its contrapuntal line and heavy notes of disharmony. The first concerns a tech elite that takes undeserved credit for things that are social products, not the work of individual genius, such as the economies of urban concentration and the progress of technology. This will be the counterpoint in chapter 1.

The second is that the high-growth economy has some very sharp downsides. One is that development is radically uneven geographically, favoring a region like the Bay Area while allowing others, such as Detroit and Stockton, to wither. Another is that the unharnessed growth leads the city on a perilous trajectory over time, a wild roller coaster ride that shakes the place and its people to their core. These are the counterpoints to chapter 2.

A third dissonant theme is the way enrichment feeds the yawning inequality in America, the worst in the developed world today, which maps all too easily onto the nation's class, race, and gender divides. The Bay Area's success undergirds the appalling enrichment of the top 1 percent and largest corporations, confirming the eternal (capitalist) principle that the rich get richer, while the poor can fend for themselves. What appears at first glance to be a high-income, high-wage economy, and thus a fairer place, is anything but. These themes are tackled in chapter 3.

The fate of the working people is a fourth oppositional theme. Millions of people in the Bay Area are doing jobs that are neither High Tech nor glamorous. One of the greatest illusions of the age is that the real producers are the highly educated and entrepreneurs, while the mass of working people are just hangers-on. Chapter 4 looks at the spectrum of jobs and wages and the fate of the emerging working class of color and shows that living in a high-wage/high-cost city is no bed of roses; hence, working people have to get organized and fight for a better life, here as elsewhere.

Meanwhile, urban space is being radically reconfigured by the greater concentration of business and well-paid techies and professionals rushing to live in San Francisco and other urban centers of the region. As a result, a tsunami of displacement has washed people out of their homes and working families have been shuffled off to the far exurbs. We take up these themes, and the fights over urban space that have broken out, in chapter 5.

The sixth peril of prosperity is the absurdly high price of housing, which makes it impossible for so many people to live in the Bay Area. Rents are among the worst in the world and make the region one of the least affordable of cities. Chapter 6 will consider the sources of the housing bubble, including effects of rapid growth, extreme wealth, and loose money on housing markets. Under current arrangements, the bay region can never solve the fundamental "housing question" of the working majority.

A seventh downside of bay urbanization is how it sprawls over the land, leaves workers commuting insufferable distances, and divides people by class and race. With rapid urban transformation, the cards in the deck are reshuffled at a furious rate; and while the game pays off nicely for developers, it repeatedly leaves the least favored households counting their losses. These are the counterthemes in chapter 7.

Another note of discord is the environmental effect of untrammeled city building and the massive energy budget, water consumption, and pollution load of a huge metropolis such as the Bay Area. Despite its past record, the bay region has not come to grips with its own environmental footprint and with global warming and its consequences, from wildfires to rising sea levels. This is dealt with in chapter 8.

Another disquieting fact is the fearsome naiveté in Tech World about the ways the new technologies actually make things worse for ordinary folks by erasing jobs, fomenting falsehood, invading privacy, and diminishing democracy. Tech World may appear open, transparent and liberatory on the surface, but it rests on the hidden power of algorithms and corporations who play by the skewed rules of the game of markets, profit-making, and capital accumulation. These perplexities are taken up in chapter 9.

The final foray into the contradictions of success comes in chapter 10, which considers the political legacy of the Bay Area. Despite its liberal reputation, the region has nurtured some ugly tendencies, and some of that has infused the supposedly progressive politics of the new elite. The city's legacy is being sorely tested today, and, while it remains a vanguard of resistance to the Far Right, it has been compromised in many ways by its own success.

★　★　★

Such a whirlwind tour through the greater San Francisco–San Jose–Oakland metropolitan region necessarily covers a lot of ground. To make it easier for the reader to follow along through ten chapters, a quick road map will help. In the spirit of the tripartite core cities of the Bay Area, the book is divided into three parts. Part I lays the foundation of the political economy of the region: the astonishing growth of the vanguard tech sector in chapter 1, the broader division of labor and uneven development in chapter 2, the enrichment of the elite and widening social divide in chapter 3, and the world of work and workers in chapter 4.

Not surprisingly for a study of an urban region, the book pivots, in Part II, through three chapters on the geography and built environment of the metropolis. The rush to build up the city centers features in chapter 5, the housing bubble and its malignant effects in chapter 6, and the outward explosion of the city-region in chapter 7. Part III of the book, by contrast, shifts from the spatial to the temporal to consider the future prospects of the metropolis, in three regards. Chapter 8 looks at whether the green legacy of the region can survive in the face of so much growth, chapter 9 reflects on the futuristic and sometimes unhinged ideas of the leading thinkers of Tech World, and chapter 10 wraps things up by considering the future of the Bay Area's progressive politics.

In sum, this book is not a boosterish tale of progress so much as a disquisition on the perils of prosperity. That contradiction brings to mind the work of a local and more recent writer than Dickens or Marx. The dark undertones of Lawrence Ferlinghetti's "Pictures of the Gone World" have haunted San Francisco since the 1950s, when the Beats made the city their home and shocked a country that had sunk into an age of deep cultural conservatism after the upheavals of the Depression, New Deal, and Second World War. The poem reproduced here seems remarkably pertinent to the present. The Bay Area is, indeed, a wonderful world if your place in the new Gilded Age is secure; but it looks a lot more hostile if you drive an Uber car through massive traffic jams or cannot find a decent rental within fifty miles of your job. And it appears positively ghastly from the perspective of a homeless person on the sidewalks of San Jose or a young black man facing police armed to the teeth in Oakland. So much has changed since 1950, but the city by the bay is, despite so many good people and ferocious struggle, still far from a shining City on a Hill in terms of equality and social justice, planning and democracy, and private virtue and the public good.

Part I
The Golden Economy
Beneath the Glitter

INTRODUCTION TO PART I

THE BAY AREA HAS JUST EXPERIENCED AN EXTRAORDINARY PERIOD OF PROSPERITY IN the 2010s, the latest of a long series of boom times in the age of High Tech electronics. That roaring economy is the basis for so much that has happened in the region in the last few years, and over the last half century, for better or worse. The state of jobs, incomes, housing, transportation and, moreover, the foundations of everyday life, rest on the way the local economy performs. Hence the opening part of this book is devoted to dissecting the bay's economy and its major limbs: the tech sector that is the leading industry, the sharp ups and downs of growth, the income and wealth generated and their distribution, and the kinds of jobs and the people who do them.

When times are good and the economy is perking along, most people try not to think about it very much beyond their own work and home, spending money and purchases. They treat the economy as a kind of sleeping dragon that is better left undisturbed and rightly consider economics to be dull reading and duller conversational material. Yet at times the beast rears its ugly head and shakes things up, forcing everyone to pay attention. The financial crash of 2008 and subsequent Great Recession was one of those times, as banks crashed, jobs evaporated, and houses were foreclosed. Lots of people took notice, many suffered, and many of those seethed with anger. Then the national economy began a recovery, if painfully slow, and things looked better as employment picked up, incomes rose a bit, and millions acquired smartphones and Facebook pages. Economic amnesia set in, as it so easily does among Americans.

People in the Bay Area are likely to be more forgetful about the last crisis than most, because the region quickly set off on an astonishing new upswing. Business, politicians, and media around the metropolis were upbeat as stock values rose, tax revenues rebounded, and good economic news flooded the airwaves. The atmosphere around the high peaks of High Tech was positively celebratory, especially among those profiting from the good economic times. They might be forgiven their hubris, since the Bay Area's performance was outrunning virtually every other place in the United States, even the world. Nevertheless, not all citizens of the region were impressed by the bounty of the boom and were not genuflecting to the gods of the market for favoring their piece of the planet. They, too, may be forgiven for a lack of enthusiasm for aggregate economic statistics, since so little of the manna from tech heaven fell their way.

The full story of the Bay Area's economic fortunes is not to be found in a recitation of gee-whiz statistics of growth and good times, though they are certainly abundant and must be a part of the urban story. The full picture of the Gone City must include bad fortune with the good—some of it remarkably bad, indeed. The four chapters to come will do both, each of them starting off with good news before tempering it with a strong dose of hard reality. Chapter 2 offers up the best of the boom times, then reminds the reader that one place may prosper while others stagnate and, moreover, every boom is followed by a bust—as the past experience of the Bay Area attests. Chapter 3 turns an eye toward the immense wealth piling up in the bay metropolis, then looks harder at the way that money sticks to a few favored hands but not to millions of others. Lastly, chapter 4 takes up the question of work in the regional economy, who fills the wide array of jobs in the metropolis, and their experiences riding on the undercarriage of the economy; and then it looks at how they are responding to the deprivations in their lives, from low wages to misogyny to police violence.

Assuredly, the central player in the modern spectacle of the Bay Area is information technology (IT), thanks to the bay city's good fortune to be sitting atop the Tech World. As the cornerstone of the regional economy, the tech industry occupies the opening chapter of the book. While the success of the tech sector is hailed far and wide, the Bay Area's importance is too often underreported or its success consigned entirely to Silicon Valley—mistakenly thought of as a place apart. Equally pernicious is the mythology of tech innovation and entrepreneurship in which new ideas and riches grow from the heads of geniuses, rather than out of an edifice built from the base technology, urban geography, collective effort, and the work of many. Furthermore, tech has a dark side beneath the gilded surface, which will begin to be addressed in chapter 1, concerning such matters as monopoly power, super profits, and exploitation of labor.

CHAPTER ONE

Tech City

Beyond the Myth of
Immaculate Innovation

THE SAN FRANCISCO BAY AREA IS THE TECH CAPITAL OF THE WORLD. SILICON VALLEY has long been acknowledged as the most important global center of electronics, and with the arrival of the internet it became the leading force in information technology; in the twenty-first century it quickly grabbed the lead in social media, smartphones, management software, and, most recently, artificial intelligence.[1] The Bay Area has more giant tech corporations, more web portals, more IT start-ups, more venture capital, and a more complex tech ecosystem than anyplace else on earth. As the most thorough study of the region's tech economy concludes, "San Francisco won the information age lottery, becoming the world center of that technological revolution." Or as the *Financial Times* recently put it: "In the last few years, Silicon Valley has strengthened its case as the new center of economic gravity in the United States."[2]

The presence of such a powerful pole of technology and economic force in the midst of the Bay Area colors deeply the social life of the region. One has to confront the tech elephant in the room right from the start. That task begins with simple acknowledgment of the massive size and impact of the industry, and the way Silicon Valley has swallowed its urban host as the tech economy spreads throughout the larger metropolis. It is equally vital to understand how the tech sector operates and what lies behind its astounding

---

1   The definition of "tech" is elastic, but here it refers to an industry that includes, in terms of U.S. Census categories, software and programming, electronic equipment and components, computer systems design, computer wholesalers, data processing and hosting, and semiconductor devices. For the details, see Storper et al. 2015. Medical and health technologies are also important in the Bay Area (see chapter 2) but are left to the side in this chapter.

2   Storper et al. 2015, p. 3. Popper & Dougherty 2015. The Bay Area's stature can be measured by statistics such as the location quotient—the amount of employment or output in a sector in excess of what would be expected if it were proportionate to population—but such figures are legible only to a small audience of scholars. See Storper 2013, Moretti 2012. There are, in any case, no such location quotients on a global scale; one must make do with loosely defined rankings of the world's "best" tech cities. For a typical such listing, see http://www.rankred.com/high-tech-cities/.

success. To do that, it is necessary to cut through a thicket of just-so stories about innovation and entrepreneurship, or where all the wondrous new electronic things come from.[3]

The chapter begins with the noted innovation capacity of the Bay Area and all the things it has produced in recent years, then moves to the world of start-ups that garners so much attention from commentators who repeatedly buff up the triumphant tale of the region as the promised land of entrepreneurship. Beneath the legendary land of feisty little firms lies a deeper channel of capital investment flowing freely into the tech sector, and outside the frame of the story yawns a landscape of monstrously large tech corporations spanning the globe. But that is not all. All those companies and capitalists rest on a solid foundation supported by three pillars: the tech industry's regional cluster in which the whole is greater than the sum of the parts; the social edifice of scientific and technological advance over many years; and the labor of thousands of skilled workers and millions more people working for peanuts.

The Tech Millennium

For the last generation, Silicon Valley has been the acknowledged leader in technical innovation for the United States and in the world. It led the Bay Area past New York in number of patents in the 1990s and now doubles the Big Apple's figure, with about one-sixth of all patents in U.S. cities. No other big city is close (fig. 1.1). The bay region's innovation capacity extends to many other sectors, as well, such as medicine and retail. What comes out of this torrent of new ideas is, first of all, a flood of New Things, devices that have changed personal lives, forms of communication, ways of doing business, the face of modern finance, and much more. And behind that is all the apparatus of the internet, including the software and coding that drives the applications on everything from phones to supercomputers. While it does not all issue from the Bay Area, the new Millennium of information technology rests to a surprising degree on the things imagined, designed, and created in this one spot on the map.

Millions, even billions, of people's lives are touched every day by the products spewing forth from the Bay Area. Start with the smartphone in your pocket, the fruit of Apple and the design genius of Steve Jobs. Whatever phone you own, it is almost surely running on either Apple's iOS or Google's Android operating system and it has likely become a focal point of life if you

---

3   Recent examples of the genre of breathless praise for Bay Area innovation are Johnson
     2012, Isaacson 2015, Weiner 2016.

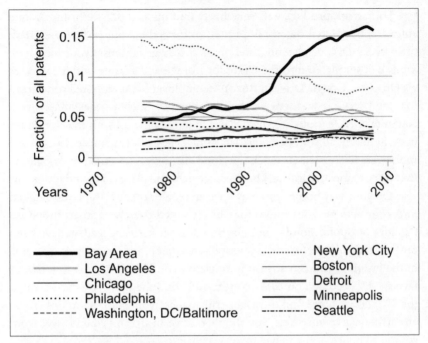

Figure 1.1: Bay Area Lead in Patents

Source: Forman et al. 2016. See also SVIndex 2016, p. 33.

are under fifty. You may use that phone to talk in the old-fashioned way but might just as well do a visual chat via WhatsApp (Facebook) or FaceTime (Apple). You will likely send your friends many texts a day but just as likely open a social media app to share photos or videos via Facebook, Instagram (acquired by Facebook), YouTube (Google), or Snapchat (in LA but started by Stanford grads). You will also likely pick up tweets (Twitter) from your favorite news feed or politician. And how about the nasty commentary you just laughed at on Reddit, the useful health tip you found on Pinterest, or the blog post you read on Tumblr (Yahoo)?

At the office, at home, or in a cafe, you surely work on a personal computer of some kind, whether desktop, laptop, or tablet. All of these use the click and menu system invented at Xerox Parc and perfected by Apple for its Mac line, guided by a mouse, trackpad, or touch screen, similarly innovated in Silicon Valley. As you work, you will plunge into the World Wide Web using a search engine like Google, Yahoo, or Ask on a web browser, such as Chrome (Google) or Safari (Apple) and, along the way, put a question to the largest online encyclopedia, Wikipedia. Your email will likely be housed on Gmail (Google) or Yahoo, and if you have your own website, the url (address) was probably issued through GoDaddy.

Your work product will very likely end up as a pdf file using Adobe software, be printed on an HP printer, or carried in your pocket on a flash drive by SanDisk. As personal and physical storage diminish, your files of all kinds will simply go into the cloud for storage and sharing with coworkers via Dropbox, Google Drive or Box. Your employer has undoubted contracted for cloud services with one of the big providers, such as Salesforce.com or NetSuite/Oracle (both of which claim to have come up with the cloud idea first). Similarly, all your personal data—messages, photos, music, videos, and more—are likely to be stored in the cloud via Apple, Facebook, or Google, so that you can move seamlessly between devices and places in your daily circuit.

On your way home, you may have an iPod or other MP3 player plugged into your ears, or your music may be streamed over your smartphone via Pandora or SoundCloud—though those former industry leaders have been outflanked by Apple, Sweden's Spotify, Sirius Radio, and other rivals. At home in the evening, you can stream a movie on Netflix or Hulu or watch your favorite TV recorded on TiVo. Netflix and YouTube may have even created the TV shows, films, and musical performances you enjoy. Should there be an earthquake or hurricane, you should receive an alert on your devices from your local police or fire department via Nixle.

The movie animations and special effects were probably created at Pixar or Industrial Light & Magic studios, founded by Steve Jobs and George Lucas. If you are a gamer, there are games to play, like Madden NFL from Electronic Arts, using graphics processing from Nvidia, the leader in virtual reality simulations. When you're on the run, there are also gaming apps for your phone by Zynga, Openfeint and Kabam, or you can pursue online gaming via Twitch (Amazon). Or if you are into the latest in virtual reality, put on a headset from Oculus Rift (Facebook).

If you feel like some exercise, you can go walking or jogging while monitoring your fitness with a Fitbit device or Apple Watch. If you're going to a party, you may have been invited through Eventbrite. If you are heading out on the town, you will probably check out bar and restaurant reviews on Yelp or get tickets for a show or ballgame through StubHub. If you need directions, refer to a Google or Apple map and get there by hailing a ride through Uber or Lyft. Today that ride will have a driver, but soon there will be self-driving vehicles guided by technologies from Waymo, Embark, or Starsky Electronics—using lidar sensors by Cruise or Velodyne.

If you are planning a business trip or vacation, you will quite likely seek out a short-term apartment or home rental on Airbnb. At home, work, the ballgame, or almost anywhere, you can order food through the app of a bevy of firms with names like Munchery, DoorDash, Grubhub, UberEats, and

Caviar. Or if you need a contractor, cleaner, or repair services, dial up Task Rabbit (IKEA) to find someone nearby. And, finally, you can pay for any of these using PayPal, Square, or ApplePay.

If you're a boss, you can hire through online listings such as Glassdoor and Craigslist, and to seek out contractors for special projects you can go through the massive hiring exchange at Odesk. You could well pay your employees with software from Oracle, track your customers with the help of Salesforce.com, and take payments through Stripe. For optimizing the performance of your distributed networks, you will want the help of Riverbed Technology. If you need to parse big data on customers and competitors, you could turn to Palantir, Quantcast, Boomerang, or Cloudera, using the Hadoop number-crunching platform. Your professional workers are very likely listed on LinkedIn (Microsoft) and use it to seek out the expertise of colleagues—including advice about seeking a better job!

If you like buying and selling through online exchanges, then you will certainly have used the marketplace giants, eBay and Craigslist. If you are rich enough, you will enjoy driving in your snazzy Tesla electric car. If you have the wealth to be an investor, you can buy stocks through Schwab, buy a mutual fund from BlackRock, or invest in a customized fund from Franklin-Templeton. If you need a loan, you can turn to the online bank Lending Club. Or if you are launching a new project, you might try crowdfunding through Indiegogo, Gigawatt, or a dozen others. When taxes come due, a good option is for online tax calculation and submission is Intuit.

★ ★ ★

The brave new world of goods and services delivered by the Bay Area's High Tech complex is impressive, but this cascade of innovations is more than a flurry of shooting stars across the consumer sky. It is a galaxy of commodities held together by the gravitational force of the internet, pivoting on Silicon Valley. The invention of World Wide Web transformed the internet into the basic integument of the electronic life, especially once Google's revolutionary search engine unlocked the infinite possibilities of the web. In the 1990s, the Bay Area became the center of the newly networked world, and no place was better positioned to take advantage of the internet: more wiring, more websites and more web users than anywhere else, on top of the fact that it produced more of the brains of the system in terms of switches, servers, and software.[4]

---

4   On the origins of the internet, see Abbate 1999, Hafner & Lyon 2006, Keen 2015. On wiring and websites, see Zook 2005.

All the devices of the networked life run on integrated circuits first developed at pioneer Silicon Valley companies, and most CPUs are still made by Intel, AMD, or Cypress Semiconductor. The routers and switches carrying all the traffic on the internet were developed companies like Cisco Systems, Juniper Networks, or Hewlett-Packard. Key switches that link devices through to the cloud are made by Arista and Brocade. The cloud itself is composed of hundreds of server farms, each housing thousands of computer servers; Google and Apple are two of the four biggest operators of server farms and builders of servers. Chip production is still done with the aid of equipment provided by Applied Materials. And many of these systems are protected by Silicon Valley companies such as Quantum backups and Symantec antivirus.

It is hard to overstate the way the internet has transformed modern life in the twenty-first century and, at the same time, the web came to be focused on the Bay Area. Today local companies' web portals dominate the World Wide Web, with seven of the world's top ten sites. Similarly, Bay Area firms occupy nine of the top ten positions in social networking in the United States (and most countries outside of China and India).

Top Ten Web Portals in the World, 2017[5]

1. Google
2. YouTube
3. Facebook
4. Baidu
5. Wikipedia
6. Yahoo
7. Reddit
8. Google India
9. QQ
10. Twitter

Top Ten Social Networking Sites in the United States, 2017[6]

1. Facebook
2. YouTube
3. Twitter
4. Reddit
5. Pinterest

---

5   http://www.alexa.com/topsites.
6   https://www.dreamgrow.com/wp-content/uploads/2017/08/top-10-social-networking-sites-by-market-share-of-visits.png.

6. Instagram
7. Tumblr (NYC)
8. LinkedIn
9. Yahoo Answers
10. Yelp

The impact of Bay Area tech firms and their hardware, software, and networks is felt far and wide. As of 2016, Apple had sold over 700 million iPhones (indeed, more people owned mobile phones than had toilets). Google handled 3.5 billion searches per day and YouTube showed its videos to 128 million monthly unique users. LinkedIn claimed over 400 million members and Twitter over 300 million active users, with Instagram running neck and neck with its elder cousin. eBay had 160 million registered users and Netflix has passed 100 million subscribers. By 2017, Facebook had over 2 billion active users around the world and its WhatsApp subsidiary was handling the chats of over a billion people.

The New New Thing
The phenomenon of tech start-ups is an essential part of the aura of electronics and the internet in the contemporary business world, and nowhere more so than in the Bay Area. If you haven't launched a start-up, you don't count as one of tech's true champions. The masters of the electronics universe are forever in search of the newest New Thing. Some start as whimsy, some with hopes to change the world, and others as practical spinoffs from research, but in the end all of them are there to make money. Tech is a thoroughly commercial enterprise.

The mythology of the plucky tech entrepreneur has diffused around the world, becoming a key element in the capitalist dream world of today. It combines the technical brilliance to dream up a new idea, the business acumen to see a viable opportunity, and the chutzpah to set out on your own. Joseph Schumpeter made the figure of the entrepreneur a staple of economic ideology, but the electronic age has turned his idea into a kind of modern Miracle Play. The tech industry has added a new twist to the old myth: Silicon Valley ethics demand that good entrepreneurs fail before they succeed, burnishing the image of the intrepid explorer on the frontiers of progress. While success is prized above all, learning by failure is part of the well-tempered entrepreneurial CV.[7]

---

7   Schumpeter 1950, García Martínez 2016, Smith 2016.

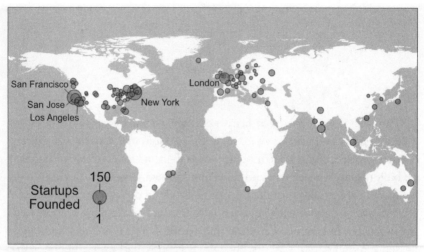

Figure 1.2: Map of Start-Ups in World Cities, 2012

Source: Zara Matheson, Martin Prosperity Institute, Toronto.

The Bay Area is acknowledged as the world's hotspot for tech start-ups (fig. 1.2). Start-ups are, indeed, a big part of the process of innovation in the tech sector. They are a compact way of giving a new idea life by immediately wrapping it in a business package and setting it loose on the market. Many good business ideas fail to be recognized within large corporations because of bureaucratic defenses of existing priorities. But good innovations can be fragile; they are like viruses, bare bits of code that cannot long survive on their own and need the warm embrace of a living cell to reproduce. The start-up is the germ cell of a viable tech company.

But if the point is ultimately moneymaking, the new companies will need outside finance to survive. To get a new company up and running requires huge infusions of cash, whether from venture capitalists, angel investors, crowdsourcing, bank loans, private equity firms, pension funds, or insurance companies. It may be possible to start small, but very soon the infant company will require more capital to make new hires, rent more space, and expand computing power. There will be new injections of cash and still greater borrowing, even as revenues grow, and then more again to keep on rising—or stave off creditors. In short, start-ups are less like nimble birds taking wing than 747s lumbering down the runway with thousands of gallons of jet fuel aboard, trying to gain lift-off speed.

Like experiments in flight, launching start-ups is inherently risky. Some schemes never get off the ground, others fail for lack of a substantial market, and others achieve instant popularity but have a hard time making their services pay. The fate of a start-up depends, in contemporary lingo, on the "burn

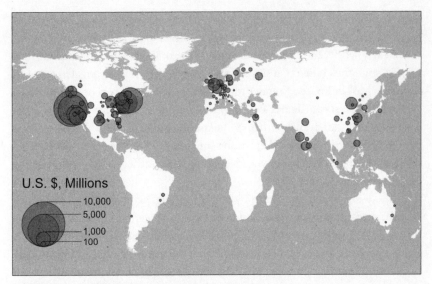

Figure 1.3: Map of Global Venture Capital Investment, 2012
Source: Zara Matheson, Martin Prosperity Institute, Toronto.

rate" at which they eat up capital and their ability to generate a "gross revenue" stream. Profits are mostly imaginary for several years, in almost every case. Because of this, tech companies and other start-ups are thrown immediately into the arms of financiers and locked in a mad dance with the world of finance.[8]

A key asset of the Bay Area is its capacity to finance start-ups. No other place in the country or across the world has such abundant funds of this kind or as large a number of venture firms. The volume of venture investment today is impressive, amounting to tens of billions of dollars, with the Bay Area holding 40 percent of the nation's venture capital pool (fig. 1.3). Venture capitalists such as Vinod Khosla, John Doerr, and Marc Andreessen are legendary figures in the Silicon Valley. Why are they here? Because this is where the action is: like-minded investors, new ideas swirling in the air, and a bevy of eager entrepreneurs.

★ ★ ★

---

8   Floum 2016b. Andrew Smith is too optimistic when he writes that start-ups are more numerous today because "the internet has demolished barriers to entering many businesses. Where once a start-up had to raise capital to pay for hardware, software, marketing, and so on, now they store files in the cloud, use open-source software, distribute through the App Store, and use Twitter for customer service and Google and Facebook for marketing" (2016, p. 9).

How to finance a start-up? In the ideal case, a couple of Stanford students, Sergey Brin and Larry Page, come up with a clever algorithm for web searches that clearly works and becomes the talk of the university computing community. Despite the choice of a silly name, Google, they find an angel investor in Andy Bechtolsheim, the founder of Sun Microsystems. Six months after that, venture capitalists at Kleiner Perkins jump on board, and five years after that the company goes public with an initial public offering (IPO) that raises over $20 billion on the stock market. In the meantime, it figures out how to raise revenues for its free services via advertising, using other clever algorithms to target users and advertisers.

Many entrepreneurs begin by bootstrapping, scraping together money from friends, family, houses, and credit cards. Recently, crowdfunding has opened up another avenue, triggered by the success of San Francisco's Indiegogo and New York's Kickstarter, which famously financed Oculus Rift. In addition, supportive investors have created warehouse incubators with cheap space to rent for potential entrepreneurs, like Hacker Dojo. But if an idea has legs, it needs to attract serious investment, and this means engaging the big players in the game, the venture capitalists, to provide money in the millions of dollars.

Venture capital firms are crucial because they consolidate funds from distant investors and put the money into carefully scrutinized investments. They have their feet on the ground of Silicon Valley and plenty of local knowledge of what is likely to work and what isn't. Even more important, they know people through their networks, making it possible to put together management teams to help innocent young entrepreneurs get their ideas operational and on the market, teams that include CEOs, CFOs, and lawyers to handle incorporations, patents, and other legal necessities. Venture capitalists also open doors to supplemental financing from angel investors and ultimately to IPOs and acquisitions. There's more to venture capitalism than simply investing and risk-taking.[9]

Angel investors have become a more popular mode of financing of late. Such "angels" are wealthy individuals, corporations, or institutions looking for high returns and willing to back unconventional people and ideas. Some such investors have joined together to create groups such as Band of Angels, Tribe of Angels, and Investors' Circle. In the past, angels were usually called in by venture capitalists to keep a new company growing, but with the rampant success stories in tech start-ups after 2010, thousands of angels—often techies

---

9   Kenney & Florida 2000, Kenney & Patton 2005, Stross 2006.

who had already struck it rich—set out hunting for opportunities on their own, and a kind of angel-investor bandwagon developed.[10]

Once a start-up is firmly established and has the expectation of making profits, its owners may decide to take the leap into an IPO. Becoming a public corporation has the advantage of raising huge quantities of money quickly on the stock markets, as well as raising the firm's profile in the world of business. But some entrepreneurs opt for the shortcut of a buyout by a large corporation such as Oracle or Facebook or by a private equity fund like Vista Equity or Thomas Bravo. This makes sense where the firm's product is a minor one that fits well into a big company's plans. It has the added advantage of turning the founders into instant millionaires—exemplified by the $2 billion take for the founders of YouTube when Google acquired it in 2006. Or it may be a respectable way out for an unprofitable start-up, of which there are many.

★   ★   ★

In talking about the IT revolution, the first thing that comes to mind is how the new technology is transforming the global economy and everyday life for billions of people. But the flip side of the tech economy is that it is all about the money. This was less so in the postwar era, when Cold War military imperatives ruled and Silicon Valley was dominated by engineers more interested in circuitry than capital. But once electronics went commercial in the PC and internet decade, money began to take over. An axiomatic shift took place with the spectacular public offering of Netscape in 1995, which hit nearly $3 billion with its IPO, followed by Google's IPO in 1997, which made geniuses of new billionaires such as Jim Clark, Marc Andreessen, and John Doerr. The "Netscape moment" launched a frenzied search for the new New Thing. No one was more vocal in declaring the digital Millennium than venture capitalist Doerr, a major backer of internet start-ups, who famously declared Silicon Valley to be the greatest legal wealth generator in the history of the world and said the tech revolution in Silicon Valley had unleashed a New Economy for the digital age.[11]

But the start-up system can go astray when blind ambition meets blinkered capital. Many an enterprising entrepreneur has convinced a venture fund or angel investor of the virtue of a bad idea, and the number of such mistakes increases exponentially as an upswing accelerates, stories of wondrous riches circulate, and more and more investors are looking for the big score. The financial crowd becomes a mob careening down Wall Street, Sand Hill Road,

10   Center for Venture Research, University of New Hampshire.
11   On the engineering culture, see Levy 1984, Saxenian 1994. On the Netscape moment, see Clark 2000, Lewis 2000. For a critical assessment, Walker 2006, Keen 2015.

and Montgomery Street, and soon bad investments, unpayable loans, and lame start-ups proliferate.

The dot-com era is the prime example of this. After the Netscape and Google launches, dot-com start-ups became more and more fanciful. A flashy website that attracted lots of viewers ("eyeballs" in the talk of the time) was enough to set investors hearts on fire. Start-up fever drove some people quite mad, with companies handing out stock to landlords in lieu of rent and burning through barrels of cash throwing lavish parties before ever having earned a dollar. The virtual life of the internet collided with the virtual valuations of finance capitalists and blew up spectacularly in 2000.[12]

When the dot-com bubble blew up, the Bay Area and its wild start-up culture came in for a good deal of well-deserved criticism for too much money chasing too many premature ideas. Yet the New Economy never died; it was reborn in a new suite of technologies. What stuck was the monetized culture of tech, the amazing riches it can produce, and the influence that money can buy. Meanwhile, the innovation machine kept rolling, and new breakthroughs arose from the wreckage.

The best start-ups are more often than not those launched in recessions or early in the business cycle when investors are fewer and cast a more critical eye on new ideas. After the washout had sobered up investors, a new group of stars began to appear in the Bay Area firmament with the arrival of Facebook in 2004. That launch was followed by Twitter in 2007, Airbnb in 2008, and Uber in 2009, though the fallout from the financial debacle of 2008 meant that no one was going overboard on these newbies, as yet. After 2010 the fireworks started going off again, and money was again the king of the digital realm.[13]

★ ★ ★

The turning point, comparable to the "Netscape moment" was the long-awaited IPO of Facebook in 2012, which netted $16 billion. A whole new generation of Bay Area start-ups became wildly successful in garnering funds. So much capital poured into start-ups that the "unicorn" era was born—the insider term for a start-up amassing over $1 billion in capital. At the peak of the start-up mania in 2015, the number of the magical beasts had leapt from a handful to over 150 worldwide, with the Bay Area in the vanguard: among the top ten were Airbnb, Dropbox, Palantir, and Pinterest (plus SpaceX in LA, started by Silicon

---

12 On the dot-com era, see Wolff 1998, Cassidy 2012. The dot-coms are the best remembered aspect of the financial bubble of the 1990s, but much bigger was the massive overinvestment in the underlying networks of fiber-optics, copper wire, and microwave transmitters. Walker 2006.

13 Cassidy 2012, García Martínez 2016.

Valley's Elon Musk), and at the pinnacle was San Francisco's Uber, the highest-valued start-up of all time at over $50 billion. Talk about virtual reality![14]

Top Ten Unicorns in 2015
(in billions)[15]

Uber $51	Flipkart $15
Xiaomi $46	Didi Kuandi $15
Airbnb $25.5	SpaceX $12
Palantir $20	Pinterest $11
Snapchat $16	Dropbox $10

By mid-2015, it was apparent that start-up values were overinflated and investors were getting nervous. There was a marked fall-off in venture capital investments and new start-ups the following year (fig. 1.4). That meant, in turn, a dearth of new unicorns and a stalled market for IPOs. After five heady years, the Bay Area start-up engine lost momentum. At the same time, there was no abrupt implosion, as in 2000, because overall stock valuations for tech companies were not dramatically out of line with profitability as they were in the 1990s and there was still a lot of investible capital looking for outlet. In fact, tech stocks as a whole kept rising over the next couple years, passing up the peak of 1999—leading to debate in the business press over whether there was or was not a new tech bubble.[16] One certainly has to wonder if a new "pets.com" moment has been reached when hundreds of millions are pouring in to back start-up Wag Labs, whose app connects dog owners and dog walkers.

In the end, the ideology of plucky start-ups runs into the hard realities of commerce and capital, and the new New Things that make the biggest splash are not so much those with the best ideas as those that generate instant riches because they attract the most capital when finance is flowing freely. When investors get nervous, start-up activity retreats and the number of start-ups falls.

Behemoths by the Bay

The myth of the entrepreneur and immaculate innovation hits another snag in the form of the mammoth corporations astride the Bay Area tech economy. Corporate giants begin as small firms with new ideas but go from minnows to whales in a generation. Meanwhile, the freethinking entrepreneurs who

---

14   Lee 2016b, Waters & Hook 2016.
15   https://www.cbinsights.com/research-unicorn-companies.
16   Lee 2015, 2016a, Waters 2015, Lien 2016, de la Merced 2016, Platt 2017, Zaleski 2017.

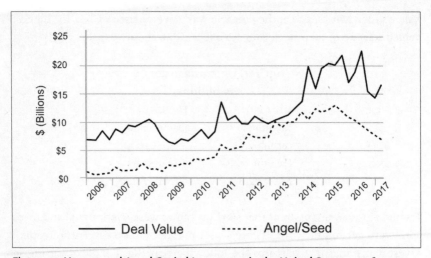

Figure 1.4: Venture and Angel Capital Investment in the United States, 2006–2017

Source: https://pitchbook.com/news/
articles/16-charts-that-illustrate-current-us-venture-capital-trends.

create successful start-ups eventually turn into corporate capitalists. Some hang on to their countercultural images by wearing tennis shoes and T-shirts into middle age. Steve Jobs was the master of image, both his own and his products', and always announced his latest triumph in jeans and a black turtleneck. Mark Zuckerberg has stepped out of the shadows to become more of a public figure alongside his wife, Priscilla Chan, yet continues to dress down in jeans and Ts. On the other hand, many of the tech executives who have been around longer come to look their part, such as Cisco's John Chambers and Oracle's Larry Ellison—who is occasionally glimpsed astride his America's Cup racing yacht.[17]

The success of Bay Area technologies has bred a succession of gargantuan corporations over the years, whose names are instantly recognized far and wide: Apple, Google, Facebook, Hewlett-Packard, Intel, and dozens more. Put them together with the remaining nontech headquarters in the metropolis and the Bay Area registers as one of the great corporate centers of the world. The Fortune 500 counts the Bay Area as home to thirty-one of the five hundred largest public corporations in the United States in 2016 (see list below). That ranks the Bay Area second only to New York among U.S.

---

17 The myth of the virtuous capitalist as small business owner who deserves the fruit of his labor goes back to John Locke's theory of property. But, as Karl Marx showed, every owner who starts with his/her own money and hard work soon has to hire helpers, whose surplus above wages helps to feed the firm's profits, and over time the work of the capitalist becomes a tiny fraction of the labor and surplus of the enterprise.

metropolitan areas. Greater New York houses eighty-eight of the Fortune 500, making it the unchallenged business center in the country. Chicago, third in population, is neck and neck with the Bay Area with thirty headquarters, followed by Houston and Dallas–Fort Worth with twenty-six and twenty-one, respectively; Los Angeles follows with twenty and Greater Boston, just behind metropolitan San Francisco in the population tables, only ten. On an international scale, the Bay Area ranks sixth in corporate headquarters, behind New York, London, Tokyo, Beijing, and Seoul.[18]

The rising number of Bay Area companies in the Fortune 500 tracks the increasing clout of electronics in the industrial mix of the American economy. In 1980, the bay region could claim sixteen of the top corporations in the United States, half of which were in the tech sector, but the largest tech firm at the time was Hewlett-Packard at only #150. The Bay Area's corporate count had surged to twenty-seven by 2000, half still in tech, and HP had risen to #13. By 2015, the total had inched up to thirty-one and Apple was in the top five. Some tech companies like HP and Intel have slipped in the rankings, while Yahoo has been dismantled and sold to Verizon—a lesson that the capitalist economy is forever churned by new inventions, competition, error, and folly. Nevertheless, the biggest tech companies have grown ever more enormous, and they now sit atop the capitalist heap as measured by stock value. The five largest companies in the world by 2017 were in the tech sector, the so-called FANG group of Apple, Google, and Facebook, plus Seattle's Microsoft and Amazon, worth $3.5 trillion at the end of 2017.[19]

Bay Area Corporations in the Fortune 500 (2015)[20]

3	Chevron	San Ramon	*Petroleum & Refining*
5	Apple	Cupertino	*Computers & Consumer Electronics*
11	McKesson	San Francisco	*Med & Health Wholesaler*
19	HP	Palo Alto	*Computers & Equipment*

---

18 A list compiled by City-Data.com reverses the Bay Area and Chicago numbers. http://www.city-data.com/forum/city-vs-city/2381480-fortune-500-2015-combined-statistical-area.html.

19 Waters 2016a, Wolf 2017. On the changing rank of all Bay Area firms, see Braithwaite 2016b. For a visualization of the value of S&P 500 companies, see http://finviz.com/map.ashx?t=sec. The term FANG was first used to refer to Facebook, Apple, Netflix, and Google (Alphabet), later adding the Seattle companies.

20 Corporate size can be measured by revenues, assets, employment, profits, and stock market value, which do not all line up. *Fortune* uses sales, which does not favor tech companies. For the annual lists, see fortune.com/fortune500/

30	Wells Fargo	San Francisco	*Commercial Banking*
40	Google	Mountain View	*Internet Services*
52	Intel	Santa Clara	*Semiconductors & Components*
60	Cisco Systems	San Jose	*Network & Comms Equipment*
81	Oracle	Redwood City	*Computer Software & Business Services*
84	Safeway	Pleasanton	*Food and Drug Stores*
118	Gilead Sciences	Foster City	*Pharmaceuticals*
172	eBay	San Jose	*Internet Services and Retailing*
182	PG&E	San Francisco	*Gas and Electric Utility*
188	Gap	San Francisco	*Retail Apparel*
220	Synnex	San Francisco	*Retail Apparel*
238	Visa	Foster City	*Financial Data Services*
242	Facebook	Menlo Park	*Internet Services and Social Media*
269	Ross Stores	Dublin	*Specialty Retailers: Apparel*
319	Applied Materials	Santa Clara	*Semiconductors & Components*
335	Franklin Resources	San Mateo	*Securities*
352	Core-Mark Holding	South San Francisco	*Wholesalers: Food and Grocery*
389	Agilent Technos	Santa Clara	*Scientific, Photo & Control Equipment*
405	Symantec	Mountain View	*Computer Software*
408	SanDisk	Milpitas	*Semiconductors & Components*
428	NetApp	Sunnyvale	*Computer Peripherals*
432	Sanmina	San Jose	*Semiconductors & Components*
435	Charles Schwab	San Francisco	*Securities*
469	Clorox	Oakland	*Household and Personal Products*
473	Adv Micro Devices	Sunnyvale	*Semiconductors & Components*
474	Netflix	Los Gatos	*Movie Streaming*
483	Salesforce.com	San Francisco	*Computer Software & Business Services*

★ ★ ★

Contrary to the mythology of start-ups, giant companies play an important role in the process of innovation. Large corporations are themselves major innovators with huge in-house R&D operations that churn out new products and improvements to old ones. Hewlett-Packard, for example, has been a leader at different times in radar tubes, large computers, laptops, and laser printers, and today the firm is leading the way in 3-D printing. Apple began

with one of the first personal computers, but its greatest hits came a generation later with iPods, iPads, and iPhones. Google went beyond search algorithms to develop the Android smartphone system and is a leader in artificial
intelligence.

At the same time, big companies reward innovators by buying up start-
ups and integrating them into larger product lines. The Bay Area leads the
way in tech acquisitions-cum-mergers, just as it does in start-ups (fig. 1.2).
The tech whales swallow start-ups like krill. Indeed, most tech start-ups
are born in the hope of a quick euthanasia via acquisition. Cisco Systems
set the pattern for corporate growth by acquisition in the 1990s, when
it ingested some seventy-five firms (a figure that has doubled since then,
including CloudLock to move into security systems). Oracle has gobbled
up well over one hundred companies, including PeopleSoft, Siebel, and Sun
Microsystems. Facebook inhaled Instagram, WhatsApp, and Oculus Rift
among its fifty or so buyouts. Even hard-pressed Yahoo bought over fifty
companies, 2010–15, including Tumblr and BrightRoll. The champion whale
is undoubtedly Google, which first ate YouTube and subsequently acquired
over two hundred competitors—eventually renaming itself as a holding
company, aptly christened as the meaningless "Alphabet." Even notoriously
self-contained Apple Corporation is looking toward acquisitions as a way to
dispose of $200 billion in loose cash and Intel has bought smaller companies
such as Nervana and Altera to better position its processor chips for the
world of artificial intelligence.[21]

Despite the reputation of the tech industry for innovation, it still makes
money in rather old-fashioned ways. On the one hand are the companies who
make solid things like phones, cars, and laptops. In this regard, Apple, Tesla,
HP, and others are heirs to capitalism's well-known ability to produce goods
and get consumers to buy them. They have been immensely successful at
commercializing electronic innovations in attractive and useful products. In
addition, the revenues of such companies are inflated by the enthusiasm of
users for cutting-edge stuff; purveyors of the new not only sell more products
but earn surplus profits on trendy items until the thrill wears off—at which
time they introduce a new model. The clothing industry is the epitome of this
phenomenon, followed closely by automakers, who have lured consumers
to pay extra for new styles from tailfins to SUVs. Apple's fortunes have been

---

21   Data are from Wikipedia entries on these companies—caveat emptor. On Intel, see Lohr
      2017.

hugely enhanced by the frenzy over the iPhone, less than a decade old but accounting for 60 percent of company revenues in 2016.[22]

A different sort of moneymaking is at work in the arena of soft tech products, such as social media and web searches. While there is a similar process of collective desire at work, in which everyone wants to join the party and be in the know, the open nature of the internet has meant that very few people want to pay for access. This has plagued many a start-up, and even mighty Google and Facebook struggled with feeble revenues in the beginning. Then they figured out the trick of inserting advertising on their pages and selling user data for marketing purposes. After that, billions of dollars were thrown at the new media, which are poised to pass up television in total advertising revenues. Google gets 90 percent of its revenue from advertising and Google and Facebook together hogged 75 percent of new digital advertising in 2015. The fact that advertising has been a staple of capitalism for well over a century takes some of the glow off the tech sector as a bastion of innovation. Websites have become electronic billboards.[23]

★ ★ ★

As a result of their prodigious growth, Google, Facebook, and Apple have become astoundingly rich and powerful corporations—the peak players of twenty-first-century capitalism in the same way that A&P, Sears Roebuck, and General Motors were at various times in the twentieth century. This raises a very old question of monopoly power that has always plagued the economists' dream world of perfect competition. Americans have been wrestling with the problem of monopolistic industries for over a century, and there is no reason to think that tech companies are any more virtuous than the railroads, Sugar Trust, or Standard Oil in the past.[24]

Google absolutely dominates internet search, for example, with over 80 percent of the traffic. Facebook is the heart of the social media universe, with 40 percent of site visits, followed closely by YouTube (Google). The irony is that Netscape and Google were the instruments used to break the previous monopoly of Microsoft over computer software and its attempt to corner the internet with its Explorer search engine. Microsoft, with help from Apple and other innovators, had previously brought the postwar giant, IBM, to its knees by replacing big computers with PCs and distributed networks. There is concern in tech circles that a place dominated by such huge corporations

---

22 Braithwaite 2016b. On surplus profit accruing to new products, see Schumpeter 1950.
23 Popper & Dougherty 2015, Garrahan 2016, García Martínez 2016.
24 Kolko 1963, White 2011.

will lose its competitive edge and innovation will suffer, in the same manner as Detroit in the mid-twentieth century.[25]

But to the rest of society, the most troubling question is not lack of innovation but the power that monopolistic corporations wield over everyone else. To what extent are the Tech Moguls extracting high prices (rents) from users? This is not immediately apparent because so many of their products are excellent and their services appear to be "free" on first glance. But the big companies systematically eliminate competitors by keeping an iron grip on intellectual property rights in key technologies. They also gobble up new rivals to nip competitors in the bud and extend their sway over emerging realms of High Tech, from videos to virtual reality. American governments have been noticeably laggard in pulling the reins in on the tech industry, but the European Union has fined Google, Facebook, and Microsoft billions for monopolistic practices.[26]

Even more troubling is the enormous power that the big tech corporations wield over everyone's personal life, public information, and the future of democracy. They hold data on the most intimate aspects of private life, daily activity, and personal finances, which they manipulate and share in ways unknown. They facilitate communication and sharing, but also the worst kinds of intrusion, harassment, and trolling. They have unprecedented sway over news and communications, but their systems are being used and abused by nefarious actors around the world to sow discord, misinformation, and anger, and generally degrade public life and civil discourse. Disillusionment with the lords of the Tech World and the new information technology has been exploding in the last few years, taking the shine off of the image of once shining knights of liberty, equality, and information for all. That will require a much-longer discussion in chapter 9.

The Industrial Geography of Tech

The Bay Area's tech firms, both large and small, rest on a much-broader foundation than their own ideas, products, and management. This is true in two dimensions. First is the global span of the tech industry, the world's largest by some measures. The Bay Area does not stand alone. A typical laptop, for example, is assembled from hundreds of parts made in dozens of locales around the world. Note that the geography of electronics is dominated by

---

25 Sobel 1983, Freiberger & Swaine 1984, Lewis 2000, Clark 2000. On the potential slowdown of innovation, Storper et al. 2015, p. 225. On Silicon Valley going the way of Detroit, see Keen 2018.
26 Baker 2016, Finley 2017, Keen 2018.

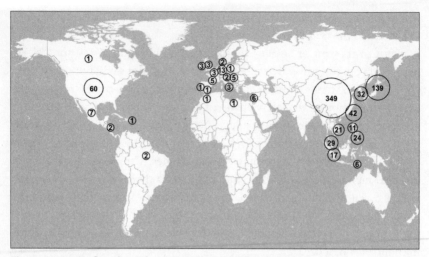

Figure 1.5: Map of Apple's iPhone Suppliers Worldwide

Source: Nitin Maurya, University of Texas, Dallas. http://www.slideshare.net/NitinMaurya5/
apple-supply-chain-analysis-57942469.

the dense links between East Asia and the west coast of North America, with
Europe as a decided outlier.

The second dimension is how global networks of High Tech are hung on
a framework erected by the largest corporations and their far-flung subsidiaries and subcontractors. The first companies to build assembly plants across the
Pacific in Southeast Asia were from Silicon Valley (National Semiconductor
and Hewlett-Packard). The Bay Area's large companies are fully global operations that integrate enormous systems of production sites, design centers,
sales outlets, and trade networks. Apple's global empire, for example, reaches
into dozens of countries (fig. 1.5).

It would be a mistake, however, to attribute globalization of tech to the
actions of international corporations alone. This was the dominant view
among economic geographers for a long time, while economists clung to
the even older notion that globalism is a matter chiefly of free trade among
nations. But economic geographers of the last generation have shown that
a third force is at work in building globalized systems of trade, production,
and corporate linkages: the collective power of industrial districts and urban
agglomerations.[27]

The big corporations have learned that the best locales for their factories
are in regional clusters of activity, and the best means of supplying components is via homegrown subcontractors embedded in cities rich in electronics

27 On the globalization of urban agglomeration, see Scott 1998.

firms, such as Shenzhen and Kuala Lumpur. Contract manufacturers such as Foxconn have become some the world's largest industrial producers, as are component makers such as Hitachi in Japan and LG in Korea (who themselves have spread dozens of factories around East Asia). By using the production capacities of East Asia (and to some extent Mexico), Bay Area tech companies are freed up to focus on the front-end functions of research, design, and commercialization. Apple does not make iPhones and HP does not make printers; they dream up new designs and operating software, work out the engineering, and then sell the finished products through the matrix of retail outlets in the wealthy countries of the Global North.[28]

The economic map of global capitalism consists of a large number of industrial districts and cities tied together through dense relations of trade, contracting, communications, management, knowledge, institutions, and cultures. Important economies of scale and scope are achieved through close interaction, specialization, and mutuality in centers of production, and such economies operate at even larger geographic scales of operation, regional, national, trans-Pacific, and global. Such high-level abstractions can be better understood if we come back to the Bay Area and its homegrown tech cluster.

★ ★ ★

The tech industry of the Bay Area is more than eye-catching products, fast-rising start-ups and megacorporations. It is a rich business ecosystem consisting of thousands of firms, large and small, interacting on a daily basis, undertaking a host of mutually supporting specialization and tied together by innumerable threads of a personal and contractual nature. It is what economic geographers call an industrial district or industrial cluster (and what previous generations of urban geographers called "agglomeration economies"). Indeed, Silicon Valley is the most famous of all industrial districts, repeatedly studied for its amazing fabric of business relations.

Cut the electronics ecosystem one way and you see a horizontal array of products and producers. This way it looks like a forest made up of many groves, each representing a sector such as telecommunications, computing, software, security, or social media, with many trees in every grove, each one marking a different company, and, finally, many specific product lines branching off every tree. It's a dense woodland, and the branches often overlap.

Cut the ecosystem another way and you see a vertical array of suppliers reaching deep into the soil to nurture the final product makers. The

---

28 Gareffi & Korzeniewicz 1994, Milburg & Winkler 2013, and especially Sturgeon 2003.

latter—usually the "brand name" firms—rely on the products of a wide array of lesser-known companies within the district. These might be makers of servers, microprocessors, and disk drives or of operations software, security systems and marketing applications. Behind those, in turn, lie many more circuit designers, chip producers and machine makers. The presence of so many buyers allows providers of highly specialized products to achieve economies of scale even with small batch and custom production.[29]

The forest is even richer than that revealed by those first two cuts. There is the internet substrate: companies building and installing the internet and microwave communications systems, microprocessor switches, and server farms supporting it all. Then there is a dense understory of supportive services: law firms specializing in contracts, incorporation, and intellectual property rights; venture capitalists and other financial wizards; and hosts of accountants, management consultancies, and other business services. Then there are the research operations within firms, in the universities, and in government, and, finally, the builders and property companies who put up factories and fit them out to order.

Furthermore, these entities do not just do business with each other; they are part of a relational ecology of social networks. They have overlapping directorates, managers, and workers who move from one to another firm, and personal connections through professional societies and extramural activities. The rather passive term "networking" does not do justice to the buzz of activity involved in making connections and making them work for people and organizations. As one study puts it, no other place in the country has such a wealth of "deal-makers" weaving their webs among the many vital parts of the ecosystem. In the same vein, the most comprehensive analysis of the Bay Area's tech economy concludes that while the advantages of a head start and clustering are vital to the region's success, "the decisive catalyst was the emergence of new organization forms and types of actors in the Bay Area" that have kept the industry from becoming sclerotic.[30]

Industrial districts are dynamic because the whole array of firms are solving practical problems of design, production, finance, and management

---

29 On industrial districts, see Scott & Storper 1986, Scott 1988, Porter 1998, Storper 1997, 2013, Duranton et al. 2010, Moretti 2012. If the organic metaphor, ecosystem, seems too loose, be assured that there are button-down economic models for the transactional networks and resulting external economies of scale that make industrial districts more productive than the sum of their parts.

30 Storper et al. 2015, p. 94, 199. On the Bay Area's networks and dealmakers, see Saxenian 1994, Kenney & Patton 2006, Feldman & Zoller 2012, Padgett & Powell 2012a, Kenney & Mowery 2014. On regional networks in general, see Storper 1997, Padgett & Powell 2012b, Benner & Pastor 2015, Kemeny et al. 2016.

every day, and doing so by working with each other, sharing ideas, and making and breaking relations. They are ecosystems of innovation, which indices such as R&D spending, patents pending, and formal contracts do not adequately capture. Their dynamism is more like tropical forests teeming with unexpected encounters and evolutionary mutations, veritable hothouses of experimentation and learning. Moreover, it you watch the ecosystem over time, you see all manner of fresh growth, new sprouts, and vines twining from tree to tree, plus the dead and dying, which leave a deep layer of detritus from past glories on which the greenery above can feed.

Industrial districts, like ecologies, are fundamentally open systems resting on a substrate of shared values and mutual trust.[31] In Silicon Valley, in particular, one of the articles of faith of participants is the belief in opensource software and open access to the internet. Such industrial cultures are reinforced by bringing thousands of people together in annual gatherings of the tribes such as the Apple Worldwide Developers Conference, the Game Developers Conference, and Salesforce.com's Dreamforce Conference—the modern equivalents of World's Fairs—or even revels such as Burning Man in the Nevada desert. Journals such as *Slate*, *Salon*, and *Macworld* published out of San Francisco have played a complementary role in building solidarity among creators and users of tech systems.

Finally, industrial districts achieve a measure of coordination from the presence of overarching industry associations. The Bay Area has some particularly well-connected business groups, such as the Silicon Valley Manufacturers Group, Silicon Valley Joint Venture, and the Bay Area Council (based in San Francisco). These are not only powerful lobbyists and publicists for big business but also organizations that build bridges among a wide range of firms and civic groups in the pursuit of regional development and that have substantial agendas in support of tech in education, research, and government.[32]

The model of industrial districts contrasts with the old standard model of industrialization, with its straight line from the steam engine to the factory to Fordism and the modern corporation. The latter captured everyone's imagination for a century but ultimately proved unable to explain why so many big corporations ran into trouble by the 1970s, how the New Economy of electronics worked, and why the open, diverse economies of cities have proved so central to capitalist development and so resilient to this day. But the industrial

---

31 On the importance such implicit values and cultures of mutuality, see Saxenian 1994, Storper 1997.

32 On the dense networks of Bay Area organizations and their favorable outlook on tech development, see Storper et al. 2015, chapters 7 and 8.

district model, too, leaves important things unsaid regarding technology and labor, to which we now turn.

The Technological Base

Something vital is missing from both the picture of entrepreneurial spirit and the framework of the industrial district, without which one cannot make sense of the immense success of electronics and information technology in the Bay Area and around the world. That missing piece is the technological foundation for the era of electronics and the internet. Electronics, like the automobile before it and machining before that, has become what a leading economic historian calls "the base technology" of the age. It permeates almost every other sector and its powers multiply exponentially over time.[33]

Capitalism has been harnessing the powers of science, engineering, and industry since the dawn of the modern era, and the resulting permanent industrial revolution has transformed the world and the human prospect. The electronic wonders of today are witness to the ongoing march of technical progress. Cotton textiles, machinery, and metals were at the core of the nineteenth century's achievements, while vehicles, assembly lines, and chemicals led the way in the twentieth century. The "High Tech" of today is no more than the latest episode in a long-running series of epochal advances in the capacity to understand, manipulate, and control nature. None of this implies that modern technology is all to the good, only that it is a powerful force developed for the benefit of capital.[34]

The electronics age may well deserve the title of a "new industrial revolution" because it has propelled modern society into domains beyond the reach of mechanical devices and chemical reactions. No previous technological base had the inherent capacity to offer up email, the smartphone, or Wikipedia. The achievement of making electrons dance to a human tune has unleashed a remarkable fund of possibilities for communications, digital computing, and automatic controls. The Bay Area tech economy is not the work of a few bright entrepreneurs but the result of wave after wave of innovation generated by the electronics revolution.

Electronics began around 1900 when tinkerers working on radio communications figured out how to alter electric current by means of electric current. The invention of the vacuum tube brought the dawn of the age of electronics, and radio grew to be a primary means of communication in

---

33 Rosenberg 1976, Womack et al. 1990.
34 On the "long industrial revolution," see, e.g., Hounshell 1984, Beniger 1986.

the first half of the twentieth century. Television, sonar, and radar joined the field in midcentury. The arrival of the silicon chip in the 1950s allowed more and more circuitry to be put on a thumbnail and the power of electronics increased at an astonishing rate, captured by Moore's law on the rapid doubling of computing power. By the dawn of the twenty-first century, the internet and its web of cables and microwave transmitters linked together computers around the world; then the smartphone gave billions of people a supercomputer that could fit in their pocket, to be used for everything from social chitchat to financial speculation.

The much-ballyhooed entrepreneurs and start-ups of today are but a thin veneer on the long arc of the electronics age. Their success rests on the accomplishments of many thousands, if not millions, of contributors to the technology of electronics over the last century. That capacity cannot simply be reduced to the discoveries of modern science and men in white coats; it is the collective achievement of a long history of research, industry, and labor, as are all modern technologies. The Bay Area played a vital part in the development of electronics for a century before the story could be told on Wikipedia, shared on Facebook, or tweeted on Twitter.

Silicon Valley has been spawning start-up electronics firms for over a century. Palo Alto's Federal Telegraph Company was founded in 1908 by Cyril Elwell, who had gained the U.S. patent rights to the arc transmitter, and he soon recruited Lee de Forest, who invented the vacuum tube—the cornerstone of all electronics. They put the Bay Area in the vanguard of the budding radio industry. Eitel-McCullough and Litton Industries of San Carlos made further advances in power tubes and tube production in the 1920s. Even more advanced tubes were developed for special effects in films by Hewlett and Packard in the late 1930s and for microwave transmission by the Varian brothers, who then went on to produce giant tubes for radar and sonar.[35]

The arrival in Palo Alto of William Shockley, co-inventor of the transistor at Bell Labs in New Jersey, introduced solid-state electronics to the Bay Area in the mid-1950s. Shockley Semiconductor recruited several of the best new graduates of U.S. engineering schools, who soon fled from the insufferable Shockley to set up their own company, Fairchild Semiconductor. That group, led by Robert Noyce, invented the integrated circuit in 1960 and began to spin off into their own firms, such as Intel and Advanced Micro Devices (AMD). They were soon joined by New York financiers such as Thomas Perkins, who

---

35   On the early history of Silicon Valley, see Sturgeon 2000, Lécuyer 2005, Leslie 1̩

collaborated with Fairchild veterans Eugene Kleiner and Don Valentine to establish the first West Coast venture capital firms.[36]

The invention of the microprocessor at Intel in 1971 led the next wave of advances in computing and communications and made possible the growing commercialization of the Valley's products, such as the first electronic games by Atari. By the 1980s, the ever-smaller, ever more powerful chips spawned the personal computer and the switches and servers driving distributed networks, allowing Silicon Valley to nurture start-ups such as Apple, Cisco, and 3Com. The moniker Silicon Valley became attached to the South Bay at the time, and its leading companies like Intel and Hewlett-Packard became known far and wide. Already apparent was the way Silicon Valley was reinventing itself with every new decade.[37]

Any narrative of heated innovation by engineers and businessmen needs to be tempered by plunging the triumph of the market in a cold bath of governmental assistance. Wartime purchases of radar and sonar tubes launched Hewlett-Packard and Varian. The development of digital computing after the war was almost entirely a project of the Department of Defense (DoD), and Cold War purchases kept the industry afloat right through the 1960s. Sales of early microprocessors and software were mostly to the aerospace industry funded by DoD. In addition, the growth of the research capacity in electronics at Stanford and Berkeley was largely funded by the National Science Foundation, a wartime creation, and other agencies of the federal government. The original internet was a DoD project called Arpanet to support war-related and interuniversity communication.[38]

The Age of the Internet launched the Bay Area onto a whole new level of mastery in the world of tech. The 1990s saw the triumph of the World Wide Web and the search engines that made it widely usable—AltaVista, Excite, and Yahoo in the early to mid-1990s, and Google launching closer to the end of the decade. Suddenly, the Bay Area became the center of the newly networked world, and no place was better positioned to take advantage of the internet: more wiring, more websites and more web users than anywhere else, on top of the fact that it produced more of the brains of the system in terms of switches, servers, and software. The test flight of the exuberant new era in the 1990s began to wobble badly in the stratosphere of the "dot-com" bubble, and the mission blew up in 2000 (see chapter 2). Nonetheless, a great

---

36 Caddes 1986, Saxenian 1994, Lécuyer 2005.
37 For the hype on early Silicon Valley see Freiberger & Swaine 1984, Levy 1984, Rogers & Larsen 1984.
38 Lowen 1997, Leslie 1993, 2000, Lécuyer 2005.

deal had been learned along the way, and some key technologies had been put in place.[39]

The twenty-first century saw three key developments coming out of the Bay Area that expanded the reach of the networked world and virtual life exponentially. The first was the meteoric rise of Google, leaving the first generation of search engines behind; Google's link-tracking algorithm was the epoch-making technology that allowed the company to shoulder aside Microsoft as the Octopus of the electronics age. Then Apple, guided by the design genius of Steve Jobs, dazzled the world with an array of new hardware—iMac, iPod, iTouch, iPhone, and iPad—backed up by superb operating systems. The third leg of the Tech Millennium was social media, led by Facebook, Twitter, and Instagram. These simple platforms allowed millions of people to link up easily to share thoughts, photos and their lives, hitting a billion participants by 2010.[40]

By the mid-2010s, the hottest new developments in High Tech were virtual and enhanced reality, self-driving automobiles and trucks, and artificial intelligence (AI) and machine learning. By then the networked life had been raised to a new level by linking every device through the internet, backed up by the massive, dispersed storage infrastructure of the cloud. The advent of home assistants, smart buildings, and even smart cities was ushering in the so-called "internet of things," which may reach unimaginable heights if the potential of 3-D printing, AI, and robotics are fully realized.[41]

Behind all the advances of the internet era lies the explosive growth of microwave networks, optical fiber cables, switches, and server farms on which the World Wide Web runs. An essential term missing from the discussion so far, and from the ideology of immaculate innovation, is "infrastructure." The internet is one of the key infrastructures of our time, along with highways, airports, and railways. The immense infrastructure of the modern economy is often unseen and little appreciated, as with electric power grids or city water supplies and sewage systems. Large-scale infrastructure is absolutely vital to the agglomeration effects that underlie urban growth, as geographers have insisted for a century.[42]

---

39 On the invention of the web and the 1990s, see Clark 2000, Hafner & Lyons 2006, Keen 2015, Isaacson 2015.

40 On Google, see Levy 2011, Hillis et al. 2012. On Apple, see Isaacson 2011, 2015. On Facebook, see Mezrich 2009, Kirkpatrick 2010.

41 On the new frontiers of transport, AI, and networking, see Glassman 2017, Stewart 2017, Cixin 2016.

42 Weber 1929, Puga 2010, Storper 2013.

The economies of sharing infrastructure are just as important to urban economics such as that of the Bay Area as the market interactions among private firms emphasized by the industrial district model. Urban infrastructure, moreover, is not a passive bunch of pipes, roadways, and wires, but a set of modern technologies that have been discovered and implemented through long years of science, hard work, and investment. The internet is a case in point, but no more so than the systems that bring clean water into the city so that everyone does not die of cholera or typhoid. Furthermore, collective infrastructure is, more often than not, provided by government, not the private market and entrepreneurial capitalists. Here again, the internet proves the point, since it was financed and encouraged for decades by the Department of Defense. Lastly, one should add another key of infrastructure to the account, that is, the buildings left by previous generations of urban dwellers and producers, which are particularly useful for nurturing start-ups, as seen clearly in the case of San Francisco.[43]

Yet one final piece of the puzzle of Bay Area tech success remains out of place: the labor force that does the work of the industry. Without the people, the picture of remains one of immaculate innovation by entrepreneurs, corporations, industrial districts, and technology on a roll.

The Labor of Tech

The goal, up to this point, has been to put the heroic entrepreneur, the start-up, and the process of innovation into a larger social context that includes global corporations, industrial districts, and a fecund base technology. All of those are collective achievements, built up over many decades. Nevertheless, the narrative still suffers from myopia as to the foundations of Tech World. You can't see the people in the silicon forest for the all the trees. What makes the Bay Area's tech sector work is ultimately the indelible element of all human enterprise, labor. The essential substrate of all industry and the economy of cities is the people who work there.[44]

---

43   Graham 2010, Schoenberger & Walker 2017.
44   A fundamental insight of classical political economy was that human labor is at the root of economic production; human beings are the initiators of all production, create the firms, and do the work of running it all. Yes, machines and chemicals, biota, fossil fuels, etc. work alongside human labor, but people design the machines, put the chemicals to work, oversee the planting, and create the knowledge behind every such act of production. Human beings always work with and on nature—materials, physical and chemical forces, and living things—to create the things that they want. This is no less true of electronics than agriculture. Smith, Ricardo, and Marx had this elemental fact of economic life right a long time ago.

Therefore, a key indicator of the importance of the Bay Area in the world of IT is the number and concentration of tech jobs in the metropolitan region. Tech is, in many regards, the largest- and fastest-growing arena of employment in the United States, since IT reaches into so many other economic domains; a loose assessment puts the number of tech jobs across all industries at twenty-five million. But the tech sector itself has no more than four to five million, and published figures can vary widely depending on the definition of the industry. Of those, roughly 10 percent, or 450,000, are in the Bay Area, which vies with New York for the top spot in aggregate tech employment. Moreover, the concentration of tech jobs in the Bay Area is still the highest of any big city at about 10 percent of total employment, with Silicon Valley leading the way at almost 30 percent of jobs in Santa Clara County.[45]

What do all these tech workers do? For simplicity, they can be divided into two groups: a higher rung of people skilled in the ways of computing and engineering (often loosely referred to as "techies") and a lower rung of people doing more well-known, common tasks, from receptionists to custodians ("ordinary workers"). Not everyone in the tech industry does "tech" work, strictly defined—far from it—and the definition of who works inside the industry and who is outside is controversial.

Starting with the first group, they are generally the ones who come up with product ideas, new software applications, better designs and engineering blueprints, and the best solutions for coding problems. Most of those workers are well educated and highly skilled, and are employed, to a significant degree, in nonroutine, creative work.[46] They occupy various kinds of office space, much of it unconventional, on the theory that such freedom of movement inspires greater collegiality and creativity. Some, however, work in very conventional offices and cubicles. Because this segment of the tech labor force is so important, some observers have gone so far as to claim that the so-called "creatives" are the principle drivers of modern urban growth. This theory of the "creative class" has the virtue that it emphasizes labor above all other sources of economic dynamism; but it goes too far and suffers from three fatal flaws.[47]

---

45 The most sophisticated assessment of the industry and its employment, using a tighter definition of tech, yielded a figure of over a quarter-million workers in IT, or about 10 percent, of the regional labor force in 2010. Storper et al. 2015, pp. 35–36. For more recent but less precise figures, see Hathaway 2012, Soergel 2017, Guedim 2017.

46 Storper et al. 2015, pp. 44–45, show that tech work is high in nonroutine tasks and is particularly so in the Bay Area. For more on skill and job quality, see chapter 4.

47 Florida 2002, 2005, Glaeser 2010. The principle example of the theory is the Bay Area.

The first error is geographic. It says that where the creatives go, economic growth will follow. The young, educated, and restless are drawn to cities by their love of cosmopolitan culture, which generates a pool of creative people, after which economic growth naturally follows. The best predictor of which cities draw creatives is said to be the number of gay people found there. This sounds very enlightened, but it is a rather "queer" theory of economic geography. If urbanity were essential to the tech industry, why was it so markedly absent from the flat plains of Silicon Valley for so long? The engineers sought by postwar tech firms were quite happy with the campus-like landscapes of Stanford Industrial Park and low-rise suburban living in Palo Alto. In fact, tech workers only flocked in large numbers to San Francisco as the demand for their labor took off in the late 1990s dot-com boom and again after 2010 (see also chapter 5).[48]

A second failure of the theory is that it gets the economic causality backwards. A mere gathering of tribes of creatives will not do much if there is no economy to work in. Growth does not arise from spontaneous combustion; there needs to be a fire already burning before adding new fuel. In cases where large numbers of creatives are drawn to a place, as with the Bay Area, the prime motivator is labor demand by firms already there. Of course, the addition of new labor keeps the flames burning brightly, and the greater the overall supply and its depth of skills, the more economies of scale in the system. Plus some will come up with fruitful ideas and found new start-ups that expand labor demand further. Nonetheless, while skilled workers may be fuel for a hot economy, there has to be a wider economic structure for them to work in: industrial districts, capital investors, and corporations.[49]

A third flaw of the theory of the creative class is that it glosses over the actual labor process of skilled workers and ignores the goals of the companies that employ them. While work tasks for favored workers are not closely defined, a lot of what passes for creative work consists of tedious coding, sales pitches, and meetings. While programmers, designers, and engineers may not be closely monitored, they are still subject to the discipline of work teams, supervisors, project deadlines, and performance reviews. In addition, they are immersed in a culture of overwork that leads to long hours at the office, even sleeping under their desks. The lovely open spaces in which they pass the day—replete with free food and beer, workout rooms, and even child-care—are also inducements to stay put and work longer. The open format also

---

48 On engineers and campus settings, see Mozingo 2011.
49 Storper 2013 provides the best analysis of why labor follows demand from growing firms rather than attracting them, in contrast to Florida and Glaeser.

allows supervisors and fellow workers to survey their movements and make sure the putative free time is not too extensive. All this pays nice dividends to the companies' owners.[50]

Most of the skilled techies are highly paid, to be sure (see chapter 3), but they, too, are exploited, just like all workers under capitalism. Their work yields more in output for the tech firms than what they are paid by their employers; if it were not so, they would be fired. Hence, a major source of the immense profits piling up in corporate hands in the tech sector is the extra work done by the techies. Their role should neither be romanticized nor excoriated; they are simply an important slice of the overall tech labor force. Moreover, they are very narrow slice in the sense that the skilled tech workforce is largely white and male, with a dollop of Indian and Chinese. The makeup of the labor force will be a major theme in chapter 4.

★　★　★

Another problem with the theory of the creative class is that it leaves out the majority of workers in the industry and their contribution to the collective enterprise. The tech industry may be the pinnacle of modern industrial sophistication, innovation, and profitability, but it still rests on a mountain of ordinary labor. A glaring absence from virtually all discussions of Tech World, whether the creative class, start-ups, or the industrial district, is the workforce beyond the engineers, managers, and other upper-end workers. The prevailing view of the tech economy is top-heavy, to say the least.

That aporia distorts the perception of what makes an industry tick and who should get the credit for its achievements. Put bluntly, the tech industry could not function without a host of people doing manual, routine, and unglamorous jobs. There are thousands who labor in machine shops, cleanrooms, warehouses, kitchens, custodial closets, and delivery trucks. Getting clear data on the percentage of workers in these categories is difficult, especially because a large percentage of supporting labor in areas such as food, security, cleaning, and landscaping is subcontracted to outside firms, which diminishes the numbers counted officially as part of the "tech sector." One study calls this "Tech's Invisible Workforce" and shows that subcontracted labor in Silicon Valley has been growing over the last twenty-five years, half again as fast as direct employment in the industry. What is more, most of the outworkers are people of color, Filipino, Vietnamese, and Latino (see chapter 4).[51]

50　Hayes 1989, Kantor & Streitfeld 2015, García Martínez 2016, Lyons 2017.
51　Silicon Valley Rising 2016, p. 4.

A last and telling oversight is the failure to mention all the labor done in and for the tech industry overseas. The global reach of the Bay Area's tech giants is motivated by one thing above all: access to cheap labor. Much of that labor works in huge factories, warehouses, and ships under deplorable conditions and at low pay. The case of the factory workers making iPhones at Foxconn's factories in Shenzhen is notorious; so many leapt to their death that the company installed nets outside dormitory windows. This is not to say that the tech corporations are not interested in skilled labor forces abroad and in the hard-earned competence of supplier firms and their associated industrial districts; but those, too, come at a discount. This is true, for example, of the giant software office-factories in Bangalore, India. The Bay Area is floating on a tsunami of surplus value produced around the world, then siphoned back to the favored metropolitan center by its global-straddling companies (for more on capital flows, see chapter 2).[52]

Conclusion

The Bay Area's tech industry is the envy of the world today in the conventional terms that define capitalist success. One sign has been the desperate efforts by policy makers to gestate local tech clusters through tax breaks, new universities, and science parks, and by cultural investments to attract the creative class. Everyone parades their local tech habitat under such silly names as Silicon Glen (Scotland), Silicon Roundabout (London), and Silicon Beach (San Diego), which would be comical if it weren't so serious to those places chasing the capitalist dream of growth through tech. Almost all of these efforts end up stillborn because they do not have the kind of industry clusters, venture capital pool, skilled labor force, and history of technological development boasted by the Bay Area.[53]

It is fine to register astonishment at the achievements of the Bay Area tech inventions, its profusion of start-ups and its globe-straddling corporations. But the essential thing is not to be taken in by the mythology of immaculate innovation, in which clever people, feisty entrepreneurs, and a dose of venture capital spontaneously combust to produce a wealth of new products, firms, and profits. This self-serving view of the masters of Tech World has become the prevailing ideology of capitalism today, as shown by this declaration in *Forbes Magazine*: "The majority of the people in the [400 richest] list are risk-takers and who have started businesses. . . . They're running businesses,

---

52 On Apple's global labor force, see Merchant 2017. On the offshoring of work, see, e.g., Castree et al. 2005, Bardhan 2009, Milberg & Winker 2013.

53 Massey et al. 1992, Storper 2013. For a map of such efforts around the world, see Kirk & Oremus 2013.

taking risks and compensated for that risk."[54] This is a pretty shaky formulation, one that attributes to individuals far more than their rightful share of the credit for the wealth they have accumulated. As this chapter has shown, the success of the region rests on broader foundations, which are too often missing from the story of Silicon Valley fever: industrial clustering and urban agglomeration, the base technology of electronics nurtured in the region, and the labor of thousands of skilled workers and millions of others.

But the story of the Bay Area does not end here. The economy of the region consists of much more than the tech sector, its success comes at a cost to other places less fortunate, and every period of rapid growth is followed by sharp downturns, as will be discussed chapter 2. Following that, the implications of the Bay Area's immense enrichment, led by tech, will be the subject of chapter 3, which will consider the ugly facts of inequality, class, and race and say more about the sources of that wealth. Then chapter 4 will take up the world of work in and out of tech, and the lives of the workers who do it. That will wrap up the first part of the book.

---

54 David Lincoln, Wealth-X's director of research, quoted at http://www.wealthx.com/articles/2011/top-10-cities-for-ultra-high-net-worth-individuals/.

CHAPTER TWO

Boom Town

Winning and Losing
the Economic Lottery

IN THE SECOND DECADE OF THE MILLENNIUM, THE BAY AREA'S BOOMING ECONOMY flashed like a supernova in the economic firmament of global capitalism. The urban region has been one of the hottest economies in the United States in recent years, and the United States has, in turn, done better than either Europe or Japan. Even China's amazing growth of the first decade of the twenty-first century slowed to single digits in the second, and countries dependent on China's insatiable appetite for natural resources have fared poorly. Meanwhile, cities such as Dubai and Lagos cooled off as the world's oil and gas economy suffered in the 2010s from overproduction and sagging demand.[1]

What does it mean to be one of the hot spots of modern capitalist system? This chapter begins to answer that question by looking at the regional economy as a whole, from what is called a "macroeconomic" perspective. The first section lays out the conventional figures on economic growth and prosperity, which are undoubtedly impressive; the gross numbers show the Bay Area not just doing well, but performing better than almost anywhere else in terms of gross domestic product and total income—even average income.

But the assessment of regional success cannot stop with a short-term slice of eye-catching figures. For one thing, the aggregate sources of growth and prosperity need to be teased out, as is done in the second section, to show that there is more to the bay economy than its leading sector, High Tech. The bay region embraces a diversified field of industry and government activities that are also quite dynamic.

The third section considers the uneven geography of macroeconomic growth and what the success of one place means for others less fortunate. The Bay Area is one of a host of large cities that are outgrowing the rest of the country and the world; but the good fortune of those cities cannot be

---

1   Floum 2016a. For details, see the World Economic Outlook reports from the International Monetary Fund (IMF) at http://www.imf.org/external/pubs/ft/weo/.

separated from the putative failure of the rest, because they are linked by a system of integrated markets, labor migration, and capital flows.

To wrap up the discussion of the macroeconomy, the last section of the chapter looks at the unevenness of growth through the lens of time—that is, the boom-and-bust pattern that characterizes all capitalist economies. The Bay Area has had a particularly rough ride in recent times. The dynamism of capitalism is not made manifest only in rapid innovation and growth, but equally in the way market economies periodically go off the rails. One cannot praise the good times without getting ready for the bad ones to come.

To put things in terms that contemporary Californians will understand—given that their lottery is now one of the biggest in the world—winning the big gamble on tech has paid off for the Bay Area. But is that the end of it? First, the diverse economic base of the metropolis cannot be overlooked; the region has not put all its bets on one horse. Second, where there are winners of the lottery, there are also losers; big cities like the Bay Area grow at the expense of other places, either by sins of commission or omission, and the plight of the losers can come back to haunt, as Trump's election victory showed. Third, instability is the name of the game in the capitalist casino, so winning today means losing when the boom blows up and the good times blow over.

The High-Flying Economy

The greater San Francisco Bay Area[2] is one of the largest regional economies in the United States. It hit a total output and income (gross domestic product, or GDP) of about $780 billion dollars in 2017. This placed it third among urban regions behind only New York and Los Angeles. If the Bay Area were a state, it would rank sixth behind Illinois. If it were a country, it would rank among the top twenty, just ahead of the Netherlands, Turkey, and Taiwan. The bay region has lately been the primary engine of growth for the state of California—despite greater Los Angeles being twice as large—and California, with a GDP of $2.5 trillion, became the sixth-largest economy in the world in 2015, passing France and Brazil and behind only the United States, China, Japan, Germany, and Britain.[3]

---

2   The Bay Area metropolis is now defined by the U.S. Census as twelve counties, but misdefinition of the urban region means that the size of the bay regional economy is frequently underestimated in popular, business, and academic discourse. For more about the definition of the urban region, see chapter 7.

3   Figures in current dollars. Bay region GDP data from the U.S. Bureau of Economic Analysis (bea.gov). Comparative data on CSAs found at http://www.city-data.com/forum/city-vs-city/2452114-2014-combined-statistical-area-gdp-released.html. Lists of state and country GDPs from Wikipedia (based on U.S. Census and national censuses). For typical misestimates (using smaller city units), see http://www.skyscrapercity.com/showthread.php?t=1489306 and http://www.worldatlas.com/articles/10-richest-cities-in-the-us.html.

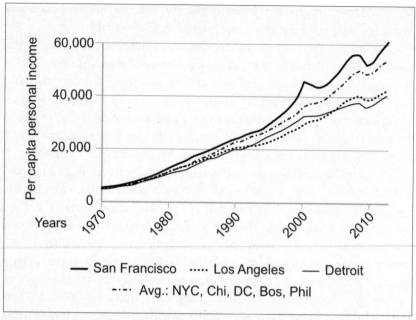

Figure 2.1: Growth of Personal Income in Major U.S. Cities
Source: Storper *et al.* 2015, p. 7.

The rate of economic growth in the Bay Area since 2010, at the low point of the Great Recession, has been astonishing. In the first five years of the decade, total output of the twelve-county region grew from approximately $550 to $750 billion, a leap of more than a third. It was still growing by 5.6 percent in 2016, double the rate for California and the rest of the country. From 2010 to 2015, the region added 553,000 jobs to a base of 3,785,300, a gain of over 15 percent. By 2013 it had regained all the jobs lost in the recession, and from 2013 to 2015, *Forbes* rated the Bay Area at the top of their list of Best Cities for Jobs.[4]

The bay economy has not just delivered the goods and jobs, but has brought with it a huge rise in aggregate income: profits to firms, personal income and household income, and tax revenues. Income per person rose from around $60,000 in 2010 to over $86,000 in 2015, the highest among large cities in the United States and among the top two or three worldwide, and the same holds if measured by household. The Bay Area contains the five richest counties in California and two of the richest in the United States (Marin and Santa Clara). Furthermore, it has outperformed every metropolis in the

---

4   Data on employment from California Economic Development Department website, http://www.labormarketinfo.edd.ca.gov. For the Forbes, list see Kotkin & Shires 2016.

country in growth of income per capita *over the last half century*, even though it already ranked first in 1970 (fig. 2.1).[5]

Without question, fate has smiled on the Bay Area. The region has been riding the high road of growth and its aggregate performance has been matched by only a handful of cities around the world, such as Singapore, Seoul, and Oslo. This is as good as it gets in terms of capitalist economic development and a source of envy from those sitting elsewhere. But tell that to a random sample of Bay Area residents and you will get some surprisingly negative responses. The conventional numbers may shine brightly, but they barely begin to tell the tale of what has transpired during the boom times by the bay.[6]

Rising average income does not lift all boats. Lots of jobs does not necessarily mean lots of good jobs with good wages. As shall be seen in chapter 3, the distribution of income matters, inequality is growing, and so is the class divide. Then chapter 4 will show what the plethora of jobs means in terms of who does what work, the welfare of working families, and the struggle to keep up in the country's most expensive city. But before getting to the incomes and lives of people, it is important to look at the dynamics of growth at the aggregate, macroeconomic, level in the rest of this chapter.

Strength in Numbers

There is a Bay Area economy beyond tech, which is conveniently forgotten by most outside observers and business cheerleaders. As one economist notes, "There are footprints of all major industry sectors in the Bay Area, but tech is the big kahuna."[7] The problem with such a formulation is that everything else gets short shrift. The reality is that the economies of great urban regions are creatures of many parts; like those of nations, they embrace a multiplicity of industries, companies, and governments. And as with IT, other sectors benefit

---

5   Income figures are for the greater Bay Area (twelve-county) from Storper et al. 2015, pp. 5–11. For similar results from the 1990s, see Galbraith & Hale 2008. City income rankings based on smaller metro units can be quite misleading; Hartford, CT, is very rich, but is comparable to Marin County not the Bay Area or New York. For bad examples, see http://www.bloomberg.com/news/articles/2015-11-05/these-are-the-20-richest-cities-in-america; http://www.worldatlas.com/articles/10-richest-cities-in-the-us.html; https://en.wikipedia.org/wiki/Highest-income_metropolitan_statistical_areas_in_the_United_States; http://www.insidermonkey.com/blog/20-richest-cities-in-the-world-by-2015-gdp-per-capita-376402/.

6   For examples of bay envy, see Madrick 2001, Hardaway 2011, Jaruzelski 2014. The prosperity of the Bay Area prompted a major study of the region by researchers at UCLA, because greater Los Angeles has lagged so badly behind its California cousin in per capita income growth. Storper et al. 2015.

7   Micah Weinberg quoted in Floum 2016a.

from urban agglomeration economies (see chapter 1). Some of these lead the way and some follow, but all are important in sustaining a viable economy in terms of employment, income, and growth. This section fills out the picture behind the Bay Area's success.

If tech constitutes 10 percent of Bay Area employment, that still leaves 90 percent to be accounted for. There are different ways of cutting up the remainder. The state employment department offers this list of the ten main sectoral clusters in the nine-county region: hospitality and tourism, information technology, health care, education retail, business services, professional and technical services, construction, social services, and finance and real estate. The Association of Bay Area Governments (ABAG) offers a somewhat different compilation, including government and dropping social services, and divides the ten sectors into two groups. The five biggest sectors are hospitality and tourism, health and education, business and professional services, manufacturing, and government; the second-tier sectors are construction, information technology, finance, retail and wholesale, transport, and utilities. The relative growth of employment in the top sectors over the last quarter century is telling (fig. 2.2).

One eye-catching fact from these figures is the size and growth of leisure and hospitality, which includes restaurants, hotels, entertainment, and tourism. Another is the size of the essential services of health care and education, and, moreover, how fast health care has grown in recent times (education's big growth came after the Second World War). More surprising is how big a share of the regional economy is still represented by manufacture, wholesale, transport, and retail—the basic goods producing, handling, and selling operations of modern industrial economies. The tenacity of manufacturing, even in decline, is striking, given that almost no one thinks of the bay region as a manufacturing center. Utilities and construction—the providers of urban infrastructure and housing—are quite significant, as well.

Notice should be taken of the continuing scale of finance in the region. San Francisco remains among the top ten financial centers in the world. The Bay Area is, in addition, one of the country's top headquarters cities (as seen in chapter 1), and those headquarters are served by a huge complex of business/management/financial services.[8] The productive nature of finance and management are hugely controversial, since they sit atop the economy. On the one hand, both are necessary to directing and controlling the operation of businesses nearby and far away. On the other hand, both extract surplus

---

8   The rest of the business and professional services group is composed of a host of small-fry serving the general public, such as dentists, tax accountants, and bank branches.

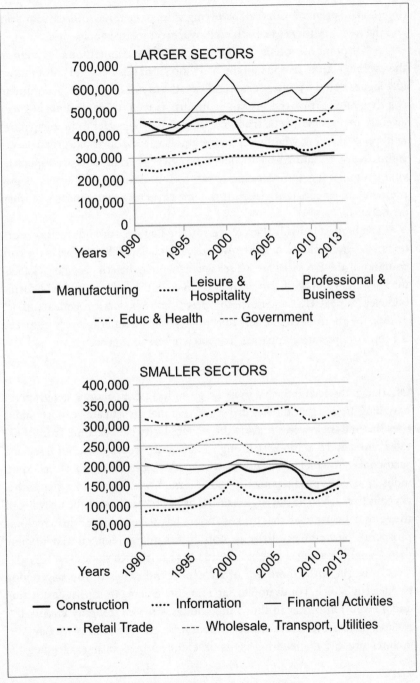

Figure 2.2: Bay Area Employment by Major Sector, 1990–2013

Source: ABAG 2015. 2-digit sectors.

(interest and profits) from the underlying work of factories, offices, transport, and the rest. In either case, both employ a great many people.

A last point of note is the importance of government employment in the overall picture. Despite all the ballyhoo from business and conservative ideologues that the private sector is always the motor of growth, government is a dynamic part of the overall economy, as well. Governments at every level are major employers, from federal and state agencies to municipalities and special districts, whether as military, police, and courts or as road pavers, transit workers, and garbage collectors. Local governments are especially vital in employing and servicing urban communities, and all levels of government are essential providers of the infrastructure that undergirds urban economies.

The biggest individual employers in the Bay Area are not tech corporations, but governments, health providers, and retailers. The top five in the core counties of the Bay Area are Kaiser Permanente (a health provider) (30,000), the City and County of San Francisco (26,900), the University of California, Berkeley (23,962), UC San Francisco (20,295), and Safeway (groceries) (18,450). In 2014, the metro area's largest thirty-five government employers outpaced the top forty private companies, 203,000 workers to 167,000.[9]

★　★　★

Of course, the tech industry must be given its due. Economic geographers have long argued that the key drivers of regional growth are "export" industries that sell their wares outside the region, bring back income from those sales, and spend that money (through wages and purchases) on "local serving" sectors. Bay Area tech is as good an example as can be found of an export industry, since its products are used all over the world. This is why many scholars consider tech to be the engine of the bay economy, and in the upswing of the 2010s it is clear to all that the tech boom has played a huge role in regional prosperity. Nevertheless, there is more to urban and regional development than a single "leading sector," no matter how brightly it shines.[10]

To begin with, there are other export industries in the bay region besides High Tech. For example, San Francisco is a major tourist destination and convention center in the United States, drawing roughly twenty-five million visitors a year to its hotels, restaurants, and entertainments. Bay Area architecture and engineering firms have done a brisk business feeding the

---

9　Cooper 2014, based on a narrow five-county Bay Area metro and publicly traded corporations.
10　The export base model figures strongly in Moretti 2012, Storper et al. 2015.

gigantic building boom in China in recent years. Local hospitals, such as UCSF, Stanford, and Benioff-Children's, draw patients from all over the world for specialized care and surgeries, given their national and global reputations, and Bay Area medical research facilities attract millions in government and corporate finance for their work.

Banks and equity funds handle trillions of dollars of wealth coming from far and wide, employing local workers in the process and investing locally, as well. Wells Fargo was the world's most valuable bank before it was hit by a raft of scandals. BlackRock is the second-largest index fund in the country and it has been shifting its key fund managers from New York to San Francisco, where almost half its business is handled. The city has offices of several major national equity funds, such as KKR, Blackstone, and TPG (former Texas Pacific Group) and many more smaller funds, like Golden Gate Capital and Blum Capital, are sprinkled around the city. Franklin-Templeton, another huge mutual fund operation, and Visa International are headquartered on the Peninsula. The large business and financial services cluster in the bay region works for corporate headquarters of all kinds, which draw profits from around the world.[11]

To focus only on export industries is a bit misleading, however. For one thing, megacities are important markets for their own goods; no place watches and obsesses over movies like Los Angeles, for example. Bay Area consumers are still the number-one target for Napa Valley wines, even though they have a worldwide reputation today. Then there are industries that are almost entirely local, by definition, such as utilities, construction, food preparation, dentistry, and commuter transit. To a significant degree, big cities bootstrap their economies by producing and consuming local commodities. This effect was more evident in the past, when goods and people did not travel as cheaply, but it is still an important factor in large urban regions today. The main advantage of export markets over local markets is that the outside world is bigger and popular products can be sold in larger numbers, opening up more scope for mass production. But, as the case of industrial districts shows, the sum of activity at what appears to be a smaller scale for each firm can offer important collective economies (see chapter 1).

A more basic problem with the export theory of development is that it rests on a strictly market exchange model that goes back to Adam Smith and David Ricardo, in which growth only comes through an expanding division of labor. While true, it only explains part of what makes economies tick, because it leaves out the three fundaments on which all markets depend:

11   For more on the thorny problem of what constitutes "services," see Sayer & Walker 1992.

production, profit, and investment. Industries develop not just by buying and selling, but by employing labor to make things, generating a profit, and reinvesting to expand operations and productivity. Local firms such as restaurants, health clinics, and law offices produce things of value, such as meals, MRIs, and legal briefs, the same as Apple does with its watches. Even though such commodities do not travel far (usually because they involve labor intensive, face-to-face interaction), they still generate profits and wages that recirculate in a growing economy.[12]

Innovation and start-ups, while vital to urban/regional dynamics, are not a monopoly of the IT industry. The Bay Area harbors innovators in every sector, as well as venture capitalists eager to fund them. The metropolitan area is known to be a leader in medical technology and health care, and its researchers and investors spawned the field of biotechnology and have maintained the region's position as the leading biotech cluster in the world. San Francisco built its position as a major financial center through innovations such as branch banking (Bank of America), the Visa card system (Bank of America), MasterCard (Wells Fargo), low-margin stock trades (Charles Schwab) and electronic trading (eTrade). There are energy sector entrepreneurs in everything from green building to solar panels (see chapter 8). The Bay Area has given birth to a number of notable ideas in retailing over the years, such as the Nature Company/Discovery Store, The North Face, and Peet's/Starbucks coffee. Even government has been an innovator, leading the nation in areas such as long-distance water supply, higher education, and building codes.[13]

Innovators pop up in every category, from construction to food products. Furthermore, a crucial dimension of innovation is spawning new sectors over time, and the Bay Area has done just that since the Gold Rush: mining equipment, farm machinery, food processing, petroleum refining, electricity, and vehicle manufacture. Electronics is doing the same today with self-driving vehicles and robotics, while biotechnology is generating whole new fields of medicine, agriculture, and environmental engineering. In this way, the region gives birth to its own diversified economy and keeps itself ahead in the competitive rat race of capitalism.[14]

The Bay Area has good reason to hope that the tech industry does not come to overwhelm everything else. Specialization can be a good thing,

---

12 The classic export-led model was applied to the regional development of the United States by Douglass North in the 1950s; and, despite his Nobel Prize in Economics, it has been disproved several times over. See Page & Walker 1991, Walker 2001.

13 Walker 1996, Kenney & Patton 2005, Kenney & Mowrey 2014, Knuth 2015.

14 See Storper et al.'s excellent treatment of the rise of biotech by the bay (2015, pp. 94–98). See also Glaeser's (2005) study of how Boston reinvented itself over time.

leading a city along a rising path of innovation and competitive survival, as the IT sector has for the Bay Area. Houston's meteoric rise is another example, founded on a concentration in oil and gas, including equipment, services, refining, and shipping. But when the energy sector sags, as it has done recently, Houston feels it strongly, and the long-term prospects for fossil fuels are not robust. The most famous case of modern-day specialization is Detroit's twentieth-century rise based on the automobile industry, becoming the fastest-growing city in the country for decades. But specialization became a liability once U.S. automakers were knocked from their perch by the Japanese in the 1970s, and Detroit headed downward.[15]

Bright Lights, Big City

As its economy has prospered, the Bay Area has grown in terms of output, income, and jobs. But can every place aspire to the same success as Greater San Francisco? Not everyone can be above average, and that holds for cities and regions, too. The unpleasant fact is that many, if not most, places in the country are doing worse—often much worse. So does the Bay Area offer a shining example to the rest, who may hope to one day follow in its footsteps, or is it a red flag to a world suffering from a serious disease of uneven development—because that is the way markets, capitalism, and power work? There are winners and losers in the new global geography, but winning and losing are not independent of one another.

The clear winners are the largest cities. It is often said that this is the age of global urbanization, now that the percentage of the human population living in cities has passed 50 percent. That threshold is hardly surprising given that capitalism has expanded around the earth, penetrating the last redoubts of nonmarket and preindustrial societies, most notably in Asia. Urbanization has evolved hand in glove with the development of the modern world over the last five hundred years, and one nation after another has seen its agrarian population dwindle and urban numbers soar. Britain passed the 50 percent urbanized mark by 1800, the United States by 1900, China in 2000. Modern cities have long served as motors of capitalist development, acting as centers of trade, finance, and government, adding manufacturing, management, and tourism along the way.[16]

The sheer scale of today's world cities boggles the mind, with several past the thirty million mark and at least three dozen over ten million. One may be delighted or horrified by these megacities, but the fact remains that they

---

15 On urban specialization and diversification, see Moretti 2012, Storper 2013.
16 Pred 1980, DeVries 1984, Cronon 1990.

dominate the scene in more and more ways. The biggest cities are the powerhouses of global capitalism: a couple dozen generate a quarter of world's
total output and the top three hundred are responsible for over 50 percent—a
proportion increasing with time. The same is true for the United States, where
the 50 largest metro areas generated almost 75 per cent of GDP growth from
2010 to 2016. The Bay Area is one of those urban conurbations favored by the
gods of the market and modernity. [17]

Meanwhile, cities across the United States have been gutted as their factories closed, agriculture industrialized, and old Downtowns dried up, and the
same is true in Europe. Once vibrant cities such as Flint, Akron, and Toledo
went into a nosedive as factory after factory closed in the 1980s and 1990s The
landscapes of industrial wreckage became so notorious that many cities paid
to demolish their own memories. Large cities such as Detroit and Cleveland
ended up hollowed out, leaving mile after mile of abandoned and demolished
neighborhoods (at one point you could drop all forty-nine square miles of San
Francisco into the empty heart of Detroit).[18]

The problem of imbalance has only been rendered worse by regional
differences. While deindustrialization ravaged much of the old industrial
heartland of America in the Midwest, the coasts—and especially the Far
West—were surging ahead. A study of economic dynamism state-by-state
over the last twenty-five years showed nine of the ten most dynamic states in
the West. Many cities in the Midwest and South have picked themselves up
and brushed off the dust of ghostly steel mills, enjoying a measure of revival
in the twenty-first century. Chicago, Pittsburgh, and Cincinnati are good
examples; but they still have not enjoyed the kind of prosperity of the coasts,
and the plight of smaller cities from Dubuque to Scranton remains grim.
One study puts the number of Americans in regions still mired in a kind of
permanent recession at over fifty million.[19]

Even in California, the contrast between the booming Bay Area and the
interior regions of the Central Valley, Imperial Valley, and mountain zones is
stark. The old lumber and mining jobs are gone from far Northern California
and the Sierra. Canneries in places like Lodi and Salinas have closed and farmworker towns such as Wasco, Pixley, and Soledad remain mired in recession
a decade after the financial crisis of 2008. Construction work has only lately

---

17 http://www.insidermonkey.com/blog/20-richest-cities-in-the-world-by-2015-gdp-per-
    capita-376402/; figure from Brooking Metropolitan Policy Program cited in Fleming 2018.
18 Perry 1987, High 2003, Gillette 2005, Keen 2015, Weaver et al. 2016.
19 On the revival in some smaller cities, see Markusen et al. 1999, Goldstein 2017. On the
    weak recovery in many regions, see Fleming & Leatherby 2017. On the general malaise
    of the national economy, see the last section of this chapter.

picked up after collapsing in the Great Recession, and tens of thousands lost their homes in the foreclosure tsunami that swept across the inland valleys. As one economist puts it, "There are many places in California that have actually been sliding backwards, the Central Valley, for example. It's not sharing in the economic success. . . . If you take the Bay Area out of California, it's doing just OK."[20]

In short, there have been plenty of losers as the industrial map of North America was redrawn over the last couple generations. There lies the taproot of pain and dislocation felt by millions of people across the country (and the same is true in Europe). They are facing a harsh reality of decline and loss in their incomes, communities, and prospects, especially for the young. Ordinary folk may crassly ascribe the source of their plight to immigrants, globalization, and big government, goaded on by demagogues such as Donald Trump and Marine Le Pen, making it all too easy for the cosmopolitan residents of prosperous cities and regions to disparage such people as hicks, dupes, and religious fanatics. But it would be well to remember that their plight is due, in no small part, to the unrelenting advance of the major urban centers and the coasts. What's wrong with Kansas, you ask? To a considerable degree, "It's the economy, stupid." [21]

When the dust settled from the national election of 2016, the facts of spatial inequality behind voting patterns became clear: the one-sixth of U.S. counties won by the Democratic presidential candidate represented two-thirds of economic output, while the results for the Republican candidate were the reverse. As a number of critics of the Democratic Party and its shocked followers on the coasts pointed out, people in the Midwest, Great Plains, and South have good reason to resent the coastal elites and to feel abandoned by the mainstream Democrats, with their oft-expressed love for Silicon Valley, the educated professionals, and the forward march of capitalist "progress."[22]

★ ★ ★

So, how to understand the widening disparity between the largest cities and the rest?

The basic idea of winners and losers in uneven spatial development was pointed out over a half century ago in a way that anyone can grasp. In brief,

---

20 Micah Weinberg, Bay Area Council Economic Institute, quoted in Floum 2016a. See Bardhan & Walker 2011.

21 Frank 2004, 2016, Callahan 2010, Williams 2017.

22 Davis 2013, 2017. Data on voting patterns at: https://www.brookings.edu/blog/the-avenue/2016/11/29/another-clinton-trump-divide-high-output-america-vs-low-output-america/. For more on the cult of progress, see chapter 9.

nothing succeeds like success, and growth tends to snowball in more developed areas. As businesses make profits, they invest and grow, which generates even more profits and investment; meanwhile, capital is attracted from low-profit, low-growth areas to high-profit, high-growth centers. Similarly, where jobs are plentiful, workers migrate from less favored places, especially declining farm regions. Moreover, as companies and worker households spend their money locally, it circulates and multiplies as it flows through the channels of growing economy. Finally, local governments tax companies and households in order to spend on their essential functions. By contrast, the losing places fall into a downward spiral of failure and loss of money, people, and business.[23]

The explanation for urban expansion favored by economic geographers today is the force of agglomeration economies. Urban agglomeration is basically the industrial district idea magnified to the scale of cities—which may, in fact, encompass several industrial districts in one giant metropolitan region, as in the case of the Bay Area (see chapter 5). The argument is that proximity yields crucial advantages by reducing distances traveled, bringing many firms into close contact, and allowing critical face-to-face interaction. On top of this, cities gather together huge pools of labor of all kinds and provide a range of buildings and infrastructure that can be shared by all. Rural areas and towns, by contrast, are less populated with people and businesses, more separate and isolated, and lacking in key infrastructure such as major airports.[24]

Though powerful, these theories of uneven development fail to explain entirely what is happening today. After all, if cities have always had an advantage, why did the Midwest previously develop a widely distributed network of small and medium-sized industrial and commercial cities? It turns out that such "systems of cities" also work quite well in terms of aggregate economies of urbanization, but they grew in relation to a healthy agrarian economy through a mutually beneficial process of agro-industrialization. That dispersed production has been undermined by the emptying out of the landscape of agriculture through gigantism in farming, merchandizing, and food processing.[25]

Globalization has further eroded the viability of the old landscape of industry in the United States and Europe. As more countries industrialized, especially in East Asia, they increased global competition. Industries and

---

23 Myrdal 1957. Myrdal's theory was based on Keynesian macroeconomics, whereas current industrial district theory is based on microeconomics that goes back to Alfred Marshall, with a bit of institutionalism thrown in. For more on migration, see chapter 4.

24 Scott and Storper 2015. On the logic of urban agglomeration, see Scott 1988, Glaeser 2010, Puga 2010, Storper 2013.

25 Page and Walker 1991. Petro-farming made for larger, capital intensive operations that displaced droves of old-fashioned farms.

workers in the developed countries came up against new rivals that whittled away their advantages. Rates of profit were hit in the late 1960s and 1970s, and large-scale plant closures and corporate failures followed in the 1980s. Lower wages in newly developing countries clobbered such labor-intensive sectors as clothing, shoes, and toys, but it was not simply cheap labor that gave the new industrializers an edge. The rapid spread of technology and industrial competence rendered overseas firms' efficiency and product quality as good or better than that in the United States. In particular, a revolution in assembly methods set in motion in Japan undermined the old order resting on Fordist mass production, hitting the auto sector especially hard. American industry has responded by raising labor productivity in export manufacturing, eliminating millions of jobs along the way, yet older factories and companies have been steadily dragged down into the vortex of recession after recession brought on by global overcapacity.[26]

Globalization cannot fully explain the upheavals in the industrial and urban landscape of the United States. That requires a hard look at the radical changes in the structure of industry and the division of labor, because permanent industrial revolution unleashed by capitalism does not consist of automation alone. Many once-popular products have simply faded away and new ones taken their place, as in the way the radial revolutionized the tire industry, plastics elevated the petrochemical industry over steel and aluminum, and canned goods were passed up by frozen, freeze-dried, and prepared foodstuffs. Similarly, Walmart and big box stores revolutionized retailing by offering thousands of goods in one place, undermining the old format of Main Streets and regional wholesalers. The Bay Area has played a part in such revolutions, as in the instance of digital photography's annihilation of the former film and photocopy capital of the country, Rochester, New York.[27]

Add to these shifts the huge expansion of health care and what might be called "auxiliary" activities that do not directly produce things like steel bars or canned fruit. Hospitals and clinics, banks and security traders, management and design are all overwhelmingly located in the biggest cities, as in the Bay Area. These expanding sectors have characteristics that lend themselves to urban concentration: they are relatively fragmented, need close proximity to

26 Martin & Rowthorn 1986, Hoerr 1988, Sayer & Walker 1992, Brenner 2002, 2006.
27 Sayer & Walker 1992, Lichtenstein 2009, Keen 2015. Big box retailers also revolutionized the handling of goods throughout their supply chains. It must be added that "globalization" previously meant the conquest and devastation of many formerly prosperous parts of the world and that today's globalization has brought a measure of economic improvement to many countries that should be celebrated. But that debate is beyond the scope of this book.

function, and require regular face-to-face contact. Moreover, activities such as business services, advanced product design and engineering, and leading-edge health practice and medical research require large numbers of highly educated, professionalized workers, who can be found most easily in big cities.[28]

These changes did not just hit the Midwest. Deindustrialization devastated the once-thriving industrial districts of San Francisco, Oakland, Richmond, and San Jose, as well. Auto plants, rolling mills, meat packers, canneries, machine shops and paint factories were shuttered, while the makers of toothpaste, soap, shredded wheat, and baby food fell before the wrecking ball of industrial progress. The difference in the Bay Area is that growing industries such as electronics, tourism, and business services replenished and renewed the economic base of the region. But they also left behind huge swaths of the inner cities that were home to the oldest and most vulnerable industries. Uneven development strikes close to home as well as far away.

Other People's Money

Perhaps the biggest oversight of agglomeration theory as an explanation for winners and losers in the geographic lottery is that it rests firmly on the grounds of production, competition, and efficiency. A basic pillar of modern economic ideology is that money earned, whether as profits, wages, or rents, is well earned by virtue of producing useful things, hard work, education, and entrepreneurial genius. This is true—up to a point. Yet why should one assume that successful people and places rest entirely on their own laurels? Perhaps they thrive on unearned incomes and the exploitation of less prosperous places?

The nineteenth-century railroad barons of San Francisco grew rich on free land, government subsidies, and monopoly pricing (not to mention cheap Chinese and Irish labor). Almost none of their vast fortunes—duly marked by palatial Victorian homes built atop Nob Hill—was earned through internal profits from railroad operations. There is no reason to think that the current crop of Bay Area capitalists is not similarly extracting resources and money from far beyond the bay region.[29]

Some of the resources flowing into big cities from outside are the fruit of the earth, such as minerals, timber, and water. In the process, rural areas have been physically devastated by being dug up, cut down, dried up, and dumped upon. The mines of the Sierra and the territory of Nevada fed America's

28 On the shift to bigger cities, see Scott 2012, Storper 2013.
29 On the railroad men, see White 2011. On the theory of surplus and cities, see Walker 2016 and Schoenberger & Walker 2017. For a discussion of direct labor exploitation, see chapters 3 and 4.

vast appetite for precious metals in the nineteenth century and made San Francisco rich in the process. Similarly, the coal mines of West Virginia yielded more riches than all the gold and silver of California yet left little in the way of economic development behind as nature's bounty fed the fortunes of Boston and New York capitalists. West Virginia continues to be hacked away and polluted by companies whose profits mostly go to places such as Durham and Pittsburgh. Chevron, PG&E, Homestake Mining, and other big companies in today's Bay Area have waxed fat on the rents accruing from oil leases, hydropower dams, and mines.[30]

Then there is the way the Bay Area and other big cities gain from the arrival of new people. Labor flows to more prosperous places in search of jobs and better wages, but there is more to it than that. One element is the "brain drain" from outmigration and "brain gain" in the receiving area. Migrants tend to be younger, so there is an age gain, as well; young people go to cities for a better education and cultural attractions, and to get a leg up on technical and industrial change. Because the Bay Area is a center of higher education and diverse learning, it benefits more than most cities, adding to its pool of educated, skilled labor. It's not so much that the free choice of "the creatives" spurs urban growth as that the cities rob the countryside of its youth. And there is another way in which migration subsidizes cities: the places of origin pay for raising the young while the cities benefit from their adult labor without paying the cost of reproduction of the labor force (see chapter 4).[31]

A third way in which the Bay Area, like other prosperous cities, lives beyond its means is a massive influx of economic surplus via financial flows. Although hard data on such flows are hard to come by, there are good reasons to think that the Bay Area and its elite are rolling in other people's money. A pretty clear indication that Bay Area companies are not simply operating as efficient machines is the vast hordes of cash that have piled up in the hands of giant corporations. Estimates of the amount of loose cash in corporate pockets are legion these days: upwards of $2 trillion for all American corporations. Not surprisingly, five of the biggest tech companies (Google, Oracle, Apple, Microsoft, and Cisco) are leading the way with a half trillion dollars in cash among them. No wonder the big boys can afford to lavish funds on multibillion-dollar buyouts such as YouTube and Oculus Rift (see chapter 1).[32]

A good deal of that surplus capital comes from investors with money burning holes in their pockets, who are trying to cash in on high returns in

30   Walker 1996, 2001, 2004, Moore 2015, Brechin 1999.
31   On the benefits of immigration, see Saxenian 2006, Peri 2010.
32   Platt 2016, W. Lee 2016.

tech in a low-interest-rate environment. Much of that money was fleeing from slowdowns in Europe, China, and Latin America. For example, foreign investment in U.S. equities more than doubled in the decade 2007–17, from less than 15 percent to more than 35 percent of gross domestic product. At the end of this huge influx of capital, the world had never been more invested in U.S. assets.[33]

Even without systematic data, there are plenty of telling stories cropping up in the business press. For example, one of the top five angel investors funding tech start-ups is Japanese. Several unicorns are awash in outside money, such as the $1.5 billion backing for Social Finance, Inc. by SoftBank Group from Japan and the $3.5 billion bet placed on Uber by the Saudi Investment Fund. GM has even put $1 billion into Lyft. SoftBank put another $9 billion into Uber in 2017 and announced a $100 billion Vision Fund (backed by Saudi money) for investment in U.S. technology companies. Chinese investment in the United States surged in 2016, with California the biggest recipient at $27 billion (chiefly in IT, real estate, and entertainment).[34]

A more systematic measure is the way the stocks of Bay Area tech corporations have shot to the top of the ranking by total capitalization. First came Cisco Systems in the late 1990s, riding the wave of the dot-com/NASDAQ bubble, discussed in the next section. Next came Google early in the twenty-first century, passing up longtime standard-bearer Microsoft. Then Apple rose to the head of the pack in the 2010s. Now it is Amazon's turn to soar, joining Apple, Alphabet (Google), Microsoft, and Facebook in the top five. It is impossible to know how much bloat there is in current stock valuations until the boom cools off. But how to account for Tesla, which makes electric cars in the thousands, surpassing the stock value of General Motors and Ford, which produce vehicles in the millions each year? Again, it is good to recall that most of the Big Four's railroad fortunes were acquired through financial shell games that kept investors buying their stocks and bonds even when they were vastly overvalued.[35]

Lastly, Bay Area corporations and billionaires engage in massive tax avoidance. The most obvious way this is done is the use of tax havens such as the Bahamas, Luxembourg, and the Channel Islands. Some 20 percent of U.S. corporate profits are held in offshore tax havens, quadruple the figure of

mas 2017, Francassa 2017, Waters 2017b. Rhodium Group at http://rhg. china-investment-monitor.
ish hoarders in tech, see Waters 2016a. On Tesla vs. Ford, see https:// m/2017/04/10/business/tesla-general-motors-stock-market.html. On ee White 2011.

thirty years ago. The names Google, Apple, Facebook, and other pillars of Bay Area prosperity keep cropping up as the leaders of the infamous pack of corporate tax evaders. Similarly, trillions of dollars—over 10 percent of U.S. personal wealth—are squirreled away in tax havens. Here is a type of globalization that has nothing to do with cheap labor, but rather the use of clever attorneys and accountants who manipulate offshore accounts, international subsidiaries, and internal pricing schemes to keep the boodle out of the hands of tax collectors.[36]

The Republican tax cutters have only made the problem worse over the last thirty-five years by favoring the rich over the rest with cuts to estate, capital gains and corporate taxes—topped off by the shameful giveaways of the 2017 legislation. That just means that more of the wealth stays in the most favored places, like the Bay Area, or flows in from investors holding bags of extra money in other parts of the country. Much has been made of the Republicans cynical ploy to hit the coastal, Democratic majority states with higher taxes, when those states already transfer income to the poorer parts of the country through federal taxation and spending. In fact, such geographic redistribution serves as a counterweight to the economic decline of the old heartland. But it is the mass of middle-income taxpayers in California and elsewhere who pay for that, while the rich people and corporations of the Bay Area gain overall from regressive tax cuts (see also chapter 3).[37]

Boom and Bust

The Bay Area economy is a supernova in the capitalist firmament, but as with exploding stars there is no telling when it will collapse back into a black hole. When the good times roll, no one wants to face the fact that booms always come to an end, even though this is an indelible aspect of modern economies. Upswings rarely last more than a decade and recessions follow like night from day. So the upbeat figures on regional economic prosperity with which this chapter began—plus the account of the fecund tech economy in chapter 1—are only half the story. A short period of rapid growth cannot simply be projected into the future. It is time to come to grips with the inevitable downturn and its implications, which will put

---

36 Data from Blair 2017, Zucman 2015. For an overview of tax havens, see Shaxson 2011, Murphy & Christensen 2012. On tech firms tax avoidance, Tang & Ngo 2012, Bowers 2015, Johnston 2016.

37 While California's taxes are higher and more progressive than in most states, they are still less so than they were in the New Deal and postwar era, leaving the state's budgets persistently in the red. Walker 1995a, 2010. On tax avoidance by the rich, see Johnston 2016.

a much-different cast on the history of the era when a full accounting is made.[38]

Recessions darken the sunny picture of capitalist growth and progress that is so prevalent in popular ideology. American historical amnesia works wonders for erasing the nightmares of major economic crises. The Great Depression of the 1930s, which followed the Roaring Twenties, is already a distant memory (and who but historians recall the depressions of the 1870s and 1890s?). Many people alive today still recall with nostalgia the Golden Age of postwar growth and American dominance over the world economy, which was barely scuffed by a couple of weak slumps in the late 1940s and 1950s. The last half century, on the other hand, has been far from golden; indeed, is has been arguably the worst epoch for growth in U.S. history. A good deal of propaganda has led memory astray, whether from the apostles of Ronald Reagan burnishing the record of the 1980s or the faithful singing praises to Bill Clinton's 1990s. The dark side of the times has been largely erased from the record.

In fact, the United States suffered five major recessions over the last fifty years. The downturn of 1973–75 marked the end of the Golden Age thanks to the revival of international competition from Japan and Europe (oil prices were a minor aspect). The recession of 1979–82 was notable for the hit taken by U.S. manufacturing, which threw millions of people out of work, as the wolf of competition devoured one obsolete factory and corporation after another and the Federal Reserve Bank squeezed out inflation. The slump of 1989–92 swept away more failing companies and factories, helped by the implosion of junk bonds, savings and loans, and real estate, plus cutbacks in military spending. The economy revived smartly in the mid-1990s, with huge gains in employment in the dawn of the New Economy, until the tech bubble burst in 2000. The subsequent recession was relatively short and mild on the national scale, thanks to strong intervention by the Fed, but low interest rates and financial deregulation fueled an enormous mortgage and housing bubble that blew up spectacularly in 2007–8. That, in turn, triggered the largest economic crisis since the Great Depression of the 1930s—hence the popular name, the Great Recession.[39]

The Great Recession has been calamitous. The official U.S. government designation of a two-year lapse in growth 2008–10 minimizes the reality. Financially, the New York Stock Exchange lost almost half its value, two

---

38 Boom-and-bust cycles color the entire history of the modern world, from the rise and fall of the Fuggers in the 1500s to the stock market frenzy of the 1920s and Great Depression of the 1930s. Kindleberger 2005.

39 The best overall treatment of global growth and crisis from World War II to the twenty-first century is by Brenner 2002, 2006. See also Gordon 2016.

major investment banks collapsed (Bear Stearns and Lehman Brothers), and the commercial banking system nearly froze up, requiring a massive federal bailout of the banks. World trade came to a near standstill in early 2009 and output fell dramatically in country after country. About eight million jobs were lost in the United States, and the unemployment rate doubled to 10 percent by the end of 2009. Employment picked up by 2010, but household incomes kept falling through 2012.

But things are actually worse than that. The Great Recession won't go away—regardless of the soaring stock market and falling unemployment. By any measure, recovery from the Great Recession was the slowest from any crisis on record, including the Great Depression of the 1930s (fig. 2.6). U.S. productivity growth remains poor overall, aggregate demand is weak because wages have barely budged, and corporations are not investing with any gusto. Loose talk of full employment by mid decade ignores the fact that so many Americans have dropped out of the labor force entirely.[40]

The situation in losing regions was decidedly worse than the national averages indicate. As of 2015, millions of workers and families still had not recovered in terms of jobs and incomes to where they were a decade earlier. Their sense of loss and abandonment was still raw when the election of 2016 rolled around. Blame fell on many quarters, from the coastal elites to the Democratic Party; unfortunately, capitalism got off scot-free, as it usually does in this country, and a billionaire developer and über-capitalist was elected president.

★ ★ ★

Regional economies can be even more unstable than the country as a whole. Some regions play a leading role in every boom, and others suffer worse in each recession. Midwest heavy industry led the way in the postwar era of prosperity, but the midwestern Rust Belt got its name from the devastation done in subsequent recessions, particularly 1979–82. The action had moved to the Sunbelt after 1975, and Los Angeles became the national center of the Reagan boom of the 1980s before being leveled by the crisis of 1989–92. The Bay Area got off lightly in that downturn but led the way in the dot-com bubble of the 1990s only to fall lower than all the rest in the recession of 2000–2002. California was the heartland of the housing boom of the early twenty-first century and epicenter of the foreclosure crisis of 2008–9, and it suffered accordingly in the Great Recession.[41]

---

40 On the Great Recession, see Shiller 2008, Gowan 2009, Roberts 2016. For more on employment and wages, see chapter 4; for more on productivity and investment, see chapter 9.

41 High 2003, Davis 1998, Bardhan & Walker 2011.

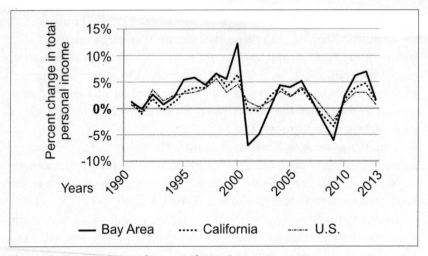

Figure 2.3: Bay Area Personal Income Fluctuations, 1990–2013

Source: ABAG 2015.

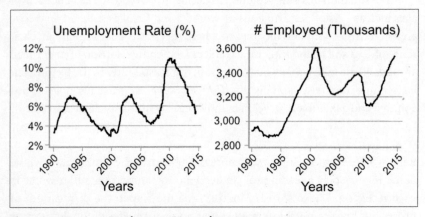

Figure 2.4: Bay Area Employment/Unemployment, 1990–2015

Source: Bay Area Council Economic Institute 2014.

The ups and downs of the Bay Area economy are readily apparent (figs. 2.3 and 2.4). Average personal income has fluctuated more in the bay region than statewide or nationally. Employment has shot up and come down hard several times. Recent Bay Area booms have been closely aligned with the introduction of innovations in High Tech, such as the microprocessor in the 1970s, PCs and networks in the 1980s, and the internet and dot-coms in the 1990s, each of which triggered waves of investment, start-ups, and competitive fever. But too little noted in the gushing histories of the new New Thing have been the downsides of every upswing: bursting bubbles, hard landings, and major shakeouts. Firms, products, and skills have been swept aside with

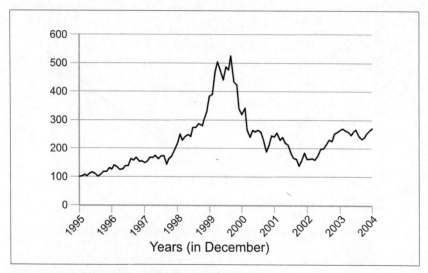

Figure 2.5: Bay Area Stock Price Index, 1995–2004
Source: Bloomberg L.P. 2005, index of 232 stocks (no longer online).

every recession, cleaning house for the next big thing. Who remembers such former tech stars as Atari, Osborne, @Home, and Pets.com?

The most spectacular blow-up came after the internet boom and dot-com mania of the 1990s. Financial mania drove the NASDAQ stock market (replete with tech company stocks) to absurd heights—from an index of fifteen hundred in 1995 to five thousand in 1999. When investors finally realized the enormity of the house of cards that had been constructed, the markets fell rapidly, erasing hundreds of start-ups and bringing some of the biggest tech companies, such as Cisco, Amazon, and HP, to their knees. A striking feature of the bubble—the largest stock frenzy in U.S. history up to that time—was the concentration of financial excess on Bay Area tech stocks (fig. 2.5).

The recession of 2000–2002 felt mild elsewhere around the United States, but it slammed the Bay Area. When the dust had settled, it was clear that Bay Area companies had been the eye of the hurricane, and collectively they lost around $7 billion of the $17 billion evaporated in the crash of the stock markets—around 40 percent of the national total. Major tech companies, such as Cisco and HP, lost 70–90 percent of their market value in the downfall of the NASDAQ. The nine-county region lost almost a half million jobs, and only crept back to the employment level of 1999 by the end of 2015.[42]

---

42 Walker 2006. Labor force participation also collapsed in the crisis of 2000 but revived better in the Bay Area than in the country as a whole.

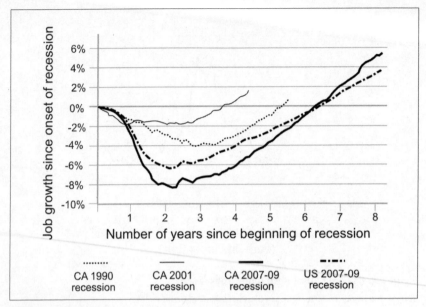

Figure 2.6: California Job Losses and Recovery, 2007–2015
Source: Allegretto 2016.

As for the housing bubble of the early twenty-first century and the Great Recession, California led the way for the nation and the world. The meltdown in California mortgages took out a host of national banks and bankrupted thousands of homeowners, while inflicting the worst budget deficit in the state's history (a one-third fall in revenues). About two million state workers lost their jobs and the unemployment rate hit 12 percent. The Central Valley and Southern California were hit the hardest. Because the Great Recession was much deeper and longer than the previous two recessions, it took six years for the state economy to make up the job losses—even though the state recovered faster than the United States as a whole (fig. 2.6).[43]

In short, the Bay Area has had a scary ride on the economic roller coaster in recent years. Because the tech sector is at the frontier of capitalist expansion today, it is more volatile than most industries and leaves the Bay Area looking, at times, more like a mining boomtown of the Old West than a stable, mature metropolis. The upshot is that no one should render judgment on the "success" of the Bay Area and its economy, past, present, or future, without a sober look at the record of business cycles and recessions.

★ ★ ★

43 Bardhan & Walker 2011.

Why do business cycles occur? They are not haphazard, but systematic in modern economies. Most people understand the laws of supply and demand, but shouldn't they also have a sense of how markets go off the rails in periods of rapid growth? Conventional economics is of little help, since it remains fixated on the idea of market equilibrium, not instability. Most economists look at business cycles as superficial waves on vast seas of well-behaved markets and gradual growth. But mainstream economists failed spectacularly to see the dangerous financial bulge of the early twenty-first century and anticipate the looming crisis of 2007–10. As a result, the Great Recession, like the Great Depression before it, led to a renewal of interest in the causes of cycles and speculative bubbles.[44]

To shine some light on the cause of business cycles, it is necessary to turn to nonmainstream theories of economics—Schumpeter, Keynes, and especially Marx—on the nature of capitalism, that is, in the dynamics of an economy guided by the profit-making, intense competition, and betting on the future. Individual firms make investments in search of profit, often with time horizons measured in years, and they do so to outflank their competitors, whose intentions and actions are unknown. The combination works well in upswings, bringing on line new products, workplaces, and technologies, with every company vying for an edge; the result can be rapid expansion of capacity and development of productive capabilities. But there comes a time when, in the supercharged atmosphere of moneymaking, competition, and ambition, companies go too far: they invest in too many factories, produce too many similar products, and start to saturate their markets. As excess capacity comes on line, they do not adjust right away, thinking that it is only a bump in the road or that their competitors will fail first. The result is overcapacity, overproduction, glutted markets, and falling profit margins. The downturn begins.[45]

Where financial bubbles are involved, business cycles are worsened: upswings become severely overheated and recessions grow to be full-fledged depressions. Credit is, of course, a normal feature of economic growth;

---

44 The Great Depression gave rise to the work of such innovative economists as Simon Kuznets (1930), John Maynard Keynes (1936), and Joseph Schumpeter (1939), now mostly ignored by mainstream economics. In the last generation, financial economists fell in love with the manifestly utopian "perfect market" theory, which states that markets always properly assess the risks presented by investing in an unknown future. For a critique, see Cassidy 2009. On economists as servants of power, see Haring & Douglas 2012.

45 On the Marxist theory of cycles, see Harvey 1982, 2017, Walker 1995c, Brenner 2006. For the Keynesian version, see Minsky 2008. The rolling pattern of boom and bust is complicated by overlapping cycles of different lengths.

companies borrow to invest, consumers borrow to buy things, and banks encourage them to do so. But as everyone warms up to prosperity they begin to borrow more and more, and the debt burden on the economy grows. As the rat race intensifies and the euphoria of a boom develops, borrowing gets out of hand—exceeding the ability of creditors to repay. Cheap credit caused by central bank monetary policy aimed at sustaining an upswing, as has been the case in the United States since the 1990s, can make matters worse.

On top of this, as profits and incomes mount up, firms, banks, and households throw their surplus funds into paper investments in stocks, bonds, mortgages, and the like. The nominal value of financial assets soars, people and firms feel even richer, and they even start to borrow to speculate in the capital markets. But the day arrives when it becomes apparent that everyone has borrowed too much, asset prices are out of line with real values, and the most overextended ones start to go bankrupt. If panic sets in, as it did in late 2008, the entire financial structure can be put in jeopardy. After the dust settles, the subsequent recession is even worse than normal slumps.[46]

Recessions are inevitable. It is not just a matter of making corrections in markets gone awry, however; recessions do a lot of dirty work to get capital accumulation back on track by purging the economy of its excesses. Excess capital shrinks as asset values tumble, companies go bankrupt, and surplus commodities are sold off at a discount. Fixed costs are reduced by closing down redundant factories and other workplaces, and labor costs are cut by laying off excess workers and driving down wages (often through threats of plant closures and more redundancies). All these things work to restore profitability—the ratio of surplus above costs to the total capital invested—and prepare the way for another round of growth. But cleaning out the Augean stables of capital means hacking away at real livelihoods and communities of working people.[47]

★ ★ ★

So what are the prospects for the boom times of the 2010s coming to an end? Reading the economic crystal ball is tricky.

First of all, the state of the global economy since the Great Recession has not been robust. Overall, growth rates peaked in 2014 and fell thereafter, while world trade plateaued (fig. 2.7). China's industrialization slowed, and government stimulus to keep the economy levitated ran up a huge debt load.

---

46 On financial crises, see Cooper 2008, Roubini & Mihm 2010, Eichengreen 2014.

47 A curious thing about the Great Recession is that it has been very poor at restoring prosperity; instead, higher profits have been redistributed to the 1% and surplus capital has been sequestered in offshore accounts. See also chapter 3.

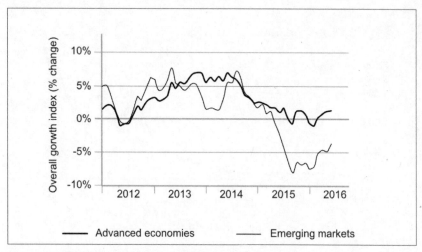

Figure 2.7: World Economic Growth Rates, 2011–2016
Source: Giles 2016.

Europe struggled with debt, austerity, and high unemployment for years. The United States did better than Europe thanks to looser monetary policy, but has hardly enjoyed a world-beating performance. Things looked better in 2017, especially in Europe. But for all the braggadocio of a boastful president, U.S. output expansion was dragging along at barely above 1 percent per year; job creation, while it continued at a good clip, peaked in 2015, and wages barely budged despite nearly full employment by standard measures.[48]

Meanwhile, financial markets have been riding high. Stocks set an upward course by 2010 and recouped all their Great Recession losses by the end of 2013, peaked in 2015, and then took a sharp dip. But that was followed by a dramatic revival in 2017, as seen in the S&P index's sharp ascent (fig. 2.8). This was due in part to capitalist euphoria over the election sweep of Republicans dedicated to massive tax cuts. Nevertheless, it was not hard to see a new bout of "irrational exuberance" at work in the development of a new asset bubble. Signs of trouble were price-earnings ratios of stocks at historically high levels, mountains of corporate and household debt piling up, and bond markets at a tipping point with long-term interest rates below short-term. More and more warning voices could be heard, despite loud braying from the political pulpits in Washington. When the bulls will finally run over the cliff is anyone's guess, but they are hurtling downward as this is written.[49]

---

48 Giles 2016, Bivens 2016, Sandbu 2016.
49 Authers 2016, 2018, McCrum 2017, Partnoy 2017, da Costa 2017, Wigglesworth 2017. The bitcoin bubble is perhaps the most freakish sign of the times.

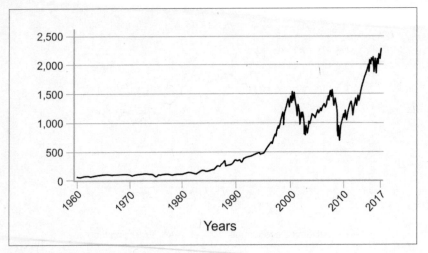

Figure 2.8: S&P 500 Stock Price Index, 1959–2017

Source: http://www.fedprimerate.com/s-and-p-500-index-history-chart.htm.

While the Bay Area economy continued to grow through 2017, job creation had fallen off by 2016, generating anxious debate in the business press.[50] The index of Bay Area stocks saw a rapid run-up to 2015, then a yearlong slump followed by a recovery in late 2016 and 2017 (fig. 2.9). By that time, commentators were warning of excess debt building up in Silicon Valley and of the perils of the bull run on tech stocks. Notably, the S&P technology index rose 21 percent in 2017, while the FANGs soared by two-thirds in value on the Dow, catapulting tech corporations into seven of the ten most valuable in the world, compared to three in 2010. This is eerily reminiscent of 1999.[51]

The sources of this kind of financial bloat are not hard to see. One is perennially low rates of interest, held down by the Fed to inflate a long, sluggish economic recovery. Another is too much money in pension and wealth funds desperate for returns in a low-interest environment. A third is excess borrowing to keep corporate performance and household consumption rising. The last is the inevitable euphoria that envelops those riding the wealth effects of soaring assets, and making more and more risky bets that the bubble with never burst. But it always does, whether in a big bang or a slower loss of gas.

★   ★   ★

50 Kotkin & Shires 2016, Warburg 2016, Avalos 2016. Employment tends to lag movements in output, while stock markets run ahead of the real economy.

51 Lee 2016a, 2017, Braithwaite 2016a, Waters & Hook 2016, Sharma 2017, Platt 2017.

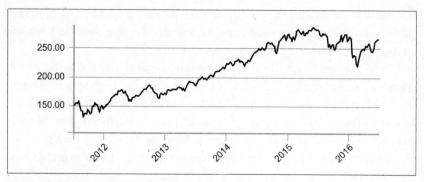

Figure 2.9: Bay Area Stock Price Index, 2011–2016

Source: Bloomberg Markets, http://www.bloomberg.com/quote/BBACAX:IND, June 23, 2016.

A recession does not seem far off as this is written. When it does arrive, the consequences will be ugly for working people and their communities—thanks to cutbacks by hard-pressed employers, lost jobs and income, foreclosed homes, and disfigured lives. Working families always suffer the worst because they have so little cushion to protect them from disaster. A parent laid off, rent payments missed, a sick child, or a grandparent in a rest home can devastate a family's finances and, even worse, send people into downward spirals of ill health, mental anguish, homelessness, and even suicide. Moreover, when businesses begin to hire again in the next upswing, they often select a new generation of workers over the old ones, whose careers are truncated and who are left to fend for themselves in a labor market unfriendly to its elders.[52]

Recessions have clear effects in terms of poverty rates, which rose sharply in the Great Recession, especially in California. Recessions also affect the health of the unemployed and their families, even as cutbacks in government aid due to budget deficits reduce healthcare services. Joblessness worsens physical and mental illness, alcohol and drug abuse, child and spouse abuse, and suicide, particularly for young men. Mortality among white working-class people with low education and poor job prospects has been rising since 2000, and the opioid crisis in depressed parts of the country, including back-country California, has hit alarming rates.[53]

The mainstream press rarely delves into the cumulative consequences of recessions, other than quoting unemployment figures. Reports on growing homelessness, poor health, and rising divorce rates are rarely connected to the hidden costs of economic recession crashing down on the heads of ordinary

---

52 Irons 2009.
53 Darity 2003, Suckler & Basu 2013, Schneider et al. 2016, Case & Deaton 2017. On Bay Area effects, see Terplan et al. 2014.

folks. But when the current economic wave breaks on the reefs of capitalist excess, a huge amount of economic and human wreckage will be revealed on the shores of the Pacific Coast's star performer.[54]

Predicting booms and busts is a notoriously tricky business, as the world discovered to its regret in the failure of all but a handful of people to foresee the financial implosion of 2007–8. But the basic fact that growth occurs in waves that rise and fall is irrefutable. The San Francisco urban region did spectacularly well in the recovery from the Great Recession, by all conventional measures, but it may just as well suffer a great fall from its new heights. Only time will tell.

Conclusion

The Bay Area economy has fared remarkably well in recent years compared to most of the United States. It became one of the brightest stars of global capitalism after the Great Recession, as Europe staggered; the luster came off the roaring economies of China and India; and the Persian Gulf, Australia, and Brazil felt the pinch of falling energy and resource prices. The high-flying bay region created lots of new products, start-ups, and jobs, while its corporations climbed the charts of sales and capital value. Aggregate wealth and income shot upward, leaving the region with some of the highest average wages and incomes in the world. Chapter 3 will look more closely at those bright, shiny income figures and their contradictions, while the concerns of this chapter have lain elsewhere.

One lesson is that while the tech sector is in the vanguard of the Bay Area's rapid growth, the regional economy is a good deal broader than IT, with strengths that run from medicine and health to tourism and entertainment, from finance and business services to ports and transportation. It is an economy that can weather many a storm and still rebound with a new burst of growth after any downturn, thanks to a mix of large companies and small, established products and new innovations, and private and public employment. Chapter 4 will investigate the nature of work and well-being of workers in that larger economy.

The Bay Area's success is not an unmixed blessing, as will be seen throughout this book. In this chapter, two of the dark sides of the region's prosperity have been investigated. One is the severity of uneven geographic development under capitalism, wherein the good fortune of the bay region goes hand in hand with the failure of other places in the United States (not to mention elsewhere in the world). As the San Francisco metropolis rolls

---

54 For more on worker precariousness, see chapter 4.

on, attracting more people, brainpower, and money, less fortunate places are evacuated of their young, their skills, and their economic surplus. They spiral down as the Bay Area and other large cities spiral upward.

The other reality that takes some of the shine off the golden economy of the last few years is that the downside of every boom is a bust. This is the temporal dimension of capitalist uneven growth, as the high-flying Bay Area has learned more than once over the last generation. It makes any statement about the future hazardous. How bad the recession to come will be for the people of the region is yet to be seen, but it will not be a picnic after a period of such overheated ambition and markets. Nor can we be sure that it will recover as briskly next time or that its long-term prospects will be as jaunty as the present state of affairs.

One might well think that the success of a place like the Bay Area is guaranteed far into the future; but nothing stays in place for long on the shifting sands of capitalism. The list of once-great cities that have stumbled and declined in the past is legion: Venice, Pisa, Augsburg, Lisbon, Liverpool, Philadelphia, St. Louis, New Orleans, Detroit, and on and on. In the famous phrase of Karl Marx and Frederick Engels, "All that's solid melts into air."[55] A changing technological base of future expansion can throw the hotshots of today's IT sector into the rubbish bin of history and even extinguish the shooting star of the Bay Area. The prospects are not dire in the short term, but predicting the future in a capitalist world is a sure-fire way to be proved wrong.

This is just the beginning of our inquiry into the dark side of the bright star of capitalism. As the following chapters will show, the fate of the working people, housing markets, racialized populations, and the environment are all put in question by rapid economic growth and the fallout from the inevitable bust. Not only that, the good times have been fed by a torrent of money that has bloated the wealth of the favored and their enterprises, a sort of malignant growth on top of what ought to be a good enough performance by the regional economy. But, again, in a world dominated by money—"Accumulate, accumulate, that is Moses and the Prophets," as Karl Marx put it—good is never enough. Nothing is ever enough.

---

55   Marx & Engels, 1849. See also Berman 1982.

CHAPTER THREE

Gold Mountain

Wealth, Inequality, and the Class Divide

THE THOUSANDS OF CHINESE WHO JOINED THE GOLD RUSH OF 1848–55 CALLED California "Gold Mountain," which was not far off the mark given the billions of dollars of precious metals that spilled out of the mountains before the gravels and mines played out. San Francisco owes its fame and fortune to the mining era launched in 1848, which propelled it into the top ten U.S. cities in a single decade. Since then, the Gold Rush has served as the Origin Myth of Northern California, repeatedly attached to good times, from World War II to the dot-com boom. The idea of a Silicon Gold Rush has appeared regularly since then in books, newspapers, and magazines around the world, and with the latest boom the phrase is again coin of the realm, from the *Huffington Post* to BuzzFeed to the *New York Times*.[1]

If the Gold Rush metaphor is going to be trotted out, however, one should recall the less appetizing aspects of the mining era that first propelled San Francisco to world prominence. The Chinese, who were every bit as much "Argonauts" as the Americans and Europeans who flooded into California, were driven from the goldfields into menial jobs, as were the Mexicans who came up from Sonora and helped teach the Anglos how to pan for gold. Meanwhile, the riches coming out of the rivers stuck to the hands of merchants more than to those of the mass of 49ers; the majority of the latter fled California when the gold ran out and the merchants clamped down on the state in the vigilante movement of 1855–56. When Comstock silver and quartz mines revived the city's fortunes in the 1860s, financial speculators were the prime beneficiaries. Meanwhile, four merchants from Sacramento took charge of the leading technology of the nineteenth century, the railroad, which in their hands was used less to conquer a continent than to corrupt a nation. Gilded Age entrepreneurial spirits were lifted more by operating in the Mining Exchange and the bond markets than by the building the New Economy of the Civil War era.[2]

---

1   See, e.g., Southwick 1999, Popper & Dougherty 2015, Alden 2015.
2   Senkiwicz 1985, Brechin 1999, White 2011.

In the contemporary tech boom-cum-Gold Rush, the Bay Area has been blessed by an unprecedented abundance of riches. As seen in the last chapter, total regional output and income shot upward much faster than population growth, resulting in a rapidly rising average income per capita (and per household). In 2017, it was heading toward $100,000 per person, one of the highest figures of any big city in the world. Moreover, average salaries and wages rose as companies rolling in revenues were able to pay more to attract employees, especially those most vital to the invention of new technologies.[3]

The narrative of a "rising tide lifting all boats" is strong in the bay region, but it is also seriously misleading. Not everyone is average. So the critical question is how has this new money been distributed up and down the social order, from owners and entrepreneurs to skilled workers and managers and thence down to the lowest ranks of workers and the poorest people? On closer inspection, the robust income and flattering averages turn out to be far from the whole story. Shine the bright light of high income through an analytical prism and it refracts into a wide spectrum of difference that colors the lovely picture of prosperity in more lurid hues.

The principal effect of the wealth erupting from the new technologies is that the Bay Area has become vastly more unequal. This new inequality features a shocking enrichment of the elite, exactly the kind of engorgement of the 1% that has been highlighted by the Occupy Wall Street movement and economists such as Thomas Piketty. The prosperity of the Bay Area elite cannot be understood only as very high incomes of the superrich; it is also an immense accumulation of wealth by a new generation of capitalists.

A second feature of the new inequality is that the salaried, professional workforce, including managers and highly skilled workers in the top 20 percent of income earners, are doing very well, indeed. That raises further questions of how closely this upper middle class is clinging to the coattails of the truly wealthy and how they relate to the mass of wage workers who are less favored. The prosperity and attitudes of this group are politically loaded matters because they are a common target of resentment by people who support right-wing demagogues—even more so than the superrich.

A third key feature of the Bay Area is that average wages for the mass of workers is higher than other cities. This ought to mean that the working people are doing well, the working middle class is growing, and poverty is rare. But working-class prosperity is much more truncated and precarious than the averages would lead one to believe. This is true primarily because

---

3   On misestimates of city incomes, see chapter 2 and on definitions of the Bay Area, see chapter 7.

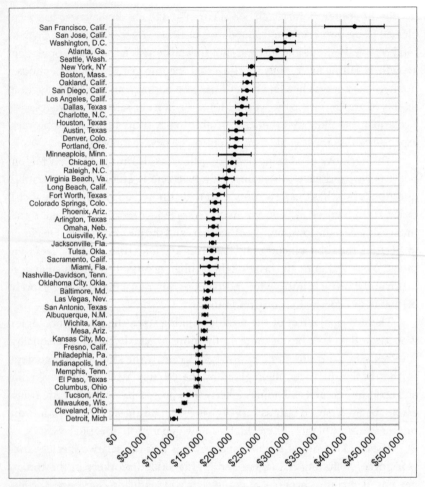

Figure 3.1: Top 5 Percent Income in 50 Largest U.S. Metro Areas, 2013

Source: Berube & Holmes 2014 (MSAs).

of the highly unequal distribution of wages, but also because a high-wage city is a place with a high cost of living—with the net result of less disposable income than might be thought.

The first three sections of the chapter consider each of these income layers in turn. Then the fourth section reflects on the significance of growing inequality for how one thinks about the hierarchy of income and wealth in the United States. The dramatic worsening of inequality even in a prosperous place such as the bay metropolis should give everyone pause, and it argues for dropping the veil of ideology—that America is a classless society—and confronting the class character of the world the New Economy has created. The chapter concludes with the disturbing topic of homelessness, which threatens

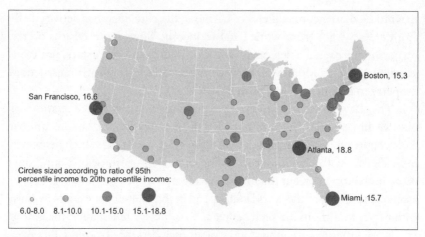

Figure 3.2: Map of Most Unequal Cities in the United States, 2012

Source: https://www.brookings.edu/research/all-cities-are-not-created-unequal.

to make a mockery, once again, of the claims that the San Francisco Bay Area is Gold Mountain and the Silicon Gold Rush is the best of all possible worlds.

The New Gilded Age

The first step in parsing the spectrum of inequality is to look more closely at the very highest incomes, and those at the top of the Bay Area's income hierarchy are very high, indeed. The top 5 percent in San Francisco's metro area are literally off the charts, with San Jose right behind; even Oakland makes the top ten (fig. 3.1). There is no data for the income of the top 1 percent in the bay region, but the top 0.5 percent in California as a whole take home just over 20 percent of state income. This figure is markedly worse than for the rest of the country, where the top 1 percent claim only 10 percent of national income.

A useful shorthand for visualizing inequality is the ratio of the income of the top 5 percent of the population to the bottom 20 percent. This measure shows the San Francisco metro area to be one of the three most unequal in the country (fig. 3.2). What is distinctive about cities like San Francisco and Boston is that the inequality is generated primarily at the top, while in other unequal cities, such as Atlanta and Miami, the main factor is the low income of the bottom 20 percent.[4]

When it comes to the topmost social strata, however, income is not a sufficient index of how rich they are. It is necessary to turn to the concentration of *wealth* in order to come to grips with the immensity of the chasm between the elite and everyone else. Wealth inequality is greater by orders of

---

4   Berube & Holmes 2014, Lehman-Frisch 2015.

magnitude than income differences. Among the elite, incomes derive chiefly from *property*, not from work. That is, income flows from returns on the ownership of capital assets such as stocks, bonds, and real estate, not from salaries and wages. Moreover, the wealthy reinvest their high incomes in more property to expand the base of their riches.

The Bay Area is characterized by an extreme concentration of ultrawealthy people. The region has led the country for years in the number and proportion of millionaires, or what the U.S. Census calls "high net worth individuals" (with or without including the value of houses). Taking only those in the top 1 percent (defined as having more than $30 million in capital assets), it is fourth in the world and second in the United States to New York, with nearly four thousand such people in 2017.[5] As for billionaires, the Forbes 400 list of America's wealthiest individuals included fifty from the Bay Area in 2016, second only to New York in number and far more per capita than any other metropolitan region, including the Big Apple.[6]

A great many of the Bay Area billionaires made their money in IT, and many of those names are common currency around the region and the country: Mark Zuckerberg, Laurene Powell Jobs, Sergey Brin, Meg Whitfield, and so on. Some captains of the tech industry are less well known, such as Larry Ellison, Thomas Siebel, or Jan Koum. Other local billionaires come from the world of finance, such as Charles Schwab, George Roberts, and Tom Steyer, or, like the Fisher family of the Gap, come out of the world of retail. George Lucas is a crossover between movies and technical effects. A few on the list are old families who made their money long ago and held onto it, such as the Haases, Goldmans, and Hearsts.

Bay Area's Fifty Billionaires, 2016[7]

Technology

No. 3	Larry Ellison $48.2 billion, Oracle Corp.
No. 10	Mark Zuckerberg $34.9 billion, Facebook
No. 12	Larry Page $31.7 billion, Google
No. 13	Sergey Brin $31.2 billion, Google
No. 28	Laurene Powell Jobs & family $16.4 billion, Apple

---

5   On millionaires, see Walker & Lohda 2013, p. 58; also Walker et al. 1990. For the 1% count, see Wealth-X 2017. That study underestimates the Bay Area by, typically, failing to add together San Francisco–Oakland and Silicon Valley. See chapter 7 on defining the Bay Area.

6   See, e.g., http://www.forbes.com/forbes-400/; http://www.forbes.com/billionaires/. The Forbes 400 only includes about three-quarters of American billionaires today; according to SFLuxe.com, the Bay Area is actually home to over seventy billionaires.

7   Source: Guzman 2016 based on *Forbes 400* annual list.

No. 47   Eric Schmidt $9.4 billion, Google

No. 53   Dustin Moskovitz $8.2 billion, Facebook

No. 60   Jan Koum $7.8 billion, WhatsApp

No. 70   Gordon Moore $7 billion, Intel

No. 97   Nicholas Woodman $5 billion, GoPro

No. 127   Reid Hoffman $3.9 billion, LinkedIn

No. 158   Brian Acton $3.4 billion, WhatsApp

No. 163   Dagmar Dolby & family $3.4 billion, Dolby Laboratories

No. 167   John Doerr $3.3 billion, Kleiner Perkins Caufield & Byers

No. 178   Evan Williams $3.2 billion, Twitter

No. 181   Marc Benioff $3.2 billion, Salesforce

No. 189   David Filo $3.1 billion, Yahoo

No. 239   Jack Dorsey, $2.6 billion, Twitter

No. 264   Romesh Wadhwani $2.5 billion, Symphony Technology Group

No. 286   Thomas Siebel $2.3 billion, Siebel Systems

No. 331   Meg Whitman $2 billion, eBay

No. 342   Jerry Wang $1.93, Yahoo

No. 345   Scott Cook $1.9 billion, Intuit

No. 350   Kavitark Ram Shriram $1.87 billion, Google

Services

No. 295   Daniel Pritzker $2.2 billion, Marmon & Hyatt Hotels

No. 325   Robert Fisher $2 billion, Gap

Real Estate

No. 109   John A. Sobrato & family $4.6 billion

No. 293   John Arrillaga $2.2 billion

No. 300   Richard Peery $2.2 billion

Finance

No. 74   Charles Schwab $6.6 billion, Charles Schwab

No. 80   Rupert Johnson $6.3 billion, Franklin Resources

No. 95   George Roberts $5 billion, KKR

No. 251   Michael Moritz $2.6 billion, Sequoia Capital

No. 301   James Coulter $2.2 billion, TPG

No. 302   Peter Thiel $2.2 billion, Facebook, Founders Fund

No. 306   Jim Breyer $2.1 billion, Accel Partners

No. 310   Douglas Leone $2.1 billion, Sequoia Capital

No. 381   Vinod Khosla $1.67 billion, Khosla Ventures

No. 387   Mark Stevens $1.62 billion, Sequoia Capital

No. 389   Thomas Steyer $1.62 billion Farallon Capital

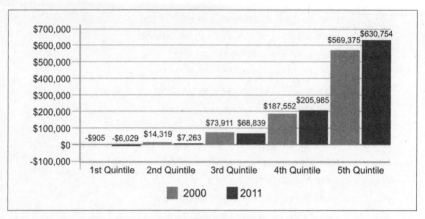

Figure 3.3: Household Net Worth in the USA, 2000 vs. 2011

Source: Marina Vornovitsky, Alfred Gottschalck & Adam Smith, *Distribution of Household Wealth in the U.S.: 2000 to 2011*, at http://www.census.gov/people/wealth/.

Ownership of wealth is concentrated almost entirely at the top of the social ladder in the United States. For the country as a whole the top 0.1 percent of households own more than one-fifth of all income-earning wealth, the rest of the top 1 percent another fifth. The next 10 percent own another two-fifths of the wealth and the rest of the top 50 percent another fifth. The lower half of the American people have no net worth at all, and the bottom 20 percent are permanently in debt. This distribution corresponds well to the Occupy Wall Street slogan that the country is split between the 1% and the other 99, though it might be more valid to speak of the 10 percent versus the rest (fig. 3.3). The share of wealth at the top has been growing markedly over the last generation (see fig. 3.9).[8]

There are no wealth distribution figures for the Bay Area alone, but the rapid growth of the West Coast, noted in chapter 2, has a parallel in the burgeoning wealth of the region. As one writer recently observed, "There has been a huge westward shift in wealth thanks to the new economy. California now has more billionaires than New York and more millionaires than the entire East Coast, from Maine to Georgia." The New Gilded Age is in full flower on the West Coast and, with it, the same old ideology of the deserving rich. As Tom Perkins, a leading Silicon Valley venture capitalist, declared with all due hubris, "The One Percent are not causing inequality—they are the job creators."[9]

---

8   Saez & Zucman 2014. Based on 2013 U.S. tax records.
9   Westward quote from Callahan 2010, p. 167. Perkins quoted in Keen 2015, p. 35.

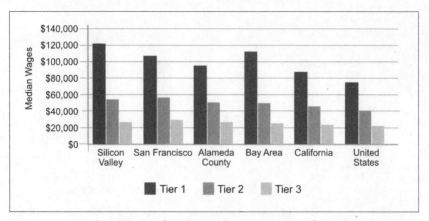

Figure 3.4: Wages by Skill Level for Silicon Valley, Bay Area, California & USA, 2014–15

Source: Massaro 2016, p. 26. Note: Tier 1 occupations (including chief executives, lawyers, accountants, physicians, and highly skilled technical occupations such as scientists, programmers, and engineers) are the highest-paying positions in the economy. Tier 2 (including teachers, librarians, administrative positions, manufacturing, and production positions such as assemblers and machinists) have historically provided the majority of employment opportunities and may be referred to as middle-wage, middle-skill positions. Tier 3 (including food service and retail positions, building and grounds cleaning positions, and personal care positions such as home health aides and child care workers) are lower-skilled service positions with lower wages that require little formal training or education. These categories correspond roughly to divisions laid out in Chapter 4.

Salaried, Skilled, and Professional

Something else has happened in the Bay Area and across the country to augment income inequality in the era of the New Economy since the 1980s: the top 20 percent of earners have done remarkably well, pulling away from the rest. These high earners are generally those in the professions, technology, and management earning monthly salaries, rather than hourly or weekly wages. They are usually highly educated, with college or higher degrees, and possess skills that are in great demand by private firms, governments, universities, and the like. Their jobs tend to be rich in what students of labor markets call nonroutine, cognitive tasks. This group also has an important degree of wealth and income from capital assets, as just noted.

The San Francisco region has an unusually high percentage of people working in skilled, salaried occupations. The Bay Area has hundreds of thousands of high-quality jobs requiring mentally challenging and unscripted tasks, about one-sixth higher than the U.S. average. This is especially pronounced in the Tech World but is true in other leading sectors such as health care, higher education, finance, and business services. Because high-quality jobs attract well-educated workers (as well as keeping local college grads here), half the local workforce has a degree from a four-year college, double the rate of Los

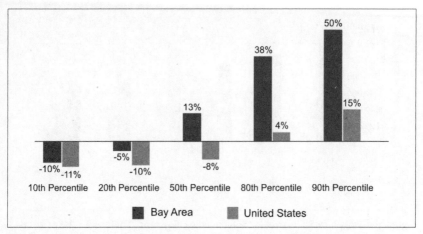

Figure 3.5: Income Gains of Upper Wage Earners, Bay Area vs. USA, 1979–2012
Source: Policy Link 2015 (5-county Bay Area).

Angeles. Only Greater Boston and Washington, DC, rival the Bay Area in the proportion of college graduates and higher degree holders.[10]

Not surprisingly, Bay Area professionals, managers and skilled workers are very well paid, with the "techies" leading the way with average salaries around $150,000 per year. Using a rough tripartite division of the labor, the top third earns more than $100,000, while the rest have lagged behind; the top tier of skilled workers earns almost five times the average of the lowest tier of unskilled workers. This is especially true of Silicon Valley and the West Bay, with the East Bay distribution slightly more equal (fig. 3.4). Moreover, the Bay Area's upper wage earners have outrun the rest of the country by a considerable margin for decades (fig. 3.5).

This is not a new story in the Bay Area, where a prosperous economy has been able to pay well and attract a large contingent of educated and skilled labor for a century and a half, and those people, in turn, made this an innovative, high-growth city long before the age of IT. The youthful techies of today hark back to the young Argonauts of the Gold Rush era or the waves of young people moving west during and after the Second World War. This has been a good place for in-migrants, who have outnumbered locally born entrants to the labor force by the end of every boom period.[11]

No wonder people in Kansas take a dim view of coastal elites. They are not so wrong to think that there's a real gulf between the two worlds. The

---

10 Figure on job quality from Storper et al. 2015, pp 44–45. Education figures (2010) from ibid., p. 52 and Walker & Lodha 2013, p. 58. For more on skill and job quality, see chapter 4.
11 Walker 1996, 2001.

youthful members of the skilled echelons of San Francisco or New York are earning outrageous salaries and living a very good life. A lot of them really do see the rest of the country as the "flyover." They think they are clever, educated, and enlightened citizens of the modern, High Tech world, and look askance at midwestern and southern workers and conservatives who cry out against gay marriage, loose morals, and immigration. Beneath these divergent worldviews lies a huge gulf in income and consumption, as well as the gap in regional development noted in the last chapter.[12]

Wage Workers

The Bay Area's high average income ought to translate into a rising tide lifting all boats, and to some degree this is true. The region's income advantage over other big cities is just as notable if only wages and salaries are considered. The same job and the same worker with the same education will be paid more, on average, in the Bay Area than anywhere else. There is clearly a knock-on effect on all wages from the enormous revenues pouring into the region.[13]

Nevertheless, most workers do ordinary jobs, are paid in wages and make anything but extraordinary incomes. The Bay Area may be a high average wage region, but millions of people still go home with middling to lousy paychecks. Moreover, inequality between different strata of the labor force has been growing, with the bulk of the improvement in the higher-skilled realms. People in humble jobs, such as custodians, security guards, and nursing aides, are not feeling the buzz.

A helpful study of the nine-county Bay Area breaks the workforce into three tiers—high, middle and low wage earners—and gives an idea of the wage ranges and percentages in each category. Only the high wage group can be considered well off, and it has been shrinking slightly for years. As for the middle tier, the economy is not generating enough new middle-wage jobs to keep the proportion of workers in that category from shrinking (fig. 3.6). Moreover, the middle tier is not secure at the lower end, since a household with two adults and two children could barely meet basic expenses in much of the region.[14]

In fact, the Bay Area and other coastal cities are not strong in creating and sustaining a middle-income group, despite their wealth. Paradoxically,

---

12 Frank 2004, 2016, Callahan 2010, Williams 2017.
13 Storper et al. 2015, table on p. 39. On income diffusion within the region, p. 79. See also Moretti 2012. Bay Area wage gains outran the rest of the country up to 2015, then fell back a bit.
14 Policy Link & PERE 2015. See also ABAG 2014, pp. 8, 20, 51.

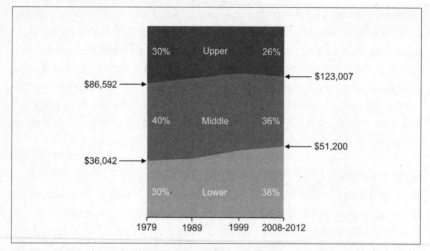

Figure 3.6: The Shrinking Middle Wage Tier in the Bay Area, 1979–2012
Source: Policy Link 2015 (5-county Bay Area).

midwestern cities do much better on this score. To put it in other terms, inequality is worsening in the region as the middle shrinks and the top and bottom income layers expand. Using another common measure of inequality, the Gini Coefficient, the Bay Area looks better than in the 95/20 measure cited above, but a sign of the times is that its Gini inequality ranking among U.S. cities has risen from number forty-five to number fifteen. Notably, the four counties of the West Bay come out much worse, ranking somewhere on a par with Guatemala, putting the heartland of High Tech neck and neck with a nation of *latifundia*.[15]

★   ★   ★

The worst aspect of the bay region's wage distribution is not the shrinking middle but the sheer number of low-wage workers (see again fig. 3.6). The hourly wage of this bottom group is less than half the regional average, two-thirds of them are paid the minimum wage, and they are half as likely to have employer-paid health care and pension plans. Low-wage work employs well over a third of the labor force, or around 1.3 million people, which translates into 3–4 million in those working families. This is only slightly better than the proportion of low-wage work in California and the nation. Another name for low-wage workers is a cheap labor, and it is shocking to see how prevalent it

---

15   Egan 2014, Knight 2014, Lehman-Frisch 2015, Berube & Holmes 2016. Midwestern workers are more likely to own homes that those in the Bay Area, too.

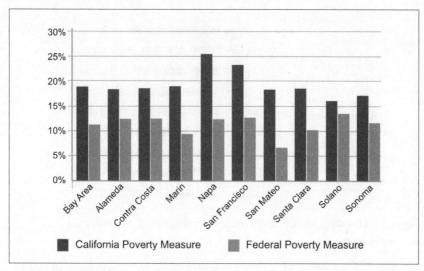

Figure 3.7: Poverty Rates in Bay Area Counties, 2011

Source: ABAG 2014.

is in the Bay Area, which is not considered a cheap labor haven like, say, Texas or Georgia.[16]

Yet another name for low-wage workers is the Working Poor. On first glance, poverty in the bay region looks mild compared to the rest of California, which had the highest rate in the country in the depths of the Great Recession. Using the federal standard, which came to around $24,000 a year in 2017, the Bay Area's poverty rate looks relatively low at about 12 percent. But that standard is a flat rate for the country, quite out of keeping with the high costs of the bay region. If the standard is adjusted for regional cost of living, as in the California Poverty Measure shown in the chart, the poverty rate shoots up close to 20 percent (fig. 3.7).[17]

Using the federal measure for eligibility for food stamps and free school lunches, which is double the basic standard, poverty hits close to one out of every four households—a startling figure for such a rich metropolis. As a consequence, large numbers of Bay Area working households have to rely on public assistance and food banks to survive, and tens of thousands of

16 Low-wage work is usually defined as below two-thirds of the median wage. The dollar figure for the low-wage threshold in California, ca. 2015, was about $14 versus approximately $20 for the Bay Area. Bernhardt et al. 2015, p. 3. ABAG 2014. There is also widespread wage theft from this group.

17 On Bay Area poverty, see Wimer et al. 2016. On California poverty, see Bohn et al., 2013, Walker & Lodha 2013, and the Stanford Center on Poverty & Inequality website: http:// inequality.stanford.edu/.

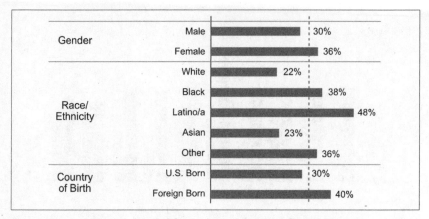

Figure 3.8: Low-Wage Work in California, by Gender, Race & Nativity, 2014

Source: Bernhardt 2014.

children feel the pinch of hunger. A recent study by a food bank in Silicon Valley showed one in four people at risk of hunger, a truly devastating figure. The booming tech economy has not solved the problem of poverty in the region by a long shot.[18]

While people of color and immigrants earn more on average in the Bay Area that other cities, and earn more at every level of education and in every industry, there is an unrelenting inequality based on gender and race. The burden of low-wage work falls disproportionately on the backs of women, racialized minorities, and immigrants, as throughout California (fig. 3.8). Upper-level jobs in the tech industry and other high-flying sectors of the Bay Area are still mostly filled by white men, with a sprinkling of educated Chinese and Indians (many of them immigrants). Conversely, those industries and the well-off elite and salaried workers depend every day on the labor of millions of ordinary workers who are overwhelmingly not white and not male (see chapter 4).[19]

None of this diminishes the greater poverty and desperation in those sections of the United States not prospering in the Age of Information, or the plight of billions of workers elsewhere in the world making even less than low-wage American workers. The Bay Area and its tech capitalism is but the tip of the iceberg of global labor exploitation and inequality. Yet even here inequality has grown to unimaginable heights, while tens of thousands of

---

18   On hunger, see Duggan 2017, Hayward 2017. On the need for public assistance by low-wage workers, see Jacobs et al. 2016. For national survey that concludes that the robust tech industry does not lower poverty rates, see Lee & Rodriguez-Pose 2016.

19   On higher average wages across the board, see Storper et al. 2015, p. 67.

working families live in poverty. That is a shocking fact of life in the Bay Area and it calls for a deeper look at the social order of the city.[20]

The American Aversion to Class

Those are the numbers, but how to interpret them? What do they tell us about the shape and significance of inequality in the Bay Area and in the twenty-first century United States? This is the point at which the discussion has to move beyond simple categories such as elite, salaried workers, and low-wage workers to confront the problem of class. Unfortunately, this is the point where most American readers become impatient and prefer to just get on with the story. Don't the numbers speak for themselves? Inequality is growing, the rich are getting richer, and a lot of people are poor. That is obvious enough.

Nevertheless, there is more that the numbers can say if the right questions are put to them. But good questions require good concepts and a framework for thinking about society and economy; class theory provides that, if given a chance. Yet class analysis is too often dismissed out of hand, for three reasons—one philosophical, one political, and one historical-geographical. Instead, Americans have averred that the country either has no permanent classes or that nearly everyone is in the "middle class."[21]

The first reason for this aversion is the long-standing belief—going back to the Classical Liberalism of John Locke, Adam Smith and John Stuart Mill, and the inspiration for American Founding Fathers like Jefferson and Madison—that a market economy provides just returns for personal merit and hard work, and is preferable to aristocratic privilege, political power, and other sources of unearned wealth. In this view, class is an attribute of precapitalist social systems and cannot resist the erosive power of the market. Classical Liberalism runs into trouble, however, because even with free markets people start from unequal positions, money buys unfair advantages, and merit is not justly rewarded. Unfortunately, that is very much what we see today, and it has sparked renewed debate over meritocracy, privilege, and power.

A second reason for a hasty dismissal of class theory is the way it was associated with twentieth-century Communism. In the hands of true believers, class was the one great social divide in the world, shoving all concerns aside, and the Socialist Revolution would sweep it away to install a veritable heaven of equality and justice. Alas, that is not quite how things worked out, and even on the Left the concept of class lost ground to race, gender, and

---

20 Elliot 2017.
21 For interesting recent discussions of class theory, see Zweig 2000, 2004, Sayer 2005, 2015, Chibber 2017. On the American liberal avoidance of class, see Tyrell 1986.

other social cleavages in the fight for a more just society. The lesson is that class is not the magic key to solve all questions of social justice. Yet class thinking has made a remarkable comeback since the Occupy movement of 2011, when people began to denounce the wealth of the 1%.

A third problem for Americans is that class seems like a concept derived from Old Europe that does not speak to the experience of this country. To an important degree, that has been true. The early Republic in the northern United States was the most egalitarian society on earth at the time and nineteenth-century growth, mass immigration, and continental expansion opened up vast opportunities for millions ordinary people to get ahead. Of course, there are a few deadly silences in that uplifting story, such as native genocide, black slavery, and Gilded Age wealth concentration, but Americans like to believe the nation righted itself through abolition, women's suffrage, and Progressive Era reforms.

In the twentieth century, the upbeat story of exceptionalism took a new form: the emergence of the Great American Middle Class in the postwar era. In the Golden Age of prosperity that followed the Second World War, there was an unprecedented bulge in the middle of the income distribution as wages improved for millions of industrial workers. The United States was once again delivering on its promise of opportunity and equality, people were moving en masse to the suburbs, and their children were going to college in unprecedented numbers. The latter was especially important in eliding class boundaries by propelling large numbers of baby-boomers into an expanding professional-technical workforce (and into the ranks of the upper middle class).[22]

There are three problems with that reassuring story, however. The first is that origins of that golden moment rested on economic crisis, world war, and intense political struggle. Inequality peaked in the 1920s and was only reversed because the upper crust were knocked down to size by the stock market crash of 1929, the Great Depression, and the New Deal of the 1930s. The wealthy took severe losses and were hit with higher taxes, while the corporations had to contend with more regulation and with industrial workers who finally gained the right to unionize. Next came the World War, which devastated Europe and Japan, leaving the United States as undisputed king of the hill, with two-thirds of the world's manufacturing capacity. The postwar middle class did not just grow out of the normal operations of U.S. capitalism.

The second problem with the story is that Blacks were still largely denied he middle class, as were most Mexicans and Filipinos. Prevailing

36, Fraser & Gerstle 1989, Beauregard 2006.

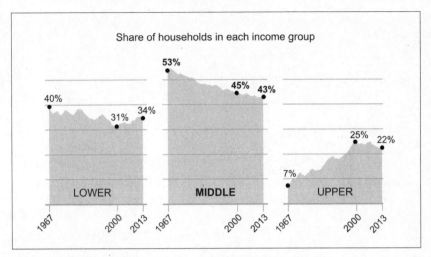

Figure 3.9: Shrinking Middle Class in the United States, 1967–2013

Source: Parlapiano et al. 2015.

White racism and the power of the southern bloc in Congress kept the New Deal order from extending to domestic and agricultural workers, and the unions, more often than not, excluded non-Whites from membership. In addition, after the war women were pushed out of the labor force back into the domestic sphere. Thanks to a long period of political struggle peaking in the civil rights and feminist movements of the 1960s, things improved; but the great postwar middle class was a largely White and male-dominated construction.[23]

Third, even that broad postwar middle class, which included large numbers of ordinary working people for the first time, did not last that long. The conditions that made it possible eroded sharply in the last quarter of the twentieth century. On the one hand, the U.S. economy faced new challenges that hurt profits and raised unemployment (see chapter 2). On the other, a new movement emerged on the Right to challenge New Deal Liberalism and the postwar order, called neoconservatism or neoliberalism (see chapter 10). As a result, the elite began to reap the bulk of gains in national income and the middle-income bulge deflated. Today it is widely recognized that the middle class is in deep trouble.[24]

The history of changes in the distribution of income and wealth are plain to see in the data for the United States assembled by a new generation

---

23 See, e.g., Lichtenstein 2002, Katznelson 2005, 2015, Milkman 1987.
24 On the history of U.S. inequality see Phillips 2002, Piketty 2011. Inattention to wealth inequality until very recently speaks volumes about the American avoidance of class. McCarty et al. 2006.

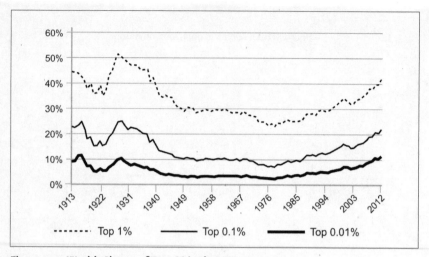

Figure 3.10: Wealth Shares of Top 1% in the USA, 1913–2012

Source: inequality.org, based on Saez & Zucman 2014,

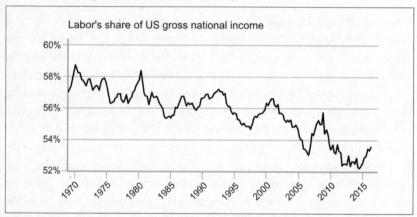

Figure 3.11: Declining Labor Share of National Income, 1967–2015

Source: https://www.theatlas.com/charts/H1iJrw3o.

of economic historians.[25] Three striking graphics now gaining wide circulation are those showing the rising share of wealth going to the 1%, the division of national income skewing back toward capital, and the shrinking middle of the income distribution (figs 3.9, 3.10, 3.11). Add to these facts the disturbing discovery that, for the first time in memory, the millennial generation is doing worse than their parents. This should be a real wake-up call for those who believe that class does not matter in America—yet the dominant

---

25 See especially Piketty 2011, Saez & Zucman 2014, Zucman 2015. Also Wolff 2014. Current studies are nicely summarized at *inequality.org*, a project of the Economic Policy Institute.

discourse, referred to many times in President Obama's speeches, is that everyone is either in or aspiring to the Great American Middle Class. Myths die hard.

Class in the New Economy

Perhaps talking about class is again permissible, as confidence about the egalitarian, classless nature of American society weakens in the face of facts on the ground. Let's revisit the previous discussion of the three major income categories to see if thinking about them in class terms can reveal more about the nature of inequality in the country and the Bay Area. Remember that class is not a passive stamp put on people by their income, but depends on matters of ownership and power, relation to other classes and to one another, and coming together around shared conditions and aspirations.

The most striking thing about the Bay Area's top 1 percent is, of course, how much richer they have become, and how fast; but that immediately points beyond mere income to an astonishing buildup of wealth. Income from wealth is not the same as income from labor; it is based on ownership of capital assets—companies, corporate stocks, real estate, and some government bonds thrown in. That is what defines a capitalist class—they are the owners of society's industrial, financial, and landed property. Moreover, what makes someone a capitalist is not just ownership but the restless reinvestment of capital to make more money. By the means of capital accumulation, wealth can build up exponentially (the miracle of compound interest). What one sees in the Bay Area's billionaires is overwhelmingly men who own the biggest companies, manage financial assets, develop real estate, and so forth, and who do so with the aim of making more profits and accumulating yet more capital. These are the new capitalist class, whether they are called the 1%, the superrich, or the business elite.[26]

One can try to argue that these people are so clever that they deserve their just reward, but as the sums mount up in amounts beyond all normal reckoning, that argument loses credibility. The bottom falls out completely when they cannot stop themselves from adding massive tax avoidance to their haul (see chapter 2). Another angle might be that these are nouveaux riches and therefore do not constitute a self-reproducing class; but Marx's definition

---

26 Marx 1863. Thomas Piketty (2011) has rightly attracted a good deal of attention with his revival of the argument that capitalist wealth will necessarily snowball if no brakes are applied to its compounding. His theory of capital is not Marxian, however. Piketty is correct that wealth tends to snowball unless derailed by war, but his theory of "capital" as a social force is very thin compared to that of Marx, and his politics of wealth control is a bit naive.

only requires that they behave in a capitalist way, as their competitive fire and continued profit-seeking show. Moreover, they soon go from youthful entrepreneur to heads of giant corporations with thousands of employees to be bossed, stockholders to be rewarded, and brand names to be burnished (chapter 1). They are giants striding the globe like the J. P. Morgans, John D. Rockefellers, and Henry Fords of the past—with Steve Jobs the iconic figure of his age. Moreover, the Tech Barons such as Mark Zuckerberg, Marc Benioff, and Sergey Brin have become highly visible in the public arena and their influence on policy and politics has grown rapidly (see chapters 9 and 10).[27]

There is more afoot in the accumulation of wealth by the 1% than the enrichment of a few capitalists. It also marks a substantial redistribution of income and wealth upward from labor to capital across the board (fig. 3.11). That redistribution is chiefly a political phenomenon brought about in two ways: by tax cuts for the rich and corporations and by systematic suppression of wages by employers. It is what some observers, including billionaire Warren Buffett, have called "class struggle from above," but most political commentators refer to as the triumph of "neoconservatism" (or, on the Left, as "neoliberalism").[28]

Next, consider the well-paid, salaried workers of the upper 20 percent of income distribution, who are especially prominent in the Bay Area. Do they constitute a class and, if so, what should they be called? There was a massive expansion of the ranks of the professions and management over the course of the twentieth century. This is particularly true in the Bay Area, with its profusion of certified professionals such as doctors and lawyers; educated managers in large firms, government, education, and health care; and, of course, the hundreds of thousands of highly educated workers in the tech sector and other industries. One proposal that makes sense is to call them "the professional-managerial-technical class," but that's a mouthful and in everyday parlance they are known as the "upper middle class." Other shorthands exist, such as "the professions," or, locally, "the techies," but these terms are too partial, so "upper middle class" will have to do.[29]

Yet the upper middle class is a contradictory crowd, so can they really be considered a class apart? Sociologists have been arguing over how to deal

---

27 Lower strata of the capitalist class are made up of small business owners in retail, tech, dentistry, and so forth who have done well for themselves and fall into the top 10 percent of wealth holders.

28 Harvey 2002. For more on the history of neoconservatism/neoliberalism, see chapter 10.

29 The professional-managerial-technical class idea was posed first by Ehrenreich & Ehrenreich (1977) and taken up by radical sociologist Erik Wright (1985, 1989) and colleagues around the world. On the rise of the professionals, see Larsen 1977, Hatch 1988.

with this group for over a century.[30] On the one hand, many of their number are workers, in the classic sense of needing to get a job to earn a living; this is true of even managers and professionals, while the bulk of this group consists simply of high-skilled workers whose talents and knowledge are scarce and in great demand—hence the elevated paychecks (professional athletes and entertainers are cases of this kind of payoff). On the other hand, their earnings can be extremely high; recall that the top 5 percent of incomes in the bay region are off the charts. While some might still consider the highest skilled workers as the upper strata of the working class, such high incomes elevates them to into the upper middle class.

And high pay is not the end of their elevated class position; members of the upper middle class are closely affiliated to the capitalist class in important ways. One is the extra rewards they regularly earn, such as the stock options that the tech industry made a normal thing for top-tier employees. Another is that high earnings are usually converted into capital assets like stocks and real estate. The fact is the top 10 percent (beyond the 1%) own a hefty two-fifths of the wealth and very likely more than that in the Bay Area. Managers and professionals also play a large role in firms and other organizations, directing the work of others, which puts them over ordinary workers. Engineers and scientists have long been close allies of upper management, and often move up into leadership positions. Politically, professionals often dominate the power structures of localities, in alliance with business.[31]

In the present environment, the upper middle class has done so much better than the rest of the working population that putting them into a broad American Middle Class is less and less appropriate (making the term 'upper middle class' even more confusing). They appear to have consolidated their collective position and pulled away from the working class below them—that is, behaved more and more like a class apart. This is quite visible in the way many Bay Area techies identify with the IT companies and aspire to join the ranks of capitalists one day. The seductions of start-ups, stock options, and the Next Big Thing are hard to resist, and the culture of moneymaking and the capitalist casino sweeps many into its arms.

Moreover, there is growing evidence that the upper middle class protect their advantages through strategies such as living in gated communities. Crucially, they dominate access to the best schools and higher

---

30   For a summary, see Giddens 1980, Giddens & MacKenzie 1982. The arguments swirl around division of labor, stratification, and class, with a strong measure of cultural valuation versus economic standing. For my own view of the intersection of class and the division of labor, see Sayer and Walker 1992.

31   Noble 1977, Cox 2016.

education—thereby undercutting the meritocracy on which their own legitimacy rests. In fairness, some of the desperation of this class to assure the
future of their children is due to the growing precariousness of employment
for the young (see chapter 4) and decline of public schools (see chapter 10).
But their response to those threats has too often been a turn toward private
solutions not public investment or better regulation of employers.[32]

Given the accumulating evidence of the decline of upward mobility
into the ranks of professionals through education of clever children of the
working class, it is not surprising that resentment has grown against the
privileges and power of the upper middle class. For various reasons, these are
feelings often more immediate and intense than those against the superrich
or capitalist class. This is hard to swallow for most Bay Area liberals—including the author—who would like to believe they not among the upper classes;
but they are.[33]

Our third group, wage workers, is by far the largest, upwards of 80
percent of the population. Can they reasonably be considered a "working
class," or is that old-fashioned term based on wishful thinking? They fit the
bill in that they overwhelmingly work for wages (some have fixed salaries but
most are paid on a time basis, i.e., wages) and have to go to work every day to
survive. At work, they are subject to the direction of employers and orders of
supervisors, whether tightly or loosely controlled. They own little property
other than a car and, for half of worker households, a house / condo. But does
the shared condition of not owning capital (property than earns money) and
doing wage work make people into a class?

The working class is split in three or four main ways that undercut a
single identity or buildup of solidarity. The first is the wide differences among
workers in wages and incomes, from quite robust to rather dismal. The wage
distribution is, to a considerable extent, based on occupations and the rewards
that come with more skilled jobs, more autonomy and greater supervisory
responsibilities. Job hierarchies tend to stratify the workforce and give more
workplace power and social prestige to those with higher skills and education.
They also have a better chance of seeing their children get a good education

---

32 On upper-middle-class strategies of self-promotion, see Golden 2006, Reeves 2017a. For
    critiques of the meritocracy and equal education, see Bowles & Gintis 1976, McNamee
    & Miller 2014, Guinier 2015, Barnes 2016. To compare class, race, and education through
    maps, see those of the Bay Area by Bill Rankin for 2010. http://www.radicalcartography.
    net/index.html?bayarea

33 On class resentment against the upper middle class, see Frank 2004, 2016, Callahan 2010,
    Geismer 2015, Williams 2017. On delusions of this class, see Ehrenreich 2005, McCarty et
    al. 2006, Reeves 2017b.

and do well. The Bay Area high average wage hides the deep divide between such favored workers and a huge low-wage workforce.[34]

A second problem is the sheer size of the working population and the deep individualism of Americans, both of which belie any easy sense of unity as a social class. It has taken unionization, stable residential communities and political struggles to bring workers together at certain times and places. A key moment in U.S. labor history was the unionization of the mass industrial work force in the middle of the twentieth century, which not only ushered millions of semi-skilled workers into the ranks of the Great American Middle Class, but provided organizational solidarity and a collective identity for working people, even as they aspired to move up to middle-class status. In the Bay Area, unions were particularly strong in the past, but are weaker today; yet they still provide a framework for working-class solidarity.[35]

A third fundamental divide is race and nationality. Racial discrimination and antagonism against immigrants have plagued U.S. history and split the American working class. Racial ordering is a fundamental inequality in it own right, with a wholly separate basis from class. The ugly reality of white racism among working people has segregated communities, poisoned unions, and cast doubt on the very idea of the "working class." The civil rights era forced the integration of recalcitrant unions and improved race relations in many places, including the Bay Area, but never completely overcame white privilege. The racial hierarchy still shows up clearly in occupational and wage differences among Bay Area workers (see fig. 3.8 and chapter 4).[36]

There is, finally, the ongoing inequality between men and women and the imprint of patriarchy on work and workers. Sexism plagues the workforce in the allocation of jobs, the prestige assigned to occupations, and the persistent wage gap suffered by women. And it goes beyond the workplace into the domestic sphere, where women are burdened with the double duty of caring for home, children, and the elderly. Women workers are persistently disadvantaged at all levels but are especially present in the low-wage workforce—and this is no less true in the well-off and liberally minded Bay Area.[37]

Despite all the barriers to the formation of a clearly defined working class, in the twenty-first century Bay Area conditions have shifted in ways that

---

34 Differences between workers in different industries also matter. Sayer & Walker 1992.
35 Davis 1986, Lichtenstein 2002, Glass 2016.
36 Davis 1986, Lichtenstein 2002, Bernhardt et al. 2015. On race versus class generally, see, e.g., Omi & Winant 1986, Balibar & Wallerstein 1991, Lustig 2004.
37 Milkman 1987, Ehrenreich 2001, 2005, Bernhardt et al. 2015, Frederickson 2015, Mount St. Marys 2015. On women and class more generally, see Hartman 1979, Federici 2012, Fraser 2014.

may well point to greater unity among the working people who make up the vast majority of the population. One is the shrinkage of the upper and middle tiers of wage-earners, even in the case of the best-paid work force in America, which has put more working people in the same boat and diminished the power of the idea of being in the Great American Middle Class.[38] Another trend is the way class and race have converged, especially in the sharp racial divide between the heavily white upper classes and bottom two-thirds of the labor force, which is made up overwhelmingly of people of color and large numbers of immigrants and their children. The same goes for the way gender aligns with class in the contemporary Bay Area, thanks to the extreme male domination of the tech industry.

These conditions have prompted a host of new movements that go beyond fighting for better wages and middle-class status—movements to defend immigrants, oppose sexism, stop wholesale criminalization, and fight for racial justice. The scope of those efforts is so great that they might well deserve the old-fashioned term "class struggles." There is so much to consider in assessing the state of the working class in the Bay Area that the whole of the next chapter is devoted to it.

★ ★ ★

A final word on class: it is not just about distribution of income and wealth, but about economic exploitation and political power. Both Classical Liberalism and American popular ideology tiptoe around these aspects of capitalist society. The socialist and labor Left, by contrast, has always insisted on the ugly side of a social order in which a relatively small percentage of people own most of the financial assets, businesses, and real estate. That ownership and the riches it delivers into a few hands gives the 1% and their allies in the top 10 percent effective control over the private economy and the right to hire and fire, direct and supervise, everyone else. And that includes the power to profit off their labor and to receive rents and interest for the use of their property.[39]

Mainstream economics considers profits to be the leftovers after labor, capital, and land have been paid their due, shrinking to zero in equilibrium. The distribution of income is determined by the market prices for goods and the contribution ("marginal productivity") of labor, land, and capital equipment. Marxian economics, by contrast, argues that the ultimate producer of output and value is labor, from which profits, rents, and interest are extracted

---

38 Smith 2012, Bernstein & Spielberg 2017.
39 For a thorough demolition of all conventional defenses of unearned wealth, see Sayer 2015.

(as "surplus value"). The idea of a labor surplus is not difficult to see: any worker who does not make more money for the company than s/he gets in wages will be fired. Of course, there is overhead, depreciation, and rent to be paid, but labor's surplus covers all that, too. At the macroeconomic scale, the same thing holds: the total national income is a product of human labor but divided up according to the relative power of the classes—which would include not just labor and capital but also the professional/managerial upper middle class. The lower the share going to wages, the higher the profit rate. Further, labor's share must be kept under control, or it will slow the accumulation of capital and generate an economic crisis (see chapter 2).[40]

There is a political side to these opposing economic theories, as well. Whereas Classical Liberalism is strong on the efficacy of markets and value of distributed property as a counterweight to state power, it is blind to the vastly unequal distribution of property and the power this gives to the 1% to buy politicians, pay lobbyists, fund think tanks, and generally steer laws and policy in their favor. A version of Classical Liberalism, called "pluralism" became popular in the United States after World War II; it projects the same idea of distributed power onto modern representative democracy, arguing that politics is the clash of innumerable private interests that balance out in the arena of public policy. But the representation of interests is not fairly distributed, and the evidence of the power of concentrated money over American politics from local governments to the national stage is piling up just like the wealth of the 1%. That power and opposition to it will feature in the rest of this book.[41]

The Human Cost of Inequality

Beyond all arguments about class and power, there is the frightful human cost of severe inequality. This is about more than the fact of exploitation and arguments about who benefits from whose labor. Nor is it just to regret the existence of poverty and the financial hardship facing those with low incomes. Paradoxically, many people around the world living in what Americans consider unacceptable poverty are actually happier and better protected by family, friends, and society than in this, the richest nation on earth. Inequality is a social relation, and the growth of inequality in the United States is a corrosive

---

40   Marx 1967. For modification of the theory to include nature and labor outside the capitalist system, see Moore 2015.

41   For critiques of pluralism, see Bachrach & Baratz 1970, Domhoff 1979. For introductions to the power of money in politics, see Drew 1999, Pierson & Hacker 2010, Meyer 2016. See also chapter 10.

force on people's minds, bodies, and survival. This goes for the Bay Area, in spades, despite its wondrous wealth and good fortune.

The social implications of inequality are dire. As public health researchers have shown through exhaustive statistical comparisons between countries and among U.S. states, inequality literally makes people sick and unhappy, and the more inequality the sicker and more miserable they are. Not surprisingly, among rich nations, the United States and Britain—where inequality is greatest—come off as the worst in measure after measure, from longevity to obesity, mental health to physical ailments. The United States and United Kingdom are notable, as well, for the strongest worship of market outcomes, the weakest social safety nets, and the harshest attitudes toward personal failure.[42]

Ironically, the same studies show that even the rich are worse off in unequal societies, not just the poor. Where capitalism rules, rich is never enough; even millionaires don't feel rich in Silicon Valley, or, as one affluent striver put it, "You're nobody here at $10 million."[43] We may not feel sorry for a miserable member of the elite, but the problem goes far deeper. It is wreaking havoc on the lives of ordinary working people who are neither millionaires nor homeless, but who are being underpaid, pushed around, and in danger of falling into penury at any time. The psychic toll of being an ordinary worker, let alone a member of the cheap labor force, can be huge (see chapter 4).[44]

Given the precarity of working people's lives, it does not take much to push some over the line. Workers and their families suffer so many blows that one more can be the punch that knocks them into disability, unemployment, and financial ruin. Some people begin spiraling down into addiction or mental illness. Families fall apart and can no longer take care of each other. The result is that thousands of people end up living in their cars or on the streets. The tattered social safety net in this country fails in all too many cases to help folks in need, whether it is interventions to protect mothers and children, paying for health care and drug treatment, or providing adequate unemployment insurance. Lack of affordable housing is, of course, a fundamental source of homelessness, and it is especially dire in the Bay Area—so much so that an entire chapter will be devoted to the problem (see chapter 6).

There are large numbers of homeless who manage, with amazing courage to continue working regular jobs, raising children, and coping with

---

42 Kawachi et al. 1999, Wilkinson & Pickett 2009.
43 Rivlin 2007.
44 Sennett 1998, Sennett & Cobb 1972, Ehrenreich 2001, 2005.

illness. Yet homelessness is a hardship from which it can be hard to recover after very much time on the streets. For many of those made homeless, physical and mental health suffer, addictions grow worse, and begging, petty crime, and prostitution become regular survival strategies. People go in and out of shelters, housing, and hospitals, not to mention jails. Some are ruined by the experience and many die from exposure. The sight of such human wreckage in the midst of plenty is heartbreaking.[45]

The numbers are homeless staggering. Official estimates taken one day a year run about 7,500 in San Francisco, 7,000 in Silicon Valley, and 5,500 in Alameda County. But that is but a screenshot of the real picture, and homeless service providers think these figures are serious undercounts because so many homeless people stay out of the way and move around in their vehicles. In any case, mere numbers do not capture the shock of so much human suffering in plain sight. It is a source of constant comment, concern, and complaint by Bay Area residents and visitors.[46]

The glow of the Bay Area's success is deeply tarnished by the tragic residue of thousands of homeless people on street corners, living out of cars, and camping under freeways. Wherever one goes in San Francisco, Berkeley, and Oakland, other than the most high-class neighborhoods, the homeless are to be found. In San Jose, the homeless are more dispersed and less visible because of the automotive landscape of Silicon Valley, but they are there, too, in creek beds, parks, and beside highways. It's not a pretty picture.

Cities around the bay have been struggling with the tidal wave of homelessness since the 1980s, trying out a variety of policies for shelter, social services, and police intervention.

San Francisco got a lot of attention with an initiative launched in 2004, called "Care Not Cash," which leased low-rent hotels to use as housing but took away people's general assistance on the tired old argument that poor people can't be trusted with money. It had little impact. A variety of public and nonprofit agencies have kept at it, providing shelters, food, medical care, and addiction clinics.

Today the city of San Francisco spends around a quarter-billion dollars a year on homeless programs, not all of them worth the money, by any means. A new initiative features "Navigation Centers," which help direct people to housing and other resources without immediately putting them

---

45 On the many paths to homelessness and the difficulty of getting back on one's feet, see Wolch & Dear 1993. See also references on unemployment and social distress in chapter 2 and the discussion of housing costs in chapter 6.

46 For numbers, see Fagan 2017a & b, Garafoli & Veklerov 2017, Kurhi 2017. On living in cars, see Orr 2017.

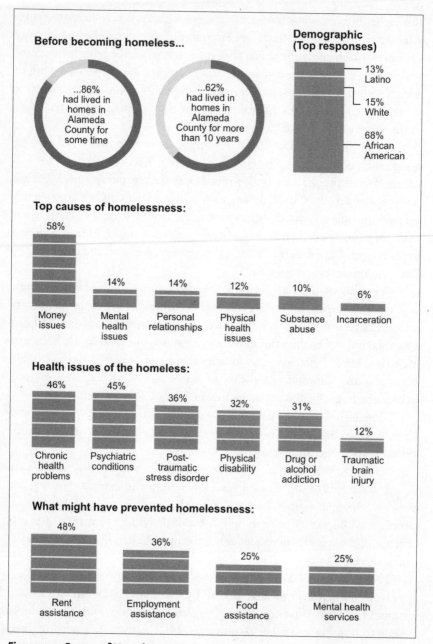

Figure 3.12: Causes of Homelessness

Source: Garafoli & Veklerov, 2017 based on data from http://everyonehome.org/wp-content/
uploads/2017/06/ALAEMDA_7–1.pdf.

into homeless shelters. A private charitable foundation called the Tipping Point Community Fund has raised $100 million from wealthy local donors to help out with mental health services, foster care, and prison release assistance. But all these efforts never get on top of the problem because there simply is not enough funding for housing.

San Jose and Santa Clara County have some of best homeless programs, but shelters and transitional housing are at capacity. Berkeley has long had excellent homeless services but faces the same Sisyphean dilemma. Oakland has often lagged in municipal efforts to help the homeless but has geared up assistance recently, including plans for villages of pod-like minihomes. Nevertheless, the numbers on the street speak volumes to how inadequate the resources for housing are and how intractable the situation has become.[47]

Along with the honorable efforts of so many homeless advocates and civil servants is a backstory of decreasing tolerance in the Bay Area for the homeless over the last thirty years. City councils have passed draconian laws against loitering, begging, sleeping, and defecating in public, which placates public opinion for a while. Some of the new princes of Tech World joined the chorus of critics of homelessness and public policy. One member of the tech elite voiced his disgust in a public statement:

> Every day, on my way to and from work, I see people sprawled across the sidewalk, tent cities, human feces, and the faces of addiction. The city is becoming a shanty town. . . . The residents of this amazing city no longer feel safe. I know people are frustrated about gentrification happening in the city, but the reality is, we live in a free market society. The wealthy working people have earned their right to live in the city. They went out, got an education, work hard, and earned it. . . . I shouldn't have to see the pain, struggle, and despair of homeless people to and from my way to work every day.[48]

A firestorm of criticism descended on this outspoken representative of the beleaguered class of "wealthy working people," but his views are quietly shared by far too many others: the idea that poor people do not work hard, the notion that the right to the city must be earned, and the belief in the fairness of the free market in housing. Each of these fallacies will be addressed directly in chapters 4, 5, and 6. What is perhaps most disturbing is the simple

---

47 On San Francisco's efforts, see Fagan 2017a & b, Knight 2017. On East Bay programs, see Garafoli & Veklerov 2017, Raguso 2017. On pod homes, see Gee 2017. On Universal Basic Income, see chapter 9.

48 Campbell 2016.

lack of humanity: that the successful should not have to witness the despair of those who have lost in the lottery of life.

When all else fails, local officials fall back on the age-old solution of expelling the unwanted, sweeping the homeless off the streets in the name of public health and decorum. Recently, San Jose cleared out "The Jungle," the largest homeless encampment in the country. Then San Francisco voters approved a ballot measure that made tent encampments illegal and allowed the city to seize tents and personal possessions. This bit of nastiness was well funded by Tech Titans such as Sequoia Capital chairman Michael Moritz and angel investor Ron Conway. Oakland has also taken to ejecting tent encampments under freeways.

None of it works. What the powers-that-be cannot admit is that the underlying causes of homelessness will never be solved in a place that runs on their most cherished principles: free markets, massive inequality, and impoverishment of the commonwealth. Those will continue to generate working lives that grind people down, perennial unemployment and debt, unaffordable housing, isolation and shattered families, and shredded public safety nets. Most of all, a society that measures itself by monetary success will continue to turn its back on "losers," in the charming term favored by the current occupant of the White House.[49]

Conclusion

Silicon Gold Rush is an overused metaphor for the current era, but it rests on real parallels to the Bay Area's past: in-rushing fortune seekers, instant riches, a boom town mentality, and a place saturated in money. It is an exciting time of technological revolution, driven by capitalism's restless need to improve, modernize, and accumulate capital. Incomes are rising on average and making this an epoch of unprecedented affluence in the region. But it is also a disturbing era of grotesque wealth, yawning inequality, and unbridled ambition that has shaken the region to its core. The Janus face of economic success is a leering mask that mocks the ideals of equality, social justice, and the collective good. In the end, a society that allows so many people to fall into public destitution in the face of abundance is a moral failure of the first order.

The growth of inequality in our time is so egregious that it demands that people take off the blinders of the old American faith in rough equality, open opportunity, and social mobility for all. Nowhere is that ideology

---

49 Fern et al. 2014, Wong 2016a, Chris Herring's commentary at https://placesjournal.org/article/tent-city-america/. On the long-term crackdown on homelessness, see Mitchell 2003.

stronger than in California, and especially in the land of gold rushes and silver booms focused on San Francisco—and not without reason. This has been a place blessed by natural wealth, abundant capital, and sustained growth, which has thrived on influxes of new arrivals, a large skilled and educated labor force, and a proliferation of new innovations and business. That good fortune continues today in the form of the tech boom and the New Economy of information. But there is more to the Bay Area than the virtuous circle of agglomeration economies; it comes joined at the hip with a vicious cycle of unabated enrichment of the upper classes. There is a strong sense today that the old model of relatively open opportunity and equitable development has gone off the rails.

That means taking seriously the deep divisions opening up in the social order and the implications of that for the inordinate power wielded by the upper classes, on the one hand, and the exploitation and hardship of the working class(es), on the other. It is hard to do that without the intellectual tools provided by a theory of class. But mere inequality is not proof of a class society, which requires a great deal more inquiry and evidence on many fronts; that is what the rest of this book will tackle. The next chapter takes up the world of work in the Bay Area and the working people who do it, and the way they experience and respond to the New Economy led by the tech industry.

CHAPTER FOUR

City at Work

Making and Fighting for a Living

THE BAY AREA AND ITS ROBUST ECONOMY IS NOT ALL ABOUT CREATIVE GENIUSES, entrepreneurial marvels, and rapid growth. The regional economy runs on the labor of three and a half million people who go to work every day, do their jobs, and get a paycheck for fulfilling their duties. Ninety percent of these are not working in the tech industry and three-quarters are not among the highly educated, skilled, and bountifully remunerated labor force. For the most part, these people are doing the conventional, unglamorous work necessary to the operation of each and every workplace, firm, and industry. They are, in short, the solid foundation of the metropolitan economy.

The previous chapter looked at the distribution of income and wealth in the bay region, with the emphasis on the enrichment at the top. It noted that despite high average wages for the bulk of working people in the Bay Area, most were not in the stratosphere of skills and earning, the middle wage group was shrinking and a huge percentage were still serving as a cheap labor force. This chapter adds another, thicker layer of evidence about what working people do and who they are. It also enlarges the scope of what it means to be "working class" and the variety of people who might be gathered under that umbrella.

The range of work being done across the bay metropolis is immense. People are employed in all types of occupations and all manner of workplaces. Most are familiar, everyday jobs in offices, stores, and classrooms, or in the city streets: secretaries, checkout clerks, teachers, nurses, trash collectors, janitors, and so on. While some are lucky to have interesting, challenging, and ever-changing work tasks, the workaday world for most people is not particularly glamorous nor do they have the chance to exercise much autonomy, creativity, or variety at work. Most workers follow a similar routine: get up and go to work every day, do what the boss asks, and do a good job or risk being replaced. For many, the work is unpleasant and working conditions terrible, and a large number have to cope with irregular and unreliable employment. The bad jobs have not all been shipped abroad—far from it.

People of color make up three-fifths of the labor force in the Bay Area,[1] creating an unprecedented conjunction of race and class compared with the past and with the almost entirely white composition of the 1 percent of the rich. Therein lies the potential for a unified opposition to the kind of inequality, instability, and corporate power created by the gilded tech economy. But working people come in all sizes and colors, hail from all corners of the globe, and face severe labor market discrimination against people of color and immigrants. More than half the workforce is female, and women face serious discrimination, as well. These differences fragment working-class identity, pit people against each other, and defeat efforts at collective mobilization for better wages and working conditions. They also make racial solidarities and gender struggles more pressing than appeals to class unity.

Nevertheless, the continuing convergence of class, race, and gender has had a profound effect on the kinds of activism that have broken out in the twenty-first century. A whole series of popular movements have arisen around employment, pay, and life chances of everyday working people. The Bay Area has long been known as a place where progressive change bubbles up from below, and this is true again today. Some of the most significant national movements of the present times have been initiated or nurtured by bay activists—battles over "living wages," immigrant rights, policing and prison reform, and gender equality. The intersection of those movements and interests lends new impulse to what used to be called "class struggles." A key theme is that the humble improvements sought by the mass of working people are just as much, if not more, important than the whizbang innovations of the tech geniuses in making the bay region and the country a better place for everyone.

The first half of this chapter lays the groundwork on the workaday world of labor in the Bay Area and the makeup of the labor force; these four sections cover the jobs people do, employment insecurity, race and racial ordering of labor markets, and the importance of immigrant workers. The second half of the chapter looks at four critical areas of activism by working people, responding to the deplorable state of working conditions, living circumstances, racial discrimination, and passage in and out of the workforce; these sections concern the movements for immigrant rights, for unions and living wages, against racialized criminal justice and against the mistreatment of women at work.

---

1   "People of color" is the preferred term among antiracist activists these days, rather than "non-Whites" or "racial minorities."

The Workaday World of the Metropolis

The focus on the tech economy in the Bay Area masks the less glamorous reality that most people are busy at the vast multitude of jobs that keep the modern city running. There are three and a half million workers in the bay region. What kind of work do they do and under what conditions? The variety of work in the modern metropolis is mind-boggling. The city is not just a place where companies and workers locate; the city is a kind of gigantic, open-ended factory embracing every kind of workplace, employer, and occupation. To get one's mind around this, it is necessary to break out of the confines of the standard categories of industrial sectors, such as were outlined in chapter 2, and think in terms of a much-larger and more complex social division of labor—a key economic term too rarely used in popular discourse.[2]

The modern urban economy is not just a collection of factories, offices, and warehouses. There is a much-larger division of labor in today's world than in the heyday of the Industrial Revolution in the nineteenth century or the Fordist era of the twentieth. The relative shrinkage of manufacturing, mining, and farming as a share of the economy rests not just on automation that eliminates jobs in those sectors; it is just as much a result of the growing complexity of every kind of social labor, whether the end product is a washing machine or a medical operation. There is a good deal of confusion about the expanding division of labor, however, because almost everything other than manufacturing has come to be called "services"—a kitchen sink term that explains nothing. The service label originally meant that the product of labor is not a material good, but in fact most of the work in today's economy produces nothing by itself; it is "intermediate" to a final result somewhere down the line.[3]

What is wanted is a closer look at occupations, not just sectors, and the way similar occupations occur across sectors—job categories such as designer, engineer, manager, custodian, food preparer, and production worker. The U.S. Census Bureau identifies over five hundred detailed occupations, which it organizes into nine major groups and twenty-three subcategories. Summarizing the data on occupations for the whole Bay Area, however, is made more difficult by the conceptual incoherence of some of the U.S. Census categories, which require a lot of massaging in order to make sense of them.

---

2   Sayer and Walker 1992.
3   Ibid., chapter 3. While stressing the expanding division of labor here, cities have always had complex economies. Hall 1982, Harvey 2003.

Here is a rough breakout of some typical Bay Area occupations by wage and job quality.[4]

High-wage and High Quality

- CEOs, corporate officers
- Science and social science researchers
- Managers, administrators, management consultants
- Financial advisors, investment managers, bank managers
- Computer and software design, engineers, architects
- Doctors, medical technicians, registered nurses
- Attorneys, psychologists, university professors

Medium-wage and Medium Quality

- Machinists, machine repairers, computer technicians
- Carpenters, plumbers, painters, drywallers, electricians
- Truckers, bus drivers, delivery drivers
- Librarians, teachers, archivists, office clerks
- Nurses, hospital staff, dental hygienists
- Performers and theater staff, athletic trainers, gym staff
- Frontline supervisors of office and admin workers
- Bookkeeping, accounting and auditing clerks, administrative assts.
- Media staff, publicists, graphic designers
- Sales and customer service reps, real estate brokers
- Car repair, maintenance specialists
- Computer support technicians, low-end coders

Low-wage and Poor Quality

- Servers, cooks, dishwashers
- Hotel maids, janitors, hospital orderlies
- Haircutters, beauticians, animal care workers
- Housekeepers, childcare providers, launderers
- Production line workers
- Landscapers, gardeners, street sweepers, recyclers
- Construction helpers
- Sales clerks, stockroom and warehouse workers
- Farmworkers

---

4   Assembled from Storper et al. 2015, Bernhardt et al. 2015, ABAG 2014, and Bureau of Labor Statistics data. These groupings do not correspond exactly to the three wage tiers in chapter 3. Allowance must be made for racial and gender discrimination, discussed below.

- Private security guards
- Secretaries, receptionists, file clerks
- Taxi drivers

Job quality is, of course, less precise than wage and salary levels, but research-ers have divined a good deal of information from census data and surveys about degree of autonomy, problem-solving, repetition, and the like in work tasks. High-quality jobs have considerable autonomy and little oversight and require more judgment about what tasks to undertake and how to go about them. Low-quality jobs are mostly routine and repetitive, closely supervised, and have little scope for initiative and creativity. Most occupations fall some-where in the middle. The education required for better jobs is higher on average, because of the need for background knowledge, exposure to a wider range of experience, and demonstrated ability to work independently; but there are many middle-level jobs with a high degree of job-specific, technical knowhow, such as machining or college administration.[5]

Nevertheless, the question of how to assess "skill" is far from obvious. Some jobs, often labeled unskilled, require a good deal of reason, acuity, and initiative, as in the case of childcare and housecleaning. By contrast, some supposedly high-skilled positions, such as store manager and software engi-neer, are occupied by people who lack much savoir faire beyond bossing and coding. The uncomfortable fact is that a lot of work is devalued by its sheer familiarity or by association with the people who do it, particularly women and people of color. Labor market discrimination does not just affect how workers are slotted into jobs but how the jobs they hold are evaluated by employers and society.[6]

*   *   *

As noted in earlier chapters, the Bay Area has an abundance of high-quality, well-remunerated jobs across every sector, which offer independence, variety, and problem-solving at work. They usually require advanced degrees or exten-sive experience and offer considerable social prestige beyond the workplace. Such jobs occupy about a quarter of the workforce, perhaps as much as a third. That is an impressive number, but it still leaves two-thirds or three-quarters of the labor force without ready access to the best jobs and wages.

The regional economy offers many middle-level jobs, however, some of which offer an extra payoff to those with more education—and even to those

---

5   Autor & Dorn 2013, Storper et al. 2015.
6   Cockburn 1985, Wilkinson 1981, Wolff 2006.

with less education who have specialized skills and knowhow acquired on the job. This middle segment constitutes roughly another third of the labor force; but job quality, like wages, tails off for the bottom half of this group. Altogether, the share of good jobs in the Bay Area probably stands at no more than half. Nevertheless, it is still greater than in cities with larger low-wage economies, such as Atlanta and Houston.[7]

Even in nominally good-quality jobs, work can still be difficult and, in some cases, intolerable. Autonomy and creativity are not incompatible with a high degree of pressure. Labs have to generate new results and patents, hospitals and clinics have keep costs down by treating more patients, and managers have to get results from those working under them. There is always another level of supervision looking down and ultimately the rigors of markets and profitability to contend with. Competition is the name of the game, and it applies to interpersonal relations as well as to firms; it is even felt by governments and nonprofits.

Work speedup has hit a wide range of professional and upper echelon occupations in recent years, whether in tech work, school teaching, university research, financial affairs, health care, or hotel management. Intensive, even frantic, work schedules are practically the norm in the tech industry, and the pressure makes tech a young person's world, as does the rate of change in technology and tasks. The industry has not been kind to older workers, brutally jettisoning those with obsolete skills, offshoring midlevel jobs, and hiring eager-beaver college grads to populate start-ups.[8]

What about the bottom third of occupations? A truly shocking aspect of work in the bay metropolis is how many lousy jobs there are in such a high-flying, sophisticated economy. The income and poverty data for low-wage work were reviewed in chapter 3, showing that the bottom third of the labor force constitutes a cheap labor pool earning less than a living income. Here the focus is on the quality of jobs, working conditions, and life chances for that bottom third—and most of the lower half of workers and their families. Good documentation about this group is actually more plentiful than for the middle and upper rungs of the laboring population.

To begin with, low-wage jobs are heavily concentrated in a few sectors, such as retail, hotels, cleaning services, food preparation, and domestic service (fig. 4.1). Jobs in these industries often come with distinct social burdens. The front end of retail requires close, fawning personal attention to clients and their desires. Hotels and hospitality jobs have similar characteristics, plus a

---

7   On the extra payoffs to middle level Bay Area workers, see Storper et al. 2015, pp. 45, 56.
8   Benner 2002, Bardhan et al. 2004, Burchell et al. 2005, Lyons 2017.

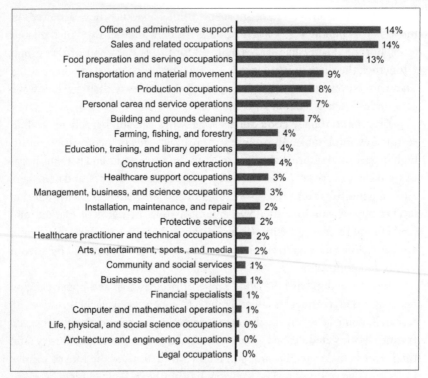

Figure 4.1: Chief Occupations of California Low-Wage Workers, 2012–2013
Source: Bernhardt 2014.

large number of back-end jobs that involve even more intimate contact with and cleaning up after guests. Domestic service, such as cleaning, childcare, housekeeping, and gardening, comes with an even higher degree of personal subordination and even humiliation—such as caring for someone else's children while one's own are latchkey kids. The Bay Area's upper classes would be hard put to get to their fancy jobs, raise their privileged kids, and enjoy evenings out on the town if their minders disappeared; but they are not always grateful for the service or respectful of domestics. Ironically, these normally invisible workers are so vital to the operation of the metropolitan economy and class system that as they are priced out of housing in boom times, a chorus of howls about their absence goes up from employers, politicians, and upper-class households.

Second, the lower echelons of the workforce suffer from a multitude of disadvantages beyond low wages. They do not, as a rule, have much autonomy at work nor are their tasks particularly creative or satisfying. The worst-paid jobs are all too often done under difficult, dirty, and dangerous conditions. Low-end jobs almost never offer the possibility of advancement and career building, and they are the most unstable, forcing people into frequent bouts of unemployment. On top of everything else, low-end workers are devalued by the rest of society for their lack of skills, education, and stability.[9]

Third, the life conditions for low-wage households are the poorest. In the expensive Bay Area housing market, many live in converted garages or their cars (see chapters 3 and 6). The children of such workers are the least likely to get a good education and get ahead. Bad jobs and unstable lives impact people's health: more physical breakdowns, mental health issues, broken families, and addiction, as well as lower life expectancy. At the same time, the proportion of low-wage workers who lack health coverage to help when they are sick or injured is much higher than for the rest of the labor force. Not only does this adversely affect their own lives, it forces them to go to work sick, where they are more likely to be injured or to infect others.[10]

Employment Insecurity and the Gig Economy
A central feature of the New Economy of the Bay Area since the 1980s has been greater contingency and insecurity of employment. The postwar regime of stable, full-time, and lifelong employment is a thing of the past. It featured, in the upper tier, career engineers at IBM in San Jose, tenured professors at California's public universities, and long-term jobs for skilled mechanics at United Airlines repair shops. In the middle were union workers with seniority at General Motors in Fremont, U.S. Steel at Pittsburg, and Lockheed in Sunnyvale. Of course, workers in the bottom tier never enjoyed much stability, but some did gain relatively permanent jobs in manufacturing, hotels, and municipal agencies. That kind of stability is much diminished over the last quarter century, and the burden of insecurity has fallen disproportionately on the young.

Companies began shifting en masse to "flexible" or "contingent" employment in the last decades of the twentieth century. This consists of putting out noncore work to subcontractors, employing temporary workers hired through outside agencies, and utilizing self-employed consultants for special projects. Silicon Valley companies were in the vanguard of the national movement to flexible/contingent labor, sporting some of the highest percentages of temp, part-time, and contract labor in the country, just as they were in

---

9 Bernhardt et al. 2015. For a portrait of low-wage work in America, see Ehrenreich 2001. On the devaluation of workers, see Jones 2016, Wise 2015. On its long history under capitalism, see Sayer 1995 and Perelman 2000.

10 Case & Deaton 2017. Recall, too, that the bottom half of the American populace have no net wealth and the bottom fifth are perennially in debt; this leaves them with no financial cushion to make up for bad wages and other aspects of precarity.

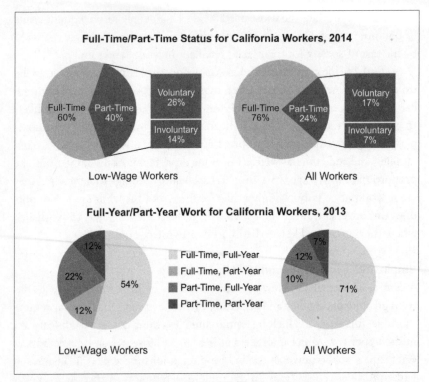

Figure 4.2: Full-Time and Part-Time Work in California, 2014

Source: Bernhardt 2014.

offshoring production and programming jobs. The transformation of employment relations has been every bit as fundamental to the New Economy as the new IT innovations.[11]

There are various estimates of the share of employment that is flexible/contingent in the Bay Area, but it appears to be between a quarter and a third of all jobs. A recent study of Silicon Valley estimates that over a quarter of jobs are subcontracted, mostly in food service, landscaping, and security work. Another study of California as a whole showed part-timers to be about 25 percent of the workforce and those with less than year-round employment closer to 30 percent (fig. 4.2).[12]

A striking aspect of contingent employment is the high correlation with low wages and lack of benefits. Workers hired through temp agencies in California, for example, earn only two-thirds of the average wages of all workers and are twice as likely to be living in poverty. Low-wage workers are

---

11 Benner 2002, Applebaum et al. 2003, Kalleberg 2009.
12 Benner 2014, Bernhardt et al. 2015.

far more likely to be part-timers, have erratic work schedules, and be laid off first in lean times, and these things make their personal lives not just flexible but chaotic. Unstable and unpredictable work has clear negative effects on income volatility, individual psychology, and family conflict. Subcontractors are also less attentive to workplace dangers and more likely to be used for hazardous work. No wonder many people have taken to calling this group of working people "the precariat."[13]

★　★　★

The new Gig Economy of the twenty-first century has received wide attention, but is greatly exaggerated in size and framed as something new and revolutionary, hailed with the usual gusto by its avatars like Travis Kalanick, who says, "It's good for everybody, it's not red or blue." In most respects, however, the Gig Economy is just an extension of flexible and contingent employment relations. While commonly touted as a kind of freedom from regular work and direct supervision, it is more like the latest twist of the rope that millions of workers hang on to for dear life.[14]

A study in San Francisco found that the proportion of gig workers—defined as independent contractors, temps, and part-timers—has not gone up in recent years. Using a more narrow definition of gig work as independent contracting, a recent study of California put the percentage in single digits, a bit higher than the country as a whole, and unchanged over time. Only a small proportion of these were based on digital platforms, such as Uber, TaskRabbit, and InstaCart—around 1 percent of the labor force (also higher than the rest of the country).[15]

The paradigmatic worker of the Gig Economy is the Uber driver, who uses a personal vehicle to provide taxi service. The key technical development is the smartphone app used by customers and drivers to coordinate with each other and make payments, which is more efficient than the old taxicab dispatcher system and more flexible than public transportation. Bringing your own car is less than revolutionary, since many workers, such as carpenters, have always supplied their own tools.

Debate is raging around the world about the pluses and minuses of the Uber system versus taxis and public transport—systems that are often all too easy to fault. Most young people like Uber because they have grown up in a world of smartphones, convenience, and contingent work. Most Uber drivers

---

13　Dietz 2012, Schneider & Harknett 2017a & b.
14　Kalanick quotation in Kessler 2013.
15　Green 2016a, Bernhardt & Thomason 2017. See also Manyika et al. 2016, though the it lumps contract work with people renting on Airbnb and trading on eBay to earn income.

like the extra income they earn off their otherwise idle cars and time—especially given the lousy state of wages in the lower half of the labor market. Cab drivers almost universally hate the competition, which lowers their take and can even eliminate their jobs entirely. In San Francisco, where cabbies once bid for expensive licenses ("medallions"), hundreds have been bankrupted.

A big question is whether the drivers are simply employees of Uber and its fellow companies, and therefore subject to normal labor market rules and regulations—which up to now they have completely avoided. In 2016, a British labor tribunal ruled that they are, indeed, employees, and in 2017 the European high court ruled that Uber is a transportation company, not just a tech platform. But gig work is not regular employment; rather, it looks a lot like alternative forms such as "inside contracting" of skilled laborers in early steel mills, self-employment by fast-food franchise operators, or independent contracting by professionals. These kinds of employment relations can offer workers a valued degree of autonomy, but demand, in turn, a huge amount of self-exploitation.[16]

Uber driving offers a certain degree of independence and flexibility, but as most drivers eventually find out, the wages don't add up to a good living. Meanwhile, Uber is skimming off a nice cut from every transaction and they are the ones setting the wage and profit rate. Ultimately, Uber controls the conditions of work through the settings on its app and leaves its drivers to shoulder all the risk of fluctuating demand, traffic conditions, and irregularity of work. This is contingent employment in new clothes.[17]

In a further twist, online platforms are being used by conventional bosses to manage the workforce: making short-term contracts, setting up weekly schedules, calling people in on short notice to fill absences, etc. As more and more employers use automated scheduling software to micromanage workers' schedules from day to day and week to week, people's home lives are being badly disrupted. This kind of unpredictable scheduling is especially hard on women workers, who bear a disproportionate share of domestic responsibilities.[18]

Something else is afoot here, too; gig work is part of the individualizing of economic life and financial responsibility. Every man, woman, and child is implored to take personal control of work, retirement, insurance, education, and so forth. Alas, greater responsibility means greater risk of failure. The Gig Economy is the antithesis of collective responsibility and class solidarity. It is furthering the expansion of the precariat.[19]

---

16 Osborne 2016, O'Connor 2017.
17 Scheiber 2017.
18 Kantor 2014, O'Connor 2016.
19 On financialization of personal life, see Martin 2002.

Workers Show Their Colors

So, with that introduction to the state of occupations and employment in the Bay Area, what about the people who fill those jobs? The first, most striking characteristic of the working class of the region is that the workers are mostly people of color. While the upper classes are overwhelmingly white—the 1% almost without exception and the top 20 percent overwhelmingly—the majority of working people are not.

A new American working class is coming into being in California and it is heavily weighted with people of color. This has enormous implications for class and race relations, but is by no means a simple fait accompli. The history of race and class in America makes such a claim immediately suspect as a gloss over the chasm between the two. Nevertheless, something unprecedented is happening here in the Bay Area and across the state, involving a substantial overlap of class and race, at a minimum, and a gradual merging of the two, at the limit. The balance of this chapter explores several ways that the two are coming together in practice.

The working population of the United States was once made up overwhelmingly of two groups: people of European descent who arrived in the north in the mass migrations of the eighteenth to early twentieth centuries and people of African origin brought to the southern states by the slave trade. As Europeans assimilated, they merged into a new identity as "white," a long process not without painful exclusion along lines of nationality and religion. Africans dispersed in large numbers during the Great Migration north and west in the mid-twentieth century, moving at last into the class of wage workers; but they remained a people apart because of white racism and Jim Crow laws.[20]

California was always different in its racial makeup, as a result of Mexico's historical overlap with the Southwest and the arrival of Asian immigrants from China, Japan, the Philippines, and India. It rejected slavery, but its racial order was often draconian. It had a wretched record on race and immigration for the first century of statehood, starting with the dispossession and slaughter of indigenous people in the Gold Rush, followed by a vicious anti-Chinese movement in the 1870s, Asian Land Laws of the 1910s, and Japanese internment in World War II.[21]

Things began to turn around after the war as a western branch of the civil rights struggle broke down restrictions on marriage, employment, schooling,

---

20 On becoming white, see Lipsitz 1998, McDermott 2006. On intra-European racism, Roediger 2005. On slavery and capitalism, Williams 1943, Rockman 1997. On the Great Migration, Gregory 2005. On the racial legacy of slavery, Roediger 2008.

21 On California's early racial order, see, e.g., Almaguer 1994, Chan 1991, Brilliant 2010.

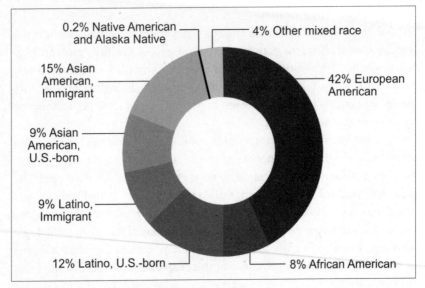

Figure 4.3: The Bay Area's Racial Mix, 2012
Source: Policy Link 2015 (5-county Bay Area).

and housing, even before the better-known U.S. Supreme Court decisions and congressional laws at the national level. California's racial makeover took off after 1965 when the harsh racial quotas of the 1924 Immigration Act were relaxed and the state became the largest point of entry for the new wave of immigration from Asia and Latin America. As a result, the state has been utterly transfigured over the last fifty years.

The racial makeup of today's California is roughly three-eighths European American, three-eighths Hispanic American (Latino), one-eighth Asian American, and one-eighth African American and Native Americans. The Bay Area's racial mix echoes that of California with one significant difference; it has a larger slice of Asian Americans and a smaller one of Latinos (fig. 4.3). Greater Los Angeles, by contrast, tilts heavily toward Latinos. Not surprisingly, California's two dominant metropolitan areas are the most diverse in the country. The United States as a whole, by contrast, is still majority white: five-eighths European American, two-eighths Hispanic/Latino, and one-eighth African American, with many fewer Asian Americans.[22]

The new immigrants and their children came looking for work and filled jobs that were opening up by the millions in the 1980s and 1990s up and down

22 For an overview of the Bay Area's racial composition, see Pastore 2008. Nothing is implied by dropping the inconvenient hyphens in speaking of various immigrant-American groups.

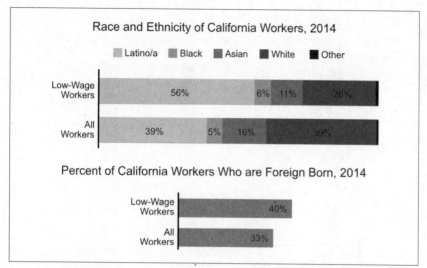

Figure 4.4: California's Workers by Race & Origin, 2014
Source: Bernhardt 2014.

the state. California's booming labor demand and immigration tailed off in the first decade of the twenty-first century, but by that time the working population had been transformed from majority White to majority Brown, with a touch of other colors. The Bay Area's working population looks similar, except that Latinos and Asians each make up about 25 percent (fig. 4.4).

★ ★ ★

If the Bay Area's labor force is such a mixture of people, how big a role do race and racism play in sorting out and splitting up the working class? Since the region prides itself on its racial tolerance, there ought to be no simple racial order among Bay Area workers. To a considerable extent this is true. The largest group in the middle-wage workforce is white, but a great many people of color can be found in that category, as well (fig. 4.5). One sees a good deal of upward mobility of workers of color into office, supervisory, and skilled jobs and some make it all the way into management and the professions. Education has a clear payoff for all workers of color, though less than for whites and Asians (fig. 4.7).[23]

Nevertheless, there is persistent inequality in the ability of racialized people to gain access to top-flight jobs and a clear disadvantage in terms of wages, regardless of education level and type of job filled (fig. 4.6). The worst jobs in the bottom third of the labor market are overwhelmingly filled

---

23   See also Storper et al. 2015.

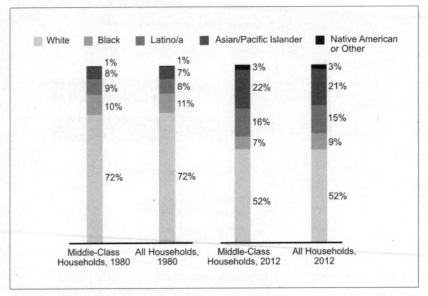

Figure 4.5: Racial Mix of Middle-Wage Workers, 1980 & 2010

Source: Policy Link 2015 (5-county Bay Area).

by people of color (although a quarter of Whites are in the low-wage work-force, too). And it should not be forgotten that people of color own much less property of every kind than white people, by an order of magnitude, and this means fewer homeowners and more indebtedness among the bottom tiers of working households.[24]

The lumpy racial categories used in most regional statistics need to be broken into finer categories to see who is doing what. The cheap labor force is made up chiefly of Mexicans and Filipinos, plus goodly numbers of Vietnamese, Chinese, and African Americans, and a smattering of Laotians, Cambodians, Koreans, East Africans, Hondurans, Guatemalans, and South Asians. Many of the lowest level workers of every origin are recent immigrants and some are undocumented, making them the most easily exploited of all because they live in constant fear of being revealed to Homeland Security's Immigration and Customs Enforcement bureau (ICE) and deported.[25]

The most deplorable exploitation is that of day laborers, who are almost exclusively Latino men. The vast majority are undocumented immigrants,

---

24 For valuable statistics on race and inequality in California, see http://www.racecounts.org/california/. On wealth by race in Los Angeles, see De la Cruz-Viesca et al. 2016. No such study exists for the Bay Area.

25 The fine divisions among and within these various communities are significant but often invisible to outside observers. On changing definitions of race, see Rodriguez 2000.

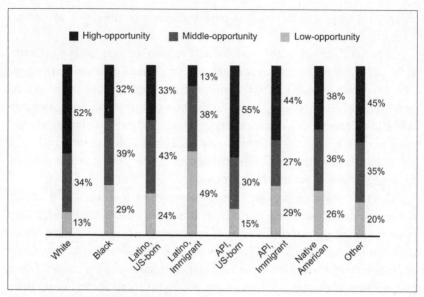

Figure 4.6: Access to Jobs by Race, 2012

Source: Policy Link, 2015 (5-county Bay Area).

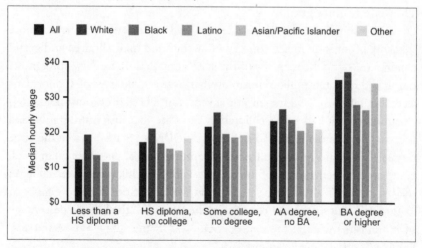

Figure 4.7: Wages by Education Level, by Race, 2008–2012

Source: Policy Link 2015 (5-county Bay Area).

and most are from native Indio groups in Southern Mexico and Guatemala (Maya, Mixtec, Zapotec) who do not always speak Spanish, let alone English. You see them standing on street corners every day of the week all around the metropolitan area, including suburbs, where they are much in demand for heavy landscaping, debris clearing, crawling under houses, and other nasty jobs. Attention to the health and safety of these workers is nil. How much (and whether) they will be paid at the end of the day is always up for grabs.[26]

Agricultural work is not much better. Farmworkers are a major presence in the outer Bay Area counties of Napa, Sonoma, Santa Cruz, and San Joaquin, where they are essential to wine, fruit, and vegetable production. They do backbreaking labor for long hours in the hot sun, often without adequate water, food, toilets, and childcare, and are frequently exposed to toxic pesticides. Some who gain a degree of permanence, as in high-end vineyards, earn a decent income; but even so the wine district of the North Bay has some of the highest rates of poverty in the region.[27]

Another arena marked by high percentages of low-wage jobs and of workers of color is construction. Beyond the better-paid crafts workers are large numbers mustered for one-off construction projects during boom times, from housing in Santa Clara County to malls in Sonoma County. They migrate in from rural counties and live in their trucks while on the job. These, too, are overwhelmingly Latinos, both immigrants and second generation, and many undocumented and working off the books.[28]

The State of Immigration

Over the last half century, California absorbed millions of immigrants, more than any other state in the country. Now they and their children and grandchildren make up the majority of the state's population. By 2015, immigrants numbered over ten million, meaning that over one-quarter of Californians were foreign-born. Children of immigrants numbered over four million, representing nearly half of all children in the state (because immigrants tend to have larger families than folks born in the United States). Given the large number of second-generation youth, the proportion of people of color is still going up. The percentages of immigrants and their children is even higher in the big cities. The Bay Area's population was about one-third foreign-born in 2015, and four of the five counties in the state with the highest percentage of immigrants were in the metropolitan area (Santa Clara, San Mateo, San Francisco, and Alameda Counties).

Immigrants are drawn chiefly by labor demand. When jobs in California were proliferating in the 1980s and 1990s, a huge influx hit the state—the greatest numbers since the late nineteenth century. After 2000 the number of immigrants fell off as the state's labor demand plateaued thanks to two major

---

26 Gonzalez 2007. See also reports of the National Day Labor Organizing Network at http://www.ndlon.org/en/.

27 Walker 2004a. See also reports of California Institute for Rural Studies, http://cirsinc.org.

28 Hsu 2014.

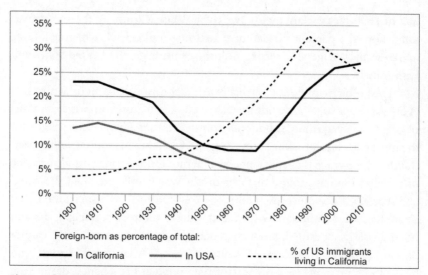

Figure 4.8: Immigration to California and USA, 1900–2010
Source: Walker & Lodha 2013.

recessions (fig. 4.8). Immigrant labor force participation is a couple percentage points higher than U.S.-born workers. Today they make up a third of the state's workforce and undocumented immigrants are one-tenth. To be sure, immigrants occupy more of the lower-ranked occupations than U.S.-born workers, but they are found in a surprisingly high percentage of upper-level jobs, as well. For example, in 2015 immigrants filled 30 percent of management, business, science and arts occupations in California versus 42 percent for U.S.-born workers.[29]

The new populace of the Golden State has come from all around the world, but the biggest contributors have been Mexico and East Asia (China and the Philippines), with substantial contingents from Central America, Southeast Asia, and Europe. There have been smaller flows from Africa, South Asia, the Middle East, and the Caribbean.

Discussions of immigrant numbers are plagued by the incoherent, unstable, and contentious categories of official statistics and popular discourse. Most figures are given by continent of origin: Asian, Hispanic, European, African, and Native American. The U.S. Census is sufficiently confounded by Latinos to have two measures, one by skin color (White, Black) and one by language (Hispanic, non-Hispanic). Why Brown is not an official skin color is not explained. This leads to some marked distortions in the figures, such as the bizarre claim that California is still 57 percent White because almost

---

29   Data from http://www.migrationpolicy.org/data/state-profiles/state/workforce/CA#.

half of Hispanics declare themselves to be White. Curiously, the 2010 census only showed 3 percent of Californians to be multiracial, which is a huge underestimate of genetic mixing over the centuries in the United States and Latin America.[30]

The problem, of course, is that race is a notoriously pseudoscientific category that slaps together crude images of physical features, imprecise notions of origin, and vague ideas about religion and culture. Racial concepts are, for the most part, literally skin deep—or go no farther than clothing and speech. But the idea of race is deeply embedded in modern thinking and the practice of racialization has profound effects on the way people are divided, slotted, and scorned. Race must, therefore, be taken seriously as a social force that establishes its own hierarchy ("a racial order") and that crosscuts class and other divisions. Because it has such important effects, the word "race" cannot be avoided, and terms such as "White," "Black," "Asian," and "Latino" can be deployed here precisely because of their popular provenance, despite the problematic character of such terminology.[31]

★ ★ ★

Do immigrants displace American-born workers? This is a politically charged question in the present atmosphere of nationalist xenophobia. It is not true, for the most part, that immigrants have taken the jobs of "native" Americans (a suspect term; "U.S.-born" is more accurate). Migrants go where there are jobs, and while jobless workers in economically stagnant regions may falsely blame immigrants for their woes, the fastest-growing regions of the country are, in fact, the ones with the largest numbers of immigrants. In the Bay Area, most migrants have come to fill new jobs, not to replace previous workers in their old jobs. This has always been a place that thrived on a influx of new labor, whether from Europe, New England, Louisiana, China, or Mexico.[32]

Nevertheless, it is true that at the same time as huge waves of new people have come into the country over the last several decades, millions of existing jobs have disappeared as old industries and occupations have shrunk. There has been a wrenching restructuring of the economy and economic geography of the United States, as noted in chapter 2, with an accompanying decimation

---

30 Rodriguez 2000, Prewitt 2013.

31 There is some genetic basis to some bodily differences among "races," such as sickle-cell anemia resistance in West Africans, but it is extremely thin. On the history of U.S. racism, see Marx 1998, McDermott 2006, Roediger 2005, 2008.

32 On migration to jobs, see Piore 1979, Storper 2013. On the history of California demography, jobs, and growth, see Gordon 1954, Walker 2001, 2008. On recent regional growth and immigrants, see Fleming & Leatherby 2016.

of working-class communities across the nation. The Bay Area, too, used to move to a very different rhythm of work on the waterfront, in warehouses and factories, and in fields and canneries. It has seen a largely white labor force replaced by people of different origins and skin tones, as the local working class was thoroughly reconstructed.[33]

The key difference is that in the Bay Area the decline of old sectors and jobs has been masked by the growth of other sectors in the social division of labor. This has been apparent since the early 1980s, when manufacturing first went into free-fall, while health care, finance, business services and tourism were rising rapidly. It became visible again in the collapse and recovery from the Great Recession, where the goods producing and handling sectors and finance fell off a cliff, while tech, health care, and tourism suffered less and recovered sooner. With every shift in the economic base, more and more immigrants and children of immigrants (and women) were hired, while older white workers lost their jobs, retired and moved away.

Of course, there are situations where immigrants have directly replaced previous workers. Many employers have been aggressive in ridding themselves of unionized and better-paid workforces; there are plenty of examples of perfectly good workers laid off and replaced by people willing to work more cheaply. But where does the fault lie—with immigrants who arrive from low-wage countries and are often in desperate straits or with the employers who make the decisions of whom to fire and whom to hire? Many companies are more than happy to break a union, undermine high wages, and exploit the needy of any race or origin. A good example is what happened to the workforce as the giant GM auto plant in Fremont became the NUMMI joint venture with Toyota and now the Tesla electric car factory.[34]

Nevertheless, no one has shown that direct replacement has been a big part of the shift to immigrant and female labor in the United States over the last forty years. Nor has immigration been the main reason that wages have grown very little over the same period; that has to do primarily with the poor performance of the U.S. economy and the decline of unions (see below). The one group who has suffered the most from the competition of immigrants and global trade is the lowest tier of labor force with the least education and fewest skills. Again, who bears responsibility for this? Is it the employers who have systematically garnered an extra measure of profits by hiring immigrants at lower wages than U.S.-born workers? Is it the neoconservatives/neoliberals

33 On the old economy of the region and local deindustrialization, see Walker 2004b, 2008 and Shapira 1986.
34 For an excellent treatment of worker displacement and immigrant recruitment, see Miraftab 2016. On Tesla's labor issues, see Hansen 2017b.

125

who have cut taxes and social spending on public education? Or is the capitalist class that has been content to reap the benefits of lower taxes and cheaper labor without investing in education and training for the American work force—of all origins and colors?[35]

The Bay Area has long had a high-road economy that offered opportunity to legions of educated and skilled people and has benefitted mightily from the contributions of the whole spectrum of migrant labor. Overall, it is clear that it has gained enormously from the labor power, skills, and extra surplus value generated by millions of immigrants.

★   ★   ★

Discussions of immigrants and race always run into the thorny question of "assimilation" or "Americanization" of people who arrive in the United States from elsewhere. New immigrants from Mexico, China, and Thailand quite naturally identify with their place of origin, just as did Italians, Irish, and Swedes when they first arrived in the United States long ago. Such identities are not continental ("Asian") or linguistic ("Hispanic"), but national, and replete with memories of old rivalries (e.g., Koreans vs. Japanese, Poles vs. Russians). Identities are even further fragmented within nations, as with the gulf among Mexicans between Mixtecs from Oaxaca, mestizo villagers from Sinaloa, and elite Chilangos from Mexico City. It is only with the passage of time in the United States, in the face of isolation and discrimination, that national and local allegiances erode and new identities begin to grow among immigrants.[36]

By the second generation, that is, those born in the United States, English becomes the primary language in 90 percent of cases. American culture also largely displaces the immigrant cultures of parents and grandparents—though usually with a strong measure of acknowledgment and respect for those roots. This is not, by any means, always a smooth process, especially where English is a second language in the home and bilingual schools are rare. Equally, the tensions within families over the transition are famously controversial and the source of a good deal of literature on the immigrant experience. Assimilation is not by any means easy, but it does happen more readily in the United States than in Europe and other receiving countries. Immigrants rarely remain cloistered in a world apart. Yet a remarkable phenomenon of

---

35 On wage effects, see Borjas 2013, Peri 2007. On the extra surplus from new labor recruits, see Moore 2015. On education cuts in California, which hit the children of immigrants the hardest, see Walker & Lodha 2013 and chapter 10.

36 For good portraits of immigrant communities, see Portas & Rumbaut 1990, Ong et al. 1994.

the new era of immigration has been the spread of Spanish as an everyday language in California.[37]

In the Bay Area, the new working class of many-hued workers, like the New Economy of work, is no longer a shock. It is the norm. This is reflected in changing attitudes at work, where people from many different origins regularly mix and socialize, and the way Spanish, Chinese, and Tagalog mingle with English in the workplace and in residential communities. This is not to say that racism is a thing of the past, but that it is in retreat. One of the key sites of integration is on the job, where the common experience of work often generates a rough sense of equality and community among working people. Not surprisingly, some employers have taken to banning speech in any language but English in order to undermine worker solidarity and organizing.

The openness of young people to the new demography and racial mixing is very encouraging. Polls showing greater liberality of the young of matters of race, immigration, sexuality, and religion are legion, and nowhere is this truer than in the socially liberal San Francisco metropolis. One of the most impressive developments in today's California is the everyday normality of interracial dating, sex, marriage, and offspring. The percentage of mixed-race children is over 5 percent and may run as high as one in ten, depending on racial self-definition. The Golden State is working hard on creating the new interracial society out of the motley crew of people from the four corners of the earth. It is, of course, still a distant ideal, but the distance traveled over the last generation or two gives hope for the future of the country.[38]

Immigrant Rights and Wrongs

The immigrant rights movement has been one of the pillars of the struggle to defend the welfare of working people in California in recent decades. The main thrust of immigrant rights work has been the legal battle for recognition of undocumented immigrants' legal status and right to live, work, and thrive in the Golden State, where around one in ten residents have entered the country without papers. The movement got off the ground in the 1980s with the effort to win amnesty for immigrants without papers, and it achieved a measure of success in the 1987 immigration act. Then the politics of immigration got dramatically worse, with Southern California as the heartland of anti-immigrant organizing in America, spawning such deplorable groups as the Minutemen and Federation for American Immigration Reform (FAIR).

---

37 Romero 2017. On Europe's resistance to assimilation, see Pred 2000.
38 One sign of improvement was the failure of the new appeal to "color-blind" treatment of everyone to take hold via ballot proposition in the early twenty-first century. Bonilla-Silva 2003. On mixed-race kids in California, see Clark et al. 2017.

Following a major recession and rioting in Los Angeles in the early 1990s, California went into a spasm of immigrant bashing. In 1994, Governor Pete Wilson (a former mayor of San Diego) pushed Proposition 187 to cut off government benefits to the undocumented, arguing that they were a major drag on a state budget already deeply in deficit. Supporters of immigrants rallied to get Prop. 187 declared unconstitutional in the courts, but the fight moved to Washington, DC, where California politicians led a new anti-immigrant drive. The reactionary Gingrich Congress and the rightward-tracking Clinton administration bought into the idea of building a wall along the California-Mexico border (Operation Gatekeeper) and passed a draconian new immigration act in 1996 aimed at deporting undocumented and criminal immigrants. California got its wall long before Trump.[39]

By the dawn of the twenty-first century, however, California was in recovery from its addiction to immigrant bashing. While the rest of the United States is still trying to get its collective head around mass immigration, California passed that point a generation ago. The demographic revolution had become clear as day by 2000, as the census showed that people of color had become the new majority in most cities in the state. A pivotal change came in the wake of Prop. 187 and its flood of xenophobic propaganda, when immigrants began to seek citizenship and voting registration in large numbers. As a result, the electorate started its dramatic shift away from dominance by upper-class Whites to a new majority with far more progressive views. Along with this, more and more Latinos and Asians were elected to city councils, mayors' offices, the legislature, and Congress (see chapter 10).

An important rallying cry in the early twenty-first century was securing universal IDs and driver's licenses for undocumented people so they could function normally. A statewide law was passed to that effect in 2003, but the recall of liberal Democrat Gray Davis immediately thereafter allowed newly elected Governor Arnold Schwarzenegger to veto it—chiefly on budgetary grounds, since the state had fallen into another deep deficit because of the dot-com meltdown. Nevertheless, immigrant activism kept moving ahead, gaining local IDs in cities such as Oakland and San Francisco, because the reality of the undocumented was not going away.

After another decade passed, and the Democrats retook the legislature and the governor's office, a statewide driver's license law was approved in 2014. A million undocumented immigrants quickly applied for the new IDs—out of the estimated 2.5 million such people in the state. Today's polls show

---

39   On Prop. 187, see Ono & Sloop 2002, Walker 1995a. On Operation Gatekeeper, see Nevins 2002.

four-fifths of public support a clear path to citizenship for the undocumented. Not only is the majority of Californians now immigrants and their children, almost all of them with family ties to undocumented individuals, the rest of the white citizenry nor longer feels threatened by the demographic transformation of the state. [40]

In the new Millennium, Los Angeles became the national center of immigrant organizing, led by the National Immigration Law Center and National Day Laborers Organizing Network. Both were active in the Bay Area, along with local groups such as the Chinese Progressive Association and East Bay Alliance for a Sustainable Economy (EBASE). Local philanthropists such as the Haas, Jr. Fund, San Francisco Foundation, Rosenberg Foundation, and Mitch and Freada Kapor were pouring money into legal challenges and immigrant rights organizing.[41]

The legal protection of immigrant rights has been led by attorneys, many of whom have been in the thick of the defense of individuals and families in the arcane corridors of the immigration courts. A number of key legal defense organizations have been formed, coming from various parts of the progressive and racial spectrum; they include the Lawyers' Committee for Civil Rights, ACLU of Northern California, Asian Law Caucus, and La Raza Centro Legal in San Francisco and the Centro Legal de la Raza in Oakland. A powerful coalition of a dozen organizations came together in 2006 as the San Francisco Immigrant Legal and Education Network.[42]

The overlap between immigrant rights and labor organizing has also been considerable in both Northern and Southern California. They came together spectacularly in May 2006 with enormous marches of immigrant workers in Los Angeles, Chicago, and other cities around the country. The rallying cry was legalization of the undocumented, defeat of the reactionary Sensenbrenner immigration bill in Congress, and protection of immigrant workers from workplace raids by ICE / Homeland Security. Unfortunately, it has been hard to follow up on the momentum gained in that moment given the growing anti-immigrant sentiment elsewhere.[43]

★ ★ ★

In the twenty-first century, mass immigration shifted away from California, after labor demand flattened out. Immigrants began to flow in large numbers

---

40 Kopetman 2016, Hayes & Hill 2017.
41 Personal communication, Ellen Widess, formerly of the Rosenberg Foundation.
42 On immigrant rights law, see Cahn et al. 2012.
43 On the origins of the mass marches and evaluation of subsequent efforts, see Voss & Bloemraad 2011.

to the eastern half of the United States, which was even less prepared to receive the new immigrants than the Golden State had been a generation earlier. Reactionary forces gathered steam in the Southeast and Midwest, and the terror attacks of 2001 triggered a spasm of xenophobia. The political atmosphere darkened across the country. The Bush administration, to its credit, resisted some of the anti-immigrant backlash and the Sensenbrenner immigration bill failed in Congress. Nevertheless, pursuit and deportation of undocumented immigrants rose to levels not seen since Operation Wetback in the 1950s.

The new strategy was the pursuit of "illegal and criminal" immigrants, with the criminality argument hardened by the redirection of the South American drug trade through Mexico and the growth of gangs of traffickers south of the border. ICE agents were set loose to round up immigrants at workplaces, arrest them at home, grab parents waiting for their kids in front of schools, and even seize people from courthouses. Many of these were demonstrably innocent of any wrongdoing: kids brought to the United States by their parents, people with traffic violations, and some simply trying to report for hearings on their refugee status.

The onset of the Great Recession brought yet another setback. Although immigrant voters contributed substantially to President Obama's election in 2008, immigration reform was soon forgotten. His administration continued deporting undocumented and criminalized immigrants in large numbers (if fewer than either the Clinton or Bush administrations), in part to reduce visible unemployment from the Great Recession (a reason too often overlooked).[44]

One branch of immigrant rights activism was quite successful under Obama, however: the "Dreamer" movement. Dreamers are the children of undocumented immigrants, who arrived as kids, grew up in the United States and are thoroughly Americanized young adults now. They are not accused of any crime but are threatened with deportation because they are not U.S. citizens. As the home of a quarter of the Dreamers, California took the lead in fighting for their rights. A California Dream Coalition came together across college campuses. This proved to be a powerful appeal to which educators and governments responded with financial support for college students.

---

44 Deportations under Obama are estimated at over five million, less than half the number under Bush and Clinton. About half were apprehended and returned at the Mexican border; the other half were full legal removals from within the United States, which are more permanent. On that score, Obama's record was worse than his predecessors. http://www.migrationpolicy.org/article/obama-record-deportations-deporter-chief-or-not.

A national organization, United We Dream, was formed in 2007 out of regional groups in Los Angeles, the Bay Area, and other big cities, to push for the DREAM act in Congress, which was defeated several times. To get around Republican opposition, the Obama administration created the Deferred Action for Childhood Arrivals (DACA) program in 2012 and signed up 750,000 Dreamers for renewable work permits. DACA was vilified by the anti-immigrant forces and promptly rescinded by President Trump after his arrival in office. Not surprisingly, a federal judge in California put that decision on hold and it is still in the courts at this writing.[45]

After 2011, Dreamer groups, led by the National Immigrant Youth Alliance, broadened their fight to take on mass deportations and to protect the rights of immigrants as a whole. The movement became dramatically more militant, breaking with mainstream efforts to secure immigration reform from Congress. They began leading protests across the country against the government's mass deportations. Their demands were backed by hundreds of mainstream labor and immigrant organizations, leading to the call for a national day of protest on April 5, 2014, under the banner Ni Una Más (Not One More). A payoff came when President Obama declared a moratorium on deportations that break up families—but that victory was overturned by the federal courts.[46]

In the face of the deportation onslaught by ICE/Homeland Security under the reactionary Trump administration, activists moved in new directions. Some focused on quick response to threats to deport specific individuals and families, through protest and providing refuge. Cities such as San Francisco, Berkeley, and San Jose reaffirmed their status as sanctuaries and some counties joined the movement.[47] Sanctuary means a refusal to cooperate with federal agents by turning over immigrants arrested locally for deportation. Some unions also joined in the move to protect their members from deportation. For example, the San Francisco hotel workers' union, UNITE HERE Local 2, began rewriting contracts so that hotels would not cooperate with ICE and threatening to stop work en masse when some owners tried to get workers to submit their papers to prove legality.[48]

---

45   On the Dreamer movement, see Nichols & Fiorito 2015.
46   Foley 2014. Thanks to Ellen Widess for insights on the immigrant rights movement.
47   This built on the Bay Area's long-standing sanctuary movement, which started in Berkeley in 1971 to protect draft dodgers and military deserters. Sanctuary was revived in force during the "Contra" wars in Central America in the 1980s, when the Bay Area was the receiving area for thousands of innocents fleeing the carnage. On sanctuary, see Cahn et al. 2012.
48   On workplace resistance, Bacon 2017.

The national battle over the future of immigration, which has been simmering for decades, burst into flame in 2018. The Trump administration's efforts to build more wall along the Mexican border, deport more "illegal" immigrants, and reduce the inflow of refugees from war-torn countries brought things to a head, as it became clear that the goal of the Far Right is to suppress mass immigration altogether and return the country to the days before 1965, when White America reigned supreme. DACA had become the focal point of the public fight over immigration policy in Washington, DC, as the Democrats, led by representatives from California, demanded permanent residency for the Dreamers.[49]

Making and Breaking the Working Middle Class

While the common American view is that most people fall into a massive middle class between the rich and the poor, that formulation is not plausible. As argued in chapter 3, the top echelons of income earners are upper class; this is clearly true of the 1%, or capitalist class, but also applies to most of the 20 percent of professionals, managers and technical workers commonly referred to as the upper middle class. This leaves the vast majority of modern society as part of the working class—still a useful category, even if workers make up a huge, disparate group.

There are, of course, a large number of middle-income wage and salary workers who might be called the middle class. The terminology is dubious, however, in that these people do not have a clear basis that sets them up as a "class" apart from other workers, as do the capitalists and propertied or the professionals and managers. True, higher-paid workers do have some significant elements of difference: more skills, education, independence, and financial security, and they are more likely to be white and work in offices (hence another favorite term, "white collar" workers). Ideologically, they quite often see themselves as above the mass of uneducated, unskilled, and impoverished workers of the bottom half of the labor force, who are much more likely to be immigrants and people of color. A reasonable compromise is to call this group the "working middle class."

Still, there are a lot of mistaken beliefs about how people arrive in the working middle class and why it has been shrinking in recent decades. The conventional view, framed by economists, is that wages are determined by education and skill, or what is known as "human capital." In this view, those with more schooling or training merit their higher payoff. Conversely, those

---

49 Berman 2018. Even the H-1B program so vital to the tech industry is in the sights of the Republicans.

who have fallen behind in earnings lack the skills and education to fill the growing number of sophisticated jobs created by the new technology. They have failed to invest the time and money to up their "human capital." This is, however, a view more congenial to the well-educated professionals like economists than to the reality of most working people's lives and labor.

In fact, skills and education do not always align closely with wages, as, for example, the college-educated high school teacher who earns a modest salary for coping with unruly students all day and the municipal sanitation worker with seniority who earns a comfortable living with benefits for going on a daily garbage route. There are three big social forces operating to elevate or depress wages in a way that has little to do with work capability and competence.

The first, as already noted, is race and gender discrimination, which lowers the payoff to workers at every skill level (see last chapter). The second is economic geography; there's payoff for the luck of the draw of where someone is born (or migrates). Regional prosperity raises the payoff for the same skills, previously shown for Bay Area. Similarly, more advanced nations pay their workforce better than poor nations. And those differences can change over time, as when the U.S. economy soared after the Second World War and workers came along for the ride. The difference in incomes is out of proportion to any gap in education—as any immigrant to the United States from Eastern Europe can attest.

The third force at work is unionization and class struggle. The reason so many working people could get on the bus for that ride to the Great American Middle Class was the mass unionization unleashed by the New Deal and labor mobilizations of the 1930s. The new industrial unions, organized under the Congress of Industrial Organizations, elevated a whole new strata of ordinary factory workers on Fordist assembly lines, in chemical works and refineries, and in trucking and dock work to a whole new level of wages and benefits, not to mention social respect (the CIO later merged with the skilled trades unions of the American Federation of Labor to form the AFL-CIO).[50]

Did those working people really move up the class ladder? No. What happened was that unions elevated the wages for a huge swath of industrial (and later, office) workers, allowing the working class to take home a larger proportion of national income than ever before (see again fig. 3.11 in chapter 3). This was not simply a passive result of national prosperity, because unionized workers make more than nonunion labor at every skill level, as well as better benefits. On top of this, the unions were an important political force driving the creation of New Deal and Great Society programs for unemployment

---

50   Fraser & Gerstle 1989, Lichtenstein 2002, Glass 2016.

insurance, Social Security, and Medicare that markedly improved the economic security of the working class as a whole. For that reason, the more prosperous middle-income group really ought to be called the unionized middle class.[51]

By contrast, the main reason the working middle class shrank over the last forty years is the decline in unionization, which has fallen from a third of the U.S. labor force to single digits. Union density has withered under the onslaught of deindustrialization of former mass production industries, the rise of new unorganized sectors, and direct employer assaults. Added to this was the decline of public education, meaning that more and more working-class kids left school with little knowledge and few skills. Even in the high-flying Bay Area, union density fell for decades and so did the wages of the bottom two-thirds of the workforce. Short-term improvements have come at the end of long upswings like the 1990s, when labor markets tighten, but the long-term decline of the working middle class is unmistakable here, as around the country.[52]

★ ★ ★

The Bay Area was a major union stronghold in the past and still has a vigorous labor movement. Labor organizing and activism began under the skilled trades unions, going back to the eight-hour movement of the 1860s. At the turn of the century, San Francisco was an almost fully unionized city and the Union Labor Party dominated politics for a decade. When mass industrial workers began to organize, San Francisco led the way with the first general strike of the epoch in 1934, inspired by the struggles of the International Longshoremen and Warehousemen's Union (ILWU). By the 1950s, unions had organized over half of San Francisco's workers, and the East Bay was not far behind.[53]

Today the Bay Area's union density is about one-sixth of the workforce, about half again that of the United States, but is no higher than the rest of California. A big reason for the decline of the unions in the Bay Area is that the booming tech sector is notoriously antiunion. Yes, tech firms pay well and hold out the possibility of striking it rich, but they have no intention of

---

51   On the union wage, see Freeman & Medoff 1984, Bernstein 2015. Another effect of mass unionization is that economists added a new category between skilled and unskilled labor, called "semiskilled," which mostly referred to unionized factory labor.

52   On union decline, see Moody 1989, Logan 2006, Western & Rosenfeld 2011. For an attempt to put lipstick on the class pig of late, see Samuelson 2017. For the opposite view, see Cohen 2017. Unions are still under assault in the courts and state legislatures, as New Deal–era rights of organizing and representation have been steadily whittled away.

53   On local union history, see Glass 2016.

yielding control over their affairs to unions. Several major efforts to organize Silicon Valley in the 1970s and 1980s came to naught. A crucial skill developed by tech executives has nothing to do with digital innovation; rather, it rests on how to outmaneuver union organizers. The disdain of tech industry leaders for unions is illustrated by the view of Paul Graham, founder of Y Combinator, who recently argued that government labor regulations create inefficient companies that overpay unionized labor and that "industries afflicted by unions are sclerotic so have left lots undone."[54]

Some of the leading unions in the bay region today are the several branches of UNITE HERE, such as Local 2 in San Francisco, Local 19 in the South Bay, and Local 28 in the East Bay. The Teamsters are well represented in trucking, delivery, and buses, represented by Local 853 and Joint Counsel 7. ILWU Local 34 is less militant than it used to be but still a presence on the waterfront. SEIU Local 1021 in San Francisco and Oakland, and the California Nurse's Association more widely, are strong advocates for healthcare workers (and patients). The building trades are still well organized by unions such as the IBEW Local 6 in San Francisco, Local 617 on BART, and Local 332 in the South Bay.

A major bulwark of unionization is government work. Unionization rates were bolstered in the late 1960s when laws against public sector unions were relaxed. Today the unionization rate for government workers is nearly 60 percent in the Bay Area—six times the rate in the private sector—and rising. Some of the biggest unions represent public workers such as public school teachers and professors (California Teachers Association, National Education Association, and American Federation of Teachers), state office staff (SEIU Local 1000), and local government workers (approximately fifty locals of the American Federation of State, County and Municipal Employees). The mix of unionized workers reflects the diverse labor force of the region, including many with college degrees.[55]

Government employment has steadily diminished with the perennial budget cuts of the last thirty years and took a dramatic dive in the Great Recession, from which it has not recovered (fig. 4.9); and this has cut into union membership.

On the other hand, union organizing in the private sector has seen renewed success around the Bay Area in recent years, thanks in part to the pressure of the cost of living and the willingness of immigrants and workers

54 On current union density, see Adler & Tilly 2014. On Silicon Valley organizing, see Hayes 1989, Pellow & Park 2002. Graham quote in Green 2016b.
55 Adler & Tilly 2014. On the rise of public sector unions, see Troy 1994; on the neoliberal counterattack, see Fletcher 2012.

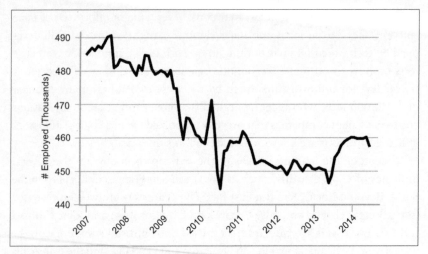

Figure 4.9: Decline of Government Jobs in the Bay Area, 2007–2015

Source: Bay Area Council Economic Institute 2014 (9-county Bay Area).

of color to organize. UNITE HERE has extended its reach from San Francisco to suburban hotels in the East Bay and Silicon Valley. The Teamsters have signed up drivers for the infamous "Google buses" run by Chariot and Bauer, warehouse workers for Google Express delivery service run by Adecco (itself a temp agency) in Palo Alto, and waste disposal workers at Genentech in South San Francisco. A coordinated union effort in Sonoma County succeeded in organizing the Graton Rancheria Casino, a major employer in the North Bay. Recently, a group of SEIU locals in the Bay Area and Los Angeles have allied under the banner of United Service Workers West to organize food service and janitorial workers at the big airports.[56]

Cooperative organizing on specific occupations and companies has proved effective. So has organizing based on locale. Working Partnerships, a nonprofit created by the Central Labor Council of Santa Clara County, has been leading creative union organizing efforts in Silicon Valley for a generation. Their latest campaign, Silicon Valley Rising, is aimed at organizing service workers at the tech giants and their subcontractors. Examples of recent success are hundreds of food service workers at Intel and Facebook who won union recognition with UNITE HERE Local 19. Silicon Valley Rising claims that some five thousand tech service workers in security, janitorial, food service, and transport have successfully unionized under their campaign. Other new campaigns are underway, such as SEIU 1877's efforts at the

---

56   Said 2017, Bennett 2016. On recent organizing in Southern California, see Milkman 2006.

two largest security firms in the Valley (not surprisingly, Apple and Google recently moved their security services back in-house).[57]

★ ★ ★

Getting a union and a contract is not the only means to higher wages. Bay Area unions are in the thick of one of the most important labor struggles of the present moment: the fight for a living wage for the bottom third of the labor force. Raising workers out of the cheap labor force is another major way of expanding the working middle class. A major landmark was the 2015 passage of a statewide $15 minimum wage by California, the first state to adopt the new target. The new minimum, which will be implemented in annual increments, raises the floor on wages by half and will affect one-third of the Golden State's labor force and a majority of working women and Latinos. Although the greater Bay Area has fewer minimum wage workers than Los Angeles and the Central Valley, one quarter of its labor force earn $15 per hour or less.[58]

That breakthrough built on efforts to establish living wage ordinances in over 150 cities across the country since the 1990s, including 34 in California. This was the only option to get around Republican control of Congress and state legislatures that made it impossible to budge the federal minimum wage and that of most states. A key idea behind the push for a living wage was to leap over the bare-bones poverty standards of existing minimum wage levels, especially when the higher costs of cities are taken into account. But they usually applied only to municipal workers and employers receiving contracts from city government.[59]

The movement took on new life after the Great Recession hit and the Occupy Wall Street movement exploded across the country in 2011. The latter's signal contribution to U.S. politics was a new focus on inequality and a new vocabulary to talk about class (the 1% vs. the 99%). Many Occupy activists in New York City came out of organized labor and afterward turned their attention to the plight of low-wage workers, spawning an upsurge among the city's worst paid, those working in restaurants and fast-food outlets. A one-day strike in late 2012 was followed by coordinated actions in cities across the country, calling for the seemingly outrageous sum of $15 per hour, double the federal minimum wage.

Out of that day came the "Fight for $15" mobilization, which dovetailed with organizing efforts at McDonald's, Walmart, and other giant corporations

---

57 Byrd & Rhee 2004, Smith 2015.
58 Adler et al. 2015.
59 On the several ways of calculating a living wage, see Luce 2015.

profiting from low-wage labor. Cities on the West Coast were the first to rally behind $15 wage floor: Seattle in 2013, then San Francisco and Los Angeles the following year. Meanwhile, the battle jumped back to the state legislatures, with over half raising their minimum wage before California's legislature made the dramatic leap to the new standard. Soon thereafter, the Bernie Sanders campaign forced the Democratic Party to adopt the $15 wage in its national platform. The Fight for $15 continues at the municipal level, with an agreement among East Bay cities to coordinate a shift to the new standard.[60]

Living wage and minimum wage campaigns are almost always part of more comprehensive agendas to reduce inequality, organize labor, and improve the welfare of the working class in general. These movements are not just the work of unions, but of labor-community organizations over the last generation, such as Working Partnerships in Santa Clara County and New Economy Working Solutions in Sonoma County. Working Partnerships has been hammering away at the need to organize around the new flexible employment relations and occupational mix in the heartland of tech, and to build broad coalitions in support of labor unions and working-class communities. In 2014, they succeeded in getting Santa Clara County to pass the most sweeping living wage ordinance yet, which includes community benefit agreements, wage theft protections, and preapprenticeship programs.[61]

Other advances in improving low-wage work conditions are quietly being made around the bay region. One example is the passage of a Living Workweek ordinance in Emeryville (an important employment cluster in the East Bay), which requires employers to give two weeks' notice of scheduling changes; this was just the third such ordinance to be passed in the country. The San Mateo County Union-Community Alliance is working to improve access to health care for poor people and immigrants. There are several city ordinances establishing minimum wages in the Bay Area's thousands of restaurants, forcing owners to pay wages and not just rely on tips. Restaurant Opportunities Centers United (ROC), a national advocacy group, has established a regional headquarters and training restaurant in East Oakland to fight the well-known racial hierarchy in restaurants—where the farther back one goes in the establishment, the darker the staff.[62]

---

60 Luce 2015, Tung et al. 2015, Bennett 2016, Dreier 2016, Rolf 2017. See also the tracking of Bay Area minimum wages at https://www.localwise.com/a/108-minimum-wage-in-the-bay-area and all such ordinances at: http://laborcenter.berkeley.edu/minimum-wage-living-wage-resources/inventory-of-us-city-and-county-minimum-wage-ordinances/.

61 Working Partnerships 2014. Thanks to Marty Bennett for his insights on the living wage movement.

62 Salian 2017, Phillips 2017.

Regional advocates are also deeply involved with state-level organizing efforts. One is the battle to improve working conditions for domestic workers such as housekeepers, nannies, and home healthcare attendants. The National Domestic Workers Alliance launched a long campaign in California to gain basic worker rights such as overtime limits and better working conditions, which was won in 2014 (and again in 2017 when sunset provisions were stripped from the original legislation). That coalition encompasses an array of immigrant rights and labor groups such as the Chinese Progressive Association of San Francisco and Filipino Advocates for Justice in Oakland. A parallel SEIU-California effort to gain overtime pay for home healthcare workers got into the state budget in 2015 and the union followed with a legislative push to gain union organizing rights for this dispersed and poorly remunerated group of workers.[63]

The Crimes of California

Crime in America is usually treated as a question of personal malfeasance and individual transgressions of the rule of law. But this view of things is based fundamentally on the Classical Liberal principle of individual responsibility for success or failure in a fair and equal market system; modern liberals soften this to allow for individuals to be led astray by bad conditions of upbringing and education. The conservative view, on the other hand, agrees on individual accountability, but sees criminality as an inherent failing of human beings, including often racist ideas about genetics and the criminal type. The Left view, by contrast, emphasizes the way crime and punishment are structured by class and racial systems that are fundamentally unequal in opportunity, power, and protection. In this view, criminals come mostly from the lower strata of the working class and the institutions of Law and Order are controlled by the upper classes.

A pillar of the neoliberal era since 1975 has been a hardening of the criminal justice system in the United States based on a mix of Classical Liberal and modern conservative thinking. That is, the more progressive liberalism of the New Deal era fell away to leave only personal responsibility shorn of context and social causality; and conservative visions of Super Predators among male youth of color, threatening all white people, reigned supreme for a time. These kinds of unsympathetic, even damning, views of other human

---

63 Butler 2017. Unfortunately, all these living wage ordinances and other health and safety laws are only as good as the enforcement effort behind them. Enforcement based on worker complaints, not government enforcement staff, is a huge challenge in nonunion environments, especially for immigrant workers who are unfamiliar with the law and undocumented workers who fear deportation.

beings made a brute-force approach to crime and punishment seem reasonable, rather than stemming from the irrational fears of the upper classes and thuggish mentality of rulers from time immemorial when faced with signs of revolt among the lower orders. Unfortunately, this outlook has filled a vast prison complex and poisoned the justice system of the country.[64]

Nowhere is this truer than in the Golden State. In fact, the Law and Order State built up over the last half century—that is, the apparatus to police the cities, crack down on malefactors, and whisk them through the courts into prison—is, to a remarkable degree, a product of California politics. It was the brainchild of the Los Angeles Police Department under Chief Darryl Gates, backed by the powerful right of postwar Southern California. It was launched at the national level under President Richard Nixon and enlarged under Ronald Reagan, both of whose political careers began in Southern California. It peaked in California under Republican Governor George Deukmejian, from the agrarian power centers of the San Joaquin Valley. It was, not surprisingly, aimed at reversing earlier legal and penal practices in the Golden State and the socially liberal trends of the postwar period (see also chapter 10).[65]

The carceral state of California catches a staggering number of people in its net, where they cycle in and out of courtrooms, police custody, youth camps, local jails, state and federal prisons, and probation offices. At the same time as the fortunes of the Bay Area were taking off in the 1980s, California was putting in place an immense prison system, going from fewer than 20,000 prisoners in 1977 to over 100,000 in the 1990s and over 150,000 by the Millennium. At times this Golden Gulag has been the largest in the world, both absolutely and relative to population size.

The most marginal elements of the working class are the most criminalized, and these are overwhelmingly men of color, black and brown. They have the least chance of finding jobs, let along good jobs, or pursuing a decent education that might lift them out of the ghettoes and barrios. They quickly fall afoul of the law when young and can rarely or ever extract themselves from the stigma. This malignant process begins with the condemnation of errant youth under stringent laws for minor drug offenses and gang membership, with excessively long terms. It continues in overcrowded prisons where young men have every opportunity to fall in with serious criminals and none at all to redeem themselves. Once let out on the streets again, mostly in the

---

64 Thanks to Tony Platt for his insights into the current state of carceral reform and the long view of the penal state. On the latter, see also Thompson et al. 1975, Hall & Scraton 1981.

65 Davis 1990, Gilmore 2007, Simon 2007, Pearlstein 2008, Alexander 2010.

poor communities of the big cities, they have little hope of finding decent jobs or escaping prison-born alliances and enmities. As a result, drugs, murderous rivalries, and death stalk the streets of places such as North Richmond, East Oakland, and Hunters Point in San Francisco on an everyday basis.

The hardline approach to Law and Order extends far beyond the prisons and gangs. Working people suffer all the time from the everyday police state installed over the last fifty years in every city across the country. Draconian drug laws have created an underground economy of dealers and suppliers that is constantly at a face-off with police, and their battles leave a bloody trail across city streets. The combination of fear and empowerment among cops too often makes the slightest encounter with an officer an unpleasant occasion, and can just as easily be deadly for young men of color. Cops are armed to the teeth and taught to shoot to kill at the least threat. Police from San Francisco and Oakland to Sonoma and San Jose have been involved in hasty killings of suspects. Even students protesting at the University of California have found out all too swiftly that police brutality does not stop at the borders of well-tended campuses.

* * *

The fight against the Law and Order State has become another vital branch of the movement to protect working people from the conservative / neoliberal onslaught. California's prison complex has come in for harsh criticism by the courts in a series of decisions from *Coleman v. Wilson*'s recognition of untreated mental health problems as "cruel and unusual punishment" under the constitution to *Brown v. Plata*, confirming that the state must reduce its overstuffed prison population by tens of thousands. These decisions rested on years of litigation challenging solitary confinement, overcrowding, poor health care, lack of mental health services, punishment by hunger, and generally insufferable conditions. They hit pay dirt with the 2009 *Brown v. Plata* decision by a special panel of Northern California federal judges, which was subsequently affirmed five to four by the U.S. Supreme Court (over the hysterical opposition of Justice Antonin Scalia).[66]

Prisoners themselves have spearheaded the attack on prison conditions, aided by activist attorneys at the ACLU, Legal Services for Prisoners with Children (LSPC), and the Center for Constitutional Rights, among others. A key moment in the fight to better their plight came in a courageous pair of collective hunger strikes in 2011 at the hellish supermax prison at Pelican Bay, which was followed by a mass strike by thirty thousand inmates up and down

---

66   For a review of court cases, see Simon 2014.

the state in 2013. After these protests, the California legislature agreed to hold public hearings, and prison officials were at last forced to relent. What came out of that was Proposition 47, passed by popular vote in 2014, to reduce penalties for a variety of crimes, allow people to expunge minor offenses from their records, and shrink jail and prison populations.[67]

The prisoners have been backed up by organizations of family members around the state, and grassroots militants have called for an end to the entire regime of caging people instead of addressing basic social needs in communities of color and working people. Critical Resistance, formed in Berkeley in 1998, is the best known of these, but others include California Prison Moratorium Project (CPMP) (Oakland to Fresno), A New PATH (Parents for Addiction Treatment & Healing) (Rancho Santa Fe), and the California Coalition for Women Prisoners (San Francisco). In 2003, a new alliance of dozens of organizations around the state was created, called California United for a Responsible Budget (CURB), to support all manner of local initiatives. One notably successful mobilization stopped the construction of new city jail in San Francisco in 2015.

The movement has expanded beyond opposition to prisons and reducing sentences to greater support for ex-convicts reentering civilian life. A recent national project launched by the LSPC is "All of Us or None," aimed at improving former prisoners' voting rights and eliminating questions about prior convictions in applications for employment, loans, apartments, government aid, insurance, and so on. The project pushed the San Francisco Board of Supervisors to enact a model ordinance to eliminate such background checks, the Fair Chance Act, in 2014.

Undoubtedly, the most important movement at present is the fight to roll back the Law and Order State on its front lines, the police and their aggressive tactics against people of color. This fight is being led by Black Lives Matter (BLM), which burst forth on the national scene after the police killing of Michael Brown in Ferguson, Missouri, in 2014. The goal of this uprising is to stop the widespread official violence by changing the culture of policing, reducing police armaments, and gaining public review of police actions. The Bay Area, too, has seen an upsurge of police shootings of African American and Latino men, including Alex Woods and Mario Nieto. Oakland has been a major node of BLM, and one of the key antecedents of the movement was the militant protests after the shooting of Oscar Grant by BART transit police in 2010. The Oakland chapter of Black Lives Matter has led several major

---

67   St. John 2013, Lovett 2015. There has been some opposition to Prop. 47, however, due to its treatment of rape and child abuse offenders.

protests, such as the mass blockade of the I-880 freeway in July 2016. It was also a local athlete, Colin Kaepernick, who started the practice of football players kneeling during the national anthem, which stirred up such anger from a certain occupant of the White House.[68]

The overall results of opposition to the Law and Order State have been mixed. In California, the state prison population has declined, but many prisoners have simply been shunted off to local authorities, leading to lots of new jail building. Nationally, libertarian and Republican Party initiatives (e.g., Right on Crime) have been at the forefront of reforms that reduce drug penalties but remain as draconian as ever in dealing with felonies. Governor Jerry Brown, very much a conservative in penal matters, follows this line. Brown has vetoed several reform bills, including one reducing minor drug infraction for immigrants to make them less at risk of deportation.

For neoliberals, reform principally means saving money by eliminating the most egregious excesses of the criminal justice system while not rethinking the basic tenets of social control by policing and imprisonment. For all too many Californians, reform of drug laws means legalization of marijuana for medical and recreational use (achieved in 2018), but not reform of the system that ensnares far too many immigrants and people of color in its net. So far, militant struggle from below and cautious reform from above have combined for a measure of progress on prisons, but resistance by police, white backlash to black protests, and the basic conservatism of the criminal (in)justice state are blunting further change.

It's a (White) Man's World

The tech elite is regularly praised to the skies for creating the wonderful world of smartphones, social media, and the sharing economy, and for the progressive potential of such free and easy communication, information, and exchange. The political views espoused by most of the top-flight owners and executives are remarkably liberal on social issues such as race and gender. Nevertheless, on closer inspection the world the tech masters have made in their own backyard is decidedly illiberal: dominated by white men, lower pay, and glass ceilings for women and people of color, and a scandalous record of sexual harassment. These failings have come under greater scrutiny recently and have prompted a growing revulsion against the tech elite.[69]

The much-heralded start-up entrepreneurs, venture capitalists, and corporate barons of tech in the Bay Area are mostly white. The main exception

---

68 Blaisdell et al. 2015, Rios 2016.
69 Rushe 2014.

is Asian American and Asian immigrant engineers, who are a regular presence among the "techies" or upper tier of technical and managerial staff of the IT companies. In addition, a large number of tech companies have been founded by Chinese and Indian immigrant engineers. Vinod Khosla is one of the most eminent venture capitalists, and there are a handful of other Asians, such as the Filipino American Dado Bonatao; but they are exceptional in the world of Sand Hill Road financiers (behind Stanford). One or two African American capitalists and executives show up in the press from time to time, but they are rare sightings. Latinos in the upper crust of tech are virtually unknown.[70]

Even among the favored Asians techies, there is widespread frustration with the limits on how far they can rise in Tech World. The best route to advancement is to work for companies owned by other Asians. On the other hand, the tech industry has never stinted on hiring people of color as production, office, and auxiliary workers; today, however, they are most likely to be working for subcontractors, not IT companies themselves. Finally, a damning case can be made against the industry for its long-standing exclusion of African American workers, currently hovering around 1 percent of the tech workforce.[71]

★　★　★

The most egregious aspect of the gender order of Tech World has been the widespread harassment of women by venture capitalists, boy entrepreneurs, and misogynist techies. As one well-placed woman in the tech industry has stated, "Silicon Valley has established itself as the boys' club of the West, just like how Wall Street has established itself as the boys' club of the East." For a long time women gritted their teeth and bore the boorish behavior of men on whom they depended for their jobs or financing. If you brought suit for sexual harassment, as did Ellen Pao against her venture capitalist employer Kleiner Perkins, it was a road to pariah status.[72]

What seems to have broken down the wall of silence is the singularly outrageous working conditions created by top management at Uber, led by notorious cofounder Travis Kalanick. As more women stepped forth to denounce the company, Kalanick was finally ousted as CEO. Soon, personal stories of harassment at other companies were pouring forth, and several more of the bad boys of tech were toppled from their digital thrones.[73]

70　Saxenian 2006, Wu 2015.
71　Wu 2015, Silicon Valley Rising 2015, Fuller 2016.
72　Quote from Natasha Lamb, director of equity research and shareholder engagement at Arjuna Capital. Wakabayaski 2017.
73　Benner 2017c, Carson 2017, Manjoo 2017, Levin 2017b.

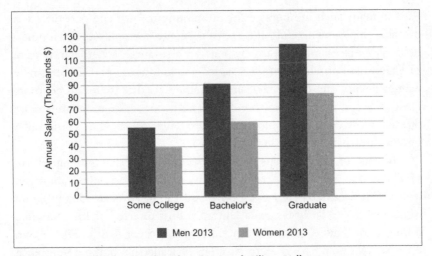

Figure 4.10: Gender Pay Gap by Education Level, Silicon Valley 2013

Source: http://peninsulapress.com/2015/02/06/gender-pay-gap-silicon-valley/.

Employees, courts, and government agencies have begun demanding that companies such as Google and Twitter reveal their internal data on hiring, pay, and promotions. These confirm the male dominance in tech. For example, of Lyft's sixteen hundred employees (excluding drivers), 42 percent are women; of Uber's global workforce of twelve thousand, 36 percent are women; Lyft's leadership is 36 percent female, Uber's 22 percent; Lyft's technical workforce is 18 percent women, Uber's 15.4 percent.[74]

This is not to say that women are well treated outside tech. Up and down the occupational hierarchy, women's pay rates are systematically lower for the same work, despite being better educated on average (fig. 4.10). Harassment and mistreatment of women workers is widespread, and it takes many forms besides sexual predation, such as differential hiring, promotion, and respect. Even more subtle kinds of misbehavior by men leave female colleagues feeling isolated and set up to fail. The persistence of gender discrimination is especially discouraging when one considers that the bay region has been an important site of agitation for women's rights in the past; this was one of the first places to put women's suffrage on the ballot, to put women in positions of authority in labor unions, and to win equal compensation for women for the same work—not to mention the Bay Area's centrality in the fight against homophobia.

The worst economic consequences are those that befall women in the bottom third of the labor force, especially single mothers and their children.

---

74 Benner 2017d, Lien 2017, Levin 2017c, Wakabayaski 2017.

Far too many such mothers get by on minimum wage and part-time and unstable employment, and a quarter of them are unemployed. Their households scrape by on meager earnings and state assistance. More than 12 percent of California households are female-led and another 12 percent are single women living alone. Children of single mothers are three to four times more likely to live in poverty than those with two parents. The problem is more dire in the low-wage economies of Southern California and the Central Valley, but the same pattern exists in the Bay Area.[75]

Because of the hardships they face, women have been in the forefront of all the movements just discussed. Marisa Franco began immigrant organizing in San Francisco before going on to be a leading advocate for immigrant rights in Arizona and Marielena Hincapié, now director of LA's National Immigration Law Center, got her start with the Legal Aid office in San Francisco. Women have risen to positions of leadership in the union movement as heads of Central Labor Councils in San Francisco (Josie Mooney), San Mateo (Shelley Kessler), and Alameda County (Josie Camacho). They have led some of the most creative union organizing efforts, like Tho Do of Local 2 of UNITE HERE, Luisa Blue of SEIU 521 and 1021, Amy Dean, Cindy Chavez, and Derica Mehrens of Working Partnerships in Santa Clara County and Maria Noel Fernandez of Silicon Valley Rising. In the fight against criminalization, Angela Davis and Ruth Gilmore have been among the leading voices for abolition, and women such as Alicia Garza, now with the Oakland office of the National Domestic Workers Alliance, have led the fight on the ground to control police violence.

Conclusion

Despite being the richest region in the richest country on earth, and currently enjoying the best of times, the Bay Area's economy still cannot deliver the goods to all its working people. While the upper echelons of the labor force do well in terms of pay, job quality, and security, conditions for those in the middle are a decidedly mixed bag. Those in the bottom third of the labor force—largely people of color and women—face a working life short on rewards and full of insecurity. For those at the very bottom—unemployed, undocumented, single with children, disabled, or trapped in the criminal justice system—the outlook is quite dire.

Fortunately, the spirit of rebellion against prevailing conditions is very much alive in the Bay Area, and efforts to raise wages, protect immigrants, equalize pay, and reduce imprisonment are making a difference in the lives

---

75 Mount St. Mary's 2015.

of millions of working families. These popular movements do not arise from thin air. They are a response to the way people enter the workforce through immigration only to be harried by a xenophobic state; how they experience work in the Gig Economy and misogynous workplaces; how they try to earn a respectable living and build a decent life by joining unions or campaigning for a living wage; and how they and their children are shunted aside by a society obsessed with crime and fearful of the unknown Other.

Some of these are classic class struggles between labor and capital, some are not; but in every case they are driven by basic concerns and dreams of the contemporary working class of the Bay Area and California. Something new is in the air, given the vast and growing inequality between the upper classes and the working people, and it is augmented by the fact that the former are so largely white and male and the latter are not. Yes, the new working class is divided by division of labor, pay, race, and gender, but there are many ties that bind it together, especially among the lower half of the labor hierarchy, such as poor wages, lousy jobs, and rising costs of living.

Nevertheless, a working class in more than name can only be made manifest through common experience, lifelong learning, and fighting for social justice. A real sense of class solidarity has to be forged through struggles such as the ones outlined here for unions, a living wage, immigrant rights, and racial justice and against harassment, criminalization, and out-of-control police.

What this chapter has shown is that in the Bay Area an emergent, multi-racial working class is on the move and is not content to accept the drippings from the banquet of the wealthy fed by the tech economic boom. Working people here are not a declining group in despair and longing for a past Golden Age, as in so many parts of the United States. They are mobilized and looking toward the future, protesting for better wages, fighting deportations and saving black lives, rather than voting for salvation by putting a Great White Hope in the White House. Therein lies real hope for the future as a multi-racial, progressive city, unloosing the shackles of ruling-class power, white supremacy, and political paralysis.

Part II
The New Metropolis
Urban Transformation and the Tech Boom

INTRODUCTION TO PART II

IN THE SECOND PART OF THIS BOOK, THE GEOGRAPHY OF THE METROPOLITAN BAY Area will be brought into focus. The political economic dramas of the tech industry, boom and bust, rich and poor, work and profit, as portrayed in the previous chapters, play out across the Bay Area metropolitan region. But they do more than just take place here; they sculpt the urban area into a new form. The city is built, rebuilt, and reshaped with every era of growth and crisis, and the opening decades of the twenty-first century are no exception. Indeed, the present decade has witnessed one of the most dramatic overhauls of the city by the bay since its founding.

At the same time, the metropolis is not a passive canvas on which are drawn the outlines of economy, polity, and society. Quite the contrary, the urban nexus is the very staff of social life, allowing for the kind of interaction so essential to technical innovation, collective labor, and the spark of new ideas. It is a principal medium in which the messages of modernity are written and cultural forms are propagated. It is also prime terrain whereupon the politics of growth and conflict are fought out. In this part of the book, the city steps forward as the main stage and essential actor in the drama of the present time. Despite the wonders of electronic miniaturization and the globe-straddling impact of the tech industry, the places bound together by the city and the everyday spaces of human-scale living still matter.

The story begins in chapter 5 with the rush to reoccupy and build up the metropolitan core of San Francisco, Oakland, and Silicon Valley—an epochal reversal of the pattern of suburban flight witnessed in the post–World War II era. In the process, massive construction schemes have been put in place, the skyline of the metropolis raised dramatically, and old social geographies redrawn. This has not been an extension of past patterns so much as the unfolding of a new era of political economy and reconceptualization of social life in the city. As the money rolls in, the favored classes move into the city center and mingle in the urban milieu, generating a much-ballyhooed revival of city fortunes. Unfortunately, the vitality of the New Urbanism that excites so many planners, urbanists, and politicians has very little place for anyone but the privileged.

In chapter 6, the ugly consequences of the Bay Area's boom economy, combined with raging inequality and the New Urbanism, are starkly revealed by a monumental housing crisis gripping the metropolis. Hundreds of thousands of people have been displaced or had their housing severely downgraded in the face of a hurricane of rent hikes and rising house prices. The Bay Area has become unaffordable for almost all of its working families, while rents extracted by owners and investors mount up, and a sense of panic has developed in the region's leadership circles. Unfortunately, the causes of housing crisis are widely misunderstood thanks to the blinders of conventional economics, and the standard cures for what ails the housing market are, despite the drumbeat of official propaganda about "housing reform," sadly insufficient.

At the same time, as chapter 7 shows, all the attention given to the New Urbanism and the housing crisis has masked even larger changes afoot in the greater Bay Area. These are staggering in their implications, as the city surges outward beyond anything previously known, workers brave astonishingly long commutes, and low-density sprawl remains the name of the game in the outer realms of the urban region. Here, too, developers harvest the gains of rising land value, while offering a restricted version of housing choice to the mass of households, too many of whom become overindebted in search of the suburban dream and lose it all to foreclosure. Meanwhile, the class and race geography of the city is being overturned from the inside out and outside in.

In short, the chickens of the tech era come home to roost on the Bay Area, and they have made a mess of things. Neither public opinion nor government policy has yet come to grips with the extent of the damage done in the course of urban restructuring on such a massive scale. As the present decade unfolded, most of what was heard in public forums was the crowing of the tech crowd, developers, and local politicians about the benefits of growth and unheard-of prosperity. By the peak times in the middle of the decade, the complaints of those paying intolerable prices for housing broke through the celebration and eventually heard in distorted form all the way to Sacramento. Sounds of hand-wringing over the disgraceful numbers of homeless and ungodly traffic also rang out over the city. But what was little heard, at least at the top of the social pyramid, were the cries of those expelled from their homes and neighborhoods to the far fringes of the metropolis or out of the city altogether.

CHAPTER FIVE

The New Urbanism
Remaking the Heart of the City

A GREAT CITY PUTS ON A NEW SUIT OF CLOTHES WITH EVERY EPOCH OF ECONOMIC growth and bears the scars of every wave of rebuilding. Urban space is created according to the technologies, tastes, and profit calculus of each generation, and then reworked into new configurations as society and economy move on to new frontiers. One era is layered onto the next like geologic deposits, uplifted to new heights and cut down again to reveal secrets of the social order. This kind of upheaval in the urban landscape has struck the Bay Area over the last quarter century, and it has meant nothing less than a wholesale transformation of the metropolitan region. Some of the changes are beautiful, others grotesque, and most highly disturbing to those who live through such remarkable changes and feel the impact on their lives and surroundings.[1]

A striking aspect of the current transformation is the resurgence of the metropolitan core—the subject of this chapter. The great metropolitan areas of the United States passed a turning point around 1980, with a marked renovation of many down-on-the-heels neighborhoods and influx of new people to the central cities, and by the twenty-first century it was apparent to all that a profound transformation was afoot. Nowhere, perhaps, has this been more dramatic than in the Bay Area. The core cities of the metropolis have acquired a new sheen of greater density, commercial revival, and cosmopolitan pleasures, a phenomenon that has come to be known as the New Urbanism. But under the superficial glitter can be found layers of lost ways of life, restricted opportunity, and mass displacement of working people of many colors.[2]

The New Urbanism and its companion, gentrification, have usually been explained in three ways. The economists justify them as the natural outcome of urban growth and rising rents at the center. Neighborhood

---

1   For the theory of urban restructuring, see Harvey 1985, Massey 2002.
2   The term "New Urbanism" also denotes a planning and architectural movement for designing denser developments with commerce, public transport, and urban amenities. It is used here in the broader sense of revival of urban centers and urbane culture, along with rising densities and more compact development.

activists denounce them as an invasion by elites looking for a good deal in housing and "authentic" urban culture. Leftists analyze them as investment strategy of capitalists profiting from the "rent gap" between run-down neighborhoods and properties repurposed for higher-income occupants. All three explanations contain important elements of truth, but a fourth factor, often overlooked, is the largest: the geography of industry and employment. What it all adds up to is, to reiterate, a thorough makeover of the metropolis by the changing political economy of the tech era.

The first section of this chapter considers the four forces remaking the heart of the metropolis and points out the shortcomings of partial explanations—especially those that treat the changes affecting the city as simply natural or positive developments of a beneficent market system. The next three sections look at the impact of the New Urbanism on the three main urban cores of the Bay Area: San Francisco, Silicon Valley, and Oakland. Each story starts with the depleted state of the cities at the end of the postwar era and early stages of revival in the late twentieth century. It then highlights the rapid redevelopment since the turn of the twenty-first century, bringing higher buildings, greater density, more money, and new people. All of these have meant a certain revitalization of the centers, which is not to be taken lightly; but they have also brought profound upheaval, distress, and displacement to huge numbers of ordinary folks who feel, justifiably, that their city has been stolen from them by the rich, the landlords, the techies, and the rest of the elites.[3]

Before any of this, however, the reader will need a quick introduction to the curious geography of the Bay Area, which gives it three heads instead of one, and therefore three main core cities feeling the impact of the New Urbanism.

★ ★ ★

The story of the New Urbanism in the Bay Area has to be a three-part tale because this is historically a tripartite metropolis. American cities are usually treated in terms of the simple metaphor of city and suburbs, and that works for nineteenth-century San Francisco. But the geography of the bay intervened, as did industrial decentralization and the rise of new, powerful business classes in outlying edge cities. In the first half of the twentieth century, Oakland and the East Bay became the fastest-growing part of the Bay Area, with its own identity. Meanwhile, San Jose had grown into a respectable town

---

3   The elephant in the room throughout this chapter will be housing prices, but a full discussion of that comes in chapter 6.

amid the orchards of the South Bay even before the postwar era of electronics hit, turning it into a third major pole of urban development in the bay region.

The result is that the Bay Area is the only metropolis in the United States with *three* central cities: San Francisco, Oakland, and San Jose. It is the mythical Cerberus of cities. None of the three dominates, even though San Francisco has historical primacy and still rules in the popular imagination. With 800,000 people San Francisco can claim less than 10 percent of the metropolitan population of 8.5 million, San Jose's 1 million amounts to about 12 percent, and Oakland is much smaller at 400,000. By contrast, New York City is unchallenged within its region, with around a third of the 24 million in Greater New York, and Los Angeles holds roughly a fifth of its urban region of 18 million souls.

The Cerberus City is a product of growth by urban agglomeration. All metropolitan areas grow through the multiplication of employment clusters, even where there is a single old core; but the process was especially fragmented in the Bay Area. San Francisco grew up around the greatest port and business complex on the West Coast, Oakland congealed around raft of heavy industries, and San Jose was the commercial and canning center of a great agricultural county. Much-larger submetropolitan areas grew up around all three, with San Francisco's suburbs extending into Marin and San Mateo Counties, the Oakland industrial belt spreading up and down the East Bay flatlands and it suburbs climbing the hills, and Silicon Valley's many factory towns sprawling across the plains of the South Bay (indeed, San Jose is not truly the center of the Valley, as will be seen). The pattern of concentration of employment today around the bay can be seen in the map (fig. 5.1); also visible is the influence transportation corridors.[4]

In local parlance, the Bay Area divides into three parts, roughly equal in population, called the West Bay (2M), East Bay (2.5M), and South Bay (2M). Yet this tripartite model of the Bay Area is too simple. The outer East Bay has a major office complex stretching along the 680 corridor from Concord to Pleasanton, home to major headquarters such as Chevron and PG&E. The North Bay (Sonoma, Napa, and Solano Counties) is an employment district dominated by the wine industry—every bit as complex a business ecology as that of electronics. Stockton, in the far edges of the bay region, has its cluster of farm-related industry and logistics.[5]

---

4   On multinodal metropolitan cities, see Muller 2001. The first geographer to speak of a "city of realms" was Vance 1964, writing on the Bay Area. On industry and metropolitan growth, see Lewis 2004. On the industrial geography of the Bay Area, see Walker 1997, 2004.

5   On 680 see Nelson 1988, Garreau 1991. On the North Bay, see Conaway 1990, Guthey 2004, Rhee & Agland 2005.

The shaping of the Bay Area by its economic geography has been firmly reinforced by separate municipal and county borders, distinct local elites, and local governments working to defend local interests. Most of all, they fiercely resisted all efforts to consolidate boundaries in the manner of New York City, in both the early and mid twentieth century. The intense fragmentation of the bay region helps explain why it is so commonly misunderstood to be two, three, or more metropolitan areas rather than a single urban region.[6]

With this introduction to the divided geography of the Bay Area, we can return to the impact of the New Urbanism on the core cities of the region.

Wellsprings of the New Urbanism

The New Urbanism of fin-de-siècle America came on the heels of a widespread emptying out of inner cities during the postwar suburban exodus. Prosperity, rising wages, guaranteed mortgages, and highway building all played a part in the bulge in outward expansion after World War II. But the critical force is the one most discussions of postwar suburbanization miss: a dramatic shift in the geography of industry and transportation. Old central factory and warehouse districts decayed and new suburban factories, offices, and employment clusters opened up, drawing with them the residential developments housing workers and professionals. This was eminently clear in the case of the Bay Area, with the rise of electronics in the South Bay, decline of food processing districts of the East Bay, and collapse of the once-great port and warehouse complex of San Francisco, among other things.[7]

As the outer edges bulged—aided by a strong dose of white flight—older neighborhoods filled up with people of color—first African Americans and then the new immigrants from Latin America and Asia—and the term "inner city" became a cipher for crime, rebellion, and racial fears. In popular and scholarly narratives from the Right, the plight of the central cities was explained chiefly in cultural and political terms: fatherless families, drug gangs, superpredators, and, of course, the failings of federal policy under the Great Society. Much of the discourse was reprehensibly racist and diverted attention from the material foundations for urban failure: chronic lack of jobs and collapsing public treasuries due to the flight of capital beyond the old civic boundaries.[8]

---

6   On the history of Bay Area municipal fragmentation, see Scott 1959. For more on defining the metropolis, see chapter 7.

7   On the old industrial geography of the Bay Area, see Walker 2004b. On industrial suburbanization in general, see Lewis 2004, 2016. For versions of American suburbanization without industry, see Walker 1981, Jackson 1984, Beauregard 2006.

8   Key conservative texts were Moynihan 1965 and Banfield 1970. For Left versions, see Walker 1981, Harvey 1973, Harrison 1974, Beauregard 2006.

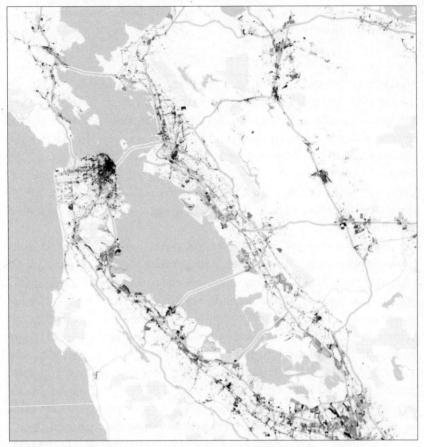

Figure 5.1: Map of Central Bay Area Employment Concentrations, 2014
Courtesy of Robert Manduca. http://www.robertmanduca.com.

With the deindustrialization of the early 1980s, central cities hit bottom, and a host of smaller cities were devastated, though the timing and the story vary from place to place (see chapter 2). By that time, studies shifted from the failings of inner cities to the rise of the Sunbelt, and from there expanded to take in the impact of globalization; serious students of economic geography realized that the problems of older cities and the Rust Belt of the northeast were caused by the shifting sands of capitalist change, global competition, and the defects of American industry. Conservative opinion, by contrast, continued to find scapegoats outside the marketplace, blaming high taxes and excessive regulation for making U.S. firms uncompetitive. Thus, instead of reinvestment in people and places damaged by economic decline, the country—led by California—got a stiff dose of neoliberal medicine: more prisons and policing, less money for schools and welfare, and mystical faith in free trade and fast finance as restoratives for economic prosperity.[9]

*   *   *

Nevertheless, many older American city centers have come back to life over the last thirty years, led by the largest metropolitan areas. What has caused this spatial transformation of U.S. cities? Four explanations stand out: growth in general (a rising rent curve), gentrification (rediscovery of urbanity), the rent gap (investor profiteering), and economic revival (tech clustering). All are partial, but put together they capture the epochal urban transformation underway, for which the ultimate driver is the unfolding of a new era of capital accumulation—which generates the growth, wealth, land investment, and clustering.

In the first case, urban land economists would say that as a metropolis grows, it necessarily drives up the "rent gradient" from the center to the edge of the city. That is, as more businesses and people move into the metropolitan area, demand for land rises and, since land is in fixed supply, its value (price) goes up (which economists call "rent" because land is not a produced commodity). Then, in turn, rising rents stimulate developers to build higher, builders to fill in vacant lots, and everyone to pack in more tightly to save space—all of which bring higher densities. Since the central city is in greatest demand (for access and prestige), it is the peak of the rent gradient, which tails off in all directions toward the suburban fringe. If the urban region has several centers or nodes, the same kind of gradient will show up around each one.[10]

While buying land near the center and building upward costs more, it allows investors to reap greater rents by packing in more tenants on valuable sites. This is why from the dawn of the twentieth century, skyscrapers have sprouted in city centers, along with high-rise apartment buildings. With every era of growth, building heights have gone up and the urban fabric has grown denser. The postwar era seems like the great exception to this rule, as metropolitan areas flattened out in the suburban boom of the 1950s; but even as the suburbia exploded outward, prosperous central cities such as New York, San Francisco, and Chicago saw a raft of new skyscrapers go up in the late 1950s and 1960s. In fact, densities in the central Bay Area held up better than both Los Angeles and San Diego at this time (fig. 5.2).[11]

---

9   On deindustrialization, see High & Lewis 2006, Vicino 2008. On finance and cities, Sbragia 1996, Weber 2015. On neoliberal California, see chapters 4 and 10.

10   On urban rent theory, see Alonso 1964, Harvey 1973.

11   On skyscrapers, see Gaines 2005, Flowers 2009, Fenske 2008. On the postwar decline of American Downtowns, see Fogelson 2001.

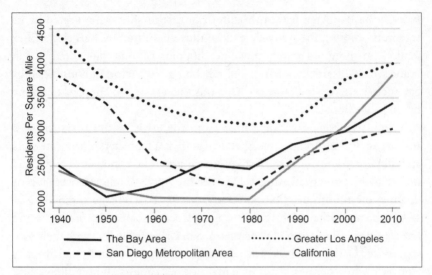

Figure 5.2: Bay Area Urban Density, 1940–2010

Source: Bay Area Council Economic Institute 2014 (9-county Bay Area).

After a pause in the crisis of the 1970s (more marked in New York than elsewhere), a new era of high rises caught hold, with phalanxes of skyscrapers shooting up in city centers of thriving regions such as the Bay Area and Southern California. There was, furthermore, a general increase in the density of buildings and population with each new wave of growth, which was particularly striking in California's notoriously sprawling cities. Shockingly, Los Angeles became the densest metropolitan area in the United States, ahead of New York, and the Bay Area was third by the end of the century.[12]

★ ★ ★

But this bare-bones explanation for rising density does not explain the kind of reversal of the suburban tide by 1980; more is required than a generic increase in the size of the metropolis and transportation advantages of centrality. Notably, there has been a rush to recolonize the urban centers by young and prosperous people, mostly white. Why has this occurred? The most popular explanation is cultural: the rediscovery of urbanity by postsuburban generations. No doubt, a major change in outlook occurred among the upper middle class, as more young Americans traveled abroad and discovered the pleasures of European and Asian cities during the "American Century."

---

12 Note that LA has long been denser than popularly thought and denser than the Bay Area. This is true regardless of the specific measure or boundary used. On the intense development of LA, see Soja 2014.

Indeed, the Bay Area was in the forefront of this shift, as indicated by its role in promoting the nouvelle cuisine movement (led by Berkeley's Chez Panisse), turning old warehouses into shopping centers (pioneered by San Francisco's Ghirardelli Square), and rehabbing old Victorian houses (led by gay men in the Castro District). This was the age of the Yuppies, or young urban professionals.[13]

Similarly, New York recovered from the crisis of the 1970s to see a massive revival of urbane living, led by fast-flying financiers, corporate suits, and the people who make the fashion and entertainment industries move, and quickly went from marketing itself as the Big Apple to massive overhauls of down-in-the-mouth neighborhoods such as the East Village and SOHO to selling the new urbane lifestyles through TV series such as *Sex in the City* and *Friends*. Other cities from Philadelphia to San Diego fell in line with their own repurposed Gaslight and Old Towne districts serving up urbanity and diversity along with microbrews, a raft of bare-brick restaurants and boutiques, and acres of new lofts and condos.[14]

A striking reimagining of urban life was taking place in a nation that had always been suspicious of—if titillated by—big cities. Young, white people were hitting the streets again, getting out of the straightjacket of the suburban castles their parents had secured in the postwar era. This was undoubtedly a positive development in many ways—a kind of transformation of the counterculture of the Sixties into urbane culture of the 1980s and 1990s. At first, the vanguard of the new urbanizers was full of those seeking alternative spaces and lives, such as the gay fixer-uppers in Cole Valley, the activists blending into the Mission District, and artists occupying warehouse lofts; and many who followed were liberally minded Whites with a genuine taste for working-class and immigrant diversity.[15]

But money, class, and race ended up trumping all that. Those with greater means have the power to choose where to live, while those without means must adapt or move out. As the wave of urbanizers grew, their incomes rose, and the chasm of class inequality expanded, they overtook entire neighborhoods and turned them into places repurposed from gritty popular districts to showcases for upper-class consumption. With this, the outcry grew over "gentrification," or wholesale seizure of urban spaces by the well-to-do (the gentry, in English terms) at the expense of the working class and people of

13 See, e.g., Zukin 1982, Hannigan 1998, Florida 2002.
14 On the reworking of New York, see Greenberg 2008, Brash 2011.
15 A similar metamorphosis occurred in Europe from the political revolutions of the mid-nineteenth century to the urbanity of fin-de-siècle Paris or Vienna. Schorske 1979, Harvey 2003.

color. The shining new vision had turned into a version of urbanity without working people or serious racial diversity.[16]

* * *

Nevertheless, culture and imagined geographies alone cannot explain the massive shift back toward the central parts of U.S. metropolitan regions— even if powered by growing income inequality. More is required. So a third explanation arose based on the logic of the property developers and their investors: the theory of the "rent gap." The argument is that there are huge profits to be made by buying undervalued inner-city properties and reselling (or renting) them to gentrifiers at elevated prices. How is this possible? On the one hand, old working-class districts and manufacturing zones declined in the postwar era, leaving deteriorated buildings, shuttered businesses, vacant properties, and elderly, poor inhabitants—areas ripe for renewal. On the other, the new demand for housing by upscale renters and buyers creates potential high prices if the neighborhoods can be reenvisioned as desirable, houses renovated, and commerce revived. This can occur piecemeal by individuals, until it reaches a threshold, or much faster if big investors and developers start buying up many properties to scale up the process of landscape transformation.[17]

Rent gap theory gets the active role of property investors right. The naive idea of conventional economists that the supply of commodities, including housing, is a passive response to consumer demand has to be rejected. Just as General Motors could sell millions on tailfins and R. J. Reynolds could do the same for death-dealing cigarettes, suppliers have the power to influence the market and shape demand. This point of who's in charge of urban growth will be revisited in chapter 7 in more depth. But while rent gap theory works on a case-by-case basis of neighborhood transition, it cannot account for the wholesale reworking of cities taking place today.

All three of the previous explanations are insufficient to explain the dramatic reurbanization of the major cities, such as New York, Miami, and Toronto. We therefore need a fourth impulse. The economies of central cities have been growing again on a foundation of new business and employment that draws in people and puts money in their pockets. In the late twentieth century, this meant, above all, having a thriving economic base of management, business services, and finance, or specializing in favored industries such

16 On spatial sorting, see Harvey 1973. On gentrification, see Lees et al. 2008. On widening class segregation, see Taylor & Fry 2012. See also chapter 7.

17 On the rent gap and redevelopment, see Smith 1996, Mele 2000. While one can welcome new thinking about the vertical geography of cities, Harris (2015) almost completely omits the most important element of all: land rent and property development.

as weaponry, oil, and tourism. New York and Chicago boosted their historical roles as corporate and financial centers, Houston and Dallas had oil, and Las Vegas and Miami had tourism. On top of this, the twenty-first century has ushered in a new era of capitalism driven by information technology; IT is overwhelmingly concentrated in the biggest metropolitan areas and is leaving its footprints all over those cities.[18]

The radical remaking of the Bay Area's urban centers has been powered, above all, by the New Economy of information technology. The tech industry has brought new companies and more jobs into the centers, and that, in turn, has drawn new people and given them the wherewithal to pay top dollar for central properties near to their workplaces. This is the primary basis of mass gentrification. San Francisco's flotilla of post-Millennium start-ups is at the heart of the city's new skyline. Tech companies have fueled San Jose's Downtown renewal and the burnishing of the corporate landscape of Silicon Valley. Oakland has been rediscovered by waves of techies, workers, and students fleeing high rents in San Francisco and the West Bay.

The New Urbanism is striking across the world's greatest cities as global capitalism works its magic, and the Bay Area, as the center of the tech industry and its riches, has felt the force of that transformation as much as, or more than, anywhere. It involves all four of the preceding forces: land markets, rent gaps, shifts in class and race composition, and restructuring of the economic base. How those work out in the three major heartlands of the bay region is the subject of the rest of this chapter. And that will prepare the way for the discussion of the housing crisis in chapter 6.

San Francisco: Revival and Metamorphosis

San Francisco's landscape has been dramatically reworked over the last generation, and its transformation has evoked the most heated commentary west of Manhattan. Observers from *Newsweek* to Reddit have decried the ruin of the much-beloved city by the bay.[19] Yet, lest we wax too nostalgic about the loss of "old" San Francisco, it is good to recall how many times the city has gone through dramatic transformations of the past: the Gold Rush city erased by the Victorian City of the silver boom, the great earthquake and fire of 1906 that ushered in the Progressive Era city, and the filling out of the Outside Lands after the First World War.

---

18 On IT jobs in big cities, see Moretti 2012 and chapter 1. On the return of corporate offices, see O'Connell 2017.

19 See, e.g., http://www.newsweek.com/san-francisco-tech-industry-gentrification-documentary-378628; https://www.reddit.com/r/sanfrancisco/comments/3s8t5m/the_hate_on_techies_and_gentrification/.

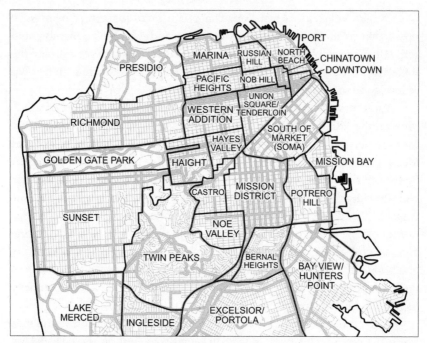

Figure 5.3: Map of San Francisco Neighborhoods

Just over the last half century, the changes have been startling. The postwar building boom of 1958 to 1975 covered Downtown with dozens of skyscrapers that announced an age of corporate headquarters and giant banks as the foundation of the city's economy: Bank of America, Transamerica, Crocker Bank, McKesson, Zellerbach, and many more. New hotel towers also sprouted up with the expanding tourism and convention sector. As older buildings fell to the wrecking ball, a movement against "Manhattanization" broke out, combining preservationists, neighborhood activists, and some of the old elite, who succeeded in halting uncontrolled demolition of historic buildings and drawing a line around Downtown to keep high rises from erasing the Tenderloin, Union Square, Chinatown, and the old Barbary Coast.

That first wave was accompanied by the freeway-building mania supported by the Highway Act of 1956, which slashed through southeast San Francisco and threatened to cut through Golden Gate Park and erect a double-deck wall along the northern waterfront. The city united in the first freeway revolt in the country to stop the latter two projects. Meanwhile, a massive state-sponsored urban renewal program erased hundreds of square blocks of the old city around Downtown in the old wholesale produce market (Embarcadero Center), Western Addition/Fillmore, Mission District, and South of Market/Skid Row (Yerba Buena Center). The cool gray city of love was a bright white city of racial cleansing, which was confronted by massive opposition from African Americans, Latinos, and Asians. The Fillmore and Yerba Buena were ultimately lost after fierce battles between activists and the Redevelopment Agency and its backers, but in the Mission and Chinatown redevelopment was brought to a standstill.[20]

A second wave of skyscrapers went up from 1975 to 1990, many of which took on the fashionable new clothes of Postmodernism: 101 California, 101 Montgomery, 345 California Center ("the roach clip"), and the Nikko and Marriott Hotels ("the jukebox"). Downtown began to push south of Market Street, after popular protest had put a stop to expansion north and west, as with Providian Financial, 50 Fremont, and 123 Mission. By this time, the ever-expanding rolls of office workers and managers had become the hip genera-tion of young urban professionals, or Yuppies, with their nouvelle cuisine and taste for boutique shopping. San Francisco was putting on urbane airs and leading the way in style for the country, with homegrown stores such as Victoria's Secret, Williams-Sonoma, Banana Republic, the Nature Company, Esprit, and Sharper Image.

When the postwar banks and corporations ran into trouble in the mid-1980s, the city was hit hard and urban revival teetered on the edge. Many familiar corporate names such as Crocker and Zellerbach disappeared into the maw of corporate mergers and buyouts, as the economy shifted into the era of high finance and hot money. Nevertheless, the Downtown cluster would weather the storm, with continued growth in securities trading, business ser-vices and conventions and tourism. When the Loma Prieta earthquake hit in 1989, causing fires in the Marina District and raising the ghosts of 1906, it did the city a backhanded favor. The temblor weakened the ugly freeways that had walled off the Embarcadero, Civic Center, and South of Market, and after a brief struggle Mayor Art Agnos succeeded in bringing the beasts down, cre-ating new open spaces. The city center and waterfront could breathe again.[21]

★   ★   ★

Then a hot wind blew in from Silicon Valley as the first internet age fired up. The blazing dot-com economy of the 1990s was centered in the South of Market district (SOMA) and achieved at a stroke what developers had been trying to pull off for a century: expanding Downtown across Market Street into territory long held by industry, warehousing, and the working class along

---

20   On the postwar boom and redevelopment, see Godfrey 1997, Walker 1998, Hartman 1984, 2002, Carlsson 2011, Howell 2015. On urban renewal's hidden racial agenda, see Weiss 1980, Freund 2007.

21   On the 1980s, see Walker et al. 1990, Walker 1998. On freeway removal, see Rubin 2011.

BARNESON
CECELY A

Wed Mar 20 2019

Pictures of a gone city : tech and the
dark side of prosperity in the San

81197016998201

p26595515

the southern waterfront. As the dot-com boom heated up, a raft of new sky-scrapers began to fill the area from Third Street east to the bay, some like 101 Second Street to provide office space for finance and management services and others such as the Paramount for high-income residences. Scores of ware-houses and factories were converted into tech offices, sweeping from Rincon Hill (where the Bay Bridge is anchored) all the way out to the Mission District.

Along with the offices came a massive build-out of residential lofts, or live/work units. Lofts began as an alternative space for artists and bohemians, but then young techies saw them as nifty digs close to work. In this they were aided by developers who saw lofts as a way to build quickly and profitably, with fewer regulations. The old landscape of industry and working-class housing South of Market began to be swept aside, along with artist spaces, nonprofit offices, and affordable housing for the poor. The dot-com boom unleashed a new urban bulldozer by means of financial speculation rather than the state.[22]

SOMA's fate was sealed by the gigantic Mission Bay project on eighty acres of fill that had long been the site of Southern Pacific's rail yards—by far the biggest new land development in the city in fifty years. Engineered by the city and its Redevelopment Agency, the project was anchored by a UC San Francisco Medical School research campus, which has subsequently attracted a host of health and biotechnology firms. Marching in bland unison around the old rail yards came block after block of boxy midrise apartment and con-dominium buildings put up by the Redevelopment Agency and eager private builders. The area's saving grace is the elegant baseball park built by the San Francisco Giants—the first professional sports facility in memory not to be built with a giveaway of public funds.

In the recovery from the dot-com crash, housing replaced commercial building as the leading edge of development—a general phenomenon in the mortgage bubble years, 2003–7. New apartment, condo, and hotel skyscrap-ers went up around SOMA, such as 555 Mission Street, the St. Regis Hotel and Residences, the fifty-eight-story Millennium Tower, and sixty-story One Rincon Hill. High-rise condominiums began filling the old industrial corridor along the bay, helped by a new light rail line—sold to the public as providing access to Downtown for the poor of Bayview–Hunters Point, but having exactly the opposite effect of opening the southeast quadrant to real estate investment. Slick new housing developments pushed into the Mission, filled gaps in the Western Addition, and popped up in every outlying district of the city. The new housing overwhelmingly targeted the well-to-do, even the

---

22 On the boom of the 1990s, see Cohen 1998, Solnit 2001, Walker 2006, Cohen & Marti 2009, Beitel 2011.

ultrarich, as developers saw their chance to cash in on the taste of the upper classes for the New Urbanism.

★ ★ ★

The tech boom of the 2010s has once again brought about a remarkable transformation of the city's landscape and life. As the vanguard of the tech industry shifted north from Silicon Valley to San Francisco—which passed the Valley in the number of start-ups in the 2000s—it brought a marked resurgence of growth in the old core city of the Bay Area. New companies began multiplying like water hyacinths in a warm pond, breeding the likes of Twitter, Quantcast, Indiegogo, and Yelp, and then the galloping unicorns such as Uber and Airbnb (see chapter 1). Some Silicon Valley companies, like Pinterest, moved to San Francisco and others, such as Google, set up branch offices there, followed by Apple and Facebook. As a result, the city experienced some of the fastest growth of any place in the country, exceeding all but four states in jobs added coming out of the Great Recession and expanding its share of the region's employment after a long period of decline (fig. 5.4).[23]

Along the way, the makeup of San Francisco's economy changed. Although finance and management are still larger than IT, they have given ground as most of the old-line companies from the twentieth century disappeared or decentralized their headquarters, as in the case of Chevron and PG&E. In finance, the towering Bank of America was swallowed by NationsBank and moved to Charlotte, North Carolina. Further losses hit the financial sector in the washout of 2007–8, in which the Bay Area took a direct hit, losing almost a quarter of the two hundred thousand jobs in that sector. As the financial heart of the region, San Francisco, suffered disproportionately.[24]

After the hiatus of the financial meltdown, the tech expansion of the 2010s set in motion a building boom that dwarfed the dot-com era of the 1990s. While the latter added about 7.5 million square feet of new office space, the latest wave is depositing a layer of square footage twice that thick. A new generation of skyscrapers shot up in SOMA, home to tech companies such as LinkedIn, Dropbox, Fitbit, and Splunk. A cluster of shafts around the intersection of Mission and First Streets now marks the peak of the skyline, topped by the city's first thousand-foot tower, the headquarters of Salesforce.com—with its lit-up nose cone. Nearby are such monsters as nine-hundred-foot-high 50 First Street, and the tallest of all is planned for the site of the

---

23 Mandel 2014, Warburg 2016.
24 Financial jobs data from BAC Economic Institute 2014. For more on the passing of the old corporate order, see Walker 1998.

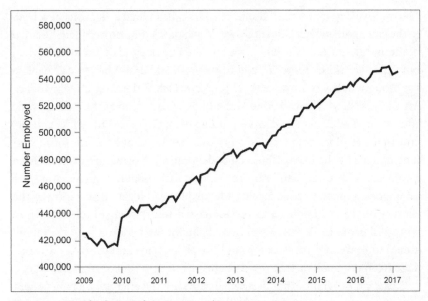

Figure 5.4: Rapid Job Growth in San Francisco, 2009–2013

Source: Warburg 2016 based on Ted Egan, San Francisco city economist.

old Transit Terminal. Just to the south, One Rincon Hill has added a second, fifty-story condominium.[25]

Downtown has been effectively recentered south of Market Street, leaving the former signature buildings north of Market—Bank of America and the Transamerica Pyramid—looking diminutive. Tech companies came to occupy about one-third of Downtown office space by 2015, twice what they filled in 2001 or 2010. Meanwhile, the Mid-Market was refashioned as a tech cluster, thanks to tax breaks granted by the city to companies such as Twitter, Zynga, Square, and Dolby—much to the benefit of the Shorenstein Company and other big landlords who had snapped up down-on-their-heels Mid-Market buildings. Property investors and developers thrived off the new generation of skyscraper offices and high-rise residences in SOMA, Mission Bay, and the old industrial southeast, especially those who had bought derelict sites in the past. While there was money to be made on refurbishing offices or Union Square commercial buildings north of Market into hotels and condos, the big scores were to be had from the huge rent gaps at the expanding frontier south of Market.[26]

★ ★ ★

25   Dineen 2016b, King 2017. For more on office construction, see chapter 6.
26   On tech leases, see Brown 2016. On Mid-Market, see Schuller 2017. For more on big investors Downtown, see chapter 6.

The massive development of South of Market has added a vigorous new layer to the city's core, which is small by world standards. The postmodern and neo-modern styles of the new high rises are often bolder and better looking than boxy postwar skyscrapers. To add to the flash and dash, the New Urbanism has brought a slew of new museum projects, such as the Museum of Modern Art and Jewish Museum around Yerba Buena Gardens in SOMA, the new de Young and California Academy of Sciences in Golden Gate Park, and the enormous Exploratorium at Pier 15. The new buildings feature some stunning designs by the likes of Herzog & de Meuron, Norman Foster, and Rem Koolhaas. As a result, San Francisco's dowdy reputation in architecture has undergone a much-needed facelift. Meanwhile, an elegant restoration of the century-old Ferry Building anchored a massive refurbishing of the waterfront from Fisherman's Wharf to the new ballpark (and soon a new basketball arena) to serve as a pleasure-ground for pedestrians and tourists—a classic page from the book of the New Urbanism.[27]

Many city neighborhoods now vibrate with the energy of a new generation of urbanites and commercial strips resonating to the abundant disposable income of the young. Retail zones are bustling, cafes filled with techies hard at work on their laptops are seemingly on every corner, and restaurants of every variety have proliferated, spilling onto sidewalks and into alleys. Houses and apartment buildings have been spruced up by new owners with more money. City planners have added pocket parks and demanded public spaces, inside and out, from office developers. A large network of bicycle lanes crisscrosses the city, along with racks of quick-rent cycles and Zipcars.

The Marina, Hayes Valley, Castro, and Upper Market are wall-to-wall cool. Mid-Market is buzzing. Whole new residential neighborhoods are blossoming around Mission Bay and Rincon Hill. The southeast is alive with new residents and businesses, plus large mixed-use developments approved for Mission Rock, Pier 70 (the old ship repair yards) and India Basin (on Islais Creek). This is the upside of gentrification and the New Urbanism, much acclaimed by those who see it as an upgrade from the scruffy landscapes of the Mission District, the Haight, the Western Addition, and the Tenderloin.

But not everyone is cheering. With growing density, commuting, and commerce, traffic is a hot mess. Many longtime residents resent the pompous skyline South of Market and deride the "silicon implants" who now dominate so much of the urban scene. The triumphant march of

27 On architecture, see Sardar 2000, King 2004, 2016a. On the waterfront, see Rubin 2011. Some of the shine came off the new SOMA high rises when it was discovered that the luxurious Millennium Tower was sinking in the muck of bay fill and a foot off kilter because its foundation is not anchored to bedrock.

gentrification has done irreversible damage to San Francisco's subcultures of artists, activists, and bohemians. It has pushed out thousands of African Americans, immigrant families, and working people in general, along with the humble shops that served their needs for low-cost food, goods, and entertainment.

The cultural and social cleansing of SOMA has been the most thorough. The southeast is now majority upper-income, except for the last black families hanging on in Bayview–Hunters Point. The Latino Mission District has been squeezed hard on all fronts, with Valencia Street now hipster way and Dolores Park overrun by the dogs of single professionals. The Tenderloin, last redoubt of the down-and-out in the city center, is being chipped away on all sides by wine bars and trendy restaurants. Mid-Market, once a working-class entertainment zone, has turned into Twitterland. And the city has plans in the works for Market–Van Ness by the Civic Center and Central SOMA west of the Moscone Convention Center.[28]

Progressive commentators have been decrying the hollowing out of city for some time now, and with good reason, and the popular press has taken up the causes in the latest boom period, as stories of teachers, firefighters, and other midwage workers—and even many young tech workers—pushed out of the city. Of course, urban restructuring is never complete, and roots of popular life and culture, like a burned-over forest, will prove to have a surprising capacity for recuperation once the latest economic and social firestorm passes. Nevertheless, the class and racial reconstitution of San Francisco is remarkable and for some a virtual whitewash of their beloved city.[29]

Silicon Valley: Geography of Nowhere to Corporate Showcase

Although Silicon Valley is one of the wonders of the industrial world, its landscape has long been derided as a faceless realm. As in the Los Angeles of yore, there is a sense of disorientation among the endless drifts of tract housing, windswept deserts of asphalt, replicant shopping centers, and ribbons of freeways and expressways running hither and yon. As one recent commentator has it, "Driving around Silicon Valley still feels like you've lain your laptop on the ground and leapt into it." One observer compared this dystopic geography to the Winchester Mystery House, a 160-room mansion west of San Jose built by the guilt-ridden heiress of the Winchester arms fortune who feared she would die if she did not keep expanding her home. Silicon Valley, in this view, is the product of a collective madness in which tech innovation and urban

---

28   Solnit 2001, 2013, Beitel 2011, Brahinsky 2011, Stehlin 2016, Schwaller 2017.
29   See, e.g., Simmons 2017, McDermid 2017.

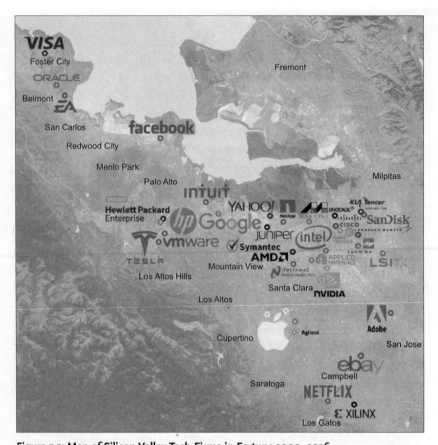

Figure 5.5: Map of Silicon Valley Tech Firms in Fortune 1000, 2016

Source: https://www.reddit.com/r/MapPorn/comments/4kwt6k/oc_silicon_valleys_largest_high_tech_companies/.

growth must continue without end, lest the ghosts of bankruptcy and ruin come a-calling.[30]

There is truth to the Winchester metaphor, given the mad pursuit of innovation and growth by tech entrepreneurs and property developers and the competitive frenzy and pursuit of accumulation that keeps them running. But there is more shape to the urban landscape than meets the eye, and it has become more clearly inscribed in the twenty-first century. The development

---

30   Kunstler 1993, quote from Smith 2016, p. 6. Winchester metaphor from Winner 1992, p. 33. Newly widowed Sarah Winchester moved to San Jose in 1884 and bought a farmhouse, to which she added new wings for forty years until her death in 1922. The house was restored and named a National Historical Landmark in the 1970s. Typical of the Valley, it is still in private hands.

of the Silicon City has been a kind of "planned sprawl" overseen by its leading businessmen, land developers, and university leaders.[31]

One of the things that made the Valley appear shapeless was the lack of a single central node, such as San Francisco's Downtown, with San Jose and Stanford—not to mention several intervening cities—vying for supremacy and stretching the core like taffy. Yet there is a core: a well-defined industrial triangle that anchors the Valley, running from Stanford south to San Jose, west to Cupertino, and back up to Stanford, taking in Palo Alto, Mountain View, Sunnyvale, and Santa Clara (fig. 5.5).

Within that triangle can be found the biggest tech companies, such as Google, HP, Intel, Apple, and Facebook, and the major industrial parks and corridors that hold most of the hundreds of other firms. The entirety of Silicon Valley overtopped this central triangle long ago, spilling west toward Santa Cruz, east into Fremont and Milpitas, and thence over to Pleasanton, and especially north up the Peninsula all the way to San Francisco. Yet the core industrial triangle still holds pride of place in the Valley after a half dozen waves of innovation, start-ups, and capital accumulation.

The story of Silicon Valley's urbanization over the last half century begins with the bipolar story of Stanford's ambitions as a university and San Jose's business elite overseeing the explosive growth of housing development; it builds up through the work of anonymous developers and real estate investors who constructed the industrial and residential landscapes; and it ends with the recent era of showcase corporate compounds and prestige buildings given to Stanford by wealthy donors. These four elements make up the rest of this section, capped by a reflection on effects of the New Urbanism around the Valley.

★　★　★

In the postwar era, the electronics industry exploded across a well-established agrarian landscape, and the Santa Clara Valley was altered beyond recognition. The scale was bigger than anything the Bay Area had seen before, twice the size of the East Bay in its period of explosive growth, five times as large as San Francisco. Residential areas spread farther with the car than the old trolleys, developers built tracts of unprecedented size, and highways such as Steven's Creek Boulevard, Central Expressway, and the Bayshore Freeway became the main streets of the new city. In the northwest corner of the Valley lay Stanford, which played a key role in the advance of electronics.

---

31 The idea of planned sprawl comes from Gottdeiner 1977. See also Hise 1997 on Los Angeles.

Popular versions of the Silicon Valley story give Stanford—and its dean of engineering, Fred Terman—far too much credit for creating the electronics mecca. Stanford University played a substantial role but less as initiator than as one gear in the transmission that drove the IT bus. The Stanford Industrial Park, regularly heralded as pioneer of the industrial landscape, was a rather ordinary piece of suburban land development, and the idea came not from Terman but the Varian brothers and their partner, Professor Ed Gintzon, who approached Stanford in 1949. Stanford's finances were shaky, and university leaders were eager to put the campus on a better financial footing by leasing some of its nine thousand acres of land. At the time Stanford's ranked low in the hierarchy of American universities; Berkeley was the prestige campus of the Bay Area and Stanford a kind of USC of the north, both better known for their football teams than their faculties.[32]

Presidents Donald Tresidder and J. Wallace Sterling wanted to upgrade the faculty and reorient the school to the needs of California industry, including oil and aeronautics as much as electronics. They succeeded beyond anyone's wildest dreams by means of four strategies.[33]

First, Stanford went to the trough of federal research grants, following the example of Berkeley's E.O. Lawrence in the 1930s and responding to Vannevar Bush's initiatives in federal support of basic research following World War II. Two-fifths of the university's budget would come from the feds at the height of the Cold War. Second, the university became the largest land developer in the Santa Clara Valley: a campus-like industrial park to house Hewlett-Packard, Varian, Kodak, and others; a shopping center that set the standard for the South Bay; offices on Sand Hill Road that became the home of venture capital; offices along El Camino that became the legal nerve center of electronics; and a medical center and biology complex that was the birthplace of gene splicing.[34]

Third, electronics moguls Bill Hewlett, David Packard, and Ed Gintzon were added to the Board of Trustees in the 1950s and began to give generously

---

32 Lowen 1997 is the best source on Stanford in this period. See also Varian 1983, Mozingo 2017. As a side note, Terman led the charge to eliminate the Department of Geography at Stanford, to his eternal shame.

33 Regime change at the university came after the grip of Herbert Hoover was broken during the war, and Tresidder's role is overlooked because of his early death. The author's father, Robert Walker, was one of Sterling's postwar faculty recruits and allies; he headed the university committee on buildings and grounds that oversaw land development in the 1950s and '60s, including the industrial park.

34 On Lawrence, see Brechin 1999. On Bush, see Lowen 1997. Hoover had previously tried to promote Stanford as a research-technical university but failed to make it a top recipient of private grants, and its reputation languished. Almost no universities accepted federal aid at the time.

of their newfound wealth; and Eitel-McCullough and Lockheed helped build up the aviation and electrical engineering departments. Fourth, the development office came up with the most audacious fundraising effort ever undertaken by a university, with a target of $1 billion, which became the model for other universities; Stanford's endowment today is second only to Harvard.[35]

In other words, government grants, land rents, electronic fortunes, and rich alumni built up Stanford more than it built Silicon Valley. While university leaders played a significant role, attributing Silicon Valley to campus visionaries is like saying John Sutter planned the California Gold Rush. Instead, Stanford was guided by mundane considerations of rising property taxes and potential lease revenues, and the campus development program evolved in tandem with electronics, changing directions several times to maximize the opportunities for rents.[36]

★　★　★

Meanwhile, the Santa Clara Valley's population was bursting the bounds of the agrarian towns, and San Jose's city fathers leapt to the forefront in seizing the opportunities presented by the massive residential expansion that accompanied the blossoming of the tech industry. The city had been the traditional commercial center of the Santa Clara Valley, one of the top agricultural regions in California. By 1900 the city was home to banks, merchant houses, and many of the big growers, and it nurtured a major packing, drying, and canning industry complex to process fruit, as well as machinery makers to supply the factories and farms. It was a modern city, willing to experiment with some of the earliest electric lighting and the first radio station in the country. Just like Los Angeles, San Jose was a booster city that first sold itself as a City of Rose Gardens and later as "the Valley of the Heart's Delight."

The postwar "growth coalition" was led by City Manager Dutch Hamann, whose fondest hope was to turn San Jose into "the Los Angeles of the North," but included other key players such as County Executive Howard Campen; Mayor Ron James, later head of the Chamber of Commerce; and

---

35　Another key trustee of the 1940s was investment banker Charles Blythe, who also led San Francisco's postwar redevelopment. On Lockheed, see Schoenberger 1997, Lowen 1997. On Stanford fundraising, see Gordon 2001, Ford 2014.

36　After the war, Stanford called on planner Lewis Mumford, who wanted a compact urban campus that left rural lands open; this was rejected in 1947 as the university saw the possibility of building housing tracts to catch the wave of suburban growth. As late as 1954, Skidmore, Owings, and Merrill wrote a campus land use plan recommending mass residential development. Yet that, too, was rejected for a mix of residential, industrial, and commercial uses. Findlay 1992, Lowen 1997. On the roles of San Jose State and Santa Clara University, see Trounstine & Christensen 1982.

former mayor Albert Ruffo, who hired Hamann, built the San Jose airport, and expanded the sewer system (while killing rent control and public housing). Chief propagandist was Joe Ridder of the *San Jose Mercury-News*, who prevented his staff from writing anything critical of growth and declared of lost orchards, "trees don't buy newspapers." Behind the scenes were the local worthies of the Progress Committee and a smoke-filled room at the St. Claire Hotel where the "Book of the Month Club"—a circle of businessmen, developers, and city officials—met to plan campaigns.[37]

The private side of the growth coalition was the land developers, who literally built the Valley. Many of them came to rank among the richest and most powerful tycoons of the region. Housing developers included Joseph Eichler, who gained fame for his Modernist designs, Stanford grads Wayne Brown and Sam Kaufman, and Robert Huff, who built high-end homes on spec—a previously unheard-of approach. As apartments grew in popularity in the 1960s, Burt Avery, George Marcus, and Gerson Bakar of San Francisco moved to the fore. Farm families such as the Nakashimas of Mountain View and Vidovichs of Sunnyvale also became developers, and San Francisco's huge Newhall Land Company joined the fray.[38]

Industrial developers slapped up utilitarian buildings in undistinguished office parks to house tech offices, research, and fabrication. The biggest were Richard Peery (who got his start developing his family's orchard land) and John Arrillaga (Peery-Arrillaga), John Sobrato and Carl Berg (Sobrato-Berg), and Ned Spieker (Crow-Spieker). Big construction companies partnered with the developers, including South Bay (Jim Mair), Avery Construction (Burt Avery), and Devcon (Gary Filizetti). Koll Corporation came north from LA to open industrial parks with local partner Drew Gibson, while Warren Epstein came south from San Francisco, and Trammell Crow from Dallas, but outside capital never pushed aside the powerhouses of the Valley.[39]

Local real estate agents prospered, too. The leading residential brokers were around Palo Alto: Cornish & Carey, Fox & Carskardon, and Hare, Brewer & Kelley. San Francisco's Coldwell Banker (now CBRE) was also

---

37 On San Jose, see Trounstine & Christensen 1982, Payne 1987. LA of the North quote from Reinhardt 1965, p. 48. George Starbird quoted in Trounstine & Christensen, p. 142, Ridder at p. 131. On Ridder, see also Rivers & Rubin 1971. On growth coalitions, see chapter 7.

38 Some public officials had their fingers in the honey pot, too: Campen and James were major San Jose landowners, and Hamann had a knack for buying properties that became shopping centers and freeway interchanges.

39 Interviews with Scott Carey, founder of C&C Commercial, June 25, 2002, and Luis Belmonte, Seven Hills Properties, June 18, 2002. On the Valley's office parks, see Mozingo 2017. There was less big capital at work in Santa Clara than in San Mateo, where wealthy families owned so many large tracts. Burns 1977, Hynding 1983, Brechin 1999.

involved, Colbert Coldwell having been real estate consultant to Stanford in the 1950s. George Marcus and William Millichap began selling apartments in 1971 and pioneered investment brokerage in this sector. San Jose, for all its frenetic growth, did not generate a dominant real estate company. Bank of America and Crocker Bank were active in financing mortgages, along with Travelers and Prudential Insurance and a host of local savings and loans.[40]

The result of all these labors was a disconnected suburban landscape that made the Santa Clara Valley the poster child of postwar sprawl long before the name "Silicon Valley" had been coined. San Jose ballooned in size, making almost fifteen hundred territorial annexations and becoming the third-largest city in the state at 175 square miles. It grabbed half the population of the county, surpassing half a million people by 1970. Hundreds of thousands of tract houses, hundreds of apartment complexes, and the scores of nondescript industrial parks were scattered across the landscape. The Valley's sprawl was widely denounced by critics of unplanned urbanization.[41]

But the critics were, in one sense, missing the point. This was not just another suburban landscape, but the archetype of the mid-twentieth century American Sunbelt city. Nor was Silicon Valley quite the madhouse portrayed by the model of the Winchester Mystery house. It was, to a large degree, a class project incorporating a broadly shared vision among men of influence that realized enormous profits from building and especially from cashing in on rising land values as farmland metamorphosed into the City of Silicon. The masters of electronics, such as Hewlett and Packard, were, like most American industrialists, content to leave the grubby politics of urban development to a willing host of local actors.

★ ★ ★

Silicon Valley began to mature as an urban landscape in the 1970s, at the time the tech industry was shifting from military contracts to commercial markets. Employment passed half a million jobs, the population hit one million and the Santa Clara Valley was mostly built over. A shift in urban growth regime was in the offing, led by a changing of the guard in the tech industry and San Jose city government.[42]

---

40 Interviews with Scott Carey, June 25, 2002, Mark Ritchie of Ritchie Commercial, June 20, 2002 (San Francisco's Ritchie & Ritchie opened a San Jose office in 1965). Coldwell's role in Findlay 1992. On insurance company investment in postwar cities, see Rubin 2012.
41 Dasmann 1966, Belser 1967, 1970, Fellmeth 1973, Downie 1973.
42 Stanford also went through a major regime shift at the time, with a de-emphasis on land development versus building the endowment and monument building (see below).

The Valley's leading capitalists got organized as over fifty companies came together in 1978 as the Silicon Valley Manufacturers Group, under the leadership of Robert Noyce and David Packard. They joined the move to a more inclusive and modulated managerialism for a new epoch of city building. Packard declared that, "San Jose and the South Bay have one overriding problem—how to manage growth in this area to provide an attractive environment for people to live in and an attractive environment for business and industry." The Manufacturers Group threw its weight behind highway construction, backing the county transportation plan and campaigning for the bond issue and tax increase. It became an advocate of affordable housing construction.[43]

When the slump of 1990–91 hit, the tech capitalists reorganized for a new policy push. Answering a call from James Morgan, chair of Applied Materials, they reorganized in 1992 as Joint Venture: Silicon Valley Network. After a shaky start, the group (renamed Joint Venture Silicon Valley) became the premier policy body in the Valley. The Silicon Valley Manufacturers (now Leadership) Group also revived in the 1990s under the direction of Carl Guardino, turning its attention once again to housing, transportation, and other urban problems. After some resistance, most developers fell in line with the new emphasis on corporate image and civic planning, aiming to glean higher rents from top-drawer development.[44]

San Jose went through a major reorganization of its urban management starting in the late 1960s, including a charter amendment to elect the mayor and the exit of Hamann and James. The new mayor, Norman Mineta, appointed a city manager and planning director who favored controlled growth, and the new regime was cemented by the mayoralty of Janet Gray Hayes, 1974–82, whose slogan was "Let's Make San Jose Better before Bigger." The city introduced the idea of an "urban services boundary," began to refuse services to developments going in too far afield, and put in place one of the first "pay as you grow" taxes (impact fees). This package became a model for cities and counties around the state. The developers tried to make a comeback in San Jose in 1978 but were quickly repudiated. Crucially, the new order had been accepted by the city's key businessmen, led by Tony Ridder of the *Mercury* (Knight-Ridder Newspapers).[45]

---

43   Saxenian 1994. Packard quoted in Trounstine & Christensen 1982, p. 119.
44   Walker 2007, Storper et al. 2015.
45   Interview with Gary Schoennauer, former planning director of San Jose, June 25, 2002. Trounstine & Christensen 1982. *Business Week*, 1970. Hayes was a conservationist linked to People for Open Space, as well as the first woman mayor of an American city over a half million. San Jose instituted tighter planning far ahead of other Sunbelt cities and even before Seattle and Portland.

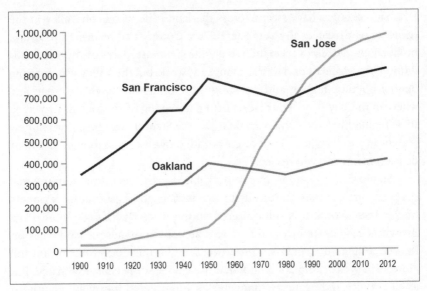

Figure 5.6: Growth of the Bay Area's Three Main Cities, 1950–2010
Source: U.S. Census data.

By the end of the century, Silicon Valley had gone through another leap in urban scale. The number of jobs peaked at well over a million in the late 1990s, San Jose topped 1 million people and the county/metro area hit 1.75 million (fig. 5.6). Consequently, a remarkable inversion occurred in the Bay Area's geography. Not only had San Jose become the largest city in the region by 1980, the Valley counted far more corporate headquarters in the Fortune 500 than San Francisco and Oakland combined. These were not housed in towering skylines such as those of Manhattan or Chicago, but neither were they former central city companies fleeing to the suburbs in search of pastoral scenes, as had been the case for much of the twentieth century. These were homegrown corporations of Silicon Valley's Tech World.

To top it off, the Bay Area was baptized in 2000 as the San Jose–San Francisco–Oakland Consolidated Statistical Area by the U.S. Census. San Jose city leaders celebrated, but no one else took the new designation seriously. Not only was San Francisco the long-standing heart of the region, it was also grabbing a big piece of the tech action. Worse, the painful truth for San Jose was that it still deferred to the power centers in the northwest county, which dominate the core triangle of Silicon Valley to this day.[46]

★ ★ ★

---

46   On corporate dispersal in the postwar era, see Mozingo 2011.

Dramatic changes have swept across the landscape of Silicon Valley in the recovery of the 2000s. By 2015 Santa Clara County had recovered to over a million jobs and almost two million people. The vast spaces of the South Bay diffused the visual impact of the changes at work, but the Valley was growing denser, building higher, and investing more in urban showplaces than any-where in the Bay Area. Four facets of the remaking of the Silicon City need to be highlighted: monument building on the Stanford campus, a bright new Downtown for San Jose, a raft of corporate showcases, and intensification of development everywhere else.

Stanford University is, to a remarkable degree, the prime monumental space of Silicon Valley and the first place visitors go to gawk at the wonders of the Tech World. It is still centered on the 1880s Quadrangle by A. Page Brown, a brilliant concoction of Richardson Romanesque and Mission Revival architecture, and the 1930s tower built for the Hoover Institution still glowers over the campus—a hulk that has gained some charm with age. But as electronics and property magnates gave more and more abundantly to the university, the campus grew larger and more elaborate, boasting a slew of magnificent new buildings named after wealthy patrons. These include the David Packard Electrical Engineering Building, Bill Gates Computer Science Building, William Hewlett Teaching Center, James Clark Center for Biomedical Engineering, John Arrillaga Family Recreation Center, Phil Knight Management Center, David and Joan Traitel Building, and Robert Bass Biology Research Building.

At the same time, San Jose was determined to claim a share of credit for the achievements of the Silicon City and to get out from under the shadow of San Francisco. In the 1980s, the city began boasting that it was "the capital of Silicon Valley." Mayor Tom McEnery, son of the largest landowner in the old urban core, pushed for a complete makeover of Downtown to comport with the city's putative standing. A program to tear down and rebuild the city's derelict center was launched by the Redevelopment Agency, directed by Bostonian planner Frank Taylor. It took twenty years, stretching into the twenty-first century, but the result was a gleaming new city center.

The long decline of San Jose's old commercial heart of the agrarian era had left a gaping hole in the middle of town. The city center, which once claimed three-quarters of the Valley's retail business, had been decimated by a ring of new shopping centers, such as Valley Fair and Eastridge (the largest mall west of Chicago when it opened). The city's one big bank, First National, had morphed into Bank of the West before it was gobbled up by BNP-Paribas. The biggest local industrial firm, FMC, moved back to Chicago. To make things worse, all the city and county offices had moved into a Modernist Civic

Center ten blocks Uptown. Even the *Mercury* jumped ship to open fields east of the city.

The new Downtown was paid for with tax revenues drawn from electronics companies by gerrymandering the redevelopment district to cover both the city center and the industrial lands of north San Jose. Some $2.5 billion was siphoned from one to the other, making the city's Redevelopment Agency the richest in California. Thanks to this massive investment, a bevy of new buildings sprang up Downtown, including a Richard Meier–designed City Hall and public library, two new hotels and a convention center, a major sports arena, and three new museums. City parks were upgraded and millions were channeled into roads tying Downtown to the freeway system. Meanwhile, the Santa Clara Valley Transportation Authority put in one of the most ambitious light rail systems in the United States. Private capitalists were motivated by all this public investment to put up skyscrapers with millions of square feet of new office space to house companies such as Adobe, Oracle, and Okta and to add several massive housing complexes such as Paseo Plaza and 101 San Fernando.[47]

The third facet of Silicon Valley's makeover is the way the big tech companies have used their immense wealth to burnish their brands by building magnificent new corporate showpieces. War profits had allowed Hewlett-Packard and Varian to construct handsome headquarters at the Stanford Industrial Park circa 1960, but newer companies shunned showy buildings. Gleaming high-rise headquarters began to appear again in the 1980s, led by Oracle's five glass cylinders in Redwood Shores, Apple's boxy complex in Cupertino, and Intel's Blue Cube in Santa Clara, opened in 1992. The 1990s brought another wave of tall, stylish buildings by the likes of Yahoo in Sunnyvale, Silicon Graphics in Mountain View, and 3Com in Santa Clara. Speculative developments were also going higher, as in the slick glass offices of Redwood City's Pacific Shores Center and Twin Dolphin Drive.

In the twenty-first century, particularly the boom of the 2010s, more grandiose plans came to fruition. For example, AMD—not exactly a household brand name—built itself a high rise designed by Pei Cobb Freed & Partners. But the big noise came, as one might expect, from the Big Three tech corporations. Google took over the Silicon Graphics campus on the bay shoreline in Mountain View, built in the 1990s, and transformed it into the world-famous Googleplex. Announced plans calling for a set of gigantic canopies of translucent glass amid a huge garden, dwarfing the present complex, have been scaled back to a single half-million-square-foot building with a

---

47   For a full study of San Jose's redevelopment, see Rhee 2007.

roof of giant solar-paneled leaves. Instead, Google acquired a huge swath of Mountain View for thousands of housing units and sites for a major office complex around Diridon rail station in San Jose.[48]

Facebook bought the 1990s complex of defunct Sun Microsystems on the baylands of East Menlo Park and reworked it into a million-square-foot corporate city-walk, featuring a main street of shops to serve their workers' every need. It then added a new west campus designed by Frank Gehry, a half-million-square-foot zigzagging building covered with a rooftop green-way. The most fabulous monument of all is Apple's three-million-square-foot headquarters in Cupertino, a gargantuan flying saucer of a building that was Steve Jobs's last fantasy. The doughnut-shaped building encircles a massive green area and is designed to emphasize horizontality and interaction among employees.[49]

Finally, the Valley's tremendous growth has been accommodated by building upward to increase density and show off the advantages of the New Urbanism. By the 1980s, developers were doing more build-to-suit work for the tech industry and putting up innovative multiuse complexes with the help of name architects. Some of the developments offered spectacular New Urbanist concoctions of residential, office, and retail space, as in the Santana Village west of Downtown San Jose. Cottle Transit Village on the old IBM office complex site on the southern edge of San Jose is only the latest New Urbanist multiuse development. Almost every town in the Valley began to reconstruct its Main Street to attract residents and shoppers and to infuse a bit of urban life into sterile suburbia.[50]

Midrise housing complexes went up all over, especially along major transportation corridors such as El Camino Real and East Santa Clara Street on the west side, and the eastern flank of the Valley came to mirror LA's endless landscape of four-to-six-story apartment buildings. For the first time, apartments, condos, and townhouses outnumbered single-family houses in San Jose in the 2000 census. The result was that Silicon Valley had become far more compact than comparable Sunbelt cities such as San Diego or Phoenix. This was no longer the age of sprawl. By 2000, greater San Jose ranked as the third-densest

---

48 Hansen 2017c.
49 Mozingo 2017.
50 Steinberg 2002, Schoennauer interview, 2002. Also Calthorpe & Fulton 2001a. Most of the old developers remained active, such as Peery-Arrillaga, Sobrato, Berg & Berg, Orchard Devcon, Cornish & Carey, BT Commercial, and Parrish. But new players appeared, as well: Coldwell Banker spinoff CB Commercial (Los Angeles), DivCo West (Canada), Cushman & Wakefield (New York), Colliers International (Canada), Archon (Dallas). Local residential brokerages, however, fell to national mergers in the 1990s, such as the Century 21 empire and CBRE, which bought up Cornish and Carey and Alain Pinel.

metro area in the United States after San Francisco and Los Angeles. Dutch Hamann's quest for parity with LA has worked out in a most unexpected way.

★ ★ ★

The impact of the New Urbanism on the people of Silicon Valley has received less attention than in San Francisco, but the same processes are at work. Without a doubt, the growing density and affluence of the Valley has brought an upgrade to many of its commercial zones. Malls such as Stanford, the Pruneyard, and Westfield Valley Fair are showcases of high-end consumption. The once sleepy Downtowns of Palo Alto, Sunnyvale, Mountain View, and Los Gatos have been turned into lively shopping and dining districts, with a gloss of bars, restaurants, and other entertainments. There are major events at sites such as Mountain View's Shoreline Amphitheater and San Jose's SAP Center, and a respectable ballet, symphony, and theater scene from Stanford to San Jose. The Valley's populace is younger and hipper than before, but the urban scene is still a far cry from San Francisco or Oakland.

Nevertheless, the rush of the upper-class people and money into the area has driven up housing prices and driven out those of lesser means. The west side of the Valley, from Palo Alto to Saratoga, has some of the most expensive real estate in the country, making it virtually impossible for workers to find anywhere to live, and the northeast corner of the Valley in the hills of Milpitas (and Fremont) is almost as bad. Former working class–friendly suburbs such as Campbell and Sunnyvale have been colonized by the well-to-do. And the pressure on central San Jose from redevelopment and gentrification will only get worse with the promised arrival of Google, bringing more office buildings and thousands more employees Downtown.

The working families of Silicon Valley have been pushed into a central band between Highways 101 and 68 and packed into apartment complexes from Mountain View to Santa Clara. The poorest households cluster in the north along the bay front and around the core of San Jose. The density of apartments buildings in East San Jose is startling. Meanwhile, tens of thousands of working people have fled to the far fringes of the region, all the way south to Hollister, over the Santa Cruz Mountains to Watsonville, and into the Central Valley. Commuter traffic is nightmarish in every direction (see chapter 7).[51]

The demographic diversity of Silicon Valley is often underappreciated. It has a higher percentage of foreign-born people than San Francisco and has become *more* diverse, not less, in recent years. Whites and Asians constitute

---

51 Mongeau 2015, Barrera 2016.

about one-third each of the populace and Latinos over one-quarter (African Americans are a miniscule one-twentieth). The presence of large numbers of upper-class Asians, as business owners, professionals, managers, and techies speaks to the importance of Chinese and Indian immigrants in the tech industry—though talk of their "dominance" is exaggerated by ignoring glass ceilings at the top and subcontracting of low-end work (see chapter 4).[52]

Cupertino, Saratoga, and Milpitas are notable for their Asian majorities and public leadership. There are, at the same time, large numbers of working-class Asians—Filipino, Vietnamese, Korean, and Chinese—on the east and south sides of San Jose, in Milpitas, and into southern Alameda County. Latinos are heavily concentrated in East and Central San Jose. Ironically, San Jose's spiffed-up Downtown is mostly used by Latinos, who create a vibrant street life in contrast to so many high-class Whites and Asians holed up in their suburban homes or at work in their tech offices.

Oaktown Rising: The New Urban Occupation

Oakland was the last of the old core cities of the Bay Area to revive, and now it, too, has been radically transformed. In the postwar era, Oakland was down on its luck, playing the poor cousin to San Francisco rather than the serious rival it had been in the early twentieth century. Its once-great industrial base melted away and Downtown withered, while prosperous Whites moved over the hills and the black ghettoes grew, bearing the burden of deindustrialization, disinvestment, and police repression. Capital withdrew from the city and refused to come back. The city and its citizens fought back gamely, without much success; then, suddenly, the new Millennium ushered in a new period of rapid growth, and Oakland was thoroughly reworked. In a sense, this was a matter of the rising tech tide of the West Bay lifting all boats—or lifeboats fleeing San Francisco's overstuffed housing market—but the East Bay economy was also growing of its own accord, with only minor incursions by the IT industry.

*   *   *

The decline of Oakland was precipitous in the 1950s and '60s. Some factories, such as the Chevy plant in East Oakland, moved to the suburbs, but most companies gradually cut back and then closed as their markets shrank, machinery became obsolete, and competitors won out. The same was true of the industrial belt north of Oakland in Emeryville, West Berkeley, and

---

52 Simonsen 2016. On Asians in the Valley, see Lung-Amam 2017. For the exaggerated view, see Nakano 2012.

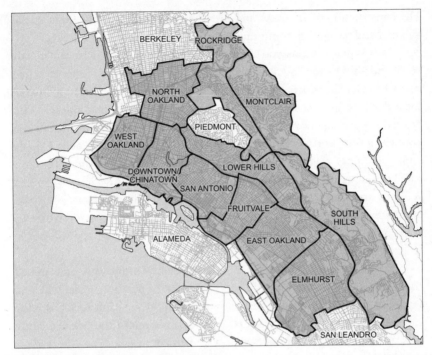

Figure 5.7: Map of Oakland Neighborhoods

Richmond. Meanwhile, the industrial suburbs to the south, such as San Leandro, Hayward, and Fremont, filled in on the strength of new factory construction accompanied by phalanxes of working-class housing tracts. The shift of the Bay Area's main container port to Oakland helped to revive the waterfront but did not stimulate much new industrial and warehousing activity.[53]

Like so many second-tier America cities, Oakland did not benefit from the corporate expansion of the postwar era. Its banks had all been bought up by the big San Francisco banks long before. Bechtel slipped away over the bridge. The city's one industrial giant, Kaiser Industries, built a large headquarters complex Uptown but then fell on hard times after its founder died. Clorox and American President Lines (the old Dollar Steamship Lines of San Francisco) participated in Downtown redevelopment, as did Wells Fargo, but Safeway kept a low profile down by the docks while Lucky Stores fled to the suburbs. Finally, Oakland's once-lively shopping scene shriveled up with the passing of the streetcars that once brought everyone Downtown.

---

53 On the industrial decline of the East Bay, see Sankalia 1999, Self 2003, McClintock 2011, Lunine 2013. Containers pass right through ports, so locating warehouses and factories near the docks no longer has a cost advantage.

The construction of freeways and BART merely facilitated the flight to the suburbs and passage of commuters straight through to San Francisco.[54]

The residents of Oakland's Downtown and flatlands districts were mostly black and poor by the end of the 1960s. Thousands of African Americans had moved to Oakland during and after the Second World War, when industrial jobs were plentiful; but they were the first to be let go as the region scaled back from the wartime boom, resulting in high unemployment rates. Meanwhile, younger white workers moved with the jobs to southern Alameda County, while the upper classes went up and over the hills. Neighborhoods deteriorated as average incomes fell, commerce dried up, banks declined to lend in redlined areas, and slumlords took over. Oakland School District's tax base shrank even as the need for funds rose, and matters were made worse by remaining white and black middle-income families pulling their kids out in favor of private schools.

The city's postwar elite, led by the Knowland family, were determined to cleanse the city of its greatly enlarged black population. West Oakland was drawn and quartered by urban renewal, freeways, and BART, driving most African Americans to East Oakland—but not out of the city. Oakland's African American population peaked at 45 percent in 1980. The elite also targeted Downtown for urban redevelopment using federal urban renewal funds, but they shot themselves in the foot by tearing out twenty square blocks in the heart of the city in the early 1970s, in what one historian wryly calls "a blitzkrieg against blight." Hundreds of businesses and people were evicted along the waterfront and up the old Washington Street shopping corridor to City Hall (Tenth to Fourteenth Streets); more of what is now branded as charming "Old Oakland" would have fallen if it were not for public protest.[55]

In a major power shift after William Knowland committed suicide, the city elected its first black mayor, Lionel Wilson, in 1977; but his administration continued the same urban renewal strategy as the city struggled to revive its sagging fortunes and racialized image. Downtown redevelopment limped along for years as a series of developers and tenants dropped in and dropped out. A couple office towers went up on Broadway, as did a hotel and convention center, and finally a major infusion of outside investment allowed it to

---

54 Self 2003, Schwarzer 2014. Schwarzer stresses the fragmentation of Downtown as a cause of its demise, yet San Francisco's core was also divided and overstretched, but the city's business activity was sufficient to overcome that; Oakland's was not. The full story of Oakland's key companies has not been told, but see Adams 1997, Walker 2004b, Lunine 2013.

55 Johnson 1993, Self 2003, Oden 2011. The same racial cleansing took place in Berkeley and Richmond.

complete the featured element of the rebuild, the City Center project, in the 1980s. City Center was an early example of New Urbanism, a mixed-use area of offices and retail around a central plaza in postmodern retro style. Oakland witnessed some revival in the 1980s, but City Center's success was mostly a zero-sum transfer of remaining businesses along Broadway to its protected confines.[56]

Then the whole redevelopment program imploded with the 1988 bankruptcy of the principal developer, Bramalea Pacific, and the onset of recession across the country. On top of the economic woes, the Loma Prieta earthquake hit in 1989, doing more damage in Oakland than anywhere else around the Bay Area. It leveled the double-decker Nimitz Freeway in West Oakland and wreaked havoc on old hotels and high-rises, many of which had to be torn down, leaving more holes in the city's fabric. Disaster struck once more in October 1991 when a giant wildfire leveled over three thousand homes in the Oakland and Berkeley hills—the largest urban conflagration in the country since 1906. In a final blow, an Uptown retail mall, which had long been a big part of the city's redevelopment plans, was shelved when the Rouse Corporation pulled out in 1992 after its West Coast president died in a plane crash. The future looked grim.[57]

★ ★ ★

Through all Oakland's trials, the focus of efforts to revive the city was on how to attract outside capital and well-to-do suburban shoppers. Both were misguided. The white upper classes and real estate developers with few exceptions wanted nothing to do with black inner cities like Oakland; they literally ran for the hills. That movement started early in the century as the Realty Syndicate and Mason-McDuffie built high-end subdivisions in places like The Uplands, Rockridge and Trestle Glen. In 1917, Piedmont cut a hole in Oakland to create a wealthy enclave smack in the middle of the city. Montclair filled in between the wars and was sealed off from the flatlands by the new postwar freeways (580 and 13). The suburbs over the hills took off after the Second World War with the opening of Highway 24 and the Caldecott Tunnel, but they were oriented toward Walnut Creek and San Francisco, not Oakland.

---

56 Oakland City Planning Commission 1969, Self 2003, Douzet 2012, Schwarzer 2015 (quote at p. 97).

57 On retail fantasies in urban renewal, see Cohen 2007. Though no one knew it at the time, Bramalea was owned by Canada's Olympia & York, the world's largest real estate developer in the 1980s, which was undone by the 1989 recession and the Canary Wharf building in London. Bramalea's head, Glenn Isaacsson, was the brains behind the revival of Jack London Square and Victorian Row, as well.

As for the corporations, they continued to cluster in San Francisco, which had ten times the square footage of office space of Oakland in the postwar era. Without many headquarters, the business services sector of the East Bay was stunted. When big companies began to move back offices to the booming 680 corridor in the 1980, they jumped right over Oakland to the far side of the hills. The new edge city of the outer East Bay soon bypassed Oakland in square footage of office space. Meanwhile, the old industrial enclave of Emeryville (which was also carved out of Oakland around 1900) completely retooled itself by attracting biotech firms, IT companies, condominiums, and three big new malls—stealing Oakland's dream of retail revival to become the new Downtown of the East Bay.[58]

The real basis of the revival of Oakland in the 1980s did not come from white people and their money. Instead, it arose from the bottom up thanks to the new immigrants from Asia and Mexico, who brought life to downtrodden neighborhoods. Chinatown swelled and Chinese spilled over the hills across Lake Merritt ("China Hill"), a new Koreatown appeared Uptown, Vietnamese filled the old San Antonio District east of the lake, and Laotian refugees ended up in far East Oakland. Meanwhile, the Fruitvale District ballooned with the influx of Latinos and their businesses, and Mexicans also began to fill in parts of West Oakland.

The prime mover of new office construction Downtown was not private capital but government, as exemplified by the twin towers of the new federal building and courthouse (later named for Ronald Dellums) and the new headquarters of the East Bay Municipal Utility District and Bay Area Rapid Transit District. There was some return of white folks to the San Antonio district in East Oakland in the 1970s and Rockridge in North Oakland in the 1980s, made up chiefly of workers from government offices and overflow from Berkeley. The era of boutiques also brought shoppers down to College Avenue from the hills. Nonetheless, after the trauma of the 1991 fire a movement arose in Montclair to secede from the city; though a failure, it highlighted the social division between the hills and the flatlands.

More changes were in store for the city as the economy revived in the 1990s. Millions in federal disaster funds and private insurance money rolled in after the earthquake and fire, spurring a wave of rehab projects Downtown and new home building in the hills. A new State Building went up (named for Mayor Elihu Harris) and the University of California built a new Office of

---

58   Garreau 1991. On Emeryville's transformation, see Hinckle & Greenwich 2003. For the impact of Emeryville on Oakland, see, e.g., Jonassen et al. 2012. On office space figures, see chapter 6.

the President. These were highly political location decisions, expressly to aid the city and to keep UC from going to Southern California. Meanwhile, the immigrant neighborhoods continued to grow in that decade, joined by the first influx of people fleeing San Francisco and Berkeley rents. But that taste of things to come was cut short by the dot-com bust.

As the twenty-first century dawned, Oakland enjoyed a growth spurt unlike anything since the Second World War, one that dramatically altered the face of the city. It had little to do with information technology, which remains concentrated in the West Bay, although Oakland gave birth to the first of the streaming apps, Pandora, and Pixar and Siebel grew up in Emeryville. The Port of Oakland and its logistics complex also benefit greatly from the trade in electronics, as well as agricultural products from the interior. The East Bay still harbors some traditional industry, such as oil refining, food processing, and machining, and South Alameda County can claim a bus maker, Gillig, and the Tesla electric car facility in Fremont. But the biggest sectors in the East Bay are health care, education, and government, along with professional services and nonprofits. The East Bay has spawned many innovative start-ups, as is typical of the Bay Area, but these are mostly in biomedical technologies, energy conservation, and business services. Oakland is especially proud of its dozens of new food product firms, most visibly breweries and distilleries.

Meanwhile, the booming Bay Area property market of the 2000s overflowed into Oakland, which had long been a doughnut hole, instead of a peak, in the rent gradient. The rent gap had grown enormous, with Oakland land values a third cheaper than in San Francisco, Berkeley, and the 680 corridor. More and more households and firms realized the savings to be had by moving to Oakland and developers looked at the profits to be made and started building condos and apartments at a feverish rate. Big capital finally came back to Oakland to invest in one of the nation's most lucrative real estate markets—about a billion dollars before the crash of 2007. High-rise condos and apartments popped up all around Downtown, from the waterfront up to the Temescal neighborhood (51st Street), peaking in the Uptown District that replaced vast acres of empty space which had never been successfully redeveloped.[59]

Jerry Brown, former and future governor of California, became Oakland's mayor from 1999 to 2007 and presided over the building boom. He was widely credited with bringing the city back to life. No doubt, his presence made a difference as he boldly declared a goal of building housing for ten

---

59   Levin 2013, Dineen 2016a. Uber also entertained the idea of moving to Oakland. Weinberg 2015.

thousand new residents in the Downtown and invited big developers, such as San Francisco's Shorenstein Company, to join the party. Mayor Brown helped break the unspoken capitalist boycott of Oakland by putting a famous white face on the city. Yet Brown's program was based on the New Urbanism idea of repopulating city centers, which was already part of Mayor Harris's redevelopment program, and the whole thing succeeded because it was carried along by the raging Bay Area economy and housing market.[60]

★ ★ ★

Oakland's boom times ushered in a remarkable civic overhaul and urban facelift. Members of the upper middle class were arriving in force. San Francisco's manic housing prices were driving all manner of young professionals, techies, teachers, and artists over the bridge. At the same time, scores of nonprofits forced out of San Francisco were setting up shop in Oakland, renting space in old Downtown office buildings. Berkeley was spilling students, staff, faculty, and bohemians over the border to neighboring towns, from Richmond to Oakland. The new arrivals added energy and money to Oakland, filling up a host of trendy bars, brewpubs, and eateries in newly hip neighborhoods such as Temescal, Uptown/Telegraph Avenue, and Grand Avenue/Adams Point.[61]

Meanwhile, the older resident population of Oakland was changing. A new working class was coming of age, featuring young people of all colors and backgrounds. By 2010, the city was about evenly represented by people of European, African, Latin, and Asian origin, and it no longer felt like a set of relatively isolated communities of color jostling for position: ghettoized African Americans, Asians confined to Chinatown, Latino Fruitvale with its own concerns. A new generation without the same identities and hang-ups had become the social dynamos of the city, establishing new cultural institutions like Destiny Arts and First Friday street fairs. As the youthful dynamism of the two Oaklands—resident working class and upper middle class arrivals—collided, there was plenty of friction but a lot of creative tension to go along with it (see also chapter 10).[62]

Today Central Oakland is a veritable showcase of the New Urbanism. The new look is due partly to the influx of people and money, partly to race and class diversity, and partly to the civic liveliness and commercial activity

---

60 DeFao 2001, Temple 2009, Elinson 2010, Douzet 2012, Schwarzer 2015.
61 Stehlin 2015, Werth 2016. Hip Oakland became a bit of a media darling, e.g., New York Times 2012. Excellent coverage of the transformation of Oakland can be found in the weekly *East Bay Express*.
62 Stehlin 2015, Werth 2016, Werth & Marienthal 2016.

those create. Urbanity is being written on the landscape, with more infill of empty spaces, higher buildings and density, more bars and restaurants, busier streets, and more foot traffic. A proliferation of bicycle lanes and dedicated streets are other markers, along with upgrades of public spaces such as the overhaul of Lake Merritt, repurposing of the Henry Kaiser Civic Auditorium, and improvements around Jack London Square. The city has further ambitions for West Oakland, Chinatown, and Auto Row in its new Downtown Specific Plan, which will streamline the approval process for development; and regional planners have jumped in to push for more growth and density.[63]

These were all signs of Oakland's rising star, but they came with strings attached. Displacement of working-class households and people of color became severe, squeezing out African Americans in particular. The foreclosure disaster that followed the housing bubble hit Oakland especially hard, with over ten thousand homes lost in the city, and speculators moved in like vultures to feast on the carcasses of neighborhoods run over by the financial bus. Just as bad as the pain of individual owners losing their homes (or renters left dangling by bankrupt landlords) was the gutting of communal life, as friends and relatives were pushed out, local businesses failed, and essential government services ran out of funds (see fig. 5.8 and chapters 6 and 7).[64]

Oakland's race and class divisions are still clearly etched on the landscape. The luster of the New Urbanism does not touch the lives of poor people in East and West Oakland, who do not frequent the trendy watering holes Downtown. Bikes lanes, rehabbed houses, and dense new developments around BART stations are signs of gentrification that is feared by many poor working-class folks. Public events such as First Fridays and Juneteenth have been narrowly proscribed over time to keep out troublesome young people of color.[65]

Eager to keep the good times rolling, Oakland's city government was slow to provide protection for tenants forced out by landlords trying to profit off the influx of higher-income renters, finally passing a Tenants Protection Ordinance in late 2014, and slow to plug loopholes in that law. Oakland did nothing while the city of Richmond tried to use eminent domain to buy underwater mortgages to keep creditors in their homes (incurring the wrath of finance capital, which boycotted the city's bonds to kill the program). A tenants' ballot measure, Renters Upgrade, lost in 2016. Meanwhile, the city turned a blind eye for years to code violations by bohemian refugees from San

---

63 Schwarzer 2015, Terplan 2015, Werth 2016.
64 Kuruvila 2011, Urban Strategies Council 2012, 2014, BondGraham 2014.
65 Stehlin 2015, Werth 2016, Wong 2017.

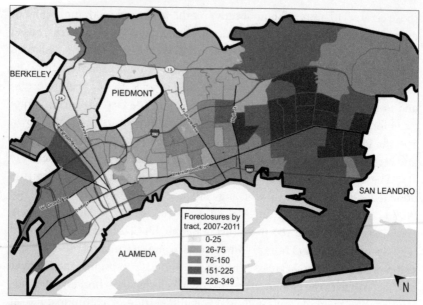

Figure 5.8: Map of Oakland Foreclosures, 2007–2011
Source: Urban Strategies Council 2013.

Francisco crowding into makeshift quarters in old warehouses—mostly for lack of resources. It seemed like a good idea to keep rents low, until a tragic fire at the "Ghost Ship" community warehouse snuffed out thirty-six lives, putting the spotlight on the plight of young artists, the abuse by rapacious landlords, and the miscarriage of duty by city departments.[66]

Conclusion

The Bay Area is not just getting denser in its old core cities; it is thickening in outlying areas and upgrading its many nodes of the New Urbanism. The outer East Bay was the first outer realm to do so, and it featured three new centers built up in the 1980s. Walnut Creek, situated at the crossroads of Highway 24 and Interstate 680, led the way thanks to a team of innovative planners and a slow-growth movement among its citizens. To the south, Bishop Ranch opened the Bay Area's premier office park, attracting the headquarters of some of San Francisco's biggest corporations: Chevron, PG&E, and PacBell (now AT&T). Walnut Creek is the commercial heart of the 680 corridor, and Bishop Ranch now has a shopping center designed by Italian architect Renzo Piano. Farther south still, Hacienda Business Park and Pleasanton teamed up to attract a herd of professional and tech offices next to a revived city center.

---

66   On the Ghost Ship fire, see https://en.wikipedia.org/wiki/2016_Oakland_warehouse_fire

In the North Bay, the city of Napa has undergone a complete makeover in keeping with the rising fortunes of the Napa Valley. In Sonoma County, Petaluma was the first to restore its old Main Street, thanks to pioneering growth controls of the 1980s. The cities of Sonoma, Healdsburg, and Sebastopol now bristle with chic restaurants and boutique shops, as do all the little towns in Marin County, such as Sausalito, Fairfax, and Mill Valley. Santa Rosa's Downtown, which was bisected by Highway 101 and gutted by redevelopment in the 1960s, is the largest and most notable of the recent success stories, and even towns with no historic centers to speak of, such as Rohnert Park and Novato, have a new sense of place. Sonoma County has just opened up its SMART train to carry commuters to San Francisco, with nodal developments around every stop.

Without a doubt, the New Urbanism has put a new shine on the metropolis, buffing up decaying old Downtowns, bringing more people together to enjoy the benefits of city life, and injecting vast amounts of money into the urban fabric and commercial zones. Rising density in city centers is, by and large, a good thing in a country that has too little taste for urban living and the benefits it brings: stimulating encounters, individual anonymity and freedom, collective living and public spaces, great cultural institutions, more tolerance for difference, and social innovation.

The Bay Area has enjoyed one of the country's most rapid and brilliant revivals of urbanity at its three big central cities, and many places beyond those, as befits a metropolitan region with one of the most dynamic and richest economies in the world. San Francisco, San Jose/Silicon Valley, and Oakland have, each in its own way, experienced a major makeover in the late twentieth and early twenty-first century. This has been a historic era of urban transformation, comparable to the Gilded Age, Progressive Era, or Postwar Epoch.

The gleaming new Bay Area of the tech era has a dark side, however. The New Urbanism can be brutal to those who lack the financial means to live well, the cultural capital to enjoy the cosmopolitan life, or the social resources to survive the competition. Most working-class people are in no position to benefit from the revival of the metropolitan cores, and indeed far too many have been driven out of their central city homes by rising rents and foreclosures and are now suffering through absurdly long commutes back to their old jobs. The impact on the young can be especially harsh, as they are forced to move back in with their parents and feel like failures if they are not techies earning six-figure incomes and living the fast life in the new city. It is even worse for the elderly, whose neighborhoods have been devastated by foreclosures or transformed by gentrification. Putting down roots is a basic aspect of human existence, and the loss of the familiar places, friends, and support of older neighborhoods can be devastating. But capitalism couldn't care less about these human tragedies in its heartless search for the new New Thing and endless accumulation of wealth.

CHAPTER SIX

Bubble by the Bay

Anatomy of a Housing Crisis

THE SAN FRANCISCO BAY AREA IS GOING THROUGH THE WORST HOUSING CRISIS IN its history. Home prices and rents have shot through the roof, becoming unaffordable for most households. It is one of the tightest and most expensive housing markets in the world. The city of San Francisco is the worst offender, but Silicon Valley, Oakland, and the rest of the region are not far behind. Here again, the Bay Area has much to teach about the dark side of the much-heralded tech economy and the boom times of the twenty-first century.

In the mythology of the Gold Rush, nuggets were there for the taking from the rivers of the Mother Lode, and everyone prospered. But history is written by the winners, who conveniently overlook the high price paid by the losers, those gold-seekers who ended up damaged, dispirited, or dead. In today's Silicon Gold Rush, the dominant narrative is about the enrichment of tech entrepreneurs, high average incomes, and urban revival, but this leaves out the unlucky ones being priced out of their homes and neighborhoods by the tens of thousands.

More than simply gentrification, the entire urban fabric is being made over by forces beyond popular control and the powers of local government. The Bay Area's landscape is in violent upheaval as real estate prices go wild, new buildings pop up everywhere, and whole neighborhoods are made over. This has come at a huge cost in displacement and disarray among working people, as this beast of a property market shakes them off like so many fleas. By the time it settles down again, the city will never be the same. The squeeze on ordinary households has produced a powerful tide of popular protest around the bay, which has stimulated a flurry of policy debate and new legislation—most of which is based on erroneous ideas about how property markets work.

Housing prices have rocketed upward in cities from Mumbai to Milan, London to Los Angeles, creating housing crises around the world that have triggered major popular struggles over the failures of property markets, the predations of speculators, and the lack of government response. As one of the world's worst cases of out-of-control housing and urban transformation, the

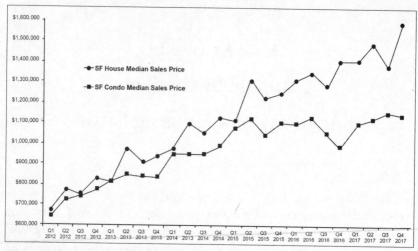

Figure 6.1: San Francisco Home Purchase Prices, 2012–2016
Source: Paragon 2016.

Bay Area has important lessons to offer about the why and wherefore of property booms, housing bubbles, and the fight for the right to dwell in the city.[1]

The chapter begins with an overview of the extremely high prices reached in the 2010s, both in relation to other U.S. cities and to movements in the recent past. The second section turns to the problem of affordability, or rather how unaffordable housing has become for the vast majority of households despite the Bay Area's high average income. The third section attempts to put the blame for the property bubble where it belongs: on overcharged demand, or too much money chasing a limited housing stock. The supply of housing matters, of course, but cannot possibly keep up in the short run when demand is so far out of whack; the way supply responds in a cyclical market is the subject of the fourth section. Finally, the last section takes a look at popular protest against runaway rents and the often-misguided response in public policy circles.

As seen in earlier chapters, trends in personal income move in close harmony with the growth of the regional economy and the geography of jobs. This means that movements in housing markets are closely linked to those in commercial real estate, such as offices, industrial, and research space. Because the recent property boom has advanced across a broad front, the discussion in this chapter will include commercial prices, demand and supply, along with the main story of the housing crisis.

---

[1]   On worldwide housing markets, see Bardhan et al. 2011. On popular responses, see Porter & Shaw 2009.

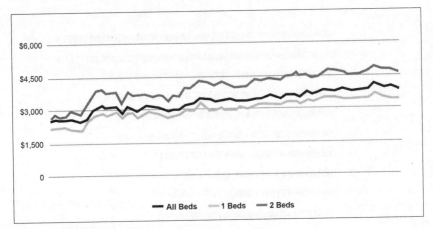

Figure 6.2: San Francisco Median Rents, 2011–2016

Source: Rent Jungle.

Markets Gone Wild

The current property boom and bubble can be observed in a number of registers. This section begins by looking at the recent run-up in the prices of home purchases, apartment rentals, and office leases in the upswing from the low point of the Great Recession. The latest price upheaval is then put into the context of the periodic cycles in property markets that last around a decade. Next, the time scale is increased again to reflect on long-term price trends of the last half century.[2]

Home purchase prices have reached astronomic heights in the recent property boom. At the nadir of the Great Recession in 2010, the average home price for the nine-county Bay Area had fallen to $460,000. Then the market revived as business recovered, hiring picked up, and incomes rose. By mid-2016, the median house price for the nine-county region had surpassed $700,000, up by two-thirds in six years. The market appeared to peak in late 2015, with prices sagging in the most expensive areas, but then lurched upward again, with the region's median price hitting $750,000 at the end of 2017 (fig. 6.1).[3]

Prices were highest in the tech-rich West Bay, led by San Francisco and San Mateo County, which both surpassed the $1 million mark by 2015; Marin and Santa Clara Counties were not far behind. The average for Alameda

---

2   The everyday term "average price" used throughout this discussion always refers to the *median* price (the point halfway between the highest and lowest), unless otherwise indicated. Prices are estimates drawn from such common sources of real estate data as Trulia, Zumper, REAL Facts, Rent Jungle, and SocketSite.

3   Pender 2018.

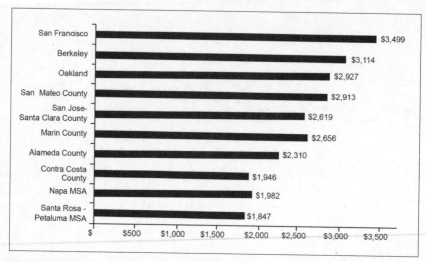

Figure 6.3: Bay Area Rents by City, 2016 (Average for all Units in Large Apartment Buildings)
Source: Paragon 2017.

County was around $750,000 and for Contra Costa, Napa, and Sonoma around a half million. Only Solano County, among the nine core counties, trailed that figure. By the end of 2017, Santa Clara County had joined the million-dollar club, while San Francisco and San Mateo Counties were over $1.2 million median price.[4]

Apartment rents have tracked home prices closely. San Francisco—where two-thirds of households rent—led the way, with average rents climbing from $2,000 per month in 2010 to $3,500 by 2015. Along the way, the city passed up Manhattan as the most expensive central metropolitan market in the country. San Mateo County was not far behind, with rents rising from around $1,500 per month in 2010 to $3,000, while Oakland and San Jose saw their rents go up in tandem, from $1,800 to $3,000, 2011–16 (figs. 6.2 & 6.3).[5]

By 2016, the three largest bay cities were all in the top five rental markets in the United States, along with New York and Boston. Then the market cooled a bit, rents leveled off through 2017, and the Bay Area fell in the rankings.[6]

---

4   Pender 2018.
5   Rent is measured in several ways, not always commensurate: mean or median, asking/paying, number of bedrooms, large and small buildings, and composite averages. For a handy survey and the varied results for San Francisco over the last ten years, see https://marthabridegam.com/sf-rent-history-chart/.
6   On the rental market cooling, see Brinkow 2016, Schenin 2016. Reports on 2017 were mixed but generally flat in San Francisco.

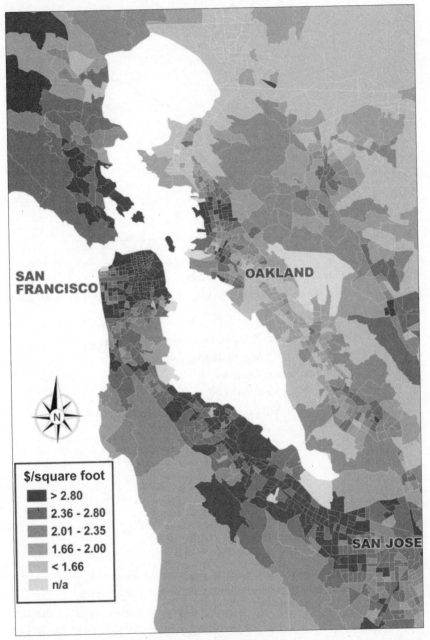

Figure 6.4: Map of Bay Area Rents by Census Tract, 2016

Source: Courtesy of Geoff Boeing. Boeing & Waddell 2017.

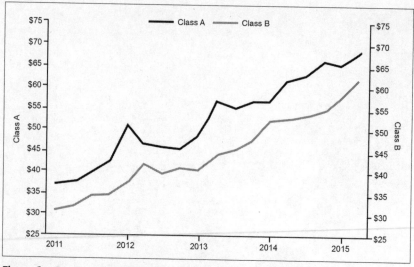

Figure 6.5: San Francisco Office Rents, 2011–2015

Source: http://www.socketsite.com/archives/2015/07/office-rents-in-s-f-nearing-all-time-high-and-absorption-slows.html.

Highest-Rent Cities in the United States, 2016[7]
(one-bedroom median)

1.	San Francisco	$3,590
2.	New York	$3,340
3.	Boston	$2,310
4.	Oakland	$2,290
5.	San Jose	$2,270
6.	Washington, DC	$2,200
7.	Los Angeles	$1,970
8.	Miami	$1,900
9.	Chicago	$1,790
10.	Seattle	$1,750

Meanwhile, San Francisco office space was soaring. From a low of around $35 per square foot in 2010, it had doubled to an average of $72 by the end of 2015. That figure topped all U.S. cities. After a pause in 2016, the office market in the city heated up again in 2017, with huge leases by Dropbox, Facebook, Adobe, Okta, and others. Rents hit an average of $74 per square foot (fig. 6.5).[8]

---

7 Source: Zumper National Rent Report, monthly, one-bedroom. https://www.zumper.com/blog/2016/.

8 Levy 2012, Wingfield 2016, Dineen 2017.

Silicon Valley office rents rose rapidly from around $30 in 2010 to an average of around $50 per square foot by 2015. In high-end enclaves such as Palo Alto and Sand Hill Road, office rents topped even those in San Francisco, coming in at around $100 per square foot in 2016; but office leases across the Valley have a wide spread, going as low as $25 in Milpitas. Industrial space is slightly cheaper than offices. Oakland's office market lagged the others but took off in 2014, hitting a new high of over $50 per square foot in 2015, compared to an average for the whole East Bay of around $35.[9]

* * *

Short-term prices do not tell the full story of rising property values. Too often commentators seize upon short-term figures to make hasty extrapolations about long-term trends, but an essential feature of all property markets is dramatic swings, or property cycles. This is how all markets work under capitalism, despite the ideology of equilibrium peddled by conventional economists, and it is particularly marked in the case of land and buildings. Property cycles last anywhere from ten to twenty-five years (see also chapter 2).[10]

The cyclic nature of property markets is evident in the Bay Area's recent history. House purchase prices, for example, have gone through four cycles over the last thirty years, with peaks in 1990, 2000, 2007, and (probably) 2017. After each peak, prices fell back—most dramatically so after the great housing bubble of the early twenty-first century burst, when midrange houses lost almost half their value. There is no reason not to expect a significant decline after the latest boom subsides, though it is unlikely to be as severe as the last collapse. It is worth noting, in addition, that the low end of the market suffers from the worst whipsaws (fig. 6.6) (see also chapter 7).

Similar cycles show up in apartment rents—shown here for the city of San Francisco only (fig. 6.7). There is an interesting difference, however, in that rents hit their highest peak in 2000 rather than in 2007, the top of the house market. This is surely due to two things: house prices were driven to new heights by the mortgage bubble of the early twenty-first century, while rents were propelled in 1990s and 2010s by the large number of new, young entrants drawn by the tech booms (and the young tend to rent first and buy

---

9   Schiada 2016. Figures are medians for all classes of office space; Class A costs roughly 50 percent more than that. Common sources of data on offices are CBRE, Cushman & Wakefield, Jones Lang Lasalle, and SocketSite. The line between office and industrial space is often blurred today, given the way tech companies lay out their operations. Kroll & Kimball 1986.

10 Essential works on property cycles are Kuznets 1930, Hoyt 1933, Burns 1935, Abramowitz 1964, Whitehand 1987, and Grenadier 1995. These economists always measure trends peak-to-peak or trough-to-trough.

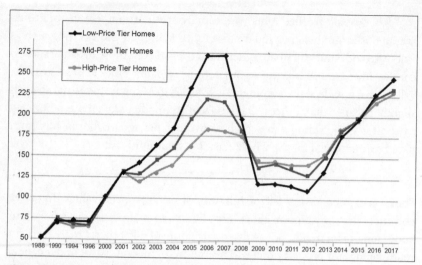

Figure 6.6: San Francisco Metro Home Price Cycles, 1988–2016

Source: Paragon 2016. Case-Shiller is the most widely used of all housing indexes.

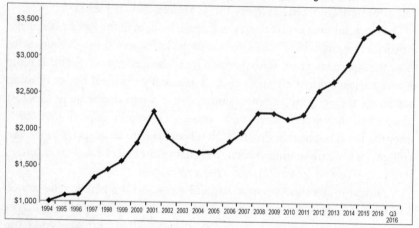

Figure 6.7: San Francisco Rent Cycles, 1994–2016

Source: Paragon 2016.

later). Rents also do not seem to fall as much in slumps, which is not welcome news for today's renters.

San Francisco office lease prices show three sharp cycles over the last generation, with peaks in 2000, 2008, and (probably) 2017. The peak of 2000 was noticeably exaggerated thanks to the dot-com bubble, while that of 2007 was relatively muted by a lack of new tech demand. The latest tech boom has driven office rents back to the same level as the 1990s bubble and even beyond in a revived leasing market in 2017—raising eyebrows as to the sustainability of such prices (see also chapter 5) (fig. 6.8).

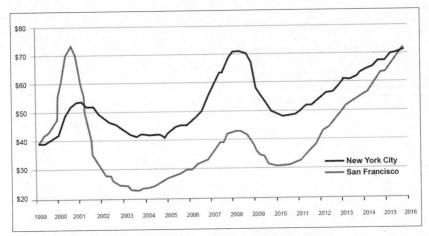

Figure 6.8: San Francisco vs. Manhattan Office Rents, 1999–2016
Source: CBRE San Francisco Market Flash, 12 January 2016. https://twitter.com/realestate4tech.

Every property cycle has its peculiarities. The Bay Area had by far the largest office bubble of the 1990s because of its role in the dot-com boom. California as a whole was the worst offender in the mortgage bubble of the early twenty-first century because it was the biggest purveyor of subprime, variable interest, and alt-A mortgages and the largest and most expensive housing market in the country (see chapter 7). In the 2010s, San Francisco is the most intense rental market in the country for both offices and apartments, with Silicon Valley and Oakland close behind, thanks to the new tech boom. How this cycle ends is unknown as of this writing—but it won't end well, that's for sure.[11]

★   ★   ★

The current boom in housing prices needs to be seen in light of a much-longer trend that has elevated Bay Area housing costs well above the average for the United States. Looking just at house purchases, the Bay Area and California have been outrunning the rest of the country since the 1970s. State home prices have been about double the national average since the late 1980s and California remains the most expensive state in the country (except for Hawaii, a statistical outlier). Bay Area prices are even more extreme: double those of California and quadruple the national average since the early twenty-first century. This is a staggering differential (fig. 6.9).

---

11   On the dot-com bubble, see Walker 2006. On the mortgage madness of the early twenty-first century, see Bardhan & Walker 2011. On the recent San Francisco office market, the coverage of the *San Francisco Chronicle* business section has been good.

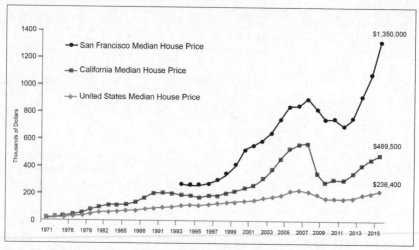

Figure 6.9: Home Prices in San Francisco, California & U.S., 1971–2013
Source: Paragon 2016.

Much noted in discussions of the housing crisis is the historic turning point around 1975, after which California started to outpace the rest of the country in housing inflation. The difference becomes dramatic over the last quarter century, led by the Bay Area. This growing divide is commonly blamed on supply shortages but is most likely due to the stunning increases in personal income and other forces on the demand side of the equation. Before taking on that argument, however, the problem of unaffordability needs to be addressed.

Housing Hell

As Bay Area prices have skyrocketed, housing has become unaffordable for most residents of the metropolitan area, as measured by comparing median purchase price and monthly rent to median household income.[12] Starting with home purchases, Bay Area houses and condos are currently beyond the means of around four-fifths of local residents, which effectively means that the entire working class has been priced out of home ownership—despite their high average incomes compared to all other cities in the country. In fact, house purchase has been beyond the means of three-quarters of households for the last three decades (fig. 6.10). Not surprisingly, homeownership rates have fallen for many years (see chapter 7).

---

12 Affordability is normally measured by the percentage of median income households that can afford to rent the median apartment or buy the median-priced house. Conversely, one can ask what percentage of the median income is consumed by the median monthly mortgage payment or apartment rent.

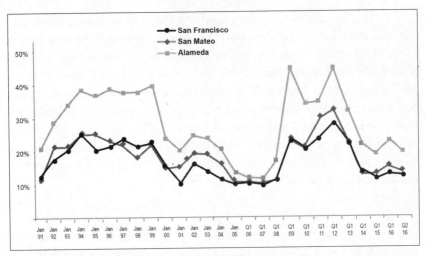

Figure 6.10: Bay Area Home Purchase Affordability, 1991–2016

Source: Paragon 2016a.

To drive the point home, some comparisons are in order. Looking at housing affordability across the country, the Bay Area is markedly worse than California, which is significantly worse than the United States as a whole; the percent of households that could afford the median-priced home purchase in 2016 was 13 percent in San Francisco, under 20 percent in the central Bay Area, just over 30 percent for California, and well over 50 percent for the United States. Not surprisingly, Bay Area cities (municipalities) captured seven of the ten top spots for least affordable in the United States in 2015, topped by Palo Alto.[13]

The Bay Area is not the worst offender for out-of-reach rents among U.S. cities, because in Miami and Los Angeles rents are not far behind and average incomes are so much lower. Nevertheless, rents in the Bay Area are barely affordable for most wage earners, with the consequence that working people spend a huge proportion of their income on housing. The average household in Silicon Valley is spending over 40 percent of its monthly income on rent, while the figure in the central Bay Area is even higher, nearly 45 percent. One study in San Francisco showed that even tech engineers were, on average, paying out 40–50 percent of their monthly pay to live in one-bedroom apartments in the heart of the city.[14]

---

13   Figures from Paragon 2016a, Gudell 2016. By contrast, at the end of the postwar golden age of homeownership, ca. 1970, two-thirds of American households could afford to buy their own home.

14   For national comparisons, see Edmiston 2016. On rent as a share of household income in the Bay Area, see Gudell 2016, Carson 2016.

Internationally, the Bay Area is among the least affordable home purchase markets, as rated by the annual *Demographia International Survey*. In 2015,
Hong Kong was the worst, followed by Sydney; San Jose metro, Auckland, and
Melbourne tied for third; then came San Francisco metro, Greater London,
San Diego, and Los Angeles. The median Bay Area house cost 4.5 to 5 times
the median household income. Comparative data on the affordability of
rental housing are harder to come by and are tricky to evaluate because of
variable definitions of the size of the average apartment and the boundaries
of metropolitan areas; still, various studies put San Francisco among the most
unaffordable cities in the world for renters.[15]

★   ★   ★

The current crop of high prices and rents has yielded a bitter harvest for
thousands of households. Purchase prices are so outrageous that there has
been little movement out of tenancy into ownership in recent years; indeed,
the percent of households renting has gone up. A small proportion of renters
are protected by rent control or kindly landlords, but most renters have experienced the pressure of rising rents and declining affordability. The unlucky
ones face four common fates: displacement from their homes, packing more
people into smaller spaces, eviction by aggressive landlords, and fleeing the
city entirely.

Displacement has become the generic term for households that have had
to move because they cannot make the rent (or house payments) where they
currently live. Tens of thousands of households move every year around the
Bay Area, and they do so for many reasons, such as changing circumstances
of work, family, and age. It is not an easy matter to sort out the effect of rising
rents from other causes, but researchers have attempted to quantify and map
displacement by high rents (fig. 6.11).

Displacement does not affect only households; it also hits commercial
lessees. The pressure for San Francisco office space has steadily pushed out
competing land uses such as warehouses and small manufacturing. High-end
restaurants and cafes and boutiques have elbowed aside older, cheaper eateries and mom-and-pop shops across the city. In the latest boom, San Francisco
nonprofits have picked up and moved en masse to Oakland (see chapter 5).[16]

---

15   Cox 2016a & b. The *Demographia* survey covers nine rich countries, but not the city-
     state of Singapore. For international rent comparisons, see https://www.rentjungle.
     com/average-rent-in-san-francisco-rent-trends/; http://ceoworld.biz/2015/10/19/top-
     50-most-expensive-cities-in-the-world-to-rent-an-apartment-2015-report/; http://www.
     pwc.com/us/en/cities-of-opportunity/2016/cities-of-opportunity-7-report.pdf.
16   Rubin 2011, Johnson 2016.

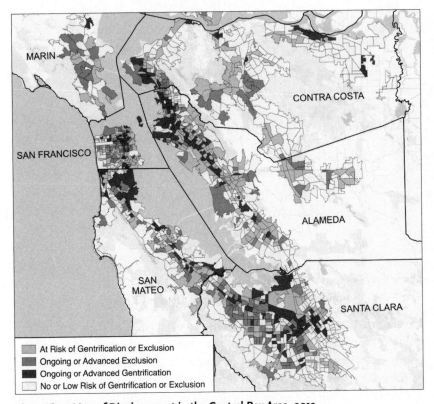

Figure 6.11: Map of Displacement in the Central Bay Area, 2013

Source: http://www.urbandisplacement.org/map/sf. Thanks to Simon Hochberg.

A second facet of the housing squeeze is overcrowding. This affects mostly immigrants, families with kids, and the young. The 2015 U.S. Census Bureau's community survey shows that overcrowding occurs in over one-fifth of San Francisco households, over one-third of rental households, and well over half of those with kids. The figures are hardly better in the South Bay or East Bay. This is particularly true for Latino and Asian working families, but it applies to many young white workers attracted by the tech boom, who survive in ways that belie their reputations for high living in the city by sharing multiple-room apartments, splitting rooms, and moving into microapartments for singles.[17]

The most appalling face of the housing crisis is eviction by landlords wishing to bring in higher-paying tenants or engage in wholesale building conversions. In many instances, it goes beyond simple nonrenewal of leases to various forms of harassment and illegal means of forcing people out. The

---

17 Kuchler 2016.

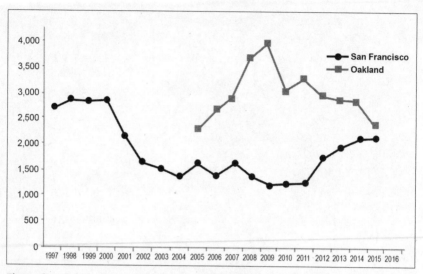

Figure 6.12: Evictions in San Francisco and Oakland, 1997–2016
Source: Sabatini 2016 and http://www.antievictionmap.com/#/oakland/.

best-known cases are "Ellis Act evictions," in which landlords get around rent controls by wholesale conversion of their buildings to condos or tenants-in-common. Nevertheless, there are ten times as many unit-by-unit evictions as Ellis Act conversions. The San Francisco Rent Board has been tracking evictions since the late 1990s, and the totals are shocking: approximately 35,000 households in the last twenty years, on a base of around 350,000 units. Evictions are also rampant in the East Bay. The Anti-Eviction Mapping Project has data for Oakland showing an even higher rate of evictions than across the Bay Bridge: more than 2,500 per year over the last ten years (fig. 6.12).[18]

A last dimension of the housing crisis is the way working-class families and people of color have been driven out of the central cities. Some of these housing refugees move across the bay from San Francisco to Oakland, north to Sonoma County, or from Silicon Valley into southern Alameda County. Many more move far across the hills to the outer East Bay, and a surprising number flee out to Central Valley towns such as Vacaville and Stockton. Similarly, the displaced move north to Lake and Mendocino Counties or south from Silicon Valley to San Benito County (see chapter 7). Then there are those who leave the Bay Area entirely, heading for Oregon, Nevada, and points east. Direct data on leavers is hard to find, but a recent poll had an astonishing one-third of respondents saying they were ready to depart for greener pastures.[19]

---

18 Dineen 2015, Sabatini 2016, www.antievictionmappingproject.net/ellis.html.
19 Fimrite 2016.

The racial implications of the housing blowout are dire. African Americans have been especially hard-pressed by the foreclosure crisis and the subsequent housing bubble. San Francisco's percentage of black households has fallen from 17 percent in 1970 to 6 percent in 2015; Oakland's share of black residents has fallen markedly, as well, from 36 percent in 2000 to 28 percent in 2010 to below 25 percent in 2015. Silicon Valley, on the other hand, never had many black folks to begin with, as in San Jose's pathetically low 3 percent. Latinos, too, have headed to the exits in large numbers, though it is harder to discern from raw data because of the continued arrival of new immigrants (see also chapter 7).

Conventional economics has nothing to say about all this, except that market solutions are always just. Inequality does not exist in their models, only choice, so displacement is entirely fair in their eyes.[20] But the people being squeezed by the housing crisis can hardly be expected to agree with this Classical Liberal economic stance and its socially conservative acceptance of wholesale displacement. They want to know why this all is happening. Why can't ordinary people afford to live in the Bay Area anymore?

How one understands the causes of the housing crisis determines what one thinks the best solutions are. The next section puts the principal blame on excessive demand, before the subsequent section takes up the problem of supply always trying to catch up with fast-moving demand.

Demented Demand

The overwhelming consensus among housing economists and in public policy circles is that the excessively high housing prices in the Bay Area (and California more generally) are due to supply restrictions due to popular opposition to new building. The answer? Expand supply by cutting restrictions and unleashing developers to build more housing, when and where they want. Recent reports by California's Legislative Analyst and popular corporate consultant McKinsey Global Institute make the case in detail.[21]

Nevertheless, runaway housing costs are not primarily due to artificial supply shortage; the problem begins with massive bloat on the demand side. There are three main forces to consider in thinking about the demand for property and urban space in the Bay Area: the tech boom and the New Urbanism, high incomes and increased wealth at the top, and expansive credit and capital flows.

---

20 McMullen 2016.

21 Taylor 2015, Woetzel et al. 2016; also Metcalf 2015, Friedersdorf 2015, Hsieh & Moretti 2017, Moretti 2017. This is by no means a new argument in the Bay Area. See Frieden 1979. For a withering critique of Hsieh & Moretti, see Bronstein 2017b.

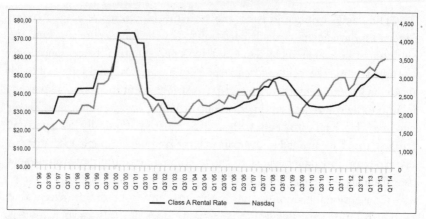

Figure 6.13: San Francisco Office Rent vs. Nasdaq, 1996–2013

Source: Paragon 2016.

The primary force driving the housing crisis, as well as high office rents, is rapid growth. The regional economy has been outrunning the rest of the country since the 1970s, and the latest upswing has been dramatic, adding well over $200 billion to GDP in five years, 2010–15. Not surprisingly, a massive surge in demand for all forms of urban property followed. The bulging demand for office space in the West Bay is a direct result of recent business expansion, augmented by the way the tech industry, finance, and business management love to cluster together in San Francisco and Silicon Valley (see chapters 1 and 2). Housing demand has followed the same logic, as business expansion creates new jobs, which have, in turn, attracted hundreds of thousands of new workers. Added to this is the New Urbanism of the last couple decades, and the degree to which so many people wish to live in an urbane environment, close to work, entertainment, and lively crowds of similarly inclined (and youthful) folks (see chapter 5).

The effect of economic booms on property demand can be illustrated by comparing San Francisco office rents to the NASDAQ stock index, which can stand in for demand for space by the tech economy. The correspondence between demand and price is strong, with both subject to dramatic peaks (fig. 6.13).[22]

The second big driver of intense housing demand is that the tech-led economy of the Bay Area is so rich. Local companies are raking in huge profits, millionaires are proliferating, and hundreds of thousands of skilled workers and managers are earning big salaries. It is hardly surprising that the

22 Especially since a financial index such as the NASDAQ is subject to more radical swings than the underlying tech economy.

nation's highest-income city has the country's most expensive housing, or that demand for housing in San Francisco and Silicon Valley is the most elevated, given that household incomes in the West Bay are nearly double the national average and higher than those in the East Bay (see chapter 7). But there is more than high *average* income at work here.

The new Gilded Age plays an essential role in exaggerating the bay region's housing crisis (chapter 3). Those with the most money drive the market, taking the best housing and bidding prices up, while the rest of the people get what's left over. As money has piled up at the top of the social order during the tech boom, both with 1 percenters and in the hands of a relatively large upper middle class of professionals, managers, and techies, it has allowed the well-to-do to overbid for houses and rentals, driving prices ever higher. Straight cash offers for million-dollar homes are not rare.

As their numbers have grown, members of the upper classes have spread out into former working-class neighborhoods, easily outcompeting average wage earners. This is the classic process of gentrification, and it works like falling dominoes. The rich grab elite spaces such as Pacific Heights and Palo Alto; the upper middle class fill up favored areas such as the Marina and Los Altos; those in the working middle class seeking more affordable places look to Oakland, San Bruno, or Richmond; and the rest of the working class and poor take the leavings or move out. Displacement proceeds apace.

The third major force bloating demand is excess capital and credit. That is, money is flowing into the Bay Area that goes beyond simply corporate earnings and individual incomes in a prosperous economy. This is the hardest part of the equation to get a handle on because of a paucity of data on regional capital flows and the way real estate investments can be hidden behind false-front companies in California. Nevertheless, there are indicators. Looking back at the dot-com bubble years of the 1990s, abnormal spikes in Bay Area tech stock values and venture capital investments were paralleled by rocketing property prices. This was clear, for example, in the exaggerated demand for office space at the time (fig. 6.13).[23]

This surely happened again in the boom of the 2010s. As noted in chapter 2, a flood of risk capital into the Bay Area led to the ridiculously high valuations of tech start-ups and unicorns. In the long stock market run-up of the decade, tech stocks have been price leaders, rising 21 percent in 2017 alone. And that is modest compared to money pouring into the high-flying FANGs, as seen in chapter 1. While those high valuations do not put money directly into anyone's pockets, high asset prices pump up the apparent wealth of tech

---

23   Walker 2006.

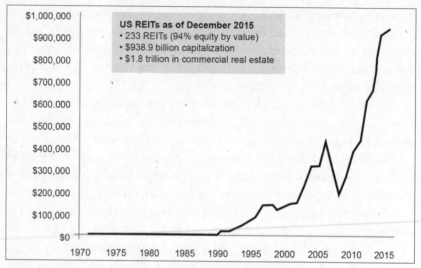

Figure 6.14: Growth of REITs in the United States, 1970–2015

Source: Knuth 2017.

owners and investors, not to mention the large numbers of upper managers and skilled workers with stock options. There is a well-known wealth effect on spending, and asset holders can cash out or borrow any time to buy property.

One of the key signs of capital rolling into local property markets is the explosion of REITs (real estate investment trusts) in the twenty-first century. REITs agglomerate funds from wealthy investors, which they put into real estate such as office towers and apartment high rises. The data on the growth of REITs in the United States is striking (fig. 6.14), indicating a host of wealth holders and fund managers with capital to burn because of a lack of alternative investment options and a growing proclivity for making profits out of land rents (see also chapter 2).[24]

REITs such as Boston Properties and Hudson Pacific moved into San Francisco in force during the Great Recession, elbowing aside traditional players such as Shorenstein Company as the leading owners of Downtown office buildings. Other REITs such as Alexandria and Prologis, which bought out original land owner Catellus, are big players in the development of Mission Bay. Residential REITs such as Essex Property Trust have gobbled up apartment buildings all around the Bay Area.[25]

---

24 On the growing attraction of rents over real investment, see Sayer 2015, Hudson 2015. On real estate as an investor's refuge from low returns, see Authers & Manibog 2017.

25 Dineen 2013, Knuth 2015, Kenney 2016, Cariaga 2016. On national trends, see Knuth 2017. For a list of largest REITs operating in the Bay Area, see http://www.bizjournals.com/sanfrancisco/subscriber-only/2015/12/11/reits.html.

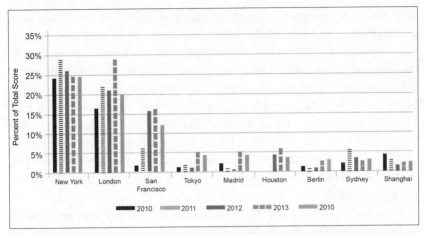

Figure 6.15: Ranking of World Cities for Real Estate Investment, 2010–2015
Source: http://www.afire.org/files/2015%20Data%20Charts.pdf.

There are other clues as to an influx of easy money into California and the Bay Area. A favorite means of parking riches for the world's wealthy is buying urban real estate. Acquiring pieds-à-terre in global cities, a practice that is well known in New York and London, is now appearing in San Francisco. A survey of global real estate investors shows San Francisco to be the third most popular target in the world. Wealthy Chinese, in particular, have put billions in newly won riches in hotels and residential properties in the United States, with about one-third of such money flowing into California. As the chief economist for the National Association of Realtors has observed, "Without a doubt foreign investors are pushing up the prices in Florida and California."[26]

Credit flows are another driver of housing demand, because homes are large purchases that households cannot normally afford without a loan. Mortgages are the principal form of loans to homebuyers. As is now well known, credit markets ran wild in the bubble of the early twenty-first century, allowing mortgage peddlers to issue millions of loans that were too large or too risky for most buyers; California was ground zero of that fiasco.[27] Is it possible that loose mortgage lending is a factor in the bloated property values of the 2010s?

Recent housing demand appears to be levitated by abundant mortgage credit. Persistently low interest rates, held down by the Federal Reserve

---

26 On New York and London, see Booth & Bengston 2016. On Chinese investment, see Agence France-Presse 2016, Munshi 2016, Badger 2017. Quotation in Badger 2017. See also examples in Selna 2010, Pender 2015a, 2016b.

27 All this is well documented by Shiller 2008, Sander 2008, and Ramirez 2013. See Bardhan & Walker 2011 for a summary. See also chapter 7.

Bank to keep a sluggish economy going since the Great Recession, have led to cheaper and larger mortgages. Although the volume of mortgage loans nationally is well below the peak of 2006, the amount of lending in California is striking; in 2014 the state garnered about $167 billion of a total of $631 billion in new and refi loans in the United States, or over 25 percent of the national total—double the state's share of population or income. That corresponds with California's inflated house prices, which are double the national average. While there is little sign of an excess of subprimes and other high-risk mortgages in the 2010s, at the very least abundant lending means that credit has not put a ceiling on the high values in the recent housing boom.[28]

It is harder to prove that more credit than necessary is flooding the state and exaggerating housing demand. One sign, however, is the lubrication of a new generation of mortgage lenders by outside investors. A good example is the $1 billion invested in online lender Social Finance in 2015, which used the money to move into home mortgages. Another indication is a surge in the fast-money operators that borrow from investors or banks to make riskier loans, which they resell to the Federal National Mortgage Association (Fannie Mae). California-based nonbank mortgage companies such as Quicken Loans, PennyMac, and AmeriHome Mortgage have risen like phoenixes to be among the nation's biggest originators in the 2010s. Such nonbank lenders were responsible for 35 percent of mortgages in 2005, fell to 10 percent of the U.S. total by 2010, and were back close to 50 percent of the market in 2016. Meanwhile, conventional banks, such as First Republic, are once again making jumbo loans with no down payments—a common practice in the last bubble.[29]

In short, the imprint of raging demand is all over contemporary property markets in the Bay Area, driving prices to unprecedented heights. Given the evidence, nothing could be more absurd than the argument made by certain economists that supply shortages are choking off regional growth. This gets causality fundamentally backwards. Housing costs do not drive the location of firms in the tech industry or other dynamic urban sectors; otherwise, cities would not exist and economic activity would spread out evenly across the country—which is evidently not the case. On the contrary, agglomeration

28 http://mortgage.nationwidelicensingsystem.org/about/Reports/2014-Annual-Mortgage-Report.pdf; http://www.urban.org/sites/default/files/publication/85991/november_chartbook_final_1.pdf. Kavanaugh 2016.
29 Pender 2015b, 2016c, Koren 2015. Several were founded by alumni of the defunct Countrywide Savings and IndyMac, the biggest purveyors of subprime mortgages in the last bubble.

economies and capital accumulation are the fount of urban growth, with housing costs as a residual.[30]

Yet even if excess demand is the primary driver of the property bubble, it must still be paired with supply shortages in order to generate the kinds of bursts in prices, gentrification, and displacement observed in the Bay Area. But where do those shortages come from? The essential source is that the supply of new urban space (land and buildings) does not respond well to price signals, no matter how high they go. Construction always plays catch-up, comes too late to halt the price bubble, and never seems to arrive at equilibrium with demand.

Sluggish Supply

If ever there was a market that does not conform to the simple models of the economists, the property market is it. Land and buildings are not like smartphones, where production can be geared up quickly to meet rising demand. Demand may shoot up, but the supply of urban space does not respond quickly and efficiently. On the one hand, urban land is a limited resource that can only be expanded at the city's edge through massive infrastructure investment or occasionally near the center through strategies such as bay fill. On the other hand, buildings are huge objects whose production is slow and expensive—all the more so as they get bigger and go higher.

As a consequence, property markets are rarely at equilibrium, as assumed in conventional models of supply and demand. They are easily knocked out of kilter by rapid change, and they follow a cyclic pattern of ups and downs in prices and construction activity that is typically more exaggerated than general business cycles. Builders try to catch up with demand, but there is normally a long lag time in construction, and sometimes it even overshoots demand. In the long run, supply and demand will tend to match up, but not by simply repeating the same building forms, as styles and densities change over time (see chapter 7). None of this has anything to do with local regulations or popular opposition, which get so much of the blame for poor supply response in conventional economic models.[31]

This section looks at four dimensions of supply and market failure: short-term shortfall during an upswing, lagged response over several years, the

---

30 On the theory of urban economies, see Storper 2013, Walker 2016, and other sources cited in chapters 1 and 2. For a trenchant critique of Hsieh & Moretti's (2017) ridiculous figures on lost growth, see Bronstein 2017b.

31 The dramatically cyclic nature of building has been known at least since the work of Kuznets 1930, Hoyt 1933, and Burns 1934.

problems created by the cyclic nature of supply, and long-term trends in housing over several cycles.

★   ★   ★

A short-term view of supply considers only one upswing of a property cycle, normally about five to eight years. It can be very misleading because demand in boom times grows so much faster than builders can respond. This is a common error that leads to panicky reactions of the kind observed recently in the Bay Area by advocates of the build-anything-anywhere school of thought represented by the YIMBY movement (discussed in the next section).

How does this work? As business revives from a recession, a new cycle begins, and demand for space—whether office, industrial, commercial, or residential—ticks up. At first, excess space from the last downturn has to be absorbed, which delays new building; then, as vacancy rates decline, prices start their upward course as businesses and households bid for the remaining space. As demand keeps rising, bidding gets more intense against a limited supply of buildings or units, and prices may shoot up even more rapidly, resulting in exaggerated values at the peak of the boom.

As price signals kick in, developers and builders finally spring into action, but their response is always delayed because new building takes so much time. Land must be purchased, plans and designs drawn up, and permits secured. Then, too, financing has to be arranged, contractors assembled, and production put in motion. Moreover, large developments require connection to urban infrastructure of roads, water, and power systems, which takes coordination with utilities and city agencies. As a result, building generally lags business cycles by at least a year or two, and often much longer. This time lag exists quite apart from any delays in obtaining permits or planning approval—which get far too much of the blame for slow supply response.[32]

Three other characteristics of housing markets are likely to exaggerate the increase in prices during an upswing. One is that existing units come on the market slowly because households do not move that often—and if rents are rising fast, they cling to existing apartments and leases even more firmly. A small percentage of houses or rentals come on the market in any year, and in the Bay Area in recent years the vacancy rates have fallen to negligible levels for single-family homes and a scant 2–3 percent for apartments. This scarcity creates a supply "bottleneck" that squeezes prices, like the narrow opening on a tube of toothpaste. Even though prices may eventually readjust to a long-term trend that is closer to overall economic growth, the short-term price and

---

32 Hoyt 1933, https://www.census.gov/construction/nrc/lengthoftime.html.

vacancy squeeze hits buyers and tenants hard and can lead to massive social disruption, as in the case of the Bay Area in the 2010s.[33]

Another aspect to short-term supply response is landlord intervention and speculation. Unlike the myth of the free market, landlords are not passive suppliers of housing; they intervene to work things to their advantage. On the one hand, they break leases and evict tenants so they can raise rents or sell to those who can pay more; this unsavory practice tends to free up rental units faster at the upper end of the market but reduce the supply at the low end. Similarly, investors jump in to buy buildings in an upswing, evict tenants, and release or resell to those who can pay more. Some speculative landlords and investors will even leave buildings empty for long periods in order to realize the most gain by not entering into long-term leases too soon in the bubble; this reduces overall supply. In the 2010s, a new kind of speculative landlord entered the picture, thanks to Airbnb, evicting long-term tenants in order list their apartments for more lucrative short-term vacation rentals. Such commercial vacation rentals allowed speculators to effectively take around two thousand apartments out of the rental market through the boom years.[34]

A third factor that impedes rapid response to demand is the difficulty of securing building sites in densely built-up parts of the metropolis. In order to build, plots must be found, purchased, cleared of former uses, and building permits secured. The difficulty is magnified where large projects are concerned and a developer must deal with a diverse array of sellers and more complex planning approvals. The result is greater short-term pressure on prices in dense areas, as can be seen in comparing office space rents in Downtown San Francisco against Silicon Valley, which is more spread out; both have experience major price spikes, but San Francisco's are worse (fig. 6.16). In today's market, the tilt toward the metropolitan center is compounding the price spike, in contrast to the 1950s when most people wanted to move to the suburbs and builders were able to provide new housing more easily where demand was highest at the urban fringe.

★   ★   ★

The next step in evaluating supply response is to move beyond the short-term spike in prices as a boom takes off and to look at midrange response by builders. Given a few years, the supply of housing, offices, and commercial space

---

33 Ng 2016.
34 On speculative landlords, see Kwong 2014. On misuse of Airbnb listings, see Barmann 2015. When more effective regulations took hold in 2018, the number of short-term listings dropped by half, proving critics of commercial operators right. Said 2018.

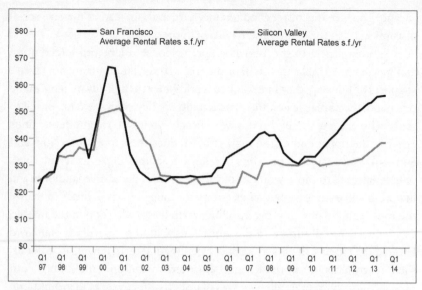

Figure 6.16: Office Rents in San Francisco & Silicon Valley, 1997–2014
Source: Roose 2014.

does, indeed, expand. So how has supply behaved in the boom of the 2010s in the Bay Area? As it turns out, not too badly.

Office building was the quickest to respond and has been on the upswing for several years. Rising prices and vacancy rates falling into single digits triggered a slew of new projects as early as 2012. In San Francisco, 4.5 million square feet of floor space were under construction in 2015, and most of that hit the market by 2017, when another 6.6 million square feet were in the pipeline. Those figures add to a base of about 75 million square feet in the Downtown area.[35]

In Silicon Valley, 5.5 million square feet were under construction in mid-2016 on a base of 70 million square feet in Santa Clara County. By contrast, the East Bay saw only a modest amount of new office construction, given lower demand and a backlog of vacancies. Oakland's total office space amounted to 24 million square feet and the 680 corridor about 28 million square feet in 2016.[36]

Nationally, new home construction in the upswing was relatively sluggish in the 2010s, given the collapse of the home purchase market in the Great Recession (fig. 6.17). The foreclosure crisis threw millions of homes onto

35 Li 2017, Dineen 2017.
36 Schiada 2016. Total office space of all classes around the nine-county Bay Area is around four hundred million square feet. San Francisco has roughly half the Class A space in the Bay Area but only one-fifth of total office space. Seifel 2008.

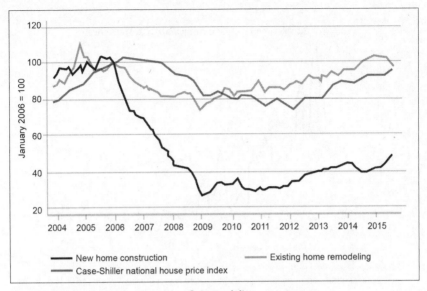

Figure 6.17: U.S. Home Construction & Remodeling, 2004–2015

Source: Cookson 2016.

the market, many developers went belly-up, and demand in the bottom half of the market never recovered from the blow. Tens of thousands of former working-class homes were gobbled up by speculative investors and switched over to rentals.

Nevertheless, Silicon Valley had one of the best recoveries from the Great Recession in single-family home construction and remodeling in the country. The San Francisco–Oakland metro area did less well, although remodeling was robust, thanks to former working-class houses being sold to higher-class buyers with the money to refurbish their homes (fig. 6.18).

More important than house construction was apartment construction, as more households sought to rent rather than buy. The building of multiple units development recovered smartly and was roaring by the middle of the decade. In the central Bay Area, the rental housing stock grew by over four thousand units per year in 2014 and 2015 and over nine thousand in 2016.[37] (fig. 6.19).

In terms of total units added to the housing stock in the 2010s, the Bay Area comes out in the middle of the pack among large U.S. cities. San Francisco–Oakland metro (the Central Bay Area) built about two thousand units per million residents in 2016. Some much-larger metros, such as New York, Los

---

37 https://sf.curbed.com/2016/8/10/12430444/sf-apartment-construction-rate-high-housing.

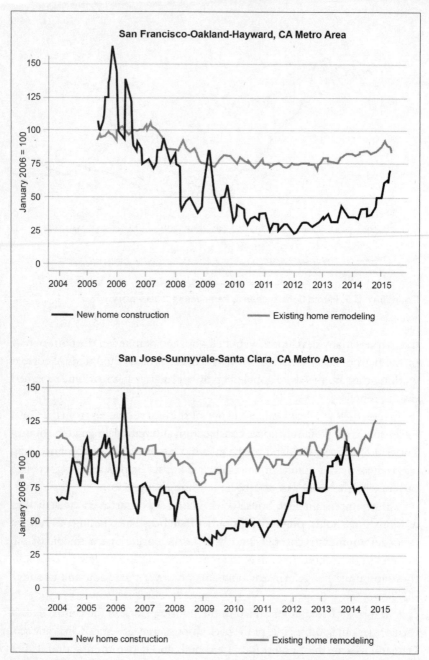

Figure 6.18: House Construction and Remodeling, 2004–2016, San Francisco & San Jose Metro Areas
Source: Cookson 2016.

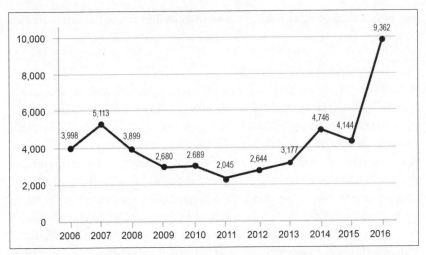

Figure 6.19: New Apartment Units, San Francisco–Oakland Metro Area, 2006–2016
Source: Otet 2016.

Angeles, and Chicago, did much worse; and two metro areas roughly comparable in size, Phoenix and Boston, also did worse. San Jose metro (Silicon Valley), which built around three thousand units per million people, outperformed all the larger cities just listed, plus San Diego and Atlanta, and did as well as Seattle and Washington, DC. A handful of cities such as Houston, Austin and Denver beat the band—but who would defend all the unbridled building in the lowlands of Houston after Hurricane Harvey?[38]

It is clear, furthermore, that lack of permit approvals is not the reason for laggard supply response; the delay comes from the time needed to actually put permitted buildings up. As one report put it, "spikes in permitting activity are echoed by spikes in new construction three to five years later." Although rents leveled off in the city by 2016, building was still accelerating, as one would expect. Yet headlines continued to cry wolf, as if somehow construction must catch up instantly and completely. This is wishful thinking, especially given the bloated state of demand.[39]

In short, the numbers on new construction do not support the conservative notion that housing supply is uniquely unresponsive in the Bay Area. In fact, out in the Sacramento and Stockton metro areas, where permits are usually much easier to obtain and building takes less time, construction has been slow to recover from the Great Recession because the bottom fell

---

38 Figures from chart on twenty top cities for new apartments in Otet 2016.

39 Quote from SPUR 2012. On the leveling off of prices, see Carmiel 2016, Richter 2016. A recent report from UCLA confirms the futility of building your way out of the current housing crisis. Fimrite 2017.

out of housing demand after the mass foreclosures in the last bust (see also chapter 7).[40]

★ ★ ★

A third facet of the supply problem is the cyclic nature of demand and supply. Ironically, given the shortfall of supply in boom times, building almost always overshoots the mark at the peak of the cycle. In the upswing, builders scramble to catch up with demand, then everyone jumps in hoping to beat the pack; no one knows when the market will turn, so collectively they end up creating too much office space and too many housing units. This bandwagon effect is made worse by swings in finance. Building takes a huge amount of credit, as developers borrow too much in hopes of making a killing and lenders lend too much in their enthusiasm to cash in on the boom; as a result, financial bubbles normally exaggerate the peaks of building booms—and the crashes in property values that regularly follow.

The problem of overshoot has plagued property markets since the founding of the United States, whether building too many canals in the 1830s or selling too many speculative lots in the Florida Land Boom of the 1920s. A famous icon of overshoot is the Empire State Building, planned to catch the office wave of the 1920s but finished in the midst of the Great Depression in 1931 and taking years to fill up with tenants. The overbuilding of single-family houses in the mortgage bubble of the 2000s is another clear case, but how quickly people forget.[41]

The normal property cycle thus generates undersupply relative to fast-rising demand in the upswing and oversupply after the peak on the downside of the boom. In the San Francisco office market, for example, vacancies were starting to rise by late 2016; yet there were still millions of square feet due to open in 2017 through 2021. When the good times turn sour, and too many buildings come on line, vacancies rise and prices fall back to earth. Falling prices and inability to sell surplus houses or lease excess office space will bankrupt some developers and builders and drive investors away for the duration of the slump. This impedes further supply expansion and the makes the recovery of building slower in the next upswing, until oversupply is absorbed and developers pull themselves together again. Then the whole crazy process takes off once more.[42]

In short, the property cycle is an inefficient way to organize the long-term supply of housing and urban building. Instead of a steady growth in

---

40 On the slow recovery of construction in Sacramento and Stockton, see Otet 2017.
41 The problem of overshoot was first pointed out in the 1930s by Hoyt 1933 and Sakolski 1932.
42 On signs of oversupply in San Francisco offices, see Li 2017.

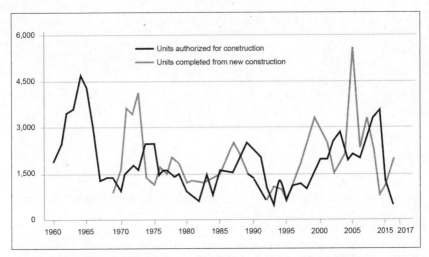

Figure 6.20: Housing Construction in San Francisco (City), 1960–2012

Source: SPUR 2012.

supply, the market generates a series of peaks and troughs, which zigzag around some long-term trend. The vagaries of the building cycle make it difficult to discern just how well supply is responding to demand in the longer term. The paths of housing construction in San Francisco illustrates the dramatic ups and downs of the market (fig. 6.20; see also figure 6.16 on offices, above). In general, the response to every period of economic growth has been robust. The 1960s were particularly favorable, but building in the 2010s hit peaks higher than that supposedly golden age of housing.

An important caveat on all discussions of housing supply is that the raw quantity of new building is not the necessarily the most important aspect of market performance. Just as important is the question: who is the housing for? In an ideal market, builders ought to supply housing up and down the range of prices and incomes; but they are, in fact, biased toward building units for the well-to-do because profits are higher per unit. In present circumstances, where demand is bloated at the top and developers are more in the thrall of financial returns, the upward tilt of housing supply is even worse. Indeed, one of the few times that large developers ever targeted working-class buyers was the postwar Golden Age, when the working middle class had good wages and mortgages were abundant and cheap—which brings us now to the very long-term view.[43]

★   ★   ★

---

43   On the history of low-income housing development in San Francisco, see Groth 1994, Howell 2015.

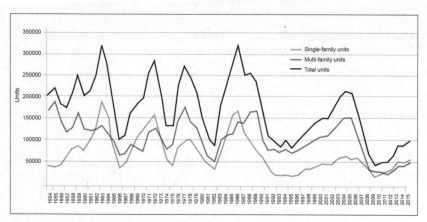

Figure 6.21: California Housing Construction, 1954–2016

Source: Construction Industry Research Board, http://www.mychf.org/
uploads/5/1/5/0/51506457/chart_pic_2016.png.

At the time scale of fifty to seventy-five years, theories about failures of supply are much harder to prove. A common accusation is that the state of California has not kept up with long-term population growth, and there is some truth to this. The state ranks forty-ninth in housing units per capita. But when did it start falling behind and what exactly has gone wrong? Was it really due to popular opposition to new housing, the explanation favored by conservative commentators? Not very likely.

There is a break point around 1970 when California housing prices start to outrun the rest of the country. How to explain this is not obvious. Because 1970 corresponds with the beginning of the era of strong environmental regulation and land conservation, first in the Bay Area and then spreading to Southern California, many critics attribute the price climb to a supply bottleneck caused by environmentalists and other local opposition to building, or what are called "NIMBYs" (not in my backyard).[44]

Looking at the data on housing construction rather than prices, however, one finds no sign of a marked slowdown circa 1970. On the contrary, construction falls off considerably in the 1990s and the decades that follow, even in the midst of the great housing bubble. The key breakpoint in housing supply appears to be 1990, not 1970 (fig. 6.21).[45]

Something has gone haywire since 1990. On the supply side, the drop-off of multiple units (apartments and condos) is striking and mostly explains the

---

44 McKinsey 2016, LAO 2015, Freiden 1971.
45 National data do not, however, show the same slowdown in the early twenty-first century as in California. Wissoker 2016, p. 7, fig. 2.

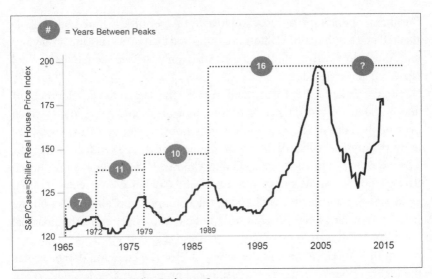

Figure 6.22: U.S. House Price Cycles, 1965–2015

Source: McLaughlin 2015. (Based on Case-Shiller index).

reduced number of housing units built. This might be due to the difficulty of rebuilding the metropolis at a higher density as it grows more populous—which might be ascribed to popular opposition (see below) or to changes in the homebuilding industry brought on by financialization: greater concentration in large firms, more pursuit of short-term financial targets, and self-generated lending to keep up sales of overpriced homes in the bubble of the early twenty-first century.[46]

The sea change in housing prices corresponds even more strongly to developments on the demand side. Notably, price cycles after that point are out of all proportion to the earlier postwar era, as shown by the Case-Shiller house purchase price index of the last fifty years (fig. 6.22). This is a national phenomenon, which corresponds to two critical political economic shifts already discussed in this book. One is the rapid growth in inequality, which has put too much money in the hands of the upper classes who are the main buyers of single-family houses. The other is the growth of finance in relation to industry and the resulting excesses of credit and free-floating capital.

The leading role of California in these developments could well explain the even more exaggerated prices and price cycles in the Golden State. Inequality was presented in chapter 3, but the development of fast finance deserves further consideration. Mortgage markets first began to run wild in the 1980s. At that time, Michael Milken of the investment bank Drexel

---

46 Wissoker 2016. On financialization of housing in general, see Davis 2009.

Burnham, operating from Rodeo Drive in LA, set off the junk bond bubble that inflated a number of California savings and loans, such as Lincoln Savings and American Savings, to humungous sizes, only to have them burst and collapse late in the decade.

In the wake of that fiasco, California led the way in the development of another form of fast finance, subprime mortgages and Alt-A loans, which became the coin of the realm in the long housing run-up of the 1990s and early twenty-first century. Many of the key mortgage lenders in that disaster were based in California, such as Countrywide Savings, Long Beach Savings (bought by Washington Mutual), and Golden West Savings (bought by Wachovia). Backed by Wall Street, they pumped up California's housing market to absurd heights before that bubble, too, deflated in the financial mortgage bond meltdown of 2007–8 (see also chapter 7).[47]

In sum, a critical look at the supply side of the equation demonstrates the highly imperfect nature of housing and property markets. They do not respond in a simple way to price signals and, therefore, will resist simplistic solutions to releasing more supply—as if it were a gusher waiting to happen if one just drills in the right place. Supply does, of course, come on line in response to rising prices, but it does so with considerable time lag and over jagged cycles that make easy judgments about longer trends a risky proposition. Yet easy judgments and simplistic solutions are the order of the day, so it is necessary to consider the politics of housing policy and the debates shaking the Bay Area to its core today.

Popular Resistance to a Broken Housing Market

The housing crisis of the 2010s in the Bay Area has made life miserable for hundreds of thousands of households, helped to rearrange the geography of the city, and prompted a huge amount of popular resistance. People are looking for answers, popular movements have sprung up, and political leaders have responded with various kinds of public policies. What is curious, however, is how often those who are being hurt by the injustices of the market are blamed for the housing crisis and how much political opposition is mobilized against them, when the popular resistance is more often right than wrong in its prescriptions to protect ordinary households from the depredations of developers and landlords.[48]

---

47 Robinson 1990, Stein 1992, Shiller 2008, Sanders 2008, Bardhan & Walker 2011.
48 For a similar critique of New York City's policies and defense of popular measures, see Capelle 2017. Both the policies and the criticisms resonate across the country, as shown by the *New York Times* publishing boilerplate attacks on popular inference with an idealized housing market by Berkeley economist Enrico Moretti. Hsieh & Moretti 2017.

Housing is the foundation of urban life, and it is no surprise that people fight for their homes, their neighborhoods, and cities they know and love. Housing is so essential to everyone's well-being that one can hardly expect people to simply accept the judgment of the market as to who should live where and how much they should pay to have a roof over their heads. The struggle over urban space is unavoidable, and the Bay Area, especially San Francisco, is hallowed ground for generations of urban dwellers who have fought for their place in the city. This section reviews past housing movements before tackling the current wave of resistance and policy conflicts at the local, regional, and state level.

★   ★   ★

Housing struggles have repeatedly lit up the Bay Area and been a pillar of local politics. Local housing advocates were early supporters of public housing in the 1930s and built the first integrated public housing project in the United States in Marin City. The New Deal mortgage finance programs became a pillar of the state's postwar suburbanization and expansion of working-class home ownership (see chapter 7). But they also solidified white-only neighborhoods, which the civil rights movement fought for years, finally winning open housing legislation in 1963, sponsored by Oakland's Byron Rumford. In a notorious moment of white backlash, that law was overturned by popular referendum in 1964 (which was then thrown out by the state Supreme Court).[49]

Another notorious housing war of the 1960s and '70s was over the urban renewal projects sweeping across the central bay cities, erasing much of the black Fillmore District, West Oakland, and South Richmond. Thousands of housing units were demolished and only about half as many built anew. These battles helped overturn the political order of San Francisco and Oakland. Huge swaths of South of Market were lost in San Francisco, and the Mission District, Tenderloin, and Chinatown were all under threat. Chinatown and the old Barbary Coast were saved by zoning limits on office expansion northward, while the Tenderloin was protected by controls on conversion of buildings to tourist hotels. At the same time, a new set of nonprofit housing developers arose that would build thousands of apartments and refurbish dozens of hotels for low-income occupancy.[50]

Rent control was also in the forefront of housing struggles in the late 1970s, with notable successes in Berkeley, San Francisco, and Santa Monica in

---

49   Casstevens 1967, Freund 2007, Brilliant 2010, Miller 2010.
50   Hartman 1984 (2002), Self 2003, Brahinsky 2011, Howell 2015.

Southern California (Oakland and San Jose have very weak rent control). But the landlord associations mobilized to halt any further such impiousness, following on their success in detaxing real property under Proposition 13 in 1978 (see chapter 10). They garnered the Ellis Act in 1985 and Costa-Hawkins Act in 1995, blocking further local rent control, ending commercial controls, and allowing owners to defenestrate tenants wholesale for sell-offs. That reversal of rent control is a touchstone of recent tenant movements.[51]

Nevertheless, San Francisco housing activists achieved some notable victories in the 1980s, led by Proposition M's limits on permits for office buildings. Less well known were aspects of Prop. M and related city legislation that protected residential areas and charged new fees on office development that could be channeled into housing and neighborhood improvements. This was followed in 1992 by the first inclusionary housing ordinance, requiring a 10 percent "set-aside" of units for low-income renters in order to get a permit for a new development.[52]

The 1990s ushered in two threats to renters, the dot-com bubble and Clinton administration public housing policies. The latter set in motion intense conflicts between negligent and heavy-handed public housing agencies in San Francisco, Oakland, and Richmond and their tenants, heightened by misguided federal efforts to improve and disperse public housing while privatizing new projects. Ad hoc tenants' groups formed and were aided by militant organizations such as the Eviction Defense Network, but hundreds of low-income families lost their homes in the process.[53]

The dot-com boom led to a housing crunch, as tech companies expanded into San Francisco's South of Market, young techies moved into converted condos and warehouse lofts, and rents spiked in a hail of property investment (see chapter 5). The young and hip took over the Valencia Street corridor in the working-class Mission. Displaced tenants, including Anglo artists and Latino workers, organized rapidly to hold back the tide, and thanks to the work of groups such as the Mission Housing Development Corporation and Mission Anti-Displacement Coalition, the district held on to its character. In addition, the city's voters passed a $100 million bond issue for low-income housing, the first of its kind in the country, in a campaign led by the CCHO (Council for Community Housing Organizations), representing the nonprofit housing movement.[54]

51 Slater 1998, Rosen & Sullivan 2012.
52 Walker 1998, Rosen & Sullivan 2012.
53 Tracy 2014.
54 Solnit 2001, Beitel 2011, Rosen & Sullivan 2012, Tracy 2014, Howell 2015, Stehlin 2015.

The Millennium brought another round of political upheaval. In San Francisco, the prodevelopment regime overseen by Mayor Willie Brown ran into a wall with the recession and the elections of 2000, in which the Left gained a majority on the Board of Supervisors. They were able to tamp down on the worst planning abuses and pass stronger inclusionary housing rules (20 percent low income) before the economy heated up again. Meanwhile in Oakland, Jerry Brown—former and future governor—took the helm from 1999 to 2007 and rode the revival of that city full tilt with his 10K housing plan. Mayor Brown and the city's elite didn't give a damn who moved into the new housing and resolutely refused to legislate inclusionary housing.[55]

But Oakland's popular housing rights movement was getting organized, finally securing the first eviction controls with Measure EE in 2002 and low-income set-asides from city government. The movement also used direct action to stop hundreds of evictions and foreclosures. It was led by Just Cause, a tenants' rights group, which merged in 2010 with St. Peter's Housing Committee in San Francisco's Mission District to create a cross-bay organization called Causa Justa::Just Cause, which was later joined by POWER, or People Organized to Win Employment Rights. The Alliance of Californians for Community Empowerment (ACCE) has also been active in the city.[56]

★ ★ ★

The housing bubble of the 2010s sparked the latest round of protests. One element that attracted a lot of national attention was blockading the buses transporting thousands of tech workers from San Francisco homes to jobs in Silicon Valley—the so-called "Google Buses." The huge, unmarked buses with tinted windows became popular symbols of the takeover of the city by the tech industry and its well-paid workers—even though most techies work in the city itself. Another twist to the movement was the use of online maps to highlight the history of Ellis Act evictions and Google bus routes through San Francisco. Activists succeeded in getting the city government to charge the buses for using Muni stops and helped the drivers of those buses to unionize.[57]

The CCHO, San Francisco Tenants Union, and other groups demanded stronger rent and eviction controls, more inclusionary housing, and more money for low-cost housing. They won several victories in San Francisco but

55   Solnit 2001, Carlsson 2004, Beitel 2011, Tracy 2014. SF's inclusionary housing act was softened again in 2010 under Mayor Gavin Newsom. Rosen & Sullivan 2012. For more on local politics, see chapter 10.
56   Causa Justa::Just Cause 2014.
57   On tech buses, see Solnit 2013. For maps, see http://sfnewdevelopments.com/beautiful-map-of-tech-shuttle-bus-routes-from-san-francisco-to-silicon-valley/.

were also turned back on other proposals. One notable success was a 2016 popular vote to raise the inclusionary housing rate to 25 percent—though it was subsequently whittled down to 18 percent in negotiations among the Board of Supervisors. Inclusionary housing percentages are a valuable tool to increase the number of lower-rent units, though they have to piggyback on market-rate projects and the definition of "moderate income" households is often stretched too far. Another victory was getting the city to limit Airbnb rentals to sixty days, curbing abuse by commercial landlords. The most controversial proposal was a call for a moratorium on new building in the Mission District, on the argument that new market-rate units set a higher rent standard that would prompt further gentrification of the neighborhood; that proposal failed at the polls. Oakland voters passed Measure JJ in 2016, organized by an alliance called the Committee to Protect Oakland Renters. Berkeley imposed taxes on short-term Airbnb rentals. Meanwhile, new rent control proposals popped up in cities around the region, passing in Mountain View, Pacifica, and Richmond and beaten back in Santa Rosa, Alameda, and San Mateo.[58]

Rent and eviction controls are excellent local policies because they slow down the rate of change in the overheated market of a boom and clamp down on speculators. Against the argument that rent control freezes the market at artificial price levels, good rent control ordinances—as in Berkeley—allow yearly rent increases and higher rents to repay improvements, while limiting move-ins and sublets, and they have an oversight board and means of appeal. Despite intense landlord opposition, Berkeley's rental housing market works very well, but it does not cover all rental units and cannot stop the overall rise in rents over time.[59]

These efforts to control housing markets are generally opposed by those who believe that the solution to the housing crisis is to build more. The intellectual purveyors of this position could be found in the Legislative Analyst's Office, business consultants McKinsey Global Institute, and the nonprofit group San Francisco Planning and Urban Research (SPUR). They offer some reasonable suggestions, such as filling empty lots, building higher density near transit, and making it easier for homeowners to add "in-law" apartments.

---

58 On Airbnb rules, see Barba 2017, Zahniser 2015. For favorable assessments of San Francisco's popular housing proposals, see Rosen & Sullivan 2012 and CHPC 2014. Some elements of the Mission ballot measure were adopted by the supervisors later. On Oakland, see Causa Justa::Just Cause 2014. On new rent control ordinances, see Streitfield 2016a, Gutierrez 2016, Singh 2017.

59 On the benefits of preserving low-cost housing by rent control and inclusionary housing, see Zuk & Chapple 2016.

Their position is, nevertheless, based on a conventional faith in market solutions that does not accord with the reality of how housing operates.[60]

The build-at-all-costs banner has been picked up and promoted by a new group who oppose all restrictions on building. They adopted the provocative name BARF (Bay Area Renters' Federation) and quickly became a force in San Francisco politics, fighting against the 25 percent inclusionary proposal and the Mission moratorium. Their slogan that NIMBYism is running amok in the Bay Area proved so effective the movement spread around California under the generic label, the "YIMBYs" (yes in my backyard). The YIMBYs have the support of developers and conservatives, as one might expect, but also attract libertarians opposed all government restrictions on principle and naive techies and young people fed up with the housing crisis.[61]

The fact is, however, that most of the essential policies needed to reform the housing market cannot be done by local governments. They cannot stop the tech boom; nor can they seriously tax the rich, the corporations, and real estate; nor can they reduce the baleful influence of fast finance on mortgages. Can that, perhaps, be achieved at the regional or state level?

★　★　★

One sign of concern is the effort of the state, regional authorities, business groups, planning advocates, and environmentalists to promote more high-density developments linked to public transit and major roadways in the bay region. A focus of this effort is the attempt to come up with a comprehensive "Plan Bay Area 2040" by ABAG (Association of Bay Area Governments) and MTC (Metropolitan Transportation Commission)—in accordance with the state's energy conservation policy (SB 375) (see chapter 8). The drafts of Plan Bay Area have done much to reveal glaring holes in regional housing policy. First, MTC is awash in federal funds for transportation, but the feds give only peanuts for housing—indeed, federal housing funds have dropped precipitously in recent years. Second, Plan Bay Area seeks to channel development into existing high-density cores, while ignoring low-density enclaves such as Lafayette and Palo Alto.[62]

In 2017, MTC convened a regional committee on housing, CASA (Committee to House the Bay Area) to try to reach some kind of political consensus on

---

60　See citations at footnote 42.

61　On YIMBYs, Narefsky 2017, Bronstein 2017a, Chen 2017. To their credit, the YIMBYs also sued the suburb of Lafayette to open up its housing, but the lawsuit failed because the courts support the right of local governments to regulate land use (which is granted by the state). Swan 2016.

62　ABAG & MTC 2017.

housing strategies. Paid for by the state Transportation Commission and the San Francisco Foundation, the committee brought together mayors, planners, developers, and scholars. Their task is daunting. Regional authorities have relatively little power to impose solutions on local governments, along with their lack of serious money for affordable housing. MTC is a dubious candidate for regional planner, given its devotion to transportation over all other considerations (see chapter 7).

While so much attention has been focused on popular opposition to new condos and apartments by popular movements in San Francisco, Oakland, and other cities, there has been surprisingly little attention to another kind of barrier: municipal and zoning boundaries around elite housing enclaves, such as Atherton and Danville. Wealthy enclaves from Mill Valley to Orinda occupy something like a fifth of all prime urban land in the Bay Area, and they systematically oppose new developments that increase density and bring in lower-class households.[63]

There is a logic to local control of land use, of course. The reality of spatial interaction in urban environments is that one person's actions affect others all around, and communities try to control what goes on around them. Such "neighborhood effects" are an irreducible element in housing markets and another reason why housing does not conform to the standard model of fluid supply and demand. Indeed, such effects are what local government and politics in the United States are all about: collective governance of local geography. So it is inevitable that building decisions are controversial and often require lengthy political negotiations. This logic applies equally to central city neighborhoods fighting for their place in the city and to suburban jurisdictions.

But there is a crucial difference between the two kinds of local politics. The well-to-do are able to cordon off exclusive retreats that protect their class and race privileges very effectively; they are the biggest NIMBYs of all—as even YIMBY activists recognize. Working-class residents, by contrast, have rarely been able to create jurisdictions that they dominate, and their neighborhoods in big cities like Oakland are almost always the weakest politically. The argument that opposition from such neighborhoods is the chief cause of malfunctioning housing markets is absurd.[64]

Two final comments on regional markets are in order. Political barriers to development are much less at the urban fringe, where fewer people live and politics are more in flux, which is why suburban growth is so popular with

---

63 On elite enclaves, see Marcuse 1997, Blakely & Snyder 1997, Fogelson 2005, Hirt 2014, Cox 2015.
64 See, e.g., Chen 2017.

developers. Contrary to what some critics of Bay Area housing restrictions say, there are almost no social restraints on building at the outer fringes of metropolitan area (see chapter 7).[65]

Lastly, not all restraints on suburban building are political. There are the material constraints of topography and hydrology, such as the bay, ocean, and rivers, which is why the Bay Area does not look like the LA basin. The bay region's many hills are also not amenable to mass construction, making it profitable only for low-density, high-value homes. This is why the common argument that the large open spaces of the Bay Area cause higher property values is bogus.[66]

★ ★ ★

As the battle over housing heated up, it moved to the state level, where efforts to intervene in California's housing crisis ramped up in 2016. One new law that year made it easier to convert spare rooms or garages into in-law apartments, following the lead of many cities. This is a fine idea, as long as it is not abused to create substandard units, but the state failed to provide more funds to local governments for housing inspections. A thoroughly misconceived solution was Governor Brown's idea of fast-tracking projects by weakening environmental and other necessary reviews of new developments, which went down to defeat that year.[67]

But the legislature came back with a bundle of new bills in the 2017 session, fifteen of which were signed into law by the governor. They are a decidedly mixed bag. On the positive side, some aimed to increase funding for low-income housing, both by adding new developer fees and by putting a $4 billion bond measure on the ballot in 2018. Others made it easier for local governments to insist on set-asides for low-income renters in new apartment complexes and for foundations to buy older buildings to keep such renters in their homes. Yet others aimed to encourage local governments to improve plans for more housing and provide financial incentives to cities to plan for new developments and grants to cover costs of environmental reviews. Some encouraged higher-density zones near transit hubs and gave cash incentives for it.[68]

---

65 Cox 2016a & b. Wendell Cox overlooks everything said here about supply restraints; even worse, he equates housing demand in morbid economies such as Cleveland and Detroit with those in California cities.

66 Santos et al. 2014.

67 Dineen 2016.

68 Quoted in Murphy & Tolan 2017. Dillon 2017. Transit hub developments have been fought by local residents for both good and bad reasons; the good reasons are how such projects contribute to gentrification by introducing higher-income housing in the name of higher density and transit planning.

Ironically, the most dubious legislation came out of the progressive strongholds of San Francisco and the East Bay. State Senator Nancy Skinner's bills streamline local approval of building permits, a standard bromide beloved of business, and her statement at the bill's signing mouthed the YIMBY line of the need to "tackle the NIMBY obstacles that keep housing from being built." A companion bill makes it easier for developers to prove "bad faith" on the part of local officials and hits local governments with a stiff fine if they refuse a court order to allow development. San Francisco senator Scott Wiener's bill, SB 35, forces local jurisdictions to meet their fair share targets of regional housing growth—something that housing justice advocates have been trying to achieve since the 1970s—but does so without regard to the stark differences between heavily impacted central cities and exclusionary suburbs.

Despite the cheering among the Bay Area's political leaders such as Mayor Libby Schaaf of Oakland and Carl Guardino, chair of the Silicon Valley Manufacturers Group, there are good reasons to criticize the new legislation. More funds for housing is a good thing, but the amount of money is an order of magnitude less than what is actually needed for low-income housing around the state. While efforts to build more housing restrictive enclaves is welcome, the new laws give developers and their allies too much power to beat back legitimate objections to gentrification, bad plans, and ugly designs. They also allow end runs around the California Environmental Quality Act, a pillar of environmental protection from damaging development for the last fifty years.[69]

Furthermore, two old skeletons in the housing closet have not been touched. One is Proposition 13, which gutted property taxes in 1978, forcing local governments to make up the lost revenues by imposing higher development fees and favoring shopping centers over housing in their plans. Another is the Costa-Hawkins Act's suppression of local rent control on single-family homes, rental units built after 1995, and vacancies. A bill to do that never made it out of committee, so ACCE started gathering signatures to put a proposition on the state ballot in 2018, called the Affordable Housing Act, which would overturn Costa-Hawkins and allow local rent control across the state once more. One can only hope that it succeeds.[70]

Conclusion

The housing crisis in the Bay Area—and in big cities around the world—is a predictable result of how property markets work in a capitalist economy; they

---

69 For a critique of the new laws, see Bronstein 2017c.
70 Brinklow 2017.

do not have the flexibility to adapt rapidly, and they are subject to big swings in prices, investment, and construction activity. Housing supply simply cannot respond quickly enough to relieve the steam in the boiler, leading to runaway prices, rampant speculation, and a general sense of crisis. In fact, the Bay Area is a worst-case scenario for housing market failure: a raging economic boom inflamed by enormous enrichment, egregious inequality, and financial bloat. Even as housing supply responds to price signals, developers build for the upper classes, not the people most adversely affected by the crisis.

The present crisis is not only a temporal but a spatial/geographic problem, because the bay metropolis is being dramatically rearranged by the same hyperactive property markets. Evictions and displacement have taken place on a huge scale, enormous numbers of people have had to change residence, and entire neighborhoods and communities have been upended. None of this has been smooth, gradual, or a fair process of "adjustment," as in the idealized models of the economists; instead, it has been a quite violent shakeup of people's lives and a profound source of distress and misery for hundreds of thousands of Bay Area residents.

While it is true that cities are dynamic systems that cannot be frozen in time or space, the wholly reasonable response of working-class people is to cry foul, try to protect themselves from the ravages of a housing market gone wild, and protest the urban upheavals going on around them. Are there solutions to the contemporary housing crisis? Not that are simple, quick, or perfect, to be sure. Thanks to popular struggle and progressive local governments, however, many sensible policies are already in use to hold the line against profit-hungry landlords, property speculators, and bulldozing developers and keep the lid on the pressure cooker of an overheated market.

In a growing city, it is inescapable that more housing needs to be built somewhere, sometime. How is that to be done? In fact, housing supply is increasing through such reasonable means as infill development, higher-density buildings, and more in-law units. Although there are always objections to any new development, letting them be heard is part of the political process in a democracy, and it often leads to adjustments in plans that improve the quality and equity of developer proposals. The number of good projects in San Francisco, Berkeley, or San Jose that get stopped for no valid reason is scant, despite the propaganda of the YIMBYs. There is no reason to panic and shove bad projects down the throats of local communities.

Nevertheless, it is past time to get tough with exclusionary enclaves from St. Francis Woods to Alamo and force them to accept substantial increases in multiunit housing among the palatial mansions and large lots. Let them continue to decide where, but not whether, such housing should be built.

Spatial equity is as important to democracy and livable cities as is income equalization through wealth redistribution.

When it comes to providing enough low-cost housing, however, market solutions are simply inadequate, as countries around the world have found again and again. For this, more radical tools are necessary. One is for the federal government to give the same tax subsidies to middle-income renters as it does to house buyers who get the interest-rate deduction (a regressive tax benefit for the upper classes). For the bottom quarter of the population, there need to be massive infusions of federal and state funds for construction of low-cost units comparable to the billions that now go into highways and mass transit. That was the original intention of the New Deal public housing act, which was distorted and ultimately destroyed over the postwar era. Public housing does not have to be huge towers that concentrate the poor; as has been proven in Berkeley and San Francisco, dispersed, midrise public housing fits better into the urban fabric. There are lots of nonprofit developers and managers in the Bay Area ready to provide good quality housing for working people.[71]

An extreme strategy is to take more housing out of the market entirely. One method is to create housing trusts to buy land and buildings, which can be rented out at whatever price the trust wishes. Land trusts are already major players in buying land for parks and open spaces around the Bay Area (see chapter 8). Another approach is partial removal from the market, as in historic preservation designations on buildings; where it is important not to destroy the legacy of the past, owners are limited as to alterations to historic structures. A similar logic can apply to whole neighborhoods, such as the Tenderloin, Chinatown, and Mission districts in San Francisco, which have regulations that restrict use, demolition, and redevelopment. This is no less reasonable than park protections or suburban zoning regulations.

A popular slogan among housing activists is the idea of "The Right to the City," a phrase coined in postwar Paris and propagated by radical geographers, which was adopted by tenants' rights group for a national Right to the City Alliance. It is a fine slogan but cannot be taken literally as some kind of natural law under the rubric of human rights. Its meaning is always shaped by national laws, local traditions, and class privileges and put to the test by political mobilizations and struggles. The upper classes in their well-guarded enclaves have long staked their claim to preferred parts of the metropolis, and

---

71 On tax subsidies to housing, see Kwak 2015. Homelessness is clearly worsened by the housing crisis, too, but is a more complex problem with its own set of quandaries. See chapter 3.

their right to the city is well established. For the working class and millions of people of color, that right, like so many, is slippery and easily lost. For them, the right to the city is a call to action and a claim to social justice—or, as it has been put by some, a fight for *spatial* justice. What the housing crisis shows in no uncertain terms is that in the contemporary Bay Area, social and spatial justice have a long way to go.[72]

---

72 On the alliance, see http://righttothecity.org. Lefebvre 1970 coined the term. Smith 1996, Mitchell 2003, and Harvey 2012 have done essential work spreading the notion. For a valuable critical assessment, see Holston 2008. On the idea of spatial justice, see Soja 2009, Marcuse 2009.

CHAPTER SEVEN

Metro Monster
Size, Sprawl, and Segregation

THE TWO PREVIOUS CHAPTERS HAVE SPOKEN TO THE INTENSE RECOLONIZATION OF the core cities of the Bay Area and the astonishing bubble in housing prices. Yet the recent economic booms have sent waves of urbanization outward in all directions, blowing up the old metropolis and sending it sprawling into the Central Valley. Urban expansion, while less debated than gentrification and housing, is every bit as important to the overall story of the Bay Area. This chapter provides a wide-angle view of the geography of the metropolitan region, which has grown to immense proportions, been reconfigured in important ways, and has remained firmly divided along lines of race and class. These changes have made it harder than ever to get one's head around the whole of the bay metropolis and to see the unity knitting together the fragments.

The Bay Area reveals fundamental forces at work in U.S. cities, such as suburbanization, property capital, and segregation, despite the peculiarities of the region. Some things never seem to change in American cities: outward sprawl at low density, the power of developers and their allies, and the crazy quilt of race and class. But these elements of urbanization have taken new forms with the explosive growth of the twenty-first century, which has brought greater scale, higher density, and geographic inversions. Viewed at this scale, the Bay Area's dynamics—and contradictions—take on new shapes. The tech industry plays second fiddle to the property developers, boom-and-bust cycles are written into the landscape, and suburban sprawl betrays the promise of dense central cities. Meanwhile, class inequality carves its own topography and racial injustice reaches all the way to the farthest outskirts of the metropolis.

The chapter begins with a look at the mega-urban region of today, reaching all the way into the Inland Empire of the north, and how its immense scale poses problems for traffic and planning; those topics take up the opening two sections. The third section describes the evolving geography of race and class across the entire metropolis and the reversal of older patterns. After that, sections four and five deal with the process by which the metropolis grows, beginning with the suburban dynamic in general and following with the role of developers and growth regimes in building the city. The final section reflects on the massive wave of suburbanization in the housing bubble of the early twenty-first century and the catastrophic losses that followed.[1]

The Elusive Metropolis

The Bay Area is a gargantuan metropolitan region but hard to get one's head around. It is a definitional nightmare that confounds the U.S. Census Bureau and residents alike, thanks to its vast sprawl, strange geographic footprint, and efflorescence of governments—plus its multinodal character, as discussed in chapter 5. As a consequence, it is commonly dismembered, underestimated, and misjudged by news reports, business plans, and government studies. Statistics about the region are almost always wrong and it or its parts often appear far down the lists of the largest cities in the United States and the world. No other U.S. city is as definitionally challenged.

In fact, the Bay Area is the fourth-largest city in the United States; only Greater New York, Los Angeles, and Chicago are larger in territory and numbers. The urbanized area of the metropolitan region extends more than 150 miles north to south and over 50 miles east to west, or around 7,500 square miles—an area larger than Connecticut and Rhode Island combined. The nine-county population in 2015 was about 7.5 million; the twelve-county population 8.7 million. As its population grew over the last quarter century, the Bay Area passed up Greater Philadelphia, jockeyed for position with Washington, DC, and Greater Boston, and kept a nose ahead of fast-rising Dallas-Fort Worth and Houston.[2]

Part of the confusion about the size of the Bay Area is due to the Census Bureau's use of three different definitions for U.S. cities: municipalities within a single border, metropolitan statistical areas (MSAs), and consolidated statistical areas (CSAs). San Francisco is a city; San Francisco-Oakland-Hayward is an MSA made up of five counties; and San Jose–San Francisco–Oakland is a CSA made up of twelve counties. No single city in the Bay Area is very large, compared to Chicago or Houston, so using San Francisco or San Jose for comparison is meaningless. MSAs are better—and frequently used in national urban statistics—but still slice and dice the Bay Area. Silicon Valley is usually equated with the San Jose MSA (one county plus bits of two others),

---

1   This chapter leans on joint work with Alex Schafran, who I thank for his insights. Walker & Schafran 2015. For town names, refer to Frontispiece map.

2   https://www.census.gov/popest/data/metro/totals/2014/CSA-EST2014-alldata.html.

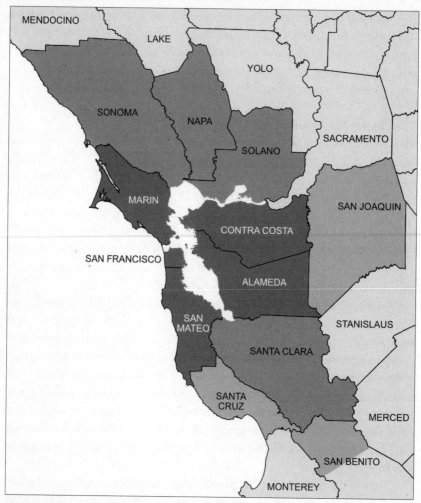

Figure 7.1: Map of the 5, 9 and 12-County Bay Areas

but the South Bay has historically been no more independent than Oakland and the East Bay, which no longer merits its own MSA. To make matters worse, the Census Bureau splits the North Bay into three mini-MSAs—Santa Rosa (Sonoma County), Napa (Napa County), and Vallejo-Fairfield (Solano County).[3]

By inventing the category of CSAs in 2000, the bureau finally brought the North, South, and Central Bay together officially as one megacity of nine counties. Then the region grew so much that the bureau expanded the CSA

---

3   The North Bay is as much a hinterland of San Francisco as northern LA County is to Los Angeles, yet the latter are conjoined as a single MSA.

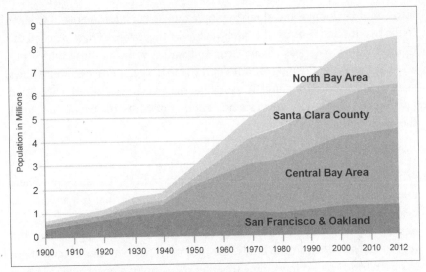

Figure 7.2: Outward Spread of Bay Area Population

Source: www.newgeography.com/
content/004165-the-evolving-urban-form-the-san-francisco-bay-area.

in 2010 to included twelve counties, adding San Joaquin, Santa Cruz, and a piece of San Benito (fig. 7.1). Unfortunately, the new twelve-county definition is rarely invoked, and the nine-county definition of the Bay Area metropolis remains popular among local planners and media.[4]

Physical geography adds to the confusion about what constitutes the Bay Area. San Francisco Bay, roughly eight hundred square miles and the largest inlet on the West Coast, sits in the middle of the metropolis, and the estuary continues upriver into the equally large Sacramento–San Joaquin Delta. The Coast Ranges encircle the region and split the inner bay area from its outer realms. The bay and hills create distinct climates and residential enclaves, all linked by narrow transportation corridors spanned by bridges and tunnels. Topography has not stopped the onrush of urbanization but sent it shooting up valleys and through gaps in the hills like flares from a wildfire.

As it swept outward, the Bay Area expanded in chunks from the nine-teenth-century core of San Francisco. In the first half of the twentieth century, the burgeoning East Bay, including Alameda and Contra Costa Counties, filled up rapidly. After World War II, Santa Clara County was the fastest-growing area, and San Mateo County suburbs filled in. By the 1970s rapid suburbanization spilled over the Oakland-Berkeley hills (the 680 corridor), up Highway 101

---

4   For unknown reasons, Wikipedia uses a thirteen-county region, just to add to the confusion.

into Sonoma County, and along the Interstate 80 corridor in Solano County. In the twenty-first century, the outer realms of the Bay Area have reached the Central Valley to the east, Santa Cruz and San Benito Counties to the south, and Lake and Mendocino Counties in the north. In the process, entire cities, such as Stockton, Tracy, and Watsonville, have been swallowed whole, and previously independent areas are being integrated into the economic life of the metropolitan area.

★　★　★

Why should anyone think about the Bay Area as a whole? Urban geographers may declare it to be a unified metropolitan region, but that is by no means evident to everyone—and for good reason. The underlying networks of economic relations can be hard to see or document, while the fragments of the region are inscribed in the landscape by municipal boundaries, and there has been little success in welding together metropolitan governments. Local identities mostly grow up within the spaces people inhabit on an everyday basis, such as neighborhoods and towns, not across long commutes, paths of logistics, or industrial districts.

There are, of course, important unifying threads of metropolitan life. The simplest is the physical presence of the city as buildings, density of occupation, and major infrastructure, such as highway networks and airports; the city ends where the open countryside begins (but this, too, is complicated by the huge open spaces incorporated into the Bay Area's urban fabric). Another defining element and unifying force is commuting fields and delivery of goods and services; these things are strongly nodal, as previously indicated, but the modern metropolis has an exceptionally high degree of cross-commuting and intraregional commercial traffic. This is felt not just in traffic flows but in diffusion effects through regional markets for goods and labor, such as the way that high wages in tech and other leading sectors echo through the metropolitan area, raising average wages for many more people. Then there are all the dense business networks of the city that involve face-to-face contact, meetings, and continuity among the various players.[5]

Nevertheless, most people in the Bay Area have only a vague notion of the whole metropolitan region. As they settle into their work and home lives, they develop a sense of place and local identity. History and habit build up along with the city. Places are not just where things happen; they develop a character of their own that accretes over time, feeds on itself, and affects all who pass through. Despite ties across the region and cross-commuting, people

---

5   On metropolitan networks and spread effects, see Storper 2013, Storper et al. 2015.

remain deeply attached to place, and this separates them. San Franciscans have a very strong identity, and they can be as insular as the denizens of Manhattan. Oakland, Berkeley, and other East Bay cities enjoy a fierce loyalty from their inhabitants, who bristle against the arrogant dismissals by "The City" across the bay. Silicon Valley has a strong local identity around the tech industry, to be sure, but also finds itself carved into scores of smaller communities. Many in the North Bay think they are still living in a rural paradise, far away from the urbanized Bay Area.[6]

Furthermore, local differences are inscribed in a political landscape ruled over by a dozen counties and 125+ municipalities, which are what most people mean by the word "city" in everyday life. The fragmentation of U.S. metropolitan areas by hundreds of municipal boundaries has been decried for a century, but it remains an essential feature of American government and urban life. Urbanists and planners insist on thinking regionally about transit, housing, and open space, but the everyday politics of local government subdivides the metropolis into tiny pieces. Government does not hold the region together or give it direction. Regional governance gets surprisingly short shift in public debate and politics.

A case can be made for the democratic virtue of having many small-scale governments, but it is countered by three negatives of miniaturization. One is the scale of infrastructure provision, which has required larger governmental units called special districts to be carved out for water supply, parks, and bus services. The Bay Area is replete with entities such as the East Bay Municipal Utility District, Santa Clara County Water Conservation District, and the Bay Area Rapid Transit District. Such special districts outnumber municipalities fourfold, with upward of five hundred in the metropolitan region. They often have more power to shape urban life and development than municipalities but are usually much less democratic than ordinary civic governments.[7]

There are two other effects of municipal miniaturization that loom large in the social order of the city and the process of urbanization, both of which figure prominently in this chapter. One is to help lock in spatial segregation by race and class, which is endemic to the Bay Area and all American cities. Another is to render local polities ripe for the picking by powerful developers and corporations, making governance by business a resilient dimension of U.S. federalism. There will be much more to say about both of these phenomena in sections to come.

---

6 On attachment to place and landscape, see Tuan 1974.
7 On special districts, see Bollens 1957, Dyble 2009, K. Cox 2016.

Efforts to create regional government in the Bay Area have failed miserably, as they have in most big American cities. The Association of Bay Area Governments (ABAG) is a useful forum for research and debate, but is toothless, lacking money to spend and enforcement powers. It was created in the early 1960s to blunt the progress of legislation for regional government moving through Sacramento. The Metropolitan Transportation Commission (MTC) was created at the behest of Washington to dole out billions of federal dollars for highways and mass transit, and it works with Caltrans and BART on transportation planning, but it has not otherwise been a force for enlightened urban policy. Even worse, MTC just took control of ABAG. The Bay Conservation and Development Commission (BCDC) plans for the bay but not the city around it (see chapter 8).[8]

The most serious efforts at regional oversight have come from business organizations, chiefly the Bay Area Council in San Francisco, the Silicon Valley Manufacturers Group, and Silicon Valley Joint Venture. They have woven together a fabric of business and government leaders in pursuit of regional growth, mostly by supporting the tech industry as the engine of regional advantage. Their chief purview is the pursuit of economic growth and technological innovation, which is a narrow remit in light of the complex problems and overall needs of a great metropolis, but they have also weighed in on housing, transportation, and environmental policy.[9]

The recent joint effort by ABAG and MTC to come up with Plan Bay Area 2040 aptly demonstrates the difficulty of enacting regional governance in service of social goals. In the spirit of the New Urbanism and California climate change policy, Plan Bay Area maps out a strategy to build much-needed housing and increase regional density. But it reinforces the geographic status quo by directing all the new high-density projects to San Francisco, Oakland, and San Jose, while bypassing low-density, wealthy suburbs such as Palo Alto and Alamo. To add insult to injury, MTC makes no promises about reshaping transit policy to fit housing goals. Thus, in the end Plan Bay Area is pretty weak tea, mostly confirming the existing trajectory of piecemeal development. If a regional agency has such blinkered vision, one can hardly blame the citizenry for thinking locally and looking to their own parochial interests.[10]

---

8   For more on regional planning history, see Scott 1985, Walker 2007.
9   Storper et al. 2015.
10   ABAG & MTC 2017.

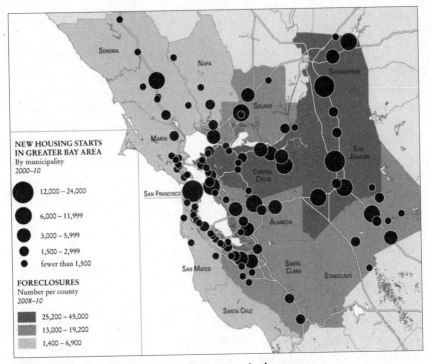

Figure 7.3: Map of New Housing in the Bay Area in the 2000s

Source: Walker & Lodha 2013. Data from RAND Corporation; cartography by Darin Jensen & Isabelle Lewis.

The Bay Area Overflows

The hyperexpansion of the Bay Area has been spilling into the topographic zone of the Central Valley for a generation. Tens of thousands of families have moved east to San Joaquin, Modesto, and Madera Counties, as well as northeast into Yolo County and Sacramento County. New housing developments have spread far and wide to accommodate this dispersion, and the Central Valley has been the leading edge of regional housing construction in the twenty-first century (fig. 7.3). As a result, thousands upon thousands of workers commute west to jobs in the old Bay Area every day, creating horrendous traffic jams.

This spread of big cities to gargantuan proportions is now normal across the United States. Southern California already has its Inland Empire in Riverside and San Bernardino Counties, which has been the fastest-growing part of greater Los Angeles for the a generation. It now boasts over four million people and is a classic edge city with its own economic base, especially a massive logistics cluster. People around Southern California are well aware of the Inland Empire, even if they never go there; but few people in Northern

California realize that they, too, have an Inland Empire. No one calls it that yet, but recognition is dawning.[11]

The Inland Empire is not the coastal Bay Area, full of well-heeled professionals, tech start-ups, and New Urbanist streetscapes, and it gets very little press compared to the gentrification of San Francisco and Oakland, but the geography of class is being rewritten there, too. The unaffordable housing in the central Bay Area has driven working people—especially couples with growing families—farther and farther out in search of the American dream of joining the (working) middle class. The personal cost of the exploding metropolis is borne by the people who must commute long hours back to inner reaches of the Bay Area for work. These are not professionals working long-distance by internet and coming in once a week to the office. They are bus drivers, teachers, mechanics, police officers, and other ordinary workers, and they pay a stiff price in time lost on crowded freeways.

The Bay Area's Inland Empire is paving over hundreds of square miles of Central Valley farmlands (see chapter 8). The urban fringe swallows up rural towns, such as Lathrop, Los Banos, and Gilroy, just as it once did places like Niles and Walnut Creek. Indeed, the scale of the metropolitan tidal wave is such that it is colliding and blending with Stockton and Sacramento, preexisting metropolitan areas of one and two million people, respectively. Sacramento is the center of California state government and Stockton an old agro-industrial center, including wineries, canneries, farm equipment, and pesticides, and both have substantial logistics operations (much of it serving agricultural exports) and construction firms (feeding the demand for urban expansion).[12]

The collision has led to speculation about a new Northern California "megapolis" of fifteen, seventeen, or twenty-one counties. Some geographers and planners see an urban region of ten million people, encompassing almost one-quarter of all Californians and embracing more than ten thousand square miles of territory all the way to the Sierra Nevada. If true, this city-on-steroids is bigger than greater Chicago and almost the size of greater Los Angeles, America's largest mega-metropolis. In the 1950s, urbanists such as Jane Jacobs famously decried the "exploding metropolis," and geographer Jean Gottmann used the term "megalopolis" to describe the emerging Boston-to-Washington corridor. One rarely hears either term today, because metropolitan gigantism

---

11 On the United States, Berube et al. 2006. On Southern California, DeLara 2009, Walker & Lodha 2013.

12 Some twenty thousand people a year are moving to Sacramento from the Bay Area. Murphy 2017.

has become so normalized and twenty-first-century urban regions exceed the scale of postwar cities by a degree of magnitude.[13]

★ ★ ★

Traffic is more than a unifying force in the metropolis; it is a daily burden and menace to millions of commuters, truck drivers, and delivery people. With every economic upswing, traffic mounts up on streets and highways until it seems like the integument of the Bay Area will burst at the seams. MTC reports that traffic congestion is up 80 percent since 2010. The streets of San Francisco have never seemed as unnavigable, roadways in Silicon Valley are mobbed, and regional freeways are jammed to the guardrails. Traffic on the bridges is already thick by 4:00 a.m. The Bay Area can boast a handful of the most pernicious highway bottlenecks in the country, led by the I-80 and I-580 approaches to the Bay Bridge. In terms of time spent in traffic congestion, San Francisco metro ranked third worst in the country after LA and New York—and fourth worst in the world. As one reporter put it, "The Bay Area seems like a special kind of hell for commuters" (fig. 7.4).[14]

As for mass transit, BART carries almost a half million passengers a day, AC Transit buses handle some two hundred thousand, and Santa Clara VTA one hundred thousand. SF Muni carries as much as the others combined—second in California only to LA's Metro bus system. Rail commuting is also thriving, though the numbers are much smaller: CalTrain runs sixty thousand people up the Peninsula, ACE takes five thousand per day over Altamont Pass, Amtrak carries thousands more on the Sacramento corridor. Yet, curiously, per capita transit ridership is down over the last twenty years.

Things are particularly dire for those commuting in and out of the Inland Empire on Interstates 80 and 580 (or by train). They suffer through eye-popping commutes of up to two hours each way, in order to reach workplaces in the East Bay, Silicon Valley, and even San Francisco. The Bay Area has the highest amount of "megacommuting" in the United States, defined as people who travel ninety or more minutes and fifty or more miles to work. Some employers have moved first shifts back to 4:00 a.m. or allowed flexible shift so that workers have an easier commute. And while some Bay Area leaders

---

13   Editors of Fortune 1958, Gottmann 1961, Morrill 2012. This kind of hyperurbanism had led some theorists to think that the entire globe is now urban. Brenner 2013. For a rebuttal, see Walker 2015.

14   Quote by Baldassari 2017. See also Marquis 2017. Inrix 2016 commute time rankings at http://inrix.com/scorecard/. Average commute time rankings by the U.S. Census use counties, not CSAs, for no good reason; in those rankings the Bay Area falls far down the list.

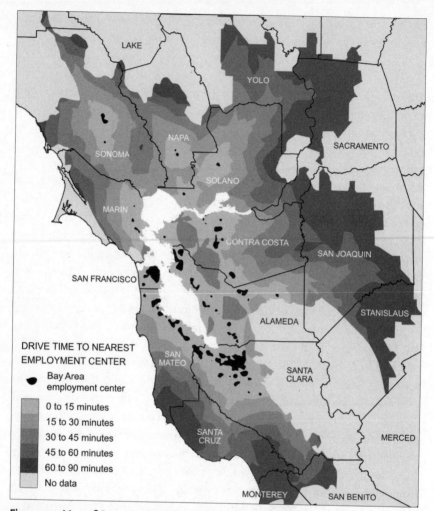

Figure 7.4: Map of Commuting Times in the Bay Area, 2008

Source: http://gis.mtc.ca.gov/home/images/motm/motmo8.pdf.

are pinning their hopes on high-speed rail to whisk workers back to the metropolitan centers, that dream is still many years off.[15]

Meanwhile, commuting patterns have been altered. For over a century, people commuted from the East Bay or the Peninsula into San Francisco's Downtown; today they go both way in huge numbers, a classic web of cross-commuting in the modern metropolis. Huge numbers commute south from San Francisco to Silicon Valley, but also north and east (fig. 7.5). Others go

---

15   Rapino and Fields 2013, Rae 2015. See the blog of Carl Guardino, head of the Silicon Valley Leadership Group: http://svlg.org/ceo_blog/2016/02/i-am-now-high-on-high-speed-rail/.

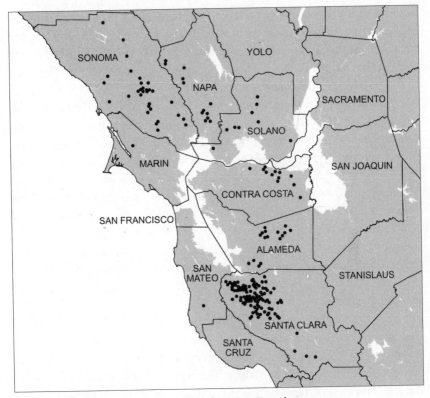

Figure 7.5: Map of Outward Commuting from San Francisco, 2015

Source: Rae 2015.

from Oakland to Walnut Creek and Fremont, from San Jose to Mountain View and Palo Alto, or from Marin to Santa Rosa and Berkeley. The result is massive traffic flows in every direction and at every hour. Peak commute traffic hours have become less and less defined, with choke points such as the Bay Bridge and Highway 237 around the south end of the bay jammed at every hour of the day.[16]

Given the traffic congestion in the Bay Area, it is disheartening to see how little is being done about it. High-velocity lanes are at a standstill. Freeway lanes are added here and there, as in the extensions of Highway 4 in Contra Costa County, but they simply fill up as fast as they are completed, pushing the traffic jams a bit farther down the line. Meanwhile, BART is creaking along on aged equipment, hoping to hang on until new cars arrive; a $3.5 billion bond approved in 2016 helps but is far from sufficient to solve the underlying problems in dilapidated roadbed, crooked rails, and outdated computers. One

---

16   For more detail, see the fine animations of Bay Area commuting in Rae 2015.

bright spot is the North Bay's SMART train, but it is a drop in the regional bucket. Some regional planners like SPUR and business groups like the Bay Area Council and Silicon Valley Leadership Group understand how bad things are, but that has yet to translate into public policy—and they too often leap to the defense of more freeway spending.[17]

Future prospects are for continued growth of car travel and little increase in mass transit. California's climate change legislation demands a stern reduction in vehicle emissions by 2030 (see chapter 8), but the state has left the job of traffic planning to regional agencies. A close look at Plan Bay Area 2040 shows that it does not reduce vehicle use at all and does not mesh traffic planning with the injunction in new climate laws to accommodate everyone who works in the metropolis to live there. Instead of ramping up mass transit, MTC continues to nickel-and-dime bus systems, even though they are by far the most efficient forms of mass transit. By way of contrast, LA's growing light rail and subway systems, which just got another injection of $120 billion in bonds, are putting the Bay Area's disconnected and overburdened transit network to shame.[18]

The Segregated Metropolis

A fundamental aspect of metropolitan geography in the United States is the way people are sorted out socially across the city, and this is no less true of the Bay Area. The urban fabric is divided into scores of municipalities and thousands of neighborhoods, and these fragments are strongly differentiated by class and race. The social divides illuminated in previous chapters are more than abstract differences of income, wealth, and opportunity; they are inscribed on the urban landscape and are part of the lived experience of everyone in the metropolis. Curiously, Americans find it difficult to think about class in the abstract, but they have a pretty clear idea of how it works in spatial terms.[19]

The microgeographies of class and race are complex, nuanced, and dynamic, but one can discern some reasonably clear patterns. The West Bay has long been richer than the East Bay, and this has continued with the rise of the tech industry, which has made the west side of Silicon Valley wealthy, as well. Rich people prefer to live on the hills, while industry and transportation

17 Cadelago 2017, http://www.bayareacouncil.org/news/bay-area-agencies-must-work-together-to-improve-transit-system/kl.

18 Thanks to Matt Williams, Sierra Club, for enlightening me on transportation planning. For more data, see ABAG & MTC 2017 and the accompanying EIR at http://2040.planbayarea.org/sites/default/files/2017-07/PBA%202040%20DEIR_0_1.pdf.

19 On urban spatial sorting in general, see Marcuse & van Kempen 2002.

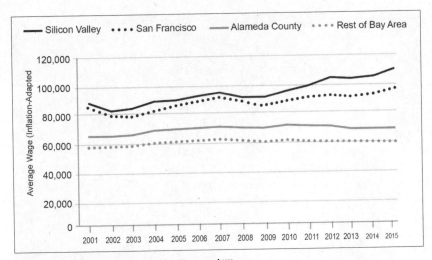

Figure 7.6: Bay Area Wage Divide, East and West

Source: Massaro 2016.

have traditionally lined the flatlands around the bay, and worker housing has stayed nearer to those employment corridors. These patterns show up clearly on a map of the Central Bay Area: the divide west and east of the bay and the prosperous highlands on both sides (figs. 7.6 and 7.7). Another salient feature of the Bay Area's geography of class is that the well-to-do occupy an enormous amount of territory; they own large houses on capacious lots, gather in spacious jurisdictions and move high in the hills to satisfy their taste for greenery and open vistas.[20]

A look at the West Bay reveals a spine of rich neighborhoods running from Marin County through the hilly center of San Francisco (Pacific Heights, West Portal, St. Francis Woods), then down along the hillsides of San Mateo in places such as Hillsborough, Woodside, and Los Altos Hills. There are also some exceptionally wealthy cities on the flats, such as Atherton, Menlo Park, and Palo Alto. All of these areas have grown richer, but not denser. The west side and southern districts of San Francisco were traditionally working class but have seen a fair measure of gentrification—though far less than the northeastern parts of the city. A band of working-class residence lines the Highway 101 corridor in San Mateo County, featuring such towns as Brisbane, South San Francisco, Redwood City, and East Menlo Park. The upper middle class lies in between but has expanded well into the old working-class strongholds, which have grown denser.

---

20 On upper-class tastes in landscapes, see Jackson 1985, Duncan & Duncan 2004, Walker 2007.

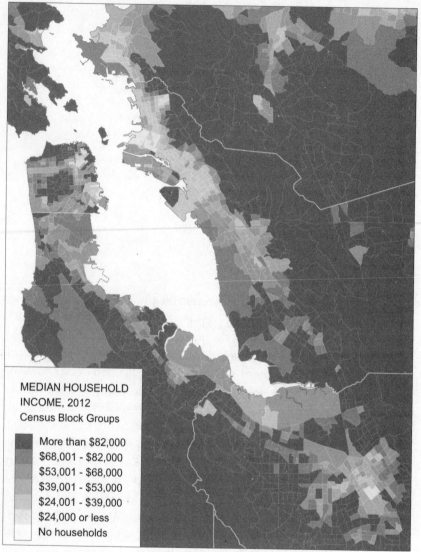

MEDIAN HOUSEHOLD
INCOME, 2012
Census Block Groups

More than $82,000
$68,001 - $82,000
$53,001 - $68,000
$39,001 - $53,000
$24,001 - $39,000
$24,000 or less
No households

Figure 7.7: Map of Bay Area Household Income, 2015

Source:https://story.maps.arcgis.com/home/item.html?id=8d2e1d77366c4d2ab16957b0547d
6ca1. B&W version by Alicia Cowart.

The East Bay has fewer enclaves of the truly rich, but the same pattern holds of the upper classes seeking the heights along the East Bay hills from Kensington down to Oakland. Over the hills, a central wedge of well-to-do residential areas runs east through Orinda and Lafayette to Alamo and Danville. Those areas have filled in with the growth of professional-managerial ranks in the Bay Area economy. The mass of working families traditionally occupied the flatlands from Hercules to Hayward, with better-off workers moving up the hillsides from Richmond down to Castro Valley. There has been considerable gentrification of those old working-class districts, from El Cerrito and Berkeley down to Union City and Fremont. East of the hills, the old industrial shore of Contra Costa County is still largely working class in towns such as Concord, Pittsburg, and Antioch. The 680 office centers of Walnut Creek, San Ramon, and Pleasanton are mixed but gradually gentrifying, while Dublin and Livermore remain mostly working class.

The South Bay extends the patterns established around the central bay region. The far west side of Silicon Valley is the richest and whitest, including Los Gatos, Saratoga and Monte Sereno. Downhill lie towns such as Cupertino, Campbell, and Sunnyvale that used to be mostly working class but now have a wide streak of upper-middle-class professional, technical, and managerial types. Working people are mostly found on the flats along Highway 101, from Mountain View to San Jose. That working-class band continues around the south end of the bay to Milpitas and up again into Newark and Union City in Alameda County. Fremont has developed a large upper-class contingent in the hills. East San Jose is almost entirely working class and the southern parts of San Jose and Santa Clara County are a mix of working-class and some upper-middle-class enclaves.

In a market system, those with money get first choice of location while the rest have to make do with the leftovers; but residential segregation is not just a result of income differences. Urban space plays a lively role in the process of class formation in America. Spatial concentration of the well-to-do is a means of showing off wealth and defending it against the lower classes. The rich gather together to share their bounty, give mutual aid, and keep up property values.

Municipal boundaries have allowed the well-heeled to defend their spaces with police and local ordinances, while elite housing developments such as Blackhawk use gates and guards to keep out the masses. While the egregious policing of dark bodies is well known, the more subtle effects of downzoning and building controls are largely invisible. Municipalities such as Saratoga, Alamo, and Ross use large lots and building height limits to keep out multiple-unit buildings that might allow the riffraff to move into their sanctuaries.[21]

Schools are absolutely central to the process of residential segregation, given that access to education is so vital to the reproduction of the upper classes (see chapter 3). By concentrating in their own municipalities and school districts, they can keep better control over public schools, provide

---

21   Squires 2002, Duncan & Duncan 2004, Katz & Rosen 1980, Hirt 2014.

more funding (from a larger tax base and more private giving), and keep out the disruptive kids from the lower orders. Palo Alto's public schools are superb. By contrast, Oakland and Richmond schools suffer from any number of deficits, like lower test scores and higher dropout rates. Their students are drawn from working-class and disadvantaged communities, and they are perennially short of resources, with their school districts going in and out of receivership.

The Bay Area ranks in the middle of U.S. cities in terms of residential segregation by income, as one might expect because of its relatively large upper middle class and working middle class. Yet as inequality has increased in the Bay Area, so has class segregation. The jump in measures of class segregation by *income* is less than many other cities because inequality in the bay region is so heavily weighted by the extreme *wealth* of a relatively small number of superrich. Nor is class segregation simply a matter of income and wealth inequality. In many U.S. cities, the upper classes have separated and walled themselves off more aggressively than in the Bay Area for historic reasons of stronger class antagonism and, crucially, more draconian racial orders.[22]

★ ★ ★

The racial map of the Bay Area overlaps the class map to a large degree, as do race and class in general (see chapter 4); but race adds its own twists and turns to the social geography of the metropolis. Racial segregation was clearly worse in the past. San Francisco's Chinatown was notorious as the only place of refuge during the raging anti-Chinese movement in the nineteenth century. Japantown in the Western Addition was the focus of city life for most Nissei before it was wiped out by the forced internment of the Second World War. Mexicans lived mostly in a few agricultural barrios around the region. In the postwar era, a "white noose" of suburbs surrounded the African American ghettoes in San Francisco, Oakland, and Richmond. Blacks were intentionally excluded from the American suburban dream and homeownership by the racism of home builders, realtors, and white neighbors.

After the civil rights laws of the 1960s, many African Americans were able to move into better neighborhoods, particularly in Oakland, Asians moved out of the confines of Chinatowns and Japantowns, and Latinos out of the traditional barrios. But the old neighborhoods are still there, like Chinatown and the Mission in San Francisco, Chinatown and Fruitvale in Oakland, and the Filipino neighborhood next to the old Alameda Naval Air Station. The black ghettoes of Hunters Point–Bayview and Fillmore in San Francisco

---

22   On spatial inequality in U.S. cities, see Taylor & Fry 2012, especially p. 6. Also Samara 2016.

and of East and West Oakland are greatly diminished but remain, and the same goes for Marin City, Southwest Berkeley, and Richmond. Over the hills, longtime racialized neighborhoods are few, like the black part of Pittsburg. In the South Bay, a small East San Jose barrio originally anchored the eastward expansion of Mexican Americans. East Palo Alto, long an African American ghetto, is now mostly Latino.[23]

But people have been on the move, and the Bay Area has undergone a profound reworking of its racial geography. The growth of the immigrant communities over the last three decades has been so massive that it has overwhelmed old racial boundaries. Most notably, former white working-class areas have been largely replaced by immigrant neighborhoods. Older studies showed the Bay Area to be the least-segregated big city in the United States on a block-by-block and census tract basis, but it is not clear if that reputation is still merited. Nevertheless, the changing demographics throughout the region have ushered in a new measure of diversity despite the strong forces at work keeping people of color at bay and sorting out various racial groups. A recent study comparing the Bay Area and Los Angeles found that a much-larger population share is living in highly diverse neighborhood types (31 percent in the San Francisco Metropolitan Area, 18 percent in Los Angeles), and a much-lower share of the population is living in homogenous neighborhoods (19 percent in the San Francisco Metropolitan Area, 33 percent in Los Angeles). This is consistent with the idea of a more racially unified working class put forth in chapter 4 (see fig. 7.8).[24]

San Francisco is majority people of color and one-third Asian. The Sunset and Richmond Districts are close to majority Chinese and the southern arc of neighborhoods shelter a mix of Latinos, Filipinos, and Chinese, along with remaining Whites. San Mateo County is half people of color, split about evenly between Asian and Latino, with few African Americans. Daly City is majority Asian, especially Filipinos; South San Francisco and San Bruno are divided about evenly among Asians, Latinos, and Whites; and Redwood City and San Mateo are mostly Latino and White.

In the North Bay, there is a concentration of Latinos in San Rafael's Canal District, in overwhelmingly white Marin County. Sonoma and Napa are about

---

23 On the history of segregation in the Bay Area, see Johnson 1993, Walker 1995b, Godfrey 1988, Self 2003. An obvious problem with regional maps is that Whites are much more spread out, so their residential areas are disproportionately large compared to their share of the population.

24 For an earlier evaluation of the degree of segregation, see Massey and Denton 1993. The recent figures are from Clark et al. 2017. For racial distribution maps of the Bay Area in 1990 and 2000, see http://geogdata.csun.edu/. For 2010, see http://www.radicalcartography.net/index.html?bayarea

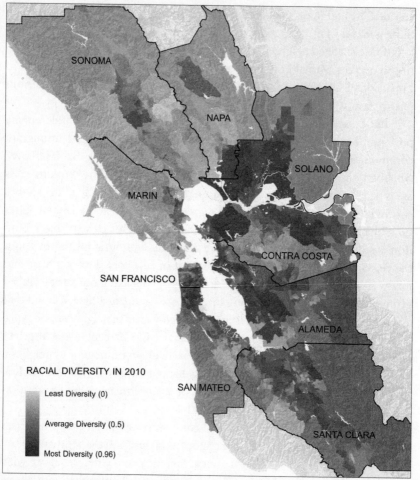

Figure 7.8: Map of Bay Area Racial Diversity, 2012

Source: Kearny Smith. http://gis.mtc.ca.gov/home/motmo12.html (9-county Bay Area).

a quarter Latino today, with concentrations in the cities on the east side of Sonoma County, like Santa Rosa and Healdsburg, and the southern end of Napa County in the city of Napa and American Canyon. Asians are much fewer. Solano County is about half people of color, with large communities of Latinos and Filipinos, but it still maintains a significant Black community in Vallejo, its most diverse city.

In the East Bay, Latinos loom large in Richmond and west Contra Costa County towns like San Pablo. Richmond has a big Laotian community, and Hercules is a majority Asian suburb. Chinese and Vietnamese are an important presence in El Cerrito and Albany. Berkeley remains two-thirds White, with distinct minorities of Blacks, Asians, and Latinos. Oakland is much

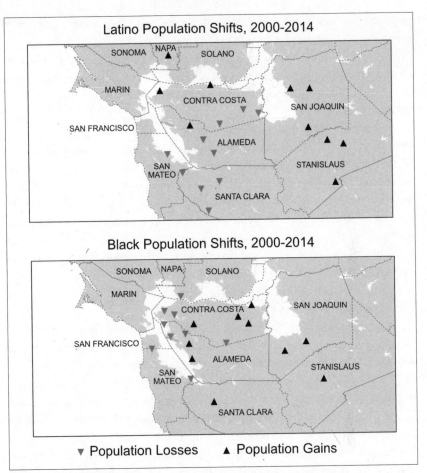

Figure 7.9: Map of Shifting Latino and African American Residence, 2000–2014

Source: Samara 2016. (11-county Bay Area).

more diverse: Central Oakland is dominated by Chinese, Vietnamese, and Koreans, far East Oakland is still majority African American, and Fruitvale in the middle of East Oakland has a growing Latino community. Latinos are strongly represented in the southern Alameda County suburbs like Hayward, and Asians have a large presence there—almost half the population of Union City. South Asians are a significant part of the generically Asian demographic. There are also significant pockets of African Americans in south county towns.

In the South Bay, Latinos occupy most of the east side of Silicon Valley and southern Santa Clara County. They make up a third of San Jose's population. In the northeast part of the Valley, Milpitas has a significant population of Filipinos, and there is a notable upper-middle-class group of Chinese and South Asians in the hills of Fremont. San Jose is one-third Asian, with notable communities of Vietnamese, Koreans, and other Asian immigrants, especially on its southeast flank. On the west side of the Valley, Asians are an important presence everywhere, with major concentrations of Chinese in Cupertino and South Asians in Sunnyvale and Santa Clara. Latinos are to be found in number in all but the most elite towns, but African Americans are scarce everywhere.[25]

As previously noted, large numbers of working-class people of color have been expelled from the central areas of the region by the preferences of the upper classes for the urban core and raging house prices, and many of those have fled to the outer suburbs of the metropolis. The postwar African American neighborhoods of San Francisco, Oakland, Berkeley, and Richmond have shrunken severely, while large black communities have sprung up in formerly white working-class suburbs, such as Antioch, Brentwood, and Pittsburg in the outer East Bay; many African Americans have moved to Stockton, as well. Latinos have also moved to the outer suburbs in large numbers, even though their inner Bay Area communities have continued to grow (fig. 7.9).[26]

Upper-class Whites have expanded their territory over time, despite their shrinking proportion of the overall population. Marin has become a super-suburb for the white upper classes, the richest county in the United States; but it was not always that way, having once supported a bohemian population in places such as Sausalito and Fairfax. Western Sonoma County and Napa County have been taken over by residences and second homes of the elite. The upper-class wedge of the East Bay has filled in and pushed outward to Blackhawk and all around the foot of Mount Diablo. In Silicon Valley, an emerging elite of Asian capitalists, managers, and top engineers has joined the white upper classes in places like Palo Alto, Los Gatos, and Menlo Park. More and more well-to-do Asians have migrated to the outer East Bay, as well, in towns such as Pleasanton, Danville, and San Ramon.

Having drawn a rough portrait of the social geography of the new Bay Area, we now turn to the process of suburban development that created the sprawling metropolis and continues to drive its fringes outward.

Suburbia Redux: Why the City Expands

Across the country most talk about the twenty-first-century urban scene focuses on city centers and the New Urbanism, but through it all metropolitan

---

25 Once again, nothing is implied by use of the shorthand names of racial/immigrant groups, which drop the tedious hyphenations. On Asian suburbs in Silicon Valley, see Lung-Amam 2017.
26 Schafran 2013, Schafran & Wegmann 2015.

areas just keep growing outward, as they always have. Low-density suburban sprawl has been the name of the game in American urbanization for a long time, with California leading the way in the twentieth century. Los Angeles is notorious for its far-flung suburbs, yet the Bay Area is equally one of the most suburbanized cities in the country. The vast majority of the built-up area is low-rise, rarely over two stories. Visitors are easily fooled by the core of San Francisco, which is an old city nestled in the heart of a Sunbelt metropolis; most of the Bay Area is a vast sea of suburbia—even the outer realms of San Francisco itself.[27]

Understanding the exploding metropolis that is the Bay Area today means taking a longer look at the processes that create suburbia and low-density sprawl in U.S. cities. At the macroeconomic level, there are five major forces at work: industrial decentralization, transportation change, the single-family home, high incomes, and mortgage finance. These are discussed in this section, where it is argued that the Bay Area has not only been strongly shaped by these forces, it has been an innovator in decentralizing practices. The following section will offer a complementary look at the microeconomic level of land development and the private and public actors who facilitate it.[28]

The most common account of suburbia can be called "the American dream" story, and it takes suburbanization to be the free choice of household-ers and their cultural preferences for automobiles and elbow room. This rings true up to a point, since Americans clearly love cars and spacious homes; but positing an existential American love for suburbia is a weak reed unless it is backed up with reasons why these desires came to be. Since people so often learn to love the landscapes they grew up in, as geographers have long pointed out, suburbia may be more of an acquired habit than part of the DNA of American life. Otherwise, how to explain New Yorkers' preference for dense urban living without personal automobiles? Or changing preferences over time, as seen in the rush to embrace the New Urbanism?[29]

The first problem with the naturalized explanation of suburbia is that many people have moved to the suburbs to be closer to jobs, as industries have kept relocating farther and farther out from the urban cores. Decentralization has been a fact of U.S. industrialization from the outset, as nineteenth-century

---

27 "Sprawl" is a rough shorthand for the spreading out of low-density development. Hayden 2004, Bruegmann 2005.

28 For critical overviews of U.S. suburbanization and the forces behind it, see Walker 1981, Hayden 2003, Schoenberger 2015.

29 For the conventional view, see Jackson 1985, Bruegmann 2005. The scholarly siren of sprawl, Robert Bruegmann, hails from the suburbs of the outer East Bay. On love of place, see Tuan 1974.

factories located at sources of water power beyond the boundaries of Boston, New York, and Philadelphia and noxious industries sought out refuge from city-dwellers' complaints on the fringes of cities. The first factories in the East Bay, for example, were dynamite producers fleeing San Francisco, and they were joined ca. 1900 by oil refineries, slaughterhouses, and paint works. Just as important to subsequent decentralization was the search for less militant labor forces, better transport, and cheap land. The switch from water and steam power to electricity flattened out factories, leading them to build on larger sites at the urban fringe, such as the General Motors assembly plant built in East Oakland in 1917. And growing scale, along with the change from rail to truck transport by 1950, pushed factories farther and farther away.[30]

A second factor in suburbanization is transportation, and it long precedes the automobile as a facilitator of urban sprawl. Transport development is what first allowed settlement to move outward from San Francisco. Bay suburbanites were already commuting by ferry and rail to San Francisco in the 1860s from such idyllic enclaves as Alameda, Menlo Park, and San Rafael. Much of the region's long-term framework was established along the rail lines and bayside ports of the time, a chain of depots, industrial satellites, and farm towns connected by transport networks owned by San Francisco capitalists.[31]

Onto this foundation were mapped some of the nation's most extensive trolley systems. San Francisco built a streetcar network that opened up its first major extensions in the Western Addition and the Mission District, then used public ownership and municipal bonds in the early twentieth century to drive the world's longest streetcar tunnel through Twin Peaks to develop the Sunset District. The East Bay's Key System and Sacramento Northern created the second longest system of trolleys and interurbans in the country after Los Angeles. The trolley systems were richly financed, most notably by Oakland's resident millionaire, Francis Marion Smith, the "Borax King." The result was a sprawling region even before the automobile became king.[32]

In the interwar era, cars and highways transformed the Bay Area into an autocentric urban world. Cars greatly extended the range and flexibility of individual commutes, beyond the linear corridors laid down around trolleys. Car culture developed quickly here, aided by high rates of automobile ownership and an expansive state road system. California was a pioneer in gas taxes and state funding of paved highways, and the state built freeways long

---

30 Lewis 2004, Walker 2004b, Lunine 2013.
31 Vance 1964, Scott 1985.
32 Perles 1981, Demoro 1985, Scott 1985.

before most of the world. In the 1930s, the New Deal constructed thousands of miles of new roads around the state, and then, in the postwar era, the interstates, new tunnels, and BART provided an ever-larger framework for regional expansion.[33]

A third element of the suburban push has been the American ideal of the single-family home and the detached house. This idea had roots in the agrarian world of the early Republic and the small towns dotted across the country in the nineteenth century, then carried over to the big cities as the upper classes sought suburban shelter from crowded industrial cities and their immigrant working-class districts. The house in an ample garden in the "middle landscape" of the suburbs became the American version of the pastoral idyll. It was built into plans for Garden Suburbs around every major city by the turn of the twentieth century, protected by deed covenants, zoning ordinances, and neighborhood associations.[34]

The bay region was always a mecca of the single-family home, despite the reputation of San Francisco as a city of apartments. The nineteenth-century Victorian city had hundreds of blocks of row houses and workers' cottages, which were originally suburban homes in areas such as the Mission, Western Addition and Inner Richmond. In the first half of the twentieth century, the western and southern flanks of the city (the so-called Outside Lands) filled in with two-story homes in Mediterranean styles popular at the time (again, mostly row houses). Oakland was always a city of freestanding homes laid out on spacious lots on wide streets, and its outer districts of the first half of the twentieth century were classic "streetcar suburbs" fanning out along radial trolley lines. It had an ample stock of workers' cottages as well as middle-class homes: first in Victorian style, then neoclassical and crafts-man, and then Mediterranean. San Jose was famously a city of commodious residences and bungalows with ample gardens.[35]

The Bay Area is awash in detached suburban dwellings. In 2010, it had almost 1.5 million single-unit detached houses and close to a quarter-million single-unit attached dwellings—more than 60 percent of the total housing stock. A majority of these were built in the postwar era, 1945–80. In 1970, only San Francisco had a housing stock that was majority multiple units, while all the outer counties had a median single-unit housing rate of over 70 percent. Single-family detached houses are notorious space eaters that make for an

---

33   On the history of California automobility, see Scott 1985, Sabin 2005, Nelson 2009.
34   On the single-family home, see Hayden 2003, Archer 2005. On the uniqueness of U.S. zoning in protecting the single-family home, see Hirt 2014. On covenants, see Gotham 2000a, Fogelson 2005.
35   On Bay Area housing styles, see Bagwell 1982, Walker 1995b, Groth 2004, Ungaretti 2012.

expansive suburbia, and they have only gotten worse with the taste for bigger homes (the median size of the single-family house today is two thousand square feet, about double what it was in the postwar era).[36]

A fourth characteristic of the suburban ideal has been homeownership. Before World War II, it was out of reach for the lower half of city dwellers. Working-class families mostly lived in rental units, whether row houses, apartment buildings, or three-deckers; Philadelphia and Baltimore were distinctive in having a goodly percentage of working-class homeowners in brick row houses. The Bay Area was even more of a haven for homeowners. Income is too often overlooked in discussions of the single-family detached house and the car in the driveway, but the ability to pay for those things was a critical foundation for suburbia. American workers had higher wages than in Europe until recently, and the Bay Area has had even higher wages and salaries than the rest of the country, going back to the Gold Rush.[37]

Lastly, San Francisco was a major financial center that could offer abundant mortgage credit to home buyers. Everyone knows how important the low-cost, thirty-year, government-backed mortgage was to the mass suburbanization after World War II, but mortgage finance was crucial to urban development long before that. In the Bay Area, ample credit for homeownership goes back to the Building and Loan Societies of the nineteenth century and took off in the first half of the twentieth with A.P. Giannini's Bank of America, which led the way in branch and consumer banking in the United States. High wages and ample credit are why Boston's working class lived in three-decker apartments while Oakland's lived in California bungalows, with homeownership rates as high as Los Angeles in the 1920s.

The financing of housing and transportation is not just an economic phenomenon; it is political, and the macroeconomics of suburbanization has been the business of the federal government for most of the last century. The 1913 income tax amendment introduced the deduction for interest paid, which became a major subsidy for homeowners. In the 1920s, Herbert Hoover, as secretary of commerce, eagerly promoted the new regime of zoning and planning by local governments by issuing model ordinances. But the biggest interventions came with the New Deal, which stabilized the whole system of mortgage lending by regulating savings and loans (S&Ls), guaranteeing bank deposits, creating a secondary market for mortgages through the Government National Mortgage Association (and later Federal National

---

36 Figures for the nine-county region; the twelve-county figures are similar. Minnesota Population Center 2011.

37 Walker 1995b, 2001. On working-class suburbs back East, see Warner 1962, Harris 1996.

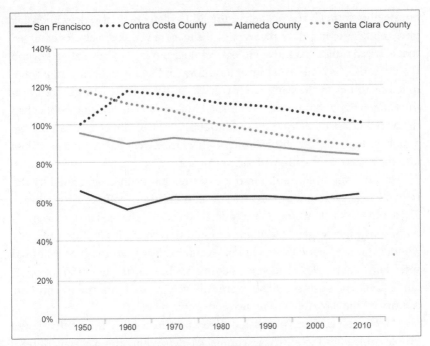

Figure 7.10: Bay Area Homeownership Rates, 1950–2010

Source: U.S. Census, Minnesota Population Center 2011. Courtesy of Alex Schafran.

Mortgage Association, or Fannie Mae), and insuring mortgages through the Federal Housing Administration (FHA) (joined later by the Veterans' Administration).[38]

California was the national leader in the development of the postwar S&L industry, which was the dynamo behind growing homeownership and suburban expansion, and the Bay Area was home to some well-established players, such as Bay View Federal Savings and Eureka Federal Savings, that became high flyers in the postwar era. San Mateo's astronomical homeownership rates in the 1950s are evidence of the era's well-financed suburbs. Indeed, virtually every corner of the Bay Area had high homeownership rates until recently.[39]

The curtain came down on the postwar era in the crisis of the 1970s, and thereafter finance entered a new, exaggerated phase that has altered the housing market of the Bay Area. Of critical importance was the rapid expansion of the secondary mortgage market in the 1980s, which funded a huge

---

38   On the housing programs, see Gelfand 1975, Freund 2007.
39   On the postwar era in California, see Burns 1975, Weiss 1987, Walker 1995b, Abrahamson 2013.

housing boom in California before the S&Ls blew up. It also drove housing prices higher, so that in the recovery of the 1990s new, riskier vehicles emerged that allowed California buyers to extend their buying power—often beyond their means. As Wall Street invented more and more elaborate mortgage-based securities in the early twenty-first century, it fed a lending frenzy in the Golden State that ultimately crashed in 2007–8. The housing bubble had the added effect of driving more households out of the center toward the periphery to find affordable housing—where they went deeper in debt to buy into the American dream, with dire results.[40]

In sum, suburbanization in the Bay Area has been exaggerated by the region's advanced state of industrial decentralization, trolleys and highways, and abundant stock of single-family detached houses, backed up by the area's bounty of high wages and finance capital that made it all affordable. No wonder the metropolis sprawled outward, no less than the better-known spread of Los Angeles. And while density has been rising in both metropolitan regions, the skids of sprawl were still well greased into the twenty-first century by the Bay Area's affluence and ample finance.

Nevertheless, rising prices and declining affordability meant that fewer people could afford to purchase a home, so ownership rates have fallen steadily (fig. 7.10). At the same time, households had to settle for less space and higher density, even far out into the suburban realms, and suburban developments featured higher-density townhouses, condos, and apartments. Yet the city is still expanding outward, and not even horrific traffic has put the brakes on suburbanization. What did bring it to a shuddering halt for a time was the catastrophic failure of the mortgage markets in 2007–8. That will be the topic of the last section of the chapter.

Who Builds the City?
Who builds the city? This seemingly innocent question is too little asked. The facile assumption is that what the buyer wants, the buyer gets, whether it is houses or televisions. This is the great American fiction of consumer sovereignty, which ignores that what you choose depends on what is on offer. No one believes this in the world of tech (are consumers panting after self-driving cars?), so why take it as gospel when it comes to urban housing? It is well known that the wonders of technological innovation, combined with the design genius of Steve Jobs, made us all eager buyers of smartphones and digital tunes. If the builders of Tech World can create new worlds of needs, desires, and style, why not the purveyors of urban life?

---

40 On California's financial excesses, see again chapter 6.

New housing is created by financiers who invest in land development, developers who assemble and prepare land, and construction companies that build houses, assisted by real estate agencies, mortgage companies, and private utilities. Together they constitute what can be called the urban development industry or property sector. In the postwar era, property-related firms accounted for 5–6 percent of all U.S. jobs, a number that rose to over 7 percent from 1995 to 2006. In California, it peaked at around one million jobs during the housing boom of the early twenty-first century. Nevertheless, the development industry has never received attention from economists commensurate with its size—perhaps because it is so dispersed and fragmented.[41]

This section takes a closer look at the microeconomics of city building. It begins with the evolution of the development sector and its rapid advance in California. It then asks what developers build and where, and how they steer the growth and shape of the city for their own gain, rather than simply responding to consumer demand. Lastly, it turns to the way local governments work hand in hand with developers to facilitate growth. The outcome is more rapid suburbanization, as well as changing styles and shifting submarkets.[42]

California's development sector has long been a step ahead of the rest of the country because the state has always been capital-rich, highly urbanized, and with a clean slate of private property. Its capitalists had a penchant for investing in land, the money to back large-scale development, and a ready market for housing. The prevailing story of American suburbanization is that large unified housing schemes emerged at the turn of the twentieth century in places such as Kansas City's Country Club District and Baltimore's Roland Park; then, after World War II, big developers such as Levitt became dominant around New York and Philadelphia. California is hardly mentioned in this East Coast version of urban history. Yet San Francisco already had mass home building in the nineteenth century, as the Realty Associates built thousands of standardized Victorian row houses. Large, planned residential developments emerged in the early 1890s at Burlingame and Mill Valley, and after 1900 such schemes proliferated, built by companies such as Baldwin & Howell in San Francisco, Mason-McDuffie in Berkeley, and the Realty Syndicate in Oakland, probably the nation's largest developer of the time.[43]

---

41 Figures from Wissoker 2016, p. 6; Bardhan & Walker 2011. On the building sector as an industrial district, see Buzzeli & Harris 2006.

42 For overviews, see Walker 1981, Knox 2008, Cox 2016. The same principles apply to commercial development, which has its own rich history. Bloom 2004.

43 Hildebrand 1981, Moudon 1986, Brechin 1989, 1999, Walker 1995b, Loeb 2002, Horiuchi 2007. Duncan McDuffie was one of the first presidents of the National Association of Real Estate Boards.

In other words, California was already a field of dreams for big develop-ers in the early twentieth century. The scale of developments continued to rise, and by the end of World War I the Golden State could boast the biggest array of New Community developers in the country, such as Doelger, Bohannon, and Eichler in the Bay Area and Kaiser-Burns, Leimert, and Kaufman & Broad in Los Angeles. This new generation of developers unified the city-building process by buying, subdividing, improving, and building upon large parcels of land (though they usually subcontracted actual construction). Only Florida could compare with California in the realm of giant housing developers, and some big Florida operators moved into California in the 1960s, such as T. Jack Foster, developer of Foster City. California also generated some of the world's biggest realty companies, such as the Bay Area's Coldwell Banker (CBRE), Ritchie & Ritchie, and Cornish & Carey (see chapter 5).[44]

In recent years, the largest Bay Area developers have sprouted in the Central Valley, such as Shea Homes, Seeno/Discovery (now merged), and Wilson Homes. They have been major builders of the new Inland Empire of the north. Southern California developers have been very active here, as well, including KB Home (formerly Kaufman & Broad) and Shappell (bought by Toll Brothers of Pennsylvania). Outside developers, such as D.R. Horton and Pulte, have rushed to take advantage of California's massive housing market, and Florida-based Lennar Corporation has grabbed the Bay Area's biggest infill developments: the old navy installations at Mare Island, Hunters' Point, and Treasure Island. Given the size of the product, a house, even the largest developers build only a few hundred or a couple thousand units per year, out of the tens of thousands added to California's housing stock annually; so small developers remain important. But the big ones lead the way in style, innovation, and political clout.[45]

Behind the developers are the financiers. Here again, the ample financial resources of California have been available to developers to assemble, improve, and build on large parcels. In the nineteenth century, San Francisco million-aires bought huge tracts of land with their mining wealth, which were later subdivided, as in the case of Millbrae (James Mills), Sharon Heights (William Sharon estate), and Oakland's China Hill (Borax Smith estate). Groups such as the Mission Housing Association were another avenue by which land was bought, subdivided, and built upon. Banks became more involved over time,

---

44   Burns 1975, Weiss 1987, Brechin 1990, Walker 1995b, Hise 1997.
45   Lists of the biggest California developers are published by Professional Builder. Shea homes is in the national top ten, Seeno/Discovery in the top twenty-five. On Lennar, see Horiuchi & Sankalia 2017. Ironically, Lennar entered California by buying out Oakland's bankrupt Bramalea in 1995.

which made it possible for developers such as Mason-McDuffie or Doelger to operate on a larger, unified scale. A key innovation of the postwar savings and loan industry, led by Home Savings in Los Angeles, was to lend to both the tract developers and then people buying the newly built homes, with developers acting as intermediaries. This was the time when big insurance companies also became investors in urban land development.[46]

In the contemporary era, financialization of real estate development has gone further, aided by an influx of institutional funds from insurance companies and REITs (see chapter 6). This has brought rapid consolidation of the leading national homebuilders through mergers and acquisitions, especially in the largest urban markets such as the Bay Area. The top firms, such as Lennar, Pulte, and KB Home, became multibillion-dollar operations by the early twenty-first century. And to pay off their investors, they drove up profits by breaking unions, standardizing and prefabricating supplies, and outsourcing work—as well as pushing in-house lending to home buyers.[47]

★   ★   ★

Where do developers prefer to invest in land and build, and why do they favor fringe development over more compact forms? Are they providing consumers what they wanted or, instead, creating the city according to their own logic of profits and after their own ideas of style? There is every reason to think that suburban sprawl is a dynamic based heavily on a logic of property investment and capital accumulation that has little to do with the American suburban dream.[48]

The first thing to realize is that it is in the interest of property capital to stretch suburbia as far as possible because the highest profits come from land value appreciation, not from building houses. That is, the key to maximizing rents is to buy land cheaply and convert it to urban use. Sprawl pays, because city land is more valuable than farm or ranch land by an order of magnitude, and it pays even more if you can leapfrog beyond other developments to buy land before farmers catch on to rising property values. Today the best gains are to be made by jumping out to places in the Central Valley, Lake County, or San Benito County. In a region as hilly as the Bay Area, it also pays to keep to sites that are easy to bulldoze and build on, so suburbanization shoots out like flares along highway corridors such as Interstate 80, I-580, and U.S.

---

46   Hanchett 2000, Rubin 2012, Abrahamson 2013.
47   Wissoker 2016.
48   For systematic arguments to this effect, see Walker 1981, Beauregard 2006, Knox 2008, Gonzales 2009, Schoenberger 2015.

101, following the lay of the land along the Valley floors flanked by the coast ranges.[49]

Second, it is more profitable to develop large swaths of land in order to internalize the gains from mutually reinforcing land uses and to top it off by giving major developments brand names like Bishop Ranch or Blackhawk. As developers have grown larger, they have been able to add bigger and bigger chunks to the edge of suburbia, all the way up to entire towns. Levittown, New York, and Lakewood (near LA) are notorious examples, and the Bay Area is replete with such wholesale developments, such as Daly City, El Cerrito, and Redwood Shores. Today the same process is being repeated in new subdivisions such as Mountain House near Tracy (by Shea Homes), Mission Village in Los Banos (by DR Horton), and Riverwalk near Lathrop (by Woodside Homes)—and even more spectacularly at Treasure Island and Hunters Point in San Francisco (by Lennar).[50]

Third, large developers have emphasized simplicity of construction and repetition of forms to keep down costs, while increasing revenue through such strategies as model designs and revamped interiors. This has led to many innovations in floor plans, fixtures, and construction, some of which look quite brilliant in retrospect (Eichler's postwar tract homes are the gold standard for that). Nevertheless, the numbing redundancy of large-scale housing tracts is strikingly evident from Doelger's postwar boxes in Daly City to the minimansions of the early twenty-first century at Gale Ranch in the East Bay's Dougherty Valley.[51]

Fourth, developers popularize styles of housing, and the styles developed in the Bay Area have been distinctive. The San Francisco Stick homes offered by the Realty Associates were an exuberant twist on prevailing Victorian architecture of the late nineteenth century, enhanced by cheap lumber and capable millwrights. Craftsman and shingle-style flourished in California from 1895 to 1914, as builders offered a different kind of bohemian vibe amid woody abundance in developments such as Berkeley's Elmwood District. Between the wars, the Mediterranean style flourished—a pastiche of Spanish baroque, Mexican ranchero, Pueblo Indian, and Italian renaissance—as builders started covering wood framing with stucco to get a bright, sunny look. Some developers, such as Charles MacGregor of Albany (just north of Berkeley), made stucco compatible with Hansel and Gretel–style houses. In the postwar era, Bay Area developers toyed with Modernism such as Eichler's flat-roofed boxes

---

49 Clawson 1971, Walker 1981, 2007, Knox 2008. On the general capitalist search for cheap inputs, see Moore 2015.
50 Brechin 1990, Walker 1995b, Loeb 2002, Ungaretti 2012, Horiuchi & Sankala 2017.
51 On developer cost controls and standardization, see Hise 1997, Loeb 2002.

or went with regional retro ranch houses, usually clad in redwood siding. In the 1980s, neo-Tuscan style became the rage, with tile roofs, stucco siding, minimal eaves, and bloated footprints. Most such developer-bred styles were drawn up by in-house architects working within narrow cost constraints.[52]

Finally, developers take rising land values into account and respond to their own best interests. In the case of infill on expensive central city land, they build upward to increase rental space, as previously noted; and as the whole urban area has risen in value, they have built more densely everywhere. Since the 1980s, new suburban landscapes have looked very different from those of the 1950s, with more two-story, tightly packed detached houses, townhouses around communal garden spaces, and mixed developments of high-rise and low-rise buildings—plus commercial space, if possible. Builders have also sought to maximize floor space versus yards for busy professionals and altered internal floor plans to suit households with fewer children. The previous fashion for ample backyards, welcoming lawns fronting the street, and lack of fences is long gone. People want—and are getting—more interior space, larger entries and master bedrooms, home entertainment centers, and more. Privacy and protection are maintained less by personal distance than by sturdy fences, gated communities, and security guards. This is no longer your grandparents' suburbia.

Waves of urban growth lay down rings like those of a tree, each with a distinctive look based on the styles, scale, and scope of development at the time. The current wave will be distinguished by lots of minimansions packed into large-scale, uniform developments, often with gated entries, since in an era of high-priced land and high incomes developers are targeting the upper end of the housing market. This is no longer the age of building for the mass of a (working) middle class, as in the 1950s, when land was cheap, incomes more equal, and finance more restricted. Even where homes have been built expressly for working-class families moving to the far urban fringes, the tendency has been to build overly large (if cheaply built) homes that could only be purchased with huge mortgages.[53]

★ ★ ★

Developers do not make the city by themselves. They have enablers among the ranks of local governments, which are the key units of the U.S. federal system

---

52 Many styles of houses developed in the Golden State spread around the country: the California bungalow in the 1910s–20s, ranch house and split-level 1930s–50s, redwood look 1960s–70s, neo-Mediterranean 1980s–90. Moudon 1986, Woodbridge 1976, King 1974, Harris & Dostrovsky 2008.

53 On waves of building and urban rings, see Whitehand 1987.

overseeing land use decisions and urban development. Suburbanization requires improvements such as roads, water, and electricity, and those, in turn, demand some degree of planning and public investment. This has made local urban government the pivot of land use politics and urban management. In order to secure approval for land use change and the extension of infrastructure, developers lobby intensely, capture local officials, and corrupt local politics to get want they want. This phenomenon has been called "the local growth machine."[54]

As a result, it makes sense to speak of "planned sprawl," because it is an outcome desired by those in positions of power, public and private. San Jose and the Santa Clara Valley had an archetypal suburban growth regime in the postwar era (see chapter 5). Yet despite the way histories of the area feature public figures such as Dutch Hamann and Fred Terman, growth regimes are driven more by private developers than public officials. The South Bay growth regime was quite undemocratic, as Nader's Raiders pointed out at the time, contrary to the theoretical blandishments of economists and political scientists about the participatory demos of the suburbs. Ordinary people were too busy scrambling to find housing, settling down in their new environs, and commuting to work to have their voices heard. This discrepancy of power was augmented by gender and racial divides, as well as the class structure.[55]

Things changed dramatically with the revolts against untrammeled growth that hit the Bay Area in the 1960s to 1980s, when the region developed a powerful conservation movement. As a result, millions of acres of parks and open spaces were protected within the nine-country urban region. Despite that success, however, suburban sprawl proceeds unabated to this day, for two reasons. One is that insofar as growth controls have been successful in the core Bay Area, developers simply jump out to the far fringes to build; the way Marin County's strict growth limits have squeezed more development up to Sonoma County (and now beyond) is a case in point. Another is that the jurisdictions at the urban fringes, from Vacaville to Merced to Watsonville, are still hungry for new development to fill municipal coffers and enrich local

---

54 Molotch 1976, Mollenkopf 1983, Logan & Molotch 1987, Elkin 1987. For a recent assessment, see Cox 2016. The same phenomenon could be found earlier in San Francisco in the Progressive Era, Oakland in the 1920s to 1950s, Marin and San Mateo Counties in the postwar era, and the 680 corridor in the 1970s and '80s. Brechin 1999, Self 2003, Rhomberg 2004, Walker 2007.

55 Planned sprawl comes from Gottdeiner 1977. Postwar liberals tried to defend local politics as a fair expression of civic democracy, as in Tiebout 1956 and Dahl 1961 (also Peterson 1981, Schneider 1989), but were rebutted by Sixties radicals, such as Bachrach & Baratz 1970 and Domhoff 1978.

landowners, lawyers, and merchants; newly urbanizing places have always been the weak link in the chain of growth control and open space conservation. Contrary to the beliefs of both advocates and critics of growth controls, the spigot of suburban sprawl has never been turned off in the Bay Area.[56]

Suburbia Devours Its Children

As the pressure of rising housing prices grew by the end of the twentieth century,[57] a mass migration of working-class households of color to the outer realms of the Bay Area was underway. This wave was led by African Americans and Latinos, particularly children of immigrants starting their own families and looking for more room to raise children; but it included a good number of Asian families, as well. In the process, many former white working-class towns such as Antioch and Concord, known for their racial barriers, have nonwhite majorities today. The pattern of racial settlement, segregation, and inequality has been inverted in the Bay Area, as in many other American metropolitan areas. The same forces that have made the region so dynamic have flipped its racial geography upside down.[58]

Unfortunately, the housing bubble and financial crisis of the early twenty-first century revealed the fragility of these open-housing era suburbs. Developers built large houses expressly for this cohort, and their bigger families and mortgage companies gleefully offered working-class households financial packages they could not afford. They did so by the sleight of hand of variable interest rates, zero down payments, and jumbo loans, while making no effort to scrutinize family finances or consider risk of unemployment. The reality was that many, if not most of these suburban dreamers did not have the means to purchase such homes and pay off the mortgages. Working-class wages in California, as in the rest of the country, had been flat for a generation, while housing prices were flying high on the wings of demand driven by a booming economy, upper-class incomes, abundant capital. The only way to make up the difference was credit, which looked cheap and easy in the moment but turned out to be costly and ruinous when the economy turned down (see chapter 6 and fig. 7.11).[59]

---

56 On Bay Area conservation and growth controls, see Walker 2007. On the marginal net effects of growth controls, see Warner & Molotch 2000. The bogus argument that growth controls created the housing crisis was dealt with in chapter 6.

57 Self 2003, Brahinsky 2012, Schafran 2009. On race and the FHA rules, which were written by representatives of the National Association of Realtors, see Gothan 2000b, Hornstein 2005, Freund 2007.

58 Compare Davis 2002, Niedt 2013. On the suburban dream for Asian Americans, see Lung-Amam 2017.

59 On the economics of the housing bubble, see Bardhan and Walker 2011.

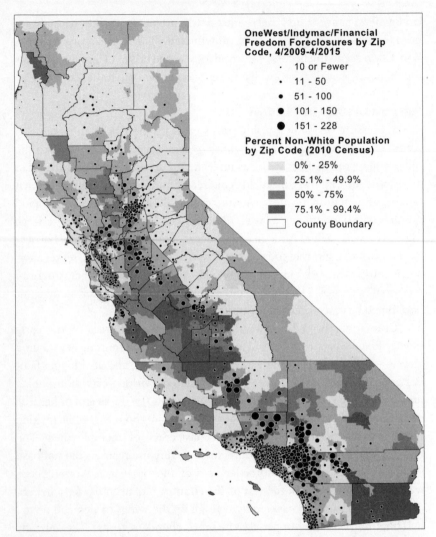

Figure 7.11: Map of Foreclosures in California, 2009–2015 (vs. Share of Non-White Population)
Source: Courtesy of Steve Spiker of Urban Strategies Council.

The financial meltdown on Wall Street in 2007–8 brought down the mortgage banks in California, such as Countrywide Savings and Washington Mutual, and laid waste to the dream of homeowners across the Golden State. Just as California had been the highest flyer in the housing bubble, it was the heart of the housing bust: one million foreclosed homes, six million underwater mortgages, and $3 trillion loss in home values. The locus of the state's meltdown was the Inland Empires of the north and south. As the financial house of cards toppled, Central Valley counties such as San Joaquin, Modesto,

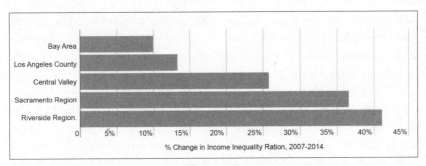

Figure 7.12: Growth of Inequality in California Regions, 2007–2014

Source: Levin 2016. Data from the Public Policy Institute of California.

and Merced topped the charts nationally, reaching astounding foreclosure rates of 30–50 percent and house price declines of 40–50 percent.

The housing collapse and financial crisis triggered the Great Recession across the country, but nowhere worse than in California, which lost two million jobs and reached an unemployment rate of 12 percent (18 percent if discouraged and part-time workers were counted). In the Central Valley counties and Inland Empire of the south, rates of unemployment, hunger, and impoverishment reached levels akin to the Great Depression of the 1930s. Topping things off were the spectacular bankruptcies of the cities of Stockton and San Bernardino, which had also borrowed too much and then saw their revenues shrink along with the economy.[60]

The situation in the Bay Area's Inland Empire was nothing short of calamitous, and depressed conditions persisted through the 2010s. As a result, inequality grew much more rapidly inland than along the coast. Yet the suffering of the Central Valley was generally seen as something apart from the prosperity of the inner Bay Area, even though they are two sides of the same coin of inequality and unequal development of the region, and the prosperous blue counties along the coast wonder why the interior counties of the state are dyed a deep red to this day (see fig. 7.12).

What is more, the fate of the bankrupt suburbs of the Inland Empire is deeply colored by race. People of color were overrepresented in high foreclosure areas such as eastern Contra Costa County and the Inland Empire of the North. Their dreams of a new suburbia built on color-blind opportunity were dashed on the shoals of the Great Recession. Whereas millions in the white working class saw themselves lifted into a suburban middle class during the postwar American Century, communities of color got on the bus too late.

---

60 On the crash in California, see Bardhan & Walker 2011, Lewis 2011, Schafran 2013, Schafran & Wegmann 2015.

Crucially, the former was based on rising wages, modest-sized homes, and sober mortgages from local S&Ls, while the latter rested precariously on stagnant incomes, predatory debt, reregulated financial markets, and mountains of risky mortgage-based securities (see again figure 7.11, above).

The older working-class districts of the inner Bay Area were also hammered when the bubble burst: East Oakland, Richmond, Union City, Hercules, San Pablo, San Francisco's Bayview, San Rafael, East Palo Alto, and so on. Even sadder than the young families striving for the American dream were the older homeowners who had taken out new loans to help the younger generation get an education, set up businesses, and move to the suburbs. Over ten thousand owners lost their homes in Oakland alone between 2007 and 2011, some 10 percent of the city's total stock of owner-occupied housing. Most of these homes were concentrated in areas that are heavily African American, Asian, and Latino. As the banks foreclosed, they resold the houses to speculative investor-landlords, who turned houses into rentals or sold them off to gentrifiers (see also chapter 5).[61]

After years of apparent progress for immigrants and racial minorities, the foreclosure crisis resulted in the greatest loss of wealth for people of color in recent U.S. history. This was not just a set of personal tragedies or the impoverishment of whole communities, it was a catastrophe for racial justice and the new working class of color. Recall that the economic foundation of class and race inequality in America is not simply wage discrimination but also wealth—Whites have it and people of color do not. That only got worse in the crash, and the Bay Area's notorious inequality and housing bloat acted like lead weights around the feet of the latter. For all its vaunted prosperity, opportunity, and high average incomes, the bay region has become more racially unequal rather than more, and that injustice is written deep in the landscape of the metropolis.[62]

Conclusion

The Bay Area's succession of economic boom times has not only stimulated the New Urbanism at the center and wildly inflated housing prices, it has driven a gargantuan expansion of the metropolis. As a result, the Bay Area of today is barely recognizable to those who grew up here in the postwar era, whether in population numbers, spatial extent, traffic jams, or the look of the urban landscape. It is not surprising, therefore, that people have a

61 Urban Strategies Council 2012, Bond-Graham 2014.
62 On the losses to foreclosures nationally, see Rivera et al. 2008, Wyly et al. 2009, Ashton 2012.

hard time getting their minds around the scale of the new metropolitan area as it sprawls ever farther afield and collides with Sacramento and Stockton. Nevertheless, it behooves citizens of the region to raise their eyes to the new horizons of today's Bay Area and consider how their piece of the city fits into a much-larger puzzle.

The bay region has welcomed millions of new residents as it has grown, offering work and opportunity to many, but it remains a highly unequal metropolis. Spatial segregation by class and race is the calling card of American cities and suburbs, and the Bay Area has not escaped that fate despite its liberal reputation. The pieces of the puzzle may have been reshuffled as the metropolitan area expanded, inverting patterns of the past, but sharp inequalities of class and race are still etched deeply on the face of the city. The housing calamity that struck so many working-class households and families of color in the Great Recession has only made things worse.

It is important for people who care about the fate of the Bay Area to look beyond the tech industry and its impacts on the region or do more than bemoan the housing crisis and fight for tenants' rights and affordable housing in the central cities. They need to understand the process by which the metropolis is constructed, and the development industry that profits off it, if they are to ever take democratic control of the city and shape it better to the needs of its citizens. This has long been apparent to conservationists fighting to control growth and protect open spaces from rampant development; but, despite their achievements, it threatens to escape again and wreak havoc because of the sheer scale of urbanization and environmental change today. That will be the subject of the next chapter.

Part III
Facing the Future
Dreams, Nightmares, and
Political Realities

INTRODUCTION TO PART III

IN PREVIOUS CHAPTERS, IT HAS BEEN ARGUED THAT THE BAY AREA IS A SPECIAL PLACE but one turned upside down by its own success. In Part I, it was portrayed as one of the country's, if not the world's, most important cities in terms of its domination of High Tech, economic performance, and accumulation of riches, but also as a place facing a growing class divide and working-class mobilization to heal glaring wounds in the social fabric. Part II treated the Bay Area in terms of its geography, showing that it is a leading example of contemporary urbanization, in view of its enormous footprint, social and spatial restructuring, and property investment and bubble. The downsides of those transformations were also made clear in terms of massive displacement, uncontrolled sprawl, and unaffordable housing.

Part III turns the spotlight on three other arenas in which the Bay Area stands out: environmental protection, living with information technology, and progressive politics. The next three chapters take a hard look at the future through those optics, by considering what damage the boom times have wrought on the well-being of the bay region, the nation, and the world. While the Bay Area has an admirable record in conservation, innovation, and politics, one cannot be sanguine about the prospects ahead. Can the citizens of the metropolis salvage the best of their heritage going forward? To do so, it will be necessary to cope with dramatic environmental change in an age of global warming, to save the best of the IT revolution from the hubris of its avatars and abuse of its platforms, and to maintain the progressive spirit of the Left Coast in the face of the dismal political tenor of the age.

Chapter 8 considers the future of the Bay Area in terms of the natural environment and the challenges of climate change. Some of the most dire effects of urban growth are to be found in and around the metropolis itself, especially as it pushes far into the interior of California. But the biggest questions of the present age concern energy use, carbon emissions, and global warming, which extend far beyond local geographies of the metropolis. While the Bay Area has an admirable record of conservation and environmental activism over the years, local achievements are insufficient to cope with the worldwide challenge of climate change, and even though the State of California has taken some important steps to control carbon emissions, the country and the world are falling far short of what is needed. As a result, conditions are changing fast, but the state has done too little to cope with the future of water supply, rising seas, and wildfires.

Chapter 9 turns to the new Tech World created by the information technology revolution birthed by Silicon Valley. It questions the utopian faith of the tech propagandists about the wonderful future given to humanity by IT and shows the dark side of clever ideas loosed on the world with too little forethought, too much hubris, and too rapacious an interest in profit. This has proved true in one domain after another: disruption and automation, the sharing economy and on-demand economy, the wealth of information on the internet and social media. The unanticipated costs of Tech World are adding up, and the public is becoming more aware of the dangers of the Brave New World of unlimited information, communication, and commerce via the internet. Calls are mounting for the lords of tech to rein in their platforms, but there is a long way to go for society to get on top of the monsters that have been unleashed.

Finally, chapter 10 pivots to politics in general. Long known as the Left Coast for its progressive politics and social movements, the Bay Area has faced two major challenges to its progressive reputation. One came from outside in the form of the neoliberal/neoconservative counterrevolution in California, by which the Golden State's favorite son, Ronald Reagan, succeeded in overthrowing the New Deal order that gave the postwar era a vital measure of social equality, worker power, and welfare programs. The other challenge came from within, as the booming tech industry has reconfigured the Bay Area and its politics. At the end of the day, the metropolis is still very much on the Blue Coast of America, as California has turned into a bulwark against the triumphant Right, but the mantle of the Left Coast has mostly slipped away, making the Bay Area less politically distinctive than it once was.

CHAPTER EIGHT

Saving Greenland

Environmentalism in the Age of Global Warming

CITIES ARE WONDERFUL THINGS, FULL OF BUSTLING PEOPLE, GREAT INSTITUTIONS, new experiences, and innovative ideas. But they are creatures of nature. Cities make massive demands on resources and have an immense impact on the natural environment. Humans and their cities have been exploiting, transforming, and damaging the earth for millennia. While the environmental problems of today, such as global climate change, are not without precedent, they are intensifying with the ever-greater size of cities, throughput of industry, and global reach of the capitalist system. By virtue of leading place in the today's world economy and technology, the Bay Area is deeply implicated in the fate of the earth.

Furthermore, the Bay Area has long been an international beacon of conservation and nature protection. The region's environmental movements have passed legislation and instilled a conservation ethic into the fiber of the urban community, and their achievements have transformed the physical fabric of the metropolis. They have reshaped this place into a uniquely green metropolis, where the bay is the centerpiece, open space is close by, beautiful views rise around every corner, and people find ample room for recreation. This is the collective accomplishment of thousands of people, hundreds of organizations, and scores of laws and regulations. And it resonates in a political culture that runs deep and springs up again and again among the young and new arrivals.

The Bay Area is, therefore, a kind of urban "Greenland," something in which its citizens can rightfully take pride. The opening section of this chapter begins on that positive note. But praising past achievements is no longer enough. Protecting one metropolitan island is a fine thing and provides a model for others, but today the problem of environmental protection has moved to larger scales, right up to the earth itself. Therefore, this chapter moves outward and upward from the old Bay Area to consider four dimensions of environmental impact and urgent needs for enlightened policies to save this metaphorical Greenland and, ultimately, the real one in the North Atlantic.

The inquiry begins by recognizing that even a putatively green city has a profound impact on the surrounding environment that is only becoming more intensive as the metropolis grows. With the explosion of the greater Bay Area outward, a vast new battlefront has opened up far inland that requires renewed attention to parks, open space, and pollution controls. That is the subject of the second section.

Moving outward to the whole of the California, the third section looks at the water supply system that feeds the Bay Area. The state's plumbing critically affects the geographic core of the region, the San Francisco Bay estuary, including the Sacramento–San Joaquin Delta. The growth of the metropolitan area, combined with global climate change's effect on California's rain and snowfall regime, is forcing a fundamental reconsideration of the historic path of water development—how water is stored, how it is used, and how the system is governed throughout the state. Whether California can break with its water-guzzling past is up in the air, but here, too, the example of water conservation in the bay region can provide a model.

In the fourth section, the topic will be energy and energy conservation, a global topic that revolves chiefly around the opposition between California's progressive efforts and the revanchism of the United States government. As the latter has worsened under the current Republican administration, the state has redoubled its efforts to contain carbon emissions through greater energy efficiency. At the same time, the Bay Area has taken the lead in certain forms of energy technology, from electric cars to battery storage to smart buildings. But much remains to be done, especially in transportation planning.

The fifth section arrives at an irreducibly global problem: rising sea levels. Given the modern world's fossil fuel mania and resulting global warming, the ice caps are melting, including that of the real Greenland (an oxymoron in name but no less real for that). As the ice melts and warmer water expands, the oceans rise. In a metropolis touched by water on every flank, this is no small consideration. Change in one Greenland is about to clobber another.

The last section concerns the impact of global warming on land, as California becomes more exposed to the dangers of wildfires. Although the state already has a Mediterranean regime of dry summers, hot fall winds, and frequent droughts that render it prone to wildfires, things are getting worse fast and Northern California is becoming more like the hotter, drier, and intensely flammable southland. Yet, despite horrendous fires in recent years, understanding of the causes and dynamics of wildfires, especially the intrusion of cities into the wildland interface, is far too limited among Bay Area urbanites.

The question, then, is whether Bay Area green politics and green tech are up to the several challenges of urban growth and environmental change at every scale. We may hope that the collective genius of the city—aptly illustrated by its tech industry, research and educational institutions, and outstanding environmental movement—rises to the occasion to help lead the way out of the age of fossil fuels, water waste, automobiles, and helter-skelter urban expansion. Can the one Greenland perhaps save its icy twin? Signs are promising, but there are still all too many crevasses to cross.

Greening the Old Bay Area

Nature made the Bay Area rich, but the plunder of California was rapid and unrelenting. It evoked quick revulsion against the rapine of land, forests, and rivers and gave rise to a nascent conservation movement led by groups such as the Sierra Club, Sempervirens Fund, and Save the Redwoods League. John Muir raised the clarion call for environmental preservation for the first time around the turn of the last century. While much of the conservationists' attention was directed toward the glories of the Sierra Nevada and the redwood forests, it also focused on more humble places nearer to home, such as Big Basin, Mount Tamalpais, and the Berkeley Hills. The result was to start building a ring of parks around the region and to root a love of nature in the city's culture and politics.[1]

Bay Area conservationists added to their reputation and to the regional greenbelt through the era of building national and state park systems in the twentieth century. Several local visionaries, such as Stephen Mather, Horace Albright, and Duncan McDuffie, led the way in creating the National Park Service and California State Park Commission. The number of parks around the region multiplied rapidly, first because of low land prices in the Depression and then owing to greatly increased budgets after the Second World War. But new challenges arose at the same time with the rapid expansion of big water projects and spreading suburbs. A new wave of conservationists was born and the Bay Area once again took a leading role in the struggles of the times.

In the postwar era, the Sierra Club took on the dam builders on the Colorado River and ski resorts in the Sierra, while the Marin Conservation League and Committee for Green Foothills wrestled with the freeway builders and developers. Above all, Save the Bay was founded to stop incursions on the bay by garbage dumps, New Town developers, and the military, and it won absolute control over bay fill and public access to the bay shore. A host of other groups sprang up in their wake. Save the Coast gained a Coastal

---

1 Walker 2007, Vogel 2018.

Commission, Save Our Seashore garnered Point Reyes National Seashore, and the Sierra Club led the fight for the Golden Gate National Recreation Area. Hundreds of local protests blossomed to halt particular developments, from housing on San Bruno Mountain to cutting redwoods along Purisima Creek. These struggles were all marked by a degree of militancy typical of the 1960s and a willingness to buck the progrowth ethos of the age.

In the 1970s and '80s, a range of slow-growth uprisings occurred in well-established suburbs such as Petaluma, Livermore, and Walnut Creek. While these had several facets, including the defense of privileged enclaves, the results turned out to favor good planning over exclusion, with an emphasis on guarding open space through urban growth boundaries. One organization, above all, kept an eye on regional growth as a whole, and steered the fragmentary revolts toward a coherent vision of metropolitan planning and a regional greenbelt: People for Open Space / Greenbelt Alliance. Its founders, Dorothy Erskine and Jack Kent, pushed through the first region-wide plan and the first agricultural preserve, which saved the Napa Valley from being paved over. Under William Evers and Larry Orman, the group changed its name and strategy to connect directly with local activists around the Bay Area, promote good city plans, and focus on lands at risk of development.

The movement further spawned a powerful group of land trusts, public and private, such as the Trust for Public Land and Marin Agricultural Land Trust. As government taxation and funding for parks diminished in the neoconservative / neoliberal era, land trusts became a way of funneling private gifts of money and property into protected open space. A device that aided this effort was the conservation easement, or the sale by private owners of the right to develop their land. Easement are widely used around the region. In many cases, property is acquired outright by a land trust and later resold or deeded to public park and open space authorities. Conservationists and voters never gave up on public parks, passing several major tax and bond measures for park acquisition.[2]

The result of all this activity has been staggering. A quarter of the nearly 4.5 million acres in the nine-county Bay Area are under permanent protection, an area larger than Yosemite National Park. Another 2.2 million acres are covered by policies such as growth boundaries, hillside ordinances, and agricultural zoning. And there is, of course, the blue heart of the region, San Francisco Bay, covering three-quarters of a million acres. The urban hardscape occupies about the same amount of territory as the bay.[3]

---

2   For a count, see http://www.conservationeasement.us/reports/easements?report_state=California&report_type=All.

3   Figures from Greenbelt Alliance 2017.

In addition, the Bay Area conservation movement targeted places far beyond San Francisco. The Sierra Club played a critical role in the establishment of the National Wilderness Act and in protecting half of Alaska, for example. David Brower was ousted from the club and started Friends of the Earth and the League of Conservation Voters, both national and international players. Friends of the River, begun to stop a dam in the Central Valley, gave birth to International Rivers, which built alliances to stop high dams around the world. The Rainforest Action Network was launched from the Bay Area, as well.

The region also spawned a series of environmental organizations fighting to control air and water pollution, along with toxic hazards. The fight against DDT won its first victories behind the United Farm Workers union in the 1960s, and the Pesticide Action Network (PAN) was born soon after, later to become a worldwide force for controlling hazardous poisons. The Silicon Valley Toxics Network, which began with a local battle to control tech firms' contamination of groundwater, went global, as well. The Bay Area also gave birth to several groups fighting to protect communities of color in Richmond and Oakland from hazardous emissions, which became part of the wider environmental justice movement. A group that spanned white conservation and environmental justice in a unique way was Communities for a Better Environment.

Bay Area environmentalism stands on three legs. One is the high level of organizational capacity, in terms of both tenacity and expertise. Another is the degree of firm legal protections and regulations, backed by government agencies. A third is a deep culture of nature protection built on environmental education and everyday experience in the use of the green-and-blue belt around the metropolis. Behind those lies a fundamental political achievement: an unequaled degree of popular mobilization. The region was the birthplace of the first mass conservation movement, with Save the Bay, Save Our Seashore, and the Sierra Club's Grand Canyon campaign in the 1960s. While the movement has been overwhelmingly recruited from the upper classes—the kind of old money and educated professionals that have been plentiful in the region for a long time—a striking thing about the movement, and a key to its success, has been the ability to appeal to a wide public including the working class and communities of color. And that mass appeal has rested, in turn, on a clear sense of public purpose and insistence on guarding beaches, woodlands, and waters as *public* space, open to all comers.[4]

---

4   Walker 2007, forthcoming.

The Mammoth Urban Footprint

A growing metropolis such as the Bay Area makes two general kinds of marks on the land: the direct footprint of building and paving and the wider impact of its resource demands—energy, water, minerals, and air required—and the expulsion of waste products. Urbanization of the contemporary Bay Area extends into the rural countryside for over one hundred miles in every direction, and the city's metabolism extends even farther, affecting the whole state and extending in some cases to the far corners of the earth. Later sections of this chapter consider the Bay Area's appetite for water and energy; this section is confined to the impacts of land use and pollution in and around the urban region.

As the Bay Area marches outward, it scrapes, reshapes, and paves the land over thousands of square miles. The expanding scale of the city poses new threats in every direction. But most of the attention still falls within the bounds of the nine-county Bay Area. Local conservationists have trouble seeing beyond the Coast Ranges to the interior Central Valley and the Inland Empire of the metropolitan region. The Valley has been abused so long by agribusiness that it does not immediately grab the heart. Yet this vast plain was once a verdant place of grassland, oaks, wetlands, and riparian forests that supported immense herds of antelope, deer, and elk, schools of salmon and clouds of migratory waterfowl. Not all of that is gone, but threats to what remains are particularly severe where urbanization has raged in recent years.

The Greenbelt Alliance has taken the lead in guiding development away from sensitive environments, publishing periodic reports on lands at risk of development. The latest report identifies almost five hundred square miles in the nine-county Bay Area at risk of urbanization over the coming thirty years. Previous reports have been quite effective at alerting local planners and governments to act preemptively to mark off land as open space off-limits to developers. At the same time, the Greenbelt Alliance and Bay Area Open Space Council have long advocated for denser housing in built-up areas in order to save open space and have convinced business leaders of the merits of their position. But Greenbelt Alliance does not project beyond the core counties of the bay region.[5]

Another method of reining in development is to acquire land directly as city, county, and state parks, either directly by park agencies or indirectly via land trusts that later pass along parcels as government money becomes available. The East Bay Regional Park District has been especially effective at

---

5   Greenbelt Alliance 2017. Kallerman & Weinberg 2017. The latter report includes a tenth
      county, Santa Cruz.

keeping ahead of the advance wave of urbanization in Alameda and Contra Costa Counties, and Sonoma and Santa Clara Counties have followed suit pretty aggressively. Marin County has had the benefit of several state and national parks in its territory. Napa and Solano Counties have lagged in terms of parks acquisition, relying on other methods of land protection, such as agricultural zones, hillside protection ordinances, and urban growth boundaries.[6]

Parkland is scarcer in the surrounding counties: Lake, Yolo, San Joaquin, Modesto, Merced, and San Benito. The interior counties are poorly served by state and federal parks and have not created substantial systems of their own. Modesto and Merced Counties have off-road vehicle state parks, and San Benito boasts the Pinnacles National Park, but that's about it. Santa Cruz and Mendocino Counties benefit from state parks and beaches along the coast and among the redwoods, and the former gained the Cotoni-Coast Dairies National Monument, added by President Obama.

Safeguarding wildlife has become a basic feature of land management around the Bay area, since the heavy boots of urbanization eliminate and fragment habitat. Park agencies and Open Space authorities, backed by conservation groups such as Save Mount Diablo, make a concerted effort to buy and protect wildlife corridors. Similarly, the recuperation of tidal wetlands from salt ponds and pastures continues apace in the bay's large wildlife refuges, along with greater attention to the bay's aquatic conditions. As a result, wildlife and bird numbers have rebounded, so much so that urban invasions by cougars, coyotes, turkeys, and wild boars have become a regular feature of Bay Area life, as well as sightings of harbor seals, porpoises, and humpback whales.[7]

Yet some of the most outstanding wildlife habitat lies beyond the nine-county bay region in the Central Valley. The principle areas are the wetlands of the Sacramento–San Joaquin Delta and riparian zones in the flood plains of the two great rivers. Quite a bit has been done over the years to protect waterfowl along the northern Sacramento River, thanks to the combined effort of state and federal wildlife agencies, land trusts, and hunting organizations, using conservation easements and agreements with farmers (especially rice growers). The area covered by national and state wildlife refuges is not large, however. The largest protected area is the Cosumnes River Preserve on the east side of the Delta, which is twice the size of the Sacramento and

---

6   Walker 2007, 2009. Solano finally got its own parks and open space district in 2017, the last of the nine counties to do so.

7   On urban wildlife, which is often overlooked, see Sturba 2012, Steinstra 2017. A recent effort to secure a California Seamounts and Ridges National Marine Conservation Area failed in Congress.

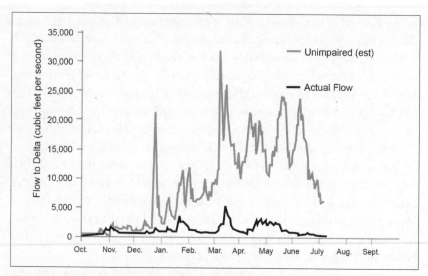

Figure 8.1: San Joaquin River Flows, Past and Present

Source: https://ww2.kqed.org/science/2016/08/19/the-biggest-california-water-decision-youve-never-heard-of/. Data from The Bay Institute.

San Joaquin National Wildlife Refuges combined. It began as a project of the Nature Conservancy and Ducks Unlimited, later joined by state and federal agencies. It combines ownership with easements on farmlands.[8]

The poor San Joaquin River is the most abused stream in the United States. Marshlands and riparian forest has been virtually eliminated, replaced by industrial farmland. There is a small wildlife refuge at the bend where the river turns north toward the Delta. So much of its flow is diverted for irrigation that the river is dry for much of the year in its lower reaches (fig. 8.1). The San Joaquin is currently the subject of ferocious political battles over its water, because environmental groups won legal cases requiring that water managers maintain a minimum summertime flow to revive decimated salmon runs. As for riverine habitat, an effort is underway to expand the San Joaquin River refuge by over twenty thousand acres. There is some local activism behind this and other river protection measures, such as a river "Blueway" for public access and recreation, by River Partners (based in Modesto) and the San Joaquin River Partnership. They could use a lot more help from the Bay Area.[9]

In western Merced County lies the Grasslands Wildlife Management Area, which combines federal and state wildlife refuges with private lands covered by easements—another joint effort of government agencies, duck

---

8   Garone 2011.
9   Pappas 2014, http://riverpartners.org.

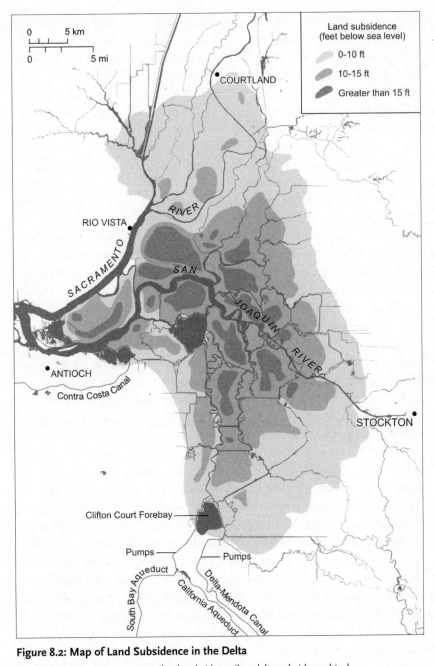

Figure 8.2: Map of Land Subsidence in the Delta

Source: https://ca.water.usgs.gov/land_subsidence/bay-delta-subsidence.html.

clubs, and land trusts. The area includes about one hundred thousand acres of the last remaining native grasslands of the Central Valley (the Grasslands Ecological Area). These were marginal lands when the project was launched in 1979, but it got a big boost from the 1982 Kesterson disaster—a large-scale die-off of waterfowl in a so-called wildlife refuge that was actually a sump for drainage of toxic runoff from irrigated lands in the Westlands Water District. All of a sudden, the state woke up to the depredations of agribusiness and there was a push to enact real wildlife protections. Ironically, the area now faces a new threat from urbanization around Los Banos on Highway 152, now within the Bay Area's commuting field.

The Sacramento–San Joaquin Delta is the keystone of conservation in the Central Valley. The Delta covers an area almost as large as San Francisco Bay and is made up of hundreds of islands and over a thousand miles of river channels and sloughs. The islands are defended by levees because the heart of the Delta is sinking as its peat soil dries out, and about two-thirds of it is below sea level (see fig. 8.2).

Why is this an urban problem? To begin with, the Delta is a large farming area, an open space used for recreation, and a wildlife resource, all of which are threatened by the explosion of urbanization around it. The Delta is encircled by the mega-urban region of the Bay Area, Stockton, and Sacramento. New housing developments have proliferated on its edges, and thousands of homes have been built below sea level by profit-hungry developers and revenue-starved localities, such as Oakley, Rio Vista, and Elk Grove, with few environmentalists and fewer scruples.[10]

The Delta began to receive serious attention because of battles over water in the 1980s. A Delta Protection Act was passed in 1992 that put the core islands off-limits to urbanization, but not the penumbra. In 2002 the legislature created the California Bay-Delta Authority, or CalFed, which supported a decade of scientific study. The U.S. Geological Survey (USGS) began monitoring subsidence, the Army Corps of Engineers the perilous condition of the levees, and the wildlife agencies the health of fisheries. Out of that came the 2009 Delta Reform Act that created a Delta Stewardship Council, which produced a Delta Plan in 2013. A large percentage of funds from a major water bond were promised for habitat restoration, to be distributed by a new Delta Conservancy. There were high hopes for a sensible approach to managing this great resource.[11]

---

10   Margolis 2005, Bliss 2015.

11   U.S. Army Corps 2011, http://deltaconservancy.ca.gov. CalFed let in critical science for a time, leading to a major bay-delta science report in 2008. Its archived website is: http://calwater.ca.gov. Dick Norgaard, personal communication.

But such optimism was uncalled for. CalFed was euthanized in 2010 because it could not solve the implacable clash between growers and environmentalists over water withdrawals. The Delta Plan suffered the same fate; in 2015 Governor Brown set the plan aside in favor of his pet Delta tunnels project, renaming it, aptly, "The California Water Fix." In an uncensored comment, the governor declared, "the Delta is a lost cause." One upshot is that restoration work was radically reduced from one hundred thousand to thirty thousand acres and from eight billion to a few hundred million dollars. Neither levee maintenance nor development controls have gone very far.[12]

Unfortunately, the Delta has always been the poor cousin to San Francisco Bay—even though they are two parts of the same great estuary—and off the radar of most Bay Area conservation organizations, starting with Save the Bay. The Bay Institute has long pushed the idea of the bay and delta as a unified estuarine system, but it does not have a high profile. A new group, Restore the Delta, was created in 2006, to combine the interests of recreational users and local farmers. The Sierra Club made the fateful blunder of supporting the Peripheral Canal project back in 1980, but is now opposed to the Water Fix, as are Friends of the River and the Planning and Conservation League in Sacramento. We return to this pivotal battle in the next section.

★ ★ ★

Although the long reach of urban resource demand is beyond the limits of what can be covered here, the local impact of urban metabolism is clearly part of the Bay Area's urban footprint. That is, metabolism implies waste products—solid, fluid, and airborne—and as the stuff comes out of urban consumption, it ends up on land, in the water, and in the air. Some wastes can be assimilated by the natural environment; but with rising masses of resource throughput, wastes become pollution hazards: heaps of garbage, outflows from sewers, and billows of smoke and particles, not to mention the toxic chemicals infiltrating all of it.

The greater Bay Area rolls in its own effluent in a number of ways, beginning with garbage. In the postwar era, mountains of solid waste were dumped into San Francisco Bay and covered with dirt. When people realized what a bad idea that was, the cities of the region looked for new places to dump their trash. They hit on a few new spots in the hills in what once seemed far away, like Altamont Pass in eastern Alameda County or Guadalupe Canyon south

---

12 https://www.californiawaterfix.com; on the opposition, see, e.g., Goode 2015, Bacher 2017.

of San Jose. The amount of trash going into landfills has diminished, however, thanks to progress in recycling.

Berkeley's Ecology Center was a pioneer back in the early 1970s in garbage separation, curbside pickups, and recycling. California took up the cause of integrated waste management in the 1980s and today claims a recycling rate of around 67 percent, double the national rate. Some cities in the Bay Area do better: Berkeley has a target of 75 percent and San Francisco an ambitious 2020 goal of zero waste. The latter has a model trash sorting and recycling facility run by Recology, a company that grew up from local roots; but Recology has been accused of fiddling the numbers to achieve the city's gaudy 80 percent recycle rate. Waste Management Corporation, which handles most of the East Bay's rubbish, has a paltry rate of 50 percent recycled, but Alameda County passed a mandatory recycling ordinance in 2012 (three years after San Francisco). No city has a curbside toxics pickup system yet, and toxic substances collected in the Bay Area are shipped to special dumps in the San Joaquin Valley, in the vicinity of poor Latino communities.[13]

Not surprisingly, the global battle to control electronic waste found one of its first advocates in the Bay Area. The Silicon Valley Toxics Coalition, founded in 1982 to fight tech companies over groundwater contamination by cleaning fluids used on silicon chips, turned to e-waste in the 1990s. They succeeded in getting California to mandate e-waste recycling in 2003, the same year as similar European legislation passed; several states have followed suit, but not the U.S. government. Despite such laws, worldwide recycling rates remain low, and two-thirds of U.S. e-waste goes to conventional dumps. As a result, the amount of toxic e-waste still getting into the environment is huge. Presently, the Toxics Coalition has turned its attention to new threats from solar power systems.[14]

Water pollution around the Bay Area fell markedly after the national Clean Water Act of 1972, which clamped down on industrial outfalls and injected billions into municipal treatment plants. Bay waters are safe for swimming today. They are, nevertheless, seriously degraded by four sources. The first is the legacy of toxics metals (chiefly mercury) washed out from mining and smelting in the nineteenth century; these still reside in bay mud, where they are picked up by bottom feeders and concentrated through the food chain, making it dangerous to eat many fish caught in the bay. The second legacy of toxics comes from past industry, especially oil refineries, but also from steel mills, pesticide plants, and the U.S. Navy; adding to this are toxic

13   Walker 2007, Leslie 2010, Minter 2014, Vogel 2018.
14   http://svtc.org, LeBlanc 2017.

leachates from former municipal landfills replete with every kind of household and business waste of the postwar era.[15]

The third major source of water pollution is current surface runoff from streets, construction, and farming. In the East Bay, for example, such runoff goes through separate storm drains into creeks and the bay untreated; it is loaded with trash, pet feces, and hazardous materials such as asbestos from car brakes. San Francisco and San Jose have combined sanitary and storm sewers, which allows for treatment; but the problem with joint systems is high storm flows, which require enormous, expensive holding tanks to allow treatment after storm peaks. Even then, such systems are subject to overflow in wet periods. Marin County is notorious for sewage expulsions from overmatched municipal systems. In recent years, the state and the Bay Area Regional Water Quality Control Board have required local governments to demand permeable pavements that allow more infiltration of rain and less stormwater runoff from new developments; but this does not force retrofitting of the old urban hardscape.[16]

The last major source of water pollution in the bay is from ships, boats, and pipelines. Every few years a ship runs into something or a pipeline breaks, spilling millions of gallons of oil; the last big one was the *Cosco Busan*, which hit the Bay Bridge in 2007. Regional agencies, from the Coast Guard to the Point Reyes Bird Observatory (now Point Blue), pitch in to clean things up and save wildlife. For thirty years, San Francisco Baykeeper has kept a close eye on discharges, errant boaters, and more. But the only good solution is prevention, and as long as petroleum and its products are transported far and wide, spills are inevitable. Of course, all these threats are going to get worse now that the Trump administration is pushing more oil drilling off the West Coast and reducing environmental regulations on toxics.[17]

Air pollution also remains a thorny problem for the Bay Area. While California has the most stringent air quality regulations in the country, they are not enough to prevent serious buildups of smog, ozone, and particulates. A recent report ranked the area sixth among U.S. cities in particle pollution and neck and neck with Shanghai. Nearly half the emissions come from transportation—automobiles, trucks, and ships—and the number of vehicles keeps going up and the commutes getting longer. As a result, the region has experienced more days when air quality exceeds state and federal safety standards, yet transportation planning under the Plan Bay Area 2040 does not adequately

---

15   Brechin 1999, Walker 2007, Horiuchi & Sankalia 2017.
16   Zito 2009, Fimrite 2017.
17   https://baykeeper.org, Lewis 2015.

address the problem (chapter 7). Furthermore, there are still serious emissions from industry, especially the five refineries in the North Bay. Worse, refineries suffer periodic accidents; the last big one was at the giant Chevron plant in Richmond in 2012, and it sent hundreds of people to hospitals.[18]

The Central Valley experiences ghastly levels of pollution. Agriculture generates a huge load of air pollutants, including dust, pesticides, and fertilizer, and the growing cities and traffic of the Valley add their share. Making matters worse, the Bay Area contributes to the mess as its smog blows inland, its trucks and trains carry goods across the Valley, and its commuting fields extend farther and farther inland. The result is the worst air pollution in the country, as emissions are trapped by the surrounding mountains and bake in temperatures that regularly exceed 100 degrees in the summer. Four of the six worst U.S. cities for ozone and particulates are in the Central Valley.[19]

As for water pollution, the Central Valley suffers from massive runoff of fertilizers, pesticides, animal wastes, and sediment from agriculture. The poor San Joaquin River is little more than a drainage ditch, and the Sacramento has a considerable toxic load, as well. From there the pollutants flow into the Delta. Other pollutants go into the soil where they contaminate aquifers; some toxics (particularly nematocides) have been found nearly a thousand feet down and in drinking water drawn from deep wells. Again, this is a problem for the core Bay Area, because the Delta's degraded waters affect San Francisco Bay water quality and so many species, such as Striped Bass, migrate in and out of the Delta.[20]

Deep Currents in California Water Policy

Water is a major concern in California and the source of profound legal and political conflict over the years. One landmark battle over water was the 1884 Sawyer decision that ended hydraulic mining, which signaled the rising power of agriculture in the state. For the next century, agribusiness ruled over California's waters, until it was blocked by the defeat of the Peripheral Canal by popular referendum in 1982. Since that time, water policy has hung in the balance between irrigators and environmentalists. The pivotal waterscape of the Central Valley is where the battle is to be won or lost—yet it remains, again, beyond the normal horizon of Bay Area concerns.

---

18 On bay air pollution, see Watkins 2016, Alexander 2017a. On the Chevron explosion, see Cuff 2017, Tepperman 2015. On Chevron's long domination of Richmond, see Early 2017. On California air pollution regulation history, see Vogel 2018.
19 American Lung Association 2016.
20 Pappas 2014, Goode 2015. The Bay Area also ships its toxic wastes to special dump sites in the San Joaquin Valley. On water pollution regulation in California, see Vogel 2018.

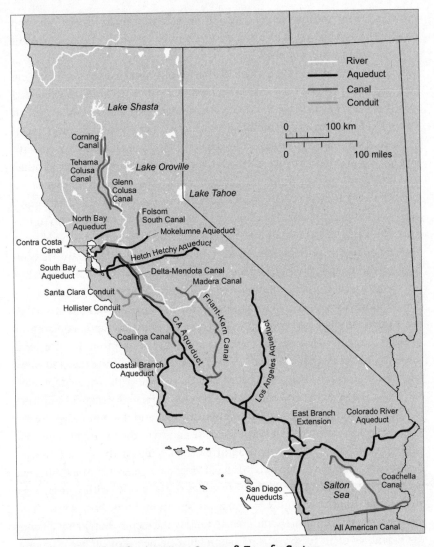

Figure 8.3: Map of California's Water Storage & Transfer System

Derived from original map by Candida Lacey in Walker & Lodha 2013.

During the century in which agriculture was king, California built the greatest water storage and transfer system in the world (fig. 8.3). It consists of hundreds of dams and thousands of miles of canals, large and small, most of which are in the Central Valley. All the rivers coming down from the Sierra Nevada have major reservoirs that supply irrigation districts and their farms on the east side of the Valley. These were, by and large, built first because the rivers and the best lands are close together there. The east side of the Valley is also endowed with one of the greatest aquifers in North America, and growers can tap groundwater easily. The humble well and submersible pump have been overshadowed by big concrete, but they provide about 40 percent of California's water supply.[21]

By the end of the 1920s, millions of acres of California farms were being irrigated. But that did not satisfy the thirst of agribusiness, which expanded into the driest parts of the southern and western San Joaquin Valley, which lack good local streams or ample groundwater. As soon as irrigation began in those areas, however, water tables started falling precipitously, so the state and federal governments were called upon to rescue lands that would otherwise have gone out of production. They built two massive water projects, the Central Valley Project (CVP) and the State Water Project (SWP), to store and carry water from the north to the south. Even worse, the soils in the marginal areas are full of heavy metals that create a toxic drainage problem, which first showed up in the aforementioned Kesterson disaster. The upshot is that the biggest, most expensive parts of the giant water system of the Central Valley are the most dubious in economic and environmental terms.

California's world-class storage and transfer system was built to overcome the natural limits of water supply. This is not a truly dry state, contrary to popular belief; its average precipitation is about that of Vermont. But precipitation is highly uneven in time and space. That is, the bulk of the rain and snow falls on the northern half of the state and they come with a huge degree of variability. The two natural phenomena are closely related, because California sits on the boundary between the wet Northwest and the desert Southwest. The redwood country of the north is a close cousin to the Olympic Peninsula, while the Mojave of Southern California is a sibling of the great Sonoran desert zone stretching deep into Mexico. Lying in between, Central California is one of the five great Mediterranean zones of the world, with winter rains, summer drought, and highly irregular precipitation from year to year. The Sierra snowpack and cool Pacific breezes modify the picture but do not change the essentials of it. In short, long before anyone heard of global warming, California had to cope with wild variability in annual rain and snowfall.[22]

All this means that it is vital to store water to tide things over the hot summers and dry years and necessary to transfer river runoff south from the wetter areas to the dry ones. This is even more desirable for irrigated agriculture because the longest, hottest summers are toward the south, allowing

21 On the history and politics of California water, see Pisani 1984, Reisner 1986, Hundley 1992, Walker 2004a.
22 Ingram & Malamud-Roam 2013, Walker & Lodha 2013. An essential dimension of California's distinct climate(s) is that it is home to a huge number of endemic (unique) species of plants and animals—more than any other part of North America.

rapid growth and multiple crops per year. As agribusiness expanded the areas of irrigated farming to the farthest extremes of the state, the size of the dams and reservoirs increased dramatically and the length of the canals, as well. Several governors, many legislators, the Department of Water Resources, and the federal Bureau of Reclamation and Army Corps of Engineers have all been good servants of the power of agribusiness, building out the system to meet every new demand.

To be sure, cities have also been major players in the development of California's immense water supply infrastructure. Los Angeles, San Francisco, and Oakland/East Bay all sought better water sources in the Sierra in the early twentieth century, building some of the world's longest aqueducts to bring that water to the coast. Later, greater Los Angeles, organized as the Metropolitan Water District of Southern California (MWD), partnered with the Imperial Valley to grab water from the Colorado River and then got a share of the Sacramento River water rolling down the California aqueduct and over the Tehachapi Mountains. The Bay Area, it should be noted, was where key technologies of water infrastructure were invented: reinforced concrete, concrete dams, high-arch dams, rotary pumps, and long-distance electricity transmission. Finally, urban demand for electricity was critical to the development of dams and hydropower, and it paid the greatest part of the costs of the big dams such as Boulder, Shasta, and Oroville.[23]

★ ★ ★

The story of connivance in California water development was made world famous by *Chinatown*—widely acclaimed as one of the finest films of all time—but the wrong lesson is often drawn. Los Angeles is not the worst actor in the story, even among the big cities (San Francisco's rape of Yosemite National Park ranks higher). The real kings of California water are the big growers. In fact, before the city of LA even got the water from the Owens Valley aqueduct, it went to irrigate orange groves for a generation. The figure of the empire-building Noah Cross is not far off the mark.[24] We shall return to the responsibility of the cities later, but the main player has been agribusiness.

Irrigated agriculture uses 80 percent of the state's water supply, yet there is never enough for them. The reason is simple: large-scale capitalist agriculture is quite profitable in California, as long as growers can secure cheap water. They never want to (or can) pay the full cost of the water, and they never have.

---

23 Gottlieb 1988, Brechin 1999, Elkind 1998. On the technologies, see Walker 2008.

24 Arax & Wartzman 2003. It is not by accident that *Chinatown* is sometimes rated the best film ever made. See, e.g., https://www.theguardian.com/film/2010/oct/22/best-film-ever-chinatown-season.

Instead, they have gamed the system in four ways. First, many growers have legacy water rights, either as riparians who draw directly from the rivers or by having prior rights to appropriate water from streams. Second, growers have the right to pump unlimited quantities of water from the ground, regardless of their neighbors. Third, growers sign long-term contracts with irrigation districts and with state and federal agencies that charge less than the full costs of the water projects that deliver the water. Fourth, the missing revenues are made up by city taxpayers and power users.[25]

Water rights and contracts are a mess. No other state in the Southwest has such a deformed legal system and so little regulatory power over water withdrawal and use. California courts gave riparian and appropriative rights equal standing in the nineteenth century. Irrigation districts brought a measure of order to local water supply around the turn of the century but did so by handing the power over water policy to local landowners and irrigators. The Progressives tried to sort things out by creating a State Water Board (now the State Water Resources Control Board), but it had little power to impose reasonable use restrictions or restrict legacy water rights. Above all, groundwater remained unregulated, which inevitably led to falling water tables all around the state—accompanied by land subsidence. Some places in the San Joaquin Valley have sunk more than twenty feet, disrupting local roads and, ironically, irrigation canals. At long last, a law passed in 2014 to regulate groundwater extraction, but it is written in such a way as to, once again, give the regulatory power to local districts, and it puts off control over overpumping until 2042 (and even then, enforcement powers are minimal).[26]

The consequence of this mad system of multiple rights, few regulations and major subsidies is that the demand for water greatly exceeds the supply, even with the vast storage and transfer system in place. No legislature or governor has been able to buck agribusiness and the cities to rein in water use. Because there are few rational limits on water demand, growers in the San Joaquin Valley regularly complain that the supply of water delivered by the feds and the state is insufficient. When there is a major drought, as happened in 2011–16, the howls of shortage become the baying of wolves. The sacrificial lamb is the Delta. The water contractors want a "transfer facility" to get more water through the Delta and to be sure that fresh and salt water do not mingle along the way. This has been part of the California Water Plan since the 1940s.

The Delta finally found its defenders in the early 1980s battle over the Peripheral Canal, as the devastating effect of pumping on fish and wildlife

---

25 Storper & Walker 1984, Stroshane 2016.
26 Grantham & Viers 2014, Serna 2017.

led to a revolt by environmentalists against state water management. Water traveling south from the Sacramento River must get through the sinuous sloughs of the Delta to the Clifton Court Forebay, where it can be pumped into the huge state and federal ditches—the California Aqueduct and the Mendota Canal—for the trip south. Water sometimes flows backward to confuse migrating fish, the gargantuan pumps gobble up millions of fry, and massive diversions deprive the ecosystem of basic nutrients. The overall result has been catastrophic to fish and other wildlife.[27]

Success of the 1982 referendum set in motion years of scientific studies and lawsuits against the water agencies. In the early twenty-first century, it looked like reason might prevail with the CalFed agreement, mustering of good science, and a series of court rulings that demanded the return of minimum flows to the San Joaquin River. Even the State Water Resources Control Board got involved at last, issuing a draft plan to limit Delta pumping.[28]

★ ★ ★

Yet the pressure on the Delta from the growers and MWD is unrelenting. The campaign is led by the State Farm Bureau and California Association of Water Agencies (themselves the creatures of agribusiness). Many urbanites think that agriculture is a spent force in California, compared to the lords of Hollywood, Silicon Valley, and finance; but agribusiness still rules the Central Valley. The tail that wags the water dog is the Westlands Water District in western Fresno County, the biggest of all irrigation districts. Westlands has a losing combination of falling water tables and "junior" rights to Delta water, meaning it is the last to be served and the first to be cut off in low water years. It also has hundreds of thousands of acres of almonds, a high-profit export crop, and cannot go without water for long. Westlands is the worst of the water-eaters.

The state is determined to build a new kind of transfer facility to carry the Sacramento River directly to the pumps: two massive tunnels, forty feet in diameter, traveling underneath the Delta. After all the debate, lawsuits, and plans for the Delta, Governor Brown and the Department of Water Resources (DWR) have decided to steamroll every obstacle and build the tunnels. They are calling the latest plan the California Water Fix, and, indeed, the fix is in. Even though the state auditor has reprimanded DWR for failing to explain how the project will be paid for, and Westlands has pulled out, declaring that the water will be too expensive, Governor Brown forges on with this white

---

27   This was obvious forty years ago (Storper & Walker 1979), but for confirmation see the studies on the archived CalFed website: calwater.ca.gov.
28   The suits were brought by the Natural Resources Defense Council in alliance with fishermen and environmental groups with bases in both the Bay Area and the Central Valley.

elephant of a project. How could Brown, a strong advocate of carbon limits and opponent of climate change denial, take a position squarely at odds with any sort of economic, environmental, or climate rationality? Such is the power of the water boys.[29]

Things are no better at the federal level. Congressman Kevin McCarthy of Kern County is the current Republican majority leader in the House and Representative Devin Nunes of Tulare County is head of the House Intelligence Committee. Both are noisy advocates of more water delivery. Westlands's former lawyer is now assistant secretary of the interior, overseeing the Bureau of Reclamation. And even on the Democratic side, there is Dianne Feinstein, a power in the U.S. Senate, who is old friends with the largest grower in Kern County and joined with the Republicans during the drought to try to override limits on Delta pumping—much to the chagrin of retiring senator Barbara Boxer, who served on the Interior Committee. In the dying days of the Obama administration, the feds declared their support for the Delta tunnels.[30]

The keyword in the water-eaters' propaganda campaign in recent years has been "reliability" of supplies. But that is a pipe dream. There is no reliability in California's climate, and it is sure to get worse with global warming. This is the worst kind of hubris, insisting that humankind can always control nature and water can be made to spout forth in the desert. But there simply is no more water to be had out of the Sacramento and Sierra Rivers. All the good dam sites have been built on, and those reservoirs provide three to four years' storage, no matter how much it rains. Proposals to raise older dams or build off-stream storage are expensive, yield little supplemental storage, and have dire environmental effects. Droughts of any length exceed the capacity of the system, as happened in 2013–15.[31]

The only rational way to bring water supply and demand into concert is to reduce demand, especially in dry years. Californians have to live within their means, and conservation is the best way to do that. Indeed, it has been happening for the last quarter century since the defeat of the Peripheral Canal. About 20 percent of irrigated acreage, mostly used for low-value crops such as alfalfa, has gone out of production since that time. If there isn't unlimited cheap water, irrigators must adapt, and they have already. Better piping and sprinkler systems, better tracking of soil moisture and plant stress, more level fields and so on—not to mention better crop planning than jumping on

---

29 Westlands's declaration is less likely to kill off the project than to get the state to find money from elsewhere to subsidize growers. On the auditor's critique, see Rogers 2017.
30 Lockhead 2016, Bacher 2017.
31 On the effects of climate change on the state's water regime, see Moser et al. 2013.

the almond bandwagon in the midst of a drought. Agriculture in California is not going to disappear, it just has to shrink a reasonable amount; and the best way to do that is to take marginal lands such as those in Westlands out of production, putting them back into grazing.[32]

The obsession of the water industry with supply expansion is shockingly out of step with reality in another way. In the heavy rains of winter in 2017, once-empty reservoirs filled up so fast that stream flow had to be released over many dams through emergency spillways. One case stands out. At Oroville, the state's second-largest dam and reservoir, the situation became critical, as the regular spillway began to wash out from the intense flows being released over several days in February. Dam operators from DWR let water go over the emergency spillway, but the latter was so poorly designed that it immediately suffered catastrophic erosion, triggering fears of potential dam collapse. DWR quickly ordered the evacuation of the city of Oroville downstream, while the public was treated to dramatic videos of the cascading water going down the main spillway, carving out huge holes, and sending spray hundreds of feet in the air. Rebuilding the spillways cost hundreds of millions of dollars, proving that the state has billions of dollars of repair and maintenance work to do on its aging water infrastructure.[33]

★　★　★

The water agencies regularly make the claim that "25 million people rely on water going through the Delta" in order to convince the general public that the water tunnels are necessary to keep the wolf from the door. This is a sham. Cities use less than a fifth of the total supply and residences only half of that; and half of that half goes to gardening. In other words, household use is less than one-twentieth of the total water consumed in California. All the scary figure of twenty-five million people means is that a portion of Sacramento River water goes into the shared pools of urban water agencies: the Metropolitan Water District of Southern California, above all, plus some to the Santa Clara Valley Water District, Contra Costa Water District (CCWD), and East Bay Municipal Utility District (EBMUD).[34]

Nevertheless, the cities cannot be relieved of their measure of responsibility for the parlous state of water policy in California. Greater Los Angeles is the worst offender, under the suzerainty of the MWD. It has always walked in lockstep with agribusiness and continues to do so. In the fight against the

---

32　Pacific Institute & NRDC 2014.
33　Miller 2017, Alexander 2017b, Walters 2017.
34　Walker & Lodha 2013.

Peripheral Canal, it was shown that ratepayers in Southern California were subsidizing Kern County growers by selling so-called surplus water to the Kern County Water District for peanuts. When this was made public in Los Angeles, the city voted against the canal—the only part of Southern California to do so—and that was decisive for its defeat. But MWD never gave up, and it has now taken the remarkable step of buying three large islands in the northern Delta so as to acquire local water rights.[35]

But why does MWD seek more water? This is not innocent, and it is not driven by "the people." Water agencies are mostly beyond the ken of most citizens and out of the reach of democratic control. MWD's board members are all appointed by local member water agencies, and only a handful of those have elected boards. But even in cases such as that of EBMUD, the election of board members is such a minor part of the ballot that most voters haven't a clue who stands for what; as result, EBMUD reliably returns prodevelopment members to office.[36]

The drive to expand urban water supplies comes mostly from developers and their allies in local government. Water supply is one piece of the "urban growth coalitions" discussed in the previous chapter. San Francisco grabbed the Hetch Hetchy valley in Yosemite to secure the development of the Outside Lands in the city and then sold water to the growing suburbs of the Peninsula and Silicon Valley. The Santa Clara Valley went after CVP water through the San Luis Project as growth was booming in the 1960s and '70s. EBMUD was formed to solve the water supply problems of Greater Oakland, as it was then known, and it and the CCWD have been resolute in supporting the development of the outer realms of the East Bay, such as the Dougherty Valley and Brentwood.[37]

Urban water use is hardly inelastic, as recent history proves. The Bay Area made huge strides in water conservation during the 1970s, when a short but very severe drought struck. At the time, liberal Democrats were in power, led by the first coming of Governor Jerry Brown, who put several key environmentalists and visionary planners in his cabinet. State and local regulations tightened up on builders and households, and, most importantly, the citizenry was alerted to the problem and responded brilliantly. Toilets and shower heads were replaced with low-flow versions, faucets were not left running, and gardens began to sprout xerophytic plants. Changing a culture is not that difficult when people feel like their efforts make a difference because they are

35 Storper & Walker 1982, Hamilton 2016.
36 An environmental revolt in the 1980s brought a green majority to the board briefly, but many of their reforms have been subsequently reversed. On MWD, see Gottlieb 1988.
37 Logan & Molotch 1981, Brechin 1999, Elkind 1998, Walker & Williams 1982.

part of a collective effort. Per capita water use has hardly budged in the Bay Area since then.[38]

Big problems still exist with overuse, as revealed by the publication of a list of abusers during the last drought by EBMUD and other agencies. Naturally, these showed that the worst offenders were the very rich living on large estates in the far suburbs. But the larger problem is that the inland areas where most new growth is occurring in and beyond the Bay Area are hotter, the gardens are larger, and water consumption per household is higher. The state has not provided much guidance compared to the 1970s, but Governor Brown did finally clamp down by telling all urban water districts to reduce their usage by 25 percent in 2015–16. Almost all did as ordered, and their publics followed suit, once again rising to meet a crisis with minimal fuss and bother. The latest drought ended with record rainfall in 2016–17 that filled the reservoirs and replenished groundwater (but far from all aquifers). It served one good purpose in that it awakened millions of Californians to that fact that you can't always get what you want, but you can still get what you need.

Beyond Fossilized Energy Policy

Since the turn of the Millennium, California has taken a forward position among U.S. states in addressing energy conservation, greenhouse gas emissions, and global warming. The state was already in the vanguard of American responses, thanks to its stringent auto emissions rules and energy-saving measures introduced since the first Brown administration in the 1970s. Then, as the reality of climate change became crystal clear to all but believers in the Rapture, the state redoubled its efforts on every front.

A first step was to mandate periodic assessments to inform the state agencies about the latest in climate science, detailing the results of scientific studies on rising temperatures, reduced snowpack, increased wildfires, and higher sea levels. The first report came out in 2009. Two years later, the state created the Cal-Adapt website to disseminate climate information to local governments and the general public. In 2013, a second report appeared, which has been the operative document for state climate planning up to this point. Bay Area conservationists were pivotal in urging the state to issue its own climate change reports and planning guidelines.[39]

California got a head start in energy conservation, just as with water, during the 1970s in response to the energy shocks (oil price hikes) of the time. During Governor Brown's first term, the legislature created the California

---

38 Walker & Lodha 2013.
39 Moser et al. 2013. See also http://cal-adapt.org.

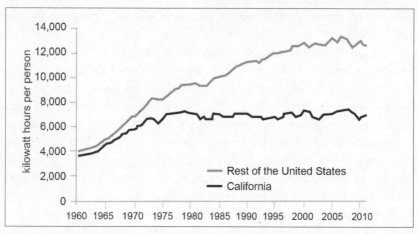

Figure 8.4: California Energy Consumption vs. the U.S., 1960–2010

Source: Walker & Lodha 2013.

Energy Commission to oversee energy policy, which included improved standards for appliances and buildings. Here again, the Golden State was able to markedly improve efficiency, as compared with the rest of the country (fig. 8.4).[40]

The state suffered another nasty shock in 2001 when several energy suppliers, including the notorious Enron, conspired to game the state and drive up prices for natural gas coming from Texas and Oklahoma; that cost California some $9 billion (and contributed to the subsequent recall of Governor Gray Davis). In response, in 2002 the legislature established the first rigorous renewable portfolio standard (RPS) for electric utilities. Four years later, it required that 20 percent of electricity be generated by renewable power sources by 2010. In 2008, Governor Arnold Schwarzenegger, who had replaced Davis, signed an executive order upping the target to one-third renewables by 2020. That was confirmed by the legislature in 2011 and later raised to one-half renewables by 2030.[41]

As for greenhouse gases, the keystone is the Global Warming Solutions Act of 2006 (popularly known as AB32), which directed the California Air Resources Board (ARB) to set emissions targets for 2020. Texas oilmen, joined by the Koch brothers, tried to overturn AB32 with a well-financed initiative in 2010, Proposition 23, but were turned back decisively by the voters. The legislature upped the ante again ten years later in a new law (SB32) that set a 2030 goal of reducing greenhouse gas emissions to 1990 levels (40 percent

---

40 Walker & Lodha 2013, https://www.greentechmedia.com/articles/read/California-Is-Proof-That-Energy-Efficiency-Works.

41 https://www.c2es.org/us-states-regions/key-legislation.

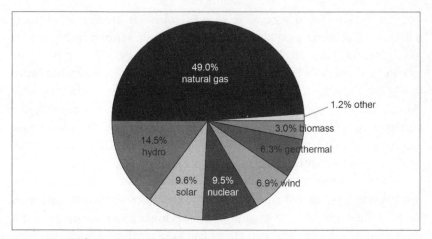

Figure 8.5: California Sources of Electricity, 2016

Source: U.S. Energy Information Administration, Electric Power Monthly, February 2016.

below trend). As part of these policies, California introduced a state "cap and trade" system for carbon similar to that adopted in Europe. Individual cities have followed suit with ambitious goals for renewable electric power, notably San Francisco's target of 100 percent renewables by 2030.

With the triumph of climate change denial in the elections of 2016 and U.S. withdrawal from the Paris Accords, California leaders became even more outspoken against national policy. Governor Brown has made his opposition visible by traveling to Europe and China to support international agreements, leading a coalition of U.S. states and cities opposed to carbon madness, and hosting a Global Climate Summit in fall 2018. [42]

★   ★   ★

As a center of innovation, the Bay Area should be expected to mobilize its resources and minds in pursuit of new energy technologies, and that has happened. Renewable energy is growing rapidly in California, and many Bay Area research centers and companies are deeply involved in the search for better ways of fueling modern life. In addition, many Silicon Valley companies are committed to sourcing from renewables. Notably, Google plans to buy enough wind and solar power to cover all its electricity use worldwide, and it is closing in on that goal.[43]

---

42 Associated Press 2017. Former governor Schwarzenegger, a Republican, has also been a vigorous critic of mainstream Republican climate denial and inaction. Goldberg 2010.

43 Baker 2016. Silicon Valley has delivered a solution to an old problem: leaking natural gas lines. Using a new detection technology from Picarro that is one thousand times more sensitive than past sensors, PG&E has been able to survey a million properties for gas leaks.

Of the handful of renewable sources, solar and wind are the leading edges of a global energy transition out of fossil fuels. Hydropower was once on the cutting edge of electric generation technology, with the Bay Area playing a leading role in its development in the twentieth century, but hydro is no longer a major source of electricity or an important part of a renewable future. The Bay Area was once a pioneer in nuclear power, too, but only one nuclear power plant is left in the state, and it is due to close. The region once led in geothermal, but good geothermal sources are few. California's last coal-powered plant was shuttered in 2015 (fig. 8.4).

California was an early leader in wind power, with about a third of the world's supply in 1990. Altamont Pass in the East Bay was the first large wind farm in the world, but the biggest state wind installations are now in Kern County and Southern California. Texas and Iowa are the U.S. leaders in wind power today, and the global centers of wind technology are in Europe and China. By contrast, the Golden State remains a major player in solar power, which provides almost 10 percent of the state's electricity and rising fast. The solar industry employs around one hundred thousand people in the state in engineering, manufacture, sales, and installation, about 40 percent of the U.S. total.[44] Solar power has become the most important renewable industry in the Bay Area, in large part because it rests on photovoltaics, an electronic technology.

There are three parts to solar electricity supply: large-scale solar farms, rooftop solar, and battery storage. All three have benefitted from state aid and local innovation of various kinds. Solar farms are the provenance of big utility companies and are located in the deserts of Southern California and the San Joaquin Valley. They generate about twice the electricity of rooftop solar in the state. The Bay Area contributes to solar farm technology with solar panels and innovations such as BrightSource's thermal solar systems that focus sunlight on large generators. Soliculture makes solar panels that absorb green light for electricity and reemits red light for plants, converting greenhouses into energy generators.

Rooftop solar is the arena of small construction firms, and it has the advantage of being widely distributed. California law allows for net metering, forcing utilities to buy back surplus electricity from distributed systems. The state has also streamlined permitting rules. While rooftop installations generate a lot of jobs, the work tends to be less well paid than for solar farms. After a boom in home installations in the 2010s, the rooftop sector saw a sharp decline in demand as government incentives fell off. This led to the

---

44　Figures from the Solar Foundation quoted in Hansen 2017a.

bankruptcy of Sungevity and buyout of SolarCity by Tesla, leaving Sunrun as the only independent left from the original trio of Bay Area solar installers.

Production of solar panels has suffered from Chinese competition, as manifested in the quick collapse of Solyndra in 2011. Yet SolarCity manufactures its own panels in Fremont. SolarCity has introduced an advanced photovoltaic roof tile for the upper end of the market, while Misolé in Santa Clara makes a flexible solar cell for uneven surfaces. A key to rooftop solar is Enphase's microconverters that turn DC into AC current.[45]

Although the cost of photovoltaics has come down rapidly, battery storage is the key to cheap, dependable solar power. Battery technology has made important strides in recent years, making handheld phones and computers ubiquitous. Batteries are also a major concern for extending the range of electric vehicles. Hence, Elon Musk's Tesla is a leading force in battery technology. Tesla pioneered stationary building storage with its Power Wall filled with lithium-ion cells, and it is promoting the idea of battery packs in homes to tide solar households through the night. Another local battery innovation is thin, flexible ZincPoly batteries made locally by Imprint Energy.[46]

A further significant facet of Bay Area green technology lies in the design and management of energy-conserving buildings and infrastructure. The area is dotted with architectural firms that can deliver LEED-certified, energy-conserving buildings of all kinds, and it is a leader in smart building technologies that use intelligent electronics to optimize lighting, air conditioning, heating, and so forth. Nest is a maker of smart thermostats. Sensity Systems optimizes large LED lighting installations. Verdegris Technologies uses AI to analyze information from electrical panels to optimize settings and predict maintenance issues. Kinestral Technologies and View make electronically regulated smart windows that change tint as the weather shifts. Stem/ Powergenics provides smart energy management systems for industry.

★ ★ ★

California can rightly claim to be one of the greenest states of the union in terms of per capita energy use and is on a par with Europe. Its recent progress at containing greenhouse gases is equally admirable. At the same time, California is so large that its total volume of carbon dioxide emitted is second only to Texas in the United States. And with rapid growth in the latest boom,

---

45 Jones 2017, Ferris 2017, Aggarwal 2017. There is a long-standing debate over the relative efficiency, social merits, and job quality of the two major forms of solar. Boronstein 2015, Jones 2017. On Solar City and Tesla's abuse of workers, see Hansen 2017b.
46 Muller 2016.

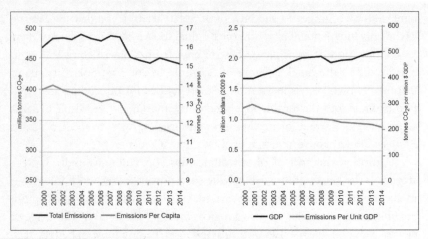

Figure 8.6: California Greenhouse Gas Emissions, 2001–2014

Source: California Air Resources Board, https://www.arb.ca.gov/cc/inventory/pubs/reports/2000_2014/ghg_inventory_trends_00–14_20160617.pdf.

it has been hard to maintain a downward trend in total greenhouse gas emissions—especially from vehicles (fig. 8.6).[47]

In short, there is no room for complacency in view of the immensity of the problem of climate change. It is clear that the advanced capitalist nations have been the most prolific consumers of energy for a long time and remain so, the Bay Area included. It is not fair that the poor nations of the world sacrifice more than the wealthy ones just because they still depend on coal and heavy industry. In fact, the efforts of China and India put the United States to shame for its recalcitrance to shoulder its share of the burden.

The Bay Area has much more to do to reduce its carbon footprint. First, it must improve transportation, which still depends overwhelmingly on cars and trucks and wastes untold amounts of fuel in traffic jams and long commutes. Locals need to figure out how to live with higher gas taxes, an easy way of reducing car usage (but one that hits working people hardest). The bus systems are sadly backward, and BART and other rail systems cover too little area.

Closely related to transport is housing, which is far too dispersed in the low-rise metropolis. Environmental and business groups have been pushing for greater housing density and transit villages, but too many local governments resist such developments. And even now that some have converted to

---

47   U.S. Energy Information Agency rankings: https://www.eia.gov/state/rankings/#/series/12 and series/226. Baker 2017a. For a critical view of California's low energy use, see Levinson 2014.

the religion of higher density, there is a dearth of federal funds to support serious housing and public transport policy.

At the same time, in a wealthy region, there is no reason why energy conservation and urban reconstruction cannot provide for living wage jobs, safe and comfortable buildings, and inexpensive, accessible public transport. Bay Area citizens have to insist that government and business follow a high road to a green future, one that takes everyone along and not just a tech and professional elite. There needs to be a broad coalition committed to both High Tech solutions and low-tech ones, to exotic innovations and practical solutions, investments in infrastructure and good jobs for ordinary workers.[48]

Conservatives may claim that good energy policy is too expensive, costs jobs, and wrecks U.S. competitiveness, but nothing could be further from the truth, and the United States is simply shooting itself in the foot. A key question for a greener future, then, is how to overcome the political obstruction of climate deniers, which threatens to take humankind down the road to the hell of a much-hotter planet. Where will the political will and mass movement come from to retake the country? We will come back to that question in the last chapter.

Global Backwash

The Bay Area's conservation movement made a huge contribution to the well-being of the region fifty years ago by stopping bay fill, saving open space, and reducing pollution, but a whole new threat has emerged from global warming. As the scenarios for polar ice melting grow more disheartening, the dangers of ocean expansion become more fearsome. Like any coastal zone, the Bay Area must cope as sea levels rise as the chickens of global warming come home to roost.

The Pacific Coast states together requested a report on climate change from the National Resources Council issued in 2012, which estimated a sea-level rise of as much as 2 feet by 2050 and 5.5 feet by 2100. In 2014, the California legislature created an independent Ocean Science Trust to further improve scientific input on global ice loss, and their report gave the most likely range of sea-level rise in California as a bit less—2 feet by 2100—but warned that it could go as high as 10 feet if there is catastrophic loss of ice from the west Antarctic sheet and Greenland.[49]

The San Francisco urban region is particularly vulnerable since it hugs the largest estuary on the western coast of the Americas. The bay is remarkably

---

48   Zabin et al. 2016.
49   Griggs et al. 2017.

shallow, with only a couple deep spots other than the canyon carved by the Sacramento River through the Golden Gate when sea levels were far lower in the past. Historically, the bay was fringed by long stretches of tidal marshes and mudflats, and the Delta was entirely marshland and sloughs until it was diked and drained. The great estuary already had a complex shoreline before U.S. conquest, but it became far more fragmented with modern attempts to alter nature to serve the gods of commerce. With good reason, one local writer called it "the broken shore."[50]

The hazards of sea-level rise are amplified by high tides and storms. Normal tides in California are four to five feet, but king tides, which usually occur in the winter, can add another foot or so; king tides already lap over the bulkheads in San Francisco and Oakland, and slosh onto roads around the bay. El Niños further augment high water. In winter storms, when strong westerly winds push water higher against the coastline, Northern California is vulnerable to powerful storm surges; surges of three feet, or 50 percent over normal tides, have been registered in San Francisco Bay. While tides are lower in the Delta, high freshwater inflows and storm surges are more dangerous, and wave action can easily breech levees.[51]

With rising sea levels from global warming, flood impacts will be significantly worse. The Union of Concerned Scientists predicts chronic inundation all around San Francisco Bay by the end of the century even under modest sea-rise scenarios, making parts of the bayside territory unlivable. If seas rise by three feet, the land area around the bay at risk from a one-hundred-year storm will double to over thirty thousand acres. Recently mapping exercises show how vulnerable the broken shore is to rising seas (fig. 8.7).[52]

★　★　★

Urban development around San Francisco Bay has been particularly aggressive in seizing the low ground. The flatlands around the bay, created by eons of sediments from the surrounding hills, are ideal for every kind of urban activity: transportation, industry, warehousing, offices, and housing. As a result, sea-level rise threatens the long-term viability of the urbanized edges of the bay shore. To make matters worse, developers of all kinds have always wanted more land, and bay fill is a cheap way to make it, so filling in the coves,

---

50　Quinn 1981.

51　A USGS 2011 report predicts that with a superstorm like that of 1861–62, there would be up to fifty levee breeches in the Delta, flooding most of the core Central Valley.

52　Bromirski & Flick 2008, U.S. Army Corps 2013, Union of Concerned Scientists 2017. Another hazard of rising sea levels is beach erosion, which will hit California's coast hard. https://www.usgs.gov/news/disappearing-beaches-modeling-shoreline-change-southern-california.

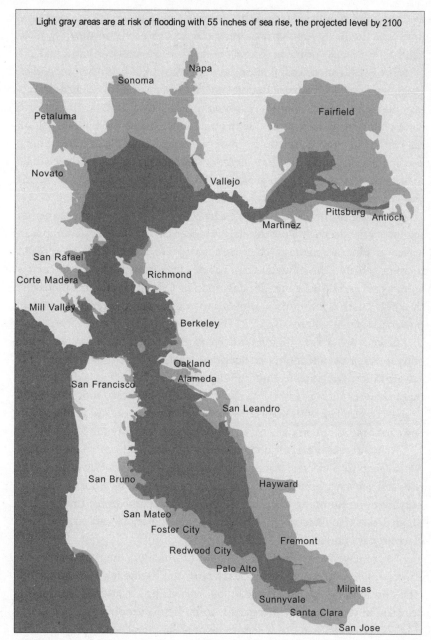

Figure 8.7: Map of San Francisco Bay Margins Subject to Flooding with Rising Sea Levels
Source: https://blog.ucsusa.org/kristy-dahl/
sea-level-rise-chronic-inundation-san-francisco-bay-area.

wetlands, and mudflats around the bay was a local pastime for a century—until Save the Bay's popular revolution put a halt to it. Unfortunately, filled lands are supremely prone to coastal flooding—not to mention earthquakes.[53]

The risks from coastal flooding are of three kinds: failures of individual buildings, failures of transportation systems, and failures of infrastructure.

Buildings on the California coast do not have to survive hurricane-force winds, but they do have to deal with inundation. In low-rise buildings flooding can undermine foundations, cause walls to fail, and ruin lower floors; keeping floodwaters out of basements is nearly impossible. Flooding can be made worse by obstructions around buildings that trap debris and impede flowing water.[54]

Flooding of surface highways, railways, and airports can cause the bay region to grind to a halt. Poor drainage, blocked culverts, and dead pumps can leave water in place for days. The worst hazards are in subways, such as BART, if water gets into the tunnels. The Embarcadero Station in San Francisco is at high risk, and BART could flood from Civic Center to Oakland, rendering the system useless for months—not just to pump out the water but to restore power and signal systems.

Sewers are at very high risk of being compromised. Flood water can enter sewer grates and infiltrated lines, overwhelming treatment systems, and sewers in low-lying areas require pumps that can fail in floods. Large treatment facilities such as EBMUD's giant plant at the eastern foot of the Bay Bridge can also fail, with huge consequences for pollution and public health. Sewage backups can, in turn, invade buildings and transit tunnels.[55]

A final threat is electrical failure, which is extremely common as floodwaters seep into electric ducts, transformers, and control boxes. In high rises and subways, hundreds of people can be stranded by electricity failure. Furthermore, pumping water out of buildings, foundations, tunnels, and flooded waterfronts in order to restore normal functions can take weeks if electricity systems are out.

There have been several attempts to estimate potential damage from storm surges with rising sea levels. In 1990, the Pacific Institute calculated losses around San Francisco Bay at $50 billion, putting a quarter-million people at risk, and the necessary investment to build protection infrastructure at $1 billion per year. A more recent report on the whole state makes an estimate of $100 billion in property at risk and a half million people forced from

53 Walker 2007, Booker 2013.
54 FEMA 2010. Rising sea levels also mean that saltwater will penetrate aquifers farther inland, eroding foundations, pipes, and ducts.
55 BCDC 2012, chapter 12 on wastewater facilities.

their homes in a one-hundred-year coastal flood, if seas rise five feet. Adding another foot or two of sea level over the next century will require billions in investment to raise bulkheads, levees, and roads.[56]

*　*　*

What is being done to respond to the threat of sea-level rise around the bay? Cities like Houston and Miami have set the bar so low that the Bay Area cannot help but look good by comparison. New York City may appear to be a model for planning after the disaster of Hurricane Sandy in 2012, but its experience is not encouraging. Despite the push to develop "resiliency plans" for the city, the rush to capitalize on the recent property boom has led to developments all around the edges of Manhattan and Brooklyn, as well as on Coney and Staten Islands, in low-lying areas that will be impossible to defend as sea levels rise.[57]

The Netherlands offers another model. They are known for their shore defenses, which have converted the ancient estuary of the Rhine and Scheldt to mostly dry land and completely reengineered the rivers' flow. This is not an acceptable solution for San Francisco Bay. Moreover, the Dutch have come to realize that just building higher levees is not the answer. Coastal areas have to live with water by expanding wetlands, pulling cities back from the coast, and raising the land—or even putting structure on pilings, as is done in tropical zones around the world.[58]

The state of California took the lead with its first scientific assessment in 2009, putting out a "California Sea-Level Rise Guidance Document" in 2010 (updated twice in light of further scientific reports). Those documents have been used by state agencies in coming up with mandated long-term plans, such as the Department of Transportation's California Transportation Plan 2040. Unfortunately, that plan is strong on warnings but short on specific responses to sea-level rise. The California Little Hoover Commission, which advises the governor and legislature on organizational matters, concluded in 2014 that thus far state leadership has been mostly advisory and not substantive.[59]

Some regional agencies are leading the way in planning. The Bay Conservation and Development Commission (BCDC), whose goal for a half

56 Gleick & Maurer 1990, Heberger et al. 2009.
57 On the blindness in Miami, see NYC Planning 2013, Baker 2010, Kevin Baker personal communication, June 16, 2017.
58 https://phys.org/news/2009-09-dutch-california-bay-area-sea.html#jCp.
59 http://www.opc.ca.gov/webmaster/ftp/pdf/docs/2013_SLR_Guidance_Update_FINAL1.pdf; http://www.dot.ca.gov/hq/tpp/californiatransportationplan2040/2040.html; Little Hoover Commission 2014.

century was to keep the bay the same, made a radical switch to regional adaptation planning after sponsoring a successful experiment in Alameda County called Adapting to Rising Tides. As the former director put it, "The challenge ahead is to protect the Bay Area from the bay, not the other way around." San Francisco Planning and Urban Research (SPUR) has teamed up with the San Francisco Estuary Institute (SFEI) and the Regional Water Quality Control Board to launch a Shoreline Adaptation Strategies project to assess the specific needs of different stretches of the bay shoreline. On the other hand, the bay region's pivotal public transportation agency, BART, seems quite unprepared for climate change. The Metropolitan Transportation Commission (MTC) has been chastised for not insisting on making sea-level rise part of the local transportation and housing plans it oversees.[60]

Save the Bay initiated a major effort to restore one hundred thousand acres of marshlands to buffer the bay shore against wave action from rising seas. The group led an impressive electoral campaign for Proposition A in 2016 to win a $25 million per year parcel tax on all property in the nine-county Bay Area, with the funds going to the San Francisco Bay Restoration Authority, launched by the state in 2008. Unfortunately, marshlands may only be effective for a foot or two of sea-level rise, and more drastic protection measures will be needed in many places. To its credit, Save the Bay has extended its vision to advocating for better planning to reduce stormwater runoff from upland areas.[61]

Encouraged by the Bay Area's passage of the wetlands measure, the Rockefeller Foundation gave $5 million for resiliency design projects for the region. These target a variety of different situations around the bay and mobilize teams of engineers, architects, planners, and ecologists to come up with creative solutions. How well these will translate into city plans remains to be seen, however, because most land development around the edge of the bay is in the hands of local governments whose level of awareness and competence varies. Can the city of Alameda cope with the reality that the entire island could be underwater with a four-foot sea rise and king tide? In short, how the Bay Area is going to cope with rising sea level remains far from clear.

San Francisco's efforts have been the most closely scrutinized. The city drew up an impressive plan in 2016 that insists on planning for sea-level rise through the end of the century, but otherwise only provides general recommendations about what exactly should be done. Meanwhile, massive new

---

60   BCDC 2012; http://www.bcdc.ca.gov/cm/2017/SLR-Policy-Recommendations.html; Will Travis quoted in King 2016b. http://www.spur.org/news/2017-07-13/new-spur-project-designing-nature-sea-level-rise. Personal communication with Matt Williams, Sierra Club, 2017.

61   Save the Bay 2015.

developments have been approved along the city's entire bay waterfront: South of Market, Treasure Island, Mission Bay, Pier 70, Hunters Point, and Candlestick Point. All of these involve large stretches of old fill that barely rise above the current water level. The private developers and their consulting engineers have come up with some creative solutions, such as leaving buffer zones in parks and wetlands, bringing in soil to raise foundations, and grading the sites toward higher ground; but whether these will be enough if sea-level goes beyond a couple feet is moot. And how the Port Commission will be able to rebuild the old seawall and the Embarcadero to deal with the inevitable tides washing over the top is going to be most interesting to watch.[62]

Burn, Baby, Burn

Global warming is coming around to bite California in another way: more wildfires. This was driven home in the most dramatic way for the Bay Area in the massive Wine Country fires of the North Bay in October 2017. There were nine separate fire ignited in a single hot, windy Sunday night, with names such as the Tubbs, Atlas, and Nunns Fire—some merging as they grew larger over several days. The fires burned 150,000 acres in the hills around the Napa, Sonoma, and Russian River Valleys and hit the city of Santa Rosa especially hard, killing forty-two people caught off guard by the speeding flames. When the smoke had cleared, nearly ten thousand houses and structures had been consumed by the blazes.[63]

The Wine Country fires reminded older Bay Area residents of the Oakland Hills fire of 1991, which had been the most devastating urban fire event of modern times (San Francisco 1906 still holds the prize as the greatest in American history). The Oakland fire devoured around thirty-five hundred homes and killed twenty-five people. It had all the same characteristics: hot fall weather, lots of dry grass, chaparral and trees, and Diablo winds blowing in from the east, dropping humidity like a stone in minutes. Such wildfires can explode into an inferno in an hour or two, feeding on abundant fuel and moving at astonishing speeds. They create their own tornadoes as the heat rises and winds whip up to over one hundred miles per hour, with the ability to jump multilane freeways to burn neighborhoods far from the wildland zones where they originate.

The Wine Country fires need to be connected to the growing number and size of wildfires across the rest of California and the Southwest. The twenty-first century has witnessed a shocking increase in giant wildfires (over one

---

62   King 2016b, Horiuchi & Sankalia 2017.
63   On the Wine Country fires, see Tolan 2017, Davis 2017b.

hundred thousand acres), including fifteen of the top twenty in the historical record. In 2015 alone, some nine thousand fires burned almost a million acres, including such infernos as the 75,000-acre (1,300-home) Valley fire in Lake County; the 150,000-acre Rough Fire in Kings Canyon; and the 65,000-acre Butte Fire in Amador and Calaveras Counties. The biggest of all, the Thomas fire that scorched 250,000 acres of Ventura and Santa Barbara Counties, hit right after the Wine Country fires. Most of the big wildfires hit the foothills of the Sierra and the mountainous terrain of Southern California, both of which are hotter and drier than the Bay Area; but something has changed for the worse, and Californians are waking up to a brutal new reality.[64]

California is naturally a land of fires. Its Mediterranean climate is characterized by wet winters and dry summers. It is a relatively temperate climate but summers get quite hot in the south and inland, regularly exceeding 100 degrees; and by fall the land is dry as a bone, no matter how wet the preceding winter. California's flora is adapted to a regime of summer drought and repeated burning; many have small, oily leaves to reduce transpiration and others have deep roots that seek and hold water. In fact, many species require fire in order to reproduce, such as the bishop pines, whose cones only open under intense heat. California is a land of recurrent drought, with a clear record of long periods of subaverage rainfall written in tree rings. The five-year drought of 2011–16 was far from abnormal.[65]

Fall is fire season in the Golden State because it is driest and windiest. Greater Los Angeles is notorious for its Santa Ana winds—a subject much bruited in Hollywood films and noir novels—but Northern California has the same phenomenon, here called "Diablo winds." Such winds are generated by huge masses of high pressure squatting inland rather than in their normal position off the coast. As air rushes from high to low pressure zones the winds blow from the east, instead of the usual pattern of the prevailing cool and moist westerlies off the Pacific Ocean. Those east winds are dry and hot, and they become drier and hotter as they compress through the canyons of the coast ranges; as a result, humidity can drop from a normal 60–80 percent to single digits in the blink of an eye.

Meanwhile, California's geography is shifting under the feet of the Bay Area, as Northern California's fire regime becomes more like that of Southern California. With global warming the fire season is getting hotter, drier, and longer, and Santa Ana/Diablo winds are growing more frequent and stronger

---

64   Krishnakumar & Fox 2017. For California's largest wildfires, see http://www.fire.ca.gov/
     communications/downloads/fact_sheets/Top20_Acres.pdf.
65   On fire around the world, see the work of Stephen Pyne; on California, see Pyne 2016.

because the high-pressure zones are larger in size and more intense. Hence, there will inevitably be more wildfires throughout the year. On top of this, the climate is likely to be more erratic, meaning that long, intense droughts will be more common. Increased winter rains, which are also likely at times with global warming, will not help; in fact, they make matters worse by leaving a buildup of fuel in trees, brush, and grass, as happened in 2017.[66]

Urban sprawl makes for a perfect storm of wildfire disasters. What the Wine Country fires, Oakland fire, and Thomas fire have in common is that California cities have pushed their tentacles far into the hill country of the Coast Ranges, Transverse Ranges, and Sierra Nevada, bringing houses into direct contact with wildlands. Housing subdivisions, surrounded by oak woodlands and chaparral, are at high risk. Farther out, idyllic housing developments for second homes and miniranches are even more exposed. The people who move into such neighborhoods love the sense of open space and contact with nature, and just to put an exclamation point on it they plant up their yards with more trees and shrubbery and fail to adequately prepare safety cordons around their houses. Such places are urban wildfires waiting to happen.[67]

When disaster strikes, local fire crews leap to the rescue. Traditional city fire departments are not prepared to deal with wildfires at the urban interface, as tragically revealed in the Oakland fire, when the equipment of firefighters from other towns would not connect to the city's hydrants—which did not matter in the end because the water supply failed when storage tanks in the hills lost power as electric lines burned. Major improvements have been made in infrastructure, equipment, and training since then, and the state now brings in CalFire crews, trucks, and planes to help in such wildfire situations. Thousands of men and women rallied to the effort in the Wine Country fires, dropping water, digging fire breaks, and lighting backfires. They eventually contained the fires.

CalFire's teams and funding are badly overstretched, however, thanks to state and federal budget cuts, and the unpleasant fact is that the future demand for their services will be worse. On the other hand, an inescapable reality of urban wildfires is that firefighters are helpless to stop advancing flames when the Diablo winds are blowing hard, especially in inaccessible backcountry canyons. As in Oakland in 1991 or Berkeley in 1923, the fires cannot be controlled until the wind shifts. Nature still has the upper hand.

---

66 On California's changing climate, see Moser et al. 2013. A good example of fuel build-up is the one hundred million dead forest trees around the state, mostly done in by the recent drought.

67 On the fire danger of the urban-wildland interface, see Davis 1998, Sagara et al. 2016, Krishnakumar & Fox 2017.

The legislature quickly passed a bill in late 2017 to put more resources into planning and preparing for wildfires, but few people have taken on board the essential lessons of wildfires. On the one hand, cities should not be built up to and into canyons and wildlands, and this means putting the brakes on developers and county officials; on the other, people should not rebuild their lost homes and communities as the insurance and FEMA money pours in—but that is exactly what happens every time, and to say so is to be branded a coldhearted brute.

Despite the hubris of mankind, nature's raw power is still apparent in the epochal changes afoot as a consequence of global warming. The earth has always been a world in flames, and human beings have, until recently, lived by lighting fires and altering landscapes through burning. But the globe has also been a place of water and ice to balance the territories dominated by desert and visited by fire. Now humans are not just burning grasslands and forests, they have set alight eons of fossil fuels trapped deep in the earth. The world is heating up faster than at any time in the geologic record, including the catastrophic end of the Permian Era—the greatest epoch of extinctions in the fossil record.

People are just waking up to the fact that the earth is not always an equilibrium system that can buffer us against our collective folly. Just in our little corner of the globe, California, the land is burning faster than ever, and the emissions from wildfires are overwhelming efforts to contain carbon emissions from human sources. Even more shocking, for the first time in human history tundra fires are breaking out in Greenland, of all places, and as the tundra emerges from its long deep freeze it releases huge quantities of methane and absorbs more sunlight. So Greenland's ice cap will only melt faster. The prospects are unnerving.[68]

Conclusion

The Bay Area has an admirable record on environmental protection and land and water conservation, and the metropolitan greenbelt, open waters of the bay, and Pacific Coast make the San Francisco urban region one of the most beautiful and livable in the world. It is an achievement to be proud of and maintain, and there are plenty of feisty organizations in place and alert citizens willing to defend what has been won from the potent forces of economic growth and property capital.

But there is a catch. The edges of the metropolitan environment do not stop at the ridges of the Coast Range; they extend far into the heart

68   For the Permian comparison, see Brannan 2017. On Greenland, see *Guardian* 2017.

of California. There they run into a very different landscape that has been reworked and degraded for 150 years, almost without limit, and into a stagnant mass of air pollution—much of it blown in from the Bay Area itself. Once over the hills, the realities of urban metabolism run smack into the massive inland waterworks built to serve agribusiness and Southern California, as well as the urban fringes of the metropolis.

Beyond California, there lies a whole other frontier of modern life and human impact on the natural environment: the ugly reality of global warming. The state, with considerable input from the Bay Area, has been wrestling with questions of energy efficiency, carbon emissions, and the politics of climate change at the national, and even international, levels. The state gets a gold star for effort, but that does not mean the Bay Area is off the hook for its massive carbon footprint. Nor does it allow for complacency in the face of an ugly national political and governmental landscape.

Finally, even if there were the political will nationally, there are still the rampaging demands of capitalism to contend with, and its insatiable appetite for natural resources, profits, and growth. Silicon Valley technology companies may look very innovative and socially progressive, but Silicon Capitalism is still the same beast. One can do worse than to heed the words of Pope Francis, who has said that capitalism "tends to devour everything which stands in the way of increased profits." Or as Edward Abbey put it a half century ago, growth for growth's sake is the ideology of the cancer cell.

CHAPTER NINE

Tech World

Utopias and Dystopias of the IT Revolution

THE PROMISE OF THE NEW INFORMATION TECHNOLOGIES ISSUING FORTH FROM THE Bay Area has come true in many ways, often beyond anyone's wildest imagining—even that of the technologists themselves. The consequences of their worldwide diffusion are equally enormous, if not always to the good, by any means. To be sure, it is amazing to be able to access encyclopedic knowledge at the touch of finger, to share dozens of digital photos instantly with friends, and to find directions anywhere through global GPS on a mobile map, all on a device that fits comfortably in a pocket or purse; but that is far from the whole story. This chapter looks at the practical impacts of the IT revolution on several areas of everyday life: disruption through automation, buying and selling over the internet, information access and privacy, and social interaction and collective governance. But it does so in view of the utopian promises made by those in Silicon Valley who developed the new technologies and the often-dystopian realities now faced by the nation and humanity.

A cynic might say that the practical results of the internetting of everything are remarkably banal: buying and selling more consumer goods, glutting the microwaves with pointless chatter, and making barrels of money for the Tech Titans and their monster corporations. But there is a disturbing side to the tech revolution in the way its tools have been put to dark effect, endangering people's jobs and privacy, modern society's hard-won knowledge and grip on reality, and even the future of popular control and democratic government. A book on the Bay Area cannot do more than touch on the wider transformation of daily life unleashed by IT, which is still in its infancy. It will take years to judge many of the most far-reaching implications of the tech revolution of these times. Nevertheless, people living in the San Francisco region are some of the most familiar with the utopian claims for the Brave New World of IT, the most practiced in its ways of doing things, and most ensnared by the temptations of what has been called "the virtual life" or "the Wired Life"—what will be called here, simply, the "Tech World."

Therefore, this discussion will put particular emphasis on the promises of the masters of Tech World, sitting on their silicon clouds around the Bay Area and looking down on the world they have shaped. The tech revolution may not have been televised, but it has been massively publicized by the avatars of High Tech via books, TED lectures, tweets, blog posts, and more. To their way of thinking, the new digital technologies have opened up vast horizons of possibility for humankind, and with evangelical fervor they have spread the gospel of cyberculture. This began in the 1990s, revived in the early twenty-first century, and won a renewed burst of enthusiasm in the boom of the 2010s. As Mike Moritz of Sequoia Capital puts it, with the modesty characteristic of the apostles of IT: "Right here between San Jose and San Francisco something remarkable has been going on, is going on and will go on. It is something that has only occurred in one or two places in the whole course of human history."[1]

The masters of the tech universe believe wholeheartedly in the potential of their wondrous inventions to deliver freedom, progress, and equality. But what do they really know about the world that they are changing? What is striking is how naive they are about the society they live in and their place in it. After all, if Reid Hoffman, founder of LinkedIn, can declaim that "Silicon Valley is a mindset, not a location," he doesn't even have a grip on the piece of turf he ought to know best and how it functions. So why would anyone expect that he and his fellow titans have a firm idea of how social media, digital networking, and smart automation are altering people, places, and practices beyond their idealized world?[2]

It is not enough to ridicule some of the outlandish things the Tech Titans say about their inventions. Their kind of thinking is indicative of a larger disconnect between the capitalists and the mass of people who end up living with the consequences of their search for profits and drive to accumulate. The bravado of the tech generation has many precedents in the long arc of Industrial Modernity, from Andrew Ure and the Crystal Palace in mid-nineteenth century Britain to Scientific Management and the cult of Henry Ford in early twentieth-century America. In the postwar era, the chief of General Motors, Charles Wilson, could declare that he had always thought that what is good for General Motors is good for the country, and vice versa. Now the

---

1   Moritz quote in Keen 2015, p. 61. An example of 1990s technotopic enthusiasm is Barlow 1996. Prescient critiques of Tech World were Carlsson 1990, Brook & Boal 1995, Barbrook & Cameron 1997.

2   Hoffman quote at https://www.brainyquote.com/quotes/keywords/silicon_valley. html. For a delightfully wacky collection of declarations by Silicon Valley gurus, see http://www.gq.com/story/the-most-bullshit-motivational-slogans-in-silicon-valley.

celebrants of Silicon Valley believe that the Millennium belongs to them and the smartphone, the internet, and the virtual life they have created. What's good for Tech World is good for America.

The ideology of the Tech Titans is the latest incarnation of a long-standing American faith in the virtues of technology and modernization. Already in the nineteenth century, the national love affair with machinery was visible to all. Americans quickly adopted the latest mechanical devices from cotton gins and reapers to Colt revolvers and rotary saws, and, moreover, they built their machines bigger and stronger than craft-minded Europeans and replaced labor with machines as quickly as possible. In the same way, they rushed to adopt the automobile, electricity, and assembly line at the turn of the twentieth century, followed by early electronic technologies such as the telephone, radio, and television. It was not by chance that so many of the key inventions of past Industrial Revolutions appeared first in the United States and were put to work so readily. One historian calls this the "American Technological Sublime," an engineering version of the ecstatic secularism found among nineteenth-century nature lovers from the Hudson River School painters to John Muir's Sierra Club. A recent observer calls the latest version of this "the digital sublime." It runs deeper in the United States than anywhere and deeper than that in the Bay Area—a reminder of Lord Bryce's aphorism that California is "America, only more so."[3]

But there is more at work here than the love of machines and technologies. The leading lights of capitalism have always sung hymns to progress—a vague but powerful promise of better things to come. In this view, Modernity is all to the good because it breaks down clotted old ways of doing things and takes humankind forward into a rosy future of greater knowledge, achievement, and prosperity. Or, as Karl Marx put it, "All that's solid melts into air." Americans have taken to the idea of progress with a passion, an article of faith that aligns nicely with a belief in national purpose and the flip side of "our remarkable, almost willful, historical amnesia."[4]

The barons of Tech World are entranced by the Future. As Justin Rosenstein puts it (unconsciously echoing *The Communist Manifesto*), "We in

---

3   Quote from Mosco 2004, p. 8. On U.S. mechanization, see Rosenberg 1972, David 1975, Hounshell 1984. On technological sublime, see L. Marx 1964, Kasson 1976, Nye 1994. On California, see Bryce 1888. This is not entirely American, of course; the adoration of technical and modernization was originally unleashed by capitalism, proclaimed by the European Enlightenment, and put into practice by the British as the Industrial Revolution. Adas 1989.

4   Marx & Engels 1848, also Harvey 2017. Amnesia quote from Mosco 2004, p. 5. For critical histories of the modern idea of progress, see Pollard 1968, Berman 1982. On the perils of American optimism, see Ehrenreich 2010.

technology have a greater capacity to change the world than the kings and presidents of even 100 years ago." One might be tempted to write off Tech World's promise to deliver a shining Future as so much fantasizing, but there is a deeply disturbing side to it. Recall the scene in the film *Chinatown* when the land baron Noah Cross is questioned about his motives and the detective Jake Gittes asks him, "Why are you doing it? How much better can you eat? What can you buy that you can't already afford?" To which Cross replies, "The future, Mr. Gittes—the *future*." Somehow the future and the fortunes of the capitalists are magically aligned in the utopia to come. As Mary Beard notes, what every ruling class seeks is "the control of time."[5]

The utopian claims of Tech World are investigated in this chapter along with the practical and often dystopian effects of their innovations. While acknowledging the immense achievements of the information revolution, the purpose of this inquiry is to balance the good against the bad—which, as in so many cases of "the shock of the new," is becoming more and more clear as time goes on. Not all the noise is coming from the Bay Area's Tech Titans, but they are the most numerous and most fulsome promoters of fabulous claims about the future of the digital age. The dire effects of their actions are surely being felt nearby and also across the country and around the world.

The first claim is that the disruption created by tech innovations is liberating, cutting through tired habits of the past to free up markets and people to work in more creative ways. The truth, however, is that what is too often disrupted are people's jobs and functioning industries, but not the workings of the capitalist economy that harnesses technologies to its purposes. A second idealistic assertion is that a "sharing economy" has been unleashed by horizontal exchanges over the internet. But the chief consequence of the new exchange has been the old capitalist goal of making money by selling more commodities and growing monster companies (and annihilating competitors).

A third utopian claim is that being plugged into the internet puts a world of information at everyone's fingertips and allows a mastery of one's life via smartphone and home assistant device. What the idealistic view overlooks is that most people are not in a position to evaluate the flood of information cascading on their heads or to protect their own data and privacy—because when we are looking out at the web, the web is looking back at us.

A fourth assertion of Tech World is that Facebook and other social media are simply ways of facilitating human contact across the vast spaces

---

5   Rosenstein quote at: http://bgr.com/2014/05/06/worst-tech-speech-ever/. Quote from Beard 2015, p. 104. For a critique of Tech World Futurism, see Niedzviecki 2015. For an uncritical account, see Johnson 2012.

of modern life, bringing people together as one big community of friends. But linking up everyone has a downside in the ability of the malign to harass, spew venom, and disperse fake information anonymously.

The final topic of the chapter is not about the implications of the IT revolution but about the personal projects of the Bay Area's Tech Titans. They have the billions to follow their dreams of saving the world, but what do they actually do with all that money? Unfortunately, their personal utopias look more like the daydreams (or nightmares) of the superrich than the wishes of ordinary people.

Disruption and the Future of Automation

The life principle of Tech World is the ability to deliver endless innovation—the new New Thing—and the ethical corollary is that innovation is virtuous by reason of its power to disrupt the existing order of things. As Mark Zuckerberg of Facebook once declared, "Move fast and break things. Unless you are breaking stuff, you are not moving fast enough." But what is the goal of speed and breakage? Why this breathless impatience with the world as it is? Zuckerberg is just the latest to mouth the Idea of Progress and the Technological Sublime.

It is a mark of the class hubris of the Tech Barons that their vision of breaking things does not include those broken by lost jobs; the breaking up of socials solidarities, rhythms of life, and points of reference; the disruption of personal lives and privacy; and much more. If some oracles of Tech World think that endless disruption is beautiful thing, many critics see it as infernal chaos. Still others see disruption as the indulgence of the powerful at the expense of the weak. In any case, the argument over disruption in the digital era is the latest chapter of a very long debate over Modernity and Machinery.[6]

The ideologues of Tech World offer three kinds of disruption as virtues: setting loose the creativity of the young, breaking up monopolies, and breaking through to a new age of automation. The celebration of youthful disruption is on full display in the hothouses of start-ups, incubators such as Hacker Dojo, Y Combinator, AngelPad, and KickLabs, which one observer calls "the soul of Silicon Valley." Here one finds smart, idealistic young people working hard, sharing ideas, and pursuing their passions. They are often dismissive of the profit motive and see themselves as fully in service of the greater good; as Hacker Dojo director Jun Wong says, "They're all trying to build something

---

6 Lewis 2000 on the frenzied pursuit of change. Zuckerberg quote at: https://www. brainyquote.com/ quotes/quotes/m/markzucker453439. For the optimists, see Downes & Nunes 2014, Sundararajan 2015. For critiques, see García Martínez 2016, Lyons 2016.

and make the world better, not like outside where people are just trying to make money." They, too, embody the relentless pursuit of the new New Thing and allegiance to the gods of technical innovation.[7]

Tech World is, in a sense, making capitalism fun again: unleashing creativity, firing young minds, and delivering the future. As one writer puts it, "Silicon Valley is to the beleaguered American dream what Hollywood was in the 1930s—a repository for the promise that hard work and superior talent and ideas will rise in the marketplace. It's a proposition without which the western model of capitalism . . . cannot presume legitimacy." This is where smart young people want to be, just as they flocked to Wall Street in the late twentieth century. Of course, this poses a further question: are Wall Street banks and IT start-ups the best use of human talent the country can come up with? At other times, young people have been drawn to Chicago, "City of Broad Shoulders," or to Detroit, "The Motor City," or Hollywood's dream machine. In the 1930s, the best and the brightest rallied to President Roosevelt's New Deal, whose goal was to serve the people by giving them jobs, public works, and education—not better apps.[8]

Monopoly is a second target of the heralds of Tech World. They believe that their innovations disrupt monopolies, break down inefficiencies, and liberate the market. A prime example is Uber's and Lyft's disruption of the taxi industry, which former Übermensch Travis Kalanick hailed as serving the public by busting up taxi monopolies. This can certainly be a good thing for lowering the cost of transportation, and many taxi companies have been effective monopolies. But the problem is that technical breakthroughs are just as likely to create new monopolies as destroy old ones, as shown by Microsoft's dominance of software in the 1980s, Google's share of web searches in the early twenty-first century, and Amazon's mastery of online shopping in the 2010s. Uber's takeover of city streets poses a similar danger. As Silicon Valley libertarian Peter Thiel admits, "Monopoly is the condition of every successful business."[9]

In fact, nothing in the workings of capitalism assures competitive markets, which is why political movements have repeatedly cropped up to demand government intervention. This is happening again with the political battles that

---

7   Quote from Smith 2016, p. 6; Wong quoted at p. 9. For more on incubators, see http://startupcalifornia.org/startup-bay-area/.

8   Quote from Smith 2016. On the New Deal, see Taylor 2009 and https://livingnewdeal.org.

9   On Kalanick and Uber, see Kessler 2013. Thiel quote from Wall Street Journal op-ed, at http://www.wsj.com/articles/peter-thiel-competition-is-for-losers-1410535536. On tech monopolies, see Keen 2015, 2018, Glassman 2017.

have broken out around the world over the regulation of Uber, Lyft, and their equivalents. Some of the fights are to protect taxi drivers and companies, as in Taipei; some are about the added traffic congestion of circling Ubers, as in San Francisco; and still others are efforts to promote public transport and reduce emissions, as in Paris. All are about establishing minimum regulations and taxes on the new transport system. The European Union has repeatedly pursued Google, Apple and others for monopolistic practices (see chapter 1).[10]

The third and most far-reaching disruption offered by Tech World is progress in automation. The advances being made in robotics, machine learning, and artificial intelligence (AI) are widely advertised today. They have quickly progressed from the realm of fantasy to practical achievements, such as self-driving cars on city streets, Smart Homes overseen by Siri and Alexa, and AI surgical and nursing assistants. The new automation has already revolutionized everyday operations such as assembling orders in warehouses, and it threatens to overturn huge domains such as trucking and customer care. It could eliminate millions of blue-collar jobs and is likely to overhaul white-collar bastions such as clinics and hospitals, classrooms and schools, and professional offices.[11]

There is, understandably, a sense of panic in some quarters. A widely quoted U.S. government report in 2016 made the bold prediction that 83 percent of the jobs paying less than $20 per hour are in danger of elimination by automation. Yet the lords of tech continue their rush to perfect self-driving vehicles, delivery bots and drones, and medical consultant apps. All they see is new potential markets looming for their products. Uber, Lyft, Tesla, Google, and start-ups such as Aurora are all vying for the lead in smart cars, and busily suing each other over stolen ideas. Amazon, Google, and DoorDash are competing to perfect robotic delivery and drones. Accenture consultants, Alphabet's DeepMind Health, and IBM's WatsonPaths are enraptured by the prospects for medical AI.

If the disruptors are remarkably blind to the unsettling effects of change on ordinary people, the history of Modernity shows repeated outbreaks of resistance from those whose lives are turned inside out. Most, like the Luddites and loom breakers of the early nineteenth century, have failed to stop the onrushing locomotive of capitalist progress—and been mocked for

---

10   Uber used a program called Greyball to send a fake version of its ride-sharing app to users to help drivers evade law enforcement agencies that were scrutinizing the service for potential violation of local laws. On traffic impacts, see Said 2017. On the EU and Google, see Birnbaum & Fung 2017. On U.S. antitrust movements, see Kolko 1963.

11   On AI, see Glassman 2017. On trucking, see Dougherty 2017. On loss of jobs, see Ford 2016, McKinsey Global 2017.

their trouble. Nevertheless, one can expect a good bit of disruption coming back to bite the disruptors today on their way to the Future. For example, several accidents drove the city of Pittsburgh to toss out Uber's self-driving cars. Drones flying near commercial aircraft have the aviation industry and regulators furiously trying to control airspace. Meanwhile, a group is mobilizing against delivery bots impeding pedestrians on the sidewalks of San Francisco.

★ ★ ★

The threat of automation may well be exaggerated, however, and the new technologies unable to live up to their promise of breaking through to a new age of robotics. Instead, the machines will continue serve their primary masters, the capitalists and the corporations. Automation has been replacing workers at a furious pace since the Industrial Revolution. The whole point of capitalist competition is to revolutionize the methods of production so as to raise the productivity of labor. Millions of workers have lost their jobs to mechanization over the last two centuries, and the same story grinds ever onward today as companies compete to stay in the running in international markets. Robots are just the new face on this long-running drama, full of personal tragedy drowned out by the brass bands celebrating progress.[12]

At the same time, rising productivity has meant steadily more total output and value, which supports rising wages and incomes, as well as a growing mass of profits and accumulation of capital. Those profits and incomes are used, in turn, to invest in machinery and to buy more consumer products, with the result that the economy spirals upward. The United States has a long-term growth rate of productivity and output of over 2 percent per year, which has yielded unprecedented employment, prosperity, and power over the long run. But something has gone wrong over the last thirty to forty years. Productivity growth has actually slowed by half to barely over 1 percent a year, and long-term output and job growth have stagnated along with it.

The surprising thing, given all the hullaballoo over the New Industrial Revolution, is that the tech industry has not fulfilled the much-advertised promise of putting the whole economy on a new, higher foundation. A wave of automation coming from Bay Area tech companies is not sweeping all before it. No doubt many mechanized production systems have been dramatically improved by computer controls, digital communications, and robotics; the evidence for this in U.S. manufacturing is incontrovertible. What IT has

---

12   For a good review of new research, see Mishel & Bivens 2017.

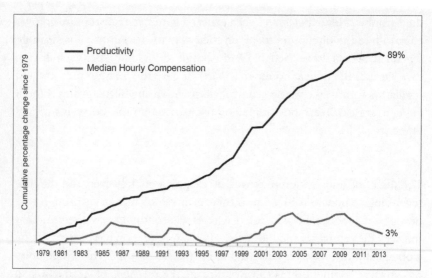

Figure 9.1: Productivity/Wage Gap in California, 1979–2013
Source: Bernhardt 2014.

manifestly not done is to raise labor productivity across the full spectrum of the division of labor and the whole of the country.[13]

The proximate cause of the productivity slowdown is that it always takes capital investment to introduce new machinery and control systems, and the capitalists have, overall, been reluctant to invest of late (like the tech giants sitting on massive piles of dollars they don't know what to do with). There are two possible reasons for this lack of enthusiasm. One is that the IT revolution is just not what it's cracked up to be, and what is missing is a new breakthrough technology that opens up vast new fields of investment—like railroads or automobiles in their heyday. A more compelling reason, however, is the feeble state of world capitalism, not the state of automation. The global economy is awash in capital, glutted with goods, and choking on excess capacity, and has been for many years now. The Great Recession only made matters worse.[14]

On top of all that, the capitalists have engaged in a massive upward redistribution of income while keeping a tight lid on wages. A simple way of showing this redistribution is the "productivity / wage gap" (fig. 9.1). The stagnation of working-class incomes is a huge brake on the economy because it suppresses mass consumption and worsens the global glut of goods and capacity. Further downward pressure is created when governments cut

---

13 On productivity stagnation, see Gordon 2016. California has done better than the nation, which is why it has grown faster, no doubt (see fig. 9.1).

14 Harvey 1982, Brenner 2006. The case for the missing breakthrough is made by Gordon 2016, a follower of Schumpeter.

expenditures because revenues fall in a weak economy (and after tax cuts), yet austerity (and tax cutting) has been the policy of the Right for years—despite the fact that it has never worked.[15]

The Sharing Economy and Business of Exchange

The IT revolution offers new ways of connecting buyers and sellers in markets for goods, transportation, and housing, not to mention entertainment, personal services, and more. It has added a new dimension to the world of exchange. The elemental form was a website for posting things to sell or auction, where buyers can survey offers and contact sellers to complete the exchange by post or face-to-face. This kind of "peer-to-peer exchange" began on sites such as Craigslist and eBay and became a huge market by the end of the 1990s.

The profile of internet-mediated, peer-to-peer exchange jumped to a new level toward the end of the first decade of the twenty-first century with the arrival of powerful new platforms using smartphones, GPS maps, and tailored apps, such as those of Uber, Lyft, and Getaround for car hires and Airbnb for apartment and house rentals. Suddenly, anyone with a smartphone could quickly solicit a ride or find a place to stay almost anywhere, any time. Importantly, these platforms include rating and review systems that allow users to have confidence in providers. Their popularity, particularly with the young, has exploded, making Uber and Airbnb household words and generating many competitors, such as France's BlaBlaCar, China's Didi Kuaidi, and India's Ola.

The avatars of Tech World have baptized the new platforms as "the sharing economy" and made typically utopian declarations about its benefits. Airbnb cofounder and CEO Brian Chesky declares that it is not about material things: "The stuff that matters in life is no longer stuff. It's other people. It's relationships. It's experience." Fellow founder Joe Gebbia has rhapsodized about the human element of vacation rentals: "The sharing economy is commerce with the promise of human connection. People share a part of themselves, and that changes everything." Enthusiastic scholar Ara Sundararajan, who has interviewed dozens of tech leaders, gushes that the sharing economy is a mix of the market and the gift-relation, a halfway house between capitalism and socialism. Or as venture capitalist Tom Perkins has said, the digital economy is a cooperative venture.[16]

---

15 Even the International Monetary Fund has come to criticize austerity as bad (Keynesian) economics. Elliot 2016.

16 Chesky quote at https://www.brainyquote.com/quotes/quotes/b/brianchesk529562.html. Gebbia quote at https://www.ted.com/talks/joe_gebbia_how_airbnb_designs_for_trust/transcript?share=171232f99a&language=en. Perkins from his autobiography, *Valley Boy*, cited by Keen 2016, p. 36. Sundararajan 2016. See also Elder-Vass 2016.

No doubt, sharing one's car or home requires an element of connection, trust, and human relationships, but enthusiasts of the sharing economy conveniently confound the essential difference between sharing and commercial transactions (which also require an element of trust). In fact, there is a lively world of cooperative, peer-to-peer endeavors on the internet, such as crowdsourced citizen science projects and crowdfunding of socially beneficial projects, but those are a far cry from the economy of car hires and apartment rentals that has emerged in recent years. Rather, the new platforms add a powerful dimension to the organization of production, exchange, and consumption in targeted commercial domains.[17]

The new platforms have proven their power to disrupt conventional practices and wreak havoc on entire industries, as in the case of Airbnb's impact on the hotel sector. About two hundred million travelers have stayed in over three million Airbnb listings in almost two hundred countries, according to the company. With hotels feeling the pinch, the American Hotel and Lodging Association has fought back, winning a number of city and state ordinances to restrict Airbnb activity, especially by commercial landlords turning apartment houses into quasi-hotels. Airbnb also became the target of a Federal Trade Commission investigation into its effects on soaring housing costs (see chapter 6).[18]

An invidious twist on the sharing economy is the way companies enlist the voluntary contributions of users of their platforms. One critic calls this the misuse of "the openness paradigm" borrowed from the idealists in software development, which is used to induce people to contribute free labor to corporations. This can be done by soliciting feedback through surveys, user groups, and chat rooms, and offering special rewards for consumer response. Some businesses even create apps in imitation of genuinely associative crowdsourcing projects. But the worst of it is the invisible gathering of data on people's patterns of use, preferences, and linkages, which enlists everyone's efforts for the corporation's benefit, whether they like it or not. A similar thing happens with professional platforms such as LinkedIn that can help companies evaluate and cull job applicants with less effort.[19]

★　★　★

17　For examples of cooperative P2P projects, see p2pfoundation.net and shareable.net. For bogus generalizing from cooperative efforts to commercial ones, see Botsman & Rogers 2010, Kirkpatrick 2010, Johnson 2012. For a critique, see Morozov 2013.

18　Benner 2017b. Also Kessler 2015.

19　Ettlinger 2014, Lyons 2016.

Beyond the hype of the sharing economy lies the real business of internet-mediated exchange, or what has come to be known as the "on-demand economy"—to wit, the purchase and delivery of goods and services via the internet and smartphones. The new technologies allow the ramping up of a very old idea of retail sales beyond brick-and-mortar stores, which began with mail-order retailing in the nineteenth century by Montgomery Ward, later joined by Sears Roebuck—which grew to be the nation's largest corporation by the 1920s. Those retailers also took advantage of the best technologies of their time, such as giant warehouses, universal postal service, a huge railroad network, and express companies that oversaw freight shipments. Consumers have long appreciated the convenience of shopping at home out of catalogs, which became icons of the mail-order era.[20]

As the internet age unfolded, people began shopping online via websites acting as modern catalogs. Virtual retailers began popping up in the 1990s, including Amazon and Priceline, but most died in the collapse of the dot-com bubble in 2000. The survivors grew rapidly after that, so brick-and-mortar stores jumped into the fray to keep up. Soon everyone was selling online. But the old-style stores were being outflanked from behind, having forgotten the principle lessons of the rise of chain stores and modern retailing—which is that the consumer interface is only half the story.

The real revolution was taking place in supply, all the way to door-to-door delivery. The on-demand economy is a misnomer that only captures the surface of selling, the smartphone apps that seem to make products appear magically at one's doorstep. But the process runs much, much deeper. The New Economy of retailing had been gestating in the 1990s with companies such as Dell Computer, which were learning how to transmit online orders along sophisticated, global supply chains managed through the internet. The new technology of computerized, internet supply chain management was, in fact, crucial to the rapid expansion of international trade in the late twentieth century. Globalization is not just about containers, ships, and overseas factories.[21]

The other great modernizer of retail supply in the late twentieth century was Walmart, followed closely by companies like Target. It, too, became a master at managing supply chains. Behind the big box stores are other big boxes: giant warehouses that are the hubs of the whole system of supply and distribution. The trick lies in managing flows in, out, and through those warehouses—receiving stock from manufacturers, sorting, shelving and

---

20 On the mail-order companies, see Tedlow 1990, Coopey et al. 2005.
21 On supply chains, see Fields 2003, Dell & Fredman 2006.

searching, assembling orders, and getting them out to retail stores—all of which demands precise tracking, communication, and transportation.[22]

All this was taking place before Amazon exploded on the scene. Recall that Amazon began in the 1990s as an online bookseller whose first accomplishment was to help Borders and Barnes & Noble decimate the old networks of local bookstores and distributors, before slaying its fellow monster booksellers, in turn. Next, Amazon branched out beyond books into recordings and then everything else. In the 2010s it became the giant of e-commerce, selling hundreds of millions of products and handling around two-thirds of all sales online, raking in over $100 billion in 2016.

The key to Amazon's success is only partly the online catalog and order platform; even more important is the immense system of supply, warehousing, and delivery Amazon has put together, building and improving upon the achievements of Dell, Walmart, and their kin. The whole point, of course, is instantaneous gratification of the consumer urge. As CEO Jeff Bezos says, "The best customer service is if the customer doesn't need to call you, doesn't need to talk to you. It just works."[23]

In the area of home delivery, Amazon is making further strides. It began by using the services of the FedEx, UPS, and DHL, which had themselves revolutionized rapid delivery systems involving aircraft, trucks, and warehouses, backed by the digital information technologies. Recently, it moved to take over deliveries and build a fleet of trucks to do so. At the same time, Amazon, Google, and other on-demand sellers are moving beyond trucks to delivery bots and drones, and one can only imagine the swarms of such devices clogging up city sidewalks and public airspace.[24]

Amazon's amazing growth mirrors Walmart in another regard: ruthless cost cutting at the expense of workers all along the supply chain. Altogether, advanced management, economies of scale, and cheap labor allow it to undercut all competitors. And if that's not enough, it keeps prices selectively below cost to drive out other retailers, which has kept Amazon from being as big a profit maker as it is an accumulator of capital. The impact on brick and mortar sales is being felt far and wide, particular in large-scale department stores, such as Sears, Penney's, and Macy's. Internet sales were 12 percent of total retailing in 2016 and rising fast, while new records were being set for bankruptcies of retailers such as American Apparel, Radio Shack, Payless Shoes, and The Limited. Along with those companies, hundreds of thousands of retail

---

22 Lichtenstein 2009.

23 Stone 2014. Quote from https://www.brainyquote.com/quotes/quotes/j/jeffbezos450020.html.

24 Birla 2005, Niemann 2007, Manjoo 2016.

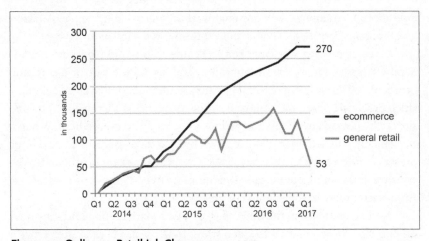

Figure 9.2: Online vs. Retail Job Change, 2014–2017

Source: http://www.progressivepolicy.org/blog/
ecommerce-job-gains-much-larger-retail-job-losses-heres/.

jobs were disappearing because e-commerce is much less labor intensive than stores (fig. 9.2).

Amazon is based in Seattle, not the Bay Area, but is always mentioned in the same breath with Apple, Google, Facebook, and Microsoft among the FANGs. Apple, as a seller of hard goods with a network of thousands of Apple Stores, employs the same kind of extensive supply chain around the world, manages it with similar information technology systems, and runs it on nonunion labor. Google has also dipped its toes into online retailing with Google Shopping, by which retailers pay to have their products advertised and sold through Google's platform. In order to challenge Amazon, Walmart has joined forces with Google to expand its online reach.[25]

Another kind of on-demand retailing is now filling up the internet and household electronics: music and video streaming. Streaming allows digital products to be shipped directly over the internet without a huge apparatus of physical supply. The internet dealt a huge blow to the music industry in the first instance, after mass reproduction and sharing of recordings became feasible in the 1990s—even though the record companies quickly shut down Bay Area start-up Napster. Then came legal downloads via Apple's iTunes and others, which began to reverse the financial losses of the industry. Two Bay Area techies came up with the algorithm for music streaming around 2000, which became commercialized as Pandora, the early leader in the field.

---

25 On the FANGs, see chapter 1. One link to the Bay Area is that John Doerr made a key investment in Amazon in 1996. Keen 2015, p. 46.

Subscription streaming now dominates music sales, led by Apple, Amazon, and Sweden's Spotify, and has stabilized revenues for the industry.[26]

Video streaming was launched in Seattle in the mid-1990s, but narrow bandwidth made mass streaming impractical, as did the lack of a common protocol. In the early twenty-first century, Adobe's Flash Player made online video practical, which was followed by the founding of Vimeo and YouTube, sites that allowed anyone to post videos to be watched everywhere. While it was quickly gobbled up by Google, YouTube has its own identity and a huge presence on the web to this day. If Web 2.0 was based on broadband, Web 3.0 is the internet of ubiquitous streaming. As Reed Hasting of Netflix says, "Broadcast TV is like the landline of 20 years ago."[27]

Netflix, launched in the mid-1990s, made its mark renting DVDs by mail, driving Blockbuster and other video stores to the wall a decade later. Once a new protocol for mass streaming was in place, Netflix shifted to a subscription service for streaming movies and TV series to home TVs, computers, tablets, and phones. Hulu, Apple (iTunes), and others followed suit in streaming services. In 2013, Netflix decided that streaming someone else's content was not enough and leapt into the business of TV and film production (following the lead of cable network HBO). Soon other tech giants jumped in, as well: Amazon, Apple, Google, and more. They are roiling the entertainment industry, but also injecting new life into Hollywood studios and indie productions.[28]

To sum up, the new sharing platforms often lead to quick taxi rides, cheap vacations, and great videos. It is not enough to denounce them for disrupting the status quo, which is not always wonderful. But there is no excuse for starry-eyed notions that the sharing economy is a new, liberating stage of collective enterprise. It is still a business, which even the tech-smitten Sundararajan admits would be better called, "Crowd-Based Capitalism." As for the business of retailing over the internet, the only one who is starry-eyed is Jeff Bezos, as he rockets to the top of the billionaires' league, passing fellow Seattle techno-capitalist Bill Gates. As Bezos succinctly sums up the present times, "Web 1.0 was making the Internet for people, Web 2.0 is making the Internet better for companies." Online shopping and rapid shipping are, without question, convenient for certain purposes, and surely the angel of Aaron Montgomery Ward is smiling down on Amazon and Co. In the end, the tech revolution may not be making the world a better place to live, but it is

26 Nicolau 2017, Greenfield 2017.
27 Zambelli 2013. Hastings's quote at: www.brainyquote.com/quotes/quotes/r/reedhastin423609.html.
28 Lev-Ram 2016. Livestreaming on Facebook and Periscope is a new and vibrant dimension of the phenomenon.

certainly making it an easier place to order shoes—from Zappos, an Amazon subsidiary—of course.[29]

Unlimited Information and the Invasion of Everyday Life

So far, engagement with the ideology of Tech World leads to the conclusion that innovation, disruption and sharing are the latest twist on tried-and-true capitalist practices and beliefs. When it comes to information and surveillance, the IT revolution goes farther, however, and poses an unprecedented set of questions about truth, privacy, and power for which the world as yet has few answers.

The Internet Age has opened up a whole new universe of communication and access to vast quantities of information. There are more than a billion websites easily discovered by means of search engines such as Baidu, Ask, Yahoo, and Bing. A new information age dawned along with the Millennium, with Google as the eye of the hurricane. The advent of its marvelous search algorithm transformed access to the wonders of the internet, becoming the gateway to the web for two-thirds of all users today. "To google" has become a verb, and conversations are regularly interrupted by someone saying, "Let's google that." Google became the octopus of the internet era, what one observer calls, "the monopolist of information."[30]

To the people who brought you Google, the potential is wonderful. As cofounder Larry Page has said, "Basically, our goal is to organize the world's information and make it universally accessible and useful." For Sergey Brin, the web might become "the third half of your brain." Miriam Rivera, an early Google employee recalls, "It was an inspiring place to be. . . . Democratizing access to information, and bringing the real world online." Brin and Page's original slogan, "Don't Be Evil," is charming if hopelessly naive, but one can hardly top CEO Eric Schmidt's claim, "To connect the world is to free the world."[31]

What could possibly go wrong with the internet as a source of information? One big drawback is the quality of what is loosely called "information," when so much of what is out there on the web is noise, or worse. The principle of open access that makes the internet such a powerful means of multiplying sources of information can also be the worst enemy of knowledge

---

29 Bezos quote from http://www.azquotes.com/quotes/topics/web-2-0.html.

30 Keen 2015, p. 57. On the rise of Google, see Levy 2011.

31 Page quoted https://www.brainyquote.com/quotes/quotes/l/larrypage173334.html. Brin quote from https://www.brainyquote.com/quotes/quotes/s/sergeybrin412532.html. Rivera quoted in 2017 at https://www.entrepreneur.com/article/283085. In fairness, Schmidt also advises people to turn their screens off and not be ruled by technology. http://www.bu.edu/news/2012/05/20/boston-university-139th-commencement-address-eric-schmidt/.

and truth. How does anyone know for sure that such and such a website is accurate? Another principle of open access is the acceptance of "comments" on web content, which is intended as a means of verifying and supplementing knowledge but regularly clogs up websites and blogs with misleading and vituperative trash talk by trolls.

Wikipedia, the online, open-source encyclopedia, is a case in point. It is a marvelous, noncommercialized resource that is one of the best and most convenient ways of searching out information (and was used in writing this book). Yet because Wikipedia is invested in the idea of veracity, it is forced to contradict the principles and practice of "openness" and "the neutral point of view" espoused by founder Jimmy Wales. It has humans who serve as gate-keepers, editing and questioning content. Even so, a good deal of questionable and factually incorrect content still gets through.[32]

In order to access all the information on the web, people turn to search engines such as Google's. Search engines that are based on sophisticated computational algorithms do much more than simply seek out key words; they look for patterns that best fit a search request or question. Pattern recognition is what the human brain does brilliantly—forming patterns out of a chaotic world of sensation, reinforcing the ones that work, and learning to recognize them in a changing universe; humans are brilliant, for example, at spotting a friend in a crowd despite changes of dress, hairstyle, and age. In order to make sense of the world beyond personal experience, however, people must have recourse to social knowledge, or collective wisdom, to filter the wheat from the chaff of random events, opinion, and other information. Search engines can travel the web instantly in response to search commands, but they are not guarantors of wisdom. In the end, human intelligence is still called for.[33]

Moreover, algorithms are opaque, and how they filter information is mostly unknown. Yet the results of such algorithms can be distorted by the assumptions of the techies who wrote the code or by poor machine learning programs that generate laughable or even harmful results. Algorithms can be misled by bogus and dangerous information, which gets picked up from false websites and starts circulating and reverberating over the internet. Or as Cathy O'Neil says, "The algorithms are making it harder and harder to get good information." In addition, there are algorithms, or "bots," that generate bogus content, such as emails from Nigerian princes, comments on webpages, and YouTube videos.[34]

32   Tkacz 2015.
33   On the effect of Google searches on people's notion of truth, see Hillis et al. 2012.
34   O'Neil quoted in Chalabi 2016. Also O'Neil 2016, Greenfield 2017. On YouTube bots, see Bridle 2017, Lewis 2018.

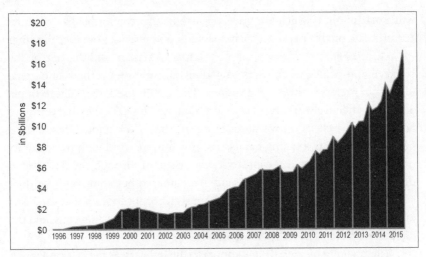

Figure 9.3: Growth in Online Advertising Revenue

Source: https://www.iab.com/wp-content/uploads/2016/06/internet-ad-revenue-chart-1996-q1–2016.gif.

Finally, the commercialization of the internet and its search engines means that a huge percentage of online content is simply advertising (fig. 9.3). Commercial ads are not the highest form of information, by anyone's standard. Tech World has actually multiplied the number of ads in play and the way they hammer at one's consciousness; an electronic billboard is harder to ignore than a wood and paper one. Google's advertising, for example, has been vastly expanded to include more banners, product listing, and video ads. Worse, Google AdWords algorithm uses keywords to make certain ads appear on pages users call up, while Facebook allows advertisers to target "lookalike audiences" spreading through user networks. As one Facebook engineer put it, "The best minds of my generation are thinking about how to make people click ads."[35]

★ ★ ★

But the quality of information coming over the internet is not the only consideration. Another set of problems arises from way the internet acts as a two-way mirror. You are looking at the world, but Google is looking back at you. That started with being plugged into the internet at home and work through personal computers, and it has expanded exponentially

---

35 Quoted in Keen 2016, p. 60. One can find all sorts of DIY handbooks on social media marketing today.

with smartphones, which are traveling spybots that cannot be used without sending data on one's contacts, whereabouts, and activities out into the ether.

Google, Facebook, Snap, Apple, Twitter, Amazon, and the rest of the big tech companies track users to gather information on them and glean hints as to preferences and dispositions. This data is used, typically, to target ads more effectively and recommend products. The data they harvest goes far beyond the clicks on websites, however; they track photos, friendships, finance, comments, reading habits, and much more. And with the ubiquity of smartphones, they can capture someone's path through the day's activities. Then they turn around and send that data to other companies for their advertising and marketing. Because these tech corporations are at the heart of internet traffic, they have the most information at their fingertips, and the temptation to harvest it for gain is irresistible.[36]

The tracking of metadata is known to the industry as the "God View." It poses fundamental threats to personal privacy. No one knows fully what data is being collected, at what degree of intimacy, from which sources, and how it is all being processed through the mysterious algorithms of the tech companies. For a time, the Federal Trade Commission put limits on the tech and communications companies' ability to cull big data and sell it for profit without the knowledge or consent of the public. But in 2017, the Republican Congress tore down that protective cover. The European Union, by contrast, has instituted a new regulation on "Algorithmic Accountability" effective in 2018.[37]

An increasingly serious problem is that the data one offers up in commercial transactions and government programs will be revealed to all at some unknown time. Notorious examples are the hacking of Yahoo, the British National Health Service, and Equifax, from which thieves extracted millions of people's secure data. Once such information gets into the wrong hands, those people are vulnerable to all kinds of misuse of their information, identity theft, and financial mischief. The silver lining for the IT industry, of course, is the explosive growth of cybersecurity firms and consultancies to help companies and individuals protect their data. Of the top 500 such companies in the world, Silicon Valley is home to 120.[38]

Even worse is the mining of personal information and big data by governments to spy on their citizens. The government works hand in hand with communications companies such as AT&T and Verizon to capture data on

---

36 On the threats to privacy, see Morozov 2011, Keen 2015, Wu 2016, Greenfield 2017.
37 On big data, see Mayer-Schönberger et al. 2013. On the issues, see datasociety.net. On European regulation see Keen 2018.
38 On international hacking, Buchanan 2017. On the cybersecurity field, see https://cybersecurityventures.com/cybersecurity-500/.

telephone calls, texts, emails, and more, and their capacity includes location tracking, activity monitoring, and tapping into electronic devices in the home. Local police forces use online data, surveillance, and social media not only to track suspects but also, more insidiously, to try to predict who will commit crimes—even though most of those being fingered have done nothing illegal. The worst Silicon Valley company in this regard is Palantir, whose data mining and predictive algorithms are used by the CIA, FBI, and military.[39]

The massive surveillance of metadata by the National Security Agency came as a shock when it was revealed by Edward Snowden in 2013—but has only become bigger and more intrusive (and Snowden is still considered a traitor instead of a hero for informing the public). More and more revelations have been made about governments around the world using the internet to spy on their citizens and suppress opposition. China's hardline regime regularly closes websites of which it does not approve, and repressive governments in Iran, Egypt, and Russia have all plumbed user data aggressively to ferret out dissidents and send them to prison or death.

★ ★ ★

Knowing all that, one of the strangest things about increased surveillance and the threats to privacy is how readily people submit to the new order in the name of Modernity and convenience. Many actively want to be connected to the internet at every possible moment and to be in the vanguard of the Wired Life, unconcerned that the better connected they are, the more transparent they become to anyone looking back through the mirror.

This is eminently true of the latest fashion, "the internet of things," which means lashing together all the devices in one's life, even wiring up the Smart Home. This can be done through Apple watches, Fitbits, or other personal activity monitors; visually through internet-linked cameras; auditorily through phones and household command centers such as Google Home and Amazon Echo; and even through biometric sensors. Certainly, lashing up everything to the web offers rapid access to the world of information, better self-awareness, and being plugged directly into the on-demand economy. But at what cost?

Tech World approves of having "computation and data communication embedded in, and distributed through, our entire environment." The wired home and person makes one's life more readable to all the data-harvesting algorithms out there. One critic calls it the "colonization of everyday life by information processing," while another argues, "This is the open secret of the internet of Things. . . . The price of connection is vulnerability [and] every

---

39   Timm 2016, Cagle 2016, Greenfield 2017, Peretti 2017.

single device that is connected to the network offers an aperture, a way in, what the security community calls an 'attack aperture.'"[40]

Slowly but surely the public is learning about the threats to privacy created by living on and with the internet. Polls show a solid majority of Americans think it is important to control who gets personal information. Even popular media such as Consumer Reports are urging people to lock down their phones and computers with encryption and secure connections. A new secure texting app, Signal, has become a favorite among young activists. The California legislature is on the verge of passing a law in opposition to the FTC's decision to let broadband companies mine and sell personal data.[41]

Social Media, False Friends, and Fake News

Predictably, the logic of unlimited connection over the internet does not necessarily lead people to seek out new horizons around the world. Instead, they love to use the new information technologies to do what humans like best: socializing (even more than online sex). This is the root of the immense success of Facebook and other social media. But along the way, social media have morphed back into immense conduits for news and information about the wide world, with profound implications for politics and democracy.

Every day a billion Facebook users link together their personal networks of friends. A third of a billion Twitter users can tweet their followers or receive the latest word(s) from their best friends or favorite entertainers. Two billion smartphone owners can add photographs to their messages, and well over a half-billion users of Instagram and Snapchat communicate principally by photo sharing. The rest of the five billion mobile phone owners have to be content with text messaging, replete with a host of emojis for every mood and sentiment. Everyone is connected now, it seems, and we are all friends, living in each other's pockets 24/7.

Naturally, the pioneers of social media are enthusiastic about what the new connectivity can offer humanity. All this digital friendliness started off with a few noble ideas for putting people together in a massively decentralized framework, such as the World Wide Web based on Chris Berners-Lee's system of individualized URL addresses. There were some experiments with bulletin boards and social networks in the 1990s, but the Facebook system took off in the early twenty-first century because of the simple logic of the "friending" system. [42]

---

40 Quotes from Greenfield 2017, pp. 31, 36, 44.
41 Angwin 2017. https://www.eff.org/deeplinks/2017/08/ab-375-californias-broadband-privacy-act-very-close-becoming-law.
42 For a celebratory history of Facebook and Zuckerberg, see Kirkpatrick 2010.

Mark Zuckerberg claims that "Facebook was not originally created to be a company. It was built to accomplish a social mission—to make the world more open and connected." That means, "There is a huge need and a huge opportunity to get everyone in the world connected, to give everyone a voice and to help transform society for the future." From there, his tone is even more prophetic: "When you give everyone a voice and give people power, the system usually ends up in a really good place. So, what we view our role as, is giving people that power."[43] But does Facebook give people meaningful voice and power?

The virtue of Facebook and other social media is that they can expand the world of friendships and regular communication among family, friends and associates over time and distance. On the other hand, social media can keep people focused on a small circle of contacts rather than looking outward. Facebook friends, online chat rooms, specialized websites, and topical feeds have a common feature of reinforcing social ties within groups. That is their intended purpose: attract people who are similar and let them hold forth to each other—the principle of the small-town sewing circle or the academic conference. Such socializing can be reaffirming, satisfying, and edifying, but it is not usually broadening—and in some cases it can be quite pernicious, as when the circle of "friends" are right-wing fanatics cementing their cockeyed worldview.[44] Indeed, the dangers of creating self-reinforcing fantasy worlds of conspiracy, violence, and sensationalism are becoming more and more apparent.

Facebook and social media can also increase unwanted social pressure on some people, especially the young and impressionable, who are made to feel worse about themselves because of the added exposure. This is amplified where friend alerts become the medium for the narcissistic and competitive to up the ante on proving how brilliant their lives are (meals, vacations, children, clothes, and so forth). If the group turns on a targeted person who becomes a pariah, things can quickly go from bad to disastrous. Bullying is common enough among school kids, but has become endemic on social media. People with malign intent can worm their way into being Facebook friends or spew venom through their Twitter feeds, but all too often the supposedly true friend is ultimately proved false. This happens in all social circles, but the

---

43 Zuckerberg quotes at https://www.brainyquote.com/quotes/quotes/m/markzucker 453428.html, also 453429, 412425.

44 For a harrowing view of the "fascosphere" on the net, see Albertini & Doucet 2016. On the dangers of YouTube's recommendation algorithm, see Lewis 2018 and AlgoTransparency, which tracks the videos YouTube's algorithm most often recommends, at https:// algotransparency.org.

question is how much more vulnerable are people on social media than in face-to-face contact?[45]

Moreover, information about individuals has a way of leaking away from protected circles of friends and spreading far and wide over the web, and it does not go away easily. Embarrassing snapshots, unguarded comments, and bad judgment have a way of clinging to everyone, hurting reputations long after the person has grown up, made amends, or moved on. The worst, of course, is intentional harassment of women through the internet and social media, and the ability of obsessive stalkers and batterers to pursue their prey even more easily over the web. Mark Zuckerberg has talked a lot about the "transparency" ushered in by the internet and social media, but transparency can mean being naked to the world.[46]

★ ★ ★

Social media have evolved in other unexpected ways, going from personal messaging to a major means of collective communication, or the New Media, surpassing newspapers, radio, and television sources of news. They have become essential means of conveying information on current events and politics, including reports from traditional news media and people passing along the latest hot topic and global gossip. Twitter, Snapchat, Instagram, Facebook, and Google are now major hubs for the diffusion and amplification of the stories that shape collective consciousness about the world. To be sure, many people love being instantly apprised of sports scores, natural disasters, and gossip on movie stars, but the thirst for trending news has, like 24-hour cable TV, created a monster that must be fed constantly. And, here again, the veracity of news depends on the quality of the origins and the machinations of algorithms, such as Facebook's News Feed.[47]

It is now well documented that the New Media are being used systematically to disperse disinformation, conspiratorial gossip, and outright lies—or fake news, as it has come to be known. Revelations about the distribution of fake stories across social media by means of false-front accounts and phony political ads in the 2016 U.S. elections have exploded. Just as disturbing as meddling by Russian and other powers has been the lackadaisical response of Google, Twitter, and Facebook to such deceptions. More disturbing than

---

45 Williams 2014, Pappas 2015.
46 Bloxham 2014. "By giving people the power to share, we're making the world more transparent." Zuckerberg quoted in Kirkpatrick 2010.
47 Which Zuckerberg and company have recently reduced in the name of protecting users from false news—a move that may backfire by shrinking the feeds from legitimate news sources.

foreign intrusions, however, is the made-in-America spew of reactionary and racist bile across the web, encouraging the expression of reactionary views, giving credence to absurd conspiracy theories, and aiding the gathering of alt-Right tribes. The misuse of the New Media has become patently obvious as the Tweeter-in-Chief proves to be one of the most inflammatory sources of disinformation in the country.[48]

In fact, the internet is awash in disinformation, falsehood, and titillation, not to mention an everyday flood of blather. The defect is systemic in the New Media because there are so many easy points of entry in the dispersed networks—the very horizontality and openness that Tech World advocates celebrate. Once a bogus idea begins to circulate, it can snowball in a matter of minutes. As a BuzzFeed report on Facebook concludes: "The best way to attract and grow an audience for political content on the world's biggest social network is to eschew factual reporting and instead play to partisan biases using false or misleading information that simply tells people what they want to hear." Indeed, the social media platforms love to see content of any kind snowball, because it generates clicks and eyeballs, in the same way they want the number of users and advertisers to grow exponentially. Meanwhile, a huge majority of Americans have become unable to distinguish fake news from the real thing.[49]

The masters of Tech World have been reluctant to face the facts about the way their digital magic carpets are being used to transport lies and fakery. Mark Zuckerberg stirred up a storm of controversy when he declared that it was "a pretty crazy idea" to suggest that fake news on Facebook helped sway the 2016 election. Since then, as evidence of abuse has mounted up, criticism has grown, and tech executives have been called before congressional committees, the big companies have been quietly tweaking algorithms and putting more people in place to monitor activity. Facebook has changed the way it tracks "trending stories" and fact-checks; Google has barred fake news websites from its AdSense advertising program; Snapchat has cracked down on misleading images; and Twitter has started banning venomous accounts. Facebook is going after violent threats and YouTube is redirecting people looking for terrorist recruitment videos to others critical of violence.[50]

48 On Russian hacking, Shane 2017, Leoning et al. 2017, https://towcenter.org/research-director-jonathan-albright-on-russian-ad-networks/. But the problem goes way beyond Russia. Hern 2017.

49 Bloxham 2014, Silverman et al. 2016, Cohen 2017. On the efficacy of fake news, see www.buzzfeed.com/craigsilverman/fake-news-survey?utm_term=.xgbgBOoqp9#. inyoeabDLW.

50 Zuckerman quoted in Silverman et al. 2016. For examples of new policies, see Wakabayashi & Isaac 2017, Lang 2017, Benner 2017a, Tsukayama 2017.

Nevertheless, the tech giants are reluctant to go too far, too fast. Too much reform might, after all, lower click rates and watch times, grow their client base more slowly, and sacrifice revenues. God forbid, they might have to submit to government regulation. Worse, they might have to admit that they are not making the world better but actually entombing people in a kind of zombie state where truth and fiction are indistinguishable and real-world engagement falls through the looking glass of their screens. The last refuge of Tech World is to claim to be the new guardians of free speech; yet the disturbing reality is that the First Amendment is being buried beneath mountains of disinformation so deep that it is getting harder and harder to dig out the truth and salvage civil discourse.[51]

Of course, fake news is not new; in their heyday U.S. newspapers and radio stations frequently engaged in the worst kind of yellow journalism and political demagoguery. Some of the current shock is due to comparisons with the high point of postwar journalism, when standards had markedly improved for big city newspapers and network TV newsrooms. Nevertheless, there may be good reason to fear for the future of democracy itself in the Information Age. How can a citizenry endlessly plied with rubbish and easily fooled by fakery capably govern themselves and monitor the powers that be? One worried commentator despairs, "What if the liberating potential of the Internet also contains the seeds of depoliticization and thus dedemocratization?"[52]

The dominance of news and public discourse by a few media monopolists is far from new in the United States, of course. The quality of mainstream journalism was already in serious doubt as newspapers, television, and radio outlets were concentrated in fewer and fewer hands, thanks to neoliberal/ neoconservative deregulation in the late twentieth century. Then the internet blasted the foundations out from under print journalism. Curiously, some Tech Titans have moved into the mainstream media, as with Jeff Bezos's purchase of the *Washington Post* and Laurene Powell Jobs's acquisition of the *Atlantic*.

Nor should one be surprised by the willingness of the elite to suppress news they do not like; Tech Moguls are no different in this regard than the powerful of every era. An egregious case was Peter Thiel's takedown of the gossip site Gawker for outing him as gay. But the message went well beyond Thiel's revenge; as venture capitalist Vinod Khosla declared, "Click bait journalists need to be taught lessons."[53]

---

51 On the danger to Free Speech, see Wu 2017.
52 Morozov quoted in Siegel 2011. See also Morozov 2011, 2013, McChesney 2014, Silverman et al. 2016, Taplin 2017.
53 On tech moving into traditional media, see Streitfeld & Isaac 2016, Rutenberg 2016. On media monopolies, see Bagdikian 1990. Khosla quoted in Silverman et al. 2016.

In short, the internet has gone in one quick generation from being the solution to better information, communication, and social relations to being one of the greatest threats to all three. Former Facebook executive Chamath Palihaptiya did not mince words when he said, "The short-term, dopamine-driven feedback loops that we have created are destroying how society works. . . . No civil discourse, no cooperation, misinformation, mistruth. . . . So we are in a really bad state of affairs right now, in my opinion." Or, as Twitter cofounder Evan Williams reflects, "I thought once everybody could speak freely and exchange information and ideas, the world is automatically going to be a better place. I was wrong about that."[54]

Want to Get Away?

The Bay Area's Titans of Tech have other dreams besides those for the internet, communication, and social media, and they have the billions to turn their ideas into reality—no matter how fantastic they might seem. These are not improvements to information technologies but visionary projects for transforming modern medicine, entire cities, and space travel. Some will surely have practical consequences down the line, while others are pie-in-the-sky. Some are utopias in Thomas More's sense of islands, while some are dystopias born of fearful minds seeking withdrawal from the ordinary world. The latter are a worrisome sign of the immense class divide in America today, but even the benign tech dreams for a better world are distorted by how the superrich think about the Future and their view of the rest of humanity.

The mildest version of Tech World escapism is the annual ritual of the Burning Man festival, which takes place in Nevada's Black Rock desert. Burning Man is a mass frolic redolent of premodern saturnalia, where thousands of people cast aside normal habits and morals for a few days of fun and fire, revels, and riotous excess. It is not a project of the Tech Barons alone, since it has a large following among the tech workers and Bay Area professionals, and it harkens back to the Human Be-Ins of the hippie generation of the Sixties. But much of its cult status derives from the early and rabid adherence of Eric Schmidt, the denizens of the Googleplex, and others among the Silicon Valley tech crowd.[55]

At the sober and virtuous end of the scale, by contrast, are the Tech Barons' philanthropic initiatives. There has been a surge in philanthropy by Bay Area billionaires in the 2010s. The Silicon Valley Community Foundation, for example, is bursting at the seams with new tech money, making it the

---

54 Palihaptiya quote in Harris 2018. Williams quote in Streitfield 2017c.
55 On Burning Man and Tech World, see Turner 2009, Bowles 2016.

largest community foundation in the country, and tech billionaires are moving up the ranks of national donors. Tech philanthropists love edgy and high-impact donations, and there is a hub, GiveWell, that helps guide the monied to leading-edge projects. They naturally believe that they are reinventing the philanthropic wheel, and venture capitalist Sean Parker has even published a manifesto calling traditional philanthropy "a strange and alien world made up of largely antiquated institutions."[56]

Nonetheless, the major gifts of the tech capitalists are very much in line with American philanthropy going back to John D. Rockefeller. Like the latter, their favorite endeavor is advancing the research component of modern medicine. Bill and Melinda Gates's commitment to global health research from their Seattle foundation is well known. Sean Parker's $600 million foundation is devoted to the cause of cutting-edge medical research. Facebook's Dustin Moskovitz and Cari Tuna started a foundation called Good Ventures, hyped as breaking new ground, but which goes down the same road by giving principally to malaria research. Marc and Lynne Benioff of Salesforce have given $250 million to the Children's Hospitals of San Francisco and Oakland, which now bear their names. While the ideal of making medical breakthroughs is consistent with the tech ideology of innovation, a cynic might suggest their obsession with medical research derives from the fact that immortality is the one thing their fortunes can't buy.[57]

While American philanthropy has much to recommend it, it has rightly been criticized for a large measure of noblesse oblige and a diversion of attention from inequality. More serious is the way foundations are used to influence social policy as a replacement for government programs funded by taxing the rich. In the case of Tech World, these characteristics are, if anything, more pronounced. Tech philanthropists share with earlier generations of wealthy donors the belief that their money, well managed and well spent, can remake society, and can do so more nimbly than public spending managed by governments and popular sovereignty. Some of the locals call this "effective altruism," or as Cari Tuna puts it, "The thing we focus on is expected value." Mark Zuckerberg and Priscilla Chan have gone one step lower by channeling their money through an "Initiative"—which translates as a private corporation, not a true foundation.[58]

---

56 On Bay Area tech philanthropy, see O'Neil 2015. Parker quote in Stanley 2015. See also Goel 2016.

57 On Rockefeller, see Brown 1979. Education is another favorite target of the Tech Titans, such as Mark Zuckerberg, Priscilla Chan, and Reed Hastings. Not surprisingly, they are advocates of wired classrooms and charter schools. Singer 2017.

58 On the history of philanthropy, see Zunz 2011. For general critiques, see Barkan 2013, 2015, McGoey 2015, Reich et al. 2016. On Zuckerberg-Chan, see Barkan 2015. Ms. Tuna quote in Goel 2016.

Another line of initiatives by tech billionaires is revisioning cities as utopian domains of High Tech business and life. Zappos CEO Tony Hsieh hopes to redevelop Downtown Las Vegas "as a hub of inspiration, entrepreneurial energy, creativity, innovation, prosperity, and discovery fueled by the Three C's: collisions, colearning, and connectedness." Google (Alphabet) has a subsidiary called Sidewalk Labs, whose mantra is, "New technologies, led by ubiquitous connectivity, can help cities tackle their biggest challenges." Y Combinator is equally ambitious; as project manager Adora Cheung declares, "If we can live in a world in which we can build cities quickly, based off mass movements of people wanting to live somewhere else, that would be amazing." Her models are Shenzhen and Dubai, built not by tech idealists but by authoritarian capitalist states. The naiveté is mind-blowing.[59]

Silicon Valley is, of course, the sine qua non for imagineers of islands of urban entrepreneurship and innovation. Peter Thiel, founder of PayPal and Palantir, thinks it should be the model for the whole of America: "Where I work in Silicon Valley, it's hard to see where America has gone wrong." At least Thiel recognizes that, "Silicon Valley is a small place. Drive out to Sacramento or even across the bridge to Oakland, and you won't see the same prosperity." The reason, of course, is the genius of the Tech Titans: "We don't accept . . . incompetence in Silicon Valley, and we must not accept it from our government." Angel investor and CEO Balaji Srinivasan has suggested that the Valley simply secede from the United States to form an independent state running on its own technology.[60]

An extreme version of Tech World utopianism is called "seasteading" and has its own institute founded by Thiel and Patri Friedman, grandson of the Chicago economist Milton Friedman, the intellectual guru of American neoliberalism. The goal is to build floating islands in the ocean to serve as ideal wired environments for entrepreneurial activity. The Seasteading Institute claims to be "working to provide a machinery of freedom to choose new societies on the blue frontier," and it envisages a kind of libertarian paradise, given that "the technology to foster the fluid mechanics of voluntary societies is at hand." Of course, what such islands promise is escape from the madding crowd of government regulators, elected politicians, and hostile workers. The Seasteading Institute has recently gained permission to

---

59 On Hsieh (who hails from the Bay Area), see http://downtownproject.com. On plans by Google and Y Combinator, see Badger 2018. Cheung quoted in Weller 2016. For critiques, see Wiig 2015, Greenfield 2017, pp. 48–59.

60 Thiel quotes from Beres 2016. Srinivasan lecture at Y Combinator, October 18, 2013, at: https://www.cnet.com/news/a-radical-dream-for-making-techno-utopias-a-reality/.

build a prototype in a Polynesian lagoon, which will, predictably, leave local residents high and dry.[61]

Such technotopian escapism is fully manifest in Elon Musk's obsession with rockets and establishing a colony on Mars. Tesla's Musk has created a space exploration company, SpaceX, to carry out his scheme. Reusable rockets, better batteries, and harvesting methane fuel on Mars are "the key[s] to making human life multi-planetary." Musk thereby joins other global billionaires such as Jeff Bezos of Amazon and Richard Branson of Virgin as Tech World's "rocket men," thrilled by the challenge, eager to one-up NASA, and fueled by their planetary-sized egos. The desire to escape the earth is a curious thing, revelatory of a fundamentally dystopian view of things as they are. If the land is too constraining, go to sea; if the earth is limited, go to Mars.[62]

Musk's escapism is topped only by the out-and-out survivalists, whose numbers are multiplying among the Bay Area's Tech Moguls. These dystopians include Steve Huffman, cofounder of Reddit, Tim Chang of Mayfield Fund, and Marvin Liao of 500 Startups. They are stockpiling food, water, and arms at hidden bunkers, ranches around the Far West and properties in New Zealand (where Peter Thiel has secretly established citizenship). These are not your everyday paranoid guys in Montana with rifles, extreme survival training, and Minuteman clubs. Instead, these wealthy men figure that if there is even a small chance of surviving the unlikely event of social breakdown or natural disaster, they have the luxury of creating that kind of personal insurance. It is a deeply creepy outlook on the world they have done so much to shape.[63]

A different kind of disquiet is to be found among those tech leaders promoting a Guaranteed Basic Income (or Universal Basic Income) for the lowest orders of society. They are aware of the nagging unemployment and low wages plaguing the U.S. economy, which they ascribe to technical change, and they believe that robotics and automation driven by machine learning and artificial intelligence will render most ordinary labor obsolete in the near future. Sam Altman of Y Combinator is so convinced of the need to provide people with an alternative means to live that he is giving one thousand Oaklanders $20,000 each for a year to see what they do with the money. It is anyone's guess how much the Tech Titans' enthusiasm for Guaranteed Basic Income is based on a humanitarian concern for those left behind by

---

61 Wong 2017. Quotes from https://www.seasteading.org.
62 Quotes from http://www.spacex.com. Vance 2015, Niedzviecki 2015, Stockton 2016, Tynan 2016. Other examples of tech space entrepreneurs are OneWeb's plan for private global satellite network and Orbital Institute's idea of gathering Big Data via satellites.
63 Osnos 2017.

the tech revolution and how much of it is motivated by fear of revolutionary upheaval by the neglected masses of unemployed.[64]

Redistribution downward is usually associated with the Left and the welfare state. Indeed, some on the Left are convinced by the case for the coming wave of automation, believing that capitalism no longer needs so many workers in the core countries, especially those with little education or skill. They call this stratum "the unnecessariat" and argue that the mass imprisonment and military enlistment of recent years have been motivated by the capitalists' desire to control the unemployed.[65]

Both Right and Left versions of this dystopia are wrong. While capitalists continuously automate older lines of production, there is no capitalist imperative to get rid of all workers. The principal causes of high unemployment (and underemployment) are a world economy has been bogged down by overproduction, bloated fortunes at the top and stagnant wages below thanks to class struggle from above, and financial excesses that periodically blow up into depressions—to which can be added government austerity policies put in place by neoliberals and backed by the tax-avoiding 1%. Blaming the state of America on the robot apocalypse is an easy way to let the rich, the Right, and the market system off the hook.[66]

A universal work program would be far more radical than a universal income, because it produces real things like houses and parks, involves care work for those in need, allows people to participate in rebuilding their communities, and involves collective action and decision-making—rather than emphasizing money, individual choice, and consumption. What the country needs is a major public works and national reconstruction effort along the lines of the New Deal in the 1930s. But serious talk of such things runs up against the resistance of the 1%, who treat progressive taxation as some kind of revolutionary seizure of property, and the Republicans, who regard all government programs other than military and police as anathema. Any Left-leaning politician, such as Bernie Sanders and Jeremy Corbyn in Britain, who advocates for serious redistribution, economic stimulus, and governmental job programs, is quickly deemed outside the sphere of acceptable politics. Unfortunately, this has left the field open to the appeal of demagogues on the Right.[67]

---

64 Waters 2017a. For critiques of GBI, see Bernhardt 2017, Greenfield 2017, pp. 202–206.
65 See, e.g., Srnicek and Williams 2016.
66 This is not to say that one shouldn't reflect on the potential nightmares of a robotic world. Turkle 2011.
67 On the kinds of programs used during the New Deal, see https://livingnewdeal.org. For a recent proposal for work programs, see Paul et al. 2017.

Conclusion

The information revolution has an immense capacity for both good and ill. It can deliver economic growth while impelling massive social disruption, allow people to share their personal lives but expose them to theft and harassment, and open up access to whole new worlds of information along with mountains of fakery. What will come of it is yet to be determined. As through the entire history of capitalist modernity, the game is on, and the fight has begun to determine the direction the IT revolution should take for humankind.

The inventions of the Tech Titans have, without question, changed the world, and it is understandable that success would go to their heads. The result has been a lot of self-congratulation and unvarnished faith in the technology they have created. Their default position is that the new capabilities are all to the good; computers, smartphones, the internet, and social media have already made the world a better place and will continue to do so unless impeded by the new Luddites of labor, government, and a resistant public. In the Tech Barons' way of thinking, problems stem from lack of the necessary information, knowledge, machinery, and apps, rather than from more basic human failings of ignorance, poverty, and malevolence. In particular, they are blind to the evils of concentrated power and their own class position, and it shows in their frequent expressions of hubris and arrogance.

Nevertheless, despite initial waves of enthusiasm for every New Thing coming out of Silicon Valley and the Bay Area, people have begun to see the digital downside and to struggle with the Tech Moguls' failed promises of greater liberty, equality, and well-being. The fetish of the digital sublime should not blind us to the fact that technical change is not a force of nature but a human product that can be controlled and steered by society. There are more and more efforts by individuals, popular movements, and governments to resist the virtual life. Those consist of any number of tactics, whether blocking ads, agreeing to pay for music, or shopping at brick-and-mortar stores; applying the brakes to car-sharing, reclassifying drivers as workers, or restricting vacation rentals; searching for privacy through encryption, rebelling against fake news, or defending the victims of digital harassment. As one critic observes, "Just a few years ago, all anyone could talk about was how to make the internet more free. Now all anyone can talk about is how to control it." There is no saying where all these initiatives will end up, and to what extent the worst effects of the new technologies can be reined in. But the bloom is off the rose.[68]

In short, Tech World does not look like utopia, but just another stage in evolution of technology, modernity, and capitalism. But the power of the

---

68   Solon 2017, Harris 2018. Quote from Siegel 2011, see also Siegel 2008.

new technology is not the sole property of the Tech Barons, nor is it their right to determine the world's future. All technology is ultimately a collective product of social labor, from the most esoteric realms of research to the practical problem encountered in every functioning application. Who decides the purpose of research and technology is an open question, and Americans might well prefer Elon Musk's battery storage innovations to his rocket ships to Mars. But the road to a democratic technology is long and hard and must be contested by workers, employers, governments, and the general public.

There are some striking recent examples of how popular movements took technology in new directions and out of the exclusive provenance of big corporations and big government. One is the way women appropriated their own health care in the 1960s and '70s and changed paradigms of medical delivery; another is the antinuclear movement's success in demystifying the technology and publicly proving its dangers; and a third is the rise of organic farming against the chemicalized monoculture of industrial agribusiness. In the end, progress will be made by those who oppose capitalism and the wonders of new technology every bit as much as by those who assert their title over progress and the Future. The first place that battle should be joined is in the Bay Area, the heartland of the information revolution.[69]

---

69 Thanks to Chris Carlsson for insisting on this point.

CHAPTER TEN

The Right Fight

What Future for the Left Coast?

THE SAN FRANCISCO BAY AREA HAS A LONG AND HONORABLE TRADITION OF POPULAR movements and progressive politics, which won it for a time the sobriquet "the Left Coast."[1] The political culture of the region represents some of the best features of American society. To an important degree it has embraced social openness and fluidity, nurtured a fierce independence and militancy among its workers, allowed subcultures to flourish outside the bounds of bourgeois morality, and encouraged people to organize, speak out, and influence collective action. It has also enjoyed an important degree of racial diversity and, at times, witnessed critical opposition to the dominant racial order of America.

This has not always been a pretty story of economic opportunity, liberal tolerance, and representative democracy. It has featured some of the fiercest class struggles, racial oppression, and political upheavals in U.S. history. The forces of progressivism and the Left have had to hone their skills against a dynamic and often ruthless capitalism, with a ruling order well practiced in domination, seduction, and repression. Given that history, there is no reason to think that the Left Coast was inevitable or that it will continue into the future in the face of repeated attacks from the Right and the massive social transformations brought about by tech capitalism.[2]

This chapter begins with the case for a distinctively progressive political culture in the Bay Area. The opening section traces key elements of that tradition back to the Gold Rush, and the next shows how that was built upon in the mid-twentieth century to arrive at the Left Coast. Having established

---

1 The "Left" is to be distinguished from "liberals;" the former refers to the Far Left and the latter to left of center like the mainstream Democrats. The Left and liberals are often at odds. The term "progressive" in everyday Bay Area parlance refers mostly to the Left but often takes in liberals.

2 The terms "Right" and "conservatives" are used here to refer to mainstream Republicans. The Far Right, by contrast, refers to the long tradition of political extremism from the John Birch Party to Tea Party and alt-Right.

that history of the city's political culture, the third section goes on to argue for the progressive element that went into the birth of the tech industry and early worldview. In laying out the story of progressive politics, however, the countervailing forces of business and political reaction in the region cannot be disregarded, nor, therefore, can the contradictions within the political outlook of Tech World.

The middle part of the chapter looks at two opposing forces to hit the Left Coast in the last quarter of the twentieth century, halting its forward progress and lessening its influence on Bay Area politics and society. The first, described in section four, is the counterrevolution of the New Right coming out of Southern California, which ushered in the age of neoconservatism and neoliberalism. The second, laid out in section five, is the impact of the expanding tech industry on the politics of the bay region. By the end of the twentieth century, the Left Coast had been considerably attenuated from its heights in the 1960s and 1970s.

The last part of the chapter turns to Bay Area political developments in the twenty-first century, in order to assess the potential for a revival of the distinctive politics of the metropolis. The sixth section takes note of the dramatic electoral shift toward the political liberalism of the Democratic Party and tries to ascertain its causes. The final section considers signs of political revolt and revival on the Left in light of the triumph of the Far Right in national politics and the presidential election of 2016.

Clearly, the progressive tradition of the Bay Area is alive and well in many respects, buttressed by the region's prosperity, skewed class structure, and racial composition, among other things. But, equally, is it under immense pressures from many directions, inside and out, and, as a consequence, the region's claim to be the Left Coast of America is mostly an exercise in nostalgia. The distinctive political culture that marked the metropolis for decades has faded, even as the region's electoral coloration has improved. There can be no clear balance sheet as yet, of course, and the potential for a new eruption against the triumph of the Far Right in American politics cannot be discounted.

Past Progressive

The Bay Area has been graced by a dynamic economy since the time of the Gold Rush. It had the good fortune of natural riches such as gold, silver, timber, crops, and oil pumping money into the metropolis. It has been a hub of transport and trade dominating the commerce of the Pacific Coast, and capital has piled up in its banks, making it the second-biggest banking center in the country by the mid-twentieth century. That capital has been reinvested not just in extraction and commerce, but also in a range of industries such as machining, food processing, wood products, and vehicles that have added their measure of surplus to the pile. That fulsome economy has supported a remarkably open social order and has benefitted from it, in turn.

No one any longer believes the simplistic idea that all places travel down a single road to modernization. One of the most interesting questions in economic geography is how different countries are launched down divergent paths of capitalist development; why, for example, did the United States not follow the path of Britain, and why did Germany overtake both Britain and France? Similar debates animate discussions of regional differences, such as that between the North and South in the United States and Brazil. The Bay Area is one among many possible capitalisms, with one of the most favorable social orders for economic development to be found anywhere.[3]

The Bay Area's social and political culture has long rested on four pillars: social fluidity, labor power, lively countercultures, and racial multiplicity. That combination has given rise to a marked streak of rebelliousness, including bohemian subcultures, class struggles, militant activism, and periodic revolts by the working class, often in alliance with elements of the upper middle class. The capitalist class has been influenced by this popular culture, and the business elite has often tolerated a large degree of nonconformity and social agitation, in part because openness and creativity have paid off in terms of innovation, profits, and growth.

The fluid society of the Bay Area is not some paradise of equality and opportunity, but it has been place in continual demographic, class, and racial flux. That flux rests on economic growth that has repeatedly drawn in people from the four corners of the earth and thrown them together to cook up new social brews. The Gold Rush of 1848–55 set the whole process in motion, combining Yankees, Latin Americans, Chinese, Europeans, and black freedmen. With the Silver Boom, 1860–75, a new batch of Irish, Chinese, and Americans rolled in. After that bubble burst, a slew of Germans, Scandinavians, and Italians arrived over the last quarter of the century. The early twentieth century brought Japanese, midwesterners, Greeks, and Portuguese. Between the wars came Okies, African Americans, and Filipinos. Following the Second World War, another wave of Whites and Blacks from the East surged into the state and, after 1975, migration was dominated by Latinos and Asians, plus lots of young Americans heading for the tech industry.

Decade after decade more people have migrated into California than were born here (a record only broken in the early twenty-first century). This

---

3   For more on comparative capitalisms, see Moore 1966, Page & Walker 1991, Walker 2001, Marx 1998, Post 2011, Acemoglu & Robinson 2013.

has meant that the social stew never congeals, as every new boom sets it boiling again with new migrants and new ingredients. This roiling has had three effects on the social order and class structure. One is that there has been real opportunity for clever and hardworking people to ply a trade, learn a profession, and move up the social ladder, with later arrivals to move in behind them; the occupational hierarchy has been quite open, and the economy has rewarded those with skill. Another is that many incomers have started businesses, built new industries, and become the nouveaux riches of the next generation. While some leading families have managed to hold position, many more have disappeared to be replaced by an upwelling of striving new capitalists. As a result, there has not been an entrenched ruling class and stagnant mass below.[4]

Of course, those kinds of class mobility have applied mostly to educated Whites. At the bottom has been a multitude of common laborers, many of them immigrants from outside the Euro-American axis. But even here the fluidity of migration has had a beneficial effect. The Bay Area never knew a huge number of poor white workers who settled at the bottom of the social order, like the Boston Irish. Nor have its racial minorities been numerous until recently, and their makeup changed from one generation to the next. Their treatment was often terrible, but it was not black slavery or brown peonage, so the racialized others did not congeal into a permanent underclass, as in the white-black divide of the rest of the country.[5]

The second determinant of Bay Area political culture has been a self-assured, organized, and militant working class—including many from the large skilled labor force—holding its ground against the power of capital. The workers became organized very early and quickly began making demands on the bosses. Carey McWilliams thought that the clash of capital and labor was quicker and sharper here than anywhere else, and he may well have been right. The first call for the eight-hour day came from San Francisco workers in the 1860s. In the 1870s, they flocked to the Workingmen's Party of the United States, an offshoot of Karl Marx's First International. In the 1880s, they gravitated to the Knights of Labor and then, in the 1890s, craft unions proliferated and bound themselves together under county based Central Labor Councils and building trades councils.[6]

An organized, skilled, and well-paid working class has repeatedly undergirded progressive political insurgencies. In the Gold Rush era, San Francisco

---

4   Walker 1996, 2001, 2004.
5   For contrasting examples of deeply racialized class systems, see Marx 1998.
6   McWilliams 1949, Shumsky 1991, Kazin 1987. In the nineteenth century, San Francisco completely dominated the state and its politics.

had, along with New York, the first elected government of Irishmen in history. A generation later, the Workingmen's Party spread so rapidly around the state it forced Democrats and Republicans to call a second Constitutional Convention in 1879 that succeeded in curbing the power of the Southern Pacific Railroad over the state legislature. Helped by the expansion of the Knights of Labor, San Francisco returned to being a Democratic city in the 1880s. Then, leveraged by the power of the trades unions, it became an early beachhead of the Progressive Era under Mayors Adolph Sutro and James Phelan in the 1890s. The labor councils became a power to be reckoned with in the city, capped off by the formation of the Union Labor Party in 1901. The ULP presided over city government for most of a decade—the first labor party to come to power anywhere in the world.[7]

Beyond class struggles, a third element was brewing by the bay: a resilient counterculture that thumbed its collective nose at Victorian mores and the family values of mainstream America. San Francisco has long been a cosmopolitan city of searchers, sailors, and sinners. Being a port city is important to the mingling and misbehaving, but that is not enough to account for the bohemian drift in the region's political culture. The Gold Rush gave birth to a dramatically open, bawdy, and boisterous urbanity, and, even after it settled down, the city attracted a motley crew of writers and journalists such as Mark Twain and Robert Lewis Stevenson through the rest of the nineteenth century. San Francisco fostered a lively mix of poets, dreamers, and bourgeois dropouts, and among the small fish swam the irrepressible Jack London, the world's most popular author of the early twentieth century. An important green branch of the counterculture, the transcendental adoration of nature cultivated by John Muir took organizational shape in the Sierra Club and other outdoor recreationists. And, curiously, a region with a persistent tilt toward men since the Gold Rush became one of the hotbeds of women's suffrage at the turn of the century.[8]

Underlying the high-minded layer of bohemia was an essential substrate of sin. Cities have always had red-light districts for drinking, brawling, dancing, and whoring, where the common people went to have a good time. In San Francisco this gained the widely recognized sobriquet of the "Barbary Coast," which was triangulated by the Downtown, Chinatown, and North Beach. Sailors and waterfront workers were far from the only ones to frequent the Barbary Coast. Blue-nosed Protestant efforts to expel the sinners fell on deaf ears, given the profits of the saloon owners and the tolerant side of

---

7   Saxton 1971, Senkewicz 1985, Issel & Cherny 1986, Lustig 2010.
8   Walker 1939, Lewis 1956.

Catholicism among the Irish, German, and Italian immigrants. When the crackdown finally came (led by Los Angeles Protestants) in the 1910s, much of the action was simply displaced to the Tenderloin District or beyond the city limits of San Francisco and Oakland. Later, North Beach and the Tenderloin would serve as essential Petri dishes for a gay subculture and the growth of gay liberation movements between the wars.[9]

A fourth consideration in the formation of the Bay Area's deep political culture is its racial multiplicity. It began with the amazing assortment of people pouring through San Francisco in search of gold, and that city had the highest percentage of foreign-born in the United States for the rest of the nineteenth century. But tens of thousands of the immigrants pouring in to look for gold, jobs, and opportunity were from East Asia and Latin America. They built a multitude of communities—Chinese, Japanese, Filipino, Mexican, and Central American—that persisted despite exploitation, rejection, and expulsion and gave the Bay Area a more international flavor and a different set of racial encounters from the rest the United States. Of course, white supremacy held sway during the first century of American California's existence, and the violent repression of Natives, Chinese, and Mexicans was ferocious at times; but a clear racial axis never became fixed here.[10]

Meanwhile, a strange thing happened to the white working class on the road to the White Republic, as they stomped on the rights of racialized Others in the nineteenth century. The mélange of European immigrants was able to forge a unified labor movement and political culture—a rarity in a country better known for its ethnic cacophony and weak working-class solidarity. That paid off in a strong working class to offset the pretensions to oligarchy among the capitalist elites. Paradoxically, the fruit of an illiberal racial order was a more liberal city in the long run because of the strength of organized labor, and that would ultimately lead to a breakthrough in racial integration in the ILWU, farmworker organizations, and a few key unions by midcentury.[11]

There were, of course, repeated revanchist efforts by the upper classes to suppress popular upheavals, from the Vigilantes of the 1850s to the Graft Trials of the 1900s. The Irish Democrats were overthrown by the Vigilantes in 1855, replaced by a so-called People's Party dominated by merchants. Twenty

---

9   Asbury 1933, Issel & Cherny 1986, Schumsky & Springer 1981, Boyd 2003, Shaw 2015. Cf. Gilfoyle 1992.
10 On white supremacy in California, see Daniels & Olin 1972, Almaguer 1994. Slaughter of the Natives was grievous, but slavery had little impact.
11 On the racism of the white working class in nineteenth-century San Francisco, see Saxton 1971, Kazin 1987, Tygiel 1992. The Chinese took the brunt of working-class aggression but persisted to play an important part in the Bay Area's racial mix.

years later, the People's Party was overthrown, in turn, by the Workingmen's Party, but the Vigilantes marched again in San Francisco and the Democrats and Republicans allied to curb the most radical aspects of the new state constitution. The Progressive Democrat, Mayor Phelan, rewrote the City Charter to diminish the power of the workers who had elected him, until they threw him out in 1902. Phelan's revenge was to bring charges of graft against the Union Labor Party leaders and have them ousted in 1906.[12]

When the ULP returned to power, the capitalists gathered in the Merchants Exchange in 1910 to plan their overthrow, led by a shipping magnate, James Rolph, who would become mayor for the next twenty years. The Union Labor Party disappeared, but its political spark carried over to the Progressive Republicans who overhauled state government under Governor Hiram Johnson in 1911. But once again the Right fought back, beating the drums of war and arresting labor leaders and anarchists, while the employers crushed strikes and rolled back the unions.[13]

Nevertheless, there has been an important degree of flexibility and open-mindedness on the part of the San Francisco ruling class. This allowed an Anglo-Scots elite to tolerate and even embrace Irish silver kings such as James Flood, Jewish merchants like Levi Straus, Democratic Party bosses such as Chris Buckley, and an Italian banker like A.P. Giannini. They even got behind a Jewish mayor in Adolph Sutro and a hard-drinking Irish one in Sunny Jim Rolph, and the city resisted the temperance movement right to the brink of Prohibition. Businessmen joined the Bohemian Club to mingle with its authors and poets, eventually taking it over, rallied to John Muir's calls to protect the Sierra, and hired bohemian architect Bernard Maybeck to design their shingle-and-redwood homes in the suburban hills.[14]

Rise of the Left Coast[15]

The latest and greatest surge of Bay Area rebellion came from the 1930s to 1970s. The upsurge was so strong across a range of progressive fronts that the Bay Area was transformed into one of the most distinctive political cultures in the United States. Only New York City could compare for the breadth and depth of political opposition at the time, but it suffered greatly from the fiscal crisis of 1973 and the blows of financiers, while the Bay Area prospered on military spending of the Vietnam War (electronics, logistics, and personnel) and fared relatively well in the downturn of the early 1970s.

---

12 Senkewicz 1985, Issel & Cherny 1986, Kazin 1987, Shumsky 1991, Tygiel 1992.
13 Frost 1968, Olin 1968, Issel & Cherny 1986, Kazin 1987, Issel 1989. See also Swatt et al. 2014.
14 Lewis 1956, Kahn & Dollinger 2003.
15 A popular term adopted by DeLeon 1992.

With the coming of the New Deal in 1933, labor began to organize across the country, but nowhere faster than in San Francisco, where the General Strike of 1934 and victory on the waterfront for the Longshoremen's Union lit a fire under the national labor movement. A pivotal development in local working-class history was the formation of the leftist and racially integrated International Longshoremen's and Warehousemen's Union (ILWU) under Harry Bridges. After that, unions became a significant voice in San Francisco city politics and public policy. Labor organizing in the fields of rural California took off, meeting ferocious resistance from growers and ultimately failing, but it inspired urban leftists such as photographer Dorothea Lange.[16]

The Second World War put a lid on political movements, though labor organizing continued in the pressure cooker of war. Further important victories came at the end the war, such as the creation of the retail clerks' union and victory over Safeway stores in Oakland. Unions were well entrenched in East Bay machining, rubber, transport, vehicles, and more, and Oakland had its own general strike in 1946. The same was true of San Jose's canneries. Despite the beginning of the Cold War, anticommunism never split the labor movement, as it did in Detroit, and Harry Bridges survived every attempt to purge him and his leftist allies in the ILWU (even though he was a closet Communist Party member). The battle with police water cannons on the steps of City Hall in 1960 put a permanent damper on the commie-baiting House Un-American Activities Committee (HUAC).[17]

The civil rights movement picked up sharply in California during and after the war, as Blacks, Latinos, and Asians, joined by the white Left, fought to make the Golden State live up to its promise of opportunity for all. Lawsuits brought an end to segregation in the shipyard unions and schools by the end of the war, and the state Supreme Court struck down segregation in housing, marriage, and employment soon thereafter. The devastating explosion of a weapons ship at Port Chicago in 1944 and the injustice of the subsequent court-martial of black sailors led to the integration of the navy. Oakland's African American community elected Byron Rumford as the first black legislator from Northern California in 1949, and he led the fight for open housing and fair employment laws. Another vital actor of the time was the Berkeley-based Committee for Fair Play, which opposed Japanese Internment in 1942 and took up the civil rights cause.[18]

---

16   Nelson 1989, Issel 1989, 2000, Glass 2016.
17   Brechin 1986, Lannon 2016, Glass 2016.
18   Self 2003, Brilliant 2010, Wollenberg 2012.

A new upsurge of the counterculture came to define San Francisco in the popular imagination and gained national attention in the 1950s with the gathering of the Beats in North Beach. Leading figures of the Beat movement, such as Jack Kerouac, Allen Ginsberg, and Lawrence Ferlinghetti (founder of City Lights Books), had fled New York's cultural and political pressure cooker for the cheap rents and laid-back cosmopolitanism of the city by the bay. Race mixing and cultural interplay of Whites, Blacks, and Asians was vital subtext of the counterculture, from the poetry readings to jazz clubs.[19]

Gays had been an essential part of the bohemian scene and Barbary Coast all along, but a new migration had begun with homosexuals conscripted for the war in the Pacific and then discharged back to the Bay Area. The Marine Cooks and Stewards Union became a famously gay unit of organized labor. Gay and lesbian bar life picked up, and the first openly homosexual advocacy groups, the Mattachine Society and Daughters of Bilitis, were founded in San Francisco and Los Angeles in the 1950s.[20]

Another dimension of the Bay Area counterculture was its green streak. Postwar poets such as Kenneth Rexroth and Gary Snyder mingled anarchism, Zen Buddhism, and a love of nature, inspiring generations of youth around Northern California. Berkeley rock climber David Brower took the helm of the Sierra Club in 1952 and revived Muir's radical vision of wildness as the savior of civilization; the club launched the first great battles of modern environmentalism by trying to stop dams on the Colorado River.[21]

In all this, the boundaries were not sharp within an ecumenical Left that mixed various currents among labor organizers and pacifists, communists and anarchists, Beats and gays, civil rights activists and conservationists. The upsurge began in the 1930s and '40s with the free-thinking intellectuals gathered around Kenneth Rexroth in San Francisco, Pacifica radio in Berkeley, and Josephine and Frank Duveneck on the Peninsula and burned brightly through the repressed 1950s, providing plenty of sparks for the social revolution of the Sixties.

★   ★   ★

The Bay Area gave birth to the New Left of the 1960s in an outburst that rested on the same four pillars that had always supported the progressive politics of the region: mobility, race mixing, counterculture, and labor organizing. While those traditions took on new forms in the political foundry of that heated

---

19   Cándida-Smith 1995.
20   Boyd 2003, Sides 2009.
21   Hammelian 1991, Halper 1991, Walker 2007.

decade, two things remained distinctive about the bay city: the intertwining of different threads of an ecumenical Left and the strength that mixture provided for local political movements.[22]

The social fluidity of mass migration into California continued through the 1960s, bringing with it Beat poets, Silicon Valley engineers, and future activists like Brooklyn's Mario Savio. A key aspect of postwar mobility, however, was the expanding opportunity for young people to go to college, as California built the country's greatest system of higher education. These were often working-class kids, but they were now training to join the professions and ranks of skilled labor for a new economic era. The postwar youth culture was robust in the Bay Area, so it not surprising that the student rebellion of the Sixties began in on the Berkeley campus and burst onto the national scene with the Free Speech Movement of 1964.[23]

Race entered the New Left through the civil rights movement, which was already active in California. The battle against racism gained new impetus from the fights against urban renewal and repression by police in San Francisco and Oakland, out of which grew the Black Panther Party, founded in 1967, and its rhetoric of community self-defense. While the guns got all the media attention, a central element of the movement was education, from better schools for inner city kids to black studies in the college curriculum—first installed at Oakland's Merritt College in 1965 (where the founders of the Black Panthers were students). Another branch of the fight for Black Power was better representation in local government, which led to Oakland's election of the first black mayor in the region in the mid-1970s.[24]

Student and race-based revolts came together in two critical battles by the bay. One was the anti–Vietnam War protests, which hit the streets of Oakland in 1966 and peaked with Nixon's bombing of Cambodia in 1970. Opposition to the war tracked the student uprising because of the military draft but took its intellectual force from the critique of American imperialism. Similarly, the struggles of African Americans, Latinos, and Asians against white domination in the United States resonated with colonial liberation movements around the world, and distaste for the war was heightened by the disproportionate draft of young men of color. Antiwar fervor swept the country, but nowhere was the combination with student protest and racial liberation more incendiary than in the Bay Area.[25]

---

22   The best overall treatment is Ashbolt 2012.
23   Rorabaugh 1989.
24   Self 2003, Brilliant 2010, Miller 2010, Bloom & Martin 2013.
25   Rorabaugh 1989, Bloom & Martin 2013.

While the Free Speech Movement was mostly white, another campus uprising was brewing among students of color, led by the Black Students Union and joined by Latino, Filipino, Native American, and Asian student organizations. It exploded in the Third World College strike at San Francisco State University in 1968 and subsequent strike at UC Berkeley in 1969—the longest student strikes in U.S. history. The strikers received a good deal of white student and faculty support, including from campus teachers' unions. On the other side, the strikers were hit by intense police action in San Francisco, and the National Guard was called to Berkeley by Governor Reagan. Nevertheless, the strikes succeeded in opening the door to the first full-scale black studies and ethnic studies departments in the country.[26]

As for the counterculture, it leapt into the mainstream in the 1960s, as the Beats morphed into the hippies of the Haight. Disdain for the conservative morals of Middle America was rife among young people, breaking out in the Summer of Love in 1967 and featuring sexual liberation, experimentation with pot and LSD, and the exuberance of West Coast rock and roll. What is more, the counterculture became a political force, as the sober militants in the Free Speech, civil rights, and antiwar movements came under the influence of the countercultural call to free oneself from a repressive culture and enjoy the festival of life.[27]

Gay and lesbian militancy also took off after a police raid on the gay New Year's Eve ball in 1965 and another on a Tenderloin club in 1967 that led to a riot—two years before New York's more famous Stonewall Riot. Then came the mass coming-out of the 1970s and a new influx of gay people to San Francisco and the gay mecca of the Castro District. The city's progressive politics were reignited by Harvey Milk's pathbreaking activism. It began with the fight against an antigay state proposition coming out of Southern California, then turned to local politics with the campaign for district elections and Milk's election to supervisor in 1976. Also emerging out of the cauldron of sexual liberation and political activism in the Bay Area was a strong countercurrent of radical feminism.[28]

Meanwhile, nature conservation moved to the center of Bay Area progressive politics. For the first time in history, environmentalism became a mass movement behind the Sierra Club, Save the Bay, Save Our Seashore, and other militant new organizations. The issues did not just concern distant places around the Far West, but also took up the defense of local environments

---

26 Cohen & Zelnick 2002, Bloom & Martin 2013.
27 Cavan 1974, Kamstra 1981, Selvin 1994.
28 Sides 2009.

threatened by freeways, housing developments, and landfills—above all, San Francisco Bay. Nature worship, practical conservation, and urban planning cross-fertilized each other to move the Bay Area to the head of American environmentalism and further confirm its distinctive progressive brand of politics.[29]

Although the labor movement is not usually associated with the New Left of the Sixties, and popular myth has it that "hardhats" hated hippies and antiwar protesters, the midcentury wave of organizing had made organized labor a bulwark of progressive politics in the Bay Area. The Sleeping Car Porters Union in Oakland was the backbone of local civil rights agitation. Many of the militant students of the Sixties came out of union families, and the unions frequently supported the same radical causes, as in the ILWU shutdowns of war materials shipments to Vietnam. As a second wave of union organizing swept the public sector, it brought into the labor movement many more women, who led the pioneering fight for equal compensation in San Jose. Above all, the struggle of the United Farm Workers under Cesar Chavez inspired the Bay Area Left and widened the spectrum of urban politics to include grape boycotts and pesticide control.[30]

Once again, it was significant that the upper classes of the Bay Area did not clamp down on the new rebellions—or failed when they tried. Labor unions became an accepted partner in the politics of San Francisco, Oakland, and San Jose. Anticommunism was not virulent among the elite and the professionals, as it was in Los Angeles, nor did the counterculture and gay liberation put fear into their hearts. Attempts at repression blew up in cases such as the obscenity trial for Allen Ginsberg's *Howl*, leaving conservatives and police on the defensive. The arrests of Free Speech activists and the antiwar movement in Berkeley helped propel Ed Meese and Ronald Reagan to national power but failed to deter those movements. The Black Panthers were destroyed by FBI assaults in many cities but survived in Oakland under Elaine Brown, who continued with community organizing and electoral politics. Meanwhile, Green politics had become a religion among the Bay Area's elite in the Sixties. By the time of the assassination of Harvey Milk in 1978, the sense of loss was not confined to the gay community but spread across a wide swath of Bay Area society.

By the end of the 1970s, then, the Bay Area had assumed the mantle of the Left Coast, a remarkably progressive and liberated metropolis in an otherwise conservative country. Yet the Left Coast was already colliding with

---

29 Walker 2007.
30 On Chavez's relation to the Bay Area and the Left, see Matthiessen 1969, Bardacke 2011.

two juggernauts that would blunt the breakthrough of the 1960s, one external and one internal. The first was the rise of what was often called, at the time, the "New Right," and known since then as neoconservatism and neoliberalism, which would sweep into power nationally in the 1980s. The second was the tech boom, which was just taking off in the 1970s and would gain national attention with the Silicon Valley fever of the 1980s. Before turning to the twin challenges to the Left Coast, the next section looks at how Silicon Valley grew out of the Bay Area and was influence by the region's progressive traditions.

The Social Roots of Silicon Valley

How to explain why the largest concentration of information technology on earth grew up in the Bay Area? The puzzle of Silicon Valley's origins is not solved by reference simply to the business ecosystem, urban agglomeration, or the luck of the draw. Every industry is embedded in a regional or national social order that goes beyond markets and firms to embrace institutions, practices, and rules of the game. Undergirding those social systems are the basic power frameworks of ownership, class, race, and gender. This raises the same historical questions previously noted with regard to the successful economic development of the Bay Area (and California) as a whole.

Only recently has the origin of Silicon Valley received serious attention. As seen in chapter 1, the growth of the tech cluster rests on agglomeration economies and the accumulation of technological innovation, but it remains to explain how the cluster got started in the first place and why here. Most of the reasons trotted out to explain Silicon Valley rest on serendipity: the home place of the Great Founder (e.g., William Shockley moving back to be near his mother), the location of a breakthrough innovation (e.g., Robert Noyce and the microprocessor), or the intervention of a visionary planner (e.g., Fred Terman inducing Hewlett and Packard to stay in the region). None of these is adequate.[31]

More satisfactory accounts try to root Silicon Valley in the social fabric of the San Francisco region. One explanation looks to the Valley's liberation from rigid corporate culture to explain why it triumphed over Boston's Route 128 as the most successful electronics center; this fits with the Bay Area's informal culture, especially after the 1960s. Yet there were lot of narrow-tie corporate types in the postwar valley at IBM, Philco-Ford, and Lockheed doing engineering for the Department of Defense, which one historian puts at

---

31 Scott and Storper, two of the best theorists of industrial clusters and cities, beg off on the initial conditions problem. Scott 1993, Storper 2013. Storper does, however, come back to try to explain how the cluster has been sustained by the local political culture. Storper et al. 2015.

the center of the Valley's success. One brilliant study combines the two strains to argue that the tech industry was the offspring of a union of Cold War cyberculture and Sixties counterculture. That is, it grew from the encounter of visionary military contractors and university computer scientists in the South Bay with the Sixties counterculture coming out of Bay Area communes, Haight-Ashbury, and Berkeley uprisings, yielding the Home Brew Club, the Whole Earth Catalog, The Well, and much more. That version of history is accurate as far as it goes, but it still leaves out too much of the social background that birthed the counterculture and the cyberculture—going back much farther than the postwar era.[32]

There are five strands to the DNA of Silicon Valley's Tech World: social openness, labor power, counterculture rebellion, and racial diversity, topped off by a strain of libertarian capitalism. These correspond to the elements of the Bay Area's progressive past and its capitalist economy, narrowed to fit the shape of one industry and its business subculture. The lesson is that the Silicon Valley success story is rooted in the social order and political culture of the Bay Area.

The first element is the fluidity of entrants into the industry, both people and firms, welcomed for the ideas and innovations they bring with them. This applies to everything from the tinkerers of the Home Brew Club to app developers working on open source platforms, and it goes back to the pioneers of electronics in the early 1900s working on long-distance electric transmission, the perfection of vacuum tubes, and radio broadcasting. Openness to all went along with a camaraderie that led to sharing of equipment, ideas, and people in the industry, still operating in the 1990s and in tech incubators—though not so much among the big monopolies today. That sense of an open, collective enterprise goes back to the mining camps of Gold Rush, the early machinery companies in San Francisco, and nineteenth-century plant breeders.[33]

The second strand of Silicon Valley's success is empowered workers— literate, skilled, educated, from the machinists of the nineteenth century to the university grads of the twentieth. The "creative class" is not new; skilled workers have long been coming up with new ways of doing things on the shop floor, in the laboratory, and at the tech incubator. And they have been unafraid to strike out on their own with start-ups. This was true of the men who left Federal Telegraph to found Eitel-McCullough in the 1920s, Hewlett and Packard setting up shop in the late 1930s, and Robert Noyce and "sainted

---

32 These accounts are owing to Saxenian 1994, Leslie 2000, and Turner 2007. See also Markoff 2005.
33 On the early tech industry in the Bay Area, see Sturgeon 2000. On other industries, see Walker 1996, 2001, 2004.

eight" who quit Fairchild Semiconductor to found their own companies in the 1960s. These workers have swum in a broad sea of freethinkers in business, arts, and politics, and they have had their own sites of discussion and learning at the Mechanics' Institute Library, Longshoremen's Hiring Hall, and university campuses. Open format offices may have replaced noisy workshops and saloons, but social interaction has been the common denominator; Steve Jobs designed the Flying Saucer headquarters for Apple with this in mind.

The third strand of the tech industry's genetic code has been a strong rebellious streak and embrace of alternatives to existing ways of doing things, which shows up in the belief that failure is a learning experience and IT can change the world. This, too, goes back to the people who pursued the dream of gold, with all its dangers and setbacks, and who worked out a remarkable degree of self-governance in the goldfields. It took new forms over the years, to be sure, resurfacing in business practices such as Giannini's adoption of branch banking and insistence that his clerks speak a second language or Henry Kaiser's construction of high-arch dams and provision of health care for his workers. The techies embrace of the 1960s counterculture continued a longer tradition of a mingling between the mainstream and bohemia in the Bay Area, and the liberal outlook of so many tech professionals and skilled workers has roots not just in the Sixties, but in the long tradition of progressive politics in the region.

The fourth strand of Bay Area progressivism, racial multiplicity, is the least evident in the origins of Silicon Valley, which grew up in the white redoubts of the South Bay. Like the railroad barons, tech capitalists have been happy to employ people of color as production workers in their factories and for auxiliary work as janitors or gardeners, but the tech companies have shunned African Americans. Nevertheless, as the country moved into the age of more open immigration, the industry started hiring large numbers of Asian-born engineers and skilled workers through the H-1B visa program, and many of those became industry leaders in their own right. Within that narrow compass, the Tech World has a significant multiracial and internationalist dimension.

The final strand in the makeup of Silicon Valley culture is the all-important element of libertarian capitalism. The counterculture meets cyberculture story is appealing, but the hard reality is that the Bay Area has always been a hotbed of capitalist enterprise. Profit making has driven industry after industry, from mining to machinery, agribusiness to resource empires, and railroads to trolley cars. Silicon Valley is just the latest in a series of eruptions of innovation and moneymaking in the capitalist mold. At the same time, as argued above, the business class has been replenished by newcomers who kept it from growing sclerotic, has been kept in check by a powerful working class, and has been influenced by the countercultures and political movements that have kept the Bay Area a relatively open, liberal society.

This combination has given the tech capitalists and legions of techies a distinctively libertarian tinge—socially liberal but economically conservative. In libertarian manner, they contrast the self-governing and innovative character of the tech industry to the blunders and immobility of governments. Brian Chesky of Airbnb puts it gently: "The community is the first recourse, the platform is the second recourse, and the government is third recourse, rather than the reverse." Scott Dadich, editor in chief of *Wired*, asserts enthusiastically that there is "a strain of optimistic libertarianism native to Silicon Valley. We value freedom: open systems, open markets, free people, free information, free inquiry. We've become even more dedicated to scientific rigor, good data, and evidence-driven thinking. And we've never lost our optimism." On the negative side of the libertarian spectrum, Basheer Janjua of Integnology takes a dim view of the U.S. government, calling it "the biggest inefficiency we have ever created." And libertarian Übermensch Peter Thiel, a follower of economists Friedrich Hayek and Milton Friedman, tacks to the Far Right in declaring, "I no longer believe that freedom and democracy are compatible."[34]

The Tech Titans' faith in libertarian capitalism has grown with the immense success and wealth of their companies, colliding with the Bay Area progressive tradition that nurtured the IT industry. But before getting to that, one needs to consider another huge challenge to the Left Coast: the triumph of neoconservatism and neoliberalism.

Right Out of California

While the Left Coast was not suppressed from within the Bay Area, it became a prime target for the New Right coming out of Southern California. The neoconservatives led by Ronald Reagan cut their teeth on the Bay Area's Left Coast as a means of conquering California. They not only moved the Golden State's politics sharply to the right from the liberal dominance of the New Deal/postwar era but also made the state into one of the crucibles of neoliberalism before carrying their program to the nation and the world with Reagan's elevation to the presidency.[35]

---

34 Chesky quote from http://venturebeat.com/2014/07/02/airbnb-ceo-spells-out-the-end-game-for-the-sharing-economy-in-7-quotes/. Dadich 2016. Janjua quoted in Lee 2016c. Thiel 2009.

35 Walker 1995a, Ethington & Levitus 2009.

There are differences between neoconservatism and neoliberalism that are often elided. To be clear, the neoconservatives are mostly concerned with social issues and political power: hatred for the New Deal's triumph, distaste for the liberalized morals of the Sixties, dislike of the lower orders (and personal failure), and fear of darker races. They defend white privilege against the civil rights revolution, promote evangelical versions of Christianity against secular rationalism, and seek stronger criminal punishment to contain unrest at the bottom. Neoliberalism is more about economics and a return to precepts of Classical Liberalism. The neoliberal's goal is to turn back the New Deal's expansion of big government, hacking it down to size through tax cuts and austerity budgets and reducing the burden of regulations to liberate the market and private enterprise. Neoliberals and neoconservatives generally agree on the need to curb the power of organized labor, reduce social welfare programs that support the undeserving poor, and enhance the wealth of the truly deserving job-creators at the top. To keep the story brief, however, the two movements will often be referred to as one: neoconservatism/neoliberalism.[36]

This section first recounts the victory of the Right in terms of state elections and leadership, then turns to the six major policy triumphs that defined the last quarter of the twentieth century.

★　★　★

California had been controlled by Republicans from the end of the People's Party to the mid-1930s, when Roosevelt's New Deal finally flipped the state to Democratic majorities in the state legislature. Even then, left-leaning Governor Culbert Olson only enjoyed one term, 1938–42, before Republican Earl Warren occupied the office for another ten years. Right-wing Republican William Knowland, whose father ran Oakland politics, became a power in the U.S. Senate through the 1950s. Yet the worm had turned, and the New Deal liberal era was launched in the Golden State, as around the country, supported by an organized working class, a mass exit of black voters from the Republican Party, and a large body of educated professionals with a progressive faith in good government.

A telling sign was Earl Warren's transformation from a conservative hack promoted by the Knowlands to a liberal statesman who espoused mass public education and racial integration—all before he was named chief justice of the U.S. Supreme Court in 1953. Liberal Republicanism prevailed in postwar

---

36　On neoliberalism, see Harvey 2005, Peck 2010. On neoconservatism, see Hardesty 1999, Frank 2004, Dochuck 2011. Both movements have been backed by big money from wealthy funders from the Coors, Mellon, Koch, and Olin families, among others. Phillips-Fein 2009, Mayer 2016.

Northern California, exemplified by U.S. Senator Thomas Kuchel, who was paired with Democratic centrist Clair Engle. In 1958, Pat Brown became the first Democratic governor in a century, and the Democratic Party majority cleaned house in a corrupt state legislature. Under Brown and the inspired legislative leadership of San Francisco's Phil Burton and LA's Jess Unruh, California became a model of Liberalism and good government. Democratic Party activist Alan Cranston took over from Kuchel in the 1970s and '80s, adding a strong liberal voice in Congress.[37]

But the New Right was building up its base in Southern California, from which they would launch their conquest of the state and the country. Their first champion was Richard Nixon, who rose to national prominence by jumping aboard the anticommunist bandwagon led by figures such as Senator Joseph McCarthy, FBI Director J. Edgar Hoover, and attorney Roy Cohn. Nixon became senator in 1950, vice president in 1952, and president in 1968. Meanwhile, an even more fervent brand of right-wing politics was gestating in Orange County in the marriage of agrarian fascism peddled by the growers such as the Welch family and suburban Cold Warriors fed by aerospace contractors. The John Birch Society was the movement's most notorious spawn, but something much wider and deeper was afoot across the region, as Southern California became the prime hearth of the Far Right in the country.[38]

Following Nixon's shattering defeat by Governor Pat Brown in 1962 and Barry Goldwater's landslide loss to Johnson in the presidential race of 1964, the southland's militants became more determined than ever to seize hold of the Republican Party. Ronald Reagan, a former Hollywood B-list actor and fallen New Dealer, was groomed to be the ideal telegenic candidate, after which he jumped directly to governor of California in 1966 and served for eight years. Reagan used his campaigns and bully pulpit to vilify the Left Coast on open housing, student protest, and black militancy; his first military engagement was sending the National Guard to take over Berkeley in 1969. Some of Reagan's worst tendencies were curbed by Democratic majority in the legislature (just as the Democratic majority in Congress put some limits on President Nixon).[39]

---

37 Putnam 1980, 2005, Jacobs 1996, Douglass 2000, Rarick 2005.
38 Schuparra 1998, McGirr 2001, Pearlstein 2008, Critchlow 2013, Olmsted 2015. In the Bay Area, by contrast, postwar Silicon Valley nurtured solid Republican Party rule in Santa Clara County, but agriculture was pushed out earlier and there were counterbalancing unions in the canneries and factories.
39 Dallek 2000, Putnam 2005, Pearlstein 2014. It should be noted that some of Reagan's key minions came from the Bay Area: Ed Meese, Caspar Weinberger, and George Shultz. Meese made his name prosecuting Free Speech protesters.

Democrat Jerry Brown (son of Pat) reclaimed the governor's office in 1974 and ushered in a brief, shining moment of Liberalism. While linked to a national rejection of the Vietnam War and Nixon presidency, the California revival of the Democrats was marked by more left-leaning policy initiatives than the Jimmy Carter administration. The Bay Area imprint on Brown's administration was notable, including energy conservation, urban planning, and toxic regulations, as well as farmworker union recognition, cabinet members such as Sim van der Rijn and Bill Press, and the appointment of a progressive majority to the state Supreme Court, including Chief Justice Rose Bird. Brown drifted back to the middle in his second term and the leftist flame in Sacramento flickered out.

Republicans held the governorship almost continuously for the next thirty years. George Deukmejian, who presided in the 1980s, was from the heartland of ultraconservative agribusiness in the San Joaquin Valley, and Pete Wilson, in the 1990s, hailed from San Diego's land of military retirees and border vigilantes. Wilson made a sharp turn to the right when his polls plunged, becoming the champion of the anti-immigrant forces. The last chapter in Republican domination was the recall of Democrat Gray Davis in 2003 and installation of Arnold Schwarzenegger for the next seven years.[40]

California's U.S. Senate seats were split between the two parties. Cranston held one, until his ties to agribusiness and S&L financier Charles Keating sullied his liberal reputation at the end of his career. The other was taken by a sequence of uninspiring conservatives—George Murphy, S.I. Hayakawa, and Pete Wilson—until the Democrats made a surprising comeback to take both seats in 1992. The assassinations of Harvey Milk and George Moscone in 1978 propelled conservative Democrat Dianne Feinstein to the mayor's office, from whence she launched herself to the Senate. Marin's Barbara Boxer was always to the left of Feinstein, but in the latter's shadow as junior senator. Meanwhile, San Francisco's Congresswoman Nancy Pelosi was rising rapidly in the Democratic Party leadership.[41]

It was a sign of the times, however, that Feinstein and Boxer in the Senate, Pelosi in the House, and Willie Brown, the power broker of the state legislature, moved into the camp led nationally by the Clintons and the Democratic Leadership Council. That is, they remained liberals on social issues but moved to the right on economic questions in hope of outflanking the Republicans. This worked for the one election that got Bill Clinton and the two women senators

---

40 On agribusiness power, see Walker 2004a; on San Diego, see Davis et al. 2003; on Prop. 187 and the border, see Nevins 2002.
41 Carlsson 2011.

into office but turned out to be a strategy that only confirmed the victory of the neoliberals. After the disastrous midterm election of 1994, Clinton seized upon a host of Republican ideas as his own, such as Workfare, immigration control, and a wall on the Mexican border, and the others followed.[42]

* * *

The neoliberal/neoconservative coalition in California pushed ahead on six main fronts: tax cutting, school revolt, law and order, anti-immigration, rolling back civil rights, and legislative restrictions. In every one of the six areas, California was in the national vanguard with policies such as tax limits, a border wall, Three Strikes, "race-blind" initiatives, and term limits, all of which were later taken up by other states and the federal government. Since the Republicans never gained firm control of the state legislature, the principal tool of the Right was to buy and sell ballot propositions, turning a putative tool of popular democracy into a blunt instrument of destruction of the postwar achievements of New Deal Liberalism and the New Left.[43]

The best-known achievement of California neoliberalism was the tax revolt begun by Proposition 13 in 1978. Prop. 13 was the brainchild of Orange County activist Howard Jarvis, head of the Southern California Apartment Owners Association, who cleverly steered popular unrest over school integration and rising house prices toward a right-wing agenda of across-the-board tax cutting. By radically cutting property taxes, it dropped the bottom out of local government and school district funding. Then, as the state took up the slack in funding schools and municipalities, it began running huge deficits with every recession. Further cuts to state income and corporate taxes followed, along with a host of regressive tax measures to keep local governments going, such as higher sales taxes, more user fees, and bigger traffic fines (property taxes are actually a progressive system that hits the wealthy harder). California dropped from one of the top states in tax effort to the middle of the pack. The starving of big government had begun.[44]

The revolt against public schools—once the pride of postwar California—began with the antibusing uprising in the San Fernando Valley of Los Angeles in the early 1970s (whereas Berkeley had been the first U.S. school system to

---

42 Nevins 2002, Packer 2013, Peters & Rosenthal 2010. Jerry Brown is another ambiguous Democrat, a liberal who has always loved austerity, thanks to his youthful training as a monk. He did little or nothing to rally opposition to the recall of his Supreme Court appointees in the mid-1980s. As California attorney general in 2007–2011 he became a law and order advocate who resisted the court-ordered reduction of California's prison population (see chapters 4 and 8).

43 On the misuse of ballot initiatives, see Schrag 1998.

44 Lo 1990, Smith 1999, Goldberg 2010. Also Walker 1995a, 2010.

fully integrate in 1966). The permanent fiscal crisis ushered in by Prop. 13 meant that per pupil spending in California schools plunged from one of the highest in the country to the bottom of the pack, down with Mississippi and Arkansas. But the discourse about why public schools were failing on measures of test performance and high school dropout rates was redirected by the neoliberals from lack of funding to the failures of teachers and need for more choice through vouchers and charter schools. Meanwhile, the cosmopolitan notion of bilingual education was killed off by Proposition 227 in 1998. In higher education, community colleges began to be pinched, followed by the state university campuses in the 1990s, and the University of California in the early twenty-first century; free tuition disappeared as an unrealistic aspiration. The starvation and privatization of public education hit just as the great wave of immigrant children were entering the system, achieving a neoliberal trifecta against public goods, people of color, and upward mobility of working-class kids through education.[45]

The neoconservative anti-immigration movement began in California as the state became the principal port of entry for Latinos and Asians in the 1970s and '80s. The intellectual core of the movement was the Federation for American Immigration Reform (FAIR), aided by naive scientists like Garrett Hardin and Paul Ehrlich. FAIR played a big role in the push for immigration reform to limit "illegal aliens" in 1986, which was blunted by the desire of agribusiness for cheap labor and a shift in the position of California unions, which had started to recruit immigrant workers. In the same year, Proposition 65 made English the official language of the state (an effort led by San Francisco's S.I. Hayakawa). The peak of anti-immigrant agitation came in 1994 with Proposition 187 denying state aid to the undocumented; although 187 was overturned by the state Supreme Court, the popular agitation stirred up by the Right led to the retrograde Immigration Act of 1996 and the Clinton administration's Operation Gatekeeper to build a wall along the California-Mexico border. The moment of mass immigration opened up by the 1965 reform act would start to close down.[46]

California was also pivotal in the national movement to roll back civil rights. The first initiative was Proposition 14 in 1964 to overturn the Fair Housing Act. Next, California became the leader in the effort to blunt affirmative action. It led off with the lawsuit by white medical student against the University of California, Davis, for reverse discrimination, which he won in

---

45 Casstevens 1967, Lo 1990, Brilliant 2010. On the neoliberal undermining of public education, see Brown 2015.
46 Walker 1995a, Ono & Sloop 2002, Nevins 2002.

a 1978 U.S. Supreme Court decision. The attack on affirmative action in the university continued under UC Regent Ward Connerly, a black Republican, who went on to lead a successful interdiction of state affirmative action by Proposition 209 in 1996. All such efforts were well funded by neoconservative donors. Then came Proposition 54, the so-called color-blind initiative to stop the state from gathering racial data on anyone; but the movement hit a rock and the proposition lost in 2002. Nevertheless, the civil rights era had passed and white recidivism was on the march across the country.[47]

A fifth pillar of the neoliberal/neoconservative drive in California was stepping up the criminalization and incarceration of the poor and dark-skinned, mostly young men. Nixon launched the national campaign for Law and Order in the early 1970s, channeling the ideas of the Los Angeles Police Department, and Reagan amplified the effort in the 1980s with the War on Drugs, while the LAPD was again leading the way with an all-out war on gangs. Meanwhile, the legislature was ratcheting up sentencing to override judges, the liberal majority on the Supreme Court was recalled in 1986, and the punitive mania reached a peak with the Three Strikes law (Proposition 184) in 1994. Governors Deukmejian and Wilson oversaw the greatest prison-building program in modern America to handle the flood of new inmates—the neoliberal version of a "public works" program—and the state achieved the dubious distinction of having the highest per capita incarceration rate in the world. Thus were the fringes of the uppity working class and racialized youth brought to heel.[48]

A final arrow in the neoliberal policy quiver was the attack on the powers of the legislature, which had been dominated by Democrats since the 1960s. A particular bête noire of the Republicans was San Francisco's Willie Brown, the powerful Speaker of the House. The buying of propositions by the monied interests was already undermining the legislative process, as was a 1930s rule requiring a two-third majority to pass the annual state budget—giving the minority GOP delegation in the legislature a veto over taxation and spending. But that was not enough, so they cooked up Proposition 14 in 1990 to impose term limits (two terms), forcing out Brown and long-serving Democratic committee chairs. A further effect was to dumb down the legislature through continuous turnover, helped along by cuts to committee staffing and the legislative research office.[49]

★　★　★

47　Chavez 1998, HoSang 2010.
48　Davis 1990, Domanick 2004, Gilmore 2007.
49　Richardson 1996, Schrag 1998, Witco 2010.

The neoliberal/neoconservative onslaught on California had a threefold effect on state and Bay Area politics. It rolled back the New Deal liberal achievements of the postwar era of modernized government, public goods, and expanded education. It blunted the radical base of the student movements, empowerment of racialized minorities, and assimilation of the new immigrants, while increasing inequality. And, by curbing effective government and muffling social alternatives, it paved the way for the kind of adoration of High Tech as the only way forward for a modern society.

Thus, even as it felt the blows of the right-wing counterrevolution, the Bay Area's political culture began to face a new challenge: the expansion of the tech industry into a capitalist behemoth. Tech growth was a mixed bag, altering the social makeup of the central cities and increasing the local power of IT companies, while adding to the region's national political clout. These changes are the focus of the next section. After that, the last two sections wrestle with the political outcome of the triangulation of Bay Area progressivism, the tech boom(s), and assault from the Right in the twenty-first century.

The Tech Tsunami Hits the Left Coast

The tech boom has dramatically changed the Bay Area, and politics is no exception. Although Tech World is rooted in the regional political culture and many of its socially progressive values, it is ultimately a business enterprise and thus bears the stamp of a capitalist perspective on the world—with a libertarian twist. Moreover, the success of the industry has altered the outlook of many participants, especially those who have hit it rich, whose commercial orientation, class arrogance, and disdain for government is far from any progressive roots. While the tech tsunami has not been all to the bad, by any means, it has had some malevolent effects, and this is true of its impact on the Left Coast. These show up in three main ways: the political slant of the techies, the regulatory evasions of the tech companies, and the growing clout of tech money in politics. Some political positives will reappear in the last two sections, however.

★　★　★

With the tech boom, tens of thousands of new people have flooded into the Bay Area to work in the industry and try to make their fortunes. Most tech workers are young, optimistic, and idealistic about open platforms, horizontal networking, and the revolutionary potential of IT. Their views on equality, race, and gender often reflect their youth and idealism, which means that they are, on the whole, more politically liberal and less sexist, homophobic, and racist than older cohorts of Americans. Overall, the growth of the tech industry might be thought to confirm the region's liberal tilt, but that is unfortunately not necessarily so.

For one thing, most of the tech minions are recent arrivals from other parts of the country and the world who have not been acculturated to the Bay Area's progressive culture and are often isolated from it by their all-embracing workplaces and work lives. Furthermore, their push into the central cities to be close to work has, as already seen, displaced many left-leaning activists, artists, students, and workers, weakening the progressive political culture of neighborhoods such as the Mission District, North Beach, and central Berkeley.

The captains of industry, themselves often young, voice similar views on equality for minorities, gays, and women; but their outlook on business's is more conservative than the run of tech workers. The top engineers are also generally to the right of lower-order coders and others of the tech workforce. Many of these hail from upper-class households and were educated at elite universities, leading San Franciscans to remark on the arrogant, "frat boy" vibe of so many of the well-heeled techies. But even the mass of coders are surprisingly apolitical believers in the meritocracy, beneficent technology, and entrepreneurism.

Then, too, there are some persistently reactionary ideas among the techies. The most obvious is the macho culture of the male-dominated worlds of engineering, finance and start-ups, noted previously. This goes along with some notoriously pseudoscientific notions about their own superiority, exemplified by Google employee James Damore's notorious memo averring that biology explains why women have less aptitude for engineering. Damore's views were backed up by Paul Graham and others, such as tech start-up investor John Durant, who declaimed that, "Charles Darwin himself would be fired from Google for his views on the sexes."[50]

* * *

The political actions of the tech capitalists speak louder than their words, and they have occasionally tried to live up to their socially liberal reputations—especially when pressed by popular disapproval. For example, where pervasive misogyny has put companies in the spotlight, they have tried to make amends. The firings of Travis Kalanick by the Uber board of directors and James Damore by Google are notable cases in point, as are the self-demotions of chief executives Mike Cagney at Social Finance and Dave McClure at 500 Startups. Some companies such as Lyft, Facebook, and Google are making

---

50   Levin 2017a. Graham and Durant quotes in Bowles 2017.

systematic efforts to improve hiring practices and work environments for women. Yet a masculinist backlash has built up in reaction to these moves.

Tech companies have also begun to take more responsibility for the malicious use of their social media platforms. They have begun to vet the worst ads, posts, tweets, and videos, but mostly because of political pushback from governments and popular anger. The libertarian outlook of tech leaders such as Mark Zuckerberg and Jack Dorsey left them looking foolish in the glare of criticism over the flood of false information, personal harassment, and fascist ravings on YouTube, Twitter, and other social platforms. Zuckerberg has even apologized for dismissing the possibility that Facebook was used by the Russians to game the 2016 elections, but he still does not want to face the fact that Facebook is not simply a platform for friendliness but a major news medium.

For the most part, the Tech Titans have felt themselves above the normal rules of the game, given their disdain for stodgy states and belief in the inherent goodness of their technologies. The greatest testament to tech arrogance is the massive tax and regulatory evasions of the tech companies. Governments have been struggling to keep up, and the big tech corporations fight almost all regulatory efforts over their actions. The European Commission is in the forefront in clamping down on the tech corporations, but the U.S. government has been reluctant to act, since it shares the same bed with tech companies over big data sharing and IT security.[51]

When it comes to local governments, the Tech Barons have been notoriously high-handed in their dealings with public officials and adept at evading control. Airbnb persistently ignored city government complaints about commercial rentals, until it forced by local officials from Paris to New York. Uber used special software called Greyball to minimize its taxes in several cities, until the ruse was uncovered. The company's refusal to play by the rules has been so egregious that Transport of London cancelled its license to operate for a time.[52]

★ ★ ★

Money talks in American politics, and Bay Area capitalists have never been shy about buying favors from politicians. Why should the Tech Titans be different? The railroad barons, silver kings, and shipbuilders of the nineteenth century were notorious for securing favors from their friends in the state

---

51 Solon & Siddiqui 2017. On tech tax evasion, see Plender 2013. On the arrogance of the industry, see Levin 2017a, Faroohar 2017.
52 Butler & Topham 2017.

capitol and U.S. Congress. Northern California irrigators, lumbermen, and highway builders secured massive state and federal investments in infrastructure in the twentieth century. The Cold War era tech industry had cozy ties to the Pentagon that kept the contracts rolling.[53]

The New Economy of the 1990s marked a turning point at which Silicon Valley became a major money trough for national politicians. Party leaders galloped between Wall Street, Hollywood, and Silicon Valley to feed party coffers, advance personal ambitions, and burnish their technological bona fides. Bill Clinton, Al Gore, and the Democratic Leadership Council eagerly embraced the abundant cash and the High Tech vision coming out of the Bay Area, giving themselves a leg up in fundraising and the appearance of the being in the economic vanguard. They extolled the Internet Age and mocked the backwardness of George H.W. Bush and Republicans who still thought the automobile and oil industries ruled the country.[54]

George W. Bush responded by outflanking Gore in Silicon Valley fundraising by two to one and equaling him in endorsements by tech leaders in the 2000 campaign. As one Bush advisor put it, "Everyone wants to associate with the future." The Democrats responded, so that in Obama's run for president in 2008 tech donors had returned to the fold. Campaign finance reform had altered the rules of the game, however, making Obama's strategy of small donations more fruitful than previous appeals to the tech corporations; hence, he benefitted from dipping deeper into the young, skilled workforce, whose predilections are more liberal than the tech elite's.[55]

In the twenty-first century, the Democrats and Tech Moguls have engaged in a long group hug, with San Francisco's Nancy Pelosi leading the charge. Pelosi's election as Speaker of the House in 2007 no doubt rested on her talents as a dealmaker and neoliberal leanings but also signaled her abilities as the party's greatest fundraiser—thanks to Silicon Valley. She is not the tech industry's only reliable voice in Congress, of course, being flanked by Anna Eshoo of Palo Alto, Zoe Lofgren of San Jose, and now Ro Khanna of Fremont. As one national observer put it: "Politicians are listening to what the people in the Bay Area are thinking about. They're not buying policy outcomes directly, but they're buying an audience." That statement is revealing, since one normally gets "an audience" not with ordinary folks but with kings and popes.[56]

As the tech industry's visibility and range increased, the big corporations jumped into the Beltway world of professional advocacy with both feet.

---

53 White 2011, Reisner 1986, Adams 1997, Brechin 1999, Leslie 2000.
54 Micklethwait 1997, Miles 2001. See also Packer 2013.
55 Quote in Wayne 2000. Green 2008.
56 On Pelosi, see Peters & Rosenthal 2010. Quote in Green 2008.

Alphabet/Google has become the largest spender on lobbying in Congress. Both the amount spent and the number of issues on which the tech companies are lobbying has spiked in the 2010s. Google funds a Beltway Think Tank, the New America Foundation, and hires former civil servants and congressional aides in droves. The split political personality of the Tech Titans is on display in their efforts to influence Washington. As one critic puts it, "The Silicon Valley billionaires and CEOs are libertarian, low-tax deregulation buddies of the Koch brothers when it comes to talking to Republicans, and dope-smoking, gay rights activist hipsters when they mix with the Democrats."[57]

The tech oligarchs have made several attempts to insinuate themselves in California state politics, with only modest success. The self-financed runs for governor by financier Ron Unz in 1994 and corporate CEO Meg Whitman in 2010 came to naught. Individual tech billionaires have backed statewide propositions over the years, notably Unz's Proposition 227 that ended bilingual education in California public schools. David Welch, founder of fiber-optic company Infinera, funded the 2014 lawsuit to end teacher tenure in California public schools—a conservative, antiunion effort which ultimately failed. The medical tech industry garnered aid for stem-cell research from state voters in 2004, after the neoconservatives pull the plug on support nationally. A handful of tech capitalists have thrown money behind efforts to rewrite California laws to allow more rapid housing development.

At the regional level, the tech industry holds sway over public policy. Business and civic organizations such as the Silicon Valley Manufacturers Group and Silicon Valley Leadership Group anchor the South Bay's regional policy and planning. The Bay Area Council in San Francisco has long given its unalloyed support to the tech industry as the economic backbone of the metropolitan area. There is a dense network of tech executives, government officials, and regional planners that is very effective at promoting the tech vision of regional development, with its high growth, rapid innovation, high salaries, and soaring property values. The tangible results are mostly seen in local willingness to accommodate tech companies' construction plans, from Sunnyvale to San Francisco, and keep taxes on business low. The levels of public investment and social services are high enough that the Bay Area has escaped the general deterioration of infrastructure that plagues the country, but the bulk of public spending goes to the classic triad of airports, highways, and transit.[58]

---

57 Fung & Shaban 2017, Quote by Robert McChesney in Solon & Saddiqqi 2017.
58 On regional associations and the tech industry, see Storper et al. 2015, chapters 7 and 8. On infrastructure in the region, pp. 130–32.

The tech boom has, on the whole, eroded the Left Coast and the progressive idealism the tech culture inherited from it. It has driven the Bay Area back toward the center, despite an influx of young, educated people espousing socially liberal views. The industry's success has swamped the metropolis with tech's libertarian ideology, tech money in politics, and the arrogance that comes with power. On the other hand, there has been a dramatic electoral reconfiguration of the region and the state away from the Right and into the arms of liberal Democrats, which seems to confirm the region's Liberalism. This is partly due to the impact of the tech industry's growth and partly to the legacy of Bay Area progressivism—and perhaps speaks to a revival of the latter tradition. The next section investigates that electoral shift.

Electoral Tectonics

Something dramatic happened by the start of the twenty-first century that would produce a decisive electoral shift toward the left in the Bay Area and California, reversing the long dominance of conservative voters in the neoliberal era. That electoral shakeup has transformed the state into a bastion of the Democratic Party, in counterflow to the domination of so much of the country's electoral power by Republicans. The electoral realignment has been so astonishing that it might seem to confirm the San Francisco region—or all of coastal California—as the Left Coast of America. But that is misleading. The shift has as much to do with the changing makeup of the electorate as with the progressive legacy of the region. This section looks at telltale election results and then seeks causes that go beyond economistic explanations.

★   ★   ★

The Reagan era in California could be blamed on popular backlash against civil rights, hippies, and student rebellion, a kind of premonition of Nixon's national coalition in 1968, but there was more at work in the state's electoral tilt to the Right at the time. The U.S. Supreme Court's "one person, one vote" decisions in the early 1960s produced a geographic reversal of power that ended the North's dominance through the state senate's rotten borough system (each county having one senator) and unleashed the full force of Southern California's demographic plurality. Reagan rode that wave into office despite the Democrats' majority in the legislature.[59]

The neoliberal/neoconservative era in California was propelled by another shift in the state's citizenry that had taken hold by the 1980s. Even as immigration was beginning to transform the state's demographics, the

---

59   On the old system, see Putnam 1980.

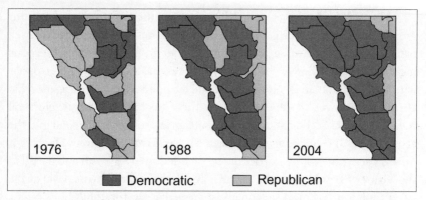

Figure 10.1: Maps of Changing Bay Area Voting Patterns, 1976–2004

Source: Lewis 2012.

electorate was shrinking and slipping backward in time. That is, the voters became older, whiter, and richer than the people of the state. Not surprisingly, that electorate was susceptible to voting for its class and race interests, which were played upon by the New Right, from racial fears of immigrants swamping their neighborhoods to fiscal fears of losing their homes to property taxes.

By contrast, the rising populace of color was effectively disenfranchised by a triple whammy of not being citizens, not yet old enough to vote, and not yet interested in U.S. politics as they settled into a new country. Latinos, in particular, counted a large percentage of undocumented and children among their number, while Asian immigrants were preoccupied with counterrevolutionary politics back home in Vietnam and China. Many immigrants were simply rendered apolitical by their experiences in their countries of origin.

Proposition 187 was the wake-up call. Applications for citizenship shot up, and voter rolls swelled with new generations coming of age and politicized by the rabid anti-immigrant politics of the 1990s. Wilson's gambit backfired spectacularly, and the vast majority of new voters were alienated from the Republican Party for life. By the early twenty-first century, the shift in the electorate propelled California fully into the Democratic Party and its progressive camp, where it now rests—well to the left of the rest of the country.[60]

The same thing happened in the Bay Area, which had been Republican for decades, outside of the working class and progressive bastions of San Francisco and the inner East Bay. The greater Bay Area could be seen as trending Democratic by the late 1980s, as exemplified by its support of Walter Mondale against George H.W. Bush for president in 1988, but bay voters could still overwhelmingly support something like Proposition 184 (the

---

60   Ramakrishnan & Baldasarre 2004, Schrag 2006, Walker 1995a, 2010.

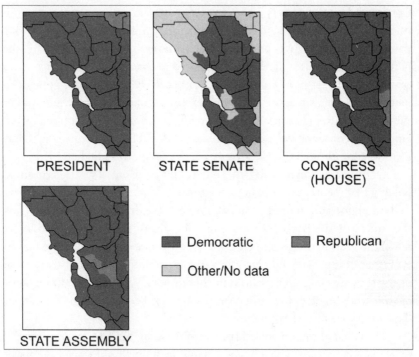

Figure 10.2: Maps of Bay Area Voting Patterns in the 2016 Election

Source: http://projects.sfchronicle.com/2016/election/.

Three Strikes initiative) in 1994. The full transition only occurred in the new Millennium (fig. 10.1).

The electoral pattern of Democratic dominance continues to the present. It holds at every level of representation, from the legislature to Congress. City offices are officially nonpartisan in California, but the same skew obtains. The number of Republicans in office around the Bay Area has diminished to the vanishing point. Meanwhile, the area has sent some of the most liberal delegations to Sacramento and Washington—including some much more Left members such as Congresswoman Barbara Lee from the East Bay, Jackie Speier from the Peninsula, and Jared Huffman from the North Bay.

In the 2016 presidential race, San Francisco voted 90 percent against Donald Trump and the nine-county Bay Area about 80 percent against. To judge by these electoral results, the Bay Area is one of the most liberal spots on the map in terms of party lines, along with New York City, Boston, and Seattle. The Bay Area is the bluest of the blue (fig. 10.2).

★   ★   ★

Confronted by the evidence about voting patterns, two questions come to mind: why the dramatic shift to the Democrats in Silicon Valley and suburban counties of the Bay Area, and does this mean that the metropolis is still the Left Coast of America? The two are related in that almost all the big cities of the country have, in color-coded terms of recent elections, gone deep blue (Democrat), while the smaller cities, towns, and rural areas are dyed-in-the-wool red (Republican). The Bay Area is by no means exceptional. Even Houston in conservative Texas and Atlanta in Republican Georgia vote solidly Democratic—though the pluralities in the bay region are higher.

One explanation for this pattern in recent elections is strictly economic, holding that income is the major determinant of recent U.S. voting patterns: well-off regions are more liberal and poorer areas more conservative. Thus, the source of the Bay Area's extreme Liberalism is to be explained by its remarkable affluence. A similar explanation is one based on differences in economic output. The red-blue split is, in this view, a direct political outcome of the striking geographic schism in contemporary economic development, in which the biggest cities and coastal states are booming while the rest of the country is going nowhere fast.[61]

The effect of this on political power in Washington is dramatic, given the U.S. federalist system. The ten bluest states, including California, have about the same population as the forty laggard states, which are solidly red. This gives the red states an 80–20 advantage in number of U.S. Senators. Similar effects give Republicans an advantage in the House of Representatives, which have been exaggerated by gerrymandering by Republican-dominated state legislatures. This is not necessarily a defect of federalism but an intended consequence of the desire by the writers of the constitution to favor smaller states and rural areas.

But there is more going on in voting preferences than income differences. One key effect is that of class (which is more than income, as discussed earlier). Upper-class people are still overwhelmingly Republican. Managers and professionals traditionally tilt toward the Republicans, but have been sliding to the Democrats in recent years as the Republican Party has been more infected by the Far Right. The working class is split between a New Deal allegiance to the Democrats (stronger in the North) and Nixon/Reagan realignment with the Republicans (stronger in the South).

---

61 On income and voting, see Gelman 2008. "The less-than-500 counties that Hillary Clinton carried nationwide encompassed a massive 64 percent of America's economic activity as measured by total output in 2015. By contrast, the more-than-2,600 counties that Donald Trump won generated just 36 percent of the country's output—just a little more than one-third of the nation's economic activity." Muro & Liu 2016. See also *Economist* 2016.

Nationally, the working class has been the backbone of the Democratic Party; but neglect of declining factory towns by party leadership and resentment of upper-class condescension has moved many to vote for Republicans. In the Bay Area, the counties that voted Democratic in 1974 were those with large working-class populations in the cities of San Francisco, Oakland, Richmond, and Vallejo, while upper-class suburbs trended Republican. The subsequent blue shift in the latter is partly because professionals have become more liberal in the mainstream sense, but also because outlying counties have become major employment centers with far greater working-class numbers.[62]

Another major force is the race effect, which is central to any account of the conservatism of large numbers of white workers, not to mention many upper-middle-class voters. Conversely, the vast bulk of new immigrants and their children reside in the biggest cities, and they tend to vote Democrat because they want more government support for education, health, transportation, and decent wages. Those who go for the Republicans are largely upper class, such as the successful business and professional elite of the Cuban community of Miami or the Mexican elite of San Antonio. In the Bay Area, the new majority of color, especially in the working class, overwhelmingly supports liberal Democrats, while the impact of conservative white workers has diminished along with their dwindling numbers.[63]

Nevertheless, politics cannot be reduced to income, class, or race; political outcomes have strictly political causes, as well.[64] The success of neoliberalism / neoconservatism in California in the late twentieth century required repeated drumbeating by the Right about the burden of taxes, the virtues of fiscal restraint, the fear of crime, and the flood of "illegals"; they were able to persuade many voters, otherwise predisposed by class, color, and age, to vote for conservative causes. By contrast, most California immigrants have been permanently alienated by the Republican tactic of blaming them for the nation's ills, driving them and their children into the arms of the Democrats. This surely helps account for the way Los Angeles has become more and more liberal over the last two generations even as its average income has *fallen* relative to the Bay Area.

Clearly, voting preferences were turned around in a short time. Nevertheless, one can make a case for continuity, too. San Francisco, Oakland, Berkeley and other parts of the region have voted Democratic and leaned well

---

62 On the importance of class to voting patterns nationally, and a rejection of the idea of a massive working-class surge for Trump and the Republicans in 2016, see Davis 2017a, Dimaggio 2017. See also Geismer 2017 on the Liberal professionals.

63 On the influence of race on voting patterns, see Phillips 2015, Davis 2017a.

64 A good statement of this is Ethington 1994.

to the Left for a long time. Bay Area's progressive tradition has surely had an influence on the liberal voting patterns of today, passed along by friends, colleagues, news media, politicians, teachers, and activist organizations—not to mention the influence of material structures of law, institutions, and geography that regulate everyday behavior. This passing of the torch is what cultural theorists call "collective memory" and economists call "path dependence."[65]

By way of contrast, a good case for political continuity can be made for the solidly red and Republican Central Valley, represented by the likes of current House Majority Leader Kevin McCarthy from Bakersfield and House Intelligence Committee Chair Devin Nunes from Tulare County. The San Joaquin Valley fits the bill as a low-income, economically depressed region, but that only touches the surface of the region's deep political conservatism. It has been a bastion of agribusiness power for a century, with strong bias toward white racism and evangelicalism brought from the South. Even as the Bay Area spills part of its working class over into the Valley, political allegiances remain stuck in the past.[66]

In short, an account of voting patterns based solely on income leaves out too many things that political theorists have wrestled with for centuries. Politics and political cultures matter, as proved by any number of examples that go against the income theory: the slave South was wealthier than the North on the eve of the Civil War; Populist farmers were poorer but more radical than urban professionals in the 1890s; workers are persistently more liberal than the upper classes; and African Americans more liberal than Whites at all income levels. Even the current red tide across rural America is a political fact inculcated by decades of right-wing propaganda, funding by wealthy donors such as the Koch brothers, and Republican maneuvering in state legislatures.

To sum up this foray through electoral politics, the Bay Area certainly registers as a bastion of mainstream Liberalism and the Democratic Party, which puts it to the left of huge swaths of the country. This is based on its economic prosperity, a class skew toward the upper middle class, and the racial makeup of the new working class, and those things are riding to a large extent on the levitating force of the tech boom. The legacy effect of Bay Area progressivism is not negligible but harder to tease out, and the same goes for the influence of Tech World ideology. In the end, the Bay Area's politics resemble other big U.S. cities today, and the distinctiveness of the city's political culture has faded since the glory days of the Left Coast.[67]

---

65 On path dependence, see Arthur 1988, Zysman 1994, David & Antonelli 1997.
66 On Central Valley politics, see Walker 2004a, Gilmore 2007.
67 Thanks to Michael Storper for insisting on this point. See also Callahan 2010.

Resistance and Renewal

Political cultures have to be renewed as circumstances change, which is why Bay Area history cannot, by itself, explain today's politics. But it is possible to trace some threads from the past to the present. The Union Labor Party and Wobblies were, no doubt, fresh in the minds of the radicals of the 1930s. When the latter aged into the Old Left of the postwar era, many on the New Left of the 1960s looked to them for models and advice. Even though the lions of the Sixties are gray-haired now, many still persist in their activism and share lessons with the young rebels of the twenty-first century. This kind of continuity has helped keep the Left vibrant in the Bay Area. Yet the situation faced by every new generation of rabble-rousers is different and calls for reconfigured goals and tactics.

This final section brings the story of metropolitan politics up to the present. It begins with a review of local developments since the turn of the century, then considers recent political directions in the tech industry, and finishes with a brief assessment of the state of the Left in the wake of the 2016 election.

★   ★   ★

In San Francisco, the assassination of Harvey Milk blunted the forward motion of the Left in electoral politics. The Chamber of Commerce and its allies quickly took away district elections, which had allowed Milk to get on the Board of Supervisors. The Left briefly regained an upper hand with the election of Mayor Art Agnos in 1987, then splintered. City Hall slipped back into the hands of the mainstream regime, neither especially Republican nor Democratic but always reliably business friendly. Uninspiring ex-police chief Frank Jordan was elected in 1991 before the probusiness coalition was salvaged by the return of charismatic Willie Brown, termed out in Sacramento and elected mayor in 1995. Brown proved to be a good servant of the developers and friend of the tech sector as he presided over the dot-com boom.[68]

Nonetheless, the new century opened up with a massive revolt against the prodevelopment policies of City Hall during the dot-com boom. Brown was nearly toppled in late 1999 by the write-in candidacy of Tom Ammiano, who had inherited the leftist mantle of Milk, and district elections were finally restored in time for the 2000 election of the Board of Supervisors, which left-wing candidates swept. Brown's chosen successor, Gavin Newsom, barely held on to the mayor's office in 2003 against a furious campaign by a left candidate.

---

68 On Milk and district elections, see Shilts 1982, Carlsson 2011, Golinger 2018. On the Brown regime, see Walker 2006, Beitel 2011. On San Francisco voting blocs, see DeLeon 1992.

Once in office, Newsom's masterstroke was to quickly approve gay marriages in defiance of a state ban, and he won further admiration for supporting striking hotel workers in the city and for instigating a major push to reduce homelessness. With a renewed economic upswing and a progressive majority with little to show, Newsom was reelected by a huge majority in 2007.[69]

When Newsom moved on to lieutenant governor in 2010, and with most of the progressive supervisors termed out, he (with the help of Willie Brown) maneuvered Ed Lee, a lifetime civil servant, into the mayor's office. Lee was supposed to be interim mayor but ran as the incumbent and won in 2011. Like Brown and Newsom before him, Lee won by appealing to the Chinese community, African Americans, and gay liberals against the white Left. Lee's first major act was to grant Twitter, Zendesk, Spotify, and other tech companies a massive tax break on the city's payroll tax for locating in the Mid-Market area—a move that has cost the city millions and is redolent of the kind of desperate policies of cities gutted by deindustrialization, not the heartland of global technology.[70]

Lee continued to bow to tech giants such as Uber and Airbnb by minimizing regulations on their operations, no doubt because tech capitalists such as Paul Graham, Michael Moritz, and Ron Conway have donated generously to city campaigns. But opposition grew, putting more Left supervisors back on the board, such as Aaron Peskin and Jane Kim. With Lee's sudden death in 2017, a new struggle erupted over who would become the interim mayor—and have a leg up as incumbent in the next elections.[71] The Left won the first round, deposing the Brown-Newsom candidate.

Berkeley, too, drifted back to the center from the halcyon days of the Berkeley Citizens' Action (BCA) uprising of the 1980s, when the city was known for stringent rent control and progressive initiatives under African American Mayor Gus Newport. Berkeley has continued to give birth to important political innovations such as healthy food in schools, taxing soft drinks, and sanctuary cities. The city has been deeply affected by the long property boom, with rising prices driving out students and people of color. Long-serving mayor Tom Bates, formerly of BCA, presided over an era of redevelopment in the early twenty-first century, as massive condo projects appeared around Downtown and in West Berkeley's old industrial areas. Controversy over such projects and the changing character of the city led Berkeley voters in 2016 to elect the city's first Latino mayor, Jesse Arroquin, and a progressive

---

69   On the elections of 1999 and 2000, see Carlsson 2004, Golinger 2018.
70   Lang 2015, McNeill 2016, Golinger 2018,
71   Green 2016b, Green et al. 2016, Schwaller 2017, Golinger 2018.

majority that promised to rethink the city's policies on development and homelessness.[72]

In the new Millennium, the mantle of the Left Coast has passed from San Francisco and Berkeley to Oakland. This was decidedly not because Oakland's elected leadership has been brilliant, but because of the deep roots of the Left in the city combined with a major social transformation due to the tech boom. The road back to political relevance has been long and hard, however. African Americans came to electoral power in the city in 1977 and presided until the end of the century under the mayoral regimes of Lionel Wilson and Elihu Harris. But given deindustrialization, they could do little with their mandates, so few were the resources available from local taxes, state transfers, or federal programs in the neoliberal era. The 1990s were the low point in the wake of the Loma Prieta earthquake and hillside fire disasters.

When former governor Jerry Brown decided to jump back into the electoral game in 1998, Oaklanders rushed to vote for him and to institute a "strong mayor" system of government. Brown's fame lent the city a bit of luster, but his success in office was mostly due to the luck of the draw, as booming San Francisco overflowed its banks. Brown welcomed developers with open arms, and his social policies were vaguely liberal but included an embrace of military charter schools. After Brown departed in 2007, two genuinely Left mayors, Ron Dellums and Jean Quan, were elected on surges of progressive activism and frustration with the effects of the Great Recession. Unfortunately, both ended up with undistinguished terms whose imprint on urban policy was slight. Dellums's term played out as farce: he did not want the job, had no plan, and was mostly an absentee mayor. Jean Quan's mayoralty was more of a tragedy. Elected under a new system of rank-choice voting, she was undone by a combination of shaky legitimacy, the Occupy protests, and her own personality. A mainstream white liberal, Libby Schaaf, was returned to office in 2015.[73]

Popular unrest in Oakland could not be quelled, however. In came waves of displaced young professionals, students and teachers, struggling artists, and techies washing up on the shores of the city. They collided with well-established African, Asian, and Mexican American neighborhoods with a strong working-class identity and history of political mobilization, who were facing police violence, foreclosures, rising rents, and massive displacement. The impact and blending of the two have generated a lively and volatile cascade of popular movements. Most notable were the large protests against

---

72 Johnson 2016, Courtright 2017.
73 East Bay Times 2009, Gammon 2011.

the killing of Oscar Grant by BART police in 2009 (well before the uprising in Ferguson, Missouri) and Occupy Oakland, which was second only to Occupy Wall Street among the mobilizations and encampments of 2011. The latter brought together labor unions, activists of every stripe and people from every racial community. At its peak, Occupy Oakland called a symbolic "general strike" and closed down the port.[74]

Popular uprisings have forced city government to move on several fronts, such as urban farming, First Friday street fairs, and banning coal shipments through the port. Oakland became a national leader in the liberalization of pot sales and use, under the spiritual lead of the aptly named Oaksterdam University. Causa Justa::Just Cause has led the fight against evictions and for rent control, finally getting results after years of inaction by the city council. At the same time, Oakland's murder rate remains intolerably high and its policing an abusively ineffective response to rampant violence, so the city has nurtured crucial protest movements such as Remember Oscar Grant, Black Lives Matter, and Critical Resistance.[75]

Progressive movements have surfaced in outlying parts of the Bay Area, as well. San Jose and the cities of Santa Clara County have benefitted from the new demographics, as well as a strong labor presence through the Central Labor Council and Working Partnerships USA. The Valley is home to some feisty grassroots groups such as Silicon Valley De-Bug and Silicon Valley Toxics Coalition, and rent control has spread to the Valley's old suburbs. In Sonoma County, labor and environmentalists have had a positive impact, as shown in liberal elected officials, construction of the SMART commuter rail line, and community benefits agreements for developments such as the Graton Casino. A persistent fact of local politics, however, is that it remains stubbornly local, and crafting alliances beyond municipal borders is always difficult. North and South Bay activists have done better in this regard than in the Central Bay, where movements are so often limited to Berkeley, Oakland, or San Francisco alone.

To a significant degree, Bay Area politics has shifted toward Sacramento with the Second Coming of Jerry Brown, (re)elected governor in 2010 and 2014, and to take advantage of the Democratic supermajorities that have taken hold in the legislature. Bay Area unions have always been more active in state than municipal politics, too. A prime example of a policy front "jumping scale" to the state level is in housing, where fifteen bills to deal with the housing

---

74 The best coverage of changing Oakland and its politics has been in the *East Bay Express*. For a snarky East Coast view of Occupy Oakland, see Mahler 2012.

75 McClintock et al. 2012, Werth 2016, Gammon 2015.

crisis were passed and signed in 2017. The results have been decidedly mixed, however, in their political thrust (see chapter 6). The emphasis on state politics has only been augmented as California has emerged as a bulwark against the Right's domination of national policy (see below).

★ ★ ★

A critical question for the future of Bay Area politics is which way the techies— capitalists, managers, and skilled workers—are bending in the political winds of the twenty-first century. The industry has some progressive roots, embodied in a liberatory ideology of openness, collective action, and sharing, and a largely youthful and liberal workforce, but it has strongly conservative tendencies, as well. The techies can contribute to the sustenance of the city's progressive tradition, but only if their best instincts are awakened through political mobilization rather than their entrepreneurial love of money and libertarian political leanings.

The politics of the denizens of the tech sector have been sorely tested by the election of President Trump and the triumph of the Far Right; but the picture that has emerged is mixed. As might be expected, the Tech Moguls have flirted with the new administration, drawn by the attractions of power, government contracts, and tax cuts. But the majority of tech workers have been hostile to the new regime and have gotten organized to make their views felt. There has been a surge of support for the Democratic Party and progressive causes.

During the presidential campaign of 2016, the big tech money was all over the political map. Few Tech Moguls supported Trump openly (Peter Thiel was a glaring exception), and 150 tech executives signed an open letter denouncing the Republican candidate's politics of hate and resentment. But most were cool toward Hillary Clinton and decidedly uninterested in Bernie Sanders. A few Democratic stalwarts such as Sheryl Steinberg of Facebook gave donations to Clinton, but others such as Elon Musk and Sean Parker flipped between candidates such as Marco Rubio and Rand Paul before landing with Clinton, and some previous Obama donors, such as Reid Hoffman and Vinod Khosla, pulled back. Surprisingly, the social libertarians at *Wired* endorsed Clinton. Tellingly, tech workers overwhelming gave their small donations to Democrats in general and Bernie Sanders in particular.[76]

By contrast, after the election a crew of Tech Moguls flew east to meet with the president-elect in what the *New York Times* called "a charmfest." Some of the biggest tech corporations fell in line with Trump's initiatives.

---

76 Streitfeld 2016b, Dadich 2016, Conger & Buhr 2016, Wilson 2016.

Intel announced that it would build a big chip factory in Arizona to comport with the administration's push for domestic manufacturing. Smaller tech firms such as Simularity and Quanergy offered to create virtual walls along the Mexican border with sensors, drones, and AI. Cisco's CEO expressed confidence in the new president, and one of Oracle's co-CEOs joined the president's transition team. Uber CEO Travis Kalanick agreed to be on a presidential advisory committee.[77]

Such moves have not been popular with many, if not most, tech users and employees. George Polisner, a senior executive at Oracle, quit over that company's collaboration with the new administration. Kalanick withdrew from the advisory commission after thousands of people erased the Uber apps on their phones. One of the strangest couplings was Elon Musk's bromance with the president, whose predilection for oil and coal run contrary to Musk's electric car and solar panel interests. Musk finally quit two of the president's business advisory councils after Trump withdrew the United States from the Paris climate agreement.

Tech workers rushed to get organized in the wake of the election. Tech Solidarity was formed in San Francisco to get things moving, and a Tech Workers Coalition was started to link employees at several large companies in Silicon Valley. Other tech workers joined Tech for Campaigns to bring coding, social media, fundraising, and data skills to help progressive electoral candidates. Another new group, TechEquity Collaborative and its project TechResistance.org, addressed people of color, including immigrants, directly. As one tech worker declared, "The things (Trump) is proposing go against everything Silicon Valley stands for: openness, equality."[78]

The ban on immigrants from Muslim majority countries was a key flash point. Thousands of workers walked out to protest at the campuses of Facebook, Twitter, and Google—and the latter were joined by company founder Sergey Brin, a Russian immigrant. Netflix's Reed Hastings denounced the ban as "so un-American it pains us all" and said "it is time to link arms together to protect American values of freedom and opportunity." Brian Chesky, chief executive of Airbnb, declared, "We must stand with those who are affected." A new grassroots organization called Tech Stands Up has been formed expressly to oppose Trump's immigration policies; a local crowd-funder, GoFundMe, quickly helped over fifty campaigns raise a million dollars to fight the travel ban; and Y Combinator created a project with the ACLU

77 Tam 2016, Wong 2016b, Stewart 2017, Thadani & Said 2017. Oracle's first client was the CIA.
78 Thadani 2017a, Swartz & Guynn 2017, Streitfeld 2017a, Kulish & Popper 2017. Quote from Wilson 2016. Of course, there are voices from the Right, gathered under the disingenuously named Lincoln Network.

to aid immigrants. As one partner observed, "I haven't seen this kind of engagement for any political action or movement as long as I have been in Silicon Valley."[79]

Over one hundred tech companies, including Apple, Facebook, and Intel, joined an amicus brief in court appeal of the administration's immigration ban. This is, of course, a matter of self-interest as much as of principle, since at least one-third of all Bay Area tech firms were started by immigrants and the industry relies so heavily on H-IB visas for recruit foreign nationals to work in the United States. The Silicon Valley Manufacturers Group, making its annual foray to lobby Congress early in 2017, reported that interest among CEOs had never been greater, with immigration a prime talking point.[80]

Nevertheless, the number-one priority of the Manufacturers Group remained "tax reform," by which they mean bringing U.S. corporate tax rates down to international rates and allowing easier repatriation of offshore profits. Tech leaders, like most other wealthy Americans, loved the massive 2017 Republican tax cuts and have not raised a peep of opposition to their obvious giveaways to the rich and the corporations. Worse, there was the supposedly liberal Marc Benioff singing Trump's praises at the 2018 Davos gathering of the rich and powerful: "I thought it was a great speech. I thought his economic narrative has become greatly enhanced now that the tax cuts have passed."[81]

In the wake of Trump's victory, a struggle broke out across the country over the future of the Democratic Party. Some have looked toward Silicon Valley to lead the party out of the wilderness, but there is good reason to doubt predictions that "Tech Democrats" are the future of national politics. Going back to the first Clinton administration, the libertarian capitalists of tech were supposed to help the party leave behind its traditional base of unionized workers and policy of government regulation for a bright new era of market liberalism with a human face. To a considerable extent, Hillary Clinton's 2016 campaign was built on the same belief that liberal tech donors, enlightened professionals, and people of color would deliver victory, without worrying about the working class and the foundations of the old New Deal coalition. That proved to be sadly mistaken.[82]

---

79 Quotes in Streitfield 2017b, Streitfield et al. 2017.
80 Wingfield & Wakabayashi 2017, Thadani 2017b
81 Ferenstein 2017. Quote from Elliot 2018.
82 For fervent declarations of the new era of Tech Democrats, see Ferenstein 2015 and Hagemann 2016. For searing critiques of the mainstream Democrats' abandonment of their old base and principles, see Packer 2013, Frank 2016, Williams 2017, Davis 2017a. For an opposing view that emphasizes race and racism in the Democrats' failure, see Phillips 2016.

After the Democrats' defeat, Mark Pincus, cofounder of Zynga, and Reid Hoffman of LinkedIn created Win the Future, or "WTF," to move the party in a new direction. Typically, WTF is not an organization but an online platform for crowdsourcing ideas, and the new direction looks a lot like the old one that failed—based on fear of the Democrats moving too far left and being insufficiently probusiness. This initiative was mocked for asserting that tech billionaires could help the party be "more in touch with mainstream America." As one critic observed, "The rich people's [mistake] is to think that the swing voter is kind of like them, which is to say progressive on social issues and regressive on corporate power." Another declared, "The weakness of the Democratic Party is not due to an underrepresentation of venture capitalists and tech company board members . . . [but] working people who are sick and tired of politics that answers to money instead of the people." The only significant voice among the Tech Moguls arguing for the Democrats to move further left is Tom Steyer, who has bluntly stated that "there is an absolute, unspoken war between corporate interests and the American people" and who started paying for a national ad campaign to impeach Donald Trump.[83]

A more promising development is the emergence of "Indivisible," which began as a Google Doc tweeted by a former congressional staffer on how to oppose the Republican agenda under Trump. The idea was to create a left-wing version of the kind of grassroots organizing done by the right-wing Tea Party. It quickly went viral and spawned a raft of protests at town hall meetings of Congress members around the country to support Obamacare. Indivisible now sports a national hub in Washington, DC, and thousands of loosely allied, volunteer chapters across the country—including a half dozen in the Bay Area. The San Francisco chapter, with 4,500 members, is one of the largest in the nation. It has raised millions of dollars through small donations via its website but has also received major donations from billionaires Reid Hoffman and Oakland mortgage banker Herb Sandler. Indivisible uses the web and attracts many techies but cannot be confined to the Tech World; it speaks to a much wider world of political organizing in the wake of 2016.[84]

★ ★ ★

---

83 Quotes from Marans 2017, Karp 2017. Steyer quote from https://mic.com/articles/182238/the-democrats-biggest-donor-says-the-party-is-blowing-it-and-should-get-behind-bernies-platform#.SOZg62eer.
84 Vogel 2017.

How has the Bay Area as a whole responded to the political challenge posed by the resurgence of the Far Right? Following the presidential election, liberals and leftists went into collective mourning but quickly rallied in opposition. There was a widespread awakening to the threats posed by the new regime in Washington to long-held rights, American democracy, and world peace. This ushered in a new sense of progressive solidarity between liberals and leftists here, as well as around the country. Some optimists began to call the widespread opposition to the Trump administration "The Resistance," borrowing a trope from Star Wars. The term may be the brainchild of George Lucas, infected by the Left Coast in his youth, but it is by no means clear that a coherent movement has emerged. Nonetheless, local organizing efforts have ramped up along lines already deeply etched in the region around health care, immigration rights, antiracism, and climate change[85]

On the electoral front, some promising organizing has emerged in pursuit of a Democratic majority in Congress in 2018. Volunteers have been heading east from the bay region to work on campaigns for a long time, but the focus now is to flip Republican house seats in California's interior, pushing the envelope of the bay blue into the red Central Valley. Close the Gap California is bent on running more women candidates for state offices. MoveOn.org, based in Berkeley, has been using its online network to promote Democratic candidates around the country, with considerable success.

Given the Democrats dominance in California, the state has become a major target of the Republicans and the Trump administration. Good examples of efforts to punish the Golden State are the limit on deductions of state and local taxes, continued enforcement of federal drug laws despite state legalization of marijuana, and ramped up ICE raids on workplaces. This has only solidified popular opposition to the new regime, putting the remaining congressional Republicans in an even more perilous situation. The Democratic-controlled state legislature has taken up any number of bills to resist directives from Washington, DC, such as state funding of health care, end-arounds to raise taxes, and protection of the coast, and the government has some forty lawsuits pending against the Trump administration.[86]

At the same time, there have been important protests in the Bay Area against the mainstream Democratic Party and its overseers, particularly Congresswoman Pelosi and Senator Feinstein. They have been taken to task for the party's treatment of Bernie Sanders, who was overwhelmingly favored

---

85 One postelection observer effused that the Resistance was rooted in the Bay Area tech community, but that is surely not the case. Garafoli 2016. On the danger posed by Trump and the Far Right to democracy, see Levitsky & Ziblatt 2018.

86 Diaz 2018.

by the Bay Area's Left and young voters in 2016. And they have been pushed to see that mainstream Democrats in Washington are more confrontational with the Republicans and Trump over issues such as Obamacare, tax cuts, Medicare, immigration policy, and the Dreamers.

The Trump administration's assault on immigrants and stepped-up deportations have inflamed passions around the Bay Area. Protesters mobbed the San Francisco airport after the announcement of the first immigrant ban. When Attorney General Jeff Sessions denounced the sanctuary movement and threatened to withhold federal dollars, it only provoked more cities to confirm their refusal to comply, and soon the California legislature declared the entire state to be a sanctuary. San Francisco joined lawsuits against the new administration over its ban on immigrants from Muslim countries, and local federal judges have repeatedly enjoined the government from enacting its plans. Defense of the Dreamers is a pillar of California politics, and the state has sued the federal government over the end of the program. Most activist energies have been taken up, however, by day-to-day efforts to defend immigrants threatened with deportation and stop seizures by ICE agents by organizing safe houses and rapid response networks.[87]

Racial tensions have been ratcheted up across the country by the aggressive posture of Trump and his alt-Right followers. The Charlottesville clash and murder of a protester in 2017 was a flash point, as were conflicts over the removal of statues of Confederate heroes. Another has been the protests by athletes over police killings of black citizens, which the Bay Area and its sports stars have been outspoken in defense of, including refusal of invitations to the White House. There were massive turnouts for the women's marches in early 2017 and 2018. The #MeToo movement against male harassment has a large following in the region, with the calling out of miscreants in the Tech World an important spark to the mobilization—though the center of the action in the state appears to be Southern California.

Another area of fierce resistance is the environment, given the Trumpian attacks on climate change science, solar energy, and national monuments and effort to open up the coast to oil drilling again. Many Bay Area professionals, university faculty, and research scientists came out on the streets for marches called by the Union of Concerned Scientists in defense of science. San Francisco has joined a dozen cities posting deleted federal climate data on their websites. Berkeley professor Dan Kammen put an exclamation point

---

87 Seipel 2017, Luna 2017. When a mass march in defense of immigrants was called for May 1, 2017, by unions and activists, almost no immigrants turned out because of the intense fear of being identified.

on it when he resigned as the scientific envoy to the State Department—with a protest letter whose bullet points spelled out "Impeach." Resistance has mostly been channeled through Sacramento, where Governor Brown has been openly defiant, declaring that, "California will resist; Trump may well create the exact opposite of what he intended, which is an aroused citizenry—and an aroused international community."[88]

A political and media circus arose over a series of confrontations created by militant Trump supporters and right-wing provocateurs targeting the Bay Area. The first incursion was a talk by Milo Yiannopoulos on the UC Berkeley campus, which was shut down by a mass demonstration and violent counterattack by Black Bloc (anarchist) militants. A subsequent mass rally by right-wing militants and white supremacists in Berkeley devolved into a brawl with "antifa" counterprotesters. Both events got a lot of national attention and criticism of Berkeley for not allowing the Far Right to exercise free speech. But a follow-up mobilization of the alt-Right called for in August was swamped by a mass turnout of peaceful left protesters. A repeat performance by Yiannopoulos in September came to naught, even as the University of California declared a "Free Speech Week," because Milo's followers failed to pay for the lecture hall. The whole bizarre farce is part of a systematic effort to embarrass liberal universities and college towns, paid for by right-wing billionaires such as Robert Mercer and Richard and Helen Devos.[89]

Frankly, the American Left is still in a parlous state and unable to launch a systematic response to the perils presented by the resurgent Far Right. If the Bay Area is any indication, the Left is still fragmented into a multitude of disparate issues, all of them virtuous but none that can generate a mass movement without wider alliances. Yet without a major mobilization around a meaningful set of radical programs—from health to housing, crime to climate, and immigration to the internet—the Left is hamstrung. Paying attention to electoral politics and supporting progressives in the Democratic Party is important but far from sufficient. Good candidates do not a movement make, and the mainstream Democrats remain in the thrall of big money and conventional nostrums for the grave social ills that plague the nation.

Conclusion

The Bay Area's progressive tilt rests on some deep social roots in the city's class structure, economic success, and renewal through in-migration, and has been cemented into the region's political culture by labor organizing,

---

88 Johnson 2017. Brown quoted in Baker 2017b.
89 For valuable perspective, see Bauer 2017.

bohemian countercultures, and periodic uprisings against unbridled capitalism, conventional morality, and state repression. The metropolis's reputation
as the Left Coast of America is often exaggerated, but it still resonates in
important ways such as voting behavior and radical mobilizations such as the
ones triggered by the Iraq invasion of 2003, the financial meltdown of 2008,
and the Trump presidential victory of 2016. Yet the city's legacy is a good deal
more ambiguous than the label "Left Coast" allows for. This is, after all, one
of the most successful and richest capitalist economies on earth, and while
smiling fortune often gives people a favorable disposition toward the poor
or the environment, it also assures that capitalism maintains a firm grip on
their allegiances.

At the heart of the Bay Area's capitalist success is the tech industry. The
social origins of Silicon Valley cannot be uncoupled from the political history
of the Bay Area. Threads of both the Cold War and the counterculture run
through the moral fiber of the tech industry, but so do threads of shared
opportunity, collective action, and rebellion, not to mention white supremacy
and crass moneymaking. Mythological accounts of Tech World as sui generis
will not stand. Economies encompass more than markets, firms, and technologies; they are, like all human practices, embedded in social orders and
inherited histories, or what geographers call "the power of place." The flow-
ering of tech has, in turn, deeply affected the course of Bay Area history and
politics, and the way the titans and the workers of IT drift in the fast-moving
political currents of contemporary California will leave a deep imprint on the
future of the region and the country.

Many leftists fear that the Bay Area is losing its way politically, led astray
by the easy riches of the tech boom and depleted of activists and alternative
cultures by the pressure of a bloated housing market. There is good reason to
be concerned, because progressive ideas and movements are relatively fragile
in the face of the headwinds of capitalism, the bluster of business, and the
recidivism of white racism. The distinctiveness of the region's political culture
has undoubtedly been blunted since the high tide of the Left Coast by the
long counterrevolution of neoliberalism and neoconservatism and diluted by
the tech tsunami that has left the region awash in money, new people, and the
dubious influence of the IT billionaires. While the Bay Area remains to the left
of the rest of the country and still offers resistance to the rightward march of
the national government, it badly needs a new upsurge of radical organizing
if it is to once again act as a beacon of social progress in a darkening time.

Bibliography

Aalbers, Manuel. 2016. *The Financialization of Housing: A Political Economy Approach*. New York: Routledge.

ABAG. 2014. *Economic Prosperity Strategy: Improving Economic Opportunity for the Bay Area's Low- and Moderate-Wage Workers*. Oakland: Association of Bay Area Governments and Metropolitan Transportation Commission.

ABAG. 2015. *San Francisco Bay Area: State of the Region—Population, Economy, Housing*. Oakland: Association of Bay Area Governments.

ABAG & MTC. 2017. *Plan Bay Area 2040*. San Francisco: Association of Bay Area Governments and Metropolitan Transportation Commission.

Abrahamson, Eric. 2013. *Building Home: Howard F. Ahmanson and the Politics of the American Dream*. Berkeley: University of California Press.

Abramowitz, Moses. 1964. *Evidence of Long Swings in Aggregate Construction since the Civil War*. New York: National Bureau of Economic Research.

Acemoglu, Daron, and James Robinson. 2013. *Why Nations Fail: The Origins of Poverty, Prosperity, and Poverty*. New York: Crown Publishing.

Adams, Stephen. 1997. *Mr. Kaiser Goes to Washington: The Rise of a Government Entrepreneur*. Chapel Hill: University of North Carolina Press.

Adas, Michael. 1989. *Machines as the Measure of Man: Science, Technology and Ideologies of Western Dominance*. Ithaca, NY: Cornell University Press.

Adler, Patrick, and Chris Tilly. 2014. *The State of the Unions in 2014: A Profile of Union Membership in Greater Los Angeles, San Francisco, California, and the Nation*. Los Angeles: Institute for Research on Labor and Employment, UCLA.

Adler, Patrick, Chris Tilly, and Trevor Thomas. 2015. *From '15 to $15: The State of the Unions in California and Its Key Cities in 2015*. Los Angeles: Institute for Research on Labor and Employment, UCLA.

Agence France-Presse. 2016. Chinese Pour $110bn into US Real Estate, Says Study. *Guardian*. May 15. https://www.theguardian.com/business/2016/may/16/chinese-pour-110bn-into-us-real-estate-says-study

Air Resources Board (ARB). 2016. *California GHG Emissions Inventory, 2016 Edition*. June 7. Sacramento: California Air Resources Board.

Albertini, Dominique, and David Doucet. 2016. *La Fachosphère: Comment l'extrême droite remporte la bataille d'internet*. Paris: Flammarion.

Alden, William. 2015. Slack Is Swept Up in Silicon Valley's Gold Rush. *BuzzFeed*. April 16. https://www.buzzfeed.com/williamalden/slack-is-swept-up-in-silicon-valleys-gold-rush?utm_term=.tiGbO7A4P#.jj5xD3Zmo

Alexander, Kurtis. 2017a. Bay Area Ranked among the Nation's Worst Spots for Air Pollution. *San Francisco Chronicle*. April 20. http://www.sfgate.com/bayarea/article/Bay-Area-ranked-among-nation-s-worst-spots-for-11082028.php

Alexander, Kurtis. 2017b. Mistrust Running High in Oroville. *San Francisco Chronicle*. June 18. https://www.pressreader.com/usa/san-francisco-chronicle/20170618/281479276407449

Alexander, Michelle. 2010. *The New Jim Crow: Mass Incarceration in the Age of Colorblindness*. New York: New Press.

Allegretto, Sylvia. 2016. *California's Labor Market: Eight Years Post-Great-Recession*. Issue Brief. May 2016. Center for Wage and Employment Dynamics, Institute for Research on Labor and Employment, University of California, Berkeley.

Almaguer, Tomas. 1994. *Racial Fault Lines: The Historical Origins of White Supremacy in California*. Berkeley: University of California Press.

Alonso, William. 1964. *Location and Land Use*. Cambridge, MA: Harvard University Press.

American Lung Association. 2016. *State of the Air*. http://www.lung.org/assets/documents/healthy-air/state-of-the-air/sota-2016-full.pdf

Angwin, Julia. 2017. How to Protect Your Digital Privacy in the Era of Public Shaming. *ProPublica*. January 26. https://www.propublica.org/article/how-to-protect-your-digital-privacy-in-the-era-of-public-shaming

Anonymous. 2016. Rent Control: Mountain View among Six Bay Area Cities Where Residents Seek Historically Elusive Statute. *San Jose Mercury News*. July 4. https://www.mercurynews.com/2016/07/04/rent-control-mountain-view-among-six-bay-area-cities-where-residents-seek-historically-elusive-statute/

Applebaum, Eileen, Annette Burkhardt, and Richard Murnane, eds. 2003. *Low-Wage America: How Employers Are Reshaping Opportunity in the Workplace*. New York: Russell Sage Foundation.

Arax, Mark, and Rick Wartzman. 2003. *The King of California: J.G. Boswell and the Making of a Secret American Empire*. New York: PublicAffairs.

Archer, John. 2005. *Architecture and Suburbia: From English Villa to American Dream House*. Minneapolis: University of Minnesota Press.

Arthur, W. Brian. 1988. Urban Systems and Historical Path Dependence. In Jesse Ausubel and Robert Herman, eds., *Cities and Their Vital Systems*. Washington, DC: National Academy Press, 85–97.

articles/2016-06-01/uber-receives-3-5-billion-investment-from-saudi-wealth-fund

Asbury, Herbert. 1933. *The Barbary Coast: An Informal History of the San Francisco Underworld*. New York: Alfred Knopf.

Ashbolt, Anthony. 2012. *A Cultural History of the Radical Sixties in the San Francisco Bay Area*. London: Pickering & Chatto.

Ashton, Phillip. 2012. "Troubled Assets": The Financial Emergency and Racialized Risk. *International Journal of Urban and Regional Research* 36 (4): 773–90.

Associated Press. 2017. China and California Sign Deal to Work on Climate Change without Trump. *Guardian*. June 7. https://www.theguardian.com/us-news/2017/jun/07/china-and-california-sign-deal-to-work-on-climate-change-without-trump

Authers, John. 2016. Irrational Exuberance Begins to Surface in US Stock Market. *Financial Times*. August 17. https://www.ft.com/content/c4406bec-6442-11e6-8310-ecfobddad227

Authers, John. 2018. US Stock Market Enters Cape Fear Territory. *Financial Times*. January 10. https://www.ft.com/content/793fbbo8-f5e5-11e7-8715-e94187b3017e

Authers, John, and Claire Manibog. 2017. Dealing with the Effects of One Bubble Creating More. *Financial Times*. August 20. https://www.ft.com/content/f3a5440a-81ee-11e7-a4ce-15b2513cb3ff

Autor, David, and David Dorn. 2013. The Growth of Low-Skill Service Jobs and the Polarization of the US Labor Market. *American Economic Review* 103 (5): 1553–97.

Avalos, George. 2016. Bay Area Job Gains Slow Sharply. *San Jose Mercury News*. April 15. http://www.mercurynews.com/2016/04/15/bay-area-job-gains-slow-sharply-but-south-bay-and-east-bay-still-grow/

BAC Economic Institute. 2014. *Bay Area Employment Statistics, July 2014*. August 15. San Francisco: Bay Area Council.

Bacher, John. 2017. Obama Administration Orders Speedy Completion of Delta Tunnels Plan. *Counterpunch*. January 17. https://www.counterpunch.org/2017/01/16/obama-administration-orders-speedy-completion-of-delta-tunnels-plan/

Bachrach, Peter, and Morton Baratz. 1970. *Power and Poverty: Theory and Practice*. New York: Oxford University Press.

Badger, Emily. 2017. When the empty apartment next door is owned by an oligarch. *New York Times*. July 21. https://nyti.ms/2tlXVCo

Badger, Emily. 2018. Tech Envisions the Ultimate Start-Up: An Entire City. *New York Times*. February 24. https://www.nytimes.com/2018/02/24/upshot/tech-envisions-the-ultimate-start-up-an-entire-city.html

Bagdikian, Ben. 1990. *The Media Monopoly*. Boston: Beacon Press. 3rd ed.

Bagwell, Beth. 1982. *Oakland: Story of a City*. Novato, CA: Presidio Press.

Baker, David. 2016. Google All-In for Wind, Sun Power. *San Francisco Chronicle*. June 12. https://www.pressreader.com/usa/san-francisco-chronicle/20161206/282205125511154

Baker, David. 2017a. California Greenhouse Gas Emissions Drop, Barely. *San Francisco Chronicle*. July 5. http://www.sfchronicle.com/business/article/California-s-greenhouse-gas-emissions-drop-8342038.php

Baker, David. 2017b. Defying Trump, California Forms Climate Alliance with Two States. *SFGate.com*. June 1. http://www.sfgate.com/bayarea/article/Defying-Trump-California-forms-climate-alliance-11189747.php

Baker, Dean. 2016. *Rigged: How Globalization and the Rules of the Modern Economy Were Structured to Make the Rich Richer*. Washington, DC: Center for Economic and Policy Research.

Baker, Kevin. 2010. Coney Island's Grand Past and Grim Future. *Village Voice*. May 25. https://www.villagevoice.com/2010/05/25/coney-islands-grand-past-and-grim-future/

Baldassari, Erin. 2017. Traffic on Major Bay Area Freeways Has Grown 80 Percent since 2010. *Mercury News*. September 20. http://www.mercurynews.com/2017/09/18/report-traffic-on-major-freeways-has-grown-80-percent-since-2010/

Balibar, Etienne, and Immanuel Wallerstein, eds. 1991. *Race, Nation, Class*. London: Verso.

Banfield, Edward. 1970. *The Unheavenly City: The Nature and Future of Our Urban Crisis*. Boston: Little, Brown.

Banham, Rainer. 1980. The Architecture of Silicon Valley. *New West* (San Jose *Mercury*) 5 (September 20): 47–51.

Barba, Michael. 2017. SF Reaches Settlement with Airbnb over Short-Term Rental Rules. *San Francisco Examiner*. May 1. http://www.sfexaminer.com/sf-reaches-settlement-airbnb-short-term-rental-rules/

Barbrook, Richard, and Andy Cameron. 1997. The Californian Ideology: A Critique of West Coast Cyber-Libertarianism. Research paper, Hyperculture Research Centre, University of Westminster. http://www.hrc.wmin.ac.uk/theory-californianideology-main.html

Bardacke, Frank. 2011. *Trampling Out the Vintage: Cesar Chavez and the Two Souls of the United Farm Workers*. London: Verso.

Bardhan, Ashok. 2008. Globalization, Job Creation and Inequality: Challenges and Opportunities on Both Sides of the Offshoring Divide. In Kira Hall, ed., *Studies in Inequality and Social Justice: Essays in Honor of Ved Prakash Vatuk*. Meerut, India: Archana Publications, 111–30.

Bardhan, Ashok, Dwight Jaffee, and Cynthia Kroll. 2004. *Globalization and a High-Tech Economy: California, the United States and Beyond*. New York: Springer.

Bardhan, Ashok, and Richard Walker. 2011. California Shrugged: The Fountainhead of the Great Recession. *Cambridge Journal of Regions, Economy and Society* 4 (3): 303–22.

Bardhan, Ashok, Robert Edelstein, and Cynthia Kroll, eds. 2011. *Global Housing Markets: Crises, Policies and Institutions*. Hoboken, NJ: John Wiley & Sons.

Barkan, Joanne. 2013. Plutocrats at Work: How Big Philanthropy Undermines Democracy. *Dissent*. https://www.dissentmagazine.org/article/plutocrats-at-work-how-big-philanthropy-undermines-democracy

Barkan, Joanne. 2015. Wealthy Philanthropists Shouldn't Impose Their Idea of Common Good on us. *Guardian*. December 3. https://www.theguardian.com/commentisfree/2015/dec/03/mark-zuckerberg-priscilla-chan-initiative-billionaire-philanthropy

Barlow, John Perry. 1996. A Declaration of the Independence of Cyberspace. February 8. https://www.eff.org/cyberspace-independence

Barmann, Jay. 2015. Study: Airbnb "Commercial Hosts" Definitely Keeping Long-Term Rental Units off the Market. May 14. *SFist*. http://sfist.com/2015/05/14/study_airbnb_commercial_hosts_defin.php

Barnes, Jack. 2016. *Are They Rich Because They're Smart? Class, Privilege and Learning Under Capitalism*. New York: Pathfinder.

Barrera, Jeff. 2016. In Search of Cheaper Housing, Silicon Valley Workers Face Long Commutes. *Peninsula Press*. April 6. http://peninsulapress.com/2016/04/06/silicon-valley-long-commutes-cost-of-living/

Bauer, Shane. 2017. What the Media Got Wrong about Last Week's Protests in Berkeley. *Mother Jones*. August 29. http://www.motherjones.com/media/2017/08/what-the-media-got-wrong-about-last-weekends-protests-in-berkeley/

Bay Area Economic Institute (BAIE). 2014. *Bay Area Employment Statistics Seasonally Adjusted*. July 2014 Update. San Francisco: Bay Area Economic Institute/Bay Area Council.

BCDC. 2012. *Adapting to Rising Tides: Vulnerability and Risk Assessment Report*. San Francisco: Bay Conservation and Development Commission.

Beauregard, Robert. 2006. *When America Became Suburban*. Minneapolis: University of Minnesota Press.

Beitel, Karl. 2011. *Local Protests, Global Movements: Capital, Community, and State in San Francisco*. Philadelphia: Temple University Press.

Beniger, James. 1986. *The Control Revolution: Technological and Economic Origins of the Information Society*. Cambridge, MA: Harvard University Press.

Benner, Chris. 2002. *Work in the New Economy: Flexible Labor Markets in Silicon Valley*. Oxford: Blackwell.

Benner, Chris, and Manuel Pastor. 2015. *Equity, Growth, and Community: What the Nation Can Learn from America's Metro Areas*. Oakland: University of California Press.

Benner, Katie. 2017a. Snapchat Discover Takes a Hard Line on Misleading and Explicit Images. *New York Times*. January 23. https://nyti.ms/2khagm3

Benner, Katie. 2017b. Inside the Hotel Industry's Plan to Combat Airbnb. *New York Times*. April 16. https://www.nytimes.com/2017/04/16/technology/inside-the-hotel-industrys-plan-to-combat-airbnb.html

Benner, Katie. 2017c. Women in Tech Speak Frankly on Culture of Harassment. *New York Times*. June 30. https://nyti.ms/2usF1td

Benner, Katie. 2017d. A Backlash Builds Against Sexual Harassment in Silicon Valley. *New York Times*. July 3. https://nyti.ms/2tGeb3Z

Bennett, Marty. 2016. California's $15 Minimum Wage Earthquake. *Sonoma County Gazette*. June 29. http://www.sonomacountygazette.com/cms/pages/sonoma-county-news-article-5378.html

Beres, Damon. 2016. Silicon Valley Is Not an American Utopia, No Matter What Peter Thiel Thinks. *Huffington Post*. July 22. http://www.huffingtonpost.com/entry/peter-thiel-rnc-silicon-valley_us_579229e8e4b00c9876cf165b

Berman, Marshall. 1982. *All That Is Solid Melts into Air*. New York: Simon and Schuster.

Berman, Russell. 2018. The Battle over DACA Reaches a Fever Pitch. *The Atlantic*. January 9. https://www.theatlantic.com/politics/archive/2018/01/daca-dream-act-immigration-congress-trump/549989/

Bernhardt, Annette. 2017. Beyond Basic Income: Claiming Our Right to Govern Technology. *UC Berkeley Labor Center Blog.* May 23. http://laborcenter.berkeley.edu/beyond-basic-income-claiming-our-right-to-govern-technology/

Bernhardt, Annette, Ian Perry, and Lindsay Cattell. 2015. *Low-Wage Work in California: 2014 Chartbook.* Berkeley: Center for Research on Labor and Employment, University of California.

Bernhardt, Annette, and Sarah Thomason. 2017. *What Do We Know about Gig Work in California? An Analysis of Independent Contracting.* June 14. Berkeley: Center for Research on Labor and Employment.

Bernstein, Jared. 2015. *The Reconnection Agenda: Reuniting Growth and Prosperity.* Washington, DC: Center for Budget and Policy Priorities.

Bernstein, Jared, and Ben Spielberg. 2017. The Whys of Increasing Inequality: A Graphical Portrait. *Washington Post.* August 14. https://www.washingtonpost.com/news/posteverything/wp/2017/08/14/the-whys-of-increasing-inequality-a-graphical-portrait/?utm_term=.a87ae2cabf18

Berube, Alan, Audrey Singer, Jill Wilson, and William Frey. 2006. *Finding Exurbia: America's Fast-Growing Communities at the Metropolitan Fringe.* Washington, DC: Brookings.

Berube, Alan, and Natalie Holmes. 2016. City and Metropolitan Inequality on the Rise, Driven by Declining Incomes. Brookings Institution. Metropolitan Report Series. http://www.brookings.edu/research/papers/2016/01/14-income-inequality-cities-update-berubeholmes

Birla, Madan. 2005. *FedEx Delivers: How the World's Leading Shipping Company Keeps Innovating and Outperforming the Competition.* Hoboken, NJ: John Wiley & Sons.

Birnbaum, Michael, and Brian Fung. 2017. E.U. fines Google a Record $2.7 Billion in Antitrust Case over Search Results. *Washington Post.* June 27. https://www.washingtonpost.com/world/eu-announces-record-27-billion-antitrust-fine-on-google-over-search-results/2017/06/27/1f7c475e-5b20-11e7-8e2f-ef443171f6bd_story.html

Bivens, Josh. 2016. Why Is the Recovery Taking So Long—And Who's to Blame? *EPI Report.* August 11. Washington, DC: Economic Policy Institute. epi.org/110211

Blackburn, Robin. 1997. *The Making of New World Slavery: From the Baroque to the Modern, 1492–1800.* London: Verso Press.

Blair, Hunter. 2017. Corporations Pay between 13 and 19 Percent in Federal Taxes—Far Less than the 35 Percent Statutory Tax Rate. *Economic Policy Institute Snapshot.* August 10. http://www.epi.org/publication/corporations-pay-between-13-and-19-percent-in-federal-taxes-far-less-than-the-35-percent-statutory-tax-rate/

Blaisdell, Katherine, Eliot Glenn, Christine Kidd, William Powers, and Rebecca Yang. 2015. Race, Place and Police: The 2009 Shooting of Oscar Grant. *Harvard Journal of African American Public Policy.* April 27. http://hjaap.org/race-place-and-police-the-2009-shooting-of-oscar-grant/

Blakely, Edward, and Mary Gail Snyder. 1997. *Fortress America: Gated Communities in the United States.* Washington, DC: Brookings Institution.

Blau, Francine, and Lawrence Kahn. 2016. *The Gender Wage Gap: Extent, Trends, and Explanations.* Cambridge, MA: National Bureau of Economic Research.

Bliss, Laura. 2015. California's "Katrina" Could Be Coming to Sacramento: You Don't Need a Hurricane to Have a Catastrophic Flood. *City Lab.* September 1. http://www.citylab.com/politics/2015/09/californias-katrina-could-be-coming-to-sacramento/402958/

Bloom, Joshua, and Waldo Martin. 2013. *Black against Empire: The History and Politics of the Black Panther Party.* Berkeley: University of California Press.

Bloom, Nicholas. 2004. *Merchant of Illusion: James Rouse, America's Salesman of the Businessman's Utopia.* Columbus: Ohio State University Press.

Bloxham, Eleanor. 2014. Facebook's Hypocritical Approach to Transparency. *Fortune.* May 27. fortune.com/2014/03/27/facebooks-hypocritical-approach-to-transparency

Boeing, Geoff, and P. Waddell. 2017. New Insights into Rental Housing Markets across the United States: Web Scraping and Analyzing Craigslist Rental Listings. *Journal of Planning Education and Research* 37 (4): 457–76.

Bohn, Sarah, Caroline Danielson, Matt Levin, Marybeth Mattingly, and Christopher Wimer. 2013. *The California Poverty Measure: A New Look at the Social Safety Net*. Policy Report/The California Poverty Measure. San Francisco: Public Policy Institute of California.

Bollens, John. 1957. *Special District Governments in the United States*. Berkeley: University of California Press.

BondGraham, Darwin. 2014. The Rise of the New Land Lords. *East Bay Express*. http://www.eastbayexpress.com/oakland/the-rise-of-the-new-land-lords/Content?oid=3836329

Bonilla-Silva, Eduardo. 2003. *Racism without Racists: Color-Blind Racism and the Persistence of Racial inequality in the United States*. Lanham, MD: Rowman & Littlefield.

Booker, Matthew. 2013. *Down by the Bay: San Francisco's History between the Tides*. Berkeley: University of California Press.

Booth, Robert, and Helena Bengtsson. 2016. The London Skyscraper That Is a Stark Symbol of the Housing Crisis. *Guardian*. May 24.

Borjas, George. 2013. Immigration and the American Worker: A Review of the Academic Literature. Washington, DC. Center for Immigration Studies. http://cis.org/immigration-and-the-american-worker-review-academic-literature

Boronstein, Saverin. 2015. Is the Future of Electricity Generation Really Distributed? *Energy Institute Blog*. May 4. Energy Institute at Haas Business School, University of California. https://energyathaas.wordpress.com/2015/05/04/is-the-future-of-electricity-generation-really-distributed/

Botsman, Rachel, and Roo Rogers. 2010. *What's Mine Is Yours: The Rise of Collaborative Consumption*. New York: HarperCollins.

Bowers, Glen. 2015. US Tech Giants Launch Fierce Fightback against Global Tax Avoidance Crackdown. *Guardian*. January 21. http://www.theguardian.com/business/2015/jan/21/us-tech-tax-avoidance-google-amazon-apple

Bowles, Nellie. 2016. "Burning Man for the 1%": The Desert Party for the Tech Elite, with Eric Schmidt in a top hat. *Guardian*. May 2. http://www.theguardian.com/business/2016/may/02/further-future-festival-burning-man-tech-elite-eric-schmidt

Bowles, Nellie. 2017. Push for Gender Equality in Tech? Some Men Say It's Gone Too Far. *New York Times*. September 23. https://nyti.ms/2ykvS87

Bowles, Samuel, and Herbert Gintis. 1976. *Schooling in Capitalist America*. New York: Basic Books.

Boyd, Nan. 2003. *Wide Open Town: A History of Queer San Francisco to 1965*. Berkeley: University of California Press.

Brahinsky, Rachel. 2011. "Hush Puppies," Communalist Politics, and Demolition Governance: The Rise and Fall of the Black Fillmore. In Chris Carlsson, ed., *Ten Years That Shook the City, 1968–78*. San Francisco: City Lights Books. 141–53.

Brahinsky, Rachel. 2012. *The Making and Unmaking of Southeast San Francisco*. Doctoral dissertation. Department of Geography, University of California, Berkeley.

Braithwaite, Tom. 2016a. Silicon Valley Risks a Worrying Debt Bender. *Financial Times*. September 30. https://www.ft.com/content/12dd9c3a-868e-11e6-bcfc-debbef66f80e

Braithwaite, Tom. 2016b. When the Outside World Intrudes on Silicon Valley. *Financial Times*. July 1. https://next.ft.com/content/66f3073e-3f52-11e6-8716-a4a71e8140b0

Brannan, Peter. 2017. When Life on Earth Was Nearly Extinguished. *New York Times*. July 29. https://nyti.ms/2u82yzz

Brash, Julien. 2011. *Bloomberg's New York: Class and Governance in the Luxury City*. Athens: University of Georgia Press.

Brechin, Gray. 1989. St. Francis Wood: A Misty Haven for San Francisco Haves. *San Francisco Focus*. September: 20–25.

Brechin, Gray. 1990. Mr. Levitt of the Sunset. *San Francisco Focus*. June. 23–26.

Brechin, Gray. 1996. Politics and Modernism: The Trial of the Rincon Annex Murals. In Paul Karlstrom, ed., *On the Edge of America: California Modernist Art, 1900–1950*. Berkeley: University of California Press, 69–93.

Brechin, Gray. 1999. *Imperial San Francisco: Urban Power, Earthly Ruin*. Berkeley: University of California Press.

Brenner, Neil. 2013. Theses on Urbanization. *Public Culture* 25 (1): 85–114.

Brenner, Robert. 2002. *The Boom and the Bubble: The US in the World Economy*. London: Verso.

Brenner, Robert. 2006. *The Economics of Global Turbulence: The Advanced Capitalist Economies from Long Boom to Long Downturn, 1945–2005*. London/New York: Verso Press.

Bridle, James. 2017. Something Is Wrong on the Internet. *Medium*. November 6. https://medium.com/@jamesbridle/something-is-wrong-on-the-internet-c39c471271d2

Brilliant, Mark. 2010. *The Color of America Has Changed: How Racial Diversity Shaped Civil Rights Reform in California, 1941–1978*. New York: Oxford University Press.

Brinklow, Adam. 2016. Bay Area Rents Drop, East Coast on the Rise. *Curbed SF*. September 1. https://sf.curbed.com/2016/9/1/12755264/bay-area-rents-drop-september-august-2016

Brinklow, Adam. 2017. Ballot Measure Would Expand Rent Control across California. *Curbed San Francisco*. October 25. https://sf.curbed.com/2017/10/25/16545952/ballot-rent-control-costa-hawkins-california

Bromirski, Peter, and Reinhard Flick. 2008. Storm Surge in the San Francisco Bay/Delta. *Shore and Beach* 76 (3): 29–37.

Bronstein, Zelda. 2017a. Inside the YIMBY Conference. *48 Hills*. July 20. https://48hills.org/2017/07/20/inside-the-yimby-conference/

Bronstein, Zelda. 2017b. When Affordable Housing Meets Free-Market Fantasy. *Dissent*. November 27. https://www.dissentmagazine.org/online_articles/hsieh-moretti-affordable-housing-free-market-fantasy

Bronstein, Zelda. 2017c. Little-Known Yimby-Developer Bills Will Have Big Impact on Local planning. *48 Hills*. December 3. https://48hills.org/2017/12/yimby-developer-bills/

Brook, Jim, and Iain Boal, eds. 1995. *Resisting the Virtual Life: The Culture and Politics of Information*. San Francisco: City Lights Books.

Brown, Eliot. 2016. Too Much Tech? Latest Boom Reshapes San Francisco. *Wall Street Journal*. August 23. http://www.wsj.com/articles/too-much-tech-latest-boom-reshapes-san-francisco-1471964867

Brown, Richard. 1979. *Rockefeller Medicine Men*. Berkeley: University of California Press.

Brown, Wendy. 2015. *Undoing the Demos: Neoliberalism's Stealth Revolution*. Cambridge, MA: MIT Press.

Bruegmann, Robert. 2005. *Sprawl: A Compact History*. Chicago: University of Chicago Press.

Bryce, James. 1889. *The American Commonwealth*. London and New York: Macmillan.

Buchanan, Ben. 2016. *The Cybersecurity Dilemma: Hacking, Trust and Fear between Nations*. Oxford: Oxford University Press.

Burchell, Brendan, David Ladipo, and Frank Wilkinson, eds. 2005. *Job Insecurity and Work Intensification*. London and New York: Routledge.

Burns, Arthur. 1935. Long Cycles in Residential Construction. In *Economic Essays in Honor of Wesley Clair Mitchell*. New York: Columbia University Press, 63–104.

Burns, Elizabeth. 1975. *The Process of Suburban Residential Development: The San Francisco Peninsula, 1860–1970*. Doctoral dissertation. Department of Geography, University of California.

Business Week. 1970. Correcting San Jose's Boomtime Mistakes. *Business Week*. September 19, 74–76.

Butler, Laphonza. 2017. Legislation Would Help Protect Home Health-Care Workers. *Sacramento Bee*. July 13. http://www.sacbee.com/opinion/op-ed/soapbox/article161241528.html

Butler, Sarah, and Gwyn Topham. 2017. Uber Stripped of London Licence Due to Lack of Corporate Responsibility. *Guardian*. September 22. http://www.theguardian.com/technology/2017/sep/22/uber-licence-transport-for-london-tfl

Buzzeli, Michael, and Richard Harris. 2006. Cities as Industrial Districts of Housebuilding. *International Journal of Urban and Regional Research* 30 (4): 894–917.

Byrd, Barbara, and Nari Rhee. 2004. Building Power in the New Economy: The South Bay Labor Council. *Journal of Labor and Society* 8 (December): 131–54.

Caddes, Carolyn. 1986. *Portraits of Success: Impressions of Silicon Valley Pioneers*. Palo Alto: Tioga Publishing Company.

Cadelago, Christopher. 2017. If You Don't Like California's Gas Tax Increase, You're Not Alone. *Sacramento Bee*. June 8. http://www.sacbee.com/news/politics-government/capitol-alert/article155169859.html

Cagle, Matt. 2016. Facebook, Instagram, and Twitter Provided Data Access for a Surveillance Product Marketed to Target Activists of Color. *American Civil Liberties Union Northern California Blog*. October 11. https://www.aclunc.org/blog/facebook-instagram-and-twitter-provided-data-access-surveillance-product-marketed-target

Cahn, Rose, et al. 2012. *Tooby's California Post-conviction Relief for Immigrants*. San Francisco: Law Offices of Norton Tooby.

Callahan, David. 2010. *Fortunes of Change: The Rise of the Liberal Rich and the Remaking of America*. Hoboken, NJ: Wiley.

Calthorpe, Peter, and William Fulton. 2001. *The Regional City: Planning for the End of Sprawl*. Washington, DC: Island Press.

Campbell, Andy. 2016. San Francisco Entrepreneur Suggests Removing "Riffraff" as Homeless Solution. *Huffington Post*. February 18. http://www.huffingtonpost.com/entry/tech-bro-cant-stand-the-riff-raff-homeless-in-san-francisco_us_56c5d579e4b0c3c55053e105

Cándida-Smith, Richard. 1995. *Utopia and Dissent: Art, Poetry and Politics in California*. Berkeley: University of California Press.

Capelle, Elizabeth. 2017. The Housing Crisis Is Not Inevitable. *Jacobin*. February 9. https://www.jacobinmag.com/2017/02/new-york-housing-gentrification-affordability-de-blasio/

Cariaga, Vance. 2016. Apartment REIT Essex Thrives in West Coast Boom Towns. *Investors Business Daily*. January 12. https://www.investors.com/research/the-new-america/technology-sector-drives-essex-property-trust-growth/

Carlsson, Chris, ed. 1990. *Bad Attitude: The Processed World Anthology*. London: Verso.

Carlsson, Chris, ed. 2004. *San Francisco: The Political Edge*. San Francisco: City Lights.

Carlsson, Chris, ed. 2011. *Ten Years That Shook the City: San Francisco, 1968–1978*. San Francisco: City Lights.

Carmiel, Oshrat. 2016. NYC, San Francisco Rental Slowdowns Hit Biggest Apartment REITs. *Bloomberg*. July 26. https://www.bloomberg.com/news/articles/2016-07-26/nyc-san-francisco-rental-slowdowns-hit-biggest-apartment-reits

Carroll, Rory. 2017. Latino laborers Fear Deportation, but Officials Tell California Farmers Not to Fret. *Guardian*. January 20. https://www.theguardian.com/us-news/2017/feb/20/deportation-fears-latino-farm-workers-trump-immigration

Carson, Biz. 2016. Some San Francisco Tech Workers Have to Spend Half Their Salary on Rent If They Want to Live Close to Work. *Business Insider*. June 28. http://www.businessinsider.com/san-francisco-tech-workers-could-spend-half-their-salary-on-rent-2016-6

Carson, Biz. 2017. Silicon Valley's Old Boy Power Structure Is Getting Toppled and the Repercussions Will Be Huge. *Business Insider*. July 1. http://www.businessinsider.com/silicon-valleys-old-boy-power-structure-is-getting-toppled-and-the-repercussions-will-be-huge-2017-7/

Case, Anne, and Angus Deaton. 2017. Mortality and Morbidity in the 21st Century. *Brookings Papers on Economic Activity*. March. https://www.brookings.edu/wp-content/uploads/2017/03/6b_cutler.pdf

Cassidy, John. 2009. *How Markets Fail: The Logic of Economic Calamities*. New York: Farrar, Straus & Giroux.

Cassidy, John. 2012. *DOT.CON: The Real Story of Why the Internet Bubble Burst*. London: Penguin.

Casstevens, Thomas. 1967. *Politics, Housing, and Race Relations: California's Rumford Act and Proposition 14*. Berkeley: Institute of Governmental Studies, University of California.

Castree, Noel, Neil Coe, Kevin Ward, and Mike Samers. 2005. *Spaces of Work: Global Capitalism and Geographies of Labour*. London: Sage Publications.

Causa Justa::Just Cause. 2014. *Development without Displacement: Resisting Gentrification in the Bay Area*. Oakland: Causa Justa::Just Cause.

Chalabi, Mona. 2016. Weapons of Math Destruction: Cathy O'Neil Adds Up the Damage of Algorithms. *Guardian*. October 27. https://www.theguardian.com/books/2016/oct/27/cathy-oneil-weapons-of-math-destruction-algorithms-big-data

Chan, Sucheng. 1991. *Asian Californians*. San Francisco: Boyd and Fraser.

Chavez, Lydia. 1998. *The Color Bind: The Battle to End Affirmative Action*. Berkeley: University of California Press.

Chen, Cathaleen. 2017. California YIMBY's Brian Hanlon on What Real Estate Insiders Can Do to Fight NIMBYism. *The Real Deal*. July 20. https://therealdeal.com/la/2017/07/20/california-yimby-brian-hanlon-on-what-real-estate-insiders-can-do-to-fight-nimbyism/

Chibber, Vivek. 2017. Rescuing Class from the Cultural Turn. *Catalyst* 1 (1): 27–56.

CHPC 2014. How San Francisco County's Housing Market Is Failing to Meet the Needs of Low-Income Families. San Francisco: California Housing Partnership Corporation. https://1po8d91kdoc03rlxhmhtydpr-wpengine.netdna-ssl.com/wp-content/uploads/2015/11/34-HousingNeedSFFINAL.pdf

Cixin, Liu. 2016. The Robot Revolution Will Be the Quietest One. *New York Times*. December 7. https://nyti.ms/2hioD56

Clark, Jim. 2000. *Netscape Time: The Making of the Billion-Dollar Start-Up That Took on Microsoft*. New York: St. Martin's Press.

Clark, William, Eva Andersson, and Bo Malmberg. 2017. What Can We Learn about Ethnic Diversity from the Distribution of Mixed-Race Individuals? *Urban Geography*. http://dx.doi.org/10.1080/02723638.2017.1308183

Clawson, Marion. 1971. *Suburban Land Conversion in the United States: An Economic and Governmental Process*. Baltimore: Johns Hopkins University Press for Resources for the Future.

Cockburn, Cynthia. 1985. *Machinery of Dominance*. London: Pluto Press.

Cohen, Lizbeth. 2007. Buying Out Downtown Revival: The Centrality of Retail to Postwar Urban Renewal. *Annals of the American Academy of Political and Social Science* 611: 82–95.

Cohen, Noam. 2017. Silicon Valley Is Not Your Friend. *New York Times*. October 13. https://www.nytimes.com/interactive/2017/10/13/opinion/sunday/Silicon-Valley-Is-Not-Your-Friend.html

Cohen, Patricia. 2017. Bump in US Incomes Doesn't Erase 50 Years of Pain. *New York Times*. September 15. https://nyti.ms/2jx5Tb5

Cohen, Peter. 1998. *Transformation in an Industrial Landscape: San Francisco's Northeast Mission*. MA thesis. Department of Geography, San Francisco State University.

Cohen, Robert, and Reginald Zelnik, eds. 2002. *The Free Speech Movement: Reflections on Berkeley in the 1960s*. Berkeley: University of California Press.

Conaway, James. 1990. *Napa: The Story of an American Eden*. New York: Avon Books.

Conger, Kate, and Sarah Buhr. 2016. Silicon Valley Shows Its Primary Colors. *TechCrunch*. June 7. https://techcrunch.com/2016/06/07/silicon-valley-shows-its-primary-colors/

Cookson, Jack. 2016. BuildZoom and Urban Economics Lab Index: First Quarter 2016. *BuildZoom Blog*. July 18. https://www.buildzoom.com/blog/index2016q1

Cooper, George. 2008. *The Origin of Financial Crises: Central Banks, Credit Bubbles and the Efficient Market Fallacy*. New York: Vintage Books.

Cooper, Julia. 2014. 3 Surprises on the 100 Largest Bay Area Employers List. *SF Business Times*. July 20. https://www.bizjournals.com/sanfrancisco/blog/2014/07/3-surprises100-largest-bay-area-employers.html

Coopey, Richard, Sean O'Connell, and Dilwyn Porter. 2005. *Mail Order Retailing in Britain: A Business and Social History*. New York: Oxford University Press.

Courtright, Emma. 2017. Berkeley's Progressive Majority Gets Serious about Homelessness Solutions. *East Bay Express*. March 21. https://www.eastbayexpress.com/oakland/berkeleys-new-progressive-majority-gets-serious-about-homelessness-solutions/Content?oid=5906279

Cox, Kevin. 2016. *The Politics of Urban and Regional Development and the American* Exception. Syracuse, NY: Syracuse University Press.

Cox, Wendell. 2016a. 12th Annual Demographia International Housing Affordability Survey: 2016. www.demographia.com/

Cox, Wendell. 2016b. Best and Worst: 2015 International Housing Affordability. January 25. http://www.newgeography.com/content/005154-best-and-worst-2015-international-housing-affordability

Critchlow, Donald. 2013. *When Hollywood Was Right: How Movie Stars, Studio Moguls, and Big Business Remade American Politics*. Cambridge: Cambridge University Press.

Cronon, William. 1991. *Nature's Metropolis: Chicago and the Great West*. Chicago: W.W. Norton.

Cuff, Denis. 2017. Oil Refinery Pollution Rules Rekindle Debate on Climate, Jobs, Protection. *East Bay Times*. March 31. http://www.eastbaytimes.com/2017/03/31/oil-refinery-pollution-rules-rekindles-debate-on-jobs-climate-protection/

da Costa, Pedro. 2017. A Key Recession Indicator Is Getting Nearer to the Danger Zone. *Business Insider*. November 19. http://www.businessinsider.com/yield-curve-flattening-could-derail-fed-interest-rate-hikes-2017-11

Dadich, Scott. 2016. *Wired* Endorses Optimism. *Wired*. August 18. https://www.wired.com/2016/08/wired-endorses-hillary-clinton/

Dahl, Robert. 1961. *Who Governs?* New Haven, CT: Yale University Press.

Dallek, Matthew. 2000. *The Right Moment: Ronald Reagan's First Victory and the Decisive Turning Point in American Politics*. New York: Free Press.

Daniels, Roger, and Spencer Olin Jr., eds. 1972. *Racism in California: A Reader in the History of Oppression*. New York: Macmillan.

Darity, William. 2003. Employment Discrimination, Segregation, and Health. *American Journal of Public Health* 93 (2): 226–31.

David, Gerald. 2009. *Managed by the Markets: How Finance Re-shaped America*. New York: Oxford University Press.

David, Paul. 1975. *Technical Choice, Innovation, and Economic Growth*. New York: Cambridge University Press.

David, Paul, and C. Antonelli, eds. 1997. The economic of path-dependence in industrial organization. *International Journal of Industrial Organization* 6 (6): 643–852.

Davis, Mike. 1986. *Prisoners of the American Dream*. London: Verso.

Davis, Mike. 1990. *City of Quartz: Excavating the Future in Los Angeles*. London: Verso.

Davis, Mike. 1998. *Ecology of Fear: Los Angeles and the Imagination of Disaster*. New York: Metropolitan/Henry Holt.

Davis, Mike. 2002. *Dead Cities, and Other Tales*. New York: New Press.

Davis, Mike. 2013. The Last White Election? *New Left Review* 79: 5–54.

Davis, Mike. 2017a. The White Working Class and the Great God Trump. *Jacobin*. February 7. https://www.jacobinmag.com/2017/02/the-great-god-trump-and-the-white-working-class

Davis, Mike. 2017b. El Diablo in Wine Country. *London Review of Books*. November 2. https://www.lrb.co.uk/v39/n21/mike-davis/el-diablo-in-wine-country

Davis, Mike, Kelly Mayhew, and Jim Miller. 2003. *Under the Perfect Sun: The San Diego Tourists Never See*. New York: New Press.

DeFao, Janine. 2001. At Midterm, Is Jerry Brown Making Grade in Oakland? *San Francisco Chronicle*. January 21. www.sfgate.com/cgi-bin/article.cgi?file=/chronicle/archive/2001/01/21/MN156017.DTL

De la Cruz-Viesca, Melany, Zhenxiang Chen, Paul Ong, Darrick Hamilton, and William Darity. 2016. *The Color of Wealth in Los Angeles*. San Francisco: The Federal Reserve Bank.

DeLara, Juan. 2009. *Remapping Inland Southern California: Global Commodity Distribution, Land Speculation, and Politics in the Inland Empire*. Doctoral dissertation. Department of Geography, University of California, Berkeley.

de la Merced, Michael. 2016. After Belt Tightening, Venture Capitalists See More Promise in 2017. *New York Times*. December 29. http://nyti.ms/2hxcleY

DeLeon, Richard. 1992. *Left Coast City: Progressive Politics in San Francisco, 1975–1991*. Lawrence: University of Kansas Press.

Dell, Michael, and Catherine Fredman. 2006. *Direct from Dell: Strategies That Revolutionized an Industry*. New York: Collins Business.

Demoro, Harre. 1985. *The Key Route: Transbay Commuting by Train and Ferry*. Glendale, CA: Interurban Press.

de Vries, Jan. 1984. *European Urbanization, 1500–1800*. Cambridge, MA: Harvard University Press.

Diaz, John. 2018. The California Resistance Intensifies. *San Francisco Chronicle*. January 28. E2.

Dietz, Miranda. 2012. *Temporary Workers in California Are Twice as Likely as Non-Temps to Live in Poverty: Problems with Temporary and Subcontracted Work in California*. Berkeley: Center for Research on Labor and Employment, University of California.

Dillon, Liam. 2017. Gov. Brown Just Signed 15 Housing Bills. Here's How They're Supposed to Help the Affordability Crisis. *Los Angeles Times*. September 29. http://www.latimes.com/politics/la-pol-ca-housing-legislation-signed-20170929-htmlstory.html

Dimaggio, Anthony. 2017. Election Con 2016: New Evidence Demolishes Myth of Trump's Blue-Collar Populism. *Counterpunch*. June 16. https://www.counterpunch.org/2017/06/16/93450/

Dineen, J.K. 2013. The REITs That Ate San Francisco. *San Francisco Business Times*. November 14. http://www.bizjournals.com/sanfrancisco/blog/2013/11/the-reits-that-ate-san-francisco.html

Dineen, J.K. 2015. Why S.F. Evictions Are on the Rise. *San Francisco Chronicle*. July 27. http://www.sfchronicle.com/politics/article/Why-S-F-evictions-are-on-the-rise-6408950.php

Dineen, J.K. 2016. S.F. Concerns over Governor's Housing Plan. *San Francisco Chronicle*. June 11, A1.

Dineen, J.K. 2016a. Price Gap Spurs S.F. Flight to East Bay: Record Numbers Relocate as Home Costs Go Skyward. *San Francisco Chronicle*. January 17, A1.

Dineen, J.K. 2016b. Building Boom Resumes as Tech Firms Crave Office Space. *San Francisco Chronicle*. August 11. http://www.sfchronicle.com/bayarea/article/Building-boom-resumes-in-S-F-as-tech-firms-crave-9135598.php

Dineen, J.K. 2017. S.F.'s Tech-Space Market Is "On Fire." *San Francisco Chronicle*. December 19. A1.

Dochuck, Darren. 2011. *Bible Belt to Sunbelt: Plain-Folk Religion, Grassroots Politics, and the Rise of Evangelical Conservatism*. New York: W.W. Norton.

Domanick, Joe. 2004. *Cruel Justice: Three Strikes and the Politics of Crime in America's Golden State*. Berkeley: University of California Press.

Domhoff, William. 1978. *Who Really Rules? New Haven and Community Power Revisited*. New Brunswick, NJ: Transaction Books.

Domhoff, William. 1979. *The Powers That Be*. New York: Vintage.

Dougherty, Conor. 2017. Autonomous Trucks Closer than They Appear. *San Francisco Chronicle*. November 14, D1.

Douglass, John. 2000. Earl Warren's New Deal: Economic Transition, Postwar Planning, and Higher Education in California. *Journal of Policy History* 12 (4): 473–512

Douzet, Frédérick. 2012. *The Color of Power: Racial Coalitions and Political Power in Oakland.* Charlottesville: University of Virginia Press.

Downes, Larry, and Paul Nunes. 2014. *Big Bang Disruption: Strategy in the Age of Devastating Innovation.* New York: Penguin.

Downie, Leonard. 1974. *Mortgage on America.* New York: Praeger.

Dreier, Peter. 2016. How the Fight for $15 Won. *American Prospect.* April 4. http://prospect.org/article/how-fight-15-won

Drew, Elizabeth. 1999. *The Corruption of American Politics: What Went Wrong and Why.* Woodstock, NY: Overlook Press.

Duggan, Tara. 2017. Hunger a Problem for 1 in 4 in the City. *San Francisco Chronicle.* May 25. http://www.sfchronicle.com/food/article/Nearly-1-in-4-San-Franciscans-struggle-with-hunger-11171678.php

Duncan, James, and Nancy Duncan. 2004. *Landscapes of Privilege: The Politics of the Aesthetic in an American Suburb.* New York: Routledge.

Duranton, Gilles. 2011. California Dreamin': The Feeble Case for Cluster Policies. *Review of Economic Analysis* 3 (1): 3–45

Duranton, Gilles, Philippe Martin, Thierry Mayer, and Florian Mayneris. 2010. *The Economics of Clusters: Experience from France.* New York: Oxford University Press.

Dyble, Louise. 2009. *Paying the Toll: Local Power, Regional Politics and the Golden Gate Bridge.* Philadelphia: University of Pennsylvania Press.

Early, Steve. 2017. *Refinery Town: Big Oil, Big Money and the Remaking of an American City.* Boston: Beacon Press.

East Bay Times. 2009. Editorial: Ron Dellums Should Not Seek a Second Term as Mayor of Oakland. December 21. http://www.eastbaytimes.com/2009/12/21/editorial-ron-dellums-should-not-seek-a-second-term-as-mayor-of-oakland/

Economist. 2016. Donald Trump's Tech Troubles. *Economist.* November 29.

EDD. 2014. *Regional Economic Analysis Profile: San Francisco Bay Area Economic Market.* February 2015. Sacramento: California Department of Employment and Economic Development, Labor Market Information Division.

EDD. 2015. *Regional Economic Analysis Profile: San Francisco Bay Area Economic Market.* June 2014. Sacramento: California Department of Employment and Economic Development, Labor Market Information Division.

Editors of *Fortune.* 1958. *The Exploding Metropolis.* New York: Doubleday.

Edmiston, Kelly. 2016. Residential Rent Affordability across U.S. Metropolitan Areas. *Federal Reserve Bank of Kansas City Economic Review.* Fourth quarter, 5–27.

Egan, Ted. 2014. Inequality in San Francisco. San Francisco: San Francisco Office of Economic Analysis. June 26.

Ehrenreich, Barbara. 2001. *Nickel and Dimed: On (Not) Getting By in America.* New York: Metropolitan.

Ehrenreich, Barbara. 2005. *Bait and Switch: The (Futile) Pursuit of the American Dream.* New York: Metropolitan Press.

Ehrenreich, Barbara. 2010. *Bright-Sided: How Positive Thinking Is Undermining America.* New York? Picador.

Ehrenreich, Barbara, and John Ehrenreich. 1977. The Professional-Managerial Class. *Radical America* 11 (2): 7–31.

Eichengreen, Barry. 2015. *Hall of Mirrors: The Great Depression, the Great Recession, and the Uses and Misuses of History.* New York: Oxford University Press.

Elder-Vass, Dave. 2016. *Profit and Gift in the Digital Economy.* Cambridge: Cambridge University Press.

Elinson, Zusha. 2010. As Mayor, Brown Remade Oakland's Downtown and Himself. *New York Times.* September 2. http://www.nytimes.com/2010/09/03/us/politics/03bcbrown.html?_r=0

Elkin, Stephen. 1987. *City and Regime in the American Republic*. Chicago: University of Chicago Press.

Elkind, Sarah. 1998. *Bay Cities and Water Politics: The Battle for Resources in Boston and Oakland*. Lawrence: University of Kansas Press.

Elliot, Larry. 2016. Austerity Policies Do More Harm than Good, IMF Study Concludes. *Guardian*. May 27. https://www.theguardian.com/business/2016/may/27/austerity-policies-do-more-harm-than-good-imf-study-concludes

Elliot, Larry. 2017. The World's Eight Richest People Have Same Wealth as Poorest 90%. *Guardian*. January 16. https://www.theguardian.com/global-development/2017/jan/16/worlds-eight-richest-people-have-same-wealth-as-poorest-50

Elliot, Larry. 2018. Donald Trump Woos Business but Attacks Media at Davos. *Guardian*. January 26. https://www.theguardian.com/business/2018/jan/26/donald-trump-booed-in-davos-as-he-woos-businesses

Ethington, Philip. 1994. *The Public City: The Political Construction of Urban Life in San Francisco, 1850–1900*. New York: Cambridge University Press.

Ethington, Philip, and David Levitus. 2009. Placing American Political Development: Cities, Regions and Regimes, 1789–2008. In Richardson Dilworth, ed., *The City in American Political Development*. New York: Routledge, 154–76.

Ettlinger, Nancy. 2014. The Openness Paradigm. *New Left Review* 89, 89–100.

Fagan, Kevin. 2017a. Nonprofit's Big Pledge for Chronic Homeless. *San Francisco Chronicle*. May 7. http://www.sfchronicle.com/bayarea/article/Nonprofit-pledges-100-million-to-aid-SF-s-11126953.php

Fagan, Kevin. 2017b. Tally Shows Successes and Failures of Outreach. *San Francisco Chronicle*. June 18.

Faroohar, Rana. 2017. The Power of the Tech Titans. *Financial Times*. https://www.ft.com/content/b2019edc-9174-11e7-a9e6-11d2foebb7f0

Federici, Silvia. 2012. *Revolution at Point Zero: Housework, Reproduction, and Feminist Struggle*. Oakland: PM Press.

Fellmeth, Robert. 1973. *The Politics of Land*. New York: Grossman.

FEMA. 2010. *Home Builders Guide to Coastal Construction: Coastal Building Success and Failure*. Technical Fact Sheet no. 1.1. Washington, DC: Federal Emergency Management Administration. https://www.fema.gov/media-library/assets/documents/6131

Fenske, Gail. 2008. *The Skyscraper and the City: The Woolworth Building and the Making of Modern New York*. Chicago: University of Chicago Press.

Ferenstein, Greg. 2015. The Age of Optimists: A Quantitative Glimpse of How Silicon Valley Will Transform Political Power and Everyday Life. https://medium.com/the-ferenstein-wire/silicon-valley-s-political-endgame-summarized-1f395785f3c1

Ferenstein, Greg. 2017. Tech CEOs Know Inequality Is Bad. So Why Does Silicon Valley Want tax cuts? *Washington Post*. November 3. https://www.washingtonpost.com/news/posteverything/wp/2017/11/03/silicon-valley-ceos-dont-want-tax-cuts-their-firms-shouldnt-lobby-for-them/?utm_term=.6cbf78a02775

Fern, Alexia, Fernandez Campbell, and Reena Flores. 2014. How Silicon Valley Created America's Largest Homeless Camp. *The Atlantic*. November 25. https://www.theatlantic.com%2Fpolitics%2Farchive%2F2014%2F11%2Fhow-silicon-valley-created-americas-largest-homeless-camp%

Ferris, David. 2017. Rooftop Solar in Tumult as Sungevity Declares Bankruptcy. *E&E News*. March 15. https://www.eenews.net/stories/1060051482

Fields, Gary. 2004. *Territories of Profit: Communications, Capitalist Development and the Innovative Enterprises of G.F. Swift and Dell Computer*. Stanford, CA: Stanford University Press.

Fimrite, Peter. 2016. One-Third Ponder Leaving the Bay Area. *San Francisco Chronicle*. May 2, C1.

Fimrite, Peter. 2017. Housing Shortage Presents Obstacles. State's costs could reach $26 billion. September 28. *San Francisco Chronicle.* http://www.sfgate.com/news/article/Severe-housing-shortage-for-Bay-Area-state-12235869.php

Fimrite, Peter. 2017. Oakland Targeted in Bid to Cut Trash Flow into SF Bay. *San Francisco Chronicle.* May 30. http://www.sfchronicle.com/science/article/Oakland-targeted-in-bid-to-cut-trash-flow-into-SF-11181110.php

Finley, Klint. 2017. Google's Big EU Fine Isn't Just about the Money. *Wired.* June 27. https://www.wired.com/story/google-big-eu-fine/

Findlay, John. 1992. Stanford Industrial Park: Downtown for Silicon Valley. In *Magic Lands: Western Cityscapes and American Culture after 1940.* Berkeley: University of California Press, 117–59.

Firth, Andrea. 2016. Living Small. *Oakland Magazine.* November 8. http://www.oaklandmagazine.com/November-2016/Living-Small/

Fleming, Sam, and Lauren Leatherby. 2017. Millions Mired in Poverty as US Upturn Passes Them By. *Financial Times.* September 25. https://www.ft.com/content/82f5f0e8-9fcf-11e7-8cd4-932067fbf946

Fleming, Sam. 2018. US Economy: The Growth Puzzle. *Financial Times.* February 19. https://www.ft.com/content/76057bd8-1342-11e8-940e-08320fc2a277

Fletcher, Bill, Jr. 2012. *"They're Bankrupting Us!" And 20 Other Myths about Unions.* Boston: Beacon Press.

Florida, Richard. 2002. *The Rise of the Creative Class: And How Its Transforming Work, Leisure, Community and Everyday Life.* New York: Basic Books.

Florida, Richard. 2005. *Cities and the Creative Class.* New York: Routledge.

Floum, Jessica. 2016a. Bay Area Economy Outpaces U.S., China. *San Francisco Chronicle.* September 26. http://www.sfchronicle.com/business/article/Bay-Area-economy-outpaces-U-S-China-9289809.php

Floum, Jessica. 2016b. Horn of Not-Exactly Plenty: Financing Isn't So Magical If Companies Aren't Profitable. *San Francisco Chronicle.* April 24, D1.

Flowers, Benjamin. 2009. *Skyscraper: The Politics and Power of Building New York City in the Twentieth Century.* Philadelphia: University of Pennsylvania Press.

Fogelson, Robert. 2001. *Downtown: Its Rise and Fall, 1880–1950.* New Haven, CT: Yale University Press.

Fogelson, Robert. 2005. *Bourgeois Nightmares: Suburbia, 1870–1930.* New Haven, CT: Yale University Press.

Foley, Elise. 2014. Immigration Activists Escalate Deportation Fight: "Not One More." *Huffington Post.* April 4. http://www.huffingtonpost.com/2014/04/04/immigration-activists-deportation_n_5093096

Ford, John. 2014. Oral history. *Stanford Historical Society Oral History Program.* Stanford Digital Repository. http://purl.stanford.edu/bk799jn0687

Ford, Larry. 2003. *America's New Downtowns: Reinvention or Revitalization?* Baltimore: Johns Hopkins University Press.

Ford, Martin. 2016. *Rise of the Robots: Technology and the Threat of a Jobless Future.* New York: Basic Books.

Forman, Chris, Avi Goldfarb, and Shane Greenstein. 2016. Agglomeration of Innovation in the Bay Area: Not Just ICT. *American Economic Review* 106 (5): 146–51. Summarized in Richard Florida, San Francisco's Increasing Dominance over U.S. Innovation. *City Lab.* May 25.

Francassa, Dominque. 2017. SoFi's Funding Round: Half a Billion. *San Francisco Chronicle.* February 25. http://www.sfchronicle.com/business/networth/article/S-F-s-SoFi-lands-another-1-billion-in-venture-6541786.php

Frank, Thomas. 2004. *What's the Matter with Kansas? How Conservatives Won the Heart of America.* New York: Metropolitan Books.

Frank, Thomas. 2016. *Listen, Liberal: Or, What Ever Happened to the Party of the People?* New York: Metropolitan Books/Henry Holt.

Fraser, Nancy. 2014. Behind Marx's Hidden Abode. *New Left Review* 86: 55-74.

Fraser, Steven, and Gary Gerstle, eds. 1989. *The Rise and Fall of the New Deal Order.* Princeton, NJ: Princeton University Press.

Fredrickson, Caroline. 2015. *Under the Bus: How Working Women Are Being Run Over.* New York: New Press.

Freeman, Richard, and James Medoff. 1984. *What Do Unions Do?* New York: Basic Books.

Freiberger, Paul, and Michael Swaine. 1984. *Fire in the Valley: The Making of the Personal Computer.* Berkeley: Osborne/McGraw-Hill.

Freund, David. 2007. *Colored Property: State Policy and White Racial Politics in Suburban America.* Chicago: University of Chicago Press.

Frieden, Bernard. 1979. *The Environmental Protection Hustle.* Cambridge, MA: MIT Press.

Frieden, Bernard, and Lynne Sagalyn. 1989. *Downtown, Inc., How America Rebuilds Cities.* Cambridge, MA: MIT Press.

Friedersdorf, Conor. 2015. San Francisco's Self-Defeating Housing Activists. *Atlantic.* May 29.

Fry, Richard, and Rakesh Kochhar. 2016. America's Shrinking Middle Class: A Close Look at Changes within Metropolitan Areas. Washington, DC: Pew Research Center. May 11. http://www.pewsocialtrends.org/2016/05/11/americas-shrinking-middle-class-a-close-look-at-changeswithin-metropolitan-areas/

Fuller, Thomas. 2016. The Loneliness of Being Black in San Francisco. *New York Times.* July 20. https://www.nytimes.com/2016/07/21/us/black-exodus-from-san-francisco.html

Gaines, Steven. 2005. *The Sky's the Limit: Passion and Property in Manhattan.* New York: Little, Brown.

Galbraith, James, and Travis Hale 2008. State Income Inequality and Presidential Election Turnout and Outcomes. *Social Science Quarterly* 89 (4): 887–901.

Gammon, Robert. 2011. Jean Quan's Big Mistake. *East Bay Express.* October 26. http://www.eastbayexpress.com/SevenDays/archives/2011/10/26/jean-quans-big-mistake

García Martínez, Antonio. 2016. *Chaos Monkeys: Obscene Fortune and Random Failure in Silicon Valley.* New York: HarperCollins.

Garofoli, Joe. 2016. The Resistance to Trump Is Rooted in the Bay Area. *San Francisco Chronicle.* December 9. http://www.sfchronicle.com/politics/article/The-Resistance-to-Trump-is-rooted-in-the-Bay-Area-10786957.php

Garofoli, Joe, and Kimberly Veklerov. 2017. Homeless Camps Becoming Entrenched in Oakland. *San Francisco Chronicle.* June 28. http://www.sfchronicle.com/bayarea/article/Homeless-camps-becoming-entrenched-in-Oakland-11240395.php

Garone, Philip. 2011. *The Rise and Fall of the Wetlands of California's Great Central Valley.* Berkeley: University of California Press.

Garrahan, Matthew. 2016. Advertising: Facebook and Google Build a Duopoly. *Financial Times.* June 23. https://next.ft.com/content/6c6b74a4-3920-11e6-9a05-82a9b15a8ee7

Garreau, Joel. 1991. *Edge City: Life on the New Frontier.* New York: Doubleday.

Gee, Alastair. 2017. Build a Wall: Emergency Housing Plan for Homeless in Silicon Valley Met with Fear. *Guardian.* August 30. https://www.theguardian.com/us-news/2017/aug/30/san-jose-silicon-valley-tiny-home-homeless-backlash

Geismer, Lily. 2015. *Don't Blame Us: Suburban Liberals and the Transformation of the Democratic Party.* Princeton, NJ: Princeton University Press.

Gelfand, Mark. 1975. *A Nation of Cities: The Federal Government and Urban America, 1933–1975.* New York: Oxford University Press.

Gelman, Andrew. 2008. *Red State, Blue State, Rich State, Poor State.* Revised edition. Princeton NJ: Princeton University Press.

Gereffi, Gary, and Miguel Korzeniewicz, eds. 1994. *Commodity Chains and Global Capitalism.* Westport, CT: Praeger.

Giddens, Anthony. 1980. *The Class Structure of the Advanced Societies*. London: Hutchinson, 2nd ed.

Giddens, Anthony, and Gavin Mackenzie, eds. 1982. *Social Class and the Division of Labour*. Cambridge: Cambridge University Press.

Giles, Chris. 2016. Global Economic Growth "Sliding Back into the Morass." *Financial Times*. October 2. https://www.ft.com/content/cd07b4fc-86f6-11e6-ad89-ba2f348161fb

Gilfoyle, Timothy. 1992. *City of Eros: New York City, Prostitution, and the Commercialization of Sex, 1820–1920*. New York: W.W. Norton.

Gillette, Howard. 2005. *Camden after the Fall: Decline and Renewal in a Post-industrial City*. Philadelphia: University of Pennsylvania Press.

Gilmore, Ruth Wilson. 2007. *Golden Gulag: Prisons, Surplus, Crisis and Opposition in Globalizing California*. Berkeley: University of California Press.

Glaeser, Edward. 2005. Reinventing Boston: 1630–2003. *Journal of Economic Geography* 5 (2): 119–53.

Glaeser, Edward. 2010. *The Triumph of the City*. Harmondsworth: Penguin.

Glass, Fred. 2016. *From Mission to Microchip: A History of the California Labor Movement*. Berkeley: University of California Press.

Gleick, Peter, and E. Maurer. 1990. Assessing the Costs of Adapting to Sea-Level Rise: A Case Study of San Francisco Bay. Oakland: Pacific Institute. http://pacinst.org/publication/costs-sea-level-rise-adaptation/

Godfrey, Brian. 1988. *Neighborhoods in Transition: The Making of San Francisco's Ethnic and Nonconformist Communities*. Berkeley: University of California Press.

Godfrey, Brian. 1997. Urban Development and Redevelopment in San Francisco. *Geographical Review* 87 (3): 309–33.

Goel, Vindu. 2016. Philanthropy in Silicon Valley: Big Bets on Big Ideas. *New York Times*. November 4. https://www.nytimes.com/2016/11/06/giving/philanthropy-in-silicon-valley-big-bets-on-big-ideas.html?_r=0

Goldberg, Lenny. 2010. Proposition 13: Tarnish on the Golden Dream. In Jeffrey Lustig, ed., *Remaking California: Reclaiming the Public Good*. Berkeley: Heyday, 41–59.

Goldberg, Suzanne. 2010. Arnold Schwarzenegger Flexes Muscles to Defend Climate Change Law. *Guardian*. October 28. http://www.theguardian.com/world/2010/oct/28/arnold-schwarzenegger-proposition23-oil-climate-change

Goldin, Daniel. 2006. *The Price of Admission: How America's Ruling Class Buys Its Way into Colleges—And Who Gets Left Outside the Gates*. New York: Random House.

Goldstein, Amy. 2017. *Janesville: An American Story*. New York: Simon & Schuster.

Golinger, Jon. 2018. *Saving San Francisco's Heart: How to Win Elections, Reclaim Our City, and Keep SF a Special Place*. San Francisco: Bay Guardian Books.

Gonzales, George. 2009. *Urban Sprawl, Global Warming, and the Empire of Capital*. Albany, NY: SUNY Press.

Gonzalez, Arturo. 2007. Day Labor in the Golden State. *California Economic Policy* 3 (3): 1–21.

Goode, Erica. 2015. Troubled Delta System Is California's Water Battleground. *New York Times*. June 24. https://www.nytimes.com/2015/06/25/science/troubled-delta-system-is-californias-water-battleground.html?_r=0

Goodell, Jeff. 2017. *The Water Will Come: Rising Seas, Sinking Cities, and the Remaking of the Civilized World*. Boston: Little, Brown.

Gordon, Larry. 2001. Father Figure. *Stanford Magazine*. March/April 2001. https://alumni.stanford.edu/get/page/magazine/article/?article_id=39478

Gordon, Margaret. 1954. *Employment Expansion and Population Growth*. Berkeley: University of California Press.

Gordon, Robert. 2016. *The Rise and Fall of American Growth: The Standard of Living Since the Civil War*. Princeton, NJ: Princeton University Press.

Gotham, Kevin. 2000a. Urban Space, Restrictive Covenants and the Origins of Racial Residential Segregation in a US City, 1900–50. *International Journal of Urban & Regional Research* 24 (3): 616–33.

Gotham, Kevin. 2000b. Racialization and the State: The Housing Act of 1934 and the creation of the Federal Housing Administration. *Sociological Perspectives* 43 (2): 291–317.

Gottdiener, Mark. 1977. *Planned Sprawl: Private and Public Interests in Suburbia*. Beverly Hills: Sage Publications.

Gottlieb, Robert. 1988. *A Life of Its Own: The Politics and Power of Water*. New York: Harcourt, Brace, Jovanovich.

Gottmann, Jean. 1961. *Megalopolis: The Urbanized Northeastern Seaboard of the United States*. New York: Twentieth Century Fund.

Gowan, Peter. 2009. Crisis in the Heartland. *New Left Review* 55: 1–33.

Graham, Stephen, ed. 2010. *Disrupted Cities: When Infrastructure Fails*. New York: Routledge.

Granovetter, Mark. 2017. *Economy and Society: Framework and Principles*. Cambridge, MA: Belknap Press of Harvard University.

Grantham, Theodore, and Joshua Viers. 2014. 100 Years of California's Water Rights System: Patterns, Trends and Uncertainty. *Environmental Research Letters* 9 (8): 1–10. http://iopscience.iop.org/article/10.1088/1748-9326/9/8/084012

Green, Emily. 2016a. Gig Work Hasn't Led to Shift in Workforce. *San Francisco Chronicle*. July 5, C1.

Green, Emily. 2016b. Top Local Donor Paul Graham: Little-Known Name with Firm Ideas. *San Francisco Chronicle*. November 2. http://www.sfchronicle.com/politics/article/Top-local-donor-Paul-Graham-little-known-name-10534378.php

Green, Emily, Joaquin Palomino, and Jessica Fluom. 2016. Elite Few Wield Big Donations in S.F. election. *San Francisco Chronicle*. November 3. http://www.sfchronicle.com/bayarea/article/Big-bucks-donors-wield-their-influence-on-SF-10535247.php

Green, Joshua. 2008. The Amazing Money Machine: How Silicon Valley Made Barack Obama This Year's Hottest Start-Up. *Atlantic*. June. www.theatlantic.com/magazine/archive/2008/06/the-amazing-money-machine/306809/.

Greenbelt Alliance. 2017. *At Risk: The Bay Area Greenbelt*. San Francisco: Greenbelt Alliance.

Greenberg, Miriam. 2008. *Branding New York: How a City in Crisis Was Sold to the World*. New York: Routledge.

Greenfield, Adam. 2017. *Radical Technologies: The Design of Everyday Life*. London: Verso.

Gregory, Jim. 2005. *The Southern Diaspora: How the Great Migrations of White and Black Southerners Transformed America*. Chapel Hill: University of North Carolina Press.

Grenadier, Steven. 1995. The Persistence of Real Estate Cycles. *Journal of Real Estate Finance and Economics* 10: 95–119.

Griggs, Gary, Joseph Arvai, Dan Cayan, Robert DeConto, Jenn Fox, Helen Fricker, Robert Kopp, Claudia Tebaldi, and Liz Whiteman (California Ocean Protection Council Science Advisory Team Working Group). 2017. *Rising Seas in California: An Update on Sea-Level Rise Science*. Oakland: California Ocean Science Trust and Ocean Protection Council.

Groth, Paul. 1994. *Living Downtown: The History of Residential Hotels in the United States*. Berkeley: University of California Press.

Groth, Paul. 2004. Workers' Cottage and Minimal Bungalow Districts in Oakland and Berkeley, CA, 1870–1945. *Urban Morphology* 8 (1): 13–25.

Guardian. 2017. Ice and Fire: Large Blaze Burns in Greenland for Two Weeks. August 19. https://www.theguardian.com/world/2017/aug/20/ice-and-fire-large-blaze-burns-in-greenland-for-two-weeks.

Gudell, Svenja. 2016. The U.S. Housing Affordability Crisis: How a Rent and Low-Income Problem Is Becoming Everyone's Problem. Zillow Research Report. April 11. http://www.zillow.com/research/housing-affordability-q4-2015-12111/

Guedim, Zayan. 2017. Top 9 US Cities Creating Most Tech Jobs. *Edgy Labs*. May 9. https://edgylabs.com/top-9-u-s-cities-most-tech-jobs/

Guinier, Lani. 2015. *The Tyranny of the Meritocracy: Democratizing Higher Education in America*. Boston: Beacon Press.

Guthey, Greig. 2004. *Terroir and the Politics of the Agro-Industry in California's North Coast Wine District*. Doctoral dissertation. Department of Geography. University of California, Berkeley.

Gutierrez, Melody. 2016. Measures Highlight Housing Anxieties. *San Francisco Chronicle*. October 30. http://www.sfchronicle.com/politics/article/Housing-turmoil-reflected-in-ballot-measures-10423852.php

Hafner, Katie, and Matthew Lyon. 2006. *Where Wizards Stay Up Late: The Origins of the Internet*. New York: Simon & Schuster.

Hagemann, Ryan. 2016. Silicon Valley Is Eating the Democratic Party. *Niskanen Center Blog Panopticontra*. September 26. https://niskanencenter.org/blog/silicon-valley-eating-democratic-party/

Hall, Peter. 1962. *The Industries of London since 1861*. London: Hutchinson.

Hall, Stuart, and Phil Scraton, 1981. Law, Class and Control. In Mike Fitzgerald, Gregor McLennan, and Jennie Pawson, eds., *Crime and Society: Readings in History and Theory*. London: Routledge & Kegan Paul, 460–97.

Halper, Jon., ed. 1991. *Gary Snyder: Dimensions of a Life*. San Francisco: Sierra Club Books.

Hamalian, Linda. 1991. *A Life of Kenneth Rexroth*. New York: W.W. Norton.

Hamilton, Matt. 2016. Southern California Water District Completes $175-Million Purchase of Delta Islands. *Los Angeles Times*. July 18. http://www.latimes.com/local/lanow/la-me-ln-delta-island-purchase-finalized-mwd-20160718-snap-story.html

Hanchett, Thomas. 2000. Financing Suburbia: Prudential Insurance and the Post–World War II Transformation of the American City. *Journal of Urban History* 26 (3): 312–28.

Hannigan, John. 1998. *Fantasy City: Pleasure and Profit in the Postmodern Metropolis*. London: Routledge.

Hansen, Louis. 2017a. Solar Industry Continues to Be Hot. *Bay Area News Group*. February 7. http://www.mercurynews.com/2017/02/07/solar-industry-continues-to-be-hot/

Hansen, Louis. 2017b. Tesla Slapped with Labor Complaint by UAW. *San Jose Mercury*. October 26. https://www.mercurynews.com/2017/10/26/tesla-slapped-with-labor-complaint-by-uaw/

Hansen, Louis. 2017c. Google-Backed Massive Housing and Office Plan Wins Approval. *San Jose Mercury*. December 12. https://www.mercurynews.com/2017/12/12/googles-massive-housing-and-office-plan-poised-for-approval/

Hardaway, Francine. 2011. What Causes Silicon Valley Envy, and How to Fix It. *Fast Company*. December 19. http://www.fastcompany.com/1802025/what-causes-silicon-valley-envy-and-how-fix-it

Hardisty, Jean. 1999. *Mobilizing Resentment: Conservative Resurgence from the John Birch Society to the Promise Keepers*. Boston: Beacon Press.

Haring, Norbert, and Niall Douglas. 2012. *Economists and the Powerful*. London: Anthem Press.

Harris, Andrew. 2015. Vertical Urbanism: Opening Up Geographies of the Three-Dimensional City. *Progress in Human Geography* 39 (5): 601–20.

Harris, John. 2018. Take from the Insiders: Silicon Valley Is Eating Your Soul. *Guardian*. January 1. https://www.theguardian.com/commentisfree/2018/jan/01/silicon-valley-eating-soul-google-facebook-tech

Harris, Richard. 1996. Chicago's Other Suburbs. *Geographical Review* 84: 394–410.

Harris, Richard, and Nadine Dostrovsky. 2008. Style for the *Zeitgeist*. The Stealthy Revival of Historicist Housing since the Late 1960s. *Professional Geographer* 60 (3): 314–32.

Harrison, Bennett. 1974. *Urban Economic Development: Suburbanization, Minority Opportunity and the Condition of the Central City*. Washington, DC: Urban Institute.

Hartman, Chester. 1984. *The Transformation of San Francisco*. Totowa, NJ: Rowman and Allenheld.

Hartman, Chester. 2002. *City for Sale: The Transformation of San Francisco*. Berkeley: University of California Press.

Hartmann, Heidi. 1979. The Unhappy Marriage of Marxism and Feminism. *Capital and Class*. 3: 45–72.

Harvey, David. 1973. *Social Justice and the City*. Baltimore: Johns Hopkins University Press.

Harvey, David. 1982. *The Limits to Capital*. Oxford: Basil Blackwell.

Harvey, David. 1985. *The Urbanization of Capital*. Baltimore: Johns Hopkins University Press.

Harvey, David. 2003. *Paris: Capital of Modernity*. London: Routledge.

Harvey, David. 2005. *A Brief History of Neo-liberalism*. New York: Oxford University Press.

Harvey, David. 2012. *Rebel Cities: From the Right to the City to the Urban Revolution*. London: Verso Press.

Harvey, David. 2017. *Marx, Capital and the Madness of Economic Reason*. New York: Oxford.

Hatch, Nathan, ed. 1988. *The Professions in America*. South Bend, IN: University of Notre Dame Press.

Hathaway, Ian. 2012. *Technology Works: High-Tech Employment and Wages in the United States*. San Francisco: Bay Area Council Economic Institute by Engine Advocacy.

Hayden, Dolores. 2003. *Building Suburbia: Greenfields and Urban Growth, 1820–2000*. New York: Pantheon.

Hayden, Dolores. 2004. *A Field Guide to Sprawl*. New York: W.W. Norton.

Hayes, Denis. 1989. *Beyond the Silicon Curtain: The Seductions of Work in a Lonely Era*. Boston: South End Press.

Hayes, Joseph, and Laura Hill. 2017. *Undocumented Immigrants in California*. San Francisco: Public Policy Institute of California.

Hayward, Diane. 2017. *Hunger in Silicon Valley More Widespread and Diverse than Previously Thought*. Second Harvest Food Bank report. December 12. http://www.shfb.org/docs/news/release/20171212_FundingGap.pdf

Heberger, Matthew, Heather Cooley, Pablo Herrera, Peter Gleick, and Eli Moore. 2009. *The Impacts of Sea-Level Rise on the California Coast*. Berkeley: California Climate Change Center.

Hern, Alex. 2017. Thirty Countries Use "Armies of Opinion Shapers" to Manipulate Democracy—Report. *Guardian*. November 14. https://www.theguardian.com/technology/2017/nov/14/social-media-influence-election-countries-armies-of-opinion-shapers-manipulate-democracy-fake-news

High, Steven. 2003. *Industrial Sunset: The Making of North America's Rust Belt, 1969–1984*. Toronto: University of Toronto Press.

High, Steven, and David Lewis. 2006. *Corporate Wasteland: The Landscape and Memory of Deindustrialization*. Ithaca, NY: IRL Press.

Hildebrand, George. 1981. *Borax Pioneer: Francis Marion Smith*. San Diego: Howell-North Books.

Hillis, Ken, Michael Petit, and Kylie Jarrett. 2012. *Google and the Culture of Search*. New York: Routledge.

Hinckle, Elizabeth, and Howard Greenwich. 2003. *Behind the Boomtown: Growth and Redevelopment in Emeryville*. California Partnership for Working Families, Oakland.

Hirt, Sonia. 2014. *Zoned in the USA: The Origins and Implications of American Land-Use Regulation*. Ithaca, NY: Cornell University Press.

Hise, Greg. 1997. *Magnetic Los Angeles: Planning the Twentieth-Century Metropolis*. Baltimore: Johns Hopkins University Press.

Hoerr, John. 1988. *And the Wolf Finally Came: The Decline and Fall of the American Steel Industry*. Pittsburgh: University of Pittsburgh Press.

Holston, James. 2008. *Insurgent Citizenship: Disjunctions of Democracy and Citizenship in Brazil*. Princeton, NJ: Princeton University Press.

Horiuchi, Lynne. 2007. Object Lessons in Home Building: Racialized Real Estate Marketing in San Francisco. *Landscape Journal* 26 (1): 61–82.

Horiuchi, Lynne, and Tanu Sankalia, eds. 2017. *Urban Reinventions: San Francisco's Treasure Island*. University of Hawaii Press.

Hornstein, Jeffrey. 2005. *A Nation of Realtors: A Cultural History of the Twentieth-Century American Middle Class*. Durham, NC: Duke University Press.

HoSang, Daniel. 2010. *Racial Propositions: Ballot Initiatives and the Making of Postwar California*. Berkeley: University of California Press.

Hounshell, David. 1984. *From the American System to Mass Production, 1800–1932*. Baltimore: Johns Hopkins University Press.

Howell, Ocean. 2015. *Making the Mission: Planning and Ethnicity in San Francisco*. Chicago: University of Chicago Press.

Hoyt, Homer. 1933. *One Hundred Years of Land Values in Chicago*. Chicago: University of Chicago Press.

Hsieh, Chang-Tai, and Enrico Moretti. 2017. How Local Housing Regulations Smother the U.S. Economy. *New York Times*. September 6. https://nyti.ms/2xNplDj

Hsu, Tiffany. 2014. 1 in 6 California Construction Workers Labors in Shadows. *Los Angeles Times*. August 31. http://www.latimes.com/business/la-fi-california-construction-underground-economy-20140829-story.html

Hudson, Michael. 2015. *Killing the Host: How Financial Parasites and Debt Bondage Destroy the Global Economy*. Petrolia, CA: Counterpunch Books.

Hundley, Norris. 1992. *The Great Thirst: Californians and Water, 1770s–1990s*. Berkeley: University of California Press.

Hynding, Alan. 1981. *From Frontier to Suburb: The Story of the San Mateo Peninsula*. Belmont: Star Books.

Ingram, Lynn, and Frances Malamud-Roam. 2013. *The West without Water: What Past Floods, Droughts, and Other Climatic Clues Tell Us about Tomorrow*. Berkeley: University of California Press.

Irons, John. 2009. Economic Scarring: The Long-Term Impacts of the Recession. EPI Briefing Paper no. 243. Washington, DC: Economic Policy Institute.

Isaacson, Walter. 2011. *Steve Jobs*. New York: Simon & Schuster.

Isaacson, Walter. 2015. *The Innovators: How a Group of Hackers, Geniuses, and Geeks Created the Digital Revolution*. New York: Simon & Schuster.

Issel, William. 1989. Business Power and Political Culture in San Francisco, 1900–1940. *Journal of Urban History* 16 (1): 52–77.

Issel, William. 2000. New Deal and Wartime Origins of San Francisco's Postwar Political Culture: The Case of Growth Politics and Policy. In Roger Lotchin, ed., *The Way We Really Were: The Golden State in the Second Great War*. Urbana: University of Illinois Press, 68–92.

Issel, William, and Robert Cherny. 1986. *San Francisco, 1865–1932: Politics, Power, and Urban Development*. Berkeley: University of California Press.

Jackson, Kenneth. 1985. *The Crabgrass Frontier: The Suburbanization of the United States*. New York: Oxford University Press.

Jacobs, John. 1995. *A Rage for Justice: The Passion and Politics of Phillip Burton*. Berkeley: University of California Press.

Jacobs, Ken, Ian Perry, and Jenifer MacGillvary. 2015. *The High Public Cost of Low Wages*. Berkeley: Center for Research on Labor and Employment, University of California.

Jaruzelski, Barry. 2014. Why Silicon Valley's Success Is So Hard to Replicate. *Scientific American*. March 14. http://www.scientificamerican.com/article/why-silicon-valleys-success-is-so-hard-to-replicate/

Johnson, Lizzie. 2016. S.F. Fund Antidote to Brutal Rent Hikes. *San Francisco Chronicle*. April 3, C1.

Johnson, Lizzie. 2017. S.F., Other U.S. Cities Will Post Purged EPA Data. *San Francisco Chronicle*. June 11. https://www.pressreader.com/usa/san-francisco-chronicle/20170611/282089161749915

Johnson, Marilyn. 1993. *A Second Gold Rush: Oakland and the East Bay in World War II.* Berkeley: University of California Press.

Johnson, Miles. 2018. US Asset Investment Surge Raises Dollar Worries. *Financial Times.* January 2. https://www.ft.com/content/2f9bf9d2-efd0-11e7-b220-857e26d1aca4

Johnson, Steven. 2012. *Future Perfect: The Case for Progress in a Networked Age.* New York: Riverhead Books (Penguin).

Johnson, Sydney. 2016. Berkeley Progressives Say Mayor Bates' Housing Plan Is a "Blueprint for Gentrification." *East Bay Express.* April 4. http://www.eastbayexpress.com/SevenDays/archives/2016/04/04/berkeley-progressives-say-mayor-bates-housing-plan-is-a-blueprint-for-gentrification.

Johnston, David. 2016. *Free Lunch: How the Wealthiest Americans Enrich Themselves at Government Expense (and Stick You with the Bill).* New York: Portfolio.

Jonassen, Wendi, John Osborn, and Alex Park. 2012. Death of Oakland's Retail Plan. *East Bay Express.* February 15. https://www.eastbayexpress.com/oakland/death-of-oaklands-retail-plan/Content?oid=3125642

Jones, Owen. 2016. *Chavs: The Demonization of the Working Class.* London: Verso.

Kahn, Ava, and Marc Dollinger, eds. 2003. *California Jews.* Boston: University Press of New England.

Kalleberg, A.L. 2009. Precarious Work, Insecure Workers: Employment Relations in Transition. *American Sociological Review* 74 (1):1–22.

Kallerman, Patrick, and Micah Weinberg. 2017. *Bay Area Balance: Preserving Open Space, Addressing Housing Affordability.* Joint report for the Bay Area Council, Greenbelt Alliance and Bay Area Open Space Council. San Francisco: Bay Area Council Economic Institute. http://www.bayareaeconomy.org/files/pdf/BayAreaBalanceOpenSpaceWeb.pdf

Kamstra, Jerry. 1981. *Stand Naked and Cool Them: North Beach and the Bohemian Dream, 1950–1980.* San Francisco: Peeramid Press.

Kantor, Jodi. 2014. Working Anything but 9 to 5: Scheduling Technology Leaves Low-Income Parents with Hours of Chaos. *New York Times.* August 13. http://www.nytimes.com/interactive/2014/08/13/us/starbucks-workersscheduling-hours.html

Kantor, Jodi, and David Streitfeld. 2105. Inside Amazon: Wrestling with Big Ideas While Working in a Bruising Workplace. *New York Times.* August 15. https://www.nytimes.com/2015/08/16/technology/inside-amazon-wrestling-big-ideas-in-a-bruising-workplace.html?_r=1

Kaplan, David. 2000. *The Silicon Boys and Their Valley of Dreams.* New York: Perennial Press.

Karp, Matt. 2017. Populism for Plutocrats. *Jacobin.* August 3. http://www.jacobinmag.com/2017/08/democrats-better-deal-midterms-clinton-2016

Kasson, John. 1976. *Civilizing the Machine: Technology and Republican Values in America, 1776–1900.* New York: Grossman.

Katz, Lawrence, and Kenneth Rosen. 1980. *The Effects of Land-Use Controls on Housing Prices.* Berkeley: Center for Real Estate Research and Urban Economics.

Katznelson, Ira. 2005. *When Affirmative Action Was White: An Untold History of Racial Inequality in Twentieth-Century America.* New York: W.W. Norton.

Katznelson, Ira. 2013. *Fear Itself: The New Deal and the Origins of Our Time.* New York: Liveright Publishing Corporation.

Kavanaugh, Michael. 2016. Lack of Interest: Ultra-Low Base Rates Have Fuelled Property Boom. *Financial Times.* May 11. https://www.ft.com/content/4da90aaa-15a7-11e6-b197-a4af20d5575e

Kawachi, Ichiro, Bruce P. Kennedy, and Richard C. Wilkinson, eds. 1999. *The Society and Population Health Reader: Income Inequality and Health.* New York: New Press.

Kazin, Michael. 1987. *Barons of Labor: The San Francisco Building Trades and Union Power in the Progressive Era.* Urbana and Chicago: University of Illinois Press.

Keen, Andrew. 2015. *The Internet Is Not the Answer.* New York: Atlantic Monthly Press.

Keen, Andrew. 2018. *How to Fix the Future: Staying Human in the Digital Age*. New York: Atlantic Books.

Kemeny, Tom, Maryann Feldman, Frank Ethridge, and Ted Zoller. 2016. The Economic Value of Local Social Networks. *Journal of Economic Geography* 16 (5): 1101–22.

Kenney, Allan. 2016. REITs Reshaping Communities: San Francisco's Mission Bay. *REIT Magazine*. May/June.

Kenney, Martin, and David Mowery, eds. 2014. *Public Universities and Regional Development: Insights from the University of California*. Stanford: Stanford University Press.

Kenney, Martin, and Donald Patton. 2005. Entrepreneurial Geographies: Support Networks in Three High-Tech Industries. *Economic Geography* 81 (2): 201–28

Kenney, Martin, and Donald Patton. 2006. The Coevolution of Technologies and Institutions: Silicon Valley as the Iconic High-Technology Cluster. In P. Braunerhjelm and M. Feldman, eds. *Cluster Genesis: Technology-Based Industrial Development*. Oxford: Oxford University Press, 38–60.

Kenney, Martin, and Richard Florida. 2000. Venture Capital in Silicon Valley: Fueling New Firm Formation. In Martin Kenney, ed., *Understanding Silicon Valley*. Stanford: Stanford University Press, 98–123.

Kessler, Andy. 2013. Travis Kalanick: Transportation Trustbuster. *Wall Street Journal*. January 25. https://www.wsj.com/articles/SB10001424127887324235104578244231122376480

Kessler, Sarah. 2015. The Sharing Economy Is Dead, and We Killed It. *Fast Company*. September 14. https://www.fastcompany.com/3050775/the-sharing-economy-is-dead-and-we-killed-it

Keynes, John Maynard. 1936. *The General Theory of Employment, Interest and Money*. London: Macmillan.

Kindleberger, Charles. 2005. *Manias, Panics and Crashes: A History of Financial Crises*. New York: Wiley.

King, John. 2004. Build It and They Will Cringe. *San Francisco Chronicle*. December 13, B1–2.

King, John. 2016a. Transbay District's Rising Expectations: New Towers, New Character for Strip That Was Mainly Bridge Access. *San Francisco Chronicle*. January 25, A1. http://www.sfchronicle.com/bayarea/article/New-construction-means-rising-expectations-for-6781242.php

King, John. 2016b. Rising Reality. A Four-Part Series on the Challenges of Sea-Level rise. *San Francisco Chronicle*. May–November. http://projects.sfchronicle.com/2016/sea-level-rise/

King, John. 2017. Bold New Neighborhood Rising among the Towers. *San Francisco Chronicle*. December 31. http://projects.sfchronicle.com/2017/transbay-terminal/the-future/

Kirk, Chris, and Will Oremus. 2013. A World Map of All the Next Silicon Valleys. *Slate*. December 19. http://www.slate.com/articles/technology/the_next_silicon_valley/2013/12/all_the_next_silicon_valleys_a_world_map_of_aspiring_tech_hubs.html

Kirkpatrick, David. 2010. *The Facebook Effect: The Inside Story of the Company That Is Connecting the World*. New York: Simon and Schuster.

Knight, Heather. 2014. Income Inequality on Par with Developing Nations. *SF Gate*. May 25. http://www.sfgate.com/bayarea/article/Income-inequality-on-par-with-developing-nations-5486434.php

Knox, Paul. 2008. *Metro-Burbia, USA*. New Brunswick, NJ: Rutgers University Press.

Knuth, Sarah. 2015. Seeing Green in San Francisco: City as a Resource Frontier. *Antipode* 48 (3): 626–44.

Knuth, Sarah. 2017. The Search for "Safe" Assets: Emerging Storylines of Property Transformation. In Asher Ghertner and Robert Lake, eds., forthcoming, *Land Fictions: The Commodification of Land in City and Country*. Ithaca, NY: Cornell University Press.

Kochhar, Rakesh, Richard Fry, and Molly Rohal. 2016. *America's Shrinking Middle Class: A Close Look at Changes within Metropolitan Areas*. Washington, DC: Pew Research Center.

Kolko, Gabriel. 1963. *The Triumph of Conservatism*. New York: Free Press.

Kopetman, Roxanna. 2016. In Program's First Year, Nearly Half of California's Driver's Licenses went to Undocumented. *Orange County Register.* January 6. http://www. ocregister.com/articles/dmv-698896-licenses-undocumented.html

Koren, James. 2015. After Subprime Collapse, Nonbank Lenders Again Dominate Riskier Mortgages. *Los Angeles Times.* November 30.

Kotkin, Joel. 2014. The World's Most Influential Cities. *Forbes.* August 14. https://www.forbes. com/sites/joelkotkin/2014/08/14/the-most-influential-cities-in-the-world/

Kotkin, Joel, and Michael Shires. 2016. The Best Cities for Jobs, 2016. *Forbes Magazine.* May 10. http://www.forbes.com/sites/joelkotkin/2016/05/10/the-best-cities-for-jobs-2016/#442342246e40

Krishnakumar, Priya, and Joe Fox. 2017. Why the 2017 Fire Season Has Been One of California's Worst. *Los Angeles Times.* October 13. http://www.latimes.com/projects/ la-me-california-fire-seasons/

Kroll, Cynthia, and Kimball, Linda. 1986. The R&D Dilemma: The Real Estate Industry and High Tech Growth. Working Paper no. 86-116. Berkeley: Center for Real Estate and Urban Economics, University of California.

Krugman, Paul. 2008. *The Return of Depression Economics and the Crisis of 2008.* New York: W.W. Norton.

Kuchler, Hannah. 2016. San Francisco Workers Forced into Cosy, Platonic Roomsharing. *Financial Times.* May 16. https://www.ft.com/content/fd489208-1117-11e6-91da-096d89bd2173

Kulish, Nicholas, and Nathaniel Popper. 2017. Crowdfunding Helps Rescue Refugees Upended by the Travel Ban. *New York Times.* February 9. https://nyti.ms/2kRspL0

Kunstler, James Howard. 1993. *The Geography of Nowhere: The Rise and Decline of America's Man-Made Landscape.* New York: Simon & Schuster.

Kurhi, Eric. 2017. San Jose: Huge Surge in Silicon Valley Homeless Youth. *San Jose Mercury News.* July 1. http://www.mercurynews.com/2017/06/30/san-jose-huge-surge-in-homeless-silicon-valley-youth/

Kuruvila, Mathai. 2011. 25% Drop in African American Population in Oakland. *San Francisco Chronicle.* March 11. http://www.sfgate.com/bayarea/article/25-drop-in-African-American-population-in-Oakland-2471925.php

Kuznets, Simon. 1930. *Secular Movements in Production and Prices.* Boston: Houghton Mifflin.

Kwak, Nancy. 2015. *A World of Homeowners: American Power and the Politics of Housing Aid.* Chicago: University of Chicago Press.

Kwong, Jessica. 2014. Report Claims Speculators Are Behind Most Ellis Act Evictions in SF. *San Francisco Examiner.* April 4. http://www.sfexaminer.com/ report-claims-speculators-are-behind-most-ellis-act-evictions-in-sf/

Lang, Marissa. 2015. Companies Avoid $34M in City Taxes Thanks to "Twitter Tax Break." *SFGate.* October 19. http://www.sfgate.com/business/article/Companies-avoid-34M-in-city-taxes-thanks-to-6578396.php

Lang, Marissa. 2017. Facebook Adjusts Trending Topics in Effort to Exclude Fake News. *SFGate.* January 25. http://www.sfgate.com/business/article/Facebook-adjusts-trending-topics-in-effort-to-10884209.php

Lannon, Albert. 2000. *Fight or Be Slaves: The History of the Oakland–East Bay Labor Movement.* Lanham, MD: University Press of America.

Larson, Magali. 1977. *The Rise of Professionalism.* Berkeley: University of California Press.

LeBlanc, Rick. 2017. E-waste Recycling Facts and Figures. *The Balance.* March 26. https:// www.thebalance.com/e-waste-recycling-facts-and-figures-2878189

Lécuyer, Christopher. 2005. *Making Silicon Valley: Innovation and the Growth of High Tech, 1930–1970.* Cambridge, MA: MIT Press.

Lee, Neil, and Andrés Rodríguez-Pose. 2016. Is There Trickle-Down from Tech? Poverty, Employment, and the High-Technology Multiplier in U.S. Cities. *Annals of the American Association of Geographers* 106 (5): 1114–34.

Lee, Thomas. 2015. Reality Check for Startup Values. *San Francisco Chronicle.* November 19. A1.

Lee, Thomas. 2016a. Unicorn Failures Are Cautionary Tales for Average Investors. *San Francisco Chronicle*. January 24, A1. http://www.sfchronicle.com/business/article/When-unicorns-fail-a-cautionary-tale-for-average-6779856.php

Lee, Thomas. 2016b. In "Unicorn" World, Some Get Nosed Out. *San Francisco Chronicle*. April 24, D1

Lee, Thomas. 2016c. Despite Politics, Silicon Valley and Trump Both Love Disruption. *San Francisco Chronicle*. December 13. http://www.sfchronicle.com/business/article/Despite-politics-Silicon-Valley-and-Trump-both-10794320.php

Lee, Thomas. 2017. No Blast from Past: New Tech Stocks Fail to Impress Wall Street. *San Francisco Chronicle*. July 15. http://www.sfchronicle.com/business/article/No-blast-from-past-New-tech-stocks-fail-to-11290292.php

Lee, Wendy. 2016. What Will Apple Do with $200 Billion? *San Francisco Chronicle*. June 5, D1.

Lees, Loretta, Tom Slater, and Elvin Wyly. 2008. *Gentrification*. New York: Routledge.

Lefebvre, Henri. 1970. *La Revolution Urbaine*. Paris: Gallimard; published in English as *The Urban Revolution*. Minneapolis: University of Minnesota Press, 2003.

Lehman-Frisch, Sonia. 2015. San Francisco: Unequal Metropolis. http://www.booksandideas.net/San-Francisco-Unequal-Metropolis.html?lang=en

Leoning, Carroll, Tom Hamburger, and Rosalind Helderman. 2017. Russian Firm Tied to Pro-Kremlin Propaganda Advertised on Facebook During Election. *Washington Post*. September 6. http://www.washingtonpost.com/politics/facebook-says-it-sold-political-ads-to-russian-company-during-2016-election/2017/09/06/32f01fd2-931e-11e7-89fa-bb822a46da5b_story.html?utm_term=.1c4c1919fd2f

Leslie, Jacques. 2010. How Gross Is My Valley? *New Republic*. June 30. https://newrepublic.com/article/75946/how-gross-my-valley

Leslie, Stuart. 1993. *The Cold War and American Science: The Military-Industrial-Academic Complex at MIT and Stanford*. New York: Columbia University Press.

Leslie, Stuart. 2000. The Biggest "Angel" of Them All: The Military and the Making of Silicon Valley. In Martin Kenney, ed., *Understanding Silicon Valley*. Stanford, CA: Stanford University Press, 48–70.

Lev-Ram, Michael. 2016. How Netflix Became Hollywood's Frenemy. *Fortune*. June 15. http://fortune.com/netflix-versus-hollywood/

Levin, Matt. 2016. California's Rich-Poor Gap: The Reality May Surprise You. CALmatters. August 11. https://calmatters.org/articles/income-inequality-in-california-may-not-look-like-you-think-it-does-and-why-that-may-be-a-good-thing/

Levin, Sam. 2013. The Nonprofit Shift. *East Bay Express*. December 25. http://www.eastbayexpress.com/oakland/the-nonprofit-shift/Content?oid=3793143

Levin, Sam. 2015. Racial Profiling at Nextdoor.com. *East Bay Express*. October 7. http://www.eastbayexpress.com/oakland/racial-profiling-via-nextdoorcom/Content?oid=4526919

Levin, Sam. 2017a. Uber's Sexual Harassment Case Shines Light on a Startup's Culture of Defiance. *Guardian*. February 21. https://www.theguardian.com/technology/2017/feb/21/uber-sexual-harassment-discrimination-scandal

Levin, Sam. 2017b. Women Say They Quit Google Because of Racial Discrimination: "I Was Invisible." *Guardian*. July 17. https://www.theguardian.com/technology/2017/aug/18/women-google-memo-racism-sexism-discrimination-quit

Levin, Sam. 2017c. Google Accused of "Extreme" Gender Pay Discrimination by US Labor Department. *Guardian*. April 7. https://www.theguardian.com/technology/2017/apr/07/google-pay-disparities-women-labor-department-lawsuit

Levinson, Arik. 2014. California Energy Efficiency: Lessons for the Rest of the World, or Not? *Journal of Economic Behavior & Organization* 107: 269–89.

Levitsky, Steven, and Daniel Ziblatt. 2018. *How Democracies Die*. New York: Crown.

Levy, Dan. 2012. SF Office Space Costs Are Soaring. *San Francisco Chronicle*. September 15, D1.

Levy, Steven. 1984. *Hackers: Heroes of the Computer Revolution*. New York: Anchor/Doubleday.

Levy, Steven. 2011. *In the Plex: How Google Thinks, Works and Shapes Our Lives.* New York: Simon and Schuster.

Lewis, David. 2015. Lessons from the Latest Spill. *Save the Bay Blog.* May 27. https://blog.savesfbay.org/tag/cosco-busan/

Lewis, Martin. 2012. The 1980s Political Transformation of California. *Geocurrents.* February 29. http://www.geocurrents.info/place/north-america/northern-california/the-1980s-geopolitical-transformation-of-california

Lewis, Michael. 2000. *The New New Thing: A Silicon Valley Story.* New York: W.W. Norton.

Lewis, Michael. 2011. California and Bust. *Vanity Fair.* November. http://www.vanityfair.com/business/features/2011/11/michael-lewis-201111.print

Lewis, Oscar. 1956. *Bay Window Bohemia: An Account of the Brilliant Artistic World of Gaslit San Francisco.* Garden City, NY: Doubleday.

Lewis, Oscar. 1980. *San Francisco: Mission to Metropolis.* San Diego: Howell-North Books.

Lewis, Paul. 2018. Fiction Is Outperforming Reality: How YouTube's Algorithm Distorts Truth. *Guardian.* February 2. https://www.theguardian.com/technology/2018/feb/02/how-youtubes-algorithm-distorts-truth

Lewis, Robert, ed. 2004. *Manufacturing Suburbs: Building, Work and Home on the Metropolitan Fringe.* Philadelphia: Temple University Press

Lewis, Robert. 2016. *Calculating Property Relations: Chicago's Wartime Industrial Mobilization, 1940–1950.* Athens: University of Georgia Press.

Li, Roland. 2017. A Historically Huge Wave of New Offices Is about to Crest in San Francisco. *San Francisco Business Times.* January 26. https://www.bizjournals.com/sanfrancisco/news/2017/01/26/san-francisco-office-construction-real-estate.html

Lichtenstein, Nelson. 2002. *The State of the Unions: A Century of American Labor.* Princeton, NJ: Princeton University Press.

Lichtenstein, Nelson. 2009. *The Retail Revolution: How Wal-Mart Created a Brave New World of Business.* New York: Picador.

Lien, Tracey. 2016. On-Demand Business Models Have Put Some Startups on Life Support. *Los Angeles Times.* June 18. http://www.latimes.com/business/technology/la-fi-tn-end-of-on-demand-snap-story.html

Lien, Tracey. 2017. Lyft Diversity Report Shows It's Mostly White, Male. *Los Angeles Times.* June 1. http://www.latimes.com/business/technology/la-fi-tn-lyft-diversity-20170601-story.html

Lind, Dara. 2017. Fewer Immigrants Being Deported under Trump than Obama: But It's Not Because Trump Isn't Trying. *Vox.* August 10. https://www.vox.com/policy-and-politics/2017/8/10/16119910/trump-deportations-obama

Lipsitz, George. 1998. *The Possessive Investment in Whiteness.* Philadelphia: Temple University Press.

Little Hoover Commission. 2014. *Governing California through Climate Change.* Report no. 221. Sacramento, CA: Little Hoover Commission.

Lo, Clarence. 1990. *Small Property versus Big Government: Social Origins of the Property Tax Revolt.* Berkeley: University of California Press.

Lockhead, Carolyn. 2016. Boxer Slams Water Bill Rider Backed by Feinstein. *SFGate.* December 5. http://www.sfgate.com/news/article/Boxer-slams-water-bill-rider-backed-by-Feinstein-10699564.php

Loeb, Carolyn. 2002. *Entrepreneurial Vernacular: Developers' Subdivision in the 1920s.* Baltimore: Johns Hopkins University Press.

Logan, John. 2006. The Union Avoidance Industry in the United States. *British Journal of Industrial Relations* 44 (4): 651–75.

Logan, John, and Harvey Molotch. 1986. *Urban Fortunes: The Political Economy of Place.* Berkeley: University of California Press.

Lohr, Stephen. 2017. Intel, While Pivoting to Artificial Intelligence, Tries to Protect Lead. *New York Times.* July 10. https://nyti.ms/2u2fhra

Lovett, Ian. 2015. California Agrees to Overhaul Use of Solitary Confinement. *New York Times.* September 2. http://www.nytimes.com/2015/09/02/us/solitary-confinement-california-prisons.html

Lowen, Rebecca. 1997. *Creating the Cold War University: The Transformation of Stanford.* Berkeley: University of California Press.

Luce, Stephanie. 2015. $15 Per Hour or Bust: An Appraisal of the Higher Wages Movement. *New Labor Forum.* Spring. http://newlaborforum.cuny.edu/2015/12/01/15-per-hour-or-bust-an-appraisal-of-the-higher-wages-movement/

Luna, Taryn. 2017. What Happens When California Becomes a Sanctuary State? *Sacramento Bee.* August 29. http://www.sacbee.com/news/politics-government/capitol-alert/article169828172.html

Lung-Amam, Willow. 2017. *Trespassers? Asian Americans and the Battle for Suburbia.* Berkeley: University of California Press.

Lunine, Seth. 2013. *Iron, Oil and Emeryville: Resource Industrialization and Metropolitan Expansion in the San Francisco Bay Area, 1850–1900.* Doctoral dissertation. Department of Geography, University of California, Berkeley.

Lustig, Jeff. 2004. The Tangled Knot of Race and Class in America. In Michael Zweig, ed., *What's Class Got to Do with It? American Society in the 21st Century.* Ithaca, NY: Cornell University Press, 45–60.

Lustig, Jeff. 2010. Private Rights and Public Purposes: California's Second Constitution Reconsidered. *California History* 87 (3): 46–64.

Lyons, Dan. 2016. *Disrupted: My Misadventure in the Start-Up Bubble.* New York: Hachette.

Lyons, Dan. 2017. In Silicon Valley, Working 9 to 5 is for Losers. *New York Times.* August 31. https://nyti.ms/2gsSUGn

Macmillan, Troy. 2016. Why San Francisco's Pacific Heights Stands Out in High-End Market. *Financial Times.* August 26. https://www.ft.com/content/3c97f92e-649e-11e6-8310-ecfobddad227

Madrick, Jeff. 2001. The Business Media and the New Economy. Research paper R-24. Shorenstein Center, Kennedy School of Government, Harvard University, Cambridge, MA. http://dev.shorensteincenter.org/wp-content/uploads/2012/03/r24_madrick.pdf

Mahler, Jonathan. 2012. Oakland, the last Refuge of Radical America. *New York Times Magazine.* August 1. http://www.nytimes.com/2012/08/05/magazine/oakland-occupy-movement.html

Mandel, Michael. 2014. *San Francisco and the Tech/Info Boom: Making the Transition to a Balanced and Growing Economy.* South Mountain Economics. https://data.bloomberglp.com/mike/sites/10/2015/06/SouthMountainEconomics_SF_TechInfo_Boom.pdf

Manjoo, Farhad. 2016. Think Amazon's Drone Delivery Idea Is a Gimmick? Think Again. *New York Times.* August 10. https://nyti.ms/2b5FoUt

Manjoo, Farhad. 2017. Uber Case Could Be a Watershed for Women in Tech. *New York Times.* July 3. https://nyti.ms/2lyopth

Manyika, James, Susan Lund, Jacques Bughin, Kelsey Robinson, Jan Mischke, and Deepa Mahajan. 2016. *Independent Work: Choice, Necessity, and the Gig Economy.* October. San Francisco: McKinsey Global Institute.

Marcuse, Peter. 1997. The Enclave, the Citadel and the Ghetto: What Has Changed in the Post-Fordist city. *Urban Affairs Review* 33 (2): 228–64.

Marcuse, Peter, ed. 2009. *Searching for the Just City: Debates in Urban Theory and Practice.* New York: Routledge.

Marcuse, Peter, and Ronald van Kempen. 2002. *Of States and Cities: The Partitioning of Urban Space.* New York: Oxford University Press.

Margolis, Jason. 2005. Housing Boom in Below-Sea-Level California Delta. *National Public Radio.* October 26. Transcript at: http://www.npr.org/templates/story/story.php?storyId=4975514

Markoff, John. 2005. *What the Dormouse Said: How the 60s Counterculture Shaped the Personal Computer Industry*. New York: Penguin/Viking.

Markusen, Ann, Yong-Sook Lee, and Sean DeGionvanna, eds. 1999. *Second Tier Cities: Rapid Growth beyond the Metropolis*. Minneapolis: University of Minnesota Press.

Marquis, Erin. 2017. San Francisco Drivers Can't Escape Legendary Traffic Even at 4 a.m. *Jalopnik*. July 28. https://jalopnik.com/tag/just-stay-home

Martin, Ron, and Bob Rowthorn, eds. 1986. *The Geography of Deindustrialization*. London: Macmillan.

Marx, Anthony. 1998. *Making Race and Nation: A Comparison of the United States, South Africa and Brazil*. Cambridge: Cambridge University Press.

Marx, Leo. 1964. *The Machine in the Garden: Technology and the Pastoral Ideal in America*. New York: Oxford University Press.

Massaro, Rachel. 2016. *2016 Silicon Valley Index*. San Jose: Joint Venture Silicon Valley, Institute for Regional Studies.

Massey, Doreen. 2005. *For Space*. London: Sage Publications.

Massey, Doreen, Paul Quintas, and David Wield. 1992. *High-Tech Fantasies: Science Parks in Society, Science and Space*. London: Routledge.

Massey, Douglas, and Nancy Denton. 1993. *American Apartheid: Segregation and the Making of the Underclass*. Cambridge, MA: Harvard University Press.

Matthiessen, Peter. 1969. *Sal si puedes: Cesar Chavez and the New American Revolution*. New York: Random House.

Mayer, Jane. 2016. *Dark Money: The Hidden History of the Billionaires Behind the Rise of Radical Right*. New York: Doubleday.

Mayer-Schönberger, Viktor, and Kenneth Cukier. 2013. *Big Data: A Revolution That Will Transform How We Live, Work, and Think*. Boston: Houghton Mifflin.

McCarty, Nolan, Keith Poole, and Howard Rosenthal. 2006. *Polarized America: The Dance of Ideology and Unequal Riches*. Cambridge, MA: MIT Press.

McChesney, Robert. 2014. *Digital Disconnect: How Capitalism Is Turning the Internet against Democracy*. New York: New Press.

McClintock, Nathan. 2011. From Industrial Garden to Food Desert: Demarcated Devaluation in the Flatlands of Oakland, California. In Alison Alkon and Julian Agyeman eds., *Cultivating Food Justice: Race, Class, and Sustainability*. Cambridge, MA: MIT Press, 89–120.

McClintock, Nathan, Heather Wooten, and Alethea Brown. 2012. Toward a Food Policy "First Step" in Oakland, California. *Journal of Agriculture, Food Systems, and Community Development* 2 (4). September.

McCrum, Dan. 2017. The Perils of Calling the Peak of the Equities Bull Run. *Financial Times*. August 16. https://www.ft.com/content/540d223c-80e0-11e7-94e2-c5b903247afd

McDermid, Riley. 2017. Tech Workers Making Six-Figures or More Sound Off about Barely "Making Ends Meet" in S.F. *San Francisco Business Times*. March 1. https://www.bizjournals.com/sanfrancisco/news/2017/03/01/tech-workers-making-six-figures-or-more-sound-off.html

McDermott, Monica. 2006. *Working Class White: The Making and Unmaking of Race Relations*. Berkeley: University of California Press.

McGirr, Lisa. 2001. *Suburban Warriors: The Origins of the New American Right*. Princeton: Princeton University Press.

McGoey, Linsey. 2015. *No Such Thing as a Free Gift: The Gates Foundation and the Price of Philanthropy*. London: Verso.

McKinsey & Co. 2016. *A Tool Kit to Close California's Housing Gap*. San Francisco: McKinsey & Co.

McKinsey Global Institute. 2017. *Jobs Lost, Jobs Gained: Workforce Transitions in a Time of Automation*. December. San Francisco: McKinsey Global Institute.

McLaughlin, Ralph. 2015. Housing in 2016: Hesitant Households, Costly Coasts, and the Bargain Belt. 2016. Trulia blog. https://www.trulia.com/blog/trends/2016-housing-predictions/

McNamee, Stephen, and Robert Miller Jr. 2014. *The Meritocracy Myth*. Lanham, MD: Rowman & Littlefield.

McNeill, Donald. 2016. Governing a City of Unicorns: Technology Capital and the Urban Politics of San Francisco. *Urban Geography* 37 (4): 494–513.

McWilliams, Carey. 1949. *California: The Great Exception*. New York: AA Wyn; reprint Santa Barbara: Peregrine Smith, 1976 ed.

Mele, Christopher. 2000. *Selling the Lower East Side: Culture, Real Estate and Resistance in New York City*. Minneapolis: University of Minnesota Press.

Merchant, Brian. 2017. *The One Device: The Secret History of the iPhone*. New York: Bantam.

Metcalf, Gabriel. 2015. What's the Matter with San Francisco? *CityLab/Atlantic*. July 23. http://www.citylab.com/housing/2015/07/whats-the-matter-with-san-francisco/399506/

Metcalf, Gabriel, and Egon Terplan. 2007. The Northern California Megaregion. *Urbanist*. November/December. https://www.spur.org/sites/default/files/publications_pdfs/SPUR_The_Northern_California_Megaregion.pdf

Mezrich, Ben. 2009. *The Accidental Billionaires: The Founding of Facebook, a Tale of Sex, Money, Genius, and Betrayal*. New York: Doubleday.

Micklethwait, John. 1997. The Valley of the Money's Delight. *Economist* 342 (March 29).

Milberg, William, and Deborah Winkler. 2013. *Outsourcing Economics: Global Value Chains in Capitalist Development*. Cambridge: Cambridge University Press.

Miles, Sara. 2001. *How to Hack a Party Line: The Democrats and Silicon Valley*. Berkeley: University of California Press.

Milkman, Ruth. 1987. *Gender at Work: The Dynamics of Job Segregation by Sex During World War II*. Urbana: University of Illinois Press.

Milkman, Ruth. 2006. *L.A. Story: Immigrant Workers and the Future of the U.S. Labor Movement*. New York: Russell Sage Foundation.

Miller, Craig. 2017. Oroville Crisis Triggers Rethinking of California Dam Management. *KQED Science*. https://ww2.kqed.org/science/2017/05/16/oroville-crisis-triggers-rethinking-of-california-dam-management/

Miller, Paul. 2010. *The Postwar Struggle for Civil Rights: African Americans in San Francisco, 1945–1975*. New York: Routledge.

Minnesota Population Center. 2011. *National Historical Geographic Information System: Version 2.0*. Minneapolis: University of Minnesota.

Minsky, Hyman. 2008. *Stabilizing an Unstable Economy*. New Haven: Yale University Press; orig. publ. 1986.

Minter, Drew. 2014. San Francisco's Recycling Claims Are Garbage. *Bloomberg.com*. July 11. https://www.bloomberg.com/view/articles/2014-07-11/san-francisco-s-recycling-claims-are-garbage

Miraftab, Faranak. 2016. *Global Heartland: Displaced Labor, Transnational Lives, and Local Placemaking*. Bloomington: Indiana University Press.

Mishel, Lawrence, and Josh Bivens. 2017. The Zombie Robot Argument Lurches On: There Is No Evidence That Automation Leads to Joblessness or Inequality. *Economic Policy Institute Report*. May 24. http://www.epi.org/files/pdf/126750.pdf

Mitchell, Don. 2003. *The Right to the City: Social Justice and the Fight for Public Space*. New York: Guilford Press.

Mollenkopf, John. 1983. *The Contested City*. Princeton, NJ: Princeton University Press.

Molotch, Harvey. 1976. The City as Growth Machine: Toward a Political Economy of Place. *American Journal of Sociology* 82: 309–32.

Mongeau, Lillian. 2015. Is Silicon Valley Driving Teachers Out? *Atlantic*. July 21. https://www.theatlantic.com/education/archive/2015/07/silicon-valley-housing-tough-on-teachers/399071/

Montgomery, Gayle, and James Johnson. 1998. *One Step from the White House: The Rise and Fall of Senator William F. Knowland*. Berkeley: University of California Press.

Moody, Kim. 1989. *An Injury to All: The Decline of American Unionism*. London: Verso.

Moore, Barrington. 1966. *The Social Origins of Dictatorship and Democracy.* Boston: Beacon Press.

Moore, Jason. 2015. *Capitalism in the Web of Life: Ecology and the Accumulation of Capital.* London: Verso.

Moore, Rowan. 2017. The Billion-Dollar Palaces of Apple, Facebook and Google. *Guardian.* July 23. https://www.theguardian.com/artanddesign/2017/jul/23/inside-billion-dollar-palaces-of-tech-giants-facebook-apple-google-london-california-wealth-power

Moretti, Enrico. 2012. *The New Geography of Jobs.* Boston: Houghton Mifflin Harcourt.

Moretti, Enrico. 2017. Fires Aren't the Only Threat to the California Dream. *New York Times.* November 3. https://nyti.ms/2hDgzSc

Morozov, Evgeny. 2011. *The Net Delusion: The Dark Side of Internet Freedom.* New York: Public Affairs Press.

Morozov, Evgeny. 2013. *To Save Everything, Click Here: The Folly of Technological Solutionism.* New York: Public Affairs Press.

Morrill, Richard. 2012. Megalopolis and Its Rivals. *New Geography.* http://www.newgeography.com/content/002788-megalopolis-and-its-rivals

Mosco, Vincent. 2004. *The Digital Sublime: Myth, Power and Cyberspace.* Cambridge, MA: MIT Press.

Moser, Susanne, Julia Ekstrom, and Guido Franco. 2013. *Our Changing Climate: 2012. Vulnerability & Adaptation to the Increasing Risks from Climate Change in California.* Summary Report of the Third Assessment from the California Climate Change Center. Sacramento: Natural Resources Agency.

Moudon, Anne. 1986. *Built for Change: Neighborhood Architecture in San Francisco.* Cambridge, MA: MIT Press.

Mount St. Mary's University. 2015. *Report on the Status of Women and Girls in California.* Los Angeles: Mount St. Mary's University.

Moynihan, Daniel. 1965. *The Negro Family: The Case for National Action* (The Moynihan Report). Washington, DC: US Department of Labor.

Mozingo, Louise. 2011. *Pastoral Capitalism: A History of Suburban Corporate Landscapes.* Cambridge, MA: MIT Press.

Mozingo, Louise. 2017. Between Power and Appearance: The Enterprise Suburbs of Silicon Valley. In Alan Berger, Joel Kotkin, and Celina Balderas Guzmán, eds., *Infinite Suburbia.* New York: Princeton Architectural Press, 622–33.

Muller, Edward. 2001. Industrial Suburbs and the Growth of Metropolitan Pittsburgh, 1870–1920. *Journal of Historical Geography* 27 (1): 58–73.

Muller, JoAnn. 2016. Elon Musk's Greatest Innovation Has Gone Unnoticed. *Forbes.* August 19. http://www.forbes.com/sites/joannmuller/2016/08/19/elon-musks-greatest-innovation-has-gone-unnoticed/

Munshi, Neil. 2016. Chinese Investors Reach for the Sky in the Windy City. *Financial Times.* May 10.

Muro, Mark, and Sifan Liu. 2016. Another Clinton-Trump Divide: High-Output America versus Low-Output America. *Brookings Brief,* 29 November.

Murphy, Katy. 2017. Bay Area Residents Seek the California Dream—in Sacramento. *Mercury News.* November 18. http://www.mercurynews.com/2017/11/18/bay-area-residents-seek-the-california-dream-in-sacramento/

Murphy, Katy, and Casey Tolan. 2017. As Jerry Brown Signs Affordable-Housing Bills, Lawmakers Promise to Stay Focused on the Crisis. September 29. *Mercury News.* http://www.mercurynews.com/2017/09/29/california-affordable-housing-bills-to-get-their-final-sign-off/

Murphy, Richard, and John Christensen. 2012. *Tax Us If You Can.* London: Tax Justice Network.

Myrdal, Gunnar. 1957. *Rich Lands, Poor Lands.* New York: Harper & Row.

Narefsky, Karen. 2017. What's in My Backyard? *Jacobin.* August 8. https://www.jacobinmag.com/2017/08/yimbys-housing-affordability-crisis-density

Nash, Gerald. 1992. *A.P. Giannini and the Bank of America*. Norman: University of Oklahoma Press.

Nelson, Bruce. 1988. *Workers on the Waterfront: Seamen, Longshoremen, and Unionism in the 1930s*. Urbana: University of Illinois Press.

Nelson, Kevin. 2009. *Wheels of Change, from Zero to 600 M.P.H: The Amazing Story of California and the Automobile*. Berkeley: Heyday Books.

Nevins, Joseph. 2002. *Operation Gatekeeper: The Rise of the Illegal Alien and the Making of the US-Mexico Boundary*. New York: Routledge.

Newcomer, Erik, and Glen Carey. 2016. Uber Receives $3.5 Billion Investment from Saudi Wealth Fund. *Bloomberg News*. June 1. http://www.bloomberg.com/news/

New York Times. 2012. The 45 Places to Go in 2012. *New York Times*. January 6. http://www.nytimes.com/2012/01/08/travel/45-places-to-go-in-2012.html?_r=0

Ng, Elaine. 2016. *Comprehensive Housing Market Analysis: San Francisco–San Mateo–San Rafael, California*. San Francisco: U.S. Department of Housing and Urban Development, Office of Policy Development and Research.

Nichols, Walter, and Tara Fiorito. 2015. Dreamers Unbound: Immigrant Youth Organizing. *New Labor Forum* 24 (Winter): 86–92.

Nicolau, Anna. 2017. How Streaming Saved the Music Industry. *Financial Times*. January 16. https://www.ft.com/content/cd99b95e-d8ba-11e6-944b-e7eb37a6aa8e

Niedt, Christopher, ed. 2013. *Social Justice in Diverse Suburbs*. Philadelphia: Temple University Press.

Niedzviecki, Hal. 2015. *Trees on Mars: Our Obsession with the Future*. New York: Seven Stories Press.

Niemann, Greg. 2007. *Big Brown: The Untold Story of UPS*. San Francisco: Jossey-Bass.

Noble, David. 1977. *America by Design*. New York: Alfred Knopf.

Noble, David. 1997. *The Religion of Technology*. New York: Knopf.

NYC Planning. 2013. *Designing for Flood Risk*. New York: Department of City Planning.

Nye, David. 1994. *American Technological Sublime*. Cambridge, MA: MIT Press.

O'Connell, Jonathon. 2017. As Companies Relocate to Big Cities, Suburban Towns Are Left Scrambling. *Washington Post*. July 16. https://www.washingtonpost.com/business/economy/as-companies-relocate-to-big-cities-suburban-towns-are-left-scrambling/2017/07/16/81c12cea-618d-11e7-84a1-a26b75ad39fe_story.html?utm_term=.8bda6727c03b

O'Connor, Sarah. 2016. When Your Boss Is an Algorithm. *Financial Times*. September 7. https://www.ft.com/content/88fdc58e-754f-11e6-b60a-de4532d5ea35

O'Connor, Sarah. 2017. Driven to Despair: The Hidden Costs of the Gig Economy. *Financial Times*. September 13. https://www.ft.com/content/749cb87e-6ca8-11e7-b9c7-15af748b60d0

O'Neil, Cathy. 2016. *Weapons of Math Destruction: How Big Data Increases Inequality and Threatens Democracy*. New York: Crown.

O'Neil, Megan. 2015. More Tech Entrepreneurs Inclined to Give Now Instead of Waiting. *Chronicle of Philanthropy*. February 8. https://www.philanthropy.com/article/More-Tech-Entrepreneurs/151769

Oakland City Planning Commission. 1969. *Oakland Central District Plan*. Oakland: Oakland City Planning Commission.

Oden, Robert. 2011. *From Black to Brown and Beyond: The Struggle for Progressive Politics in Oakland, 1966–2011*. San Diego: Cognella Publishing.

Olin, Spencer. 1968. *California's Prodigal Sons: Hiram Johnson and the Progressives, 1911–1917*. Berkeley: University of California Press.

Olmstead, Kathryn. 2015. *Right Out of California: The Big Business Roots of Modern Conservatism*. New York: New Press.

Omi, Michael, and Howard Winant. 1986. *Racial Formation in the United States*. New York: Routledge & Kegan Paul.

Ong, Paul, Edna Bonacich, and Lucie Cheng, ed. 1994. *The New Asian Immigration in Los Angeles and Global Restructuring*. Philadelphia: Temple University Press.

Ono, Kent, and John Sloop. 2002. *Shifting Borders: Rhetoric, Immigration, and California's Proposition 187*. Philadelphia: Temple University Press.

Orr, John. 2017. Working Poor Finding Homes on Four Wheels in Mountain View. *San Jose Mercury News*. July 14. http://www.mercurynews.com/2017/07/12/working-poor-finding-homes-on-four-wheels-in-mountain-view/

Osborne, Hilary. 2016. Uber loses Right to Classify UK Drivers as Self-Employed. *Guardian*. October 28. https://www.theguardian.com/technology/2016/oct/28/uber-uk-tribunal-self-employed-status

Osnos, Even. 2017. Survival of the Richest. *New Yorker*. January 30. http://www.newyorker.com/magazine/2017/01/30/doomsday-prep-for-the-super-rich

Otet, Amah. 2016. Apartment Construction at 10-Year High, Eases Pressure on Rental Prices in Booming Markets. *Real Estate News/Rental Market/RentCafé*. August 31.

Otet, Amah. 2017. Apartment Construction at Its Highest Level in 20 Years, with Denver, Nashville Joining NYC as 2017's Hottest Rental Markets. *Rent Cafe Blog*. August 2. https://www.rentcafe.com/blog/rental-market/us-apartment-construction-at-a-20-year-high-in-2017/

Pacific Institute & NRDC. 2014. *The Untapped Potential of California's Water Supply: Efficiency, Reuse, and Stormwater*. *Issue Brief*. Oakland: Pacific Institute. http://pacinst.org/app/uploads/2014/06/ca-water-capstone.pdf

Packer, George. 2013. *The Unwinding: An Inner History of the New America*. New York: Farrar, Straus & Giroux.

Padgett, John, and Walter Powell. 2012a. Why the Valley Went First: Aggregation and Emergence in Regional Inventor Networks. In Padgett and Powell, eds., *The Emergence of Organizations and Markets*. Princeton, NJ: Princeton University Press, 520–44.

Padgett, John, and Walter Powell, eds. 2012b. *The Emergence of Organizations and Markets*. Princeton, NJ: Princeton University Press.

Page, Brian, and Walker, Richard. 1991. From Settlement to Fordism: The Agro-Industrial Revolution in the American Midwest. *Economic Geography* 67 (4): 281–315.

Pappas, Stephanie. 2014. America's Most Endangered River: San Joaquin in California. *Scientific American*. April 9. https://www.scientificamerican.com/article/americas-most-endangered-river-san-joaquin-in-california/

Pappas, Stephanie. 2015. Cyberbullying on Social Media Linked to Teen Depression. *LiveScience*. June 22. https://www.livescience.com/51294-cyberbullying-social-media-teen-depression.html

Paragon Real Estate Group. 2016a. Housing Affordability in the SF Bay Area. August 15. http://www.paragon-re.com/Bay_Area_Housing_Affordability

Paragon Real Estate Group. 2016b. 30 Years of Real Estate Cycles in San Francisco. http://www.paragon-re.com/3_Recessions_2_Bubbles_and_a_Baby

Parlapiano, Alicia, Robert Gebeloff, and Shan Carter. 2015. The Shrinking American Middle Class. *New York Times*. January 25. https://www.nytimes.com/interactive/2015/01/25/upshot/shrinking-middle-class.html

Partnoy, Frank. 2017. The Sequel to the Global Financial Crisis Is Here. *Financial Times*. July 31. https://www.ft.com/content/95808118-662e-11e7-9a66-93fb352ba1fe

Pastor, Manuel. 2008. *State of the Region: The New Demography, the New Economy and the New Environment*. Los Angeles: Program for Environmental and Regional Equity, University of Southern California.

Paul, Mark, William Darity Jr., Darrick Hamilton, and Anne Price. 2017. Returning to the Promise of Full Employment: A Federal Job Guarantee in the United States. Research Brief, volume 2, June. Samuel Dubois Cook Center on Social Equity, New School for Social Research. https://socialequity.duke.edu/sites/socialequity.duke.edu/files/site-images/cook%20center_fjg_brief_2017.pdf

Payne, Stephen, with Santa Clara County Historical Heritage Commission. 1987. *Santa Clara County: Harvest of Change.* Northridge, CA: Windsor Press.

Pearlstein, Rick. 2008. *Nixonland: The Rise of a President and the Fracturing of America.* New York: Scribner.

Pearlstein, Rick. 2014. *Invisible Bridge: The Fall of Nixon and the Rise of Reagan.* New York: Simon & Schuster.

Peck, Jamie. 2010. *Constructions of Neoliberal Reason.* New York: Oxford University Press.

Pellow, David, and Lisa Park. 2002. *The Silicon Valley of Dreams: Environmental Injustice, Immigrant Workers, and the High-Tech Global Economy.* New York: New York University Press.

Pender, Kathleen. 2015a. More US Homes Being Bought by Foreign Residents. *San Francisco Chronicle.* July 6. http://www.sfchronicle.com/business/networth/article/More-U-S-homes-bought-by-foreign-residents-8344394.php

Pender, Kathleen. 2015b. S.F.'s SoFi Lands Whopping $1 Billion in Venture Capital. *San Francisco Chronicle.* September 30. http://www.sfchronicle.com/business/networth/article/S-F-s-SoFi-lands-another-1-billion-in-venture-6541786.php

Pender, Kathleen. 2016a. Bay Area Housing Prices Rose—Except in San Francisco. *San Francisco Chronicle.* June 23, C1.

Pender, Kathleen. 2016b. Chinese Buying Big Residential Projects. *San Francisco Chronicle.* March 13, D1.

Pender, Kathleen. 2016c. Nonbank Lenders Surging in California Mortgage Market. *San Francisco Chronicle.* July 12. http://www.sfgate.com/business/networth/article/Nonbank-lenders-surging-in-California-mortgage-8354881.php

Pender, Kathleen. 2018. San Jose Could Be This Year's Most Insane Housing Market. *San Francisco Chronicle.* February 1, p. A1. http://www.sfchronicle.com/business/networth/article/San-Jose-could-be-this-year-s-most-insane-12541492.php

Perelman, Michael. 2000. *The Invention of Capitalism: Classical Political Economy and the Secret History of Primitive Accumulation.* Durham, NC: Duke University Press.

Peretti, Jacques. 2017. Palantir: The "Special Ops" Tech Giant That Wields as Much Real-World Power as Google. *Guardian.* July 30. https://www.theguardian.com/world/2017/jul/30/palantir-peter-thiel-cia-data-crime-police

Peri, Giovanni. 2007. How Immigrants Affect California Employment and Wages. *California Counts: Population Trends and Profiles* 8 (3): February.

Perlberg, Heather, and Prashant Gopal. 2016. Silicon Valley Elites Get Home Loans with No Money Down. July 27. *Bloomberg.com.* http://www.bloomberg.com/news/articles/2016-07-27/zero-down-on-a-2-million-house-is-no-problem-in-silicon-valley

Perles, Anthony. 1981. *The People's Railway: The History of the Municipal Railway of San Francisco.* Glendale, CA: Interurban Press.

Perry, David. 1987. The Politics of Dependency in Deindustrializing America: The Case of Buffalo, NY. In Michael Smith and Joe Feagin, eds., *The Capitalist City.* Oxford: Basil Blackwell, 113–37.

Peters, Ronald, and Cindy Rosenthal. 2010. *Speaker Nancy Pelosi and the New American Politics.* New York: Oxford University Press.

Peterson, Paul. 1981. *City Limits.* Chicago: University of Chicago Press.

Phillips, Justin. 2017. Group Fights Segregation in Bay Area Restaurants. *San Francisco Chronicle.* April 16, A1.

Phillips, Steve. 2016. *Brown Is the New White: How the Demographic Revolution Has Created a New American Majority.* New York: New Press.

Phillips-Fine, Kim. 2009. *Invisible Hands: The Making of the Conservative Movement from the New Deal to Reagan.* New York: W.W. Norton.

Pierson, Paul, and Jacob Hacker. 2010. *Winner-Take-All Politics: How Washington Made the Rich Richer—and Turned Its Back on the Middle Class.* New York: Simon & Schuster.

Piketty, Thomas. 2014. *Capital in the 21st Century.* Cambridge, MA: Harvard University Press.

Piore, Michael. 1979. *Birds of Passage: Long Distance Migrants and Industrial Societies.* New York: Cambridge University Press.

Pisani, Donald. 1984. *From the Family Farm to Agribusiness: The Irrigation Crusade in California and the West, 1850–1931.* Berkeley: University of California Press.

Platt, Eric. 2016. US Companies' Cash Pile Hits $1.7tn. *Financial Times.* May 20. https://www.ft.com/content/368ef430-1e24-11e6-a7bc-ee846770ec15

Platt, Eric. 2017. US Tech Sector Surges Past Its Dotcom Era Peak. *Financial Times.* July 19. https://www.ft.com/content/020f0722-6cbb-11e7-b9c7-15af748b60d0

Plender, John. 2013. Apple, Google and Facebook Are Latter-Day Scrooges. *Financial Times.* December 29. https://www.ft.com/content/558894bc-68b0-11e3-bb3e-00144feabdc0

Policy Link. 2015. *An Equity Profile of the San Francisco Bay Area Region.* Oakland: Policy Link & Program in Environmental and Regional Equity at the University of Southern California.

Pollard, Sidney. 1968. *The Idea of Progress: History and Society.* New York: Basic Books.

Popper, Nathaniel, and Conor Dougherty. 2015. Wall St. Stars Join Silicon Valley Gold Rush. *New York Times.* March 25, A1. http://www.nytimes.com/2015/03/25/business/wall-st-stars-join-silicon-valley-gold-rush.html?_r=0

Porter, Libby, and Kate Shaw, eds. 2009. *Whose Urban Renaissance? An International Comparison of Urban Regeneration Strategies.* London: Routledge.

Porter, Michael. 1998. *On Competition.* Boston: Harvard Business School Publishing.

Portes, Alejandro, and Ruben Rumbaut. 1990. *Immigrant America: A Portrait.* Berkeley: University of California Press.

Post, Charles. 2011. *The American Road to Capitalism: Studies in Class Structure, Economic Development and Political Conflicts, 1620–1877.* Boston: Brill Publishers.

Pred, Allan. 1980. *Urban Growth and City Systems in the United States, 1840–60.* Cambridge, MA: Harvard University Press.

Pred, Allan. 2000. *Even in Sweden: Racisms, Racialized Spaces, and the Popular Geographical Imagination.* Berkeley: University of California Press.

Preston, William. 1981. *Vanishing Landscapes: Land and Life in the Tulare Lake Basin.* Berkeley: University of California Press.

Prewitt, Kenneth. 2013. *What Is Your Race? The Census and Our Flawed Efforts to Classify Americans.* Princeton, NJ: Princeton University Press.

Puga, Diego. 2010. The Magnitude and Causes of Agglomeration Economies. *Journal of Regional Science* 50 (1): 203–19.

Putnam, Jackson. 1980. *Modern California Politics: 1917–1980.* San Francisco: Boyd & Fraser.

Putnam, Jackson. 2005. *Jess: The Political Career of Jesse Marvin Unruh.* Lanham, MD: University Press of America.

Pyne, Stephen. 2016. *California: A Fire Survey.* Tucson: University of Arizona Press.

Quinn, Arthur. 1981. *Broken Shore: The Marin Peninsula, a Perspective on History.* Layton, UT: Peregrine Smith.

Rae, Alasdair. 2015. Mapping the Polycentric Metropolis: Journeys to Work in the Bay Area. *Under the Raedar.* July 12. Reproduced at *City Metric,* http://www.citymetric.com/transport/how-do-you-map-city-no-centre-commuting-patterns-san-francisco-bay-area-1245

Raguso, Emilie. 2017. Mayor: New Budget Is City's "Biggest Investment" Ever to End homelessness. *Berkeleyside.* June 28. http://www.berkeleyside.com/2017/06/28/berkeley-mayor-new-budget-citys-biggest-investment-ever-end-homelessness/

Ramakrishnan, Kathick, and Mark Baldassare. 2004. *The Ties That Bind: Changing Demographics and Civic Engagement in California.* San Francisco: Public Policy Institute of California.

Ramirez, Steven. 2013. *Lawless Capitalism: The Subprime Crisis and the Economic Rule of Law.* New York: New York University Press

Rapino, Melanie, and Allison Fields. 2013. Mega Commuters in the U.S.: Time and Distance in Defining the Long Commute Using the American Community Survey. U.S. Census Bureau Working Paper 2013-03. http://www.census.gov/hhes/commuting/files/2012/Paper-Poster_Megacommuting%20in%20the%20US.pdf

Rarick, Ethan. 2005. *California Rising: The Life and Times of Pat Brown*. Berkeley: University of California Press.

Reeves, Richard. 2017a. *Dream Hoarders: How the American Upper Middle Class Is Leaving Everyone Else in the Dust, Why That Is a Problem, and What to Do about It*. Washington, DC: Brookings Institution Press.

Reeves, Richard. 2017b. Stop Pretending You're Not Rich. *New York Times*. June 11. https://nyti.ms/2t6ONke

Reich, Rob, Chiara Cordelli, and Lucy Bernholz, eds. 2016. *Philanthropy in Democratic Societies: History, Institutions, Values*. Chicago: University of Chicago Press.

Reinhardt, Richard. 1965. Joe Ridder's San Jose. *San Francisco Magazine*. November.

Reisner, Marc. 1986. *Cadillac Desert: The American West and Its Disappearing Water*. New York: Viking.

Rhee, Nari. 2007. *Searching for Working Class Politics: Labor, Community and Urban Power in Silicon Valley*. Doctoral dissertation. Department of Geography, University of California,

Rhomberg, Christopher. 2004. *No There There: Race, Class and Community in Oakland*. Berkeley: University of California Press.

Richardson, James. 1996. *Willie Brown: A Biography*. Berkeley: University of California Press.

Richter, Wolf. 2016. San Francisco's Epic Condo Boom Is Turning into a Bust. *Business Insider*. April 11. http://www.businessinsider.com/san-franciscos-condo-boom-turning-into-bust-2016-4

Rios, Edwin. 2016. Hunger Strike in San Francisco Puts a Spotlight on Police Brutality. *Mother Jones*. April 27. http://www.motherjones.com/politics/2016/04/hunger-strike-san-francisco-police-shootings/

Rivera, Amaad, and United for a Fair Economy. 2008. *Foreclosed: State of the Dream 2008*. Boston: United for a Fair Economy.

Rivers, William, and David Rubin. 1971. *A Region's Press: Anatomy of Newspapers in the San Francisco Bay Area*. Berkeley: Institute of Governmental Studies, University of California.

Rivlin, Gary. 2007. In Silicon Valley, Millionaires Who Don't Feel Rich. *New York Times*. August 5. www.nytimes.com/2007/08/05/technology/05rich.html?_r=0

Roberts, Michael. 2016. *The Long Depression: Marxism and the Global Crisis of Capitalism*. Chicago: Haymarket Books.

Robinson, Melia. 2016. A Chinese Billionaire-Owned Real Estate Firm Is Building a Huge Skyscraper in San Francisco. *Business Insider*. December 12. http://www.businessinsider.my/photos-san-francisco-oceanwide-center-2016-12/

Robinson, Michael. 1990. *Overdrawn: The Bailout of American Savings*. New York: Dutton.

Rockman, Seth. 2009. *Scraping By: Wage Labor, Slavery, and Survival in Early Baltimore*. Baltimore: Johns Hopkins University Press.

Rodriguez, Clara. 2000. *Changing Race: Latinos, the Census, and the History of Ethnicity in the United States*. New York: New York University Press.

Roediger, David. 2005. *Working towards Whiteness: How America's Immigrants Became White—the Strange Journey from Ellis Island to the Suburbs*. New York: Basic Books.

Roediger, David. 2008. *How Race Survived U.S. History: From Settlement and Slavery to the Obama Phenomenon*. London: Verso.

Rogers, Paul. 2017. State Auditor Rips Jerry Brown's $17 Billion Delta Tunnels Project. *San Jose Mercury News*. October 5. http://www.mercurynews.com/2017/10/05/significant-cost-increases-and-delays-state-auditor-rips-jerry-browns-17-billion-delta-tunnels-project/

Rogers, Everett, and Judith Larsen. 1984. *Silicon Valley Fever*. New York: Basic Books.

Rolf, David. 2016. *The Fight for $15: The Right Wage for a Working America*. New York: New Press.

Romero, Simon. 2017. Spanish Thrives in the U.S. Despite English-Only Drive. *New York Times*. August 23. https://www.nytimes.com/2017/08/23/us/spanish-language-united-states.html

Roose, Kevin. 2014. The Tech Sector's New Urban Aesthetic. *New York Magazine*. May 13. http://nymag.com/daily/intelligencer/2014/05/tech-sectors-new-urban-aesthetic.html

Rorabaugh, W.J. 1989. *Berkeley at War: The 1960s*. New York: Oxford University Press.

Rose, Mike. 2004. *The Mind at Work: Valuing the Intelligence of the American Worker*. New York: Viking.

Rosen, Marcia, and Wendy Sullivan. 2012. *From Urban Renewal and Displacement to Economic Inclusion: San Francisco Affordable Housing Policy, 1978–2012*. Washington, DC & San Francisco: Poverty and Race Research Action Council and National Housing Law Project. http://www.prrac.org/pdf/SanFranAffHsing.pdf

Rosenberg, Nathan. 1972. *Technology and American Economic Growth*. New York: Harper Torchbooks.

Rosenberg, Nathan. 1976. Technological Change in the Machine Tool Industry, 1840–1910. In *Perspectives on Technology*. Cambridge: Cambridge University Press, 9–31.

Roubini, Nouriel, and Stephen Mihm. 2010. *Crisis Economics: A Crash Course in the Future of Finance*. New York: Penguin Press.

Rubin, Elihu. 2012. *Insuring the City: The Prudential Center and the Postwar Urban Landscape*. New Haven, CT: Yale University Press.

Rubin, Jasper. 2011. *A Negotiated Landscape: The Transformation of the San Francisco Waterfront Since 1950*. Chicago: Center for American Places at Columbia College Chicago.

Ruiz, Rebecca. 2013. Life, Death and PTSD in Oakland: How Violence and Poverty Are Traumatizing the City's Youth. *East Bay Express*. December 11. http://www.eastbayexpress.com/oakland/life-death-and-ptsd-in-oakland/Content?oid=3783767

Rushe, Dominic. 2014. Twitter's Diversity Report: White, Male and Just Like the Rest of Silicon Valley. *Guardian*. July 25. https://www.theguardian.com/technology/2014/jul/25/twitter-diversity-white-men-facebook-silicon-valley

Rutenberg, Jim. 2016. Behind the Scenes, Billionaires' Growing Control of the News. *New York Times*. May 27. https://nyti.ms/1U0Gbl4

Rycroft, Robert. 2015. *The Economics of Inequality, Discrimination, Poverty, and Mobility*. New York: Routledge.

Sabatini, Joshua. 2016. San Francisco Evictions Continue to Rise Since 2010. *San Francisco Examiner*. March 29. http://www.sfexaminer.com/san-francisco-evictions-continue-rise-year-since-2010/

Sabin, Paul. 2005. *Crude Politics: The California Oil Market, 1900–1940*. Berkeley: University of California Press.

Saez, Emmanuel, and Gabriel Zucman. 2014. *Wealth Inequality in the United States since 1913: Evidence from Capitalized Income Tax Data*. Cambridge, MA: National Bureau of Economic Research. Also appeared as an article in *Quarterly Journal of Economics* 131 (2) May 2016: 519–78.

Sagara, Eric, Emmanuel Martinez, and Ike Sriskandarajah. 2016. When Spark Meets Sprawl: Building in Wildlands Increases Fire Risk. *Reveal*. October 8. https://www.revealnews.org/article/when-spark-meets-sprawl-building-in-wildlands-increases-fire-risk/

Said, Carolyn. 2011. Home Prices to Hit Bottom This Year, Report Says. *San Francisco Chronicle*. February 9. http://www.smcare.org/care/news_features/news/2011/sfgate_020911.asp

Said, Carolyn. 2017. Uber and Lyft Cars Flood S.F. Streets. *San Francisco Chronicle*. June 13. http://www.sfgate.com/business/article/Uber-Lyft-cars-have-heavy-impact-on-SF-streets-11214835.php

Said, Carolyn. 2018. Airbnb S.F. Listings Halved at Deadline. *San Francisco Chronicle*. January 18, A1.

Sakolski, Aaron. 1932. *The Great American Land Bubble*. New York: Harper & Bros.

Salian, Isha. 2017. Emeryville Fair Workweek Ordinance Takes Effect. *San Francisco Chronicle*. June 30. http://www.sfchronicle.com/business/article/Emeryville-fair-workweek-ordinance-takes-effect-11259938.php

Samara, Tony. 2016. *Race, Inequality and the Resegregation of the Bay Area*. Oakland: Urban Habitat.

Samuelson, Robert. 2017. The Quiet Comeback of the Middle Class. *Washington Post.* September 3. https://www.washingtonpost.com/opinions/the-quiet-comeback-of-the-middle-class/2017/09/03/02075778-8f36-11e7-91d5-ab4e4bb76a3a_story.html?utm_term=.9be3e891a1bb

Sandbu, Martin. 2016. Debt and Demand. *Financial Times.* October 6. https://www.ft.com/martin-sandbu

Sanders, Anthony. 2008. The Subprime Crisis and Its Role in the Financial Crisis. *Journal of Housing Economics.* 17: 254–61.

Sankalia, Tanu. 1999. *Landscapes of Deindustrialization: Examining Urban Repair in West Oakland.* MA thesis. Department of City and Regional Planning, University of California, Berkeley.

Santos, Maria, James Thorne, Jon Christensen, and Zephyr Frank. 2014. An Historical Land Conservation Analysis in the San Francisco Bay Area: 1850–2010. *Landscape and Urban Planning* 127: 114–23.

Sardar, Zahid. 2000. *San Francisco Modern.* San Francisco: Chronicle Books.

Save the Bay. 2015. *2020 Strategic Plan.* Oakland: Save the Bay.

Saxenian, AnnaLee. 1994. *Regional Advantage: Silicon Valley and Route 128 in Comparative Perspective.* Cambridge, MA: Harvard University Press.

Saxenian, AnnaLee. 2004. Taiwan's Hsinchu region. In Timothy Bresnahan and Alfonso Gambardella, eds., *Building High-Tech Clusters: Silicon Valley and Beyond.* Cambridge: Cambridge University Press, 190–228.

Saxenian, AnnaLee. 2006. *The New Argonauts: Regional Advantage in a Global Economy.* Cambridge, MA: Harvard University Press.

Saxton, Alexander. 1971. *The Indispensible Enemy: Labor and the Anti-Chinese Movement in California.* Berkeley: University of California Press.

Sayer, Andrew, and Richard Walker. 1992. *The New Social Economy: Reworking the Division of Labor.* Cambridge, MA: Basil Blackwell.

Sayer, Andrew. 1995. *Radical Political Economy: A Critique.* Oxford: Blackwell.

Sayer, Andrew. 2005. *The Moral Significance of Class.* Cambridge: Cambridge University Press.

Sayer, Andrew. 2015. *Why We Can't Afford the Rich.* Chicago: Polity Press.

Sbragia, Alberta. 1996. *Debt Wish: Entrepreneurial Cities, U.S. Federalism and Economic Development.* Pittsburgh: University of Pittsburgh Press.

Schafran, Alex. 2009. Outside Endopolis: Notes from Contra Costa County. *Critical Planning* 16: 11–33.

Schafran Alex. 2013. Origins of an Urban Crisis: The Restructuring of the San Francisco Bay Area and the Geography of Foreclosure. *International Journal of Urban and Regional Research* 37 (3): 663–88

Schafran Alex, and Jon Wegmann. 2012. Restructuring, Race and Real Estate: Changing Home Values and the New California Metropolis, 1989–2010. *Urban Geography* 33: 630–54

Scheiber, Noam. 2017. How Uber Uses Psychological Tricks to Push Its Drivers Buttons. *New York Times.* April 2. https://www.nytimes.com/interactive/2017/04/02/technology/uber-drivers-psychological-tricks.html?_r=0

Schenin, Richard. 2016. Bay Area Rents: Still Rising but Leveling Off. *San Jose Mercury News.* July 21.

Schiada, Amber. 2016. San Francisco Bay Area Market Overview, Q1/2016. Chicago: Jones Lang Lasalle. http://edgeblog.jll.com/2016/04/11/san-francisco-bay-area-office-market-overview-q1-2016/

Schneider, Daniel, and Kristen Harknett. 2017a. How Work Schedules Affect Health and Wellbeing. Unpublished paper, Department of Sociology, University of California, Berkeley.

Schneider, Daniel, and Kristen Harknett. 2017b. Income Volatility in the Service Sector: Contours, Causes, and Consequences. July 7. Aspen Institute EPIC Program. https://www.aspeninstitute.org/publications/income-volatility-service-sector-contours-causes-consequences/

Schneider, Daniel, Kristen Harknett, and Sara McLanahan. 2016. Intimate Partner Violence in the Great Recession. *Demography* 53: 471–505.

Schneider, Mark. 1989. *The Competitive City: The Political Economy of Suburbia*. Pittsburgh: University of Pittsburgh Press.

Schoenberger, Erica. 1997. *The Cultural Crisis of the Firm*. Cambridge: Blackwell.

Schoenberger, Erica. 2015. *Nature, Choice and Social Power*. New York: Routledge.

Schoenberger, Erica, and Richard Walker. 2017. Beyond Exchange and Agglomeration: Resource Flows and City Environments as Wellsprings of Urban Growth. *Journal of Economic Geography* 17 (5): 935–58.

Schorske, Carl. 1979. *Fin de Siècle Vienna: Politics and Culture*. New York: Knopf/Random House.

Schrag, Peter. 1998. *Paradise Lost: California's Experience, America's Future*. New York: New Press.

Schrag, Peter. 2006. *California: America's High-Stakes Experiment*. Berkeley: University of California Press.

Schumpeter, Joseph. 1939. *Business Cycles*. New York: McGraw-Hill.

Schumpeter, Joseph. 1950. *Capitalism, Socialism, Democracy*. New York: Harper.

Schuparra, Kurt. 1998. *Triumph of the Right: The Rise of the California Conservative Movement, 1945–1966*. Armonk, NY: M.E. Sharpe.

Schwaller, Katja. 2017. *Welcome to Twitterlandia: Reshaping Work and Public Space in San Francisco's Mid-Market*. MA in Urban Affairs, University of San Francisco.

Schwarzer, Mitchell. 2015. Oakland City Center: The plan to reposition Downtown within the Bay Region. *Journal of Planning History* 14 (2): 88–111.

Scott, Allen. 1988. *Metropolis: From the Division of Labor to Urban Form*. Berkeley: University of California Press.

Scott, Allen. 1993. *Technopolis: High Technology Industry and Regional Development in Southern California*. Los Angeles: University of California Press.

Scott, Allen. 1998. *Regions and the World Economy: The Coming Shape of Global Production, Competition, and Political Order*. Oxford: Oxford University Press.

Scott, Allen. 2012. *A World in Emergence: Cities and Regions in the 21st Century*. Cheltenham: Edward Elgar.

Scott, Allen, and Michael Storper, eds. 1986. *Work, Production, Territory: The Geographical Anatomy of Contemporary Capitalism*. Boston: Allen & Unwin.

Scott, Allen, and Michael Storper. 2015. The Nature of Cities: The Limits and Scope of Urban Theory. *International Journal of Urban and Regional Research* 39 (1): 1–15.

Scott, Mel. 1985 [1959] *The San Francisco Bay Area: A Metropolis in Perspective*. Berkeley: University of California Press. (2nd ed.)

Seifel Consulting. 2016. *Downtown San Francisco: Market Demand, Growth Projections and Capacity Analysis*. San Francisco: SF Planning Department.

Seipel, Tracey. 2017. Healthcare Workers Rally to Halt Oakland Nurse's Deportation. *Mercury News*. August 15. http://www.mercurynews.com/2017/08/14/healthcare-workers-rally-to-halt-oakland-nurses-deportation/

Self, Robert. 2003. *American Babylon: Race and the Struggle for Postwar Oakland*. Princeton: Princeton University Press.

Selna, Robert. 2010. Foreign Investors Eye San Francisco Hotels. *San Francisco Chronicle*. May 26. http://www.sfgate.com/business/article/Foreign-investors-eye-San-Francisco-hotels-3187903.php

Selvin, Joel. 1994. *Summer of Love: The Inside Story of LSD, Rock & Roll, Free Love, and High Times in the Wild West*. New York: Dutton.

Senkewicz, Robert. 1985. *Vigilantes in Gold Rush San Francisco*. Stanford, CA: Stanford University Press.

Sennett, Richard, and Jonathan Cobb. 1972. *The Hidden Injuries of Class*. New York: Vintage Books.

Sennett, Richard. 1998. *The Corrosion of Character: The Personal Consequences of Work in the New Capitalism*. New York: W.W. Norton.

Serna, Joseph. 2017. San Joaquin Valley Continues to Sink Because of Groundwater Pumping, NASA Says. *Los Angeles Times*. February 9. http://www.latimes.com/local/lanow/la-me-ln-central-valley-subsidence-20170209-story.html

Shane, Scott. 2017. The Fake Americans Russian Created to Influence the Election. *New York Times*. September 7. https://nyti.ms/2xdVuXM

Shapira, Phil. 1986. *Industry and Jobs in Transition: A Study of Industrial Restructuring and Worker Displacement in California*. Doctoral dissertation. Department of City and Regional Planning, University of California, Berkeley.

Sharma, Ruchir. 2017. When Will the Tech Bubble Burst? *New York Times*. August 5. https://nyti.ms/2uuzQbS

Shaw, Randy. 2015. *The Tenderloin: Sex, Crime and Resistance in the Heart of San Francisco*. San Francisco: Urban Reality Press.

Shaxson, Nicholas. 2011. *Treasure Islands: Tax Havens and the Men Who Stole the World*. New York: Palgrave Macmillan.

Shiller, Robert. 2008. *The Subprime Solution: How Today's Global Financial Crisis Happened, and What to Do about It*. New York: Penguin.

Shilts, Randy. 1982. *The Mayor of Castro Street: The Life and Times of Harvey Milk*. New York: St. Martin's Press.

Shumsky, Neil. 1991. *The Evolution of Political Protest and the Workingmen's Party of California*. Columbus: Ohio State University Press.

Shumsky, Neil, and Larry Springer. 1981. San Francisco's Zone of Prostitution, 1880–1934. *Journal of Historical Geography* 7 (1): 71–89.

Sides, Josh. 2009. *Erotic City: Sexual Revolutions and the Making of Modern San Francisco*. New York: Oxford University Press.

Siegel, Lee. 2008. *Against the Machine: Being Human in the Era of the Electronic Mob*. New York: Profile Books.

Siegel, Lee. 2011. Twitter Can't Save You. Review of Morozov 2011. *New York Times Sunday Book Review*. February 4. http://www.nytimes.com/2011/02/06/books/review/Siegel-t.html?pagewanted=all

Silicon Valley Rising. 2016. *Tech's Invisible Workforce*. San Jose: Working Partnerships.

Silverman, Craig, Ellie Hall, Lauren Strapaglei, Jeremy Singer-Vine, and Hamza Shaban. 2016. Hyperpartisan Facebook Pages are Publishing False and Misleading Information at an Alarming Rate. *Buzzfeed News*. October 20. https://www.buzzfeed.com/craigsilverman/partisan-fb-pages-analysis?utm_term=.scVPaDeBzJ#.wsgWDPpBJQ

Simmons, Andrew. 2017. The Elusive Teacher Next Door. *Atlantic*. June 28. https://www.theatlantic.com/education/archive/2017/06/the-elusive-teacher-next-door/531990/

Simon, Jonathon. 2007. *Governing through Crime*. New York: Oxford University Press

Simon, Jonathan. 2014. *Mass Incarceration on Trial: A Remarkable Decision and the Future of Prisons in America*. New York: New Press.

Simonsen, Sharon. 2015. Asians Outnumber Whites in Silicon Valley. *SiliconValleyOneWorld*. April 20. http://www.siliconvalleyoneworld.com/2015/04/20/demographers-asians-now-outnumber-whites-in-silicon-valley/

Singer, Natasha. 2017. The Silicon Valley Billionaires Remaking America's Schools. *New York Times*. June 6. https://nyti.ms/2sMKXMN

Singh, Puneet. 2017. Bay Area Cities Implement New Eviction and Rent Control Measures. Law Offices of Kimball, Tirey & St. John. January 23. http://www.kts-law.com/bay-area-cities-implement-new-eviction-and-rent-control-measures-2/

Slater, Dashka. 1998. The Rise and Fall of Berkeley Rent Control. *East Bay Express* 21 (9): October 9.

Smith, Andrew. 2016. Inside Hacker Dojo, the Soul of Silicon Valley. *Financial Times*. July 15. https://www.ft.com/content/d2f3e8c4-49af-11e6-8d68-72e9211e86ab

Smith, Daniel. 1999. Reevaluating the Causes of Proposition 13. *Social Science History* 23 (2): 173–210.

Smith, Hedrick. 2012. *Who Stole the American Dream?* New York: Random House.

Smith, Neil. 1996. *The New Urban Frontier: Gentrification and the Revanchist City.* London: Routledge.

Smith, S.E. 2015. Silicon Valley's Labor Uprising: Unions Are Spreading like Wildfire through Tech's Low-Wage Workforce. *In These Times*. September 7. http://inthesetimes.com/article/18367/silicon-valleys-labor-uprising

Sobel, Robert. 1983. *IBM: Colossus in Transition.* New York: Bantam Books.

Soergel, Andrew. 2017. Tech Earnings, Jobs Blow Away the Rest of the Labor Market. *U.S. News & World Report*. April 3. https://www.usnews.com/news/articles/2017-04-03/tech-earnings-jobs-blow-away-the-rest-of-the-labor-market

Soja, Edward. 2010. *Seeking Spatial Justice.* Minneapolis: University of Minnesota Press.

Soja, Edward. 2014. *My Los Angeles: From Urban Restructuring to Regional Urbanization.* Berkeley: University of California Press.

Solnit, Rebecca. 2013. Diary. *London Review of Books* 35 (3): 34–35. http://www.lrb.co.uk/v35/n03/rebecca-solnit/diary

Solnit, Rebecca, and Susan Schwartzenberg. 2001. *Hollow City: Gentrification and the Eviction of Urban Culture.* London: Verso Press.

Solon, Olivia. 2017. Tech's Terrible Year: How the World Turned on Silicon Valley in 2017. *Guardian*. December 23. https://www.theguardian.com/technology/2017/dec/22/tech-year-in-review-2017

Solon, Olivia, and Sabrina Siddiqi. 2017. Forget Wall Street: Silicon Valley Is the New Political Power in Washington. *Observer*. September 3. http://www.theguardian.com/technology/2017/sep/03/silicon-valley-politics-lobbying-washington

Southwick, Karen. 1999. *Silicon Valley Gold Rush: The Next Generation of High-Tech Stars Rewrites the Rules of Business.* New York: John Wiley & Sons.

Spanger-Siegfried, Erika, Kristina Dahl, Astrid Caldas, Shana Udvardy, Rachel Cleetus, Pamela Worth, and Nicole Hernandez Hammer. 2017. *When Rising Seas Hit Home: Hard Choices Ahead for Hundreds of US Coastal Communities.* Union of Concerned Scientists. https://www.ucsusa.org/global-warming/global-warming-impacts/when-rising-seas-hit-home-chronic-inundation-from-sea-level-rise#.WkSOkxNSzok

SPUR. 2012. In San Francisco, the Boom Is Back. *Urbanist*. no. 519. December 18. http://www.spur.org/publications/urbanist-article/2012-12-18/san-francisco-boom-back

Squires, Gregory, ed. 2002. *Urban Sprawl.* Washington, DC: The Urban Institute.

Srnicek, Nick, and Alex Williams. 2016. *Inventing the Future: Postcapitalism and a World Without Work.* London: Verso.

St. John, Paige. 2013. Inmates End California Prison Hunger Strike. *Los Angeles Times*. September 5. http://articles.latimes.com/2013/sep/05/local/la-me-ff-prison-strike-20130906

Stanley, Alessandra. 2015. Silicon Valley's New Philanthropy. *New York Times*. October 31. http://nyti.ms/1KNbPND

Stehlin, John. 2015. *Business Cycles: Race, Gentrification, and the Making of Bicycle Space in the San Francisco Bay Area.* Doctoral dissertation. Department of Geography, University of California, Berkeley.

Stehlin, John. 2016. The Post-industrial "Shop Floor": Emerging Forms of Gentrification in San Francisco's Innovation Economy. *Antipode* 48 (2): 474–93.

Stein, Benjamin. 1992. *A License to Steal: The Untold Story of Michael Milken and the Conspiracy to Bilk the Nation.* New York: Simon & Schuster.

Steinberg, Goodwin. 2002. *From the Ground Up: Building Silicon Valley*. Stanford, CA: Stanford University Press.

Steinstra, Tom. 2017. How Winter's Flooding Will Create a Wildlife Rebirth in Spring. February 11. *San Francisco Chronicle*. http://www.sfchronicle.com/sports/article/How-winter-s-flooding-will-create-a-wildlife-10925995.php

Sterba, Jim. 2012. *Nature Wars: The Incredible Story of How Wildlife Comeback Turned Backyards into Battlegrounds*. New York: Crown Books.

Stewart, Jack. 2017. Mapped: The Top 263 Companies Racing toward Autonomous Cars. *Wired*. May 17. https://www.wired.com/2017/05/mapped-top-263-companies-racing-toward-autonomous-cars/

Stewart, James. 2017. Elon Musk Has Trump's Ear, and Wall Street Takes Note. *New York Times*. January 26. https://nyti.ms/2jBHmNG

Stockton, Nick. 2016. Elon Musk Announces His Plan to Colonize Mars and Save Humanity. *Wired*. September 27. https://www.wired.com/2016/09/elon-musk-colonize-mars/

Stone, Brad. 2014. *The Everything Store: Jeff Bezos and the Age of Amazon*. New York: Little Brown & Co.

Storper, Michael. 1997. *The Regional World*. New York: Guilford Press.

Storper, Michael. 2013. *The Keys to the City: How Economics, Institutions, Social Interaction, and Politics Shape Development*. Princeton, NJ: Princeton University Press.

Storper, Michael, and Richard Walker. 1979. The California Water System: Another Round of Expansion? *Public Affairs Report*. 20 (2): 1–11.

Storper, Michael, and Richard Walker. 1984. *The Price of Water: Surplus and Subsidy in the California State Water Project*. Berkeley: Institute of Governmental Studies.

Storper, Michael, Thomas Kemeny, Naji Makarem, and Taner Osman. 2015. *The Rise and Decline of Great Urban Economies: Los Angeles and San Francisco since 1970*. Stanford, CA: Stanford University Press.

Streitfield, David. 2016a. "We Almost Have Riots": Tensions Flare in Silicon Valley over Growth. *New York Times*. November 4. https://nyti.ms/2en12RW

Streitfield, David. 2016b. Specter of Trump Loosens Tongues, If Not Purse Strings, in Silicon Valley. *New York Times*. October 16. http://nyti.ms/2e8RrlN

Streitfield, David. 2017a. Tech Opposition to Trump Driven by Employees, Not Executives. *New York Times*. February 6. https://nyti.ms/2kEA9jH

Streitfield, David. 2017b. Activism Hits Even Less Flashy Tech Companies. *New York Times*. February 12. https://nyti.ms/2l4ujIz

Streitfield, David. 2017c. "The Internet Is Broken": @ev Is Trying to Salvage It. *New York Times*. May 20. https://nyti.ms/2rCf9tM

Streitfeld, David, and Mike Isaac. 2016. Tech Titans Raise Their Guard, Fight Back against News Media. *New York Times*. May 27. https://nyti.ms/1U1POzL

Streitfeld, David, Mike Isaac, and Katie Benner. 2017. Silicon Valley's Ambivalence toward Trump Turns to Anger. January 29. *New York Times*. https://nyti.ms/2jGjDy5

Stroshane, Tim. 2016. *Drought, Water Law, and the Origins of California's Central Valley Project*. Reno: University of Nevada Press.

Stross, Randall. 2006. It's Not the People You Know. It's Where You Are. *New York Times*. October 22, BU3. http://www.nytimes.com/2006/10/22/

Stuckler, David, and Sanjay Basu. 2013. *The Body Economic: Why Austerity Kills*. New York: Basic Books.

Sturgeon, Timothy. 2000. How Silicon Valley Came to Be. In Martin Kenney, ed., *Understanding Silicon Valley: The Anatomy of an Entrepreneurial Region*. Stanford, CA: Stanford University Press, 15–47.

Sturgeon, Timothy. 2003. What Really Goes On in Silicon Valley? Spatial Clustering and Dispersal in Modular Production Networks. *Journal of Economic Geography* 3 (2): 199–225.

Sundararajan, Arun. 2016. *The Sharing Economy: The End of Employment and the Rise of Crowd-Based Capitalism*. Cambridge, MA: MIT Press.

Swan, Rachel. 2016. Suing the Suburbs to Generate Housing. *San Francisco Chronicle*. May 3, A1.

Swartz, Jon, and Jessica Guynn. 2017. Tech's Latest Start-Up: Anti-Trump Activism. *USA Today*. February 7. https://www.usatoday.com/story/tech/news/2017/02/07/techs-latest-start-up-anti-trump-activism/97564884/

Swatt, Steve, Susie Swatt, Jeff Raimundo, and Rebecca LaVally. 2014. *Game Changers: Twelve Elections that Transformed California*. Berkeley: Heyday Books.

Tam, Pui-Wing. 2016. Trump's Meeting with Tech Leaders Turns into a Charmfest. December 15. https://nyti.ms/2hJZFTx

Tang, Samuel, and Kuan Ngo. 2012. *Tech Untaxed: Tax Avoidance in Silicon Valley, and How America's Richest Company Pays a Lower Tax Rate than You Do*. Berkeley: Greenlining Institute.

Taplin, Jonathan. 2017. *Move Fast and Break Things: How Facebook, Google and Amazon Cornered Culture and Undermined Democracy*. New York: Little, Brown/Hachette.

Taylor, Mac. 2015. *California's High Housing Costs: Causes and Consequences*. Sacramento: Legislative Analyst Office.

Taylor, Nick. 2009. *American-Made: The Enduring Legacy of the WPA, When FDR Put the Nation to Work*. New York: Bantam.

Taylor, Paul, and Richard Fry. 2012. *The Rise of Residential Segregation by Income*. Research Report. Washington, DC: Pew Research Center. http://assets.pewresearch.org/wp-content/uploads/sites/3/2012/08/Rise-of-Residential-Income-Segregation-2012.2.pdf

Tedlow, Richard. 1990. *New and Improved: The Story of Mass Marketing in America*. New York: Basic Books.

Temple, James. 2009. Oakland 10K Initiative: 10 Years Later. *San Francisco Chronicle*. July 12. http://www.sfgate.com/realestate/article/Economy-casts-shadow-on-Oakland-10K-plan-s-10th-3225820.php

Tepperman, Jeanne. 2015. Chevron Management Failures Led to Massive August 2012 Explosion in Richmond. *East Bay Express*. January 29. https://www.eastbayexpress.com/SevenDays/archives/2015/01/29/chevron-management-failures-led-to-massive-august-2012-explosion-in-richmond

Terplan, Egon, et al. 2014. *Economic Prosperity Strategy: Improving Economic Opportunity for the Bay Area's Low and Moderate Wage Workers*. Report to the Bay Area Regional Prosperity Plan Steering Committee. San Francisco: San Francisco Planning and Urban Research.

Terplan, Egon. 2015. *A Downtown for Everyone: Shaping the Future of Downtown Oakland*. Oakland: San Francisco Planning and Urban Research Association.

Thadani, Trisha. 2017a. More Elect to Use Tech Skills to Aid Campaigns. *San Francisco Chronicle*. March 9. http://www.sfchronicle.com/politics/article/Tech-workers-electing-to-use-skills-in-politics-10991062.php

Thadani, Trisha. 2017b. Silicon Valley Leaders Head to D.C. to Push Tech Agenda. *SFGate.com*. March 13. http://www.sfgate.com/business/article/Silicon-Valley-leaders-head-to-D-C-to-push-tech-10994003.php

Thadani, Trisha, and Carolyn Said. 2017. Bay Area Businesses Bid on Wall Despite Risk. *San Francisco Chronicle*. March 29, A1.

Thiel, Peter. 2009. The Education of a Libertarian. *Cato Unbound*. April 13. https://www.cato-unbound.org/2009/04/13/peter-thiel/education-libertarian

Thomas, Landon. SoftBank's $100 Billion Investment Fund Starts to Take Shape. *New York Times*. January 10. http://nyti.ms/2jrGzOz

Thompson, Edward, Douglas Hay, and Peter Linebaugh. 1975. *Albion's Fatal Tree: Crime and Society in Eighteenth-Century England*. New York: Pantheon Books.

Tiebout, Charles. 1956. A Pure Theory of Local Expenditures. *Journal of Political Economy* 64: 416–24.

Timm, Trevor. 2016. The Government Just Admitted It Will Use Smart Home Devices for Spying. *Guardian.* February 9. https://www.theguardian.com/commentisfree/2016/feb/09/internet-of-things-smart-devices-spying-surveillance-us-government

Tkacz, Nathaniel. 2015. *Wikipedia and the Politics of Openness.* Chicago: University of Chicago Press.

Tolan, Casey. 2017. Wine Country Fires Near Complete Containment. *San Jose Mercury News.* October 28. http://www.mercurynews.com/2017/10/28/wine-country-fires-near-complete-containment-but-rebuilding-could-take-years/

Tracy, James. 2014. *Dispatches against Displacement: Field Notes from San Francisco's Housing Wars.* Oakland: AK Press.

Trounstine, Philip, and Terry Christensen. 1982. *Movers and Shakers: The Study of Community Power.* New York: St. Martin's Press.

Troy, Leo. 1994. *The New Unionism in the New Society: Public Sector Unions In The Redistributive State.* Fairfax, VA: George Mason University Press.

Tsukayama, Hayley. 2017. Twitter May Be Getting Less Awful at Fighting Abuse. *San Francisco Chronicle.* July 21. https://www.pressreader.com/usa/san-francisco-chronicle/20170721/282084866862162

Tuan, Yi-Fu. 1974. *Topophilia: A Study of Environmental Perception, Attitudes and Values.* Englewood Cliffs, NJ: Prentice-Hall.

Tung, Irene, Yannet Lathrop, and Paul Sonn. 2015. *The Growing Movement for $15.* New York: National Employment Law Project.

Turkle, Sherry. 2011. *Alone Together: Why We Expect More from Technology and Less from Each Other.* New York: Basic Books.

Turner, Fred. 2007. *From Counterculture to Cyberculture: Stewart Brand, the Whole Earth Network and the Rise of Digital Utopianism.* Chicago: University of Chicago Press.

Turner, Fred. 2009. Burning Man at Google: A Cultural Infrastructure for New Media Production. *Media and Society* 11 (1–2): 73–94.

Tynan, Dan. 2016. Rocket Men: Why Tech's Biggest Billionaires Want Their Place in Space. *Guardian.* December 5. https://www.theguardian.com/science/2016/dec/05/tech-billionaires-space-exploration-musk-bezos-branson

Tyrrell, Ian. 1986. *The Absent Marx: Class Analysis and Liberal History in the Twentieth-Century America.* New York: Greenwood Press.

Ungaretti, Lorri. 2012. *Stories in the Sand: San Francisco's Sunset District, 1847–1964.* San Francisco: Balangero Books.

Urban Strategies Council. 2012. *Who Owns Your Neighborhood? The Role of Investors in Post-Foreclosure Oakland.* Oakland: Urban Strategies Council.

Urban Strategies Council. 2013. *Building an Indicator Base for Healthy Housing Issues in Oakland.* Oakland: Alameda County Healthy Homes Alliance and Urban Strategies Council.

Urban Strategies Council. 2014. *Housing Equity Roadmap.* Oakland: City of Oakland.

U.S. Army Corps of Engineers. 2013. *Technical Memorandum for Existing Condition Analysis for Risk Informed Decision Making for Project Alternative Selection: Delta Islands and Levees Feasibility Study, California.* Sacramento: Corps of Engineers. http://www.spk.usace.army.mil/Portals/12/documents/civil_works/Delta/DeltaStudy/Appendix%20C%20Flood%20Risk%20Management.pdf

U.S. Geological Survey. 2011. *ARKstorm Scenario. Open-File Report 2010-131.* http://pubs.usgs.gov/of/2010/1312/

Vance, Ashlee. 2015. *Elon Musk: Tesla, Space and the Quest for a Fantastic Future.* New York: Ecco/HarperCollins.

Vance, James. 1964. *Geography and Urban Evolution in the San Francisco Bay Area.* Berkeley: Institute of Governmental Studies, University of California

Varian, Dorothy. 1983. *The Inventor and the Pilot: Russell and Sigurd Varian.* Palo Alto: Pacific Books.

Vicino, Thomas. 2008. *Transforming Race and Class in Suburbia: Decline in Metropolitan Baltimore.* New York: Palgrave Macmillan.

Viviano, Frank. 1984. The Architecture of Impermanence. *San Jose Mercury, New West Magazine*, Feb. 5.10–15

Vogel, David. 2018. *California Greenin': How the Golden State Became an Environmental Leader.* Princeton, NJ: Princeton University Press.

Vogel, Kenneth. 2017. The "Resistance," Raising Big Money, Upends Liberal Politics. *New York Times.* October 7. https://nyti.ms/2yOFSH1

Voss, Kim, and Irene Bloemraad, eds. 2011. *Rallying for Immigrant Rights: The Struggle for Inclusion in 21st Century America.* Berkeley: University of California Press.

Wakabayashi, Daisuke. 2017. At Google, Employee-Led Effort Finds That Men Are Paid More than Women. *New York Times.* September 8. https://nyti.ms/2gRfSqD

Wakabayashi, Daisuke, and Mike Isaac. 2017. In the Race against Fake News, Google and Facebook Stroll to the Starting Line. *New York Times.* January 26. https://nyti.ms/2k5khq5

Walker, Frances. 1939. *San Francisco's Literary Frontier.* New York: Alfred Knopf.

Walker, Richard. 1981. A Theory of Suburbanization: Capitalism and the Construction of Urban Space in the United States. In Michael Dear and Allen Scott, eds., *Urbanization and Urban Planning in Capitalist Societies.* New York: Methuen. 383–430

Walker, Richard. 1995a. California Rages against the Dying of the Light. *New Left Review* 209: 42–74.

Walker, Richard. 1995b. Landscape and City Life: Four Ecologies of Residence in the San Francisco Bay Area. *Ecumene.* 2(1): 33–64.

Walker, Richard. 1995c. Regulation and Flexible Specialization as Theories of Capitalist Development: Challengers to Marx and Schumpeter? In Helen Liggett and David Perry, eds., *Spatial Practices: Critical Explorations in Social/Spatial Theory.* Thousand Oaks, CA: Sage, 167–208.

Walker, Richard. 1996. Another Round of Globalization in San Francisco. *Urban Geography.* 17/1: 60–94.

Walker, Richard. 1998. An Appetite for the City. In James Brook, Chris Carlsson, and Nancy Peters, eds., *Reclaiming San Francisco: History, Politics and Culture.* San Francisco: City Lights Books, 1–20.

Walker, Richard. 2001. California's Golden Road to Riches: Natural Resources and Regional Capitalism, 1848–1940. *Annals of the Association of American Geographers* 91 (1): 167–99.

Walker, Richard. 2004a. *The Conquest of Bread: 150 Years of Agribusiness in California.* New York: New Press.

Walker, Richard. 2004b. Industry Builds Out the City: Industrial Decentralization in the San Francisco Bay Area, 1850–1950. In Robert Lewis, ed., *Manufacturing Suburbs: Building Work and Home on the Metropolitan Fringe.* Philadelphia: Temple University Press, 92–123.

Walker, Richard. 2006. The Boom and the Bombshell: The New Economy Bubble and the San Francisco Bay Area. In Giovanna Vertova, ed., *The Changing Economic Geography of Globalization.* London: Routledge, 121–47.

Walker, Richard. 2007. *The Country in the City: The Greening of the San Francisco Bay Area.* Seattle: University of Washington Press.

Walker, Richard. 2008. At the Crossroads: Defining California through the Global Economy. In David Igler and William Deneven, eds., *A Companion to California History.* Hoboken, NJ: Wiley-Blackwell, 75–96.

Walker, Richard. 2009. The Lungs of the City: 75 Years and Counting for the East Bay Parks, *Bay Nature.* October–December, 18–22.

Walker, Richard. 2010. The Golden State Adrift. *New Left Review* 66: 5–30.

Walker, Richard. 2015. Building a Better Theory of the Urban: A Response to "Towards a New Epistemology of the Urban?" *City* 19 (2–3): 183–91.

Walker, Richard. 2016. Why Cities? *International Journal of Urban and Regional Research* 40 (1): 164–80.

Walker, Richard. Forthcoming. Nature's Popular Metropolis: The Greening of the San Francisco Bay Area. In Henrik Ernstson and Sverker Sörlin, eds., *Grounding Urban Natures: Histories and Futures of Urban Ecologies.* Cambridge, MA: MIT Press.

Walker, Richard, and Matthew Williams. 1982. Water from Power: Water Supply and Regional Growth in the Santa Clara Valley. *Economic Geography* 58 (2): 95–119.

Walker, Richard, and the Bay Area Study Group. 1990. The Playground of US Capitalism? The Political Economy of the San Francisco Bay Area in the 1980s. In Mike Davis, Steve Hiatt, M. Kennedy, Susan Ruddick, and Mike Sprinker, eds., *Fire in the Hearth: The Radical Politics of Place in America.* London: Verso. 3–82.

Walker, Richard, and Suresh Lodha. 2013. *The Atlas of California: Mapping the Challenge of a New Era.* Berkeley: University of California Press and London: Myriad Editions.

Walker, Richard, and Alex Schafran. 2015. The Strange Case of the Bay Area. *Environment and Planning A* 47: 10–29.

Walters, Dan. 2017. Oroville Dam Flaws Don't Bode Well for Tunnels, Train Projects. *San Francisco Chronicle.* July 26. http://www.sfchronicle.com/news/article/Bad-Oroville-Dam-design-doesn-t-bode-well-11438530.php

Warburg, Jennifer. 2016. Are We Headed for an Economic Correction? Bay Area Experts Weigh In. March 9. San Francisco: San Francisco Planning and Urban Research. http://www.spur.org/news/2016-03-09/are-we-headed-economic-correction-bay-area-experts-weigh

Warner, Kee, and Harvey Molotch. 2000. *Building Rules: How Local Controls Shape Community Environments and Economies.* Boulder, CO: Westview Press.

Warner, Sam Bass. 1962. *Streetcar Suburbs: The Process of Growth in Boston, 1870–1900.* Cambridge, MA: Harvard University Press.

Waters, Richard. 2015. Dotcom History Is Not Yet Repeating Itself, but It Is Starting to Rhyme. *Financial Times.* March 12. https://next.ft.com/content/655d167c-c89c-11e4-8617-00144feab7de

Waters, Richard. 2016a. Best Coast Tech Is Top and Looking to the Clouds for Growth. *Financial Times.* August 4. https://www.ft.com/content/3e11fdb8-5a49-11e6-9f70-badea1b336d4

Waters, Richard. 2016b. High Hopes for Tech Groups' Overseas Cash Piles. *Inside Business.* December 29. https://www.ft.com/content/d033830e-cde1-11e6-864f-20dcb35cede2

Waters, Richard. 2017a. Silicon Valley Aims to Engineer a Universal Basic Income Solution. *Financial Times.* May 2. https://www.ft.com/content/b0659404-0fea-11e7-a88c-50ba212dce4d

Waters, Richard. 2017b. Sovereign Wealth Funds Seek Closer Silicon Valley Ties. *Financial Times.* October 19. https://www.ft.com/content/ce53c1d2-b4e2-11e7-a398-73d59db9e399

Waters, Richard, and Leslie Hook. 2016. Unicorns: Between Myth and Reality. *Financial Times.* June 27. https://www.ft.com/content/3a53fb48-39f8-11e6-9a05-82a9b15a8ee7

Watkins, James. 2016. October 25. Think China's Pollution Is Bad? Try Northern California. *OZY.* http://www.ozy.com/acumen/think-chinas-pollution-is-bad-try-northern-california/71553

Wealth-X 2017. *World Ultra-Wealth Report 2017.* New York: Wealth-X Ltd.

Weaver, Russell, Sharmistha Bagchi-Sen, Jason Knight, and Amy Frazier. 2016. *Shrinking Cities: Understanding Urban Decline in the United States.* New York: Routledge.

Weber, Alfred. 1929. *Theory of the Location of Industries.* English trans. C.J. Friedrich, Chicago: University of Chicago Press; originally published as *Über den Standorts der Industrien.* Tubingen: J.C.B. Mohr. 1909.

Weber, Rachel. 2015. *From Boom to Bubble: How Finance Built the New Chicago.* Chicago: University of Chicago Press.

Weinberg, Cory. 2015. Uber Shakes Up Real Estate Market with Massive Purchase of Oakland's Former Sears Building. *San Francisco Business Times.* September 22. http://www.bizjournals.com/sanfrancisco/blog/real-estate/2015/09/exclusive-uber-oakland-sears-building.html

Weiner, Eric. 2016. *The Geography of Genius: Lessons from the World's Most Creative Places*. New York: Simon & Schuster

Weiss, Marc. 1980. The Origins and Legacy of Urban Renewal. In Pierre Clavel, John Forester, and William Goldsmith, eds., *Urban and Regional Planning in an Age of Austerity*. New York: Pergamon Press, 54–80.

Weiss, Marc. 1987. *The Rise of the Community Builders: The American Real Estate Industry and Urban Land Planning*. New York: Columbia University Press.

Weller, Chris. 2016. Silicon Valley Giant Wants to Build a Brand-New City from the Ground Up. *Business Insider*. June 27. http://uk.businessinsider.com/y-combinator-launching-research-project-to-build-brand-new-city-2016-6?r=US&IR=T

Werth, Alex. 2016. The Current Moment in Oakland. January 2. Unpublished paper. Department of Geography, University of California Berkeley.

Werth, Alex, and Eli Marienthal. 2016. "Gentrification" as a Grid of Meaning: On Bounding the Deserving Public of Oakland First Fridays. *City* 20 (5): 719–36.

Western, Bruce, and Jake Rosenfeld. 2011. Unions, Norms, and the Rise in U.S. Wage Inequality. *American Sociological Review* 76 (4): 513–37.

White, Richard. 2011. *Railroaded: The Transcontinentals and the Making of Modern America*. New York: W.W. Norton.

Whitehand, J.W.R. 1987. *The Changing Face of Cities: A Study of Development Cycles and Urban Form*. New York: Oxford University Press.

Wigglesworth, Robin. 2017. Corporate Debt Boom Will Come to a Nasty End. *Financial Times*. December 22. https://www.ft.com/content/a7b4f94c-e66a-11e7-97e2-916d4fbacoda

Wiig, Alan. 2015. IBM's Smart City as Techno-Utopian Policy Mobility. *City* 19 (2–3): 258–73, www.tandfonline.com/doi/abs/10.1080/13604813.2015.1016275

Wilkinson, Frank, ed. 1981. *The Dynamics of Labor Market Segmentation*. London: Academic Press.

Wilkinson, Richard, and Kate Pickett. 2009. *The Spirit Level: Why Greater Equality Makes Societies Stronger*. London: Bloomsbury.

Williams, Eric. 1943. *Capitalism and Slavery*. Chapel Hill: University of North Carolina Press; reprint New York: Capricorn Books, 1966 ed.

Williams, Joan. 2017. *White Working Class: Overcoming Class Cluelessness in America*. Cambridge, MA: Harvard Business Review Press.

Williams, Roy. 2014. How Facebook Can Amplify Low Self-Esteem/Narcissism/Anxiety. *Psychology Today*. May 20. https://www.psychologytoday.com/blog/wired-success/201405/how-facebook-can-amplify-low-self-esteemnarcissismanxiety

Wilson, Megan. 2016. Tech Cash Skews to Democrats. *The Hill*. June 7. http://thehill.com/business-a-lobbying/business-a-lobbying/282418-tech-cash-skews-to-democrats

Wimer, Christopher, Marybeth Mattingly, Sara Kimberlin, Caroline Danielson, and Sarah Bohn. 2016. *Poverty and Deep Poverty in California*. California Poverty Measure Policy Report. Stanford, CA: Stanford Center on Poverty and Inequality.

Wingfield, Nick. 2016. San Francisco Office Rents Pass Manhattan as Most Expensive in Country. *New York Times*. January 8. https://bits.blogs.nytimes.com/2016/01/08/san-francisco-office-rents-pass-manhattan-as-most-expensive-in-country/

Wingfield, Nick, and Daisuke Wakabayashi. 2017. Tech Companies Fight Trump Immigration Order in Court. *New York Times*. January 30. https://nyti.ms/2jPCoNp

Winner, Langdon. 1992. Silicon Valley Mystery House. In Michael Sorkin, ed., *Variations on a Theme Park: The New American City and the End of Public Space*. New York: Hill and Wang/Noonday Press, 31–61.

Wise, Tim. 2015. *Under the Affluence: Shaming the Poor, Praising the Rich, and Sacrificing the Future of America*. San Francisco: City Lights Publishers.

Wissoker, Peter. 2016. Putting the Supplier in Housing Supply: An Overview of the Growth and Concentration of Large Homebuilders in the United States, 1990–2007. *Housing Policy Debate* 26 (3): 536–62.

Witco, Christopher. 2010. The California Legislature and the Decline of Majority Rule. In Jeffrey Lustig, ed., *Remaking California*. Berkeley: Heyday Books, 60–77.

Woetzel, Jonathan, Jan Mischke, Shannon Peloquin, and Daniel Weisfield. 2016. *A Tool Kit to Close California's Housing Gap.* October. San Francisco: McKinsey Global Institute.

Wolch, Jennifer, and Michael Dear. 1993. *Malign Neglect: Homelessness in an American City.* San Francisco: Jossey-Bass Publishers.

Wolf, Martin. 2017. Taming the Masters of the Tech Universe. *Financial Times*. November 14. https://www.ft.com/content/45092c5c-c872-11e7-aa33-c63fdc9b8c6c#myft:saved-articles:page

Wolff, Edward. 2006. *Does Education Really Help? Skill, Work, and Inequality.* New York: Oxford University Press.

Wolff, Edward. 2014. *Household Wealth Trends in the United States, 1962–2013: What Happened over the Great Recession?* Cambridge, MA: National Bureau of Economic Research.

Wolff, Michael. 1998. *Burn Rate: How I Survived the Gold Rush Years on the Internet.* New York: Simon & Schuster.

Wollenberg, Charles. 2012. "Dear Earl": The Fair Play Committee, Earl Warren, and Japanese Internment. *California History* 89 (4): 24–55.

Wong, Ashley. 2017. Vast New Bay Area Bike-Share Program Is Everywhere . . . Except Deep East Oakland. *East Bay Express.* July 15. https://www.eastbayexpress.com/oakland/new-bay-area-bike-share-program-is-everywhere-except-deep-east-oakland/Content?oid=7991195

Wong, Julia Carrie. 2016a. Wealthy San Francisco Tech Investors Bankroll Bid to Ban Homeless Camps. *Guardian.* October 12. https://www.theguardian.com/us-news/2016/oct/12/san-francisco-homeless-proposition-q-tech-investors

Wong, Julia Carrie. 2016b. Ctrl+Z: Silicon Valley Leaders U-turn on Donald Trump. *Guardian.* November 11. https://www.theguardian.com/technology/2016/nov/11/silicon-valley-donald-trump-critics-tech-reactions

Wong, Julia Carrie. 2017. Seasteading: Tech Leaders Plans for Floating City Trouble French Polynesians. *Guardian.* January 2. https://www.theguardian.com/technology/2017/jan/02/seasteading-peter-thiel-french-polynesia

Woodbridge, Sally, ed. 1976. *Bay Area Houses.* New York: Oxford University Press; Salt Lake City: Peregrine Smith, 1988, 2nd ed.

Working Partnerships. 2014. *Setting Job Standards for a New Economy.* San Jose, CA: Working Partnerships USA.

Working Partnerships. 2016. *Tech's Invisible Workforce.* San Jose, CA: Working Partnerships USA & Silicon Valley Rising. http://www.siliconvalleyrising.org/TechsInvisibleWorkforce.pdf

Wright, Brian. 2016. Universal Basic Income, an Idea Whose Time Has Come. *San Francisco Chronicle.* June 20. http://www.sfchronicle.com/opinion/openforum/article/Universal-basic-income-an-idea-whose-time-has-8313798.php

Wright, Erik. 1985. *Classes.* London: Verso.

Wright, Erik, ed. 1989. *The Debate on Classes.* London: Verso.

Wu, Bob. 2015. 20 Asian Americans Dominating Technology Start-Ups. April 7. https://www.linkedin.com/pulse/20-asian-americans-dominating-technology-start-ups-bob-wu

Wu, Tim. 2016. *The Attention Merchants: The Epic Scramble to Get Inside Our Heads.* New York: Vintage Books.

Wu, Tim. 2017. How Twitter Killed the First Amendment. *New York Times.* October 27. https://nyti.ms/2iGd6Wj

Wyly, Elvin, Markus Moos, Daniel Hammel, and Emanuel Kabahizi. 2009. Cartographies of Race and Class: Mapping the Class-Monopoly Rents of American Subprime Mortgage Capital. *International Journal of Urban and Regional Research* 33 (2): 332–54.

Zabin, Carol, Abigail Martin, Rachel Morrello-Frosch, Manuel Pastor, and Jim Sadd. 2016. *Advancing Equity in California Climate Policy: A New Social Contract for Low-Carbon Transition.* Center for Research on Labor and Employment, University of California, Berkeley.

Zahniser, David. 2015. Fresh off Bay Area Victory, Tech Giant Airbnb May Set Its Sights on LA. *Los Angeles Times*. November 16. http://www.latimes.com/local/cityhall/la-me-airbnb-campaign-20151116-story.html

Zaleski, Olivia. 2017. VCs Hunt for a Food Delivery Business That's Sustainable. *Bloomberg Technology*. May 18. https://www.bloomberg.com/news/articles/2017-05-18/vcs-hunt-for-a-food-delivery-business-that-s-sustainable

Zambelli, Alex. 2013. A History of Media Streaming and the Future of Connected TV. *Guardian*. March 1. https://www.theguardian.com/media-network/media-network-blog/2013/mar/01/history-streaming-future-connected-tv

Zito, Kelly. 2009. Marin Sewage Spill to Reach 300,000 Gallons. *San Francisco Chronicle*. February 18. http://www.sfgate.com/bayarea/article/Marin-sewage-spill-to-reach-300-000-gallons-3250573.php

Zook, Matthew. 2005. The Geography of the Internet Industry: Venture Capital, Dot-Coms and Local Knowledge. Cambridge, MA: Blackwell.

Zucman, Gabriel. 2015. *The Hidden Wealth of Nations: The Scourge of Tax Havens*. Chicago: University of Chicago Press.

Zuk, Miriam, and Karen Chapple. 2016. Housing Production, Filtering and Displacement: Untangling the Relationships. *IGS Research Brief*. May. Berkeley: Institute of Governmental Studies.

Zukin, Sharon. 1982. *Loft Living: Culture and Capital in Urban Change*. Baltimore: Johns Hopkins University Press.

Zunz, Oliver. 2011. *Philanthropy in America: A History*. Princeton, NJ: Princeton University Press.

Zweig, Michael. 2000. *The Working Class Majority: America's Best Kept Secret*. Ithaca, NY: ILR/Cornell University Press.

Zweig, Michael, ed. 2004. *What's Class Got to Do with It? American Society in the 21st Century*. Ithaca, NY: Cornell University Press.

Zysman, John. 1994. How Institutions Create Historically Rooted Trajectories of Growth. *Industrial and Corporate Review* 3 (1): 243–83.

About the author

Richard A. Walker is professor emeritus of geography at the University of California, Berkeley, where he taught from 1975 to 2012. Walker has written on a diverse range of topics in economic, urban, and environmental geography, with scores of published articles to his credit. He is coauthor of *The Capitalist Imperative* (1989) and *The New Social Economy* (1992) and has written extensively on California, including *The Conquest of Bread*(2004), *The Country in the City* (2007) and *The Atlas of California* (2013).

Walker is currently director of the Living New Deal Project, whose purpose is to inventory all New Deal public works sites in the United States and recover the lost memory of government investment for the good of all. Walker now splits time between Berkeley and Burgundy.

Index

"Passim" (literally "scattered") indicates intermittent discussion of a topic over a cluster of pages.

ABOUT PM PRESS

PM Press was founded at the end of 2007 by a small collection of folks with decades of publishing, media, and organizing experience. PM Press co-conspirators have published and distributed hundreds of books, pamphlets, CDs, and DVDs. Members of PM have founded enduring book fairs, spearheaded victorious tenant organizing campaigns, and worked closely with bookstores, academic conferences, and even rock bands to deliver political and challenging ideas to all walks of life. We're old enough to know what we're doing and young enough to know what's at stake.

We seek to create radical and stimulating fiction and non-fiction books, pamphlets, T-shirts, visual and audio materials to entertain, educate, and inspire you. We aim to distribute these through every available channel with every available technology—whether that means you are seeing anarchist classics at our bookfair stalls, reading our latest vegan cookbook at the café, downloading geeky fiction e-books, or digging new music and timely videos from our website.

PM Press is always on the lookout for talented and skilled volunteers, artists, activists, and writers to work with. If you have a great idea for a project or can contribute in some way, please get in touch.

PM Press
PO Box 23912
Oakland, CA 94623
www.pmpress.org

FRIENDS OF PM PRESS

These are indisputably momentous times—the financial system is melting down globally and the Empire is stumbling. Now more than ever there is a vital need for radical ideas.

In the years since its founding—and on a mere shoestring—PM Press has risen to the formidable challenge of publishing and distributing knowledge and entertainment for the struggles ahead. With over 300 releases to date, we have published an impressive and stimulating array of literature, art, music, politics, and culture. Using every available medium, we've succeeded in connecting those hungry for ideas and information to those putting them into practice.

Friends of PM allows you to directly help impact, amplify, and revitalize the discourse and actions of radical writers, filmmakers, and artists. It provides us with a stable foundation from which we can build upon our early successes and provides a much-needed subsidy for the materials that can't necessarily pay their own way. You can help make that happen—and receive every new title automatically delivered to your door once a month—by joining as a Friend of PM Press. And, we'll throw in a free T-shirt when you sign up.

Here are your options:

- **$30 a month** Get all books and pamphlets plus 50% discount on all webstore purchases

- **$40 a month** Get all PM Press releases (including CDs and DVDs) plus 50% discount on all webstore purchases

- **$100 a month** Superstar—Everything plus PM merchandise, free downloads, and 50% discount on all webstore purchases

For those who can't afford $30 or more a month, we have **Sustainer Rates** at $15, $10 and $5. Sustainers get a free PM Press T-shirt and a 50% discount on all purchases from our website.

Your Visa or Mastercard will be billed once a month, until you tell us to stop. Or until our efforts succeed in bringing the revolution around. Or the financial meltdown of Capital makes plastic redundant. Whichever comes first.

From ◼SPECTRE▶ from PM Press

Capital and Its Discontents: Conversations with Radical Thinkers in a Time of Tumult

Sasha Lilley

ISBN: 978-1-60486-334-5
$20.00   320 pages

Capitalism is stumbling, empire is faltering, and the planet is thawing. Yet many people are still grasping to understand these multiple crises and to find a way forward to a just future. Into the breach come the essential insights of *Capital and Its Discontents*, which cut through the gristle to get to the heart of the matter about the nature of capitalism and imperialism, capitalism's vulnerabilities at this conjuncture—and what we can do to hasten its demise. Through a series of incisive conversations with some of the most eminent thinkers and political economists on the Left—including David Harvey, Ellen Meiksins Wood, Mike Davis, Leo Panitch, Tariq Ali, and Noam Chomsky—*Capital and Its Discontents* illuminates the dynamic contradictions undergirding capitalism and the potential for its dethroning. At a moment when capitalism as a system is more reviled than ever, here is an indispensable toolbox of ideas for action by some of the most brilliant thinkers of our times.

"These conversations illuminate the current world situation in ways that are very useful for those hoping to orient themselves and find a way forward to effective individual and collective action. Highly recommended."
—Kim Stanley Robinson, *New York Times* bestselling author of the *Mars Trilogy* and *The Years of Rice and Salt*

"In this fine set of interviews, an A-list of radical political economists demonstrate why their skills are indispensable to understanding today's multiple economic and ecological crises."
—Raj Patel, author of *Stuffed and Starved* and *The Value of Nothing*

"This is an extremely important book. It is the most detailed, comprehensive, and best study yet published on the most recent capitalist crisis and its discontents. Sasha Lilley sets each interview in its context, writing with style, scholarship, and wit about ideas and philosophies."
—Andrej Grubačić, radical sociologist and social critic, co-author of *Wobblies and Zapatistas*

Global Slump: The Economics and Politics of Crisis and Resistance

David McNally

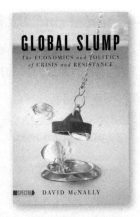

ISBN: 978-1-60486-332-1
$15.95   176 pages

Global Slump analyzes the world financial meltdown as the first systemic crisis of the neoliberal stage of capitalism. It argues that—far from having ended—the crisis has ushered in a whole period of worldwide economic and political turbulence. In developing an account of the crisis as rooted in fundamental features of capitalism, *Global Slump* challenges the view that its source lies in financial deregulation. It offers an original account of the "financialization" of the world economy and explores the connections between international financial markets and new forms of debt and dispossession, particularly in the Global South. The book shows that, while averting a complete meltdown, the massive intervention by central banks laid the basis for recurring crises for poor and working class people. It traces new patterns of social resistance for building an anti-capitalist opposition to the damage that neoliberal capitalism is inflicting on the lives of millions.

"In this book, McNally confirms—once again—his standing as one of the world's leading Marxist scholars of capitalism. For a scholarly, in depth analysis of our current crisis that never loses sight of its political implications (for them and for us), expressed in a language that leaves no reader behind, there is simply no better place to go."
—Bertell Ollman, professor, Department of Politics, NYU, and author of *Dance of the Dialectic: Steps in Marx's Method*

"David McNally's tremendously timely book is packed with significant theoretical and practical insights, and offers actually-existing examples of what is to be done. Global Slump *urgently details how changes in the capitalist space-economy over the past 25 years, especially in the forms that money takes, have expanded wide-scale vulnerabilities for all kinds of people, and how people fight back. In a word, the problem isn't neo-liberalism—it's capitalism."*
—Ruth Wilson Gilmore, University of Southern California and author, *Golden Gulag: Prisons, Surplus, Crisis, and Opposition in Globalizing California*

Stop, Thief!
The Commons, Enclosures,
and Resistance

Peter Linebaugh

ISBN: 978-1-60486-747-3
$21.95   304 pages

In this majestic tour de force, celebrated historian Peter Linebaugh takes aim at the thieves of land, the polluters of the seas, the ravagers of the forests, the despoilers of rivers, and the removers of mountaintops. Scarcely a society has existed on the face of the earth that has not had commoning at its heart. "Neither the state nor the market," say the planetary commoners. These essays kindle the embers of memory to ignite our future commons.

From Thomas Paine to the Luddites, from Karl Marx—who concluded his great study of capitalism with the enclosure of commons—to the practical dreamer William Morris—who made communism into a verb and advocated communizing industry and agriculture—to the 20th-century communist historian E.P. Thompson, Linebaugh brings to life the vital commonist tradition. He traces the red thread from the great revolt of commoners in 1381 to the enclosures of Ireland, and the American commons, where European immigrants who had been expelled from their commons met the immense commons of the native peoples and the underground African-American urban commons. Illuminating these struggles in this indispensable collection, Linebaugh reignites the ancient cry, "STOP, THIEF!"

"*There is not a more important historian living today. Period.*"
—Robin D.G. Kelley, author of *Freedom Dreams: The Black Radical Imagination*

"*E.P. Thompson, you may rest now. Linebaugh restores the dignity of the despised luddites with a poetic grace worthy of the master... [A] commonist manifesto for the 21st century.*"
—Mike Davis, author of *Planet of Slums*

"*Peter Linebaugh's great act of historical imagination... takes the cliché of 'globalization' and makes it live. The local and the global are once again shown to be inseparable—as they are, at present, for the machine-breakers of the new world crisis.*"
—T.J. Clark, author of *Farewell to an Idea*

From ■SPECTRE▶ from PM Press

Catastrophism: The Apocalyptic Politics of Collapse and Rebirth

Sasha Lilley, David McNally, Eddie Yuen, and James Davis with a foreword by Doug Henwood

ISBN: 978-1-60486-589-9
$16.00   192 pages

We live in catastrophic times. The world is reeling from the deepest economic crisis since the Great Depression, with the threat of further meltdowns ever-looming. Global warming and myriad dire ecological disasters worsen—with little if any action to halt them—their effects rippling across the planet in the shape of almost biblical floods, fires, droughts, and hurricanes. Governments warn that no alternative exists than to take the bitter medicine they prescribe—or risk devastating financial or social collapse. The right, whether religious or secular, views the present as catastrophic and wants to turn the clock back. The left fears for the worst, but hopes some good will emerge from the rubble. Visions of the apocalypse and predictions of impending doom abound. Across the political spectrum, a culture of fear reigns.

Catastrophism explores the politics of apocalypse—on the left and right, in the environmental movement, and from capital and the state—and examines why the lens of catastrophe can distort our understanding of the dynamics at the heart of these numerous disasters—and fatally impede our ability to transform the world. Lilley, McNally, Yuen, and Davis probe the reasons why catastrophic thinking is so prevalent, and challenge the belief that it is only out of the ashes that a better society may be born. The authors argue that those who care about social justice and the environment should eschew the Pandora's box of fear—even as it relates to indisputably apocalyptic climate change. Far from calling people to arms, they suggest, catastrophic fear often results in passivity and paralysis—and, at worst, reactionary politics.

"This groundbreaking book examines a deep current—on both the left and right—of apocalyptical thought and action. The authors explore the origins, uses, and consequences of the idea that collapse might usher in a better world. Catastrophism is a crucial guide to understanding our tumultuous times, while steering us away from the pitfalls of the past."
—Barbara Epstein, author of *Political Protest and Cultural Revolution: Nonviolent Direct Action in the 1970s and 1980s*